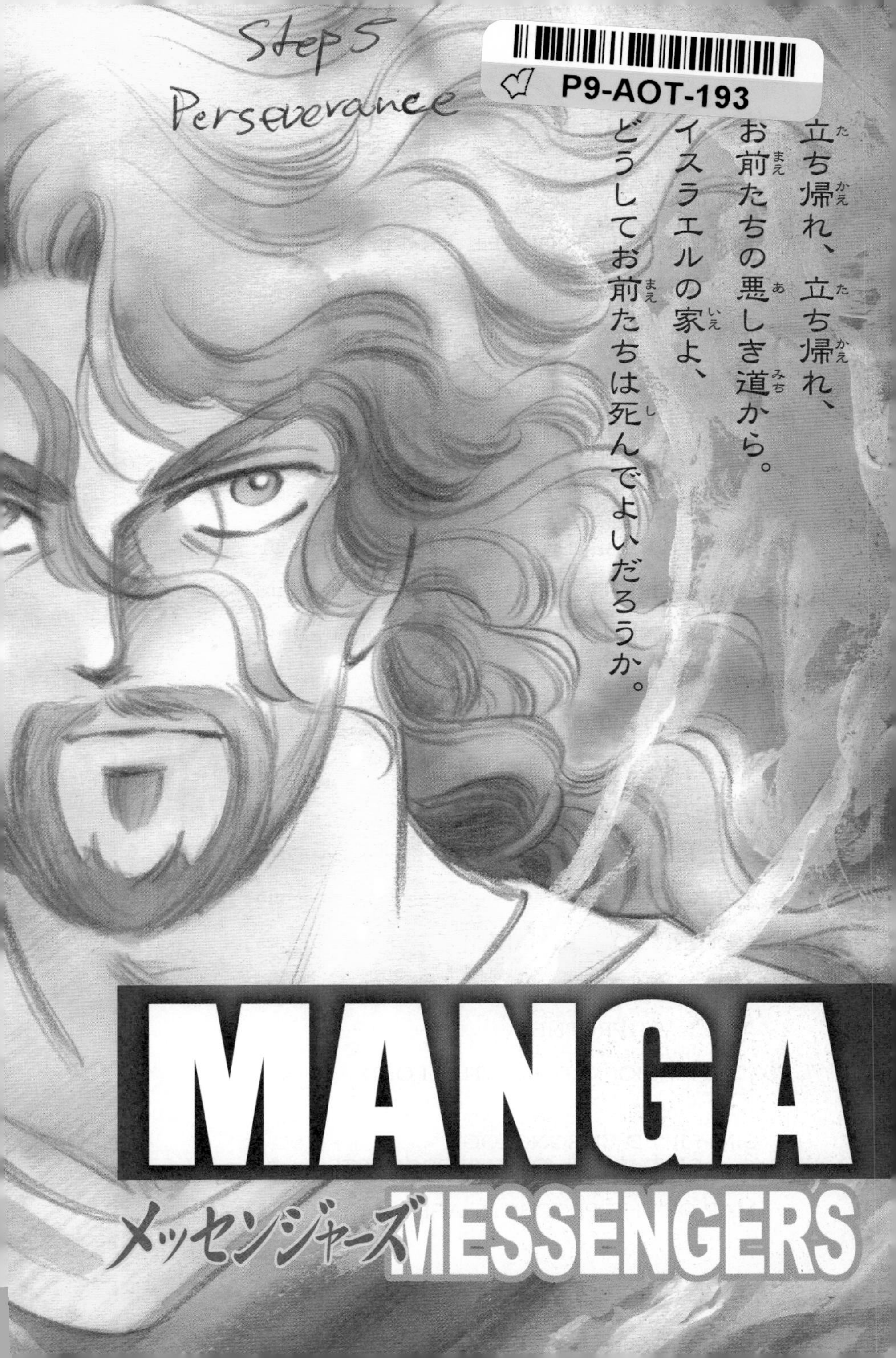
立ち帰れ、立ち帰れ、
お前たちの悪しき道から。
イスラエルの家よ、
どうしてお前たちは死んでよいだろうか。
MANGA
メッセンジャーズ
MESSENGERS

CONTENTS

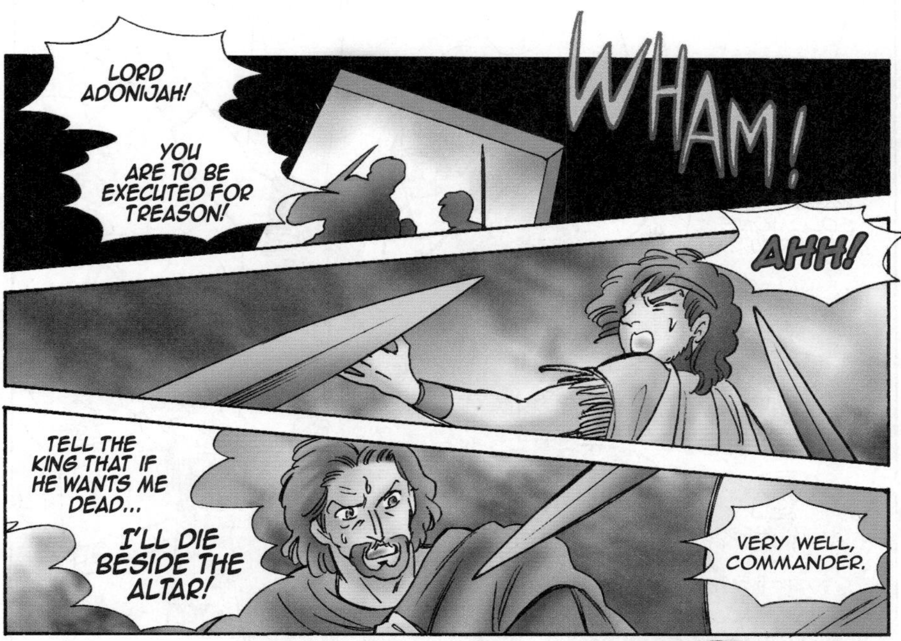
LORD ADONIJAH!
YOU ARE TO BE EXECUTED FOR TREASON!
WHAM!
AHH!
TELL THE KING THAT IF HE WANTS ME DEAD...
I'LL DIE BESIDE THE ALTAR!
VERY WELL, COMMANDER.

1. Construction of the Temple

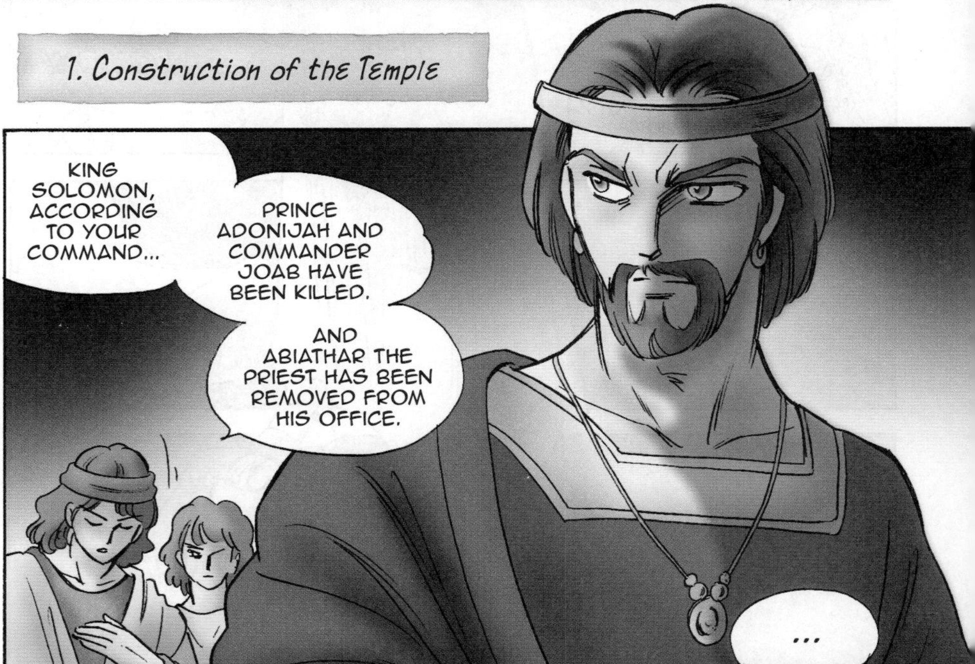
KING SOLOMON, ACCORDING TO YOUR COMMAND...
PRINCE ADONIJAH AND COMMANDER JOAB HAVE BEEN KILLED.
AND ABIATHAR THE PRIEST HAS BEEN REMOVED FROM HIS OFFICE.
...

WITH THE DEATH OF HIS RIVALS, THE KINGDOM WAS FIRMLY IN SOLOMON'S CONTROL.
HOORAY
LONG LIVE THE KING!
HURRAH
KING SOLOMON!
O LORD MY GOD, I WILL DO AS YOU HAVE REQUESTED THROUGH MY FATHER, DAVID...
I WILL BUILD THE TEMPLE OF THE LORD.
SOLOMON!

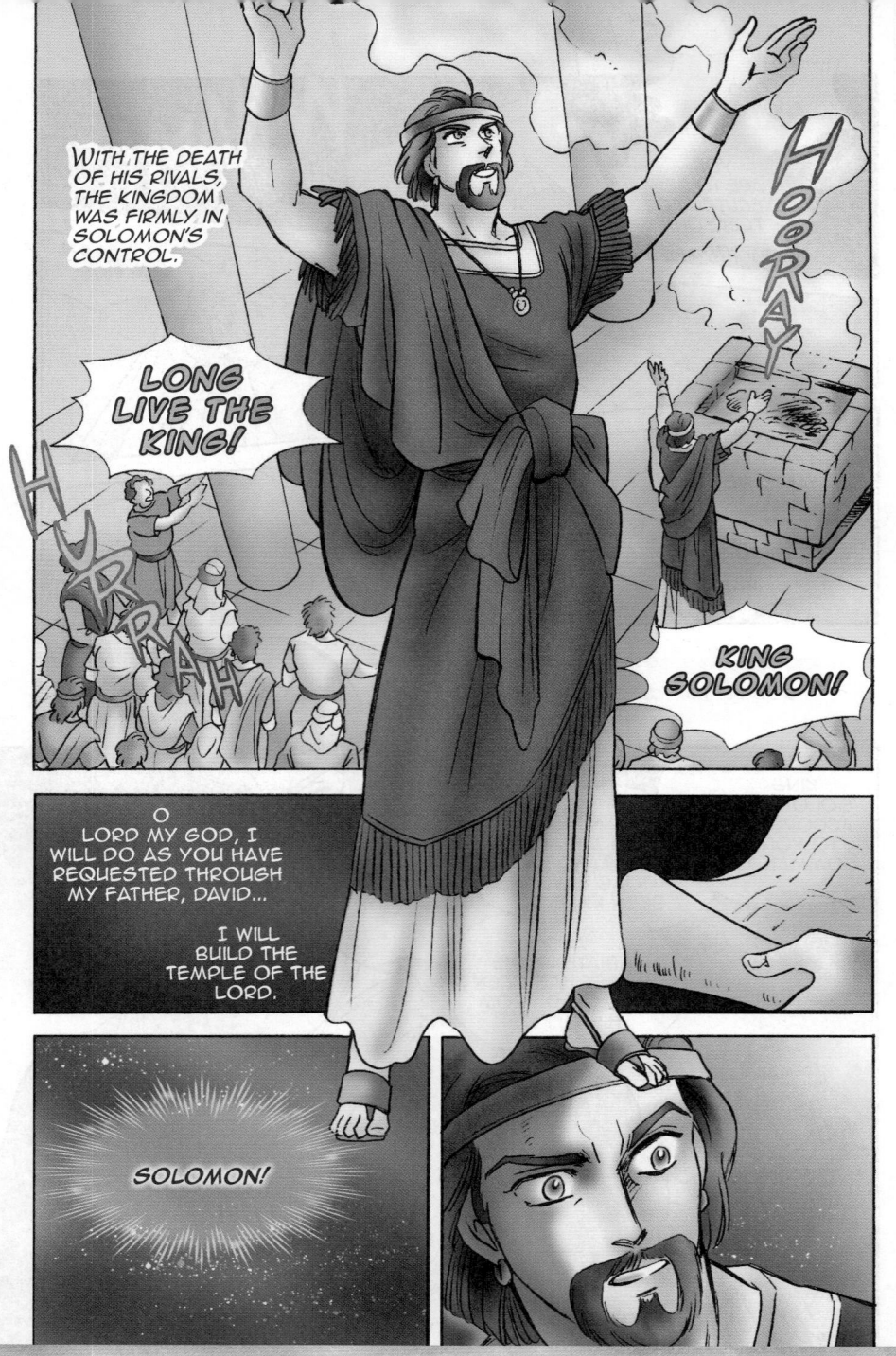

1 Kings 2:12; 3:4-15

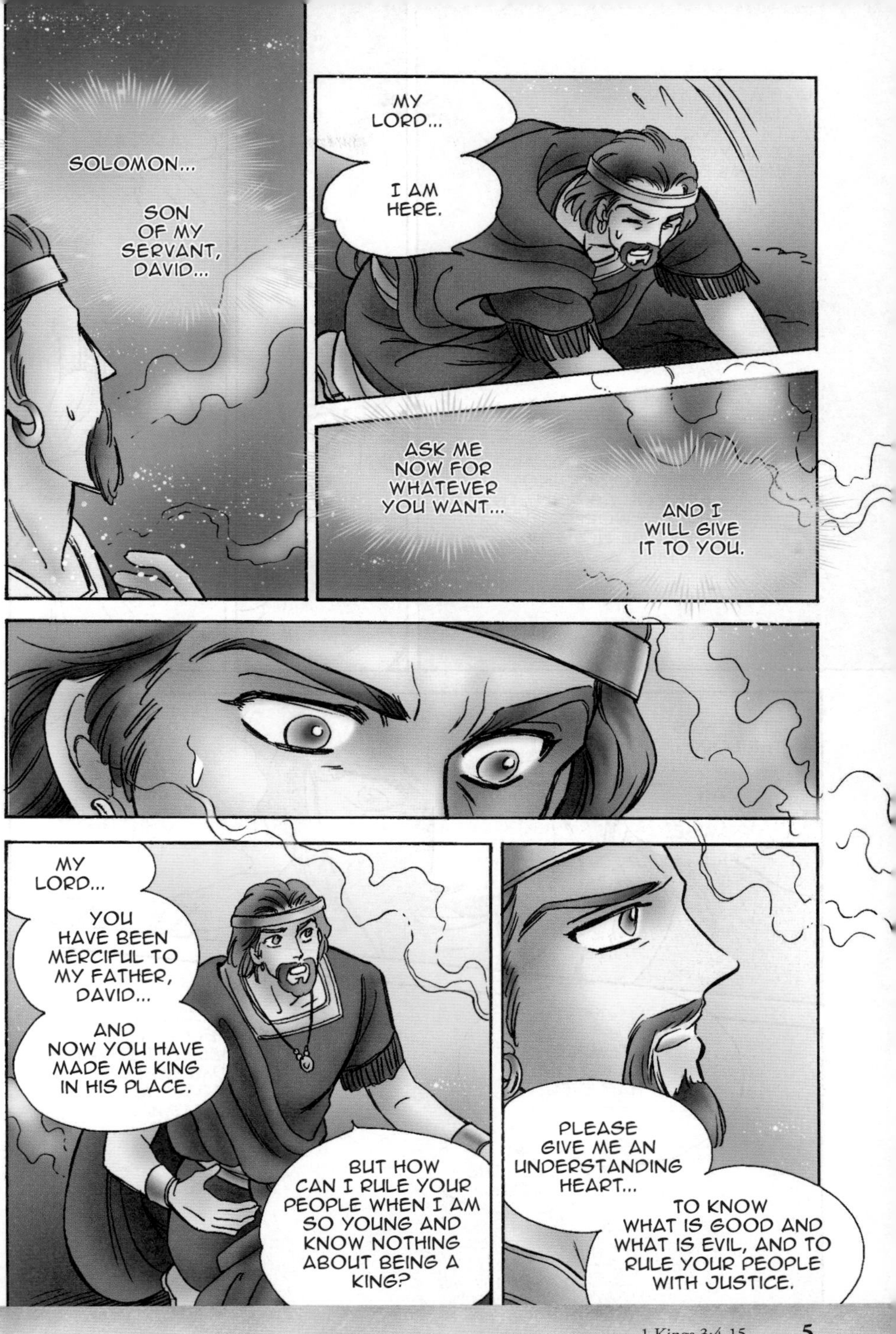
SOLOMON...
SON OF MY SERVANT, DAVID...
MY LORD...
I AM HERE.
ASK ME NOW FOR WHATEVER YOU WANT...
AND I WILL GIVE IT TO YOU.
MY LORD...
YOU HAVE BEEN MERCIFUL TO MY FATHER, DAVID...
AND NOW YOU HAVE MADE ME KING IN HIS PLACE.
BUT HOW CAN I RULE YOUR PEOPLE WHEN I AM SO YOUNG AND KNOW NOTHING ABOUT BEING A KING?
PLEASE GIVE ME AN UNDERSTANDING HEART...
TO KNOW WHAT IS GOOD AND WHAT IS EVIL, AND TO RULE YOUR PEOPLE WITH JUSTICE.

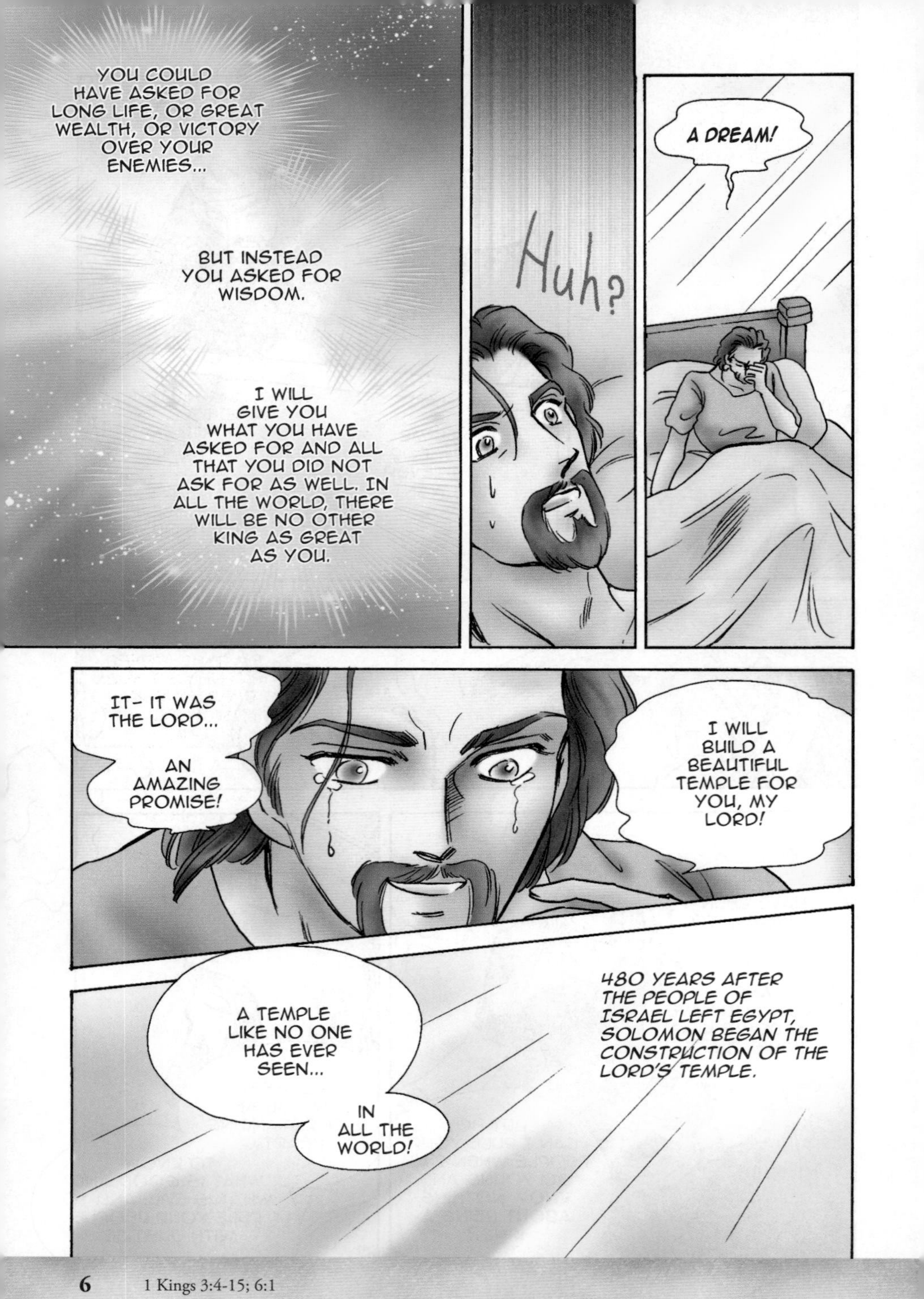
YOU COULD HAVE ASKED FOR LONG LIFE, OR GREAT WEALTH, OR VICTORY OVER YOUR ENEMIES...
BUT INSTEAD YOU ASKED FOR WISDOM.
I WILL GIVE YOU WHAT YOU HAVE ASKED FOR AND ALL THAT YOU DID NOT ASK FOR AS WELL. IN ALL THE WORLD, THERE WILL BE NO OTHER KING AS GREAT AS YOU.
Huh?
A DREAM!
IT- IT WAS THE LORD...
AN AMAZING PROMISE!
I WILL BUILD A BEAUTIFUL TEMPLE FOR YOU, MY LORD!
A TEMPLE LIKE NO ONE HAS EVER SEEN...
IN ALL THE WORLD!
480 YEARS AFTER THE PEOPLE OF ISRAEL LEFT EGYPT, SOLOMON BEGAN THE CONSTRUCTION OF THE LORD'S TEMPLE.

 1 Kings 3:4-15; 6:1

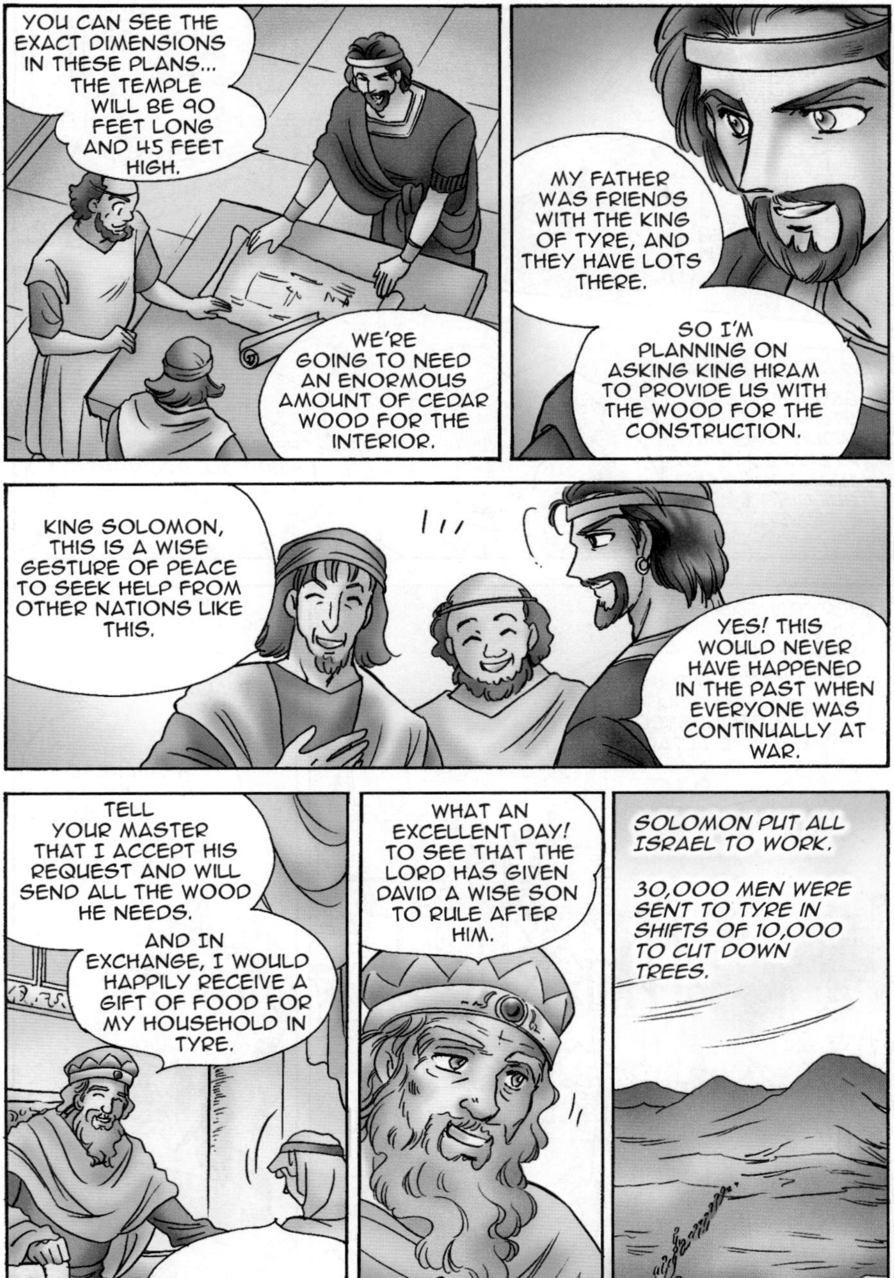
YOU CAN SEE THE EXACT DIMENSIONS IN THESE PLANS... THE TEMPLE WILL BE 90 FEET LONG AND 45 FEET HIGH.
WE'RE GOING TO NEED AN ENORMOUS AMOUNT OF CEDAR WOOD FOR THE INTERIOR.
MY FATHER WAS FRIENDS WITH THE KING OF TYRE, AND THEY HAVE LOTS THERE.
SO I'M PLANNING ON ASKING KING HIRAM TO PROVIDE US WITH THE WOOD FOR THE CONSTRUCTION.
KING SOLOMON, THIS IS A WISE GESTURE OF PEACE TO SEEK HELP FROM OTHER NATIONS LIKE THIS.
YES! THIS WOULD NEVER HAVE HAPPENED IN THE PAST WHEN EVERYONE WAS CONTINUALLY AT WAR.
TELL YOUR MASTER THAT I ACCEPT HIS REQUEST AND WILL SEND ALL THE WOOD HE NEEDS.
AND IN EXCHANGE, I WOULD HAPPILY RECEIVE A GIFT OF FOOD FOR MY HOUSEHOLD IN TYRE.
YES, SIR.
WHAT AN EXCELLENT DAY! TO SEE THAT THE LORD HAS GIVEN DAVID A WISE SON TO RULE AFTER HIM.
SOLOMON PUT ALL ISRAEL TO WORK.
30,000 MEN WERE SENT TO TYRE IN SHIFTS OF 10,000 TO CUT DOWN TREES.

70,000 MEN WERE BROUGHT TO MOVE WOOD AND STONE...

3,600 MEN SUPERVISED THE WORKERS.

80,000 MEN CUT STONE FROM THE MOUNTAINS AND PREPARED IT FOR TRANSPORT AND BUILDING.

THE STONE AND WOOD WERE ALL BROUGHT TO JERUSALEM WHERE THE TEMPLE WOULD BE CONSTRUCTED.

EVERYTHING IS PROCEEDING WELL, YOUR HIGHNESS.

WE HAVE THE GOLD YOU REQUESTED FOR THE ALTAR AND THE MOST HOLY PLACE.

THE HOLY OBJECTS WILL NEED TO BE CREATED WITH EXTRAORDINARY CARE...

WE'LL NEED HIGHLY SKILLED CRAFTSMEN.

VERY GOOD.

1 Kings 5:1–6:38; 7:13–9:9; 10:11

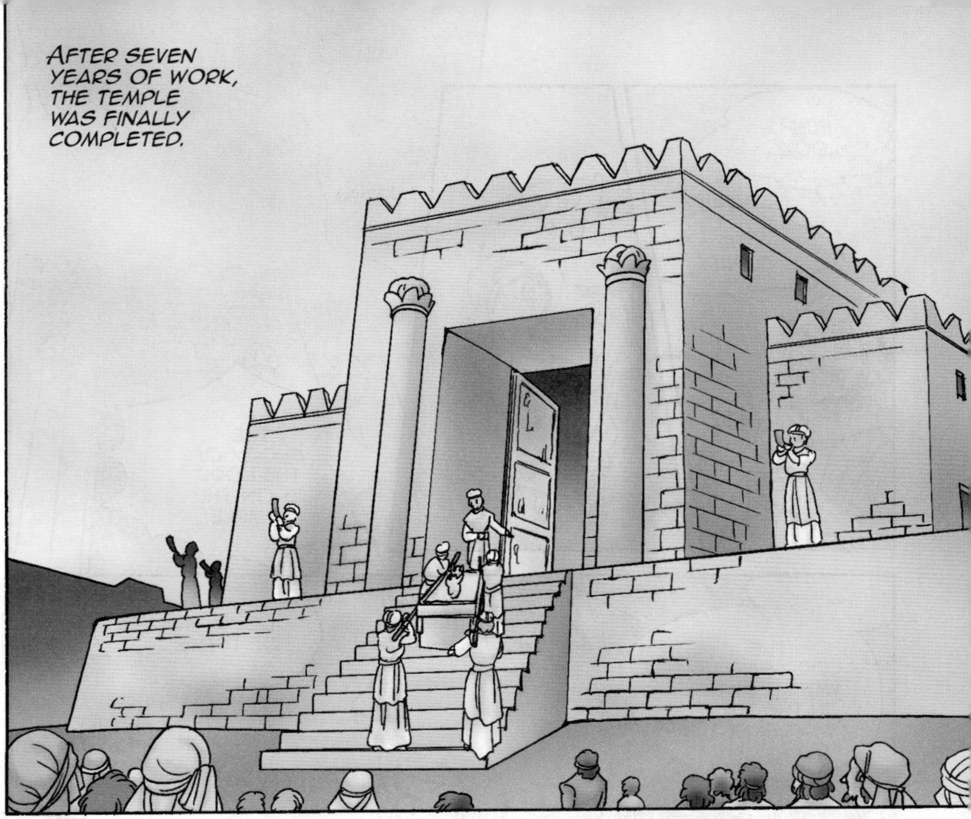
AFTER SEVEN YEARS OF WORK, THE TEMPLE WAS FINALLY COMPLETED.

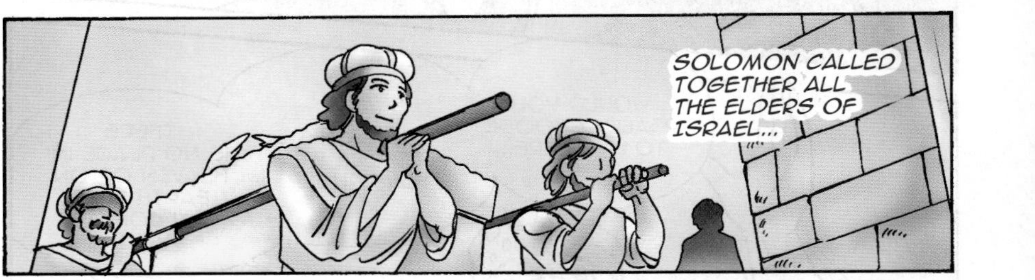
SOLOMON CALLED TOGETHER ALL THE ELDERS OF ISRAEL...

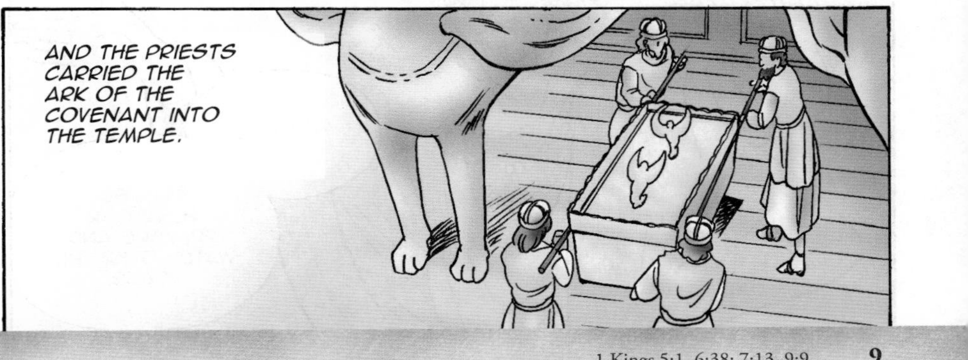
AND THE PRIESTS CARRIED THE ARK OF THE COVENANT INTO THE TEMPLE.

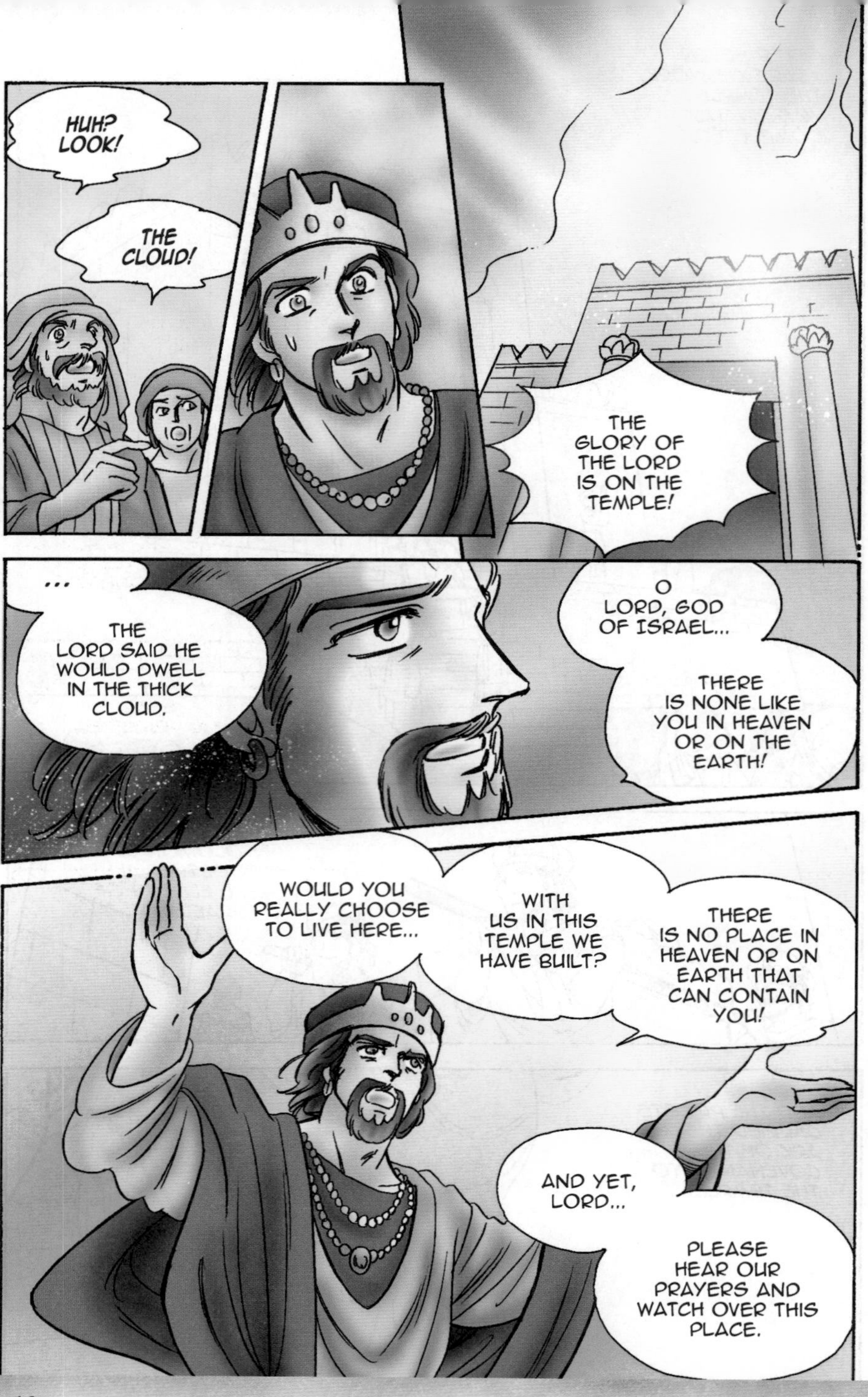
HUH? LOOK!
THE CLOUD!
THE GLORY OF THE LORD IS ON THE TEMPLE!
...
THE LORD SAID HE WOULD DWELL IN THE THICK CLOUD.
O LORD, GOD OF ISRAEL...
THERE IS NONE LIKE YOU IN HEAVEN OR ON THE EARTH!
...
WOULD YOU REALLY CHOOSE TO LIVE HERE...
WITH US IN THIS TEMPLE WE HAVE BUILT?
THERE IS NO PLACE IN HEAVEN OR ON EARTH THAT CAN CONTAIN YOU!
AND YET, LORD...
PLEASE HEAR OUR PRAYERS AND WATCH OVER THIS PLACE.

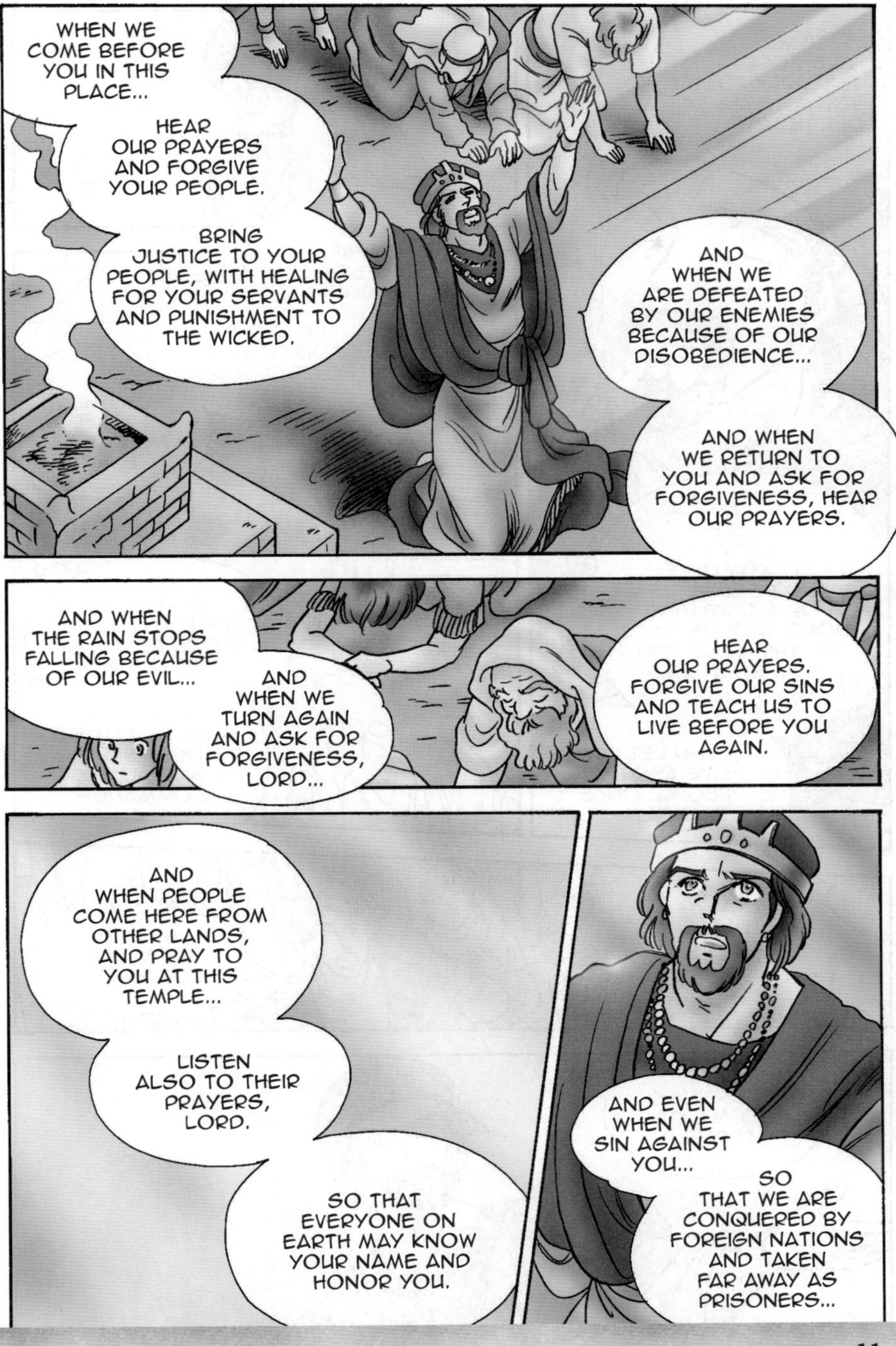
WHEN WE COME BEFORE YOU IN THIS PLACE...
HEAR OUR PRAYERS AND FORGIVE YOUR PEOPLE.
BRING JUSTICE TO YOUR PEOPLE, WITH HEALING FOR YOUR SERVANTS AND PUNISHMENT TO THE WICKED.
AND WHEN WE ARE DEFEATED BY OUR ENEMIES BECAUSE OF OUR DISOBEDIENCE...
AND WHEN WE RETURN TO YOU AND ASK FOR FORGIVENESS, HEAR OUR PRAYERS.
AND WHEN THE RAIN STOPS FALLING BECAUSE OF OUR EVIL...
AND WHEN WE TURN AGAIN AND ASK FOR FORGIVENESS, LORD...
HEAR OUR PRAYERS. FORGIVE OUR SINS AND TEACH US TO LIVE BEFORE YOU AGAIN.
AND WHEN PEOPLE COME HERE FROM OTHER LANDS, AND PRAY TO YOU AT THIS TEMPLE...
LISTEN ALSO TO THEIR PRAYERS, LORD.
SO THAT EVERYONE ON EARTH MAY KNOW YOUR NAME AND HONOR YOU.
AND EVEN WHEN WE SIN AGAINST YOU...
SO THAT WE ARE CONQUERED BY FOREIGN NATIONS AND TAKEN FAR AWAY AS PRISONERS...

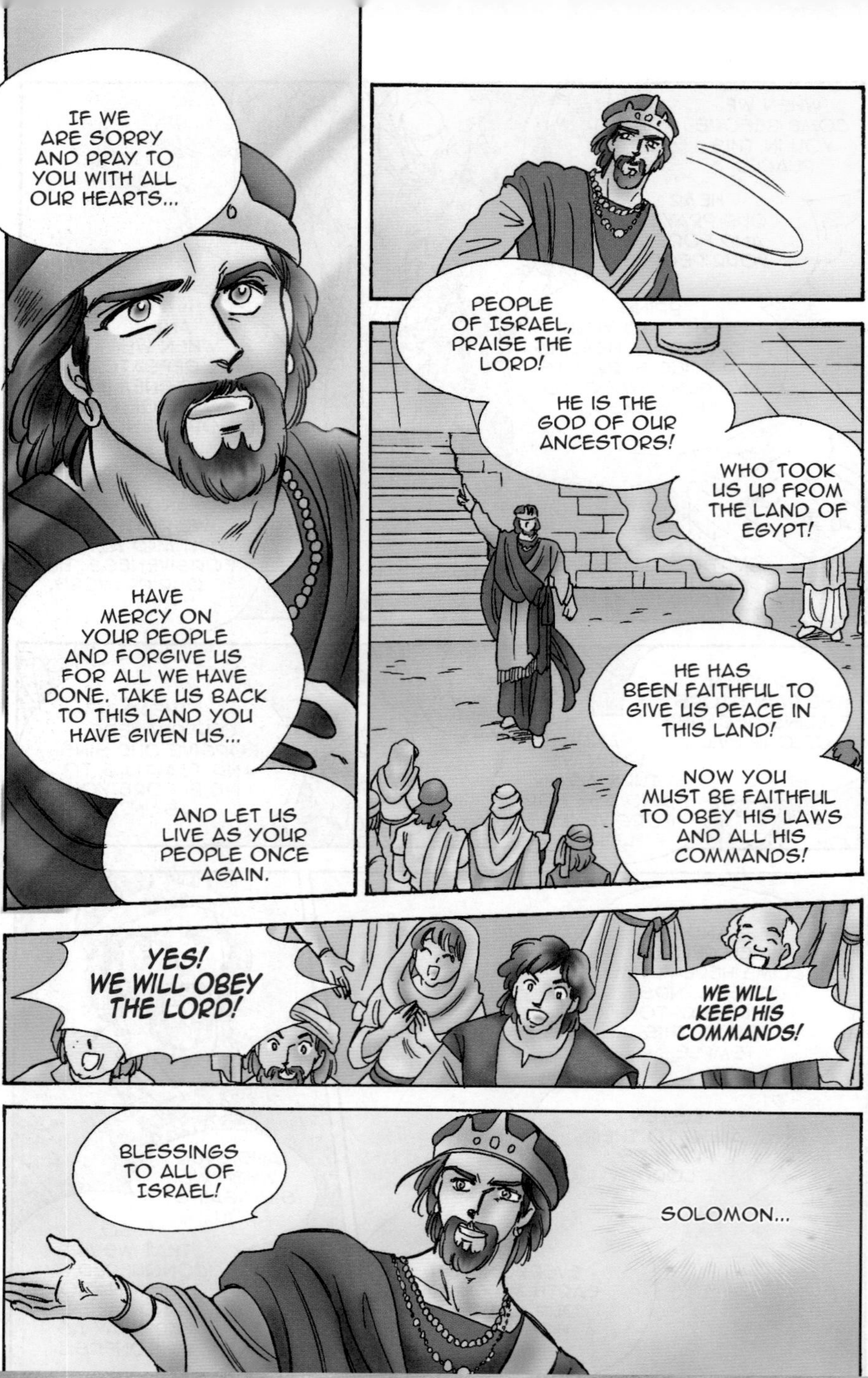
IF WE ARE SORRY AND PRAY TO YOU WITH ALL OUR HEARTS...
HAVE MERCY ON YOUR PEOPLE AND FORGIVE US FOR ALL WE HAVE DONE. TAKE US BACK TO THIS LAND YOU HAVE GIVEN US...
AND LET US LIVE AS YOUR PEOPLE ONCE AGAIN.
PEOPLE OF ISRAEL, PRAISE THE LORD!
HE IS THE GOD OF OUR ANCESTORS!
WHO TOOK US UP FROM THE LAND OF EGYPT!
HE HAS BEEN FAITHFUL TO GIVE US PEACE IN THIS LAND!
NOW YOU MUST BE FAITHFUL TO OBEY HIS LAWS AND ALL HIS COMMANDS!
YES! WE WILL OBEY THE LORD!
WE WILL KEEP HIS COMMANDS!
BLESSINGS TO ALL OF ISRAEL!
SOLOMON...

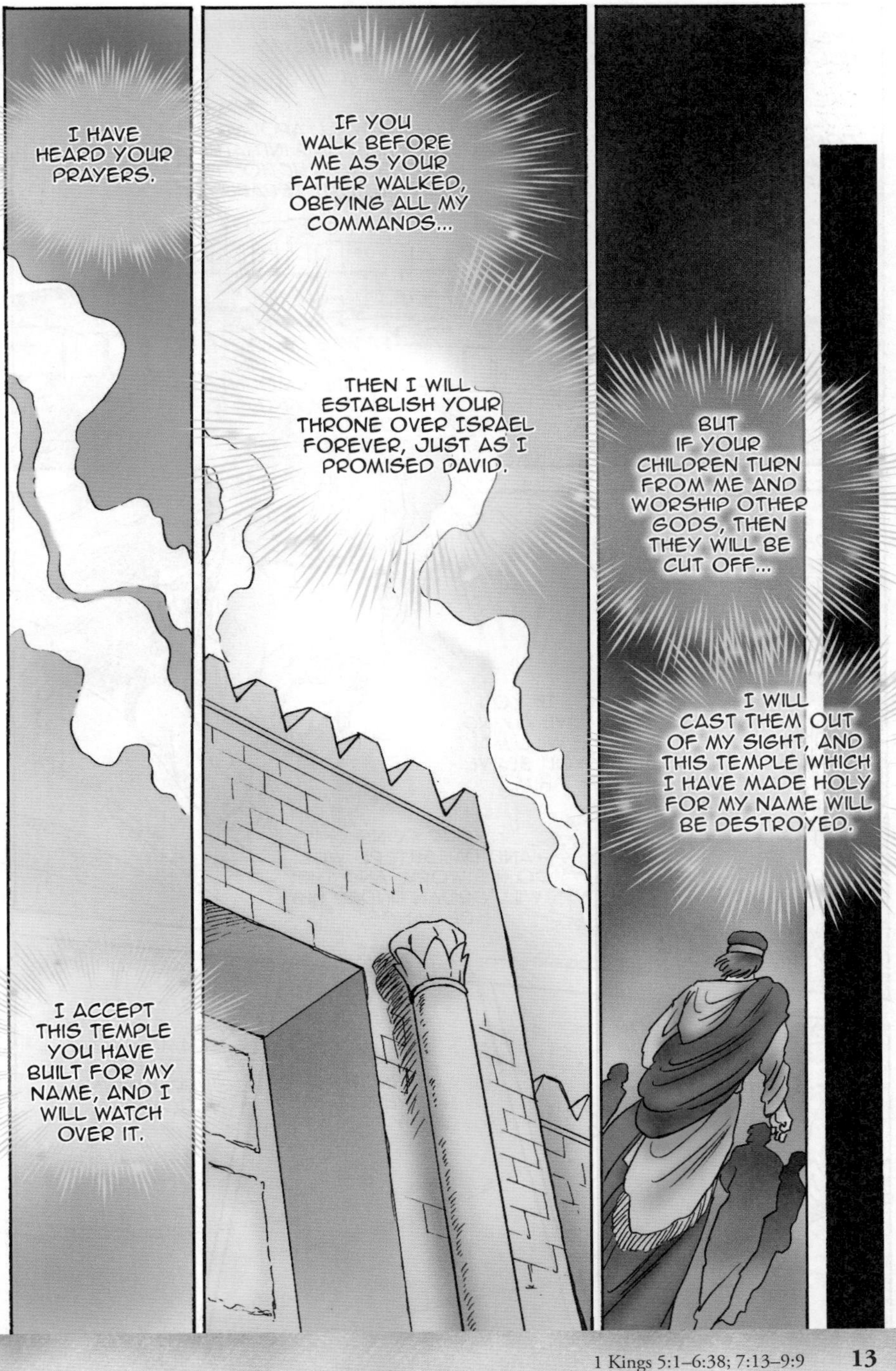

I HAVE HEARD YOUR PRAYERS.
I ACCEPT THIS TEMPLE YOU HAVE BUILT FOR MY NAME, AND I WILL WATCH OVER IT.
IF YOU WALK BEFORE ME AS YOUR FATHER WALKED, OBEYING ALL MY COMMANDS...
THEN I WILL ESTABLISH YOUR THRONE OVER ISRAEL FOREVER, JUST AS I PROMISED DAVID.
BUT IF YOUR CHILDREN TURN FROM ME AND WORSHIP OTHER GODS, THEN THEY WILL BE CUT OFF...
I WILL CAST THEM OUT OF MY SIGHT, AND THIS TEMPLE WHICH I HAVE MADE HOLY FOR MY NAME WILL BE DESTROYED.

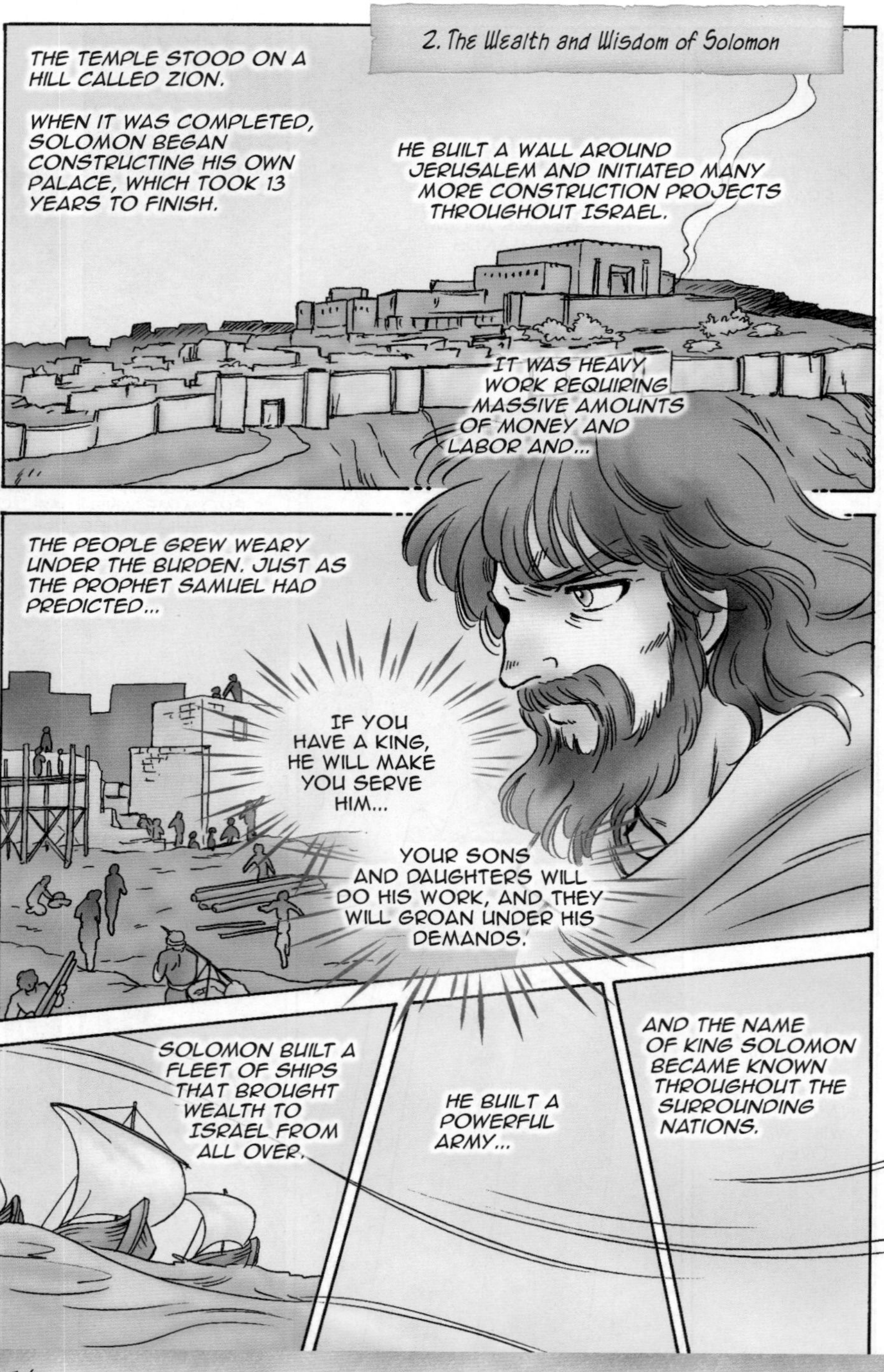
2. The Wealth and Wisdom of Solomon
THE TEMPLE STOOD ON A HILL CALLED ZION.
WHEN IT WAS COMPLETED, SOLOMON BEGAN CONSTRUCTING HIS OWN PALACE, WHICH TOOK 13 YEARS TO FINISH.
HE BUILT A WALL AROUND JERUSALEM AND INITIATED MANY MORE CONSTRUCTION PROJECTS THROUGHOUT ISRAEL.
IT WAS HEAVY WORK REQUIRING MASSIVE AMOUNTS OF MONEY AND LABOR AND...
THE PEOPLE GREW WEARY UNDER THE BURDEN. JUST AS THE PROPHET SAMUEL HAD PREDICTED...
IF YOU HAVE A KING, HE WILL MAKE YOU SERVE HIM...
YOUR SONS AND DAUGHTERS WILL DO HIS WORK, AND THEY WILL GROAN UNDER HIS DEMANDS.'
SOLOMON BUILT A FLEET OF SHIPS THAT BROUGHT WEALTH TO ISRAEL FROM ALL OVER.
HE BUILT A POWERFUL ARMY...
AND THE NAME OF KING SOLOMON BECAME KNOWN THROUGHOUT THE SURROUNDING NATIONS.

1 Samuel 8:10-18; 1 Kings 8:1; 9:10-28

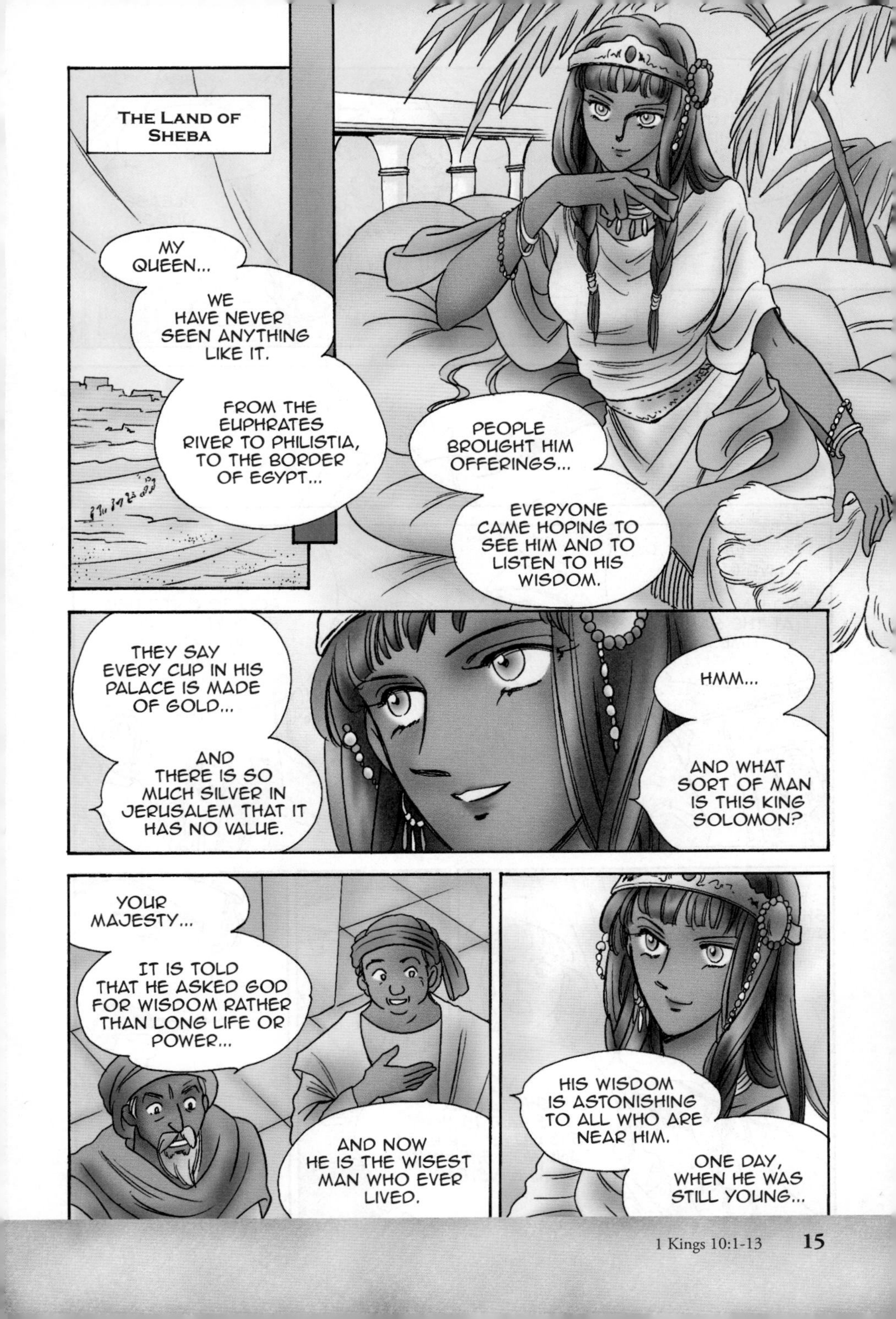

The Land of Sheba
My queen...
We have never seen anything like it.
From the Euphrates River to Philistia, to the border of Egypt...
People brought him offerings...
Everyone came hoping to see him and to listen to his wisdom.
They say every cup in his palace is made of gold...
And there is so much silver in Jerusalem that it has no value.
Hmm...
And what sort of man is this King Solomon?
Your majesty...
It is told that he asked God for wisdom rather than long life or power...
And now he is the wisest man who ever lived.
His wisdom is astonishing to all who are near him.
One day, when he was still young...

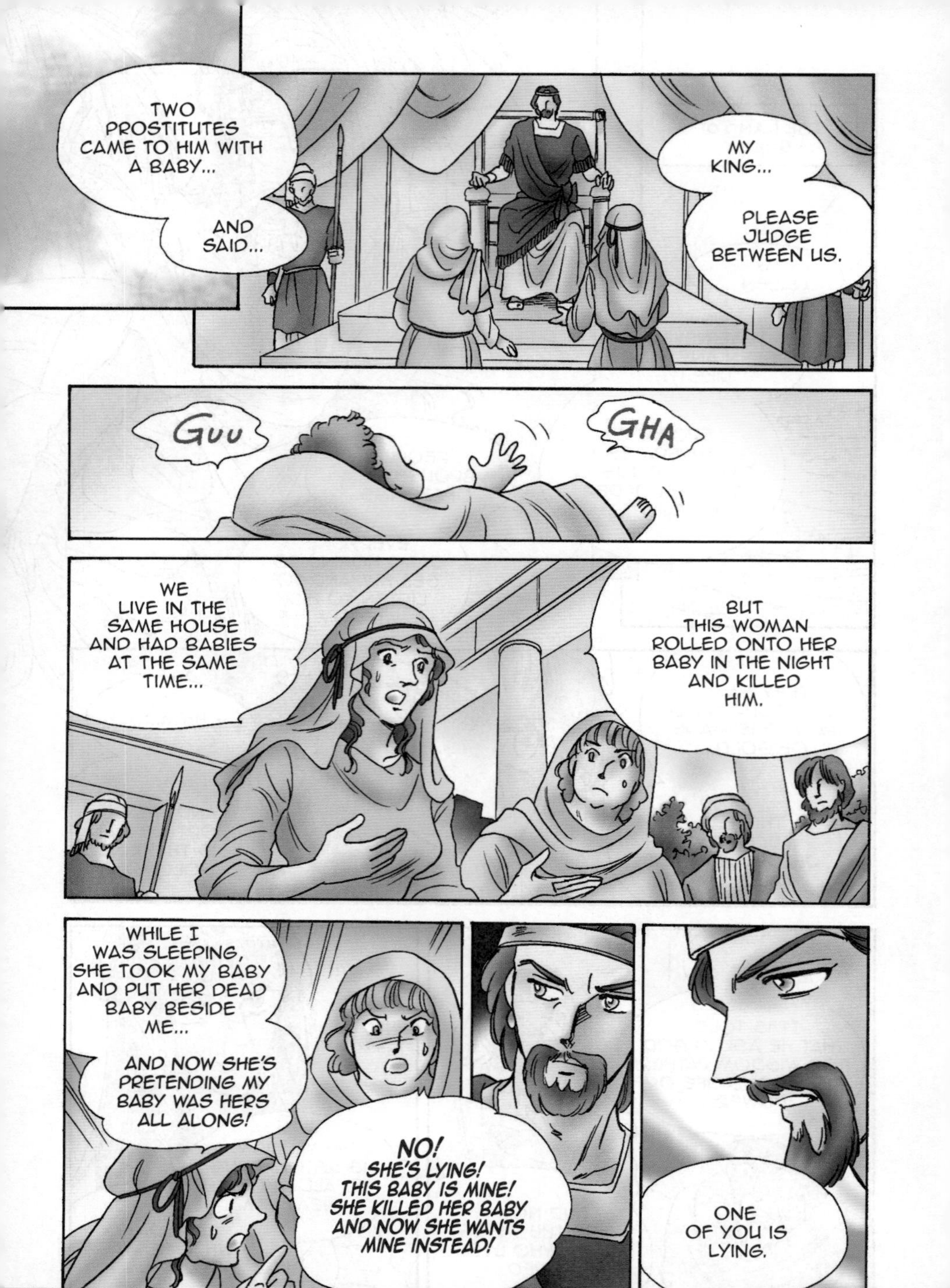
TWO PROSTITUTES CAME TO HIM WITH A BABY...
AND SAID...
MY KING...
PLEASE JUDGE BETWEEN US.
GUU
GHA
WE LIVE IN THE SAME HOUSE AND HAD BABIES AT THE SAME TIME...
BUT THIS WOMAN ROLLED ONTO HER BABY IN THE NIGHT AND KILLED HIM.
WHILE I WAS SLEEPING, SHE TOOK MY BABY AND PUT HER DEAD BABY BESIDE ME...
AND NOW SHE'S PRETENDING MY BABY WAS HERS ALL ALONG!
NO! SHE'S LYING! THIS BABY IS MINE! SHE KILLED HER BABY AND NOW SHE WANTS MINE INSTEAD!
ONE OF YOU IS LYING.

IT'S HER!

SHE'S THE LIAR!

NO! THE CHILD IS MINE!

SILENCE IN THE PRESENCE OF THE KING!

GIVE ME A SWORD!

THERE'S NO WAY TO KNOW WHICH OF YOU IS LYING.

SO, TO BE FAIR...

I WILL CUT THIS BABY IN TWO...

AND YOU CAN EACH HAVE HALF.

HUH?!

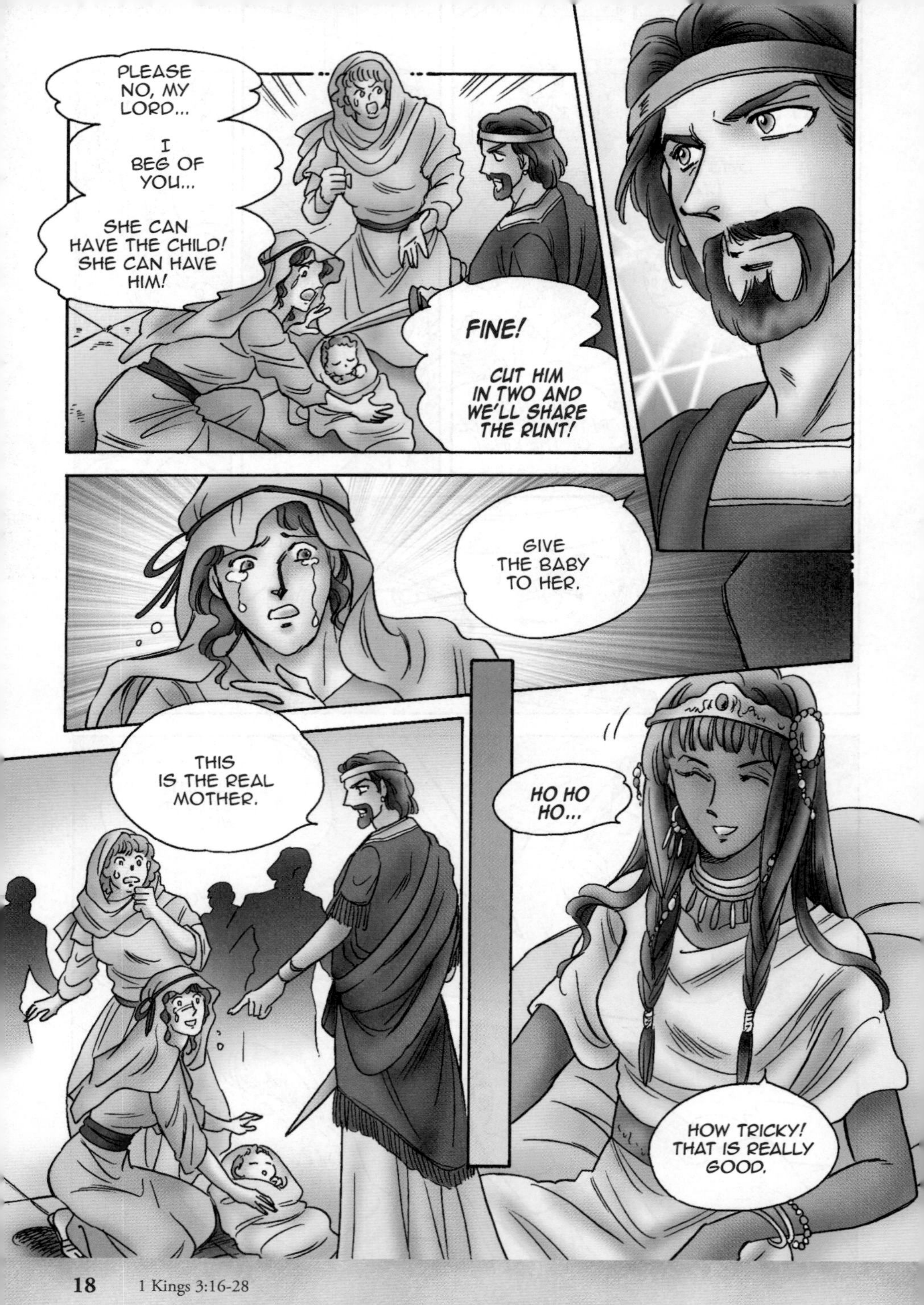
PLEASE NO, MY LORD...
I BEG OF YOU...
SHE CAN HAVE THE CHILD! SHE CAN HAVE HIM!
FINE!
CUT HIM IN TWO AND WE'LL SHARE THE RUNT!
GIVE THE BABY TO HER.
THIS IS THE REAL MOTHER.
HO HO HO...
HOW TRICKY! THAT IS REALLY GOOD.

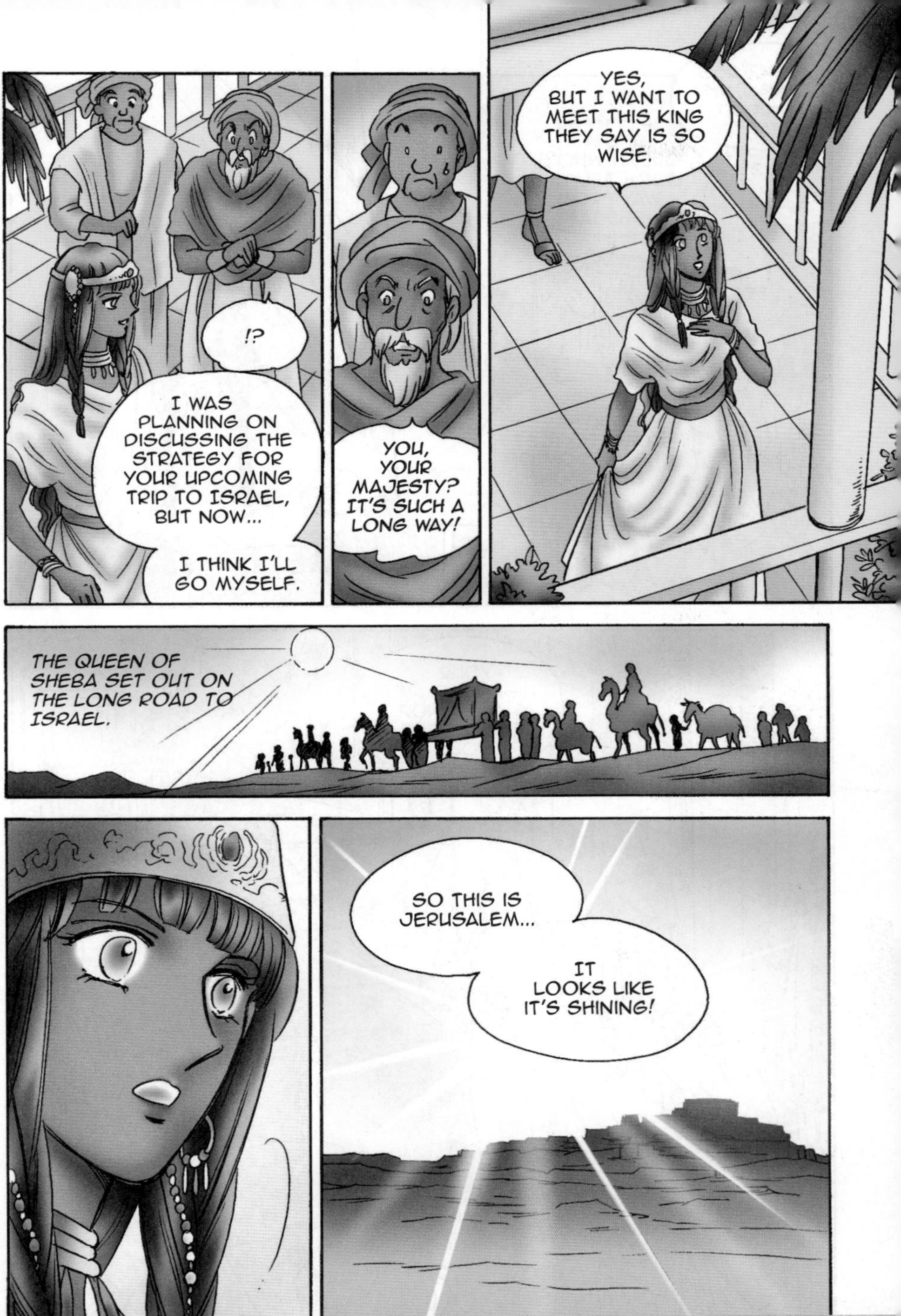
!?
I WAS PLANNING ON DISCUSSING THE STRATEGY FOR YOUR UPCOMING TRIP TO ISRAEL, BUT NOW...
I THINK I'LL GO MYSELF.
YOU, YOUR MAJESTY? IT'S SUCH A LONG WAY!
YES, BUT I WANT TO MEET THIS KING THEY SAY IS SO WISE.
THE QUEEN OF SHEBA SET OUT ON THE LONG ROAD TO ISRAEL.
SO THIS IS JERUSALEM...
IT LOOKS LIKE IT'S SHINING!

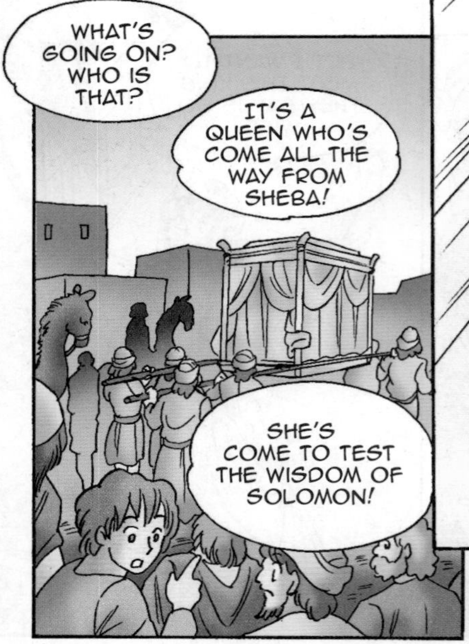
WHAT'S GOING ON? WHO IS THAT?
IT'S A QUEEN WHO'S COME ALL THE WAY FROM SHEBA!
SHE'S COME TO TEST THE WISDOM OF SOLOMON!

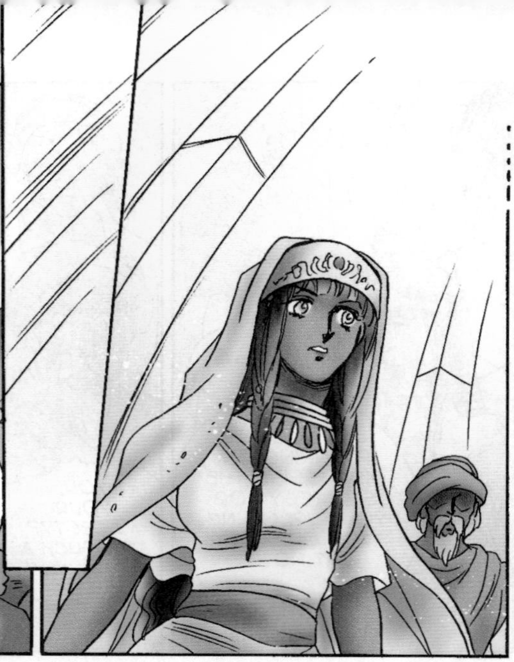

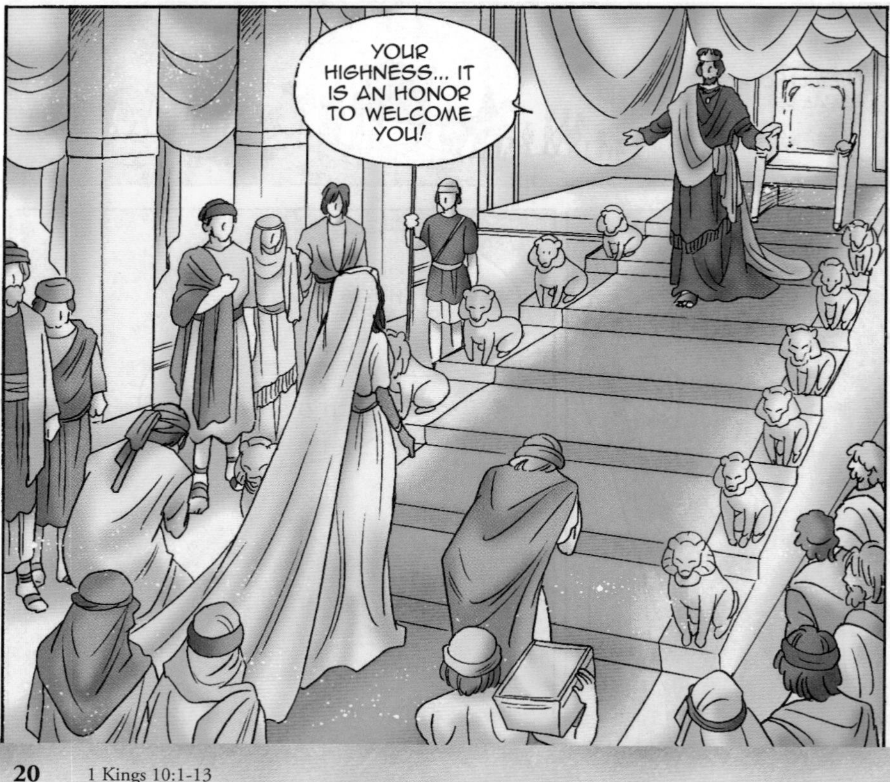
YOUR HIGHNESS... IT IS AN HONOR TO WELCOME YOU!

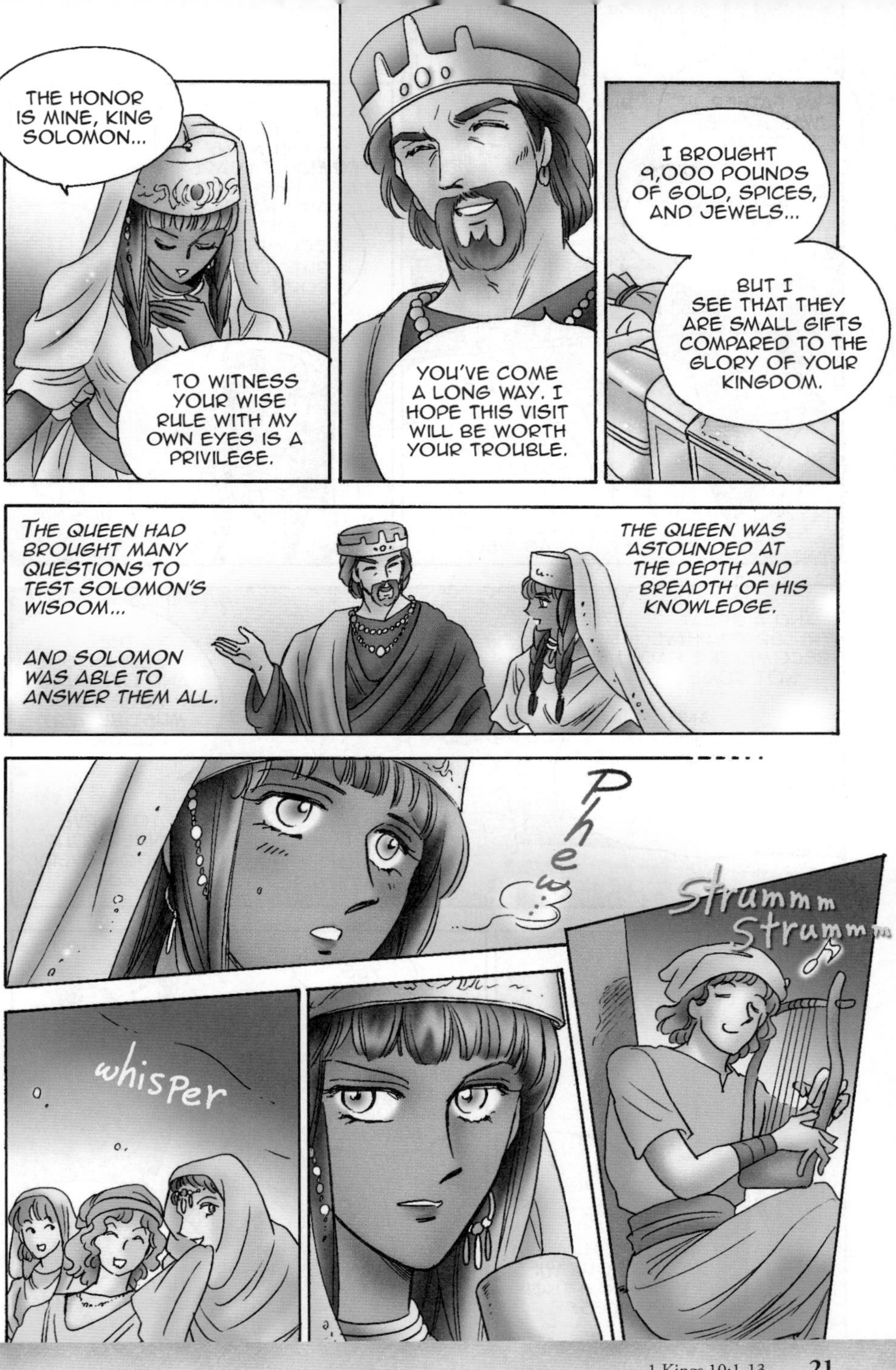
THE HONOR IS MINE, KING SOLOMON...
TO WITNESS YOUR WISE RULE WITH MY OWN EYES IS A PRIVILEGE.
YOU'VE COME A LONG WAY. I HOPE THIS VISIT WILL BE WORTH YOUR TROUBLE.
I BROUGHT 9,000 POUNDS OF GOLD, SPICES, AND JEWELS...
BUT I SEE THAT THEY ARE SMALL GIFTS COMPARED TO THE GLORY OF YOUR KINGDOM.
THE QUEEN HAD BROUGHT MANY QUESTIONS TO TEST SOLOMON'S WISDOM...
AND SOLOMON WAS ABLE TO ANSWER THEM ALL.
THE QUEEN WAS ASTOUNDED AT THE DEPTH AND BREADTH OF HIS KNOWLEDGE.
Phew
Strummm Strummm
whisper

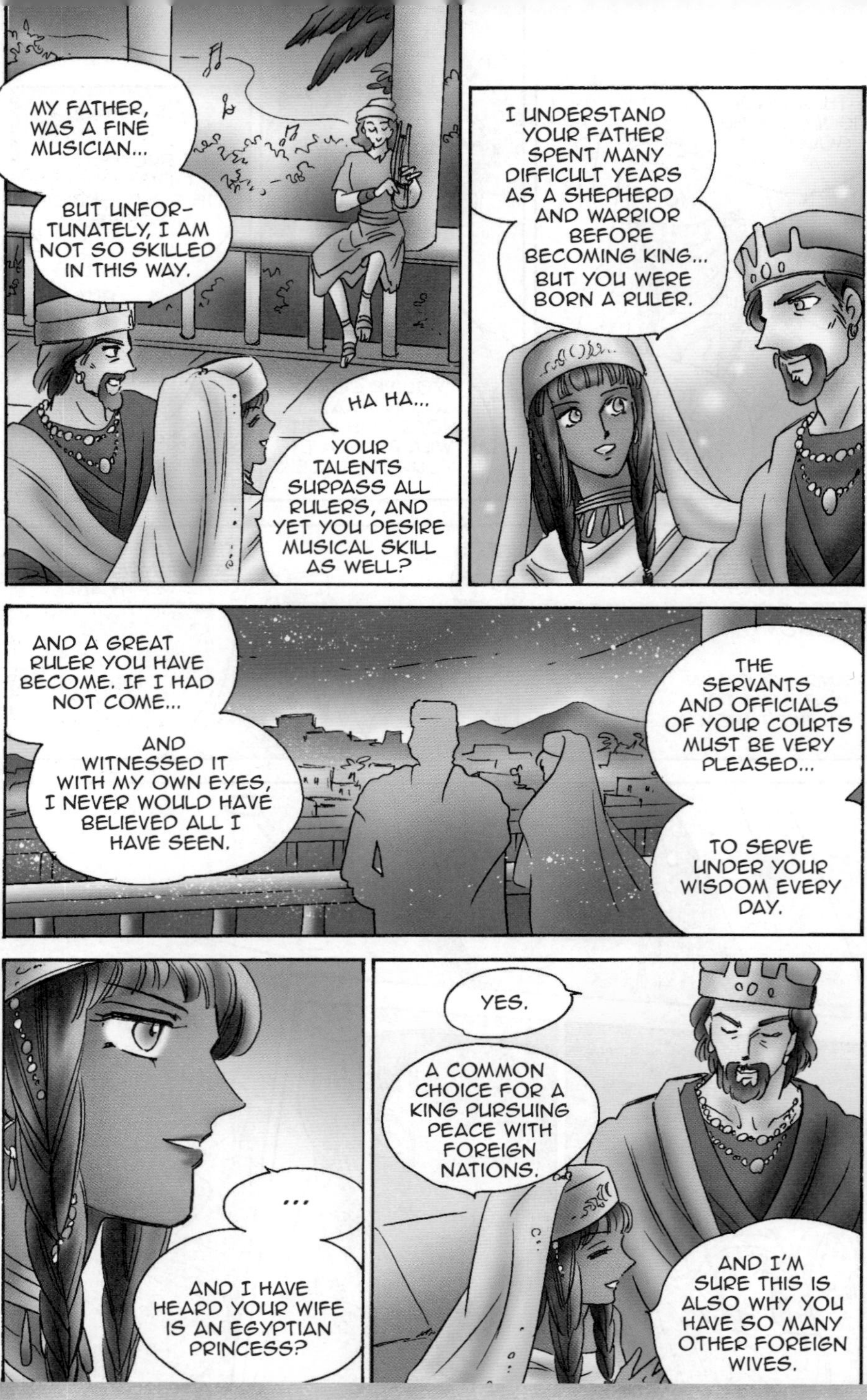
MY FATHER, WAS A FINE MUSICIAN...
BUT UNFORTUNATELY, I AM NOT SO SKILLED IN THIS WAY.
HA HA...
YOUR TALENTS SURPASS ALL RULERS, AND YET YOU DESIRE MUSICAL SKILL AS WELL?
I UNDERSTAND YOUR FATHER SPENT MANY DIFFICULT YEARS AS A SHEPHERD AND WARRIOR BEFORE BECOMING KING...
BUT YOU WERE BORN A RULER.
AND A GREAT RULER YOU HAVE BECOME. IF I HAD NOT COME...
AND WITNESSED IT WITH MY OWN EYES, I NEVER WOULD HAVE BELIEVED ALL I HAVE SEEN.
THE SERVANTS AND OFFICIALS OF YOUR COURTS MUST BE VERY PLEASED...
TO SERVE UNDER YOUR WISDOM EVERY DAY.
...
AND I HAVE HEARD YOUR WIFE IS AN EGYPTIAN PRINCESS?
YES.
A COMMON CHOICE FOR A KING PURSUING PEACE WITH FOREIGN NATIONS.
AND I'M SURE THIS IS ALSO WHY YOU HAVE SO MANY OTHER FOREIGN WIVES.

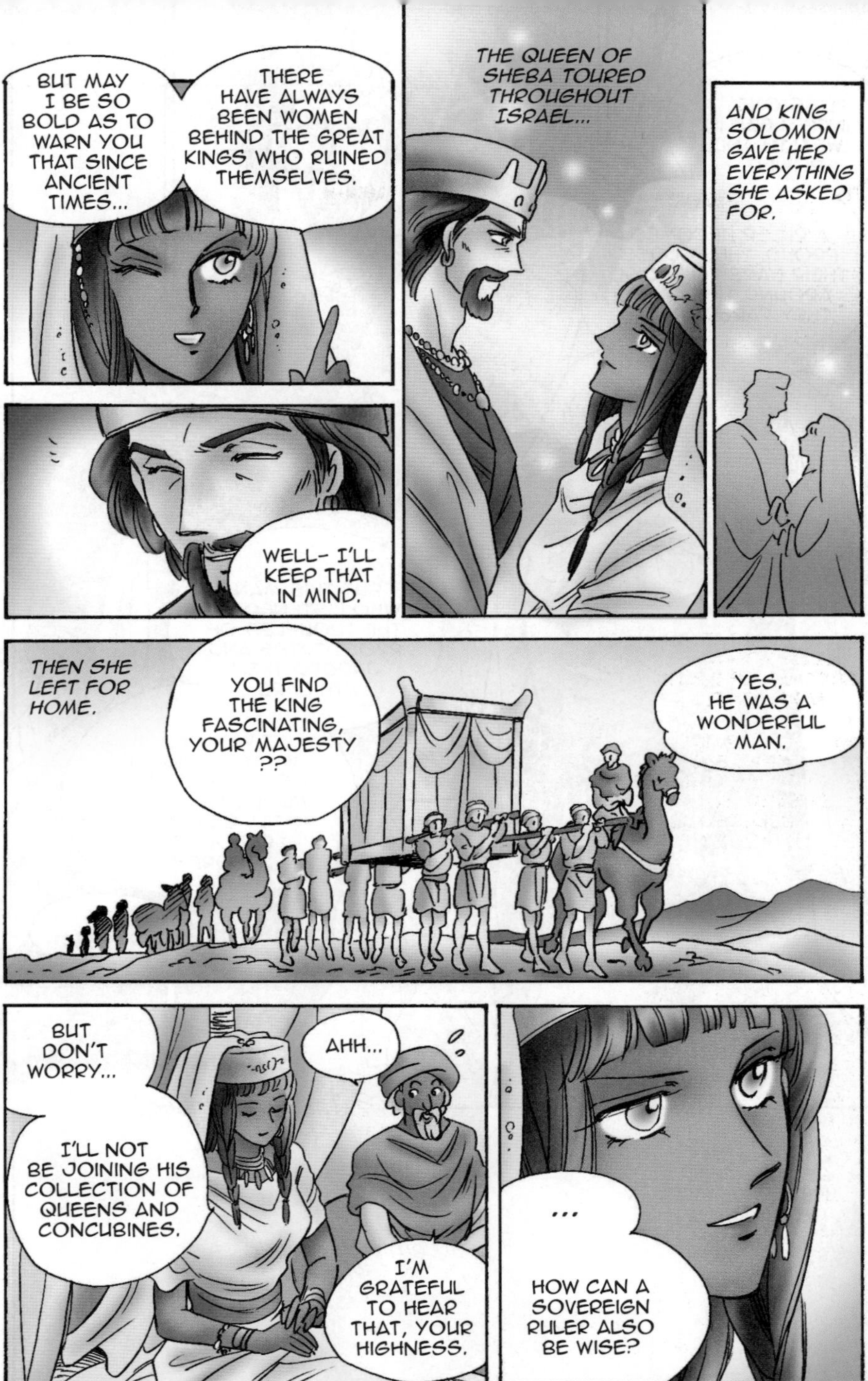

BUT MAY I BE SO BOLD AS TO WARN YOU THAT SINCE ANCIENT TIMES...
THERE HAVE ALWAYS BEEN WOMEN BEHIND THE GREAT KINGS WHO RUINED THEMSELVES.
WELL- I'LL KEEP THAT IN MIND.
THE QUEEN OF SHEBA TOURED THROUGHOUT ISRAEL...
AND KING SOLOMON GAVE HER EVERYTHING SHE ASKED FOR.
THEN SHE LEFT FOR HOME.
YOU FIND THE KING FASCINATING, YOUR MAJESTY ??
YES. HE WAS A WONDERFUL MAN.
BUT DON'T WORRY...
AHH...
I'LL NOT BE JOINING HIS COLLECTION OF QUEENS AND CONCUBINES.
I'M GRATEFUL TO HEAR THAT, YOUR HIGHNESS.
...
HOW CAN A SOVEREIGN RULER ALSO BE WISE?

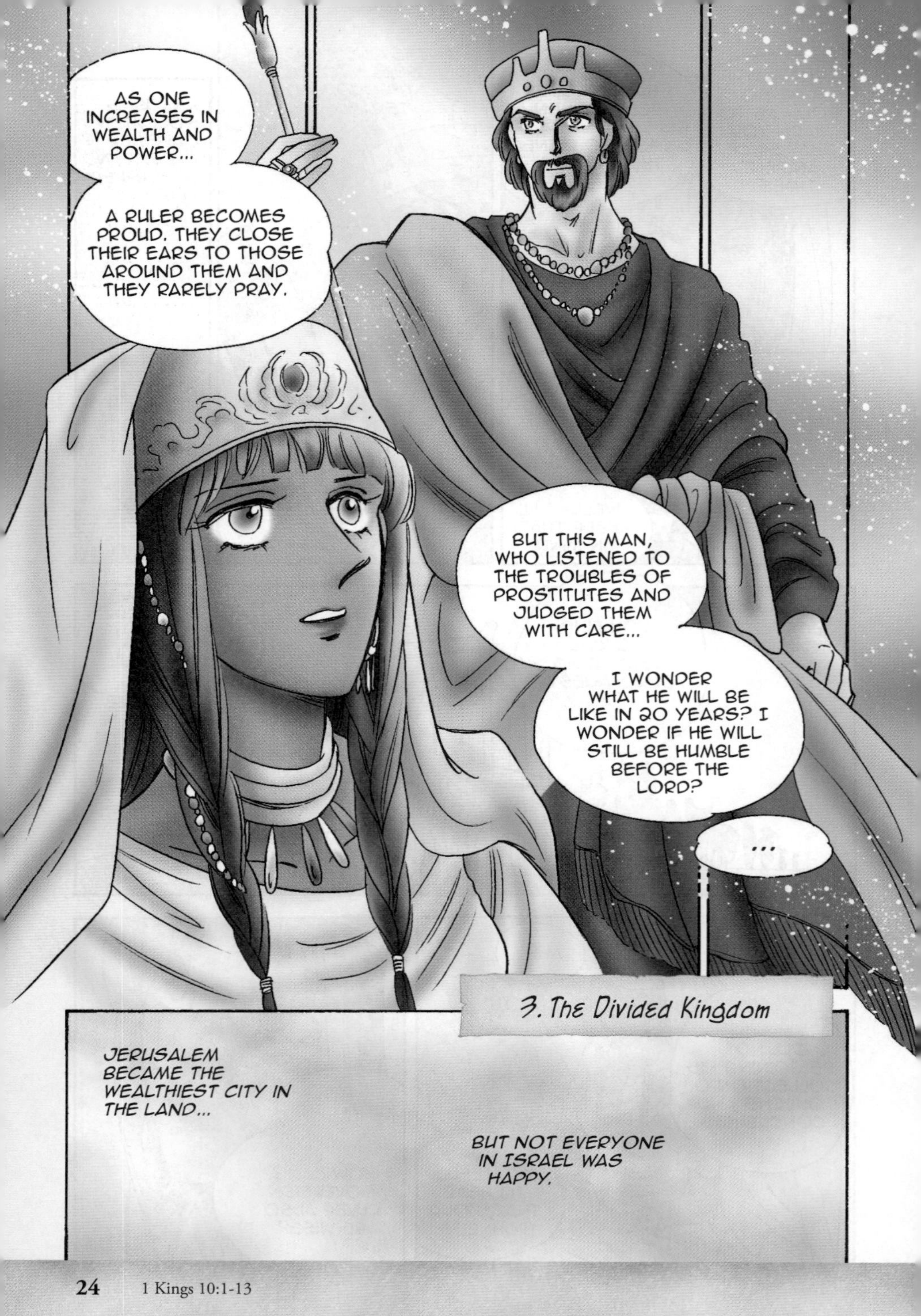
AS ONE INCREASES IN WEALTH AND POWER...
A RULER BECOMES PROUD. THEY CLOSE THEIR EARS TO THOSE AROUND THEM AND THEY RARELY PRAY.
BUT THIS MAN, WHO LISTENED TO THE TROUBLES OF PROSTITUTES AND JUDGED THEM WITH CARE...
I WONDER WHAT HE WILL BE LIKE IN 20 YEARS? I WONDER IF HE WILL STILL BE HUMBLE BEFORE THE LORD?
...
3. The Divided Kingdom
JERUSALEM BECAME THE WEALTHIEST CITY IN THE LAND...
BUT NOT EVERYONE IN ISRAEL WAS HAPPY.

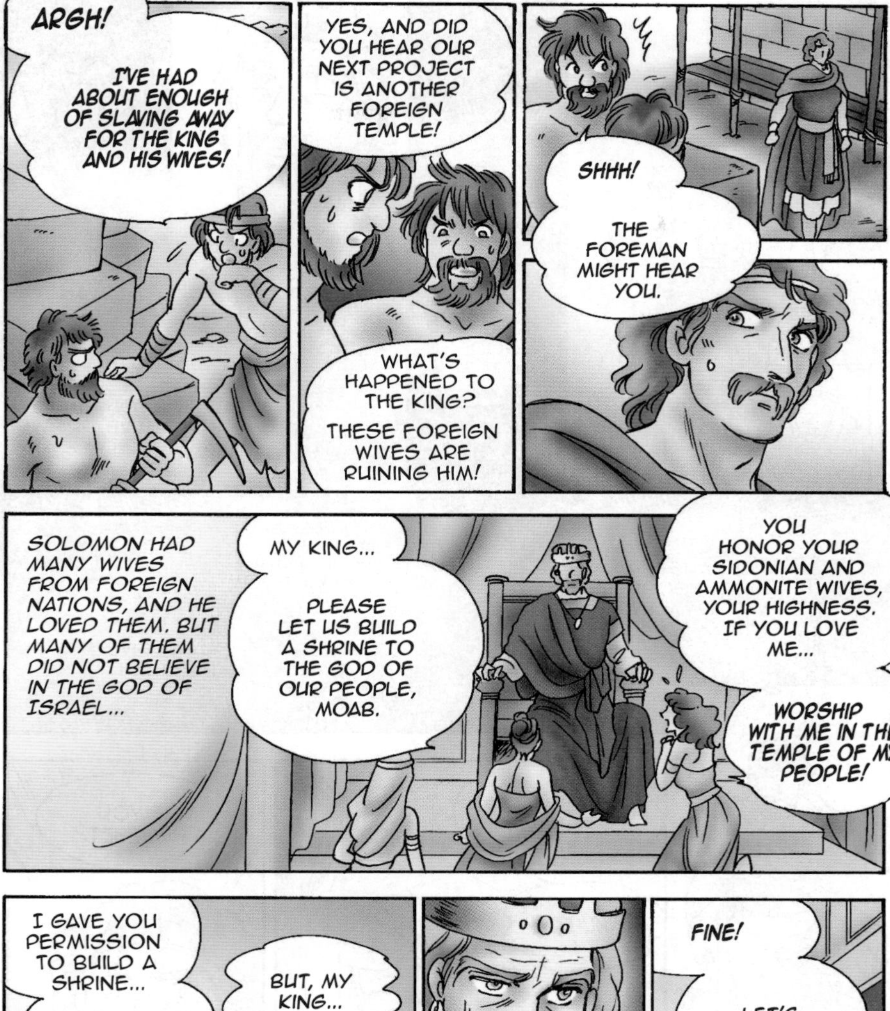
ARGH!
I'VE HAD ABOUT ENOUGH OF SLAVING AWAY FOR THE KING AND HIS WIVES!
YES, AND DID YOU HEAR OUR NEXT PROJECT IS ANOTHER FOREIGN TEMPLE!
WHAT'S HAPPENED TO THE KING?
THESE FOREIGN WIVES ARE RUINING HIM!
SHHH!
THE FOREMAN MIGHT HEAR YOU.
SOLOMON HAD MANY WIVES FROM FOREIGN NATIONS, AND HE LOVED THEM. BUT MANY OF THEM DID NOT BELIEVE IN THE GOD OF ISRAEL...
MY KING...
PLEASE LET US BUILD A SHRINE TO THE GOD OF OUR PEOPLE, MOAB.
YOU HONOR YOUR SIDONIAN AND AMMONITE WIVES, YOUR HIGHNESS. IF YOU LOVE ME...
WORSHIP WITH ME IN THE TEMPLE OF MY PEOPLE!
I GAVE YOU PERMISSION TO BUILD A SHRINE...
BUT I CANNOT WORSHIP WITH YOU.
BUT, MY KING...
DO YOU LOVE YOUR WIVES FROM SIDON MORE THAN ME?
URGH... THE LORD LOVES ME...
HE WILL CERTAINLY FORGIVE ME FOR MY WEAKNESS.
FINE!
LET'S GO.

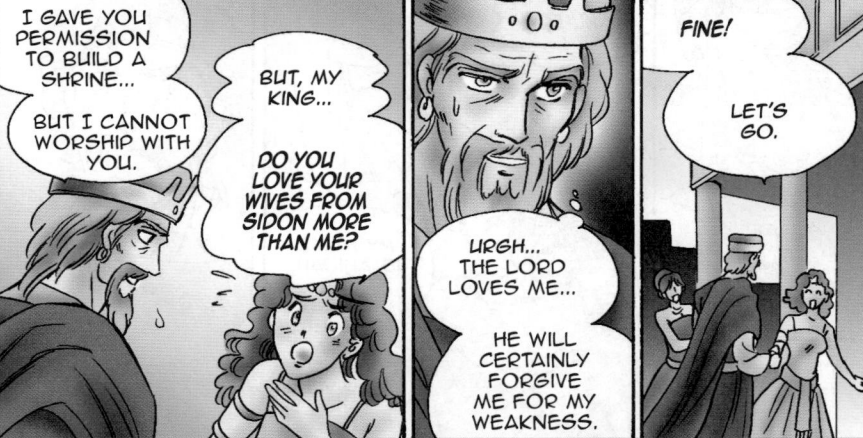

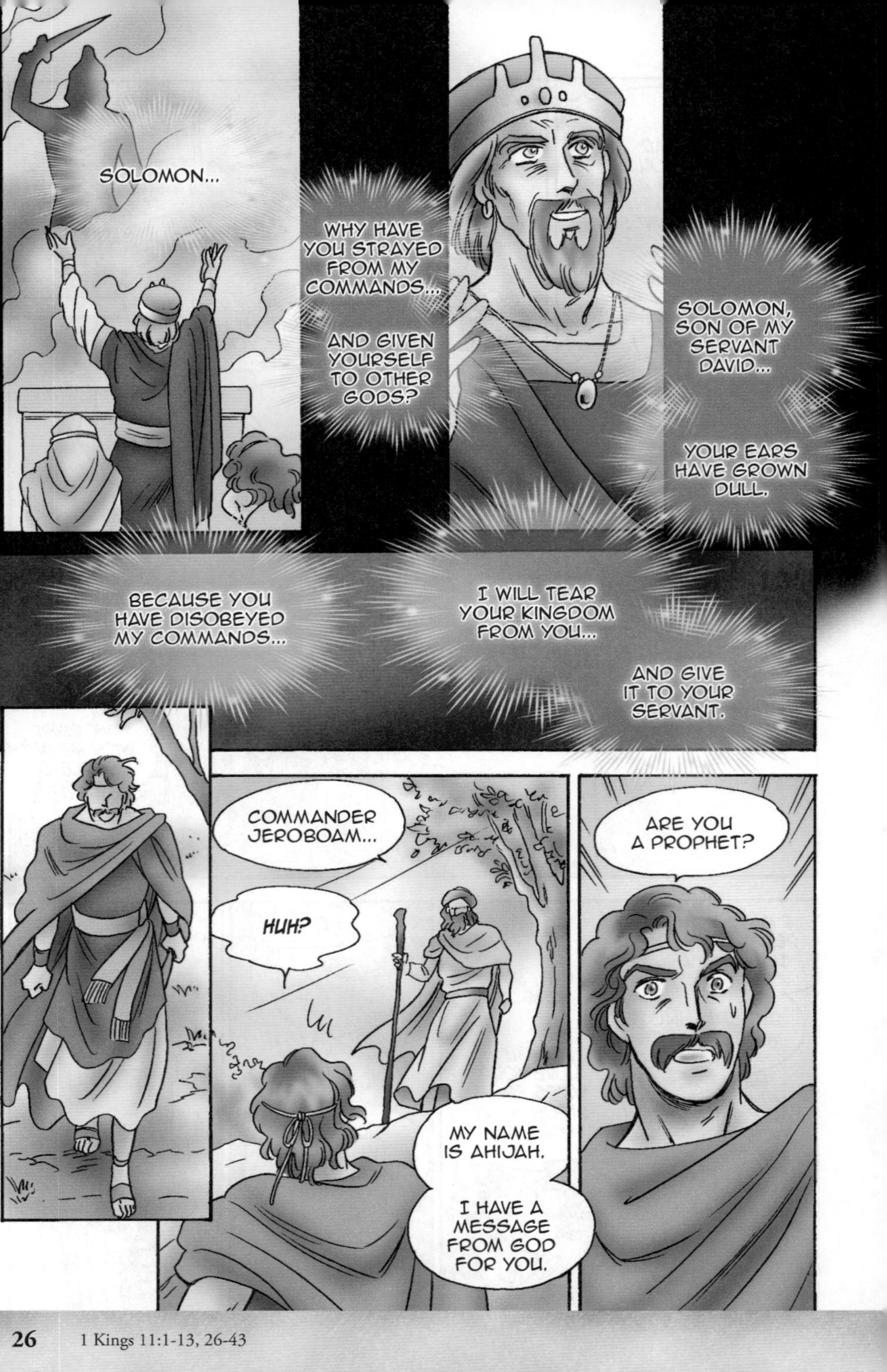
SOLOMON...
WHY HAVE YOU STRAYED FROM MY COMMANDS...
AND GIVEN YOURSELF TO OTHER GODS?
SOLOMON, SON OF MY SERVANT DAVID...
YOUR EARS HAVE GROWN DULL.
BECAUSE YOU HAVE DISOBEYED MY COMMANDS...
I WILL TEAR YOUR KINGDOM FROM YOU...
AND GIVE IT TO YOUR SERVANT.
COMMANDER JEROBOAM...
HUH?
ARE YOU A PROPHET?
MY NAME IS AHIJAH.
I HAVE A MESSAGE FROM GOD FOR YOU.

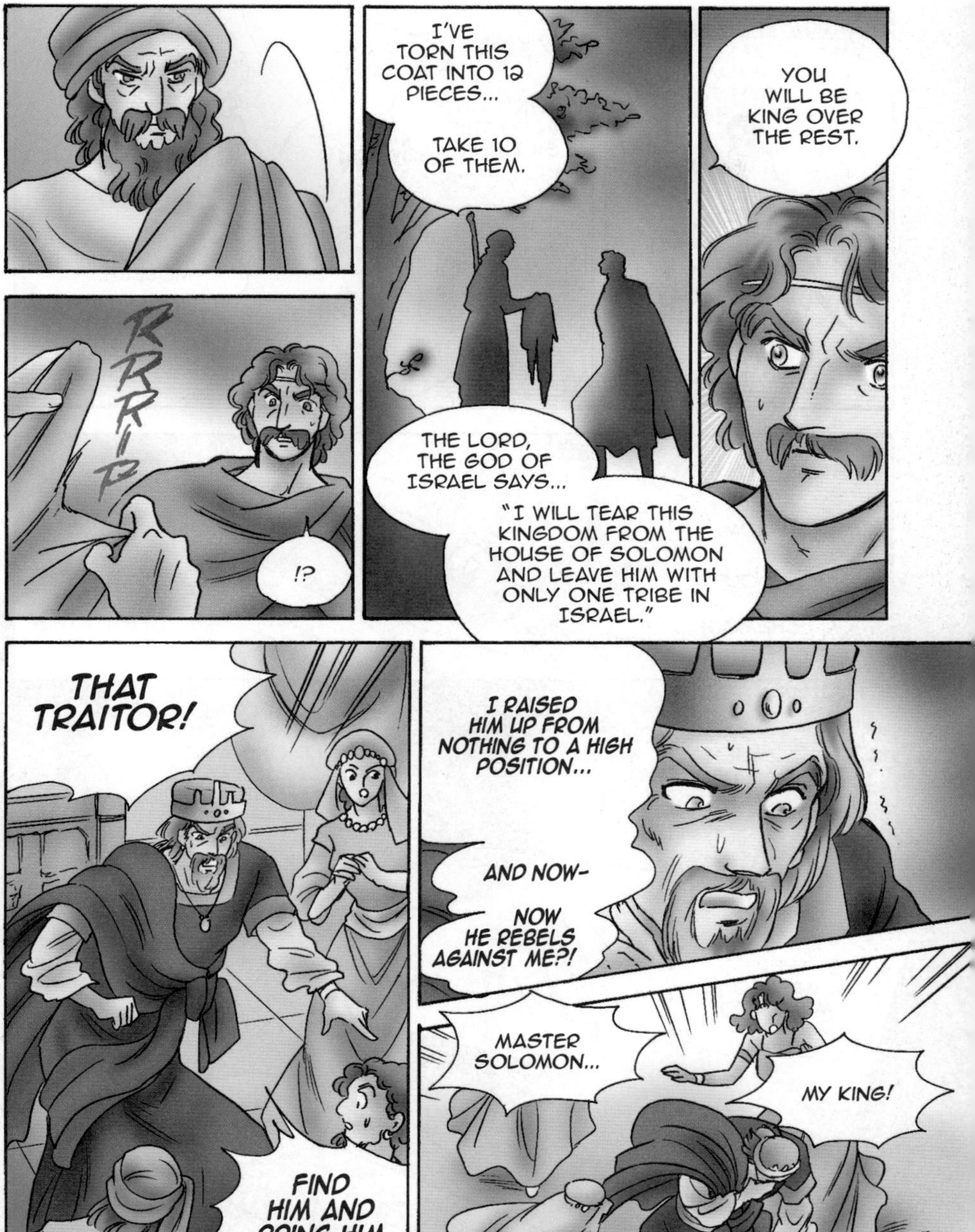

I'VE TORN THIS COAT INTO 12 PIECES...
TAKE 10 OF THEM.
YOU WILL BE KING OVER THE REST.
RRRIP
!?
THE LORD, THE GOD OF ISRAEL SAYS...
"I WILL TEAR THIS KINGDOM FROM THE HOUSE OF SOLOMON AND LEAVE HIM WITH ONLY ONE TRIBE IN ISRAEL."
THAT TRAITOR!
I RAISED HIM UP FROM NOTHING TO A HIGH POSITION...
AND NOW-
NOW HE REBELS AGAINST ME?!
FIND HIM AND BRING HIM TO ME!
MASTER SOLOMON...
MY KING!

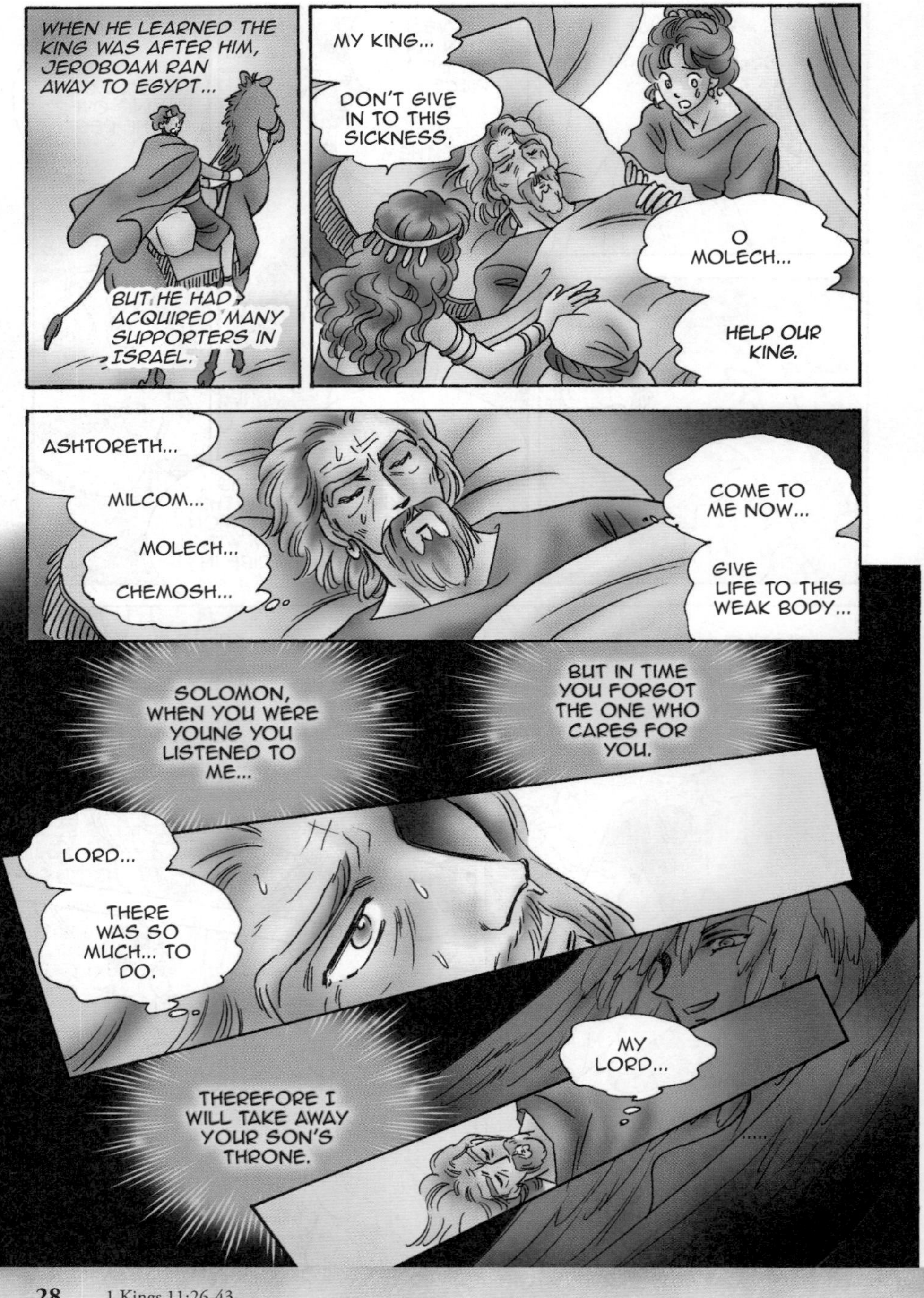
WHEN HE LEARNED THE KING WAS AFTER HIM, JEROBOAM RAN AWAY TO EGYPT...
BUT HE HAD ACQUIRED MANY SUPPORTERS IN ISRAEL.
MY KING...
DON'T GIVE IN TO THIS SICKNESS.
O MOLECH...
HELP OUR KING.
ASHTORETH...
MILCOM...
MOLECH...
CHEMOSH...
COME TO ME NOW...
GIVE LIFE TO THIS WEAK BODY...
SOLOMON, WHEN YOU WERE YOUNG YOU LISTENED TO ME...
BUT IN TIME YOU FORGOT THE ONE WHO CARES FOR YOU.
LORD...
THERE WAS SO MUCH... TO DO.
MY LORD...
THEREFORE I WILL TAKE AWAY YOUR SON'S THRONE.
.....

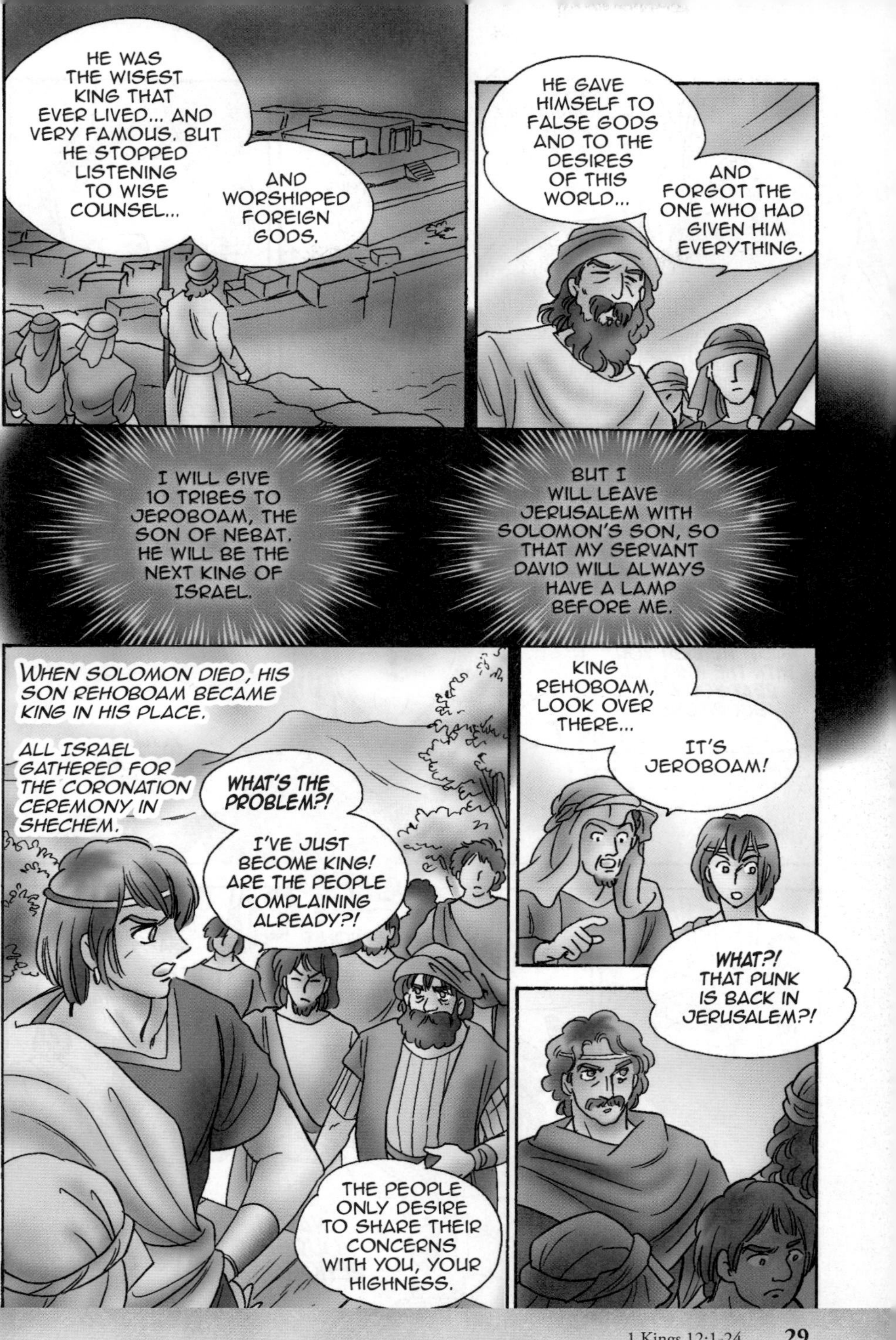
HE WAS THE WISEST KING THAT EVER LIVED... AND VERY FAMOUS. BUT HE STOPPED LISTENING TO WISE COUNSEL...
AND WORSHIPPED FOREIGN GODS.
HE GAVE HIMSELF TO FALSE GODS AND TO THE DESIRES OF THIS WORLD...
AND FORGOT THE ONE WHO HAD GIVEN HIM EVERYTHING.
I WILL GIVE 10 TRIBES TO JEROBOAM, THE SON OF NEBAT. HE WILL BE THE NEXT KING OF ISRAEL.
BUT I WILL LEAVE JERUSALEM WITH SOLOMON'S SON, SO THAT MY SERVANT DAVID WILL ALWAYS HAVE A LAMP BEFORE ME.
WHEN SOLOMON DIED, HIS SON REHOBOAM BECAME KING IN HIS PLACE.
ALL ISRAEL GATHERED FOR THE CORONATION CEREMONY IN SHECHEM.
WHAT'S THE PROBLEM?!
I'VE JUST BECOME KING! ARE THE PEOPLE COMPLAINING ALREADY?!
THE PEOPLE ONLY DESIRE TO SHARE THEIR CONCERNS WITH YOU, YOUR HIGHNESS.
KING REHOBOAM, LOOK OVER THERE...
IT'S JEROBOAM!
WHAT?! THAT PUNK IS BACK IN JERUSALEM?!

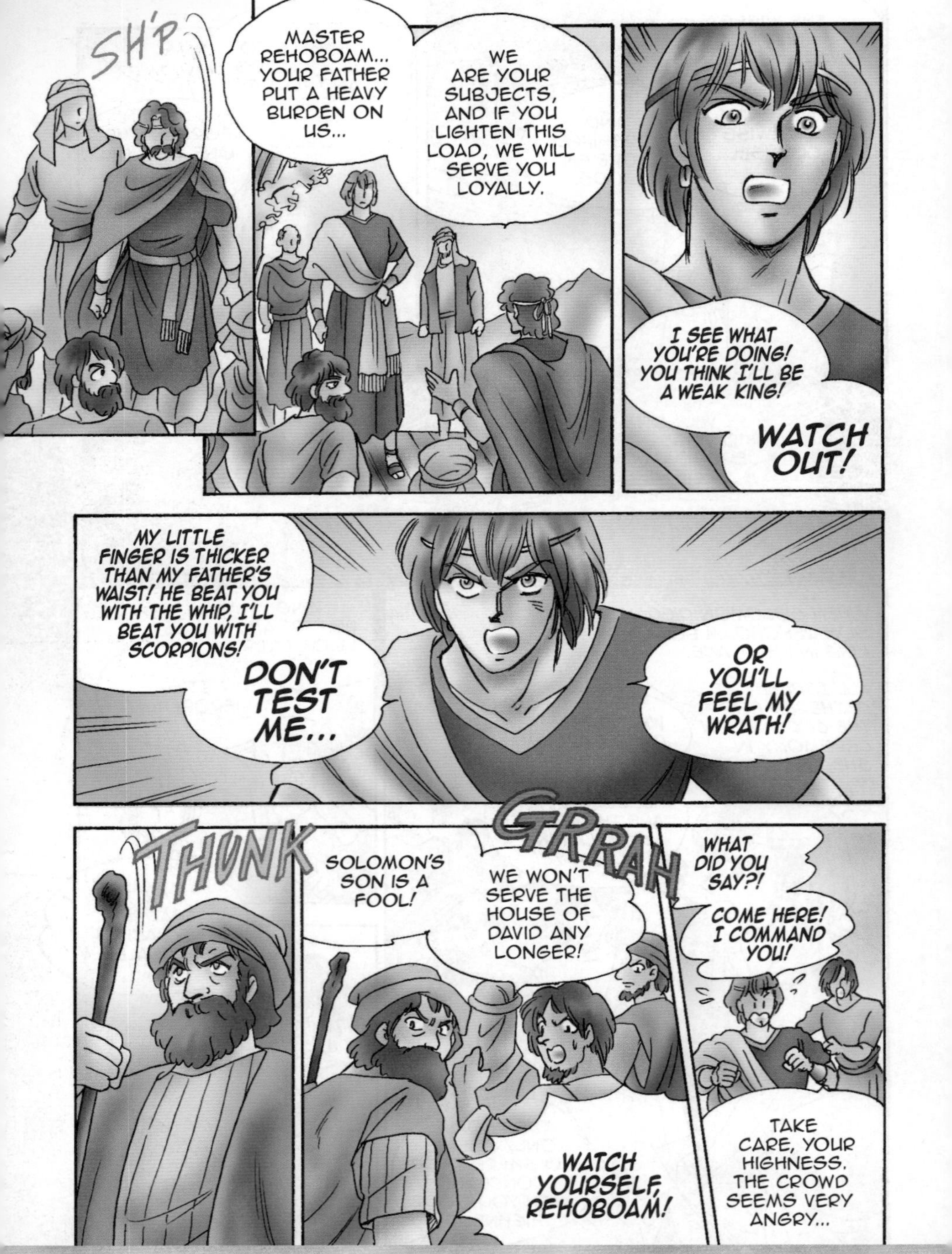
SH'P
MASTER REHOBOAM... YOUR FATHER PUT A HEAVY BURDEN ON US...
WE ARE YOUR SUBJECTS, AND IF YOU LIGHTEN THIS LOAD, WE WILL SERVE YOU LOYALLY.
I SEE WHAT YOU'RE DOING! YOU THINK I'LL BE A WEAK KING!
WATCH OUT!
MY LITTLE FINGER IS THICKER THAN MY FATHER'S WAIST! HE BEAT YOU WITH THE WHIP, I'LL BEAT YOU WITH SCORPIONS!
DON'T TEST ME...
OR YOU'LL FEEL MY WRATH!
THUNK
SOLOMON'S SON IS A FOOL!
GRRAH
WE WON'T SERVE THE HOUSE OF DAVID ANY LONGER!
WATCH YOURSELF, REHOBOAM!
WHAT DID YOU SAY?!
COME HERE! I COMMAND YOU!
TAKE CARE, YOUR HIGHNESS. THE CROWD SEEMS VERY ANGRY...

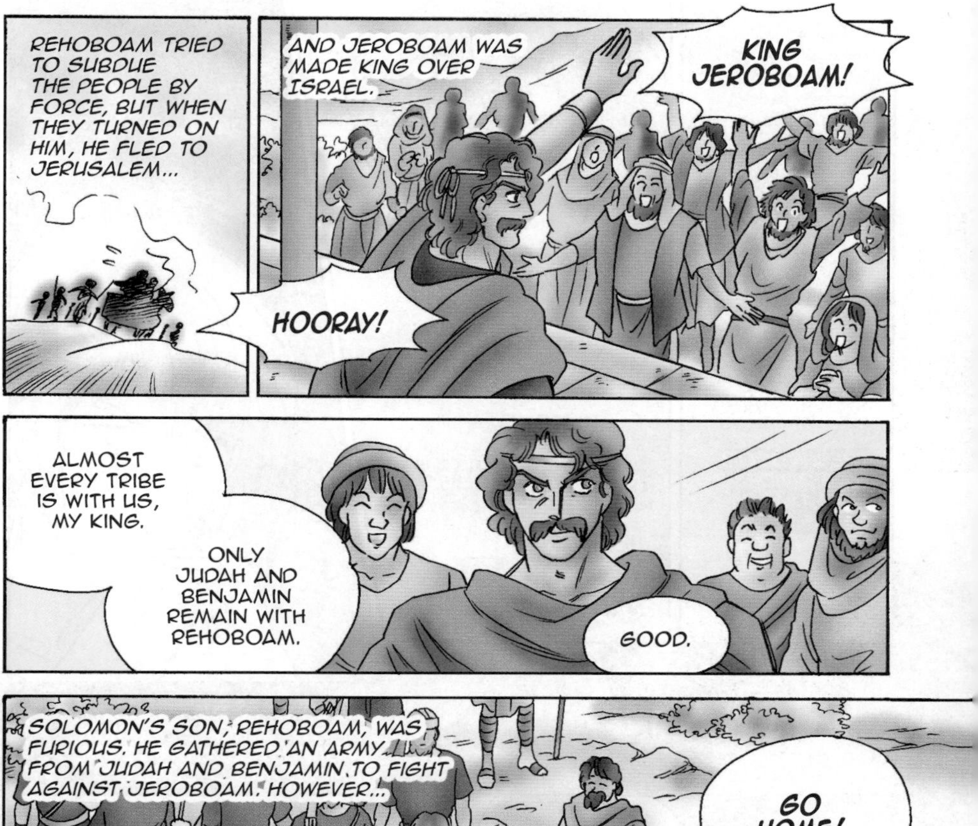
REHOBOAM TRIED TO SUBDUE THE PEOPLE BY FORCE, BUT WHEN THEY TURNED ON HIM, HE FLED TO JERUSALEM...
AND JEROBOAM WAS MADE KING OVER ISRAEL.
KING JEROBOAM!
HOORAY!
ALMOST EVERY TRIBE IS WITH US, MY KING.
ONLY JUDAH AND BENJAMIN REMAIN WITH REHOBOAM.
GOOD.
SOLOMON'S SON, REHOBOAM, WAS FURIOUS. HE GATHERED AN ARMY FROM JUDAH AND BENJAMIN TO FIGHT AGAINST JEROBOAM. HOWEVER...
GO HOME!
HUH? WHO'S THAT?
IT'S THE PROPHET, SHEMAIAH!
THE LORD SAYS, "DO NOT FIGHT AGAINST YOUR BROTHERS IN ISRAEL!
"THIS DIVISION OF YOUR KINGDOM IS FROM ME."
WHUMP

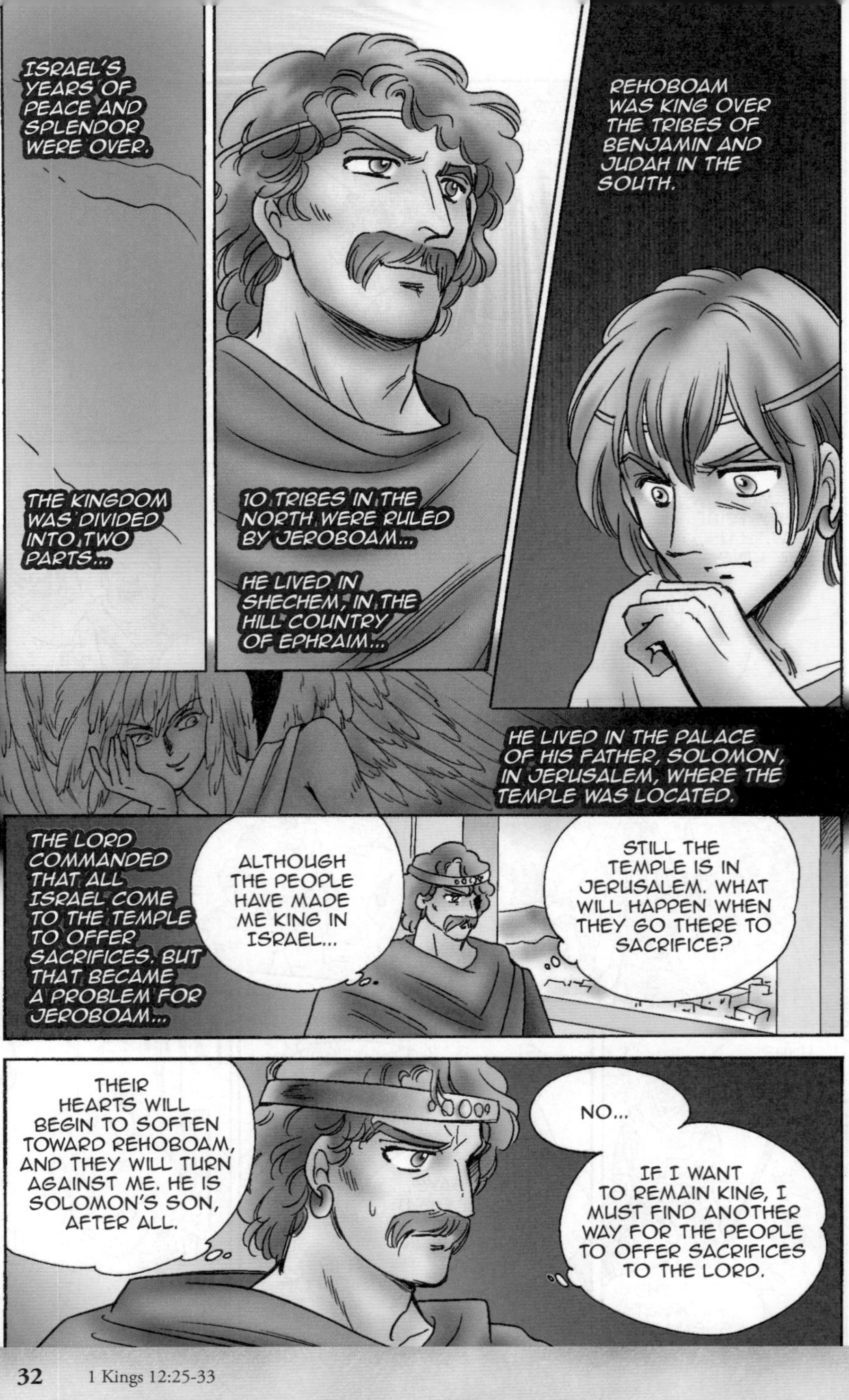
ISRAEL'S YEARS OF PEACE AND SPLENDOR WERE OVER.
REHOBOAM WAS KING OVER THE TRIBES OF BENJAMIN AND JUDAH IN THE SOUTH.
THE KINGDOM WAS DIVIDED INTO TWO PARTS...
10 TRIBES IN THE NORTH WERE RULED BY JEROBOAM...
HE LIVED IN SHECHEM, IN THE HILL COUNTRY OF EPHRAIM...
HE LIVED IN THE PALACE OF HIS FATHER, SOLOMON, IN JERUSALEM, WHERE THE TEMPLE WAS LOCATED.
THE LORD COMMANDED THAT ALL ISRAEL COME TO THE TEMPLE TO OFFER SACRIFICES. BUT THAT BECAME A PROBLEM FOR JEROBOAM...
ALTHOUGH THE PEOPLE HAVE MADE ME KING IN ISRAEL...
STILL THE TEMPLE IS IN JERUSALEM. WHAT WILL HAPPEN WHEN THEY GO THERE TO SACRIFICE?
THEIR HEARTS WILL BEGIN TO SOFTEN TOWARD REHOBOAM, AND THEY WILL TURN AGAINST ME. HE IS SOLOMON'S SON, AFTER ALL.
NO...
IF I WANT TO REMAIN KING, I MUST FIND ANOTHER WAY FOR THE PEOPLE TO OFFER SACRIFICES TO THE LORD.

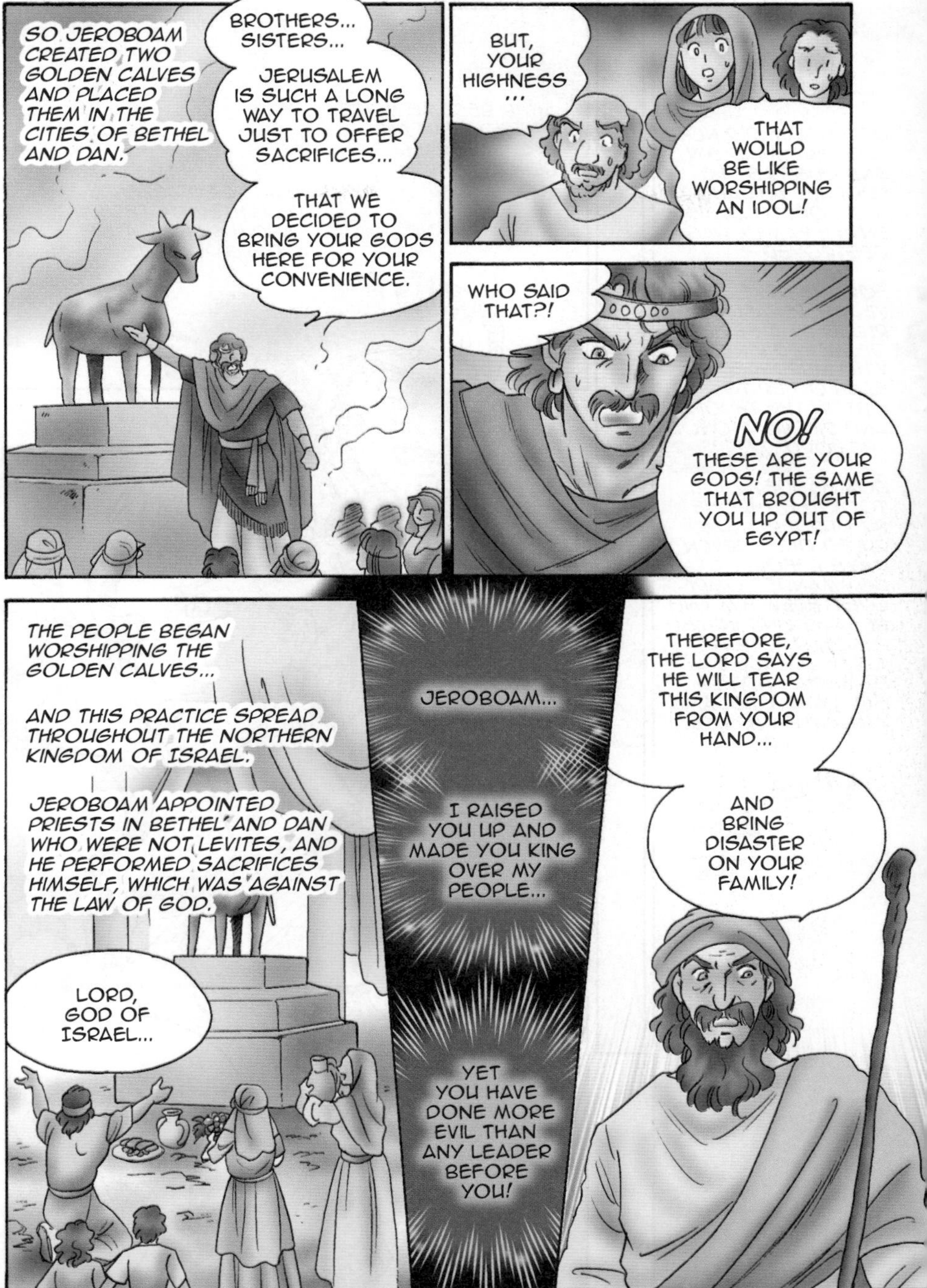
SO JEROBOAM CREATED TWO GOLDEN CALVES AND PLACED THEM IN THE CITIES OF BETHEL AND DAN.
BROTHERS... SISTERS...
JERUSALEM IS SUCH A LONG WAY TO TRAVEL JUST TO OFFER SACRIFICES...
THAT WE DECIDED TO BRING YOUR GODS HERE FOR YOUR CONVENIENCE.
BUT, YOUR HIGHNESS ...
THAT WOULD BE LIKE WORSHIPPING AN IDOL!
WHO SAID THAT?!
NO! THESE ARE YOUR GODS! THE SAME THAT BROUGHT YOU UP OUT OF EGYPT!
THE PEOPLE BEGAN WORSHIPPING THE GOLDEN CALVES...
AND THIS PRACTICE SPREAD THROUGHOUT THE NORTHERN KINGDOM OF ISRAEL.
JEROBOAM APPOINTED PRIESTS IN BETHEL AND DAN WHO WERE NOT LEVITES, AND HE PERFORMED SACRIFICES HIMSELF, WHICH WAS AGAINST THE LAW OF GOD.
LORD, GOD OF ISRAEL...
JEROBOAM...
I RAISED YOU UP AND MADE YOU KING OVER MY PEOPLE...
YET YOU HAVE DONE MORE EVIL THAN ANY LEADER BEFORE YOU!
THEREFORE, THE LORD SAYS HE WILL TEAR THIS KINGDOM FROM YOUR HAND...
AND BRING DISASTER ON YOUR FAMILY!

1 Kings 12:25-33; 14:1-20

JEROBOAM DID NOT TURN FROM HIS SIN, AND JUST AS THE PROPHET AHIJAH HAD FORETOLD, HIS ENTIRE FAMILY WAS DESTROYED.

FOR THE NEXT 30 YEARS, ISRAEL WAS RULED BY A SERIES OF WICKED KINGS WHO MURDERED EACH OTHER TO OBTAIN THE THRONE AND DID NOT HONOR THE LORD.

COMMANDER ZIMRI TOOK THE THRONE BY MURDER AND RULED ONLY SEVEN DAYS BEFORE COMMANDER OMRI OVERTHREW HIM AND BECAME KING IN HIS PLACE. OMRI BUILT A NEW PALACE IN SAMARIA AND HIS SON, AHAB, BECAME KING WHEN HE DIED.

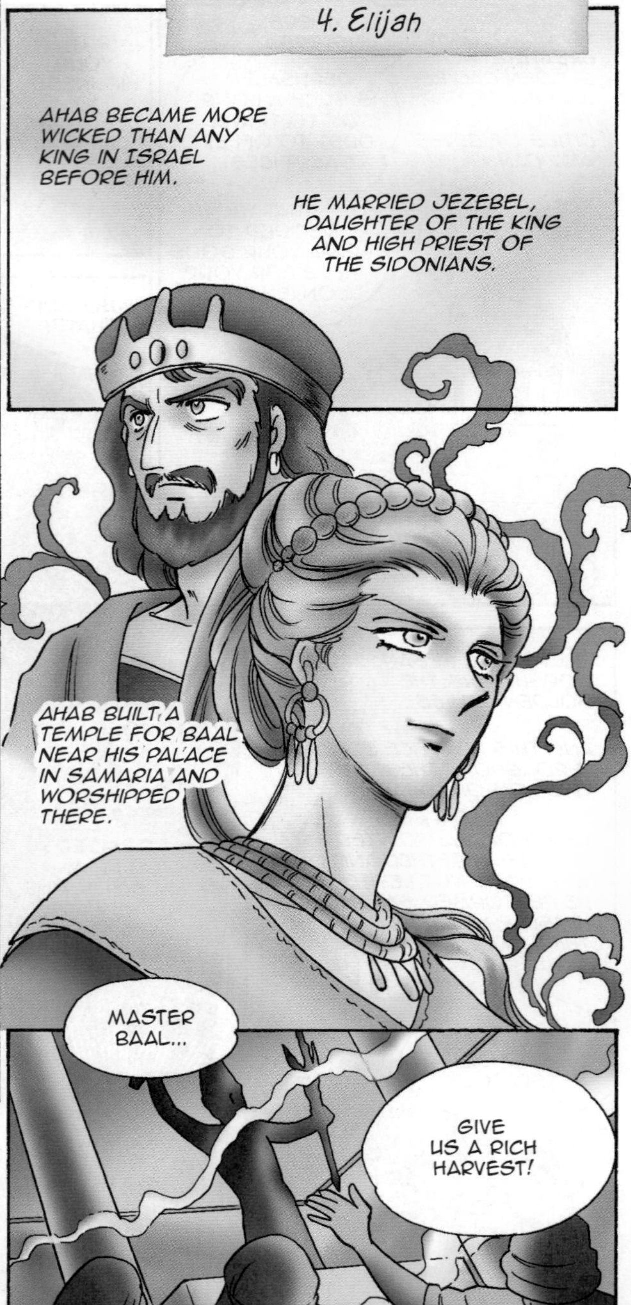
4. Elijah
AHAB BECAME MORE WICKED THAN ANY KING IN ISRAEL BEFORE HIM.
HE MARRIED JEZEBEL, DAUGHTER OF THE KING AND HIGH PRIEST OF THE SIDONIANS.
AHAB BUILT A TEMPLE FOR BAAL NEAR HIS PALACE IN SAMARIA AND WORSHIPPED THERE.
MASTER BAAL...
GIVE US A RICH HARVEST!

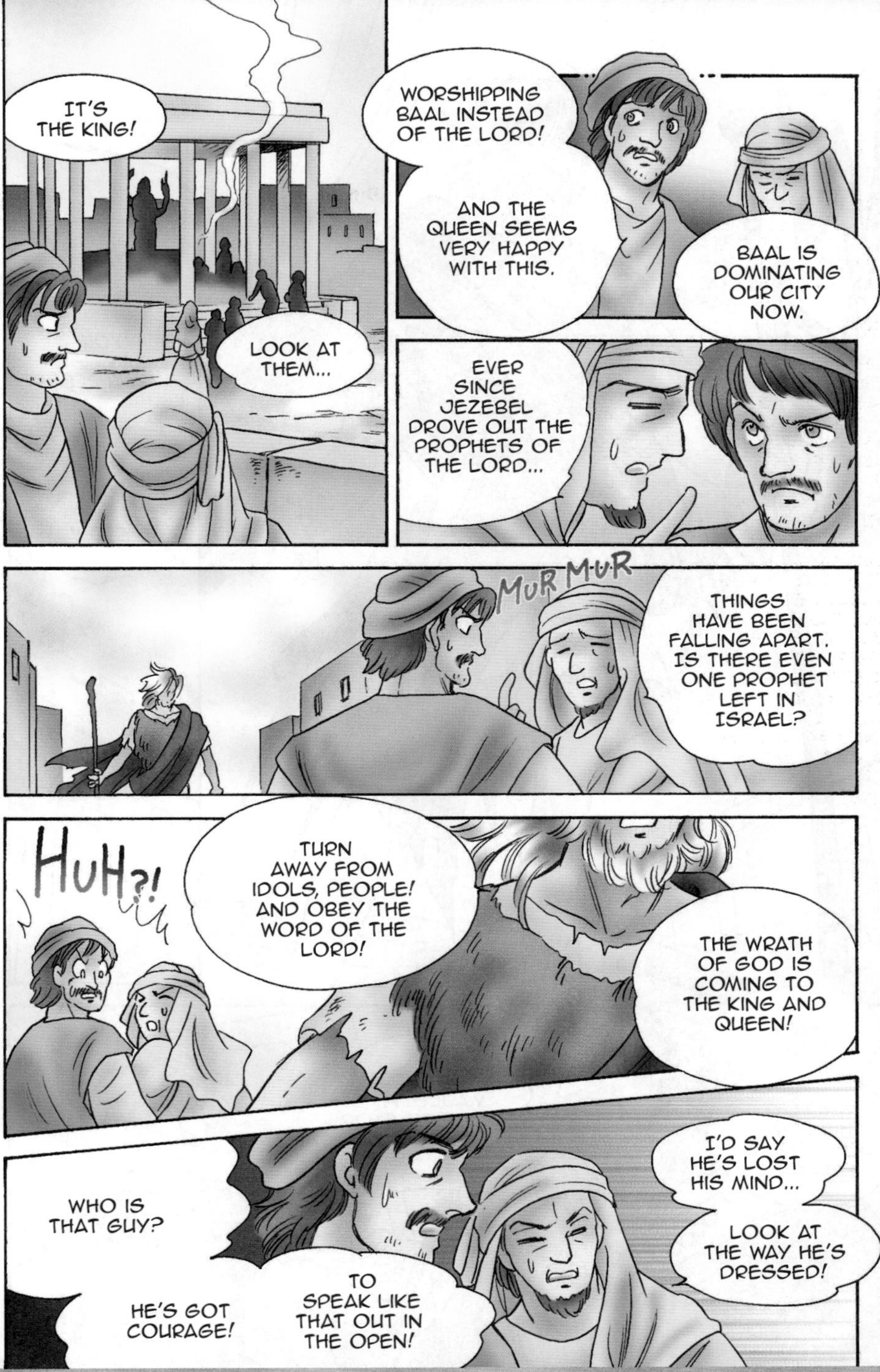
IT'S THE KING!
LOOK AT THEM...
WORSHIPPING BAAL INSTEAD OF THE LORD!
AND THE QUEEN SEEMS VERY HAPPY WITH THIS.
BAAL IS DOMINATING OUR CITY NOW.
EVER SINCE JEZEBEL DROVE OUT THE PROPHETS OF THE LORD...
MUR MUR
THINGS HAVE BEEN FALLING APART. IS THERE EVEN ONE PROPHET LEFT IN ISRAEL?
HUH?!
TURN AWAY FROM IDOLS, PEOPLE! AND OBEY THE WORD OF THE LORD!
THE WRATH OF GOD IS COMING TO THE KING AND QUEEN!
WHO IS THAT GUY?
I'D SAY HE'S LOST HIS MIND...
LOOK AT THE WAY HE'S DRESSED!
HE'S GOT COURAGE!
TO SPEAK LIKE THAT OUT IN THE OPEN!

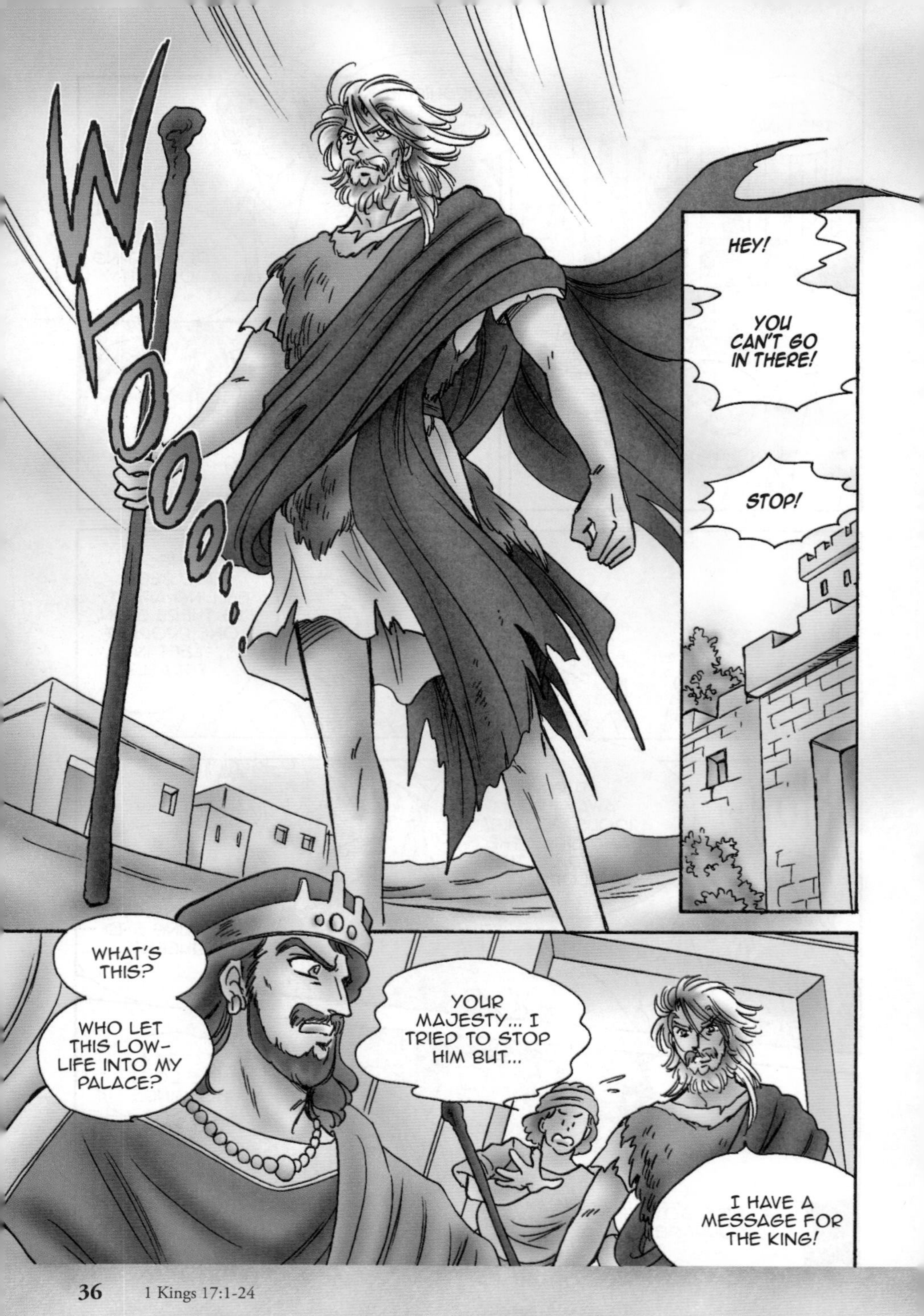
WHOOOO
HEY!
YOU CAN'T GO IN THERE!
STOP!
WHAT'S THIS?
WHO LET THIS LOW-LIFE INTO MY PALACE?
YOUR MAJESTY... I TRIED TO STOP HIM BUT...
I HAVE A MESSAGE FOR THE KING!

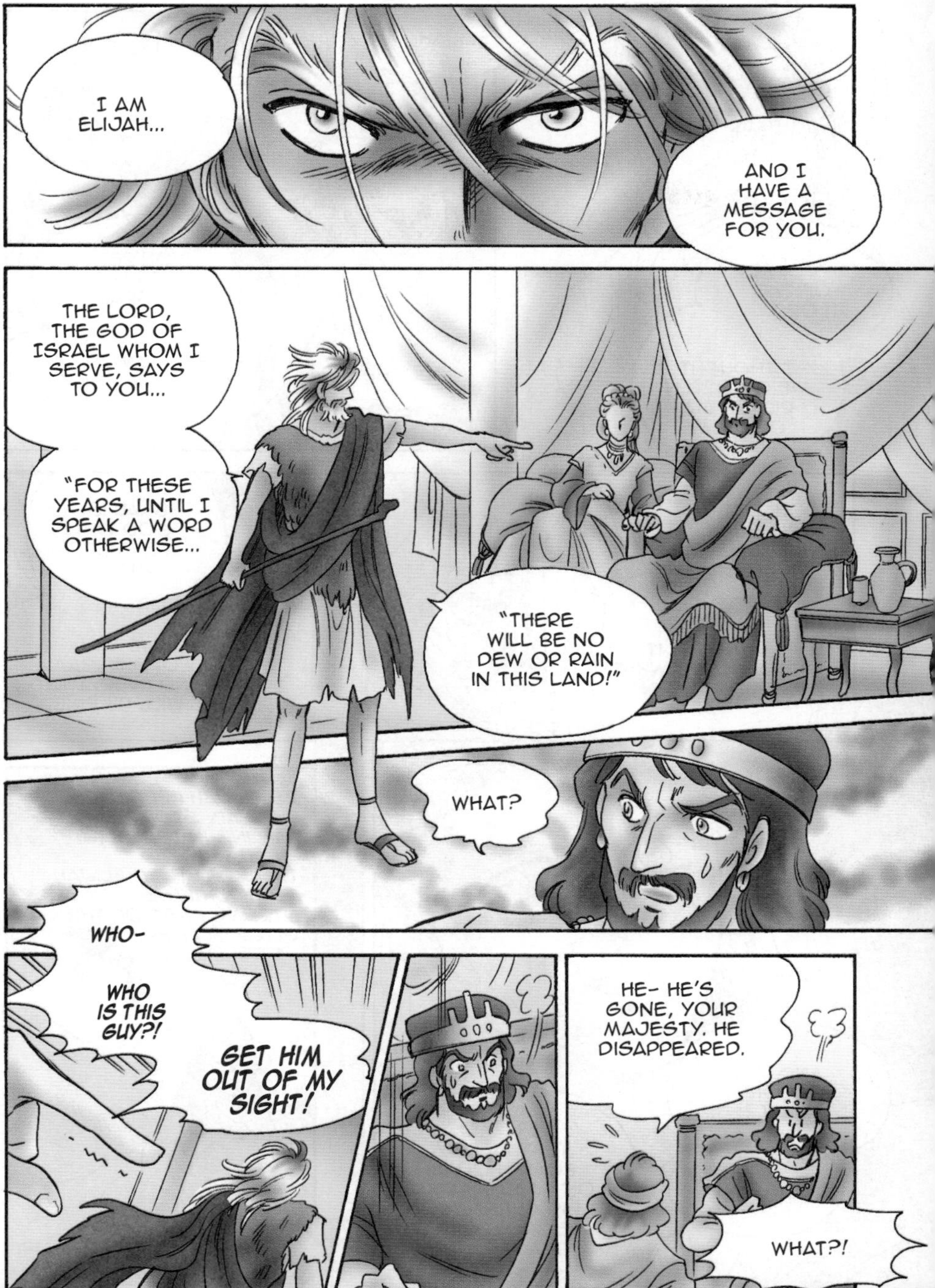
I AM ELIJAH...
AND I HAVE A MESSAGE FOR YOU.
THE LORD, THE GOD OF ISRAEL WHOM I SERVE, SAYS TO YOU...
"FOR THESE YEARS, UNTIL I SPEAK A WORD OTHERWISE...
"THERE WILL BE NO DEW OR RAIN IN THIS LAND!"
WHAT?
WHO-
WHO IS THIS GUY?!
GET HIM OUT OF MY SIGHT!
HE- HE'S GONE, YOUR MAJESTY. HE DISAPPEARED.
WHAT?!

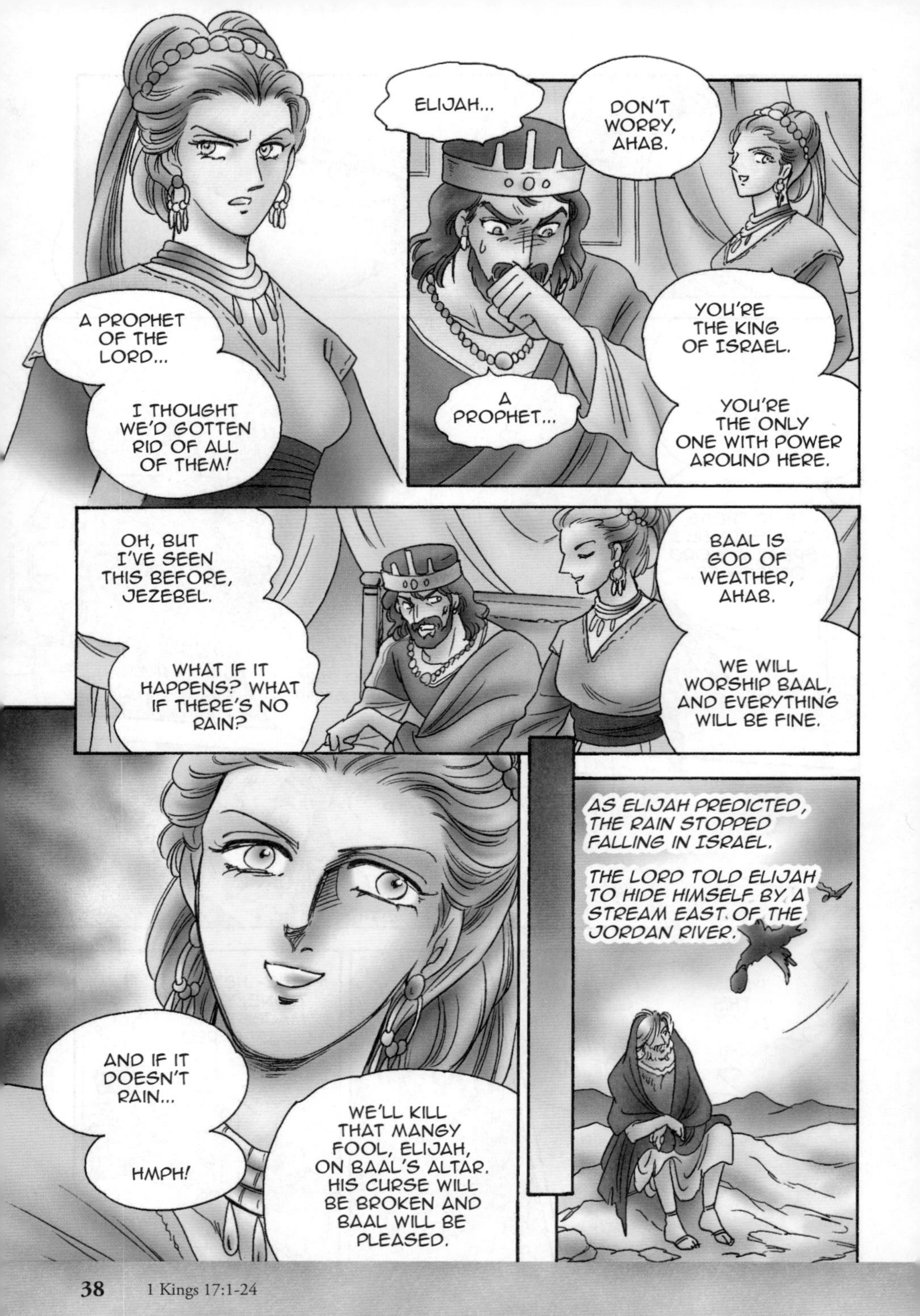
A PROPHET OF THE LORD...
I THOUGHT WE'D GOTTEN RID OF ALL OF THEM!
ELIJAH...
DON'T WORRY, AHAB.
A PROPHET...
YOU'RE THE KING OF ISRAEL.
YOU'RE THE ONLY ONE WITH POWER AROUND HERE.
OH, BUT I'VE SEEN THIS BEFORE, JEZEBEL.
WHAT IF IT HAPPENS? WHAT IF THERE'S NO RAIN?
BAAL IS GOD OF WEATHER, AHAB.
WE WILL WORSHIP BAAL, AND EVERYTHING WILL BE FINE.
AND IF IT DOESN'T RAIN...
HMPH!
WE'LL KILL THAT MANGY FOOL, ELIJAH, ON BAAL'S ALTAR. HIS CURSE WILL BE BROKEN AND BAAL WILL BE PLEASED.
AS ELIJAH PREDICTED, THE RAIN STOPPED FALLING IN ISRAEL.
THE LORD TOLD ELIJAH TO HIDE HIMSELF BY A STREAM EAST OF THE JORDAN RIVER.

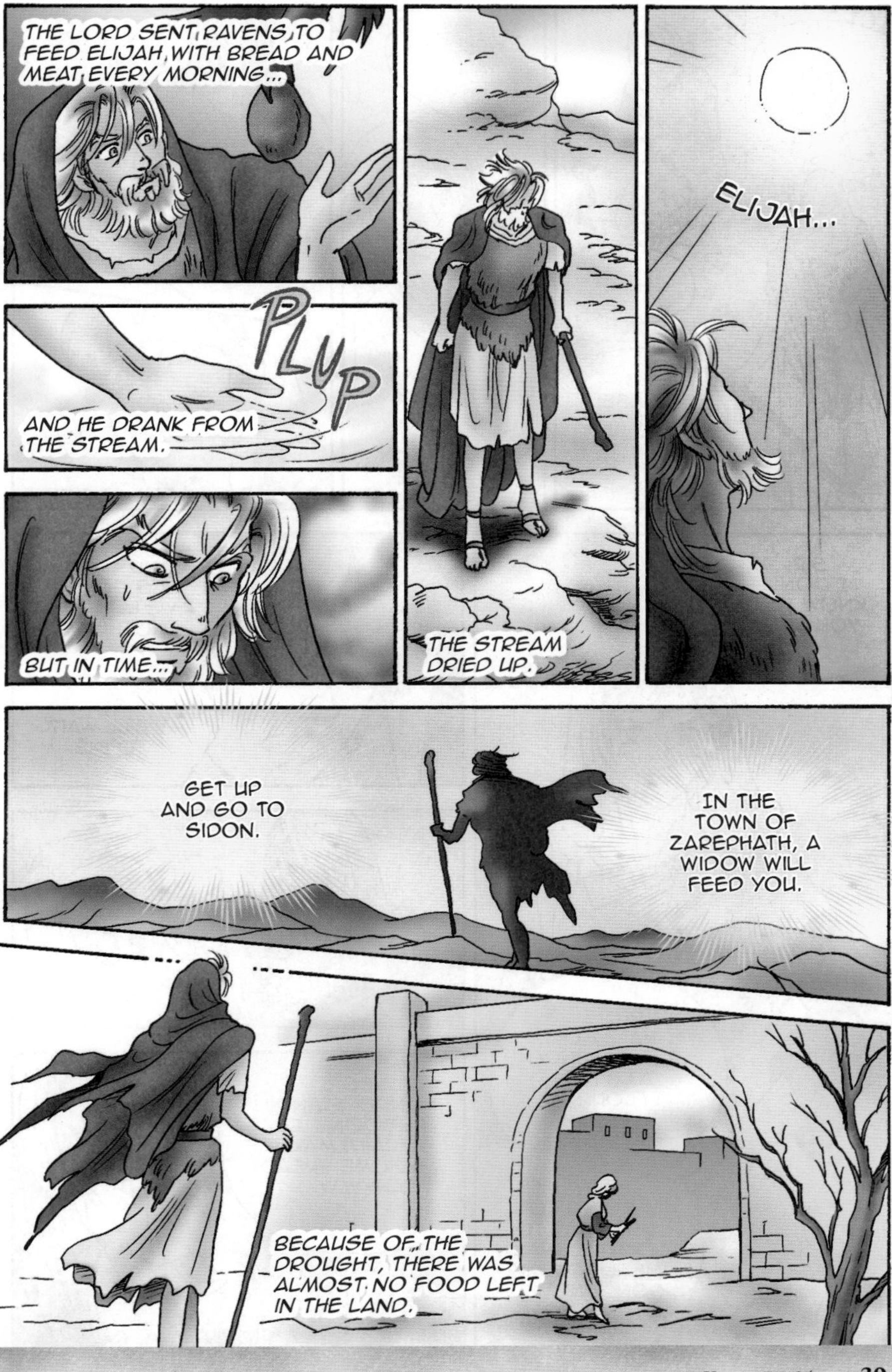
THE LORD SENT RAVENS TO FEED ELIJAH WITH BREAD AND MEAT EVERY MORNING...
PLUP
AND HE DRANK FROM THE STREAM.
BUT IN TIME...
THE STREAM DRIED UP.
ELIJAH...
GET UP AND GO TO SIDON.
IN THE TOWN OF ZAREPHATH, A WIDOW WILL FEED YOU.
BECAUSE OF THE DROUGHT, THERE WAS ALMOST NO FOOD LEFT IN THE LAND.

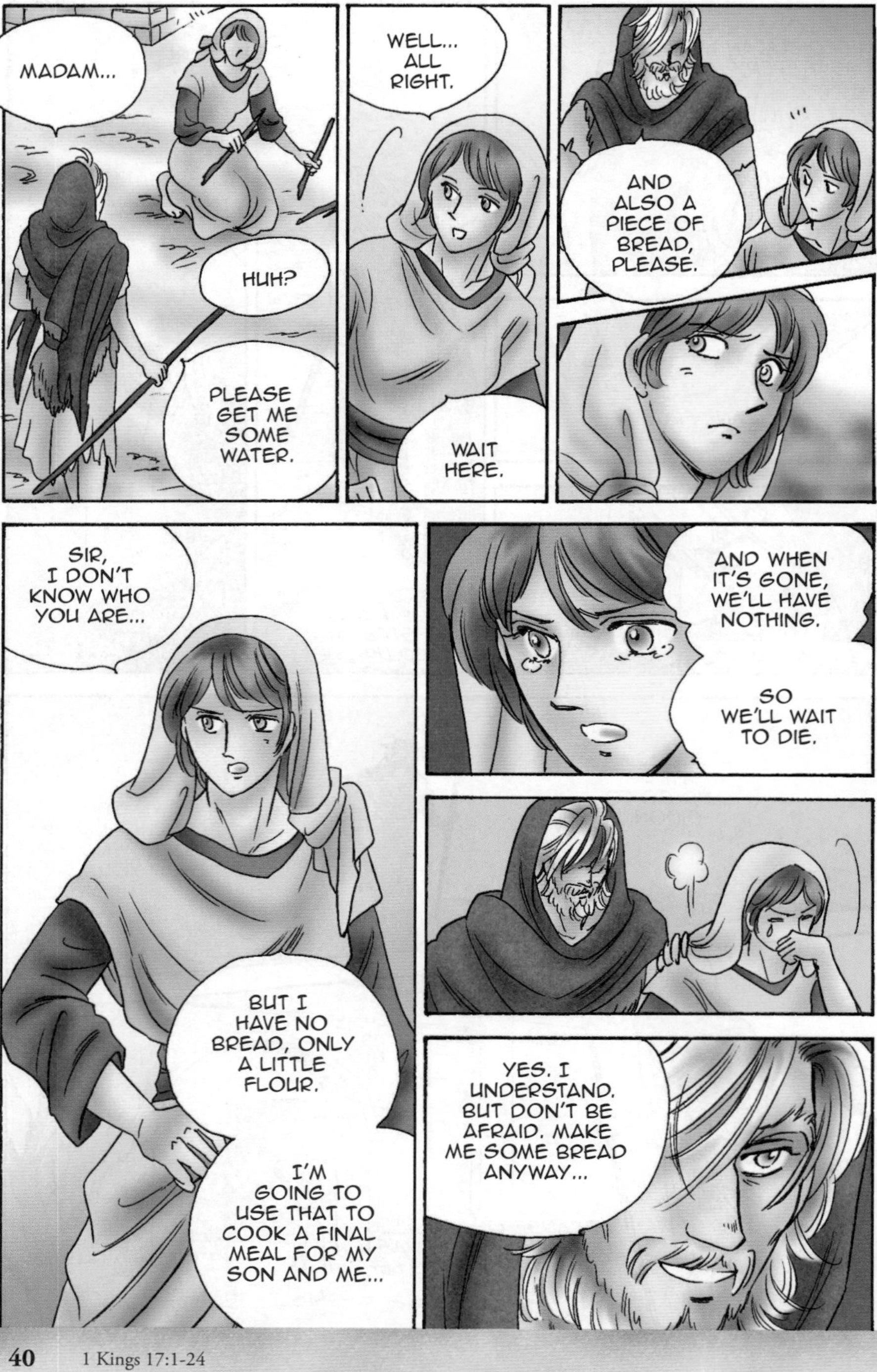
MADAM...
HUH?
PLEASE GET ME SOME WATER.
WELL... ALL RIGHT.
WAIT HERE.
AND ALSO A PIECE OF BREAD, PLEASE.
SIR, I DON'T KNOW WHO YOU ARE...
BUT I HAVE NO BREAD, ONLY A LITTLE FLOUR.
I'M GOING TO USE THAT TO COOK A FINAL MEAL FOR MY SON AND ME...
AND WHEN IT'S GONE, WE'LL HAVE NOTHING.
SO WE'LL WAIT TO DIE.
YES. I UNDERSTAND. BUT DON'T BE AFRAID. MAKE ME SOME BREAD ANYWAY...

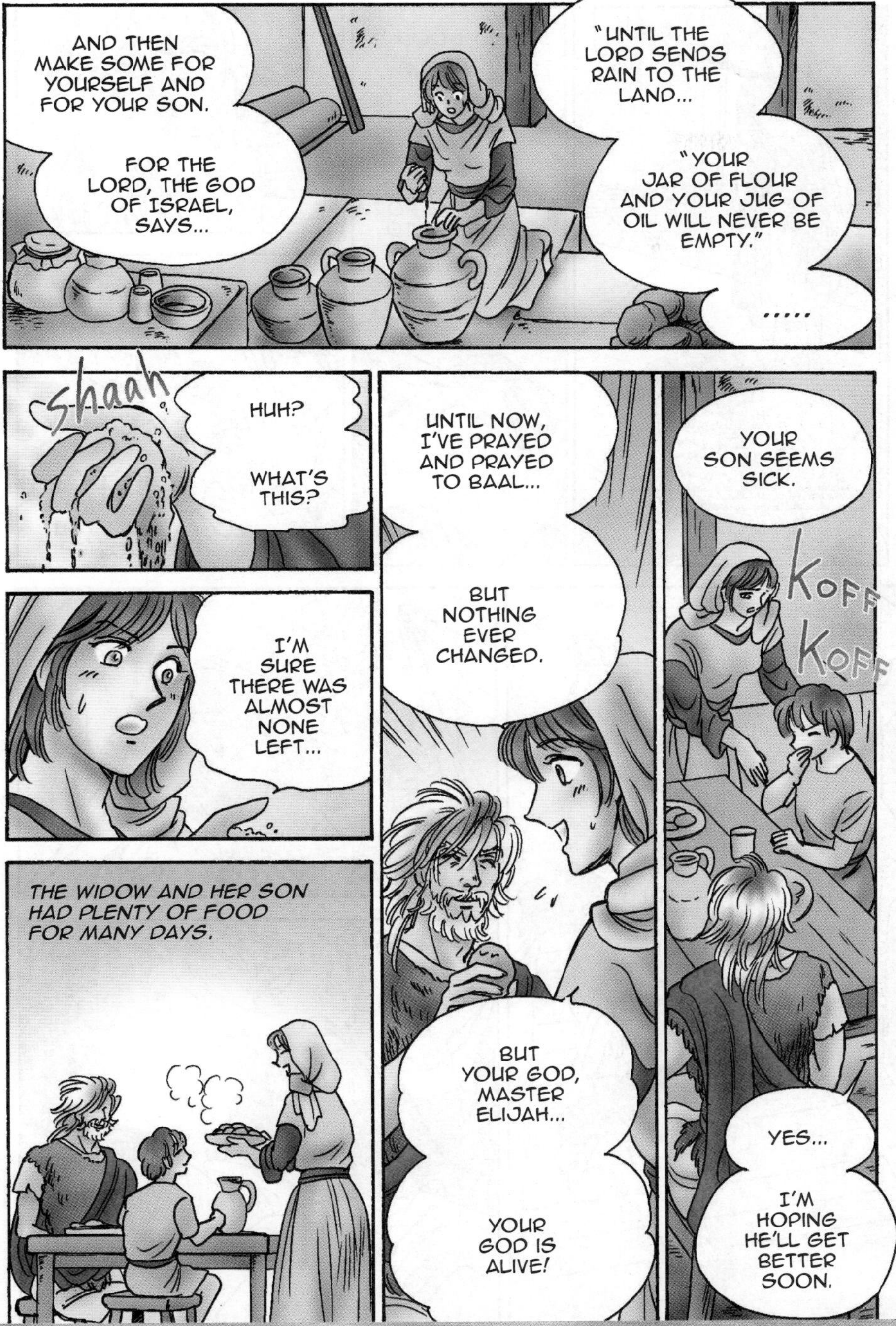
AND THEN MAKE SOME FOR YOURSELF AND FOR YOUR SON.
FOR THE LORD, THE GOD OF ISRAEL, SAYS...
"UNTIL THE LORD SENDS RAIN TO THE LAND...
"YOUR JAR OF FLOUR AND YOUR JUG OF OIL WILL NEVER BE EMPTY."
.....
shaah
HUH?
WHAT'S THIS?
I'M SURE THERE WAS ALMOST NONE LEFT...
THE WIDOW AND HER SON HAD PLENTY OF FOOD FOR MANY DAYS.
UNTIL NOW, I'VE PRAYED AND PRAYED TO BAAL...
BUT NOTHING EVER CHANGED.
BUT YOUR GOD, MASTER ELIJAH...
YOUR GOD IS ALIVE!
YOUR SON SEEMS SICK.
KOFF KOFF
YES...
I'M HOPING HE'LL GET BETTER SOON.

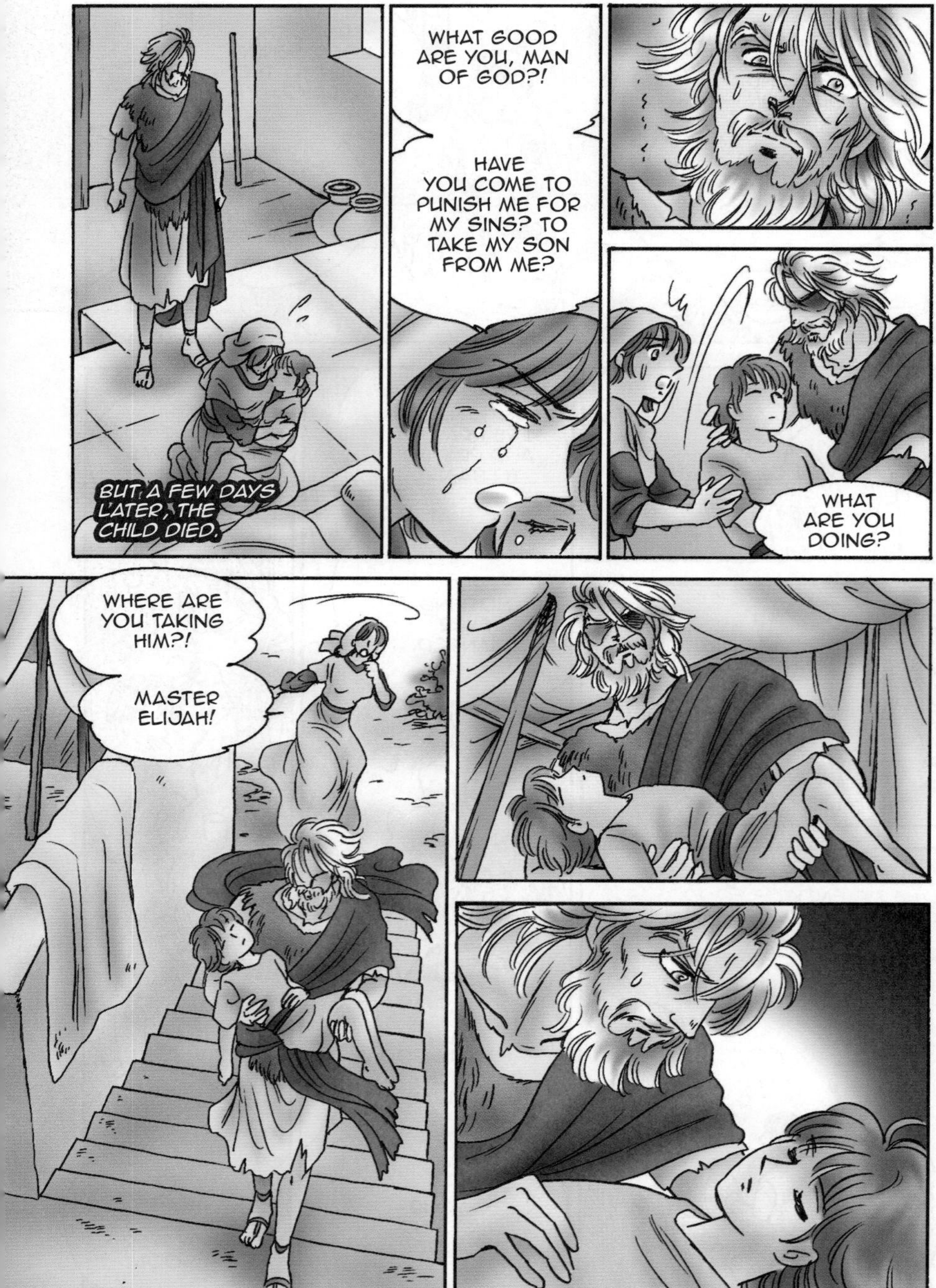
BUT, A FEW DAYS LATER, THE CHILD DIED.
WHAT GOOD ARE YOU, MAN OF GOD?!
HAVE YOU COME TO PUNISH ME FOR MY SINS? TO TAKE MY SON FROM ME?
WHAT ARE YOU DOING?
WHERE ARE YOU TAKING HIM?!
MASTER ELIJAH!

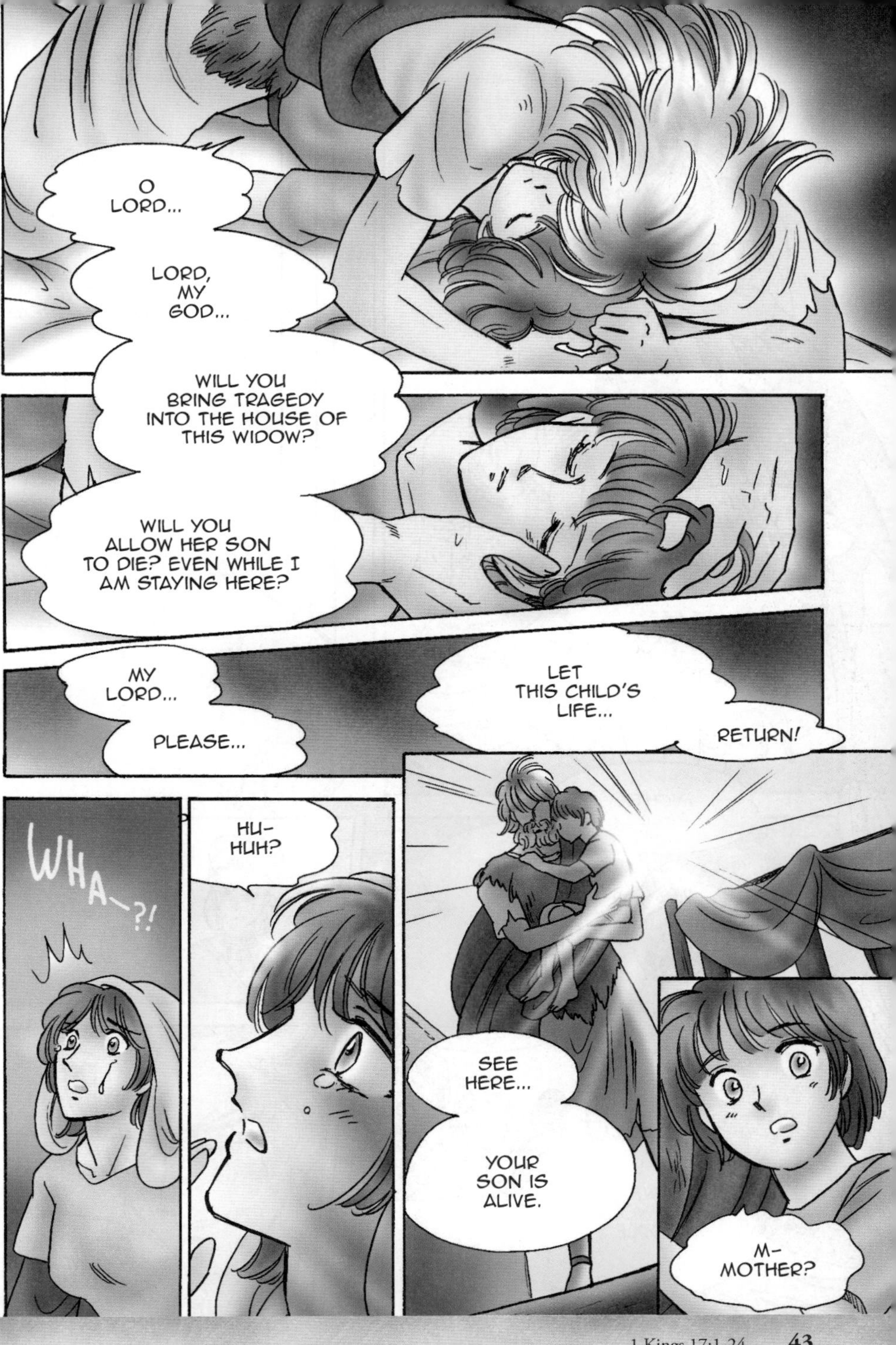
O LORD...
LORD, MY GOD...
WILL YOU BRING TRAGEDY INTO THE HOUSE OF THIS WIDOW?
WILL YOU ALLOW HER SON TO DIE? EVEN WHILE I AM STAYING HERE?
MY LORD...
PLEASE...
LET THIS CHILD'S LIFE...
RETURN!
WHA-?!
HU-HUH?
SEE HERE...
YOUR SON IS ALIVE.
M-MOTHER?

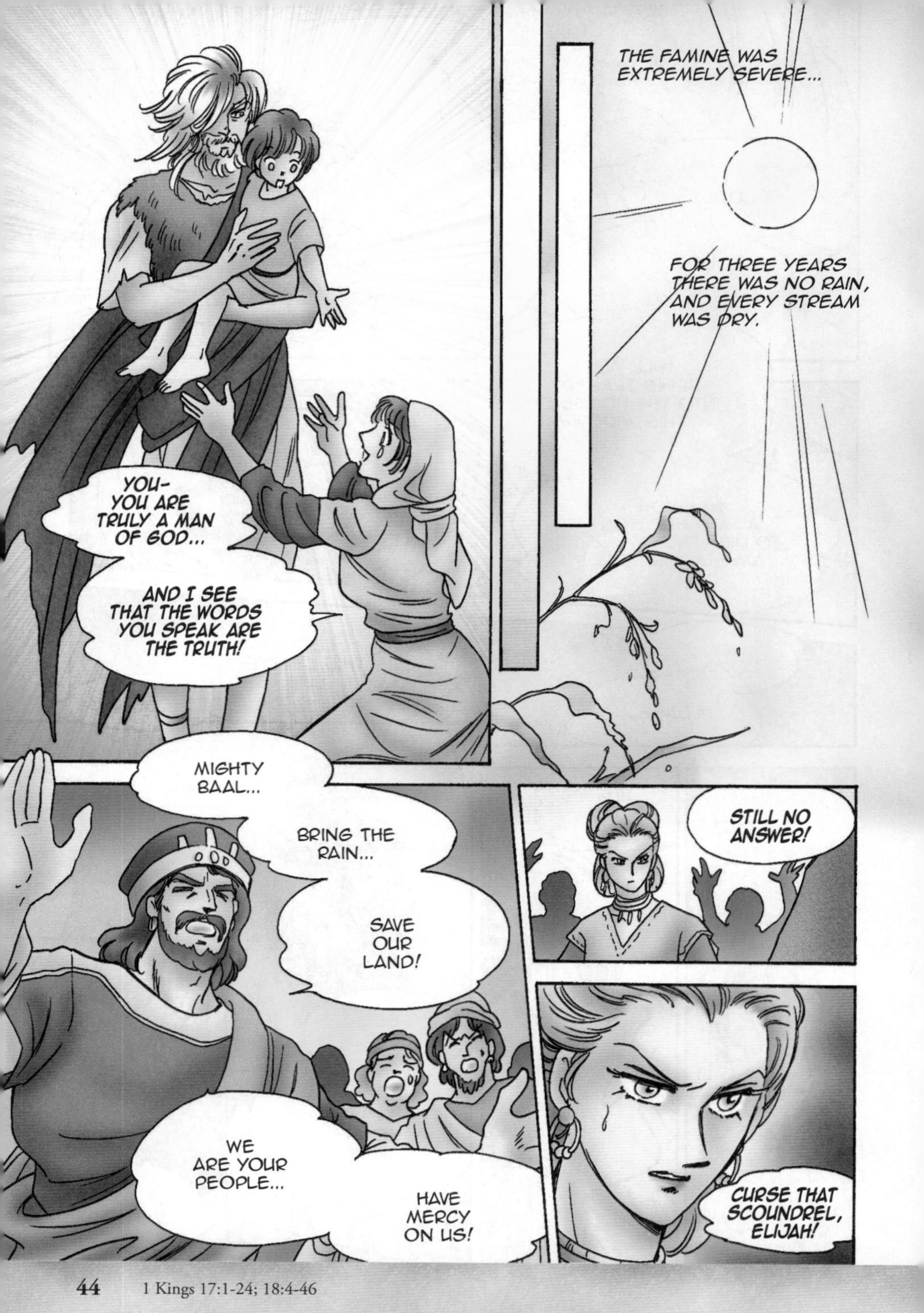
YOU-
YOU ARE TRULY A MAN OF GOD...
AND I SEE THAT THE WORDS YOU SPEAK ARE THE TRUTH!
THE FAMINE WAS EXTREMELY SEVERE...
FOR THREE YEARS THERE WAS NO RAIN, AND EVERY STREAM WAS DRY.
MIGHTY BAAL...
BRING THE RAIN...
SAVE OUR LAND!
WE ARE YOUR PEOPLE...
HAVE MERCY ON US!
STILL NO ANSWER!
CURSE THAT SCOUNDREL, ELIJAH!

SO... HAVE YOU RETURNED?

AS SURELY AS THE LORD LIVES...

I PROMISE YOU I WILL SHOW MYSELF TO AHAB TODAY.

...

YOU TROUBLER OF ISRAEL!

IT IS NOT I WHO HAVE BROUGHT TROUBLE ON ISRAEL, BUT YOU! YOU AND YOUR FATHER'S HOUSEHOLD!

YOU WHO HAVE WORSHIPPED BAAL, INSTEAD OF THE LORD.

NOW GATHER ALL THE PEOPLE OF ISRAEL ALONG WITH QUEEN JEZEBEL'S 450 PROPHETS OF BAAL...

AND MEET ME AT MOUNT CARMEL! THERE WE WILL FIND OUT WHOSE GOD IS THE TRUE GOD!

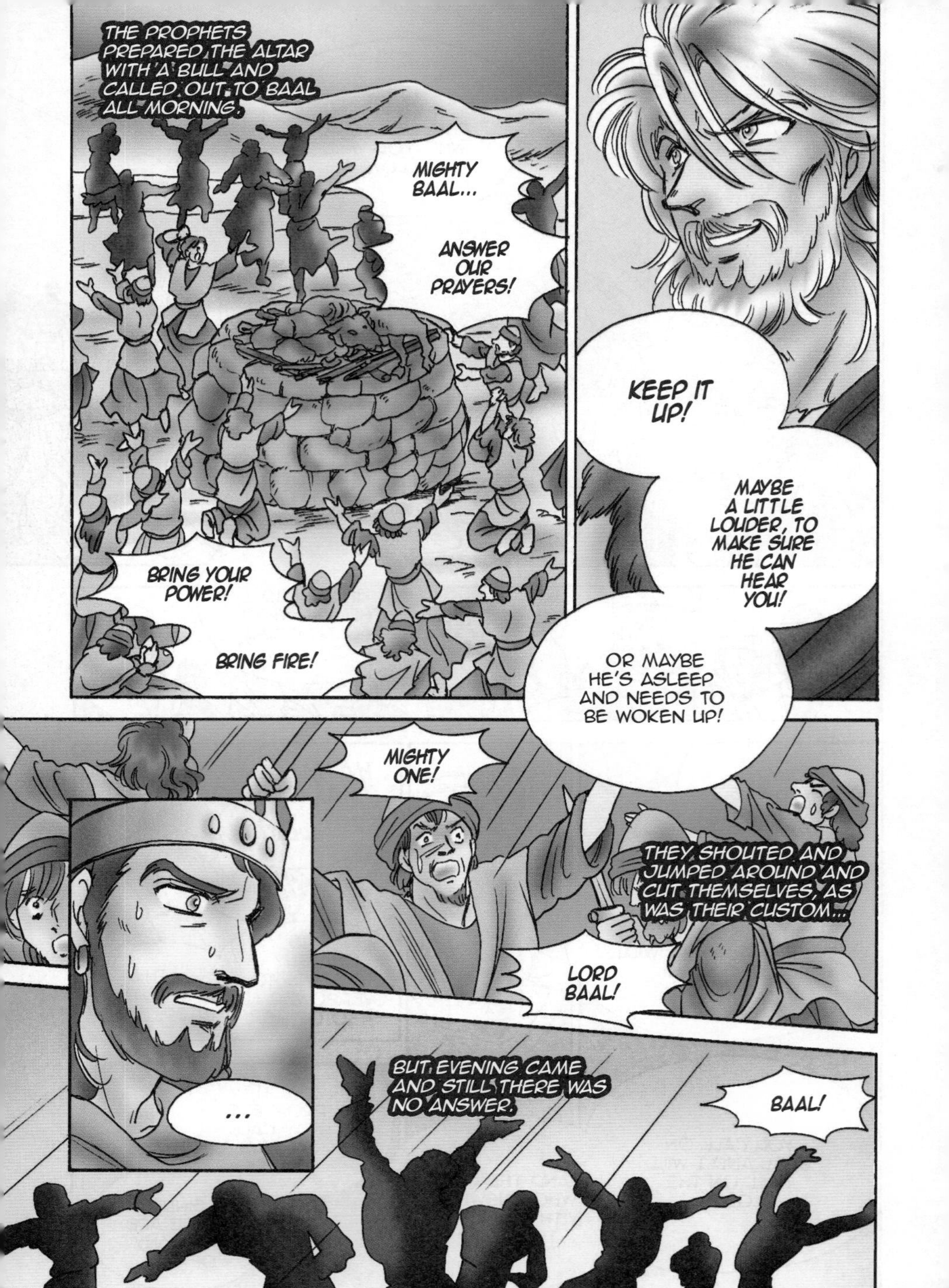
THE PROPHETS PREPARED THE ALTAR WITH A BULL AND CALLED OUT TO BAAL ALL MORNING.
MIGHTY BAAL...
ANSWER OUR PRAYERS!
BRING YOUR POWER!
BRING FIRE!
KEEP IT UP!
MAYBE A LITTLE LOUDER, TO MAKE SURE HE CAN HEAR YOU!
OR MAYBE HE'S ASLEEP AND NEEDS TO BE WOKEN UP!
MIGHTY ONE!
THEY SHOUTED AND JUMPED AROUND AND CUT THEMSELVES, AS WAS THEIR CUSTOM...
LORD BAAL!
...
BUT EVENING CAME AND STILL THERE WAS NO ANSWER.
BAAL!

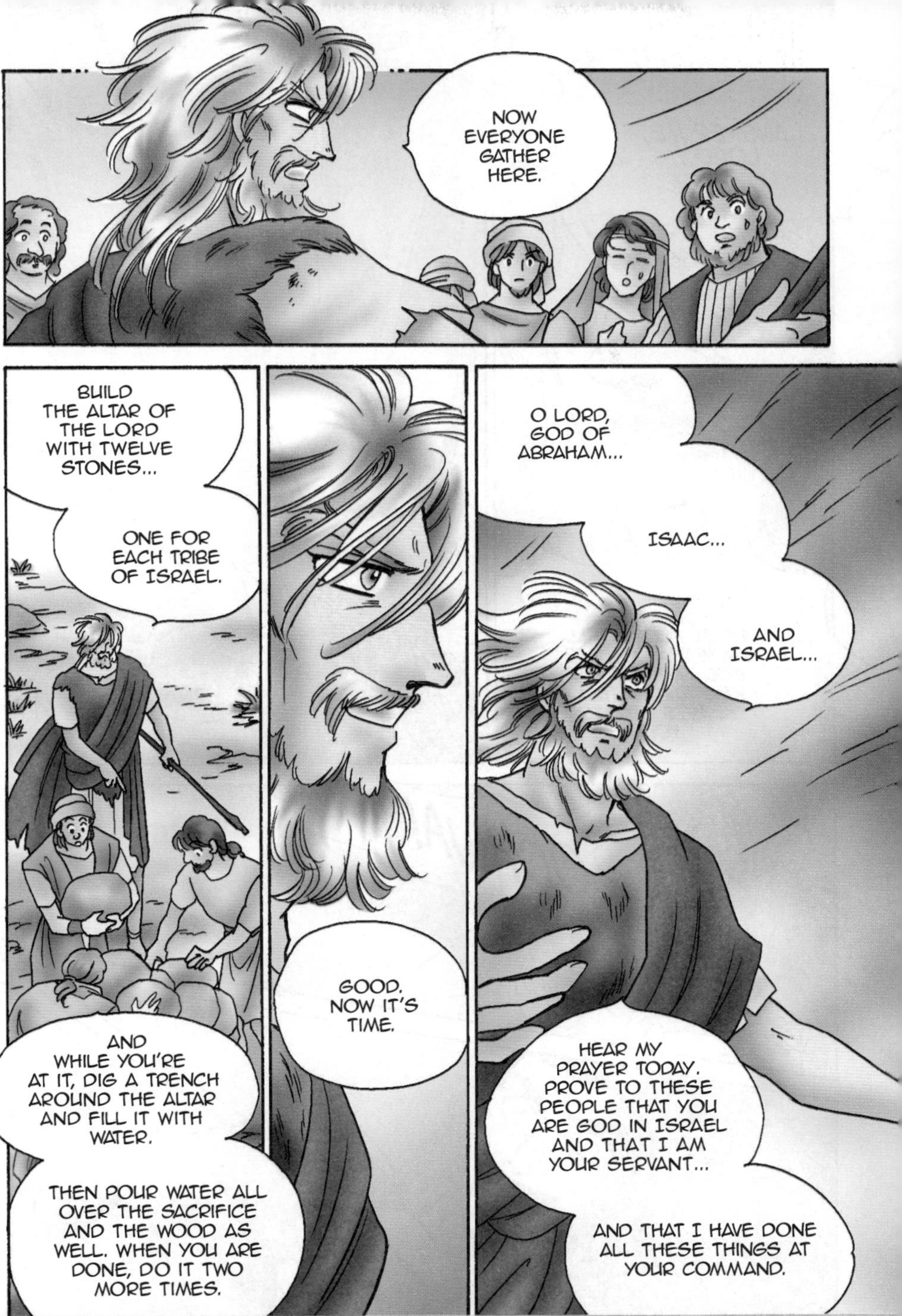
NOW EVERYONE GATHER HERE.
BUILD THE ALTAR OF THE LORD WITH TWELVE STONES...
ONE FOR EACH TRIBE OF ISRAEL.
AND WHILE YOU'RE AT IT, DIG A TRENCH AROUND THE ALTAR AND FILL IT WITH WATER.
THEN POUR WATER ALL OVER THE SACRIFICE AND THE WOOD AS WELL. WHEN YOU ARE DONE, DO IT TWO MORE TIMES.
GOOD. NOW IT'S TIME.
O LORD, GOD OF ABRAHAM...
ISAAC...
AND ISRAEL...
HEAR MY PRAYER TODAY. PROVE TO THESE PEOPLE THAT YOU ARE GOD IN ISRAEL AND THAT I AM YOUR SERVANT...
AND THAT I HAVE DONE ALL THESE THINGS AT YOUR COMMAND.

ANSWER ME, LORD...

FWOAM!

SO THAT THESE PEOPLE WILL KNOW THAT YOU ARE GOD AND THAT YOU HAVE TURNED THEIR HEARTS BACK TO YOU!

OOHWAAH

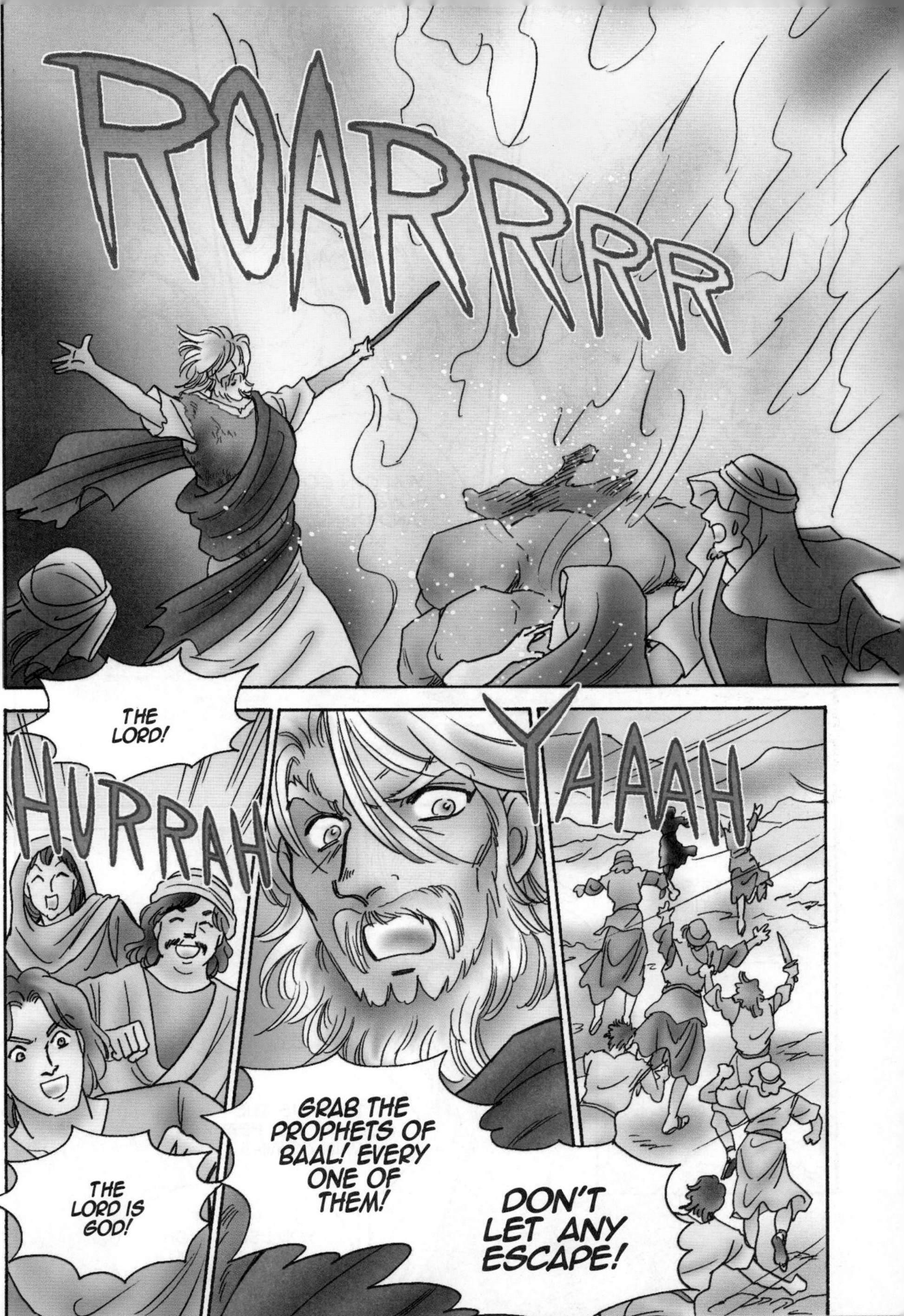
ROARRRRR
THE LORD!
HURRAH
YAAAH
GRAB THE PROPHETS OF BAAL! EVERY ONE OF THEM!
THE LORD IS GOD!
DON'T LET ANY ESCAPE!

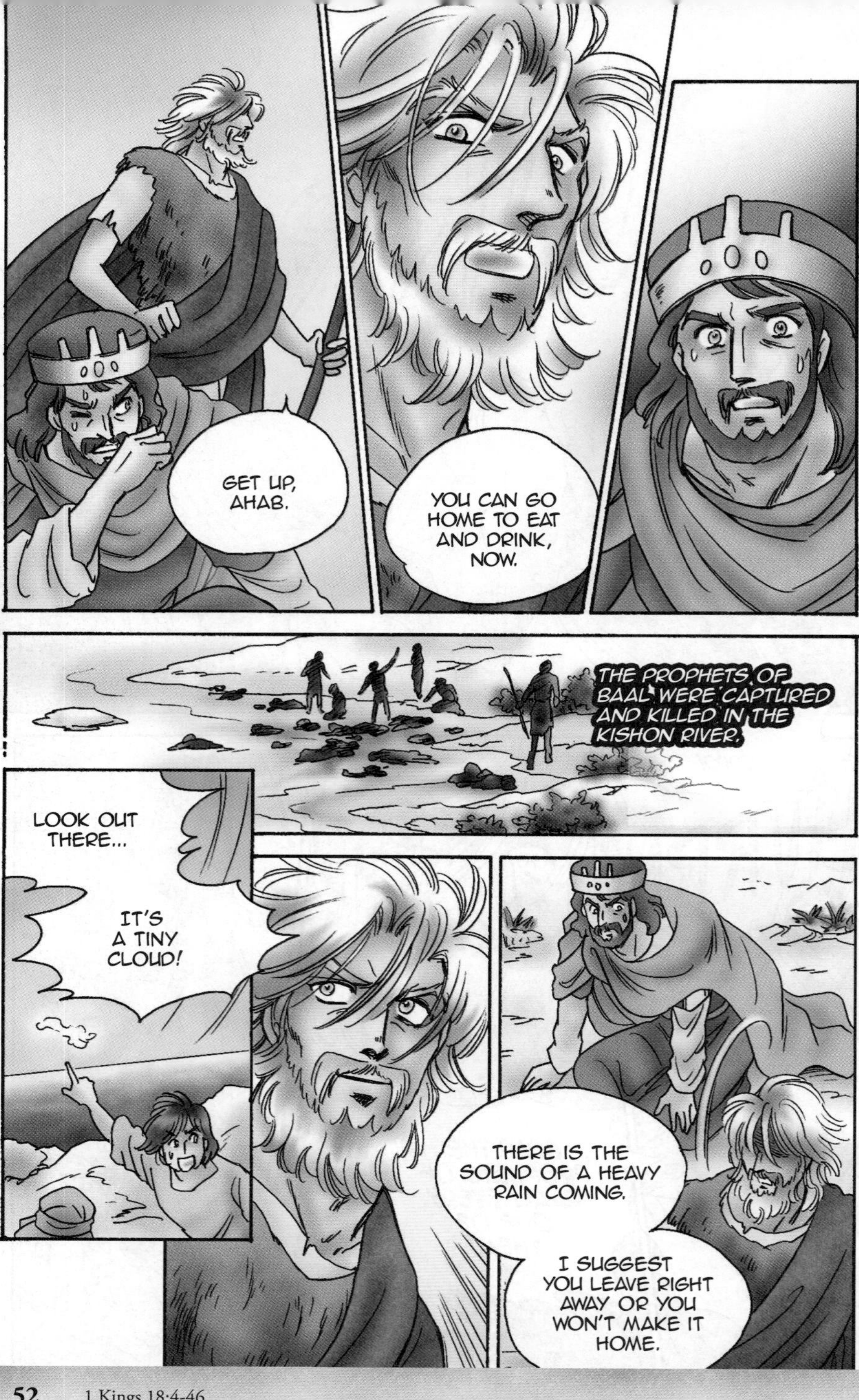
GET UP, AHAB.
YOU CAN GO HOME TO EAT AND DRINK, NOW.
THE PROPHETS OF BAAL WERE CAPTURED AND KILLED IN THE KISHON RIVER.
LOOK OUT THERE...
IT'S A TINY CLOUD!
THERE IS THE SOUND OF A HEAVY RAIN COMING.
I SUGGEST YOU LEAVE RIGHT AWAY OR YOU WON'T MAKE IT HOME.

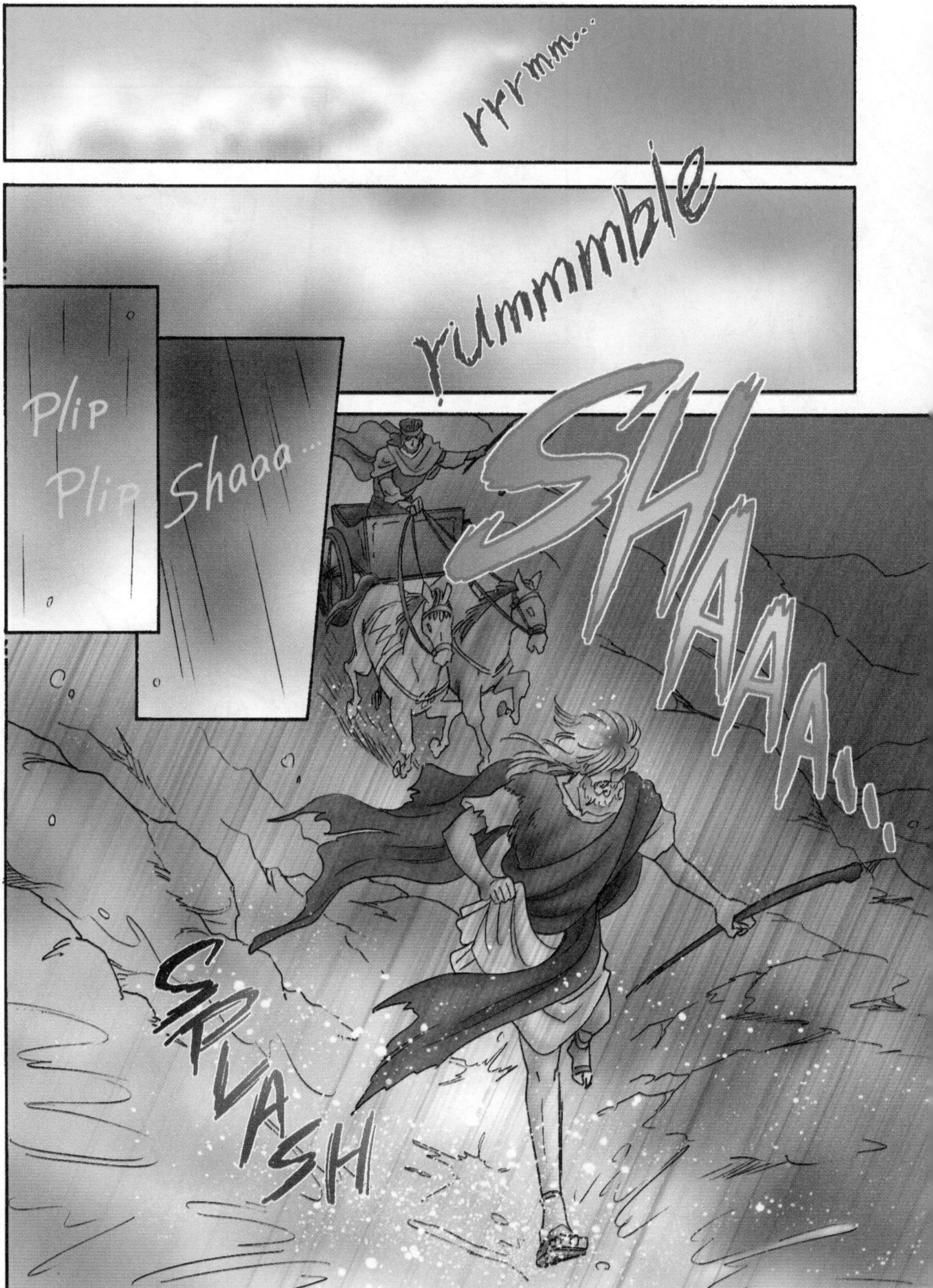
rrrmm...
rummmble
Plip
Plip
Shaaa...
SHAAAA...
SPLASH

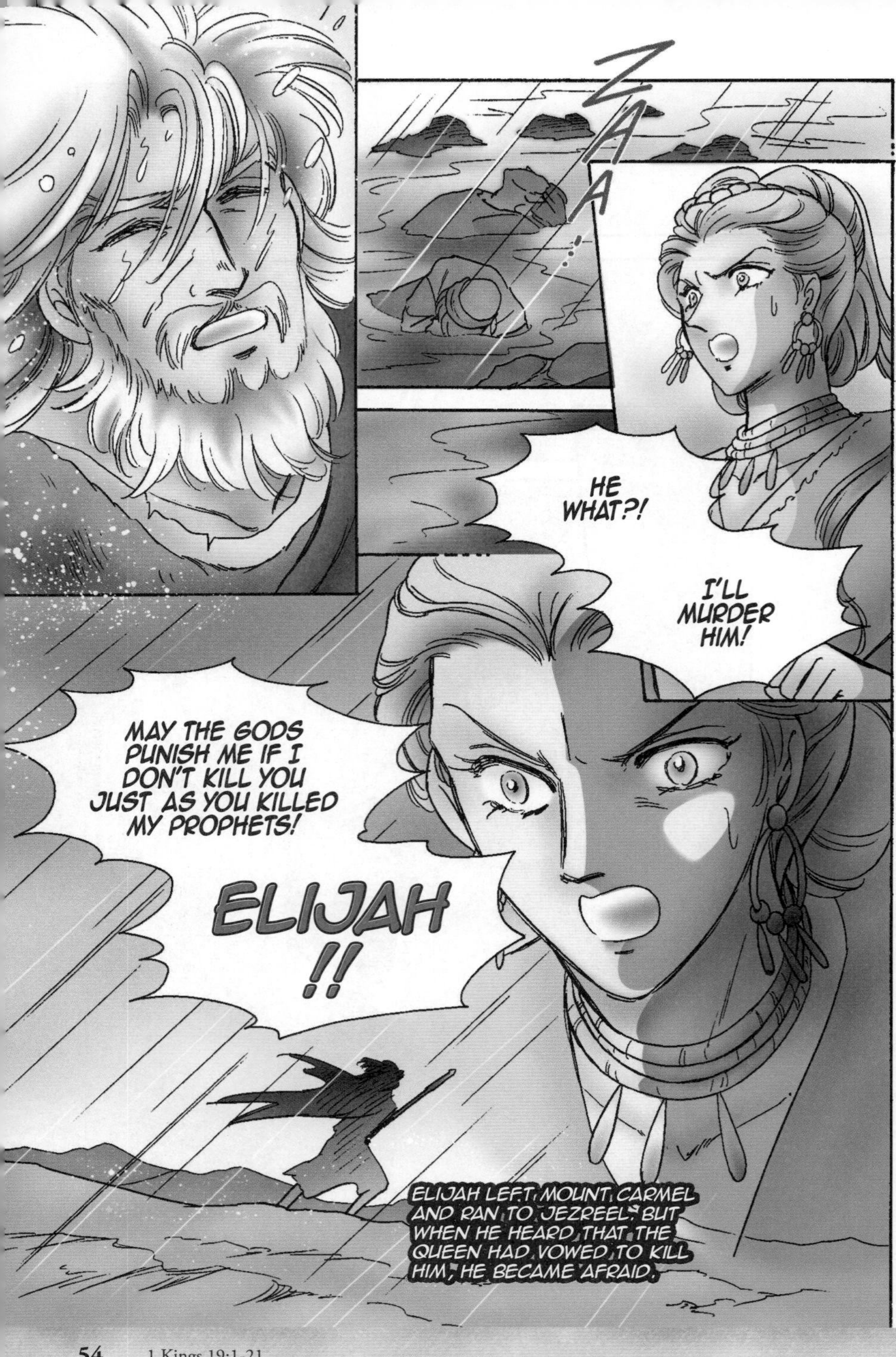
ZAAA...
HE WHAT?!
I'LL MURDER HIM!
MAY THE GODS PUNISH ME IF I DON'T KILL YOU JUST AS YOU KILLED MY PROPHETS!
ELIJAH !!
ELIJAH LEFT MOUNT CARMEL AND RAN TO JEZREEL. BUT WHEN HE HEARD THAT THE QUEEN HAD VOWED TO KILL HIM, HE BECAME AFRAID.

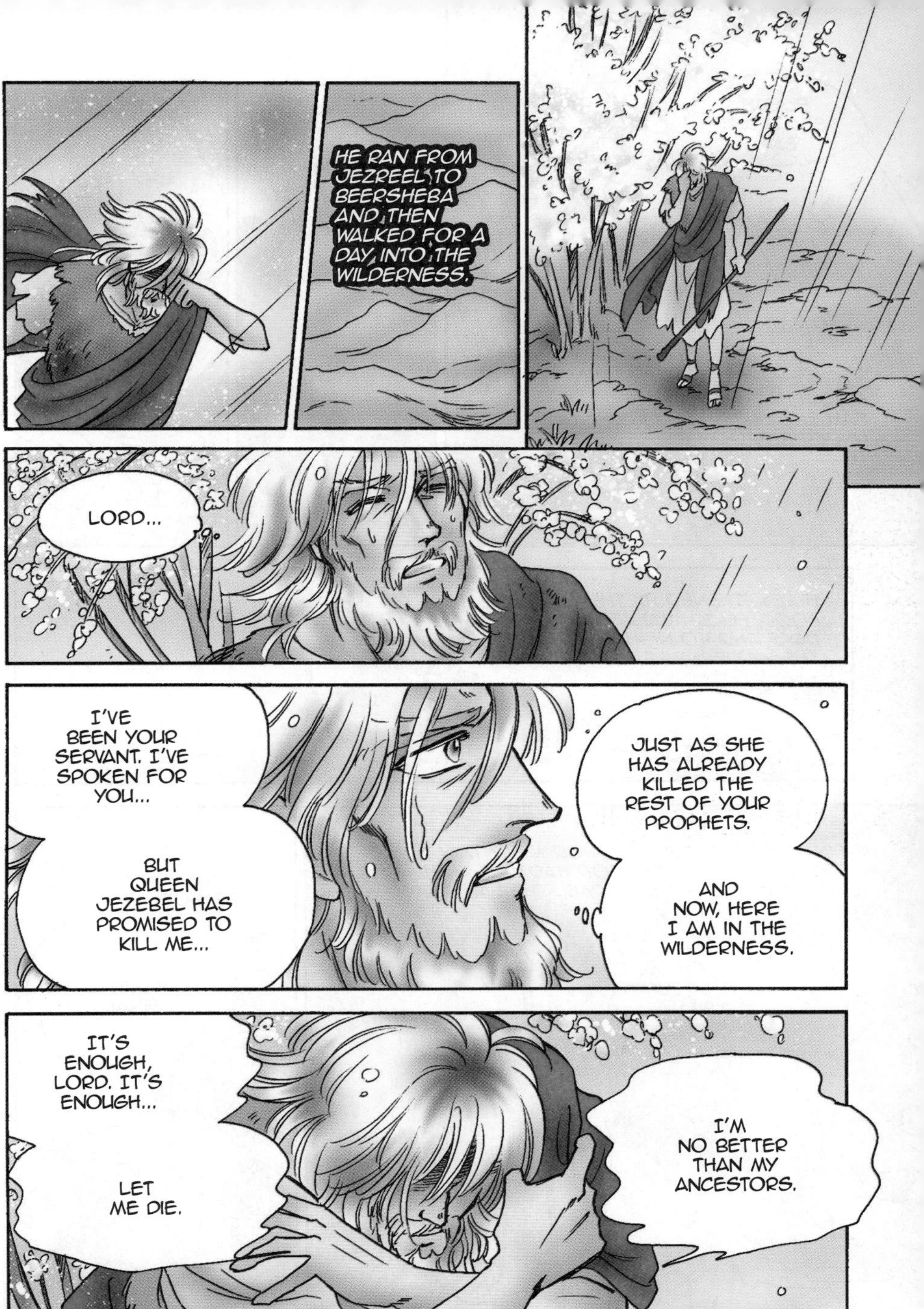
HE RAN FROM JEZREEL TO BEERSHEBA AND THEN WALKED FOR A DAY INTO THE WILDERNESS.
LORD...
I'VE BEEN YOUR SERVANT. I'VE SPOKEN FOR YOU...
BUT QUEEN JEZEBEL HAS PROMISED TO KILL ME...
JUST AS SHE HAS ALREADY KILLED THE REST OF YOUR PROPHETS.
AND NOW, HERE I AM IN THE WILDERNESS.
IT'S ENOUGH, LORD. IT'S ENOUGH...
LET ME DIE.
I'M NO BETTER THAN MY ANCESTORS.

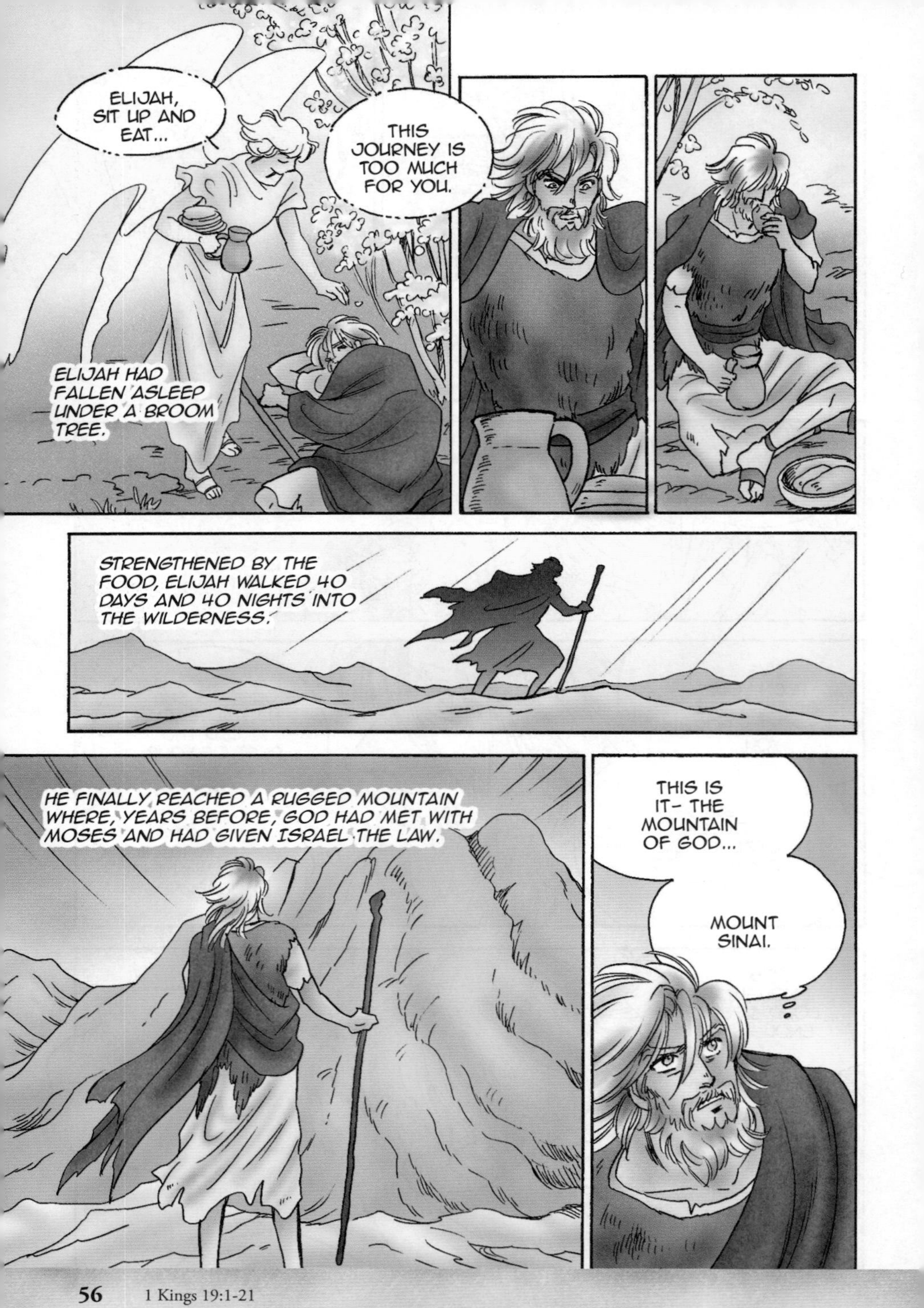
ELIJAH, SIT UP AND EAT...
ELIJAH HAD FALLEN ASLEEP UNDER A BROOM TREE.
THIS JOURNEY IS TOO MUCH FOR YOU.
STRENGTHENED BY THE FOOD, ELIJAH WALKED 40 DAYS AND 40 NIGHTS INTO THE WILDERNESS.
HE FINALLY REACHED A RUGGED MOUNTAIN WHERE, YEARS BEFORE, GOD HAD MET WITH MOSES AND HAD GIVEN ISRAEL THE LAW.
THIS IS IT- THE MOUNTAIN OF GOD...
MOUNT SINAI.

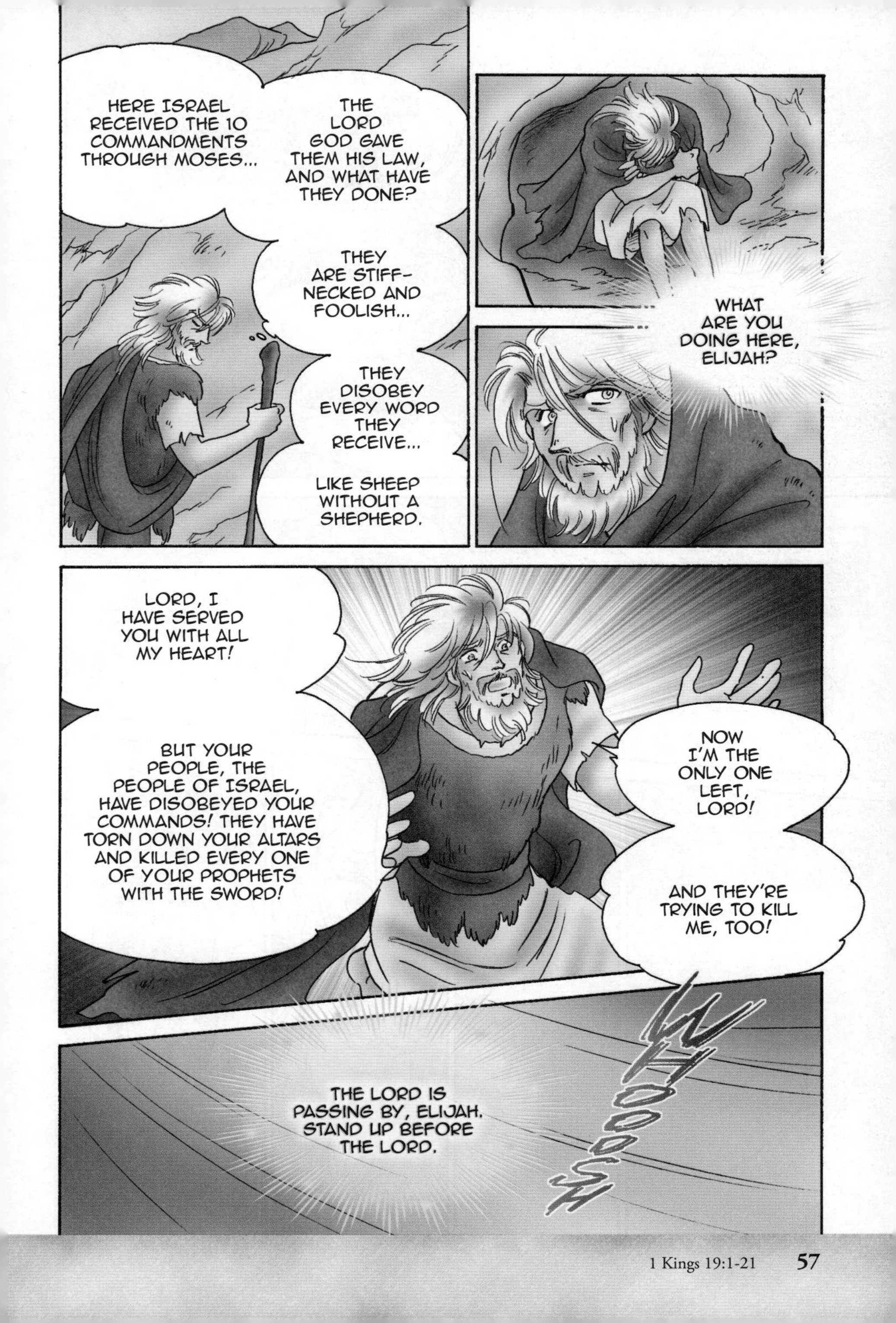
HERE ISRAEL RECEIVED THE 10 COMMANDMENTS THROUGH MOSES...
THE LORD GOD GAVE THEM HIS LAW, AND WHAT HAVE THEY DONE?
THEY ARE STIFF-NECKED AND FOOLISH...
THEY DISOBEY EVERY WORD THEY RECEIVE...
LIKE SHEEP WITHOUT A SHEPHERD.
WHAT ARE YOU DOING HERE, ELIJAH?
LORD, I HAVE SERVED YOU WITH ALL MY HEART!
BUT YOUR PEOPLE, THE PEOPLE OF ISRAEL, HAVE DISOBEYED YOUR COMMANDS! THEY HAVE TORN DOWN YOUR ALTARS AND KILLED EVERY ONE OF YOUR PROPHETS WITH THE SWORD!
NOW I'M THE ONLY ONE LEFT, LORD!
AND THEY'RE TRYING TO KILL ME, TOO!
WHOOOOSH
THE LORD IS PASSING BY, ELIJAH. STAND UP BEFORE THE LORD.

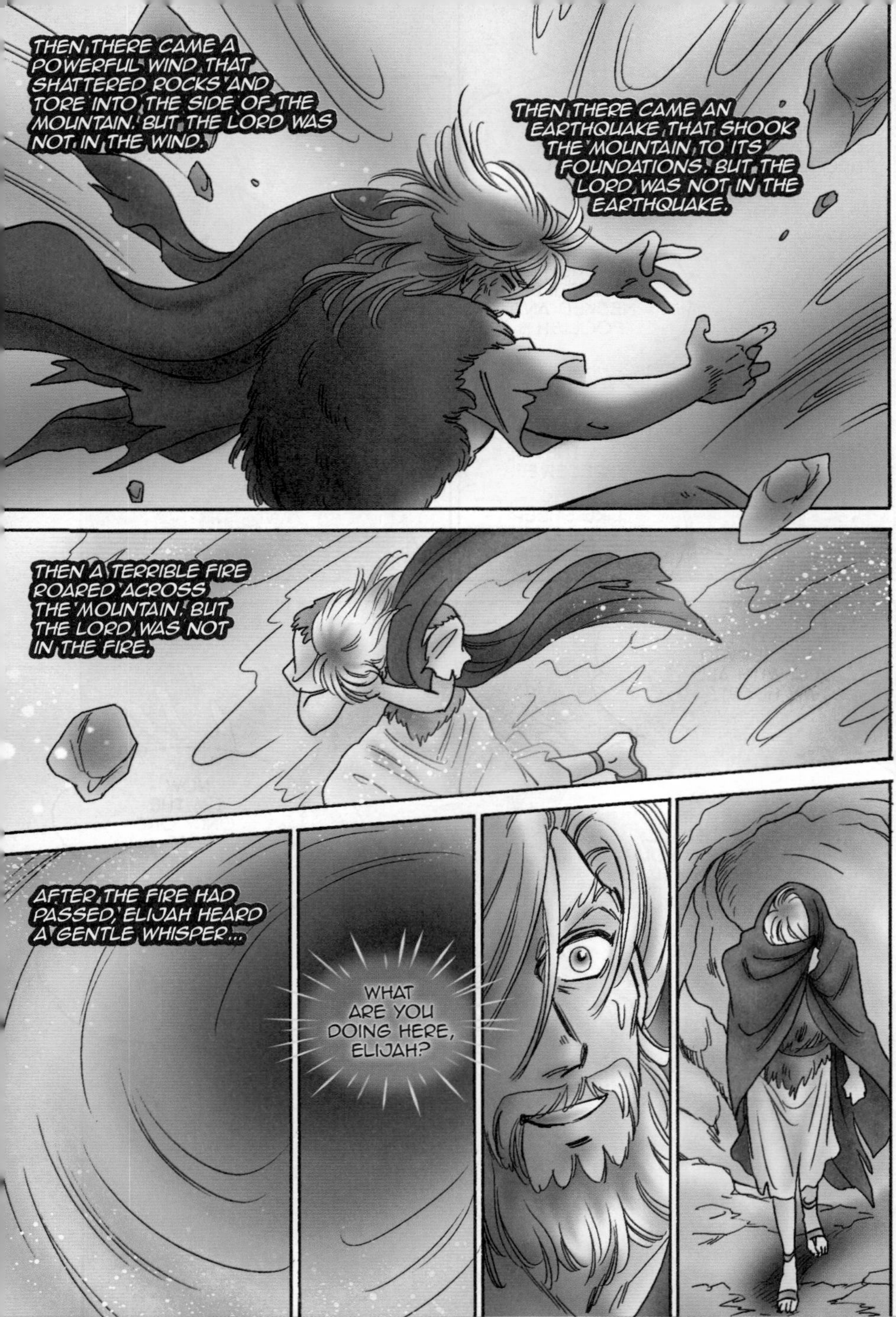
THEN THERE CAME A POWERFUL WIND THAT SHATTERED ROCKS AND TORE INTO THE SIDE OF THE MOUNTAIN. BUT THE LORD WAS NOT IN THE WIND.
THEN THERE CAME AN EARTHQUAKE THAT SHOOK THE MOUNTAIN TO ITS FOUNDATIONS. BUT THE LORD WAS NOT IN THE EARTHQUAKE.
THEN A TERRIBLE FIRE ROARED ACROSS THE MOUNTAIN. BUT THE LORD WAS NOT IN THE FIRE.
AFTER THE FIRE HAD PASSED, ELIJAH HEARD A GENTLE WHISPER...
WHAT ARE YOU DOING HERE, ELIJAH?

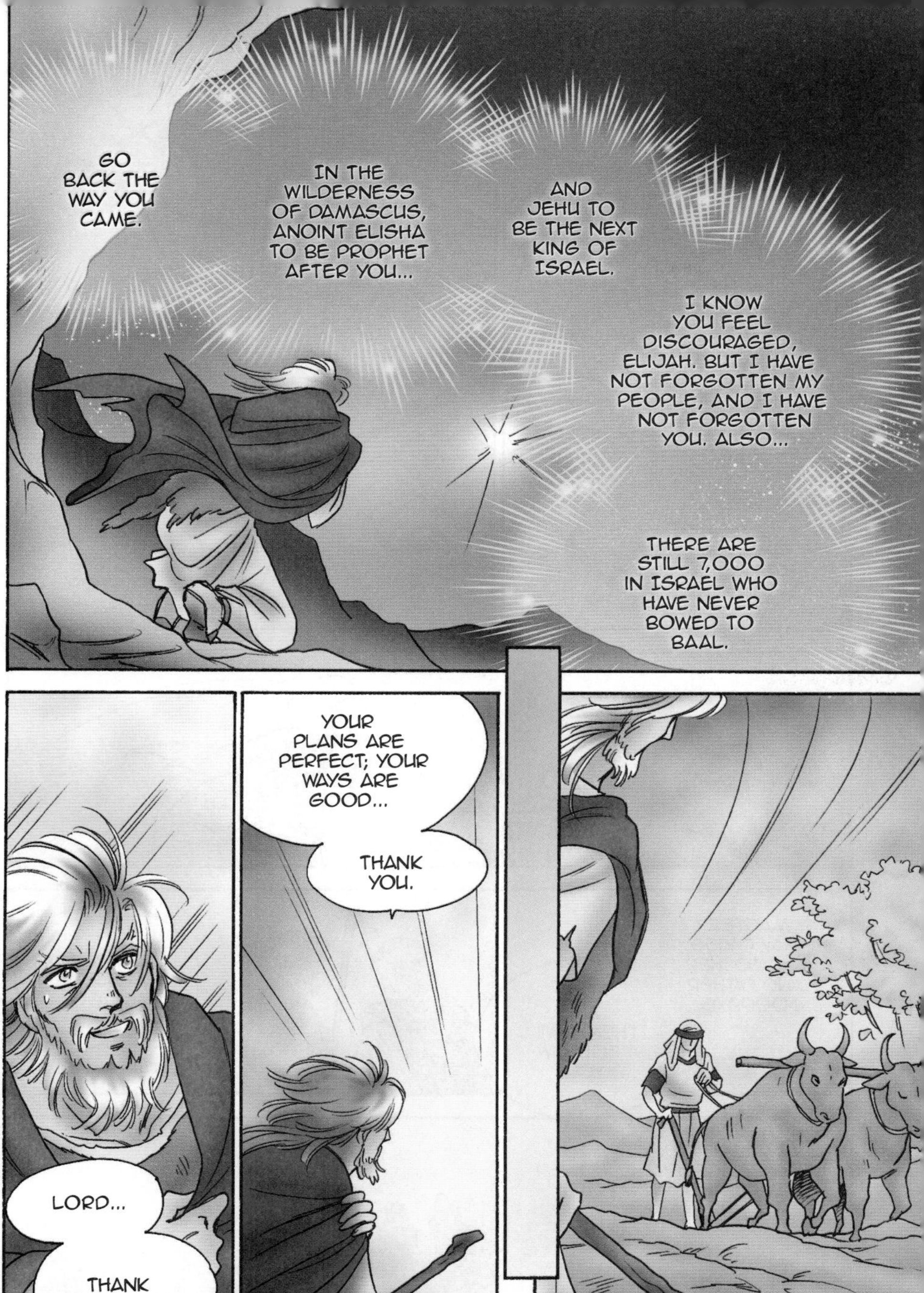
GO BACK THE WAY YOU CAME.
IN THE WILDERNESS OF DAMASCUS, ANOINT ELISHA TO BE PROPHET AFTER YOU...
AND JEHU TO BE THE NEXT KING OF ISRAEL.
I KNOW YOU FEEL DISCOURAGED, ELIJAH. BUT I HAVE NOT FORGOTTEN MY PEOPLE, AND I HAVE NOT FORGOTTEN YOU. ALSO...
THERE ARE STILL 7,000 IN ISRAEL WHO HAVE NEVER BOWED TO BAAL.
LORD...
THANK YOU.
YOUR PLANS ARE PERFECT; YOUR WAYS ARE GOOD...
THANK YOU.

ELISHA...

HUH?

YES?

CARRY THIS.

WHUH

FLAP

IT'S THE PROPHET!

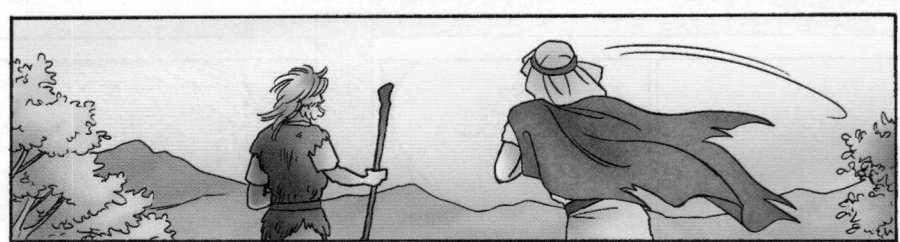

MASTER, MAY I KISS MY MOTHER AND FATHER GOODBYE...

AND THEN I WILL FOLLOW YOU?

WHY ARE YOU ASKING ME? GO!

ELISHA SAID GOODBYE TO HIS FAMILY, THEN FOLLOWED ELIJAH AND SERVED HIM.

6. Elijah's Departure

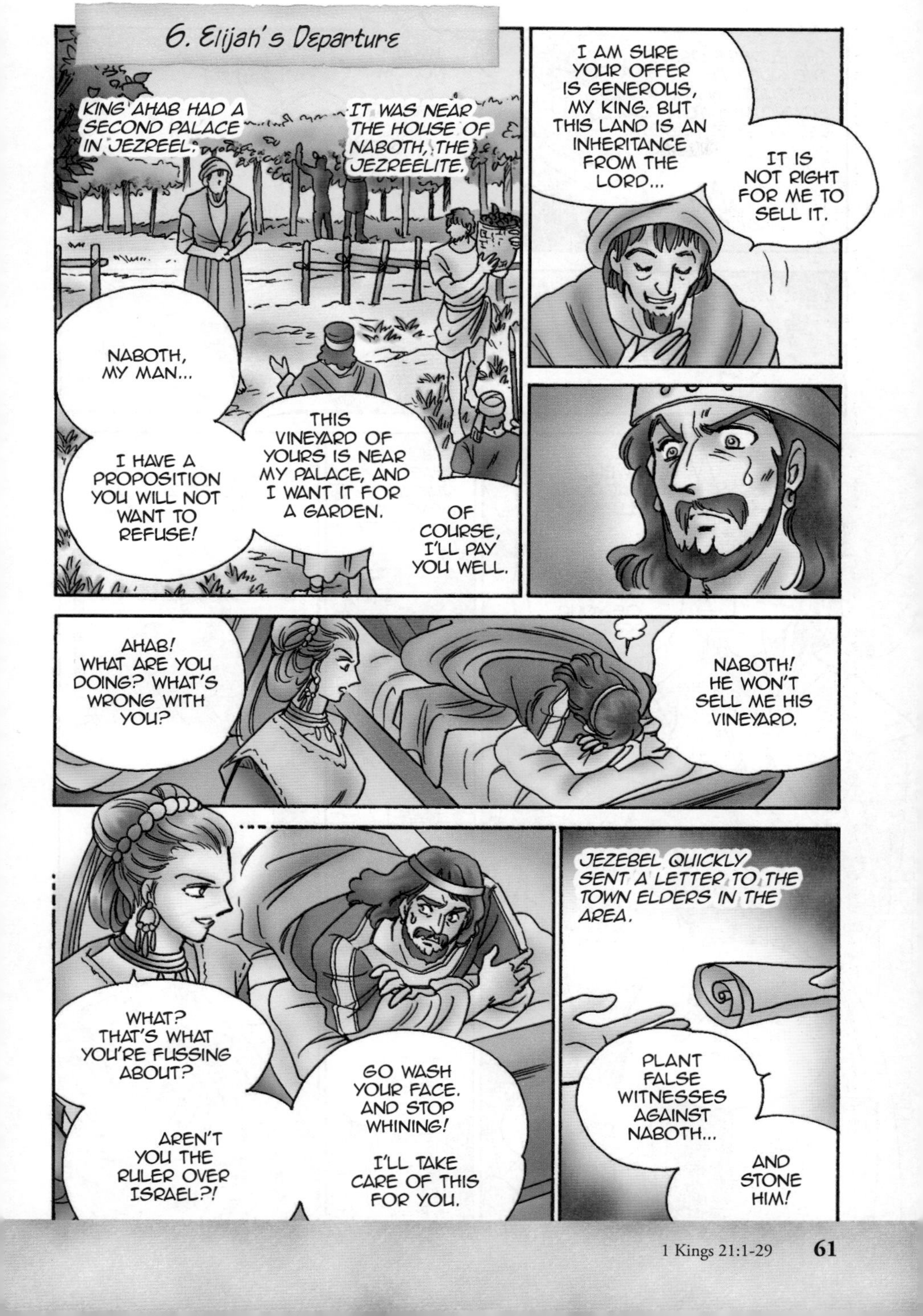
KING AHAB HAD A SECOND PALACE IN JEZREEL.
IT WAS NEAR THE HOUSE OF NABOTH, THE JEZREELITE.
NABOTH, MY MAN...
I HAVE A PROPOSITION YOU WILL NOT WANT TO REFUSE!
THIS VINEYARD OF YOURS IS NEAR MY PALACE, AND I WANT IT FOR A GARDEN.
OF COURSE, I'LL PAY YOU WELL.
I AM SURE YOUR OFFER IS GENEROUS, MY KING. BUT THIS LAND IS AN INHERITANCE FROM THE LORD...
IT IS NOT RIGHT FOR ME TO SELL IT.
AHAB! WHAT ARE YOU DOING? WHAT'S WRONG WITH YOU?
NABOTH! HE WON'T SELL ME HIS VINEYARD.
WHAT? THAT'S WHAT YOU'RE FUSSING ABOUT?
AREN'T YOU THE RULER OVER ISRAEL?!
GO WASH YOUR FACE. AND STOP WHINING!
I'LL TAKE CARE OF THIS FOR YOU.
JEZEBEL QUICKLY SENT A LETTER TO THE TOWN ELDERS IN THE AREA.
PLANT FALSE WITNESSES AGAINST NABOTH...
AND STONE HIM!

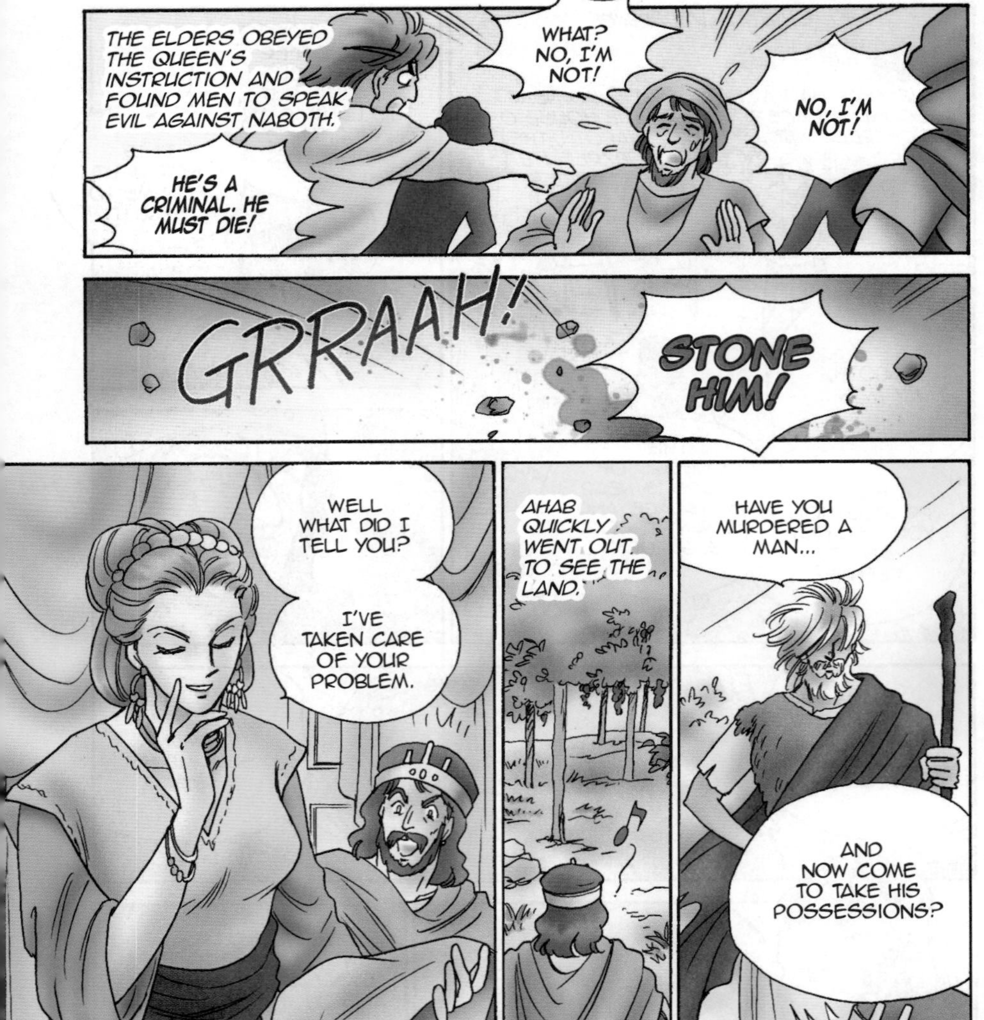
THE ELDERS OBEYED THE QUEEN'S INSTRUCTION AND FOUND MEN TO SPEAK EVIL AGAINST NABOTH.
HE'S A CRIMINAL. HE MUST DIE!
WHAT? NO, I'M NOT!
NO, I'M NOT!
GRRAAH!
STONE HIM!
WELL WHAT DID I TELL YOU?
I'VE TAKEN CARE OF YOUR PROBLEM.
NABOTH'S DEAD AND THE FIELD IS YOURS.
REALLY?!
AHAB QUICKLY WENT OUT TO SEE THE LAND.
THIS IS GREAT!
HAVE YOU MURDERED A MAN...
AND NOW COME TO TAKE HIS POSSESSIONS?
?

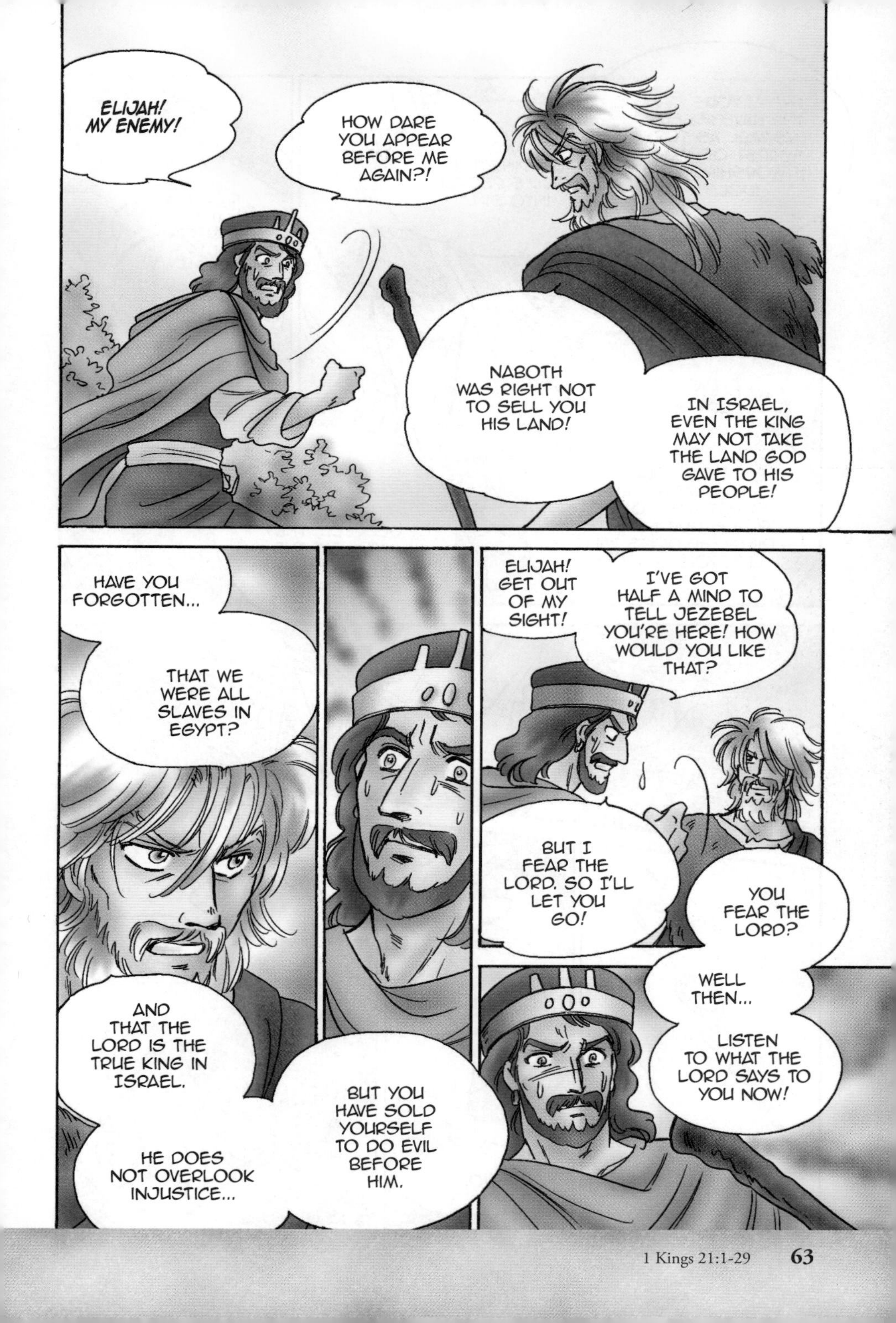
ELIJAH! MY ENEMY!
HOW DARE YOU APPEAR BEFORE ME AGAIN?!
NABOTH WAS RIGHT NOT TO SELL YOU HIS LAND!
IN ISRAEL, EVEN THE KING MAY NOT TAKE THE LAND GOD GAVE TO HIS PEOPLE!
HAVE YOU FORGOTTEN...
THAT WE WERE ALL SLAVES IN EGYPT?
ELIJAH! GET OUT OF MY SIGHT!
I'VE GOT HALF A MIND TO TELL JEZEBEL YOU'RE HERE! HOW WOULD YOU LIKE THAT?
BUT I FEAR THE LORD. SO I'LL LET YOU GO!
YOU FEAR THE LORD?
WELL THEN...
LISTEN TO WHAT THE LORD SAYS TO YOU NOW!
AND THAT THE LORD IS THE TRUE KING IN ISRAEL.
HE DOES NOT OVERLOOK INJUSTICE...
BUT YOU HAVE SOLD YOURSELF TO DO EVIL BEFORE HIM.

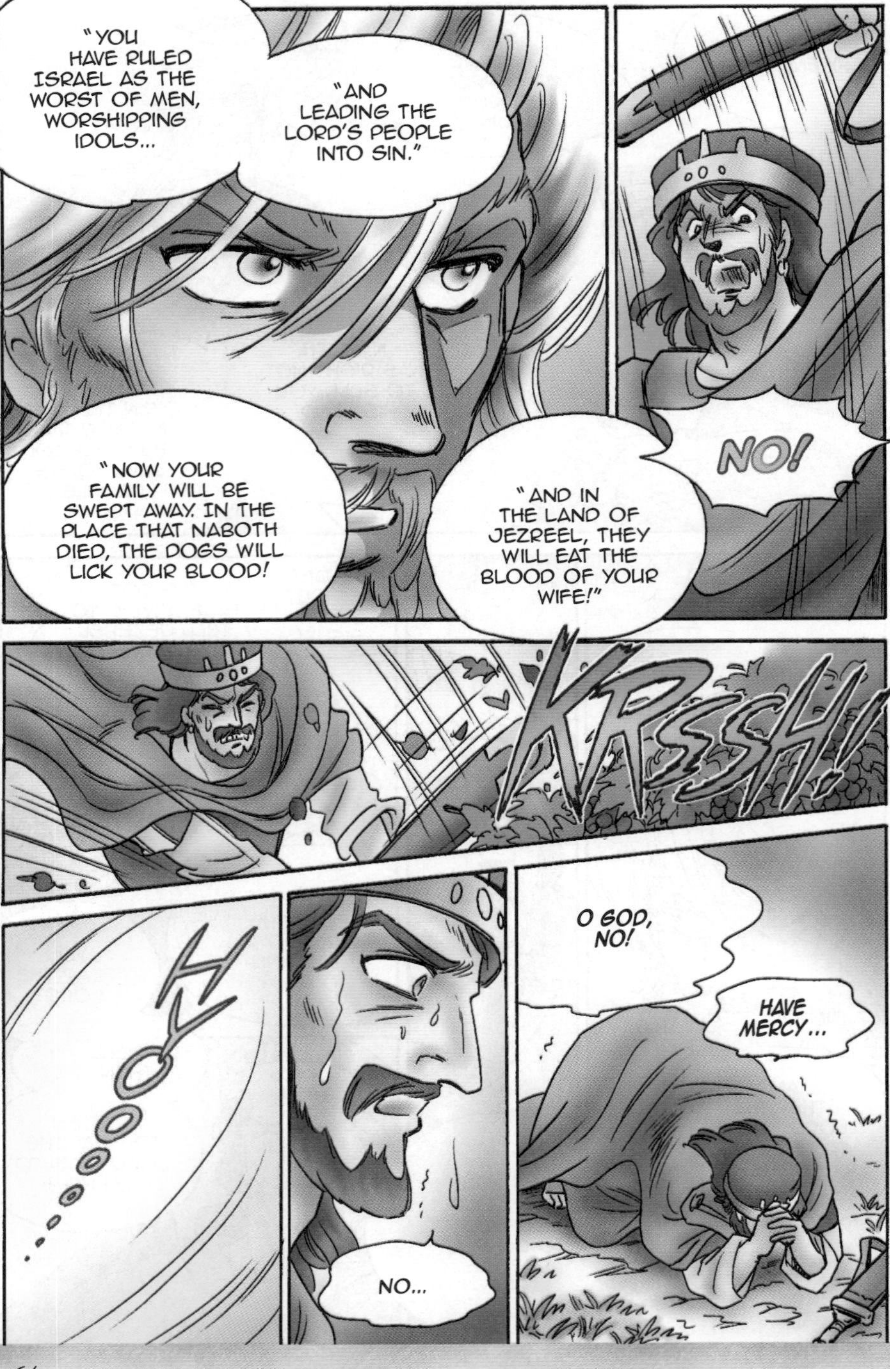
"YOU HAVE RULED ISRAEL AS THE WORST OF MEN, WORSHIPPING IDOLS...
"AND LEADING THE LORD'S PEOPLE INTO SIN."
"NOW YOUR FAMILY WILL BE SWEPT AWAY. IN THE PLACE THAT NABOTH DIED, THE DOGS WILL LICK YOUR BLOOD!
"AND IN THE LAND OF JEZREEL, THEY WILL EAT THE BLOOD OF YOUR WIFE!"
NO!
KRSSH!
HYOOOOO...
NO...
O GOD, NO!
HAVE MERCY...

NORTHERN ISRAEL AND SOUTHERN JUDAH WARRED AGAINST EACH OTHER FOR MANY YEARS.

BUT IN THE DAYS OF AHAB, THE TWO WERE RECONCILED, AND THE KING OF JUDAH'S SON MARRIED AHAB'S DAUGHTER.

NOW THE NATION OF ARAM WAS POWERFUL, AND ISRAEL WAS NOT STRONG ENOUGH TO STAND AGAINST IT.

SO AHAB JOINED FORCES WITH THE KING OF JUDAH, AND THEY WENT OUT TO FIGHT THE ARMIES OF ARAM TOGETHER.

HYAH!

BUT, IN THE MIDST OF BATTLE...

AGHH!

!!

E-ELIJAH...

AHAB, WAS TAKEN BACK TO SAMARIA AND BURIED THERE.

HIS CHARIOT WAS WASHED BY THE POOL OF SAMARIA...

AND, THE DOGS LICKED UP HIS BLOOD.

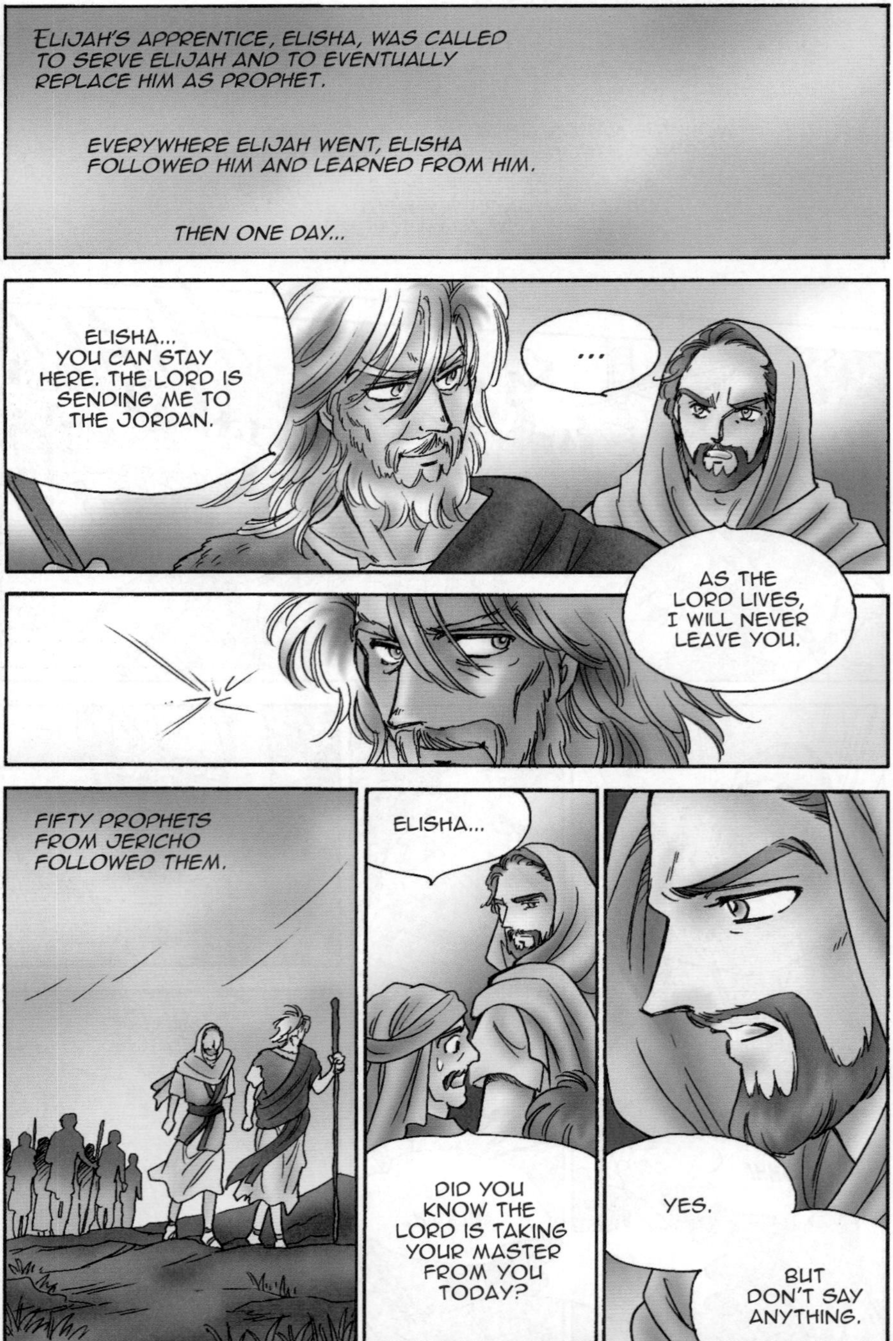
ELIJAH'S APPRENTICE, ELISHA, WAS CALLED TO SERVE ELIJAH AND TO EVENTUALLY REPLACE HIM AS PROPHET.
EVERYWHERE ELIJAH WENT, ELISHA FOLLOWED HIM AND LEARNED FROM HIM.
THEN ONE DAY...
ELISHA... YOU CAN STAY HERE. THE LORD IS SENDING ME TO THE JORDAN.
...
AS THE LORD LIVES, I WILL NEVER LEAVE YOU.
FIFTY PROPHETS FROM JERICHO FOLLOWED THEM.
ELISHA...
DID YOU KNOW THE LORD IS TAKING YOUR MASTER FROM YOU TODAY?
YES.
BUT DON'T SAY ANYTHING.

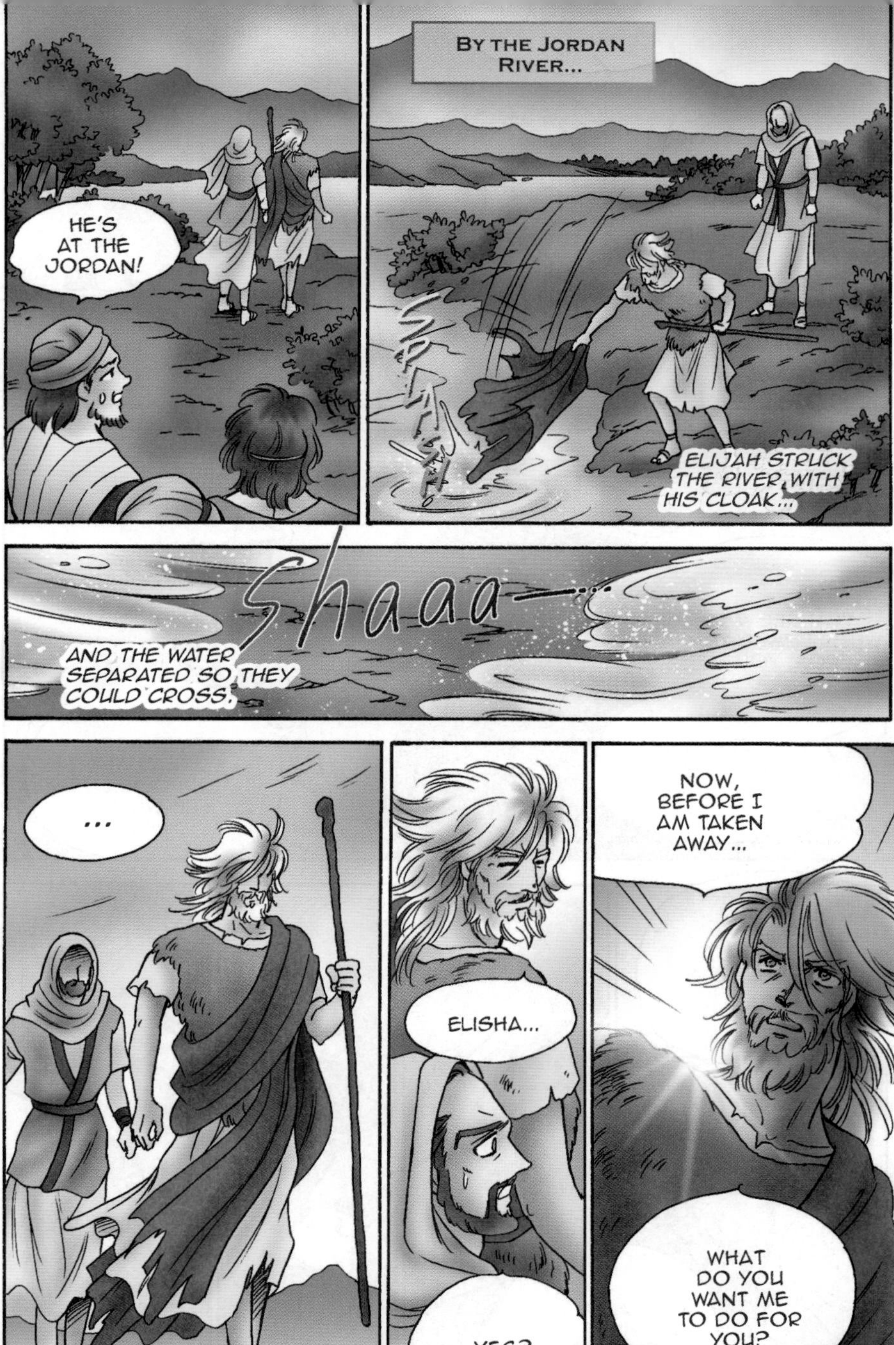
HE'S AT THE JORDAN!
BY THE JORDAN RIVER...
SPLASH
ELIJAH STRUCK THE RIVER WITH HIS CLOAK...
Shaaa—
AND THE WATER SEPARATED SO THEY COULD CROSS.
...
ELISHA...
YES?
NOW, BEFORE I AM TAKEN AWAY...
WHAT DO YOU WANT ME TO DO FOR YOU?

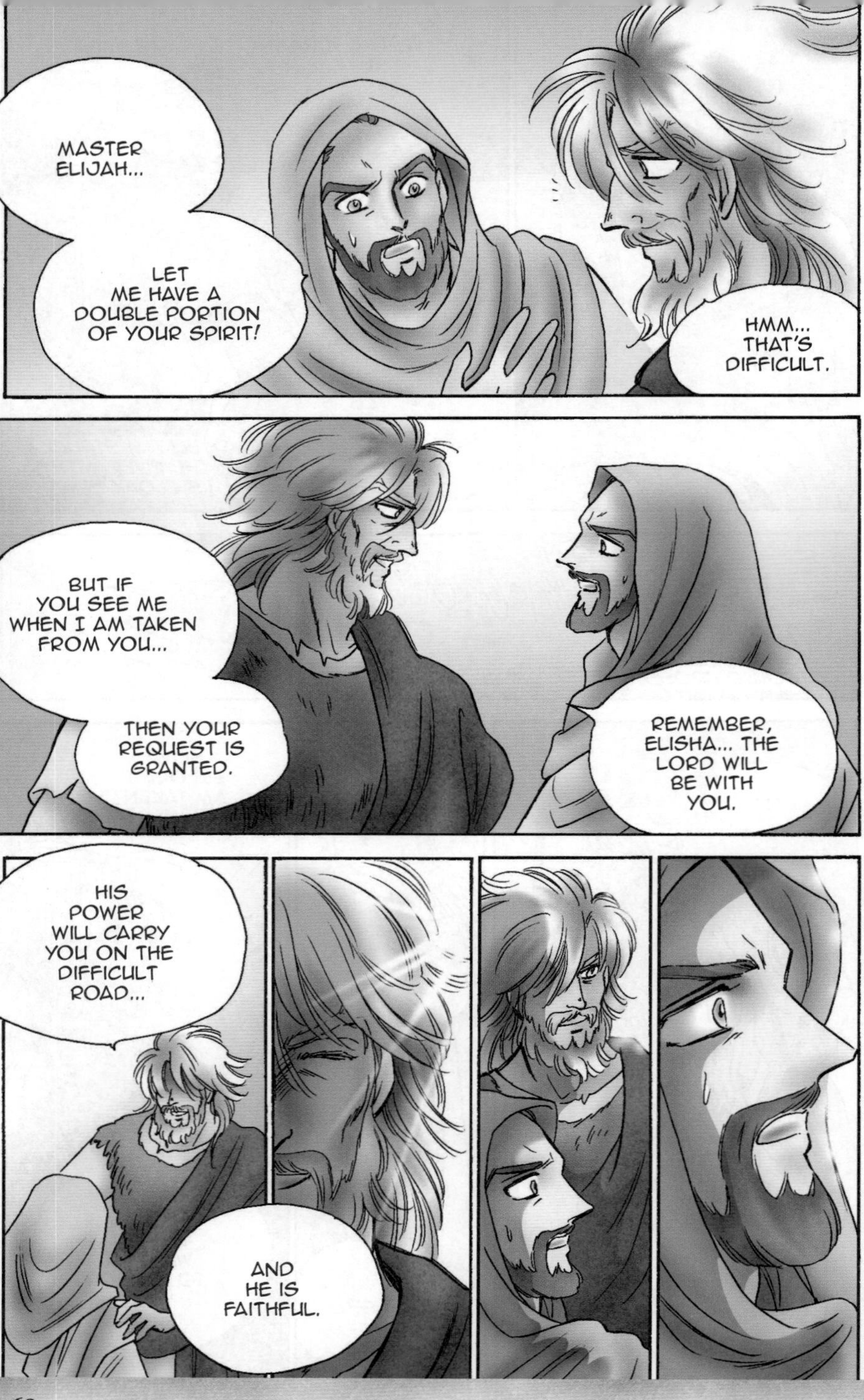
MASTER ELIJAH...
LET ME HAVE A DOUBLE PORTION OF YOUR SPIRIT!
HMM... THAT'S DIFFICULT.
BUT IF YOU SEE ME WHEN I AM TAKEN FROM YOU...
THEN YOUR REQUEST IS GRANTED.
REMEMBER, ELISHA... THE LORD WILL BE WITH YOU.
HIS POWER WILL CARRY YOU ON THE DIFFICULT ROAD...
AND HE IS FAITHFUL.

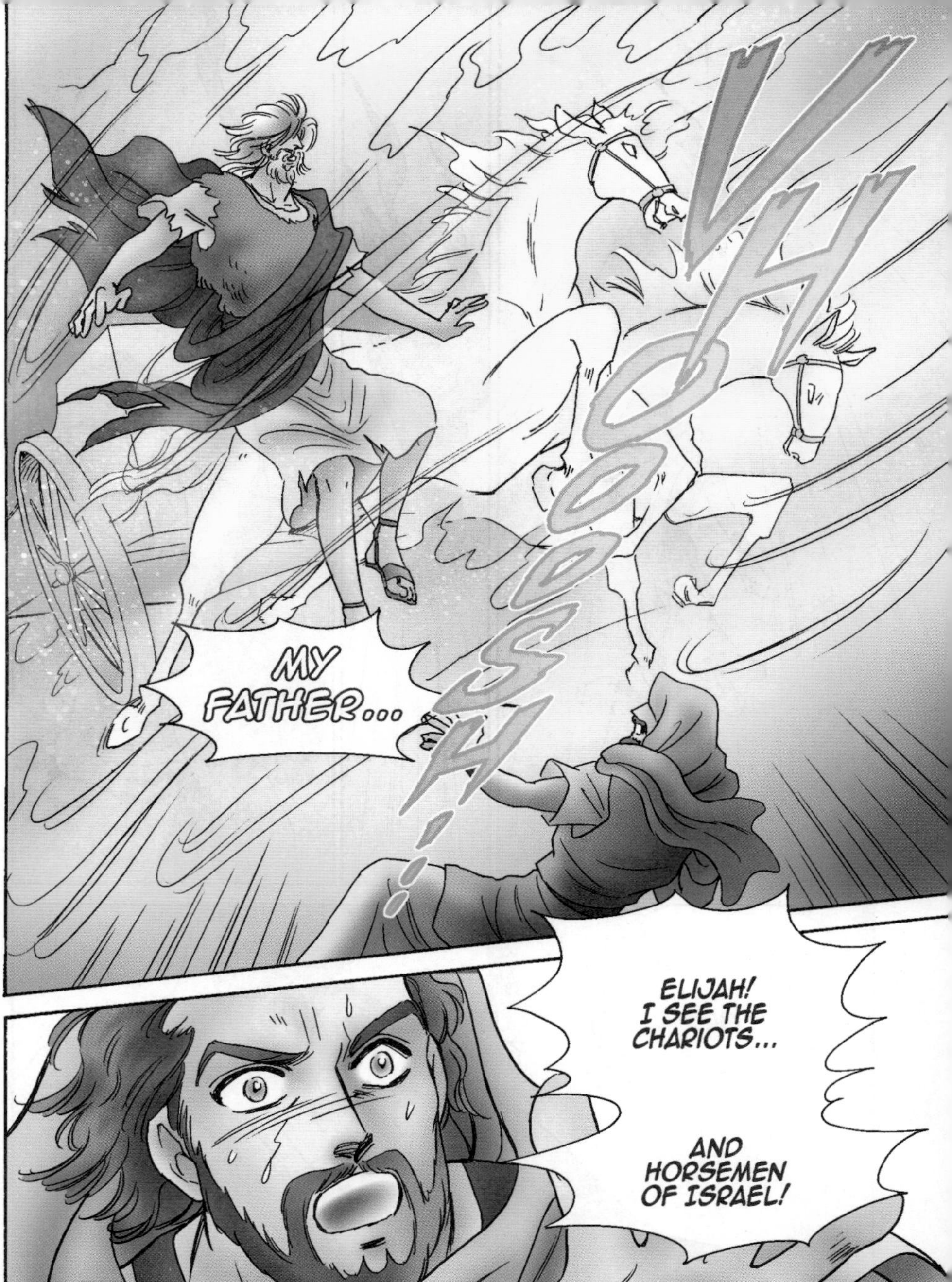
WHOOOOSH...!
MY FATHER...
ELIJAH! I SEE THE CHARIOTS...
AND HORSEMEN OF ISRAEL!

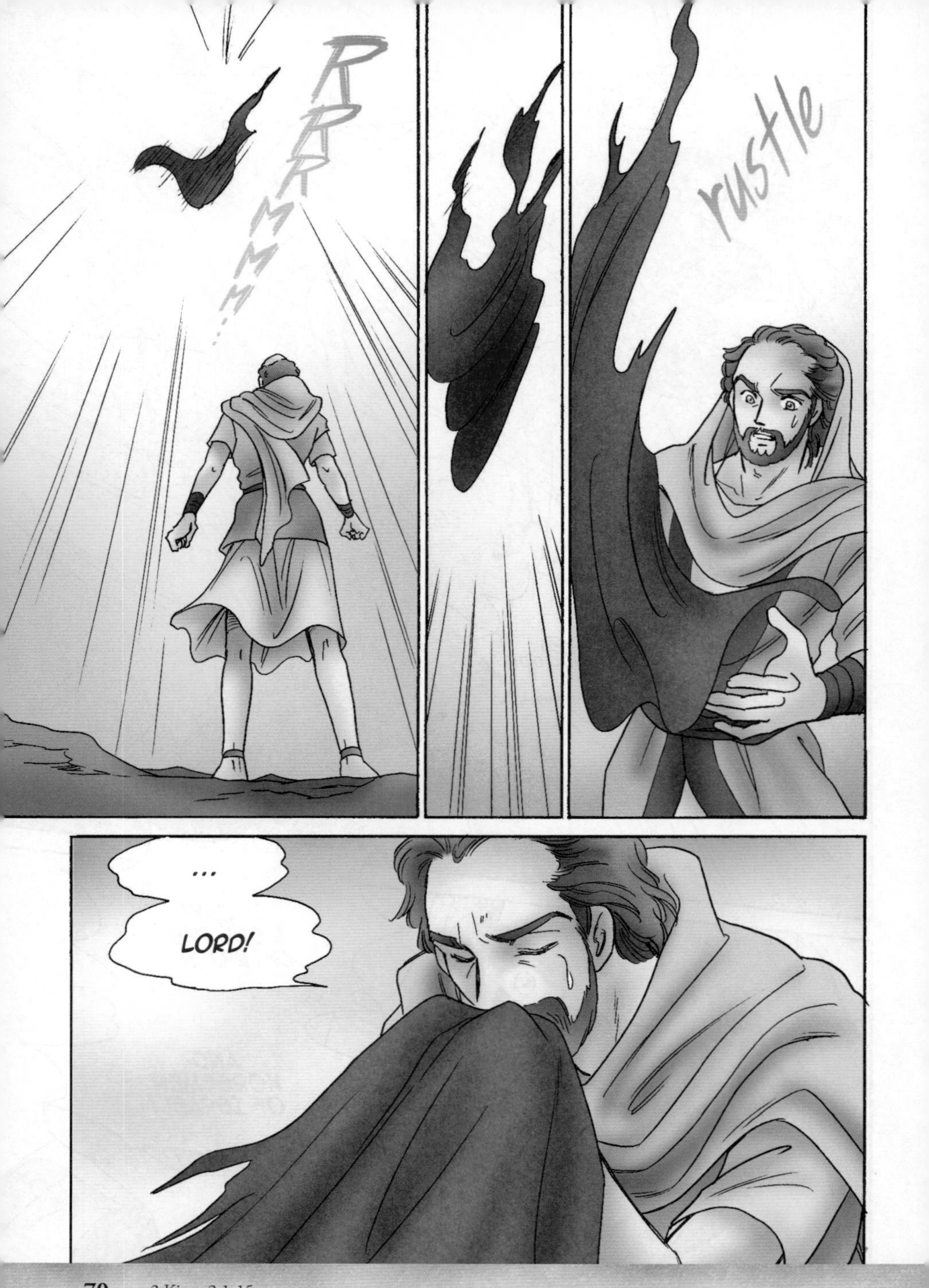
RRRMMMM...
rustle
...
LORD!

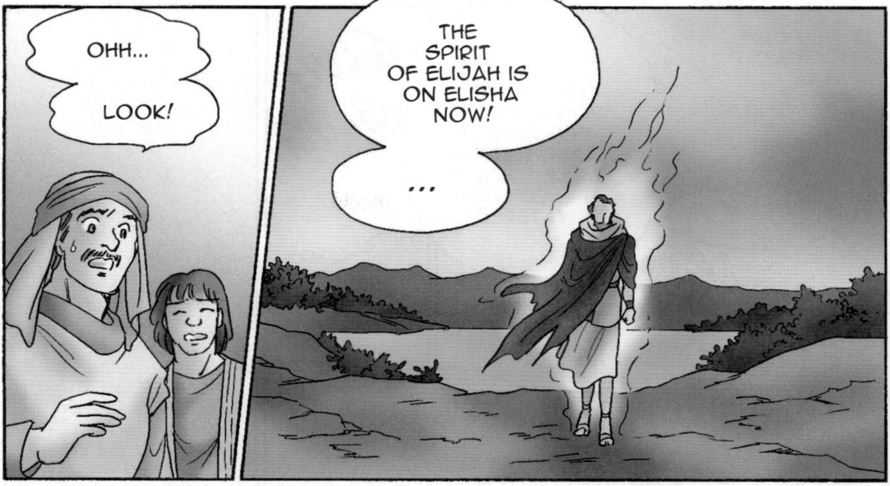
OHH...
LOOK!
THE SPIRIT OF ELIJAH IS ON ELISHA NOW!
...

7. The Power of Elisha

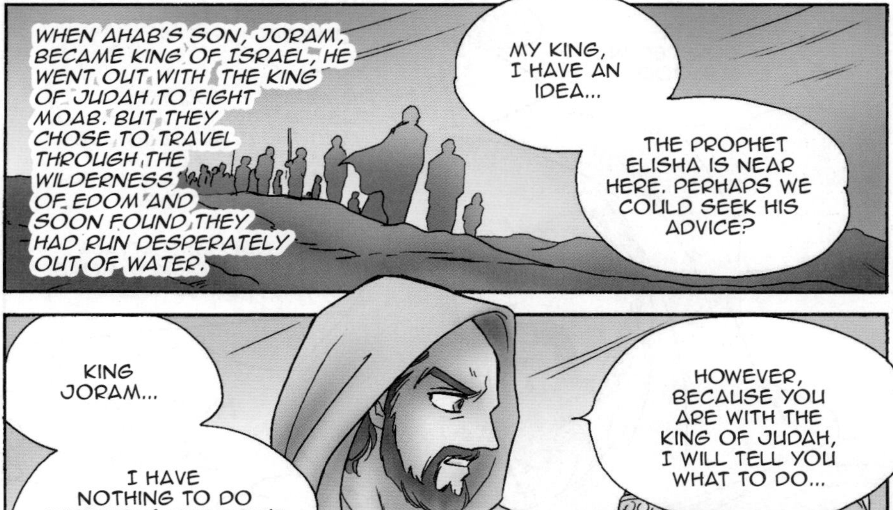
WHEN AHAB'S SON, JORAM, BECAME KING OF ISRAEL, HE WENT OUT WITH THE KING OF JUDAH TO FIGHT MOAB. BUT THEY CHOSE TO TRAVEL THROUGH THE WILDERNESS OF EDOM AND SOON FOUND THEY HAD RUN DESPERATELY OUT OF WATER.
MY KING, I HAVE AN IDEA...
THE PROPHET ELISHA IS NEAR HERE. PERHAPS WE COULD SEEK HIS ADVICE?
KING JORAM...
I HAVE NOTHING TO DO WITH YOU! WHY DON'T YOU SEEK COUNSEL FROM THE PROPHETS OF YOUR FATHER AND MOTHER!
HOWEVER, BECAUSE YOU ARE WITH THE KING OF JUDAH, I WILL TELL YOU WHAT TO DO...
URGH!

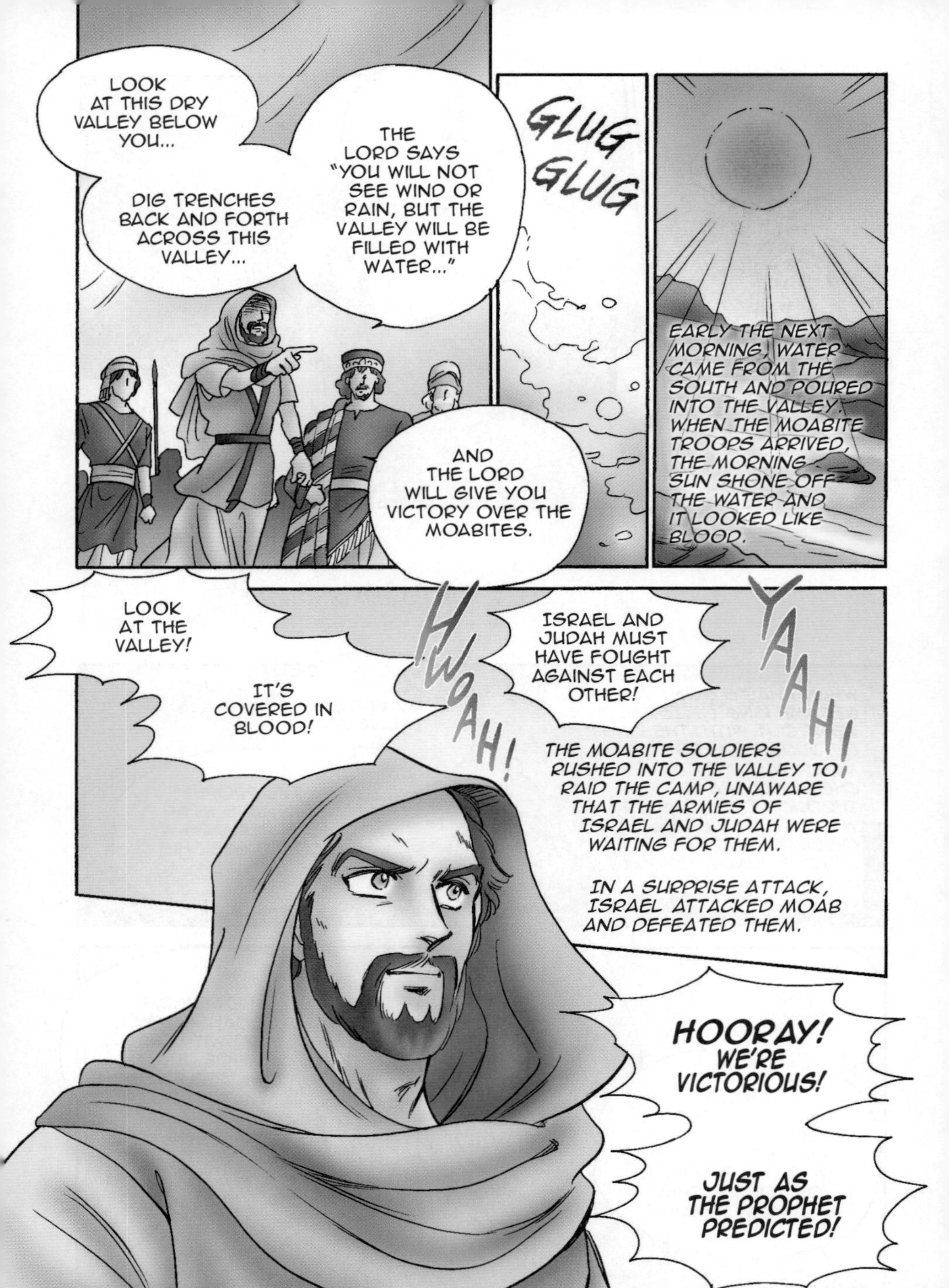
LOOK AT THIS DRY VALLEY BELOW YOU...
DIG TRENCHES BACK AND FORTH ACROSS THIS VALLEY...
THE LORD SAYS "YOU WILL NOT SEE WIND OR RAIN, BUT THE VALLEY WILL BE FILLED WITH WATER..."
AND THE LORD WILL GIVE YOU VICTORY OVER THE MOABITES.
GLUG GLUG
EARLY THE NEXT MORNING, WATER CAME FROM THE SOUTH AND POURED INTO THE VALLEY. WHEN THE MOABITE TROOPS ARRIVED, THE MORNING SUN SHONE OFF THE WATER AND IT LOOKED LIKE BLOOD.
LOOK AT THE VALLEY!
IT'S COVERED IN BLOOD!
ISRAEL AND JUDAH MUST HAVE FOUGHT AGAINST EACH OTHER!
HWOAH!
YAAH!
THE MOABITE SOLDIERS RUSHED INTO THE VALLEY TO RAID THE CAMP, UNAWARE THAT THE ARMIES OF ISRAEL AND JUDAH WERE WAITING FOR THEM.
IN A SURPRISE ATTACK, ISRAEL ATTACKED MOAB AND DEFEATED THEM.
HOORAY! WE'RE VICTORIOUS!
JUST AS THE PROPHET PREDICTED!

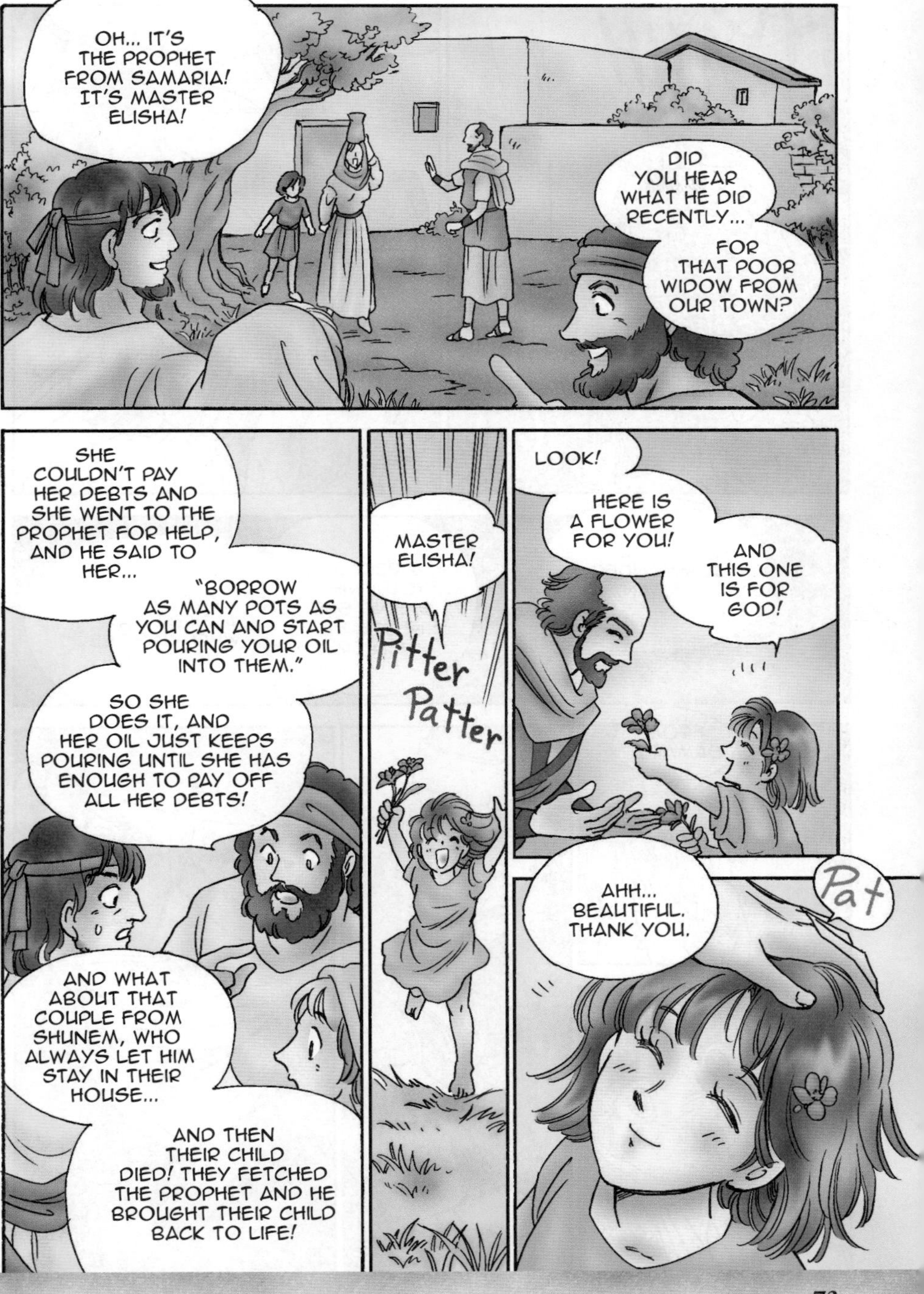
OH... IT'S THE PROPHET FROM SAMARIA! IT'S MASTER ELISHA!
DID YOU HEAR WHAT HE DID RECENTLY...
FOR THAT POOR WIDOW FROM OUR TOWN?
SHE COULDN'T PAY HER DEBTS AND SHE WENT TO THE PROPHET FOR HELP, AND HE SAID TO HER...
"BORROW AS MANY POTS AS YOU CAN AND START POURING YOUR OIL INTO THEM."
SO SHE DOES IT, AND HER OIL JUST KEEPS POURING UNTIL SHE HAS ENOUGH TO PAY OFF ALL HER DEBTS!
AND WHAT ABOUT THAT COUPLE FROM SHUNEM, WHO ALWAYS LET HIM STAY IN THEIR HOUSE...
AND THEN THEIR CHILD DIED! THEY FETCHED THE PROPHET AND HE BROUGHT THEIR CHILD BACK TO LIFE!
MASTER ELISHA!
Pitter Patter
LOOK!
HERE IS A FLOWER FOR YOU!
AND THIS ONE IS FOR GOD!
AHH... BEAUTIFUL. THANK YOU.
Pat

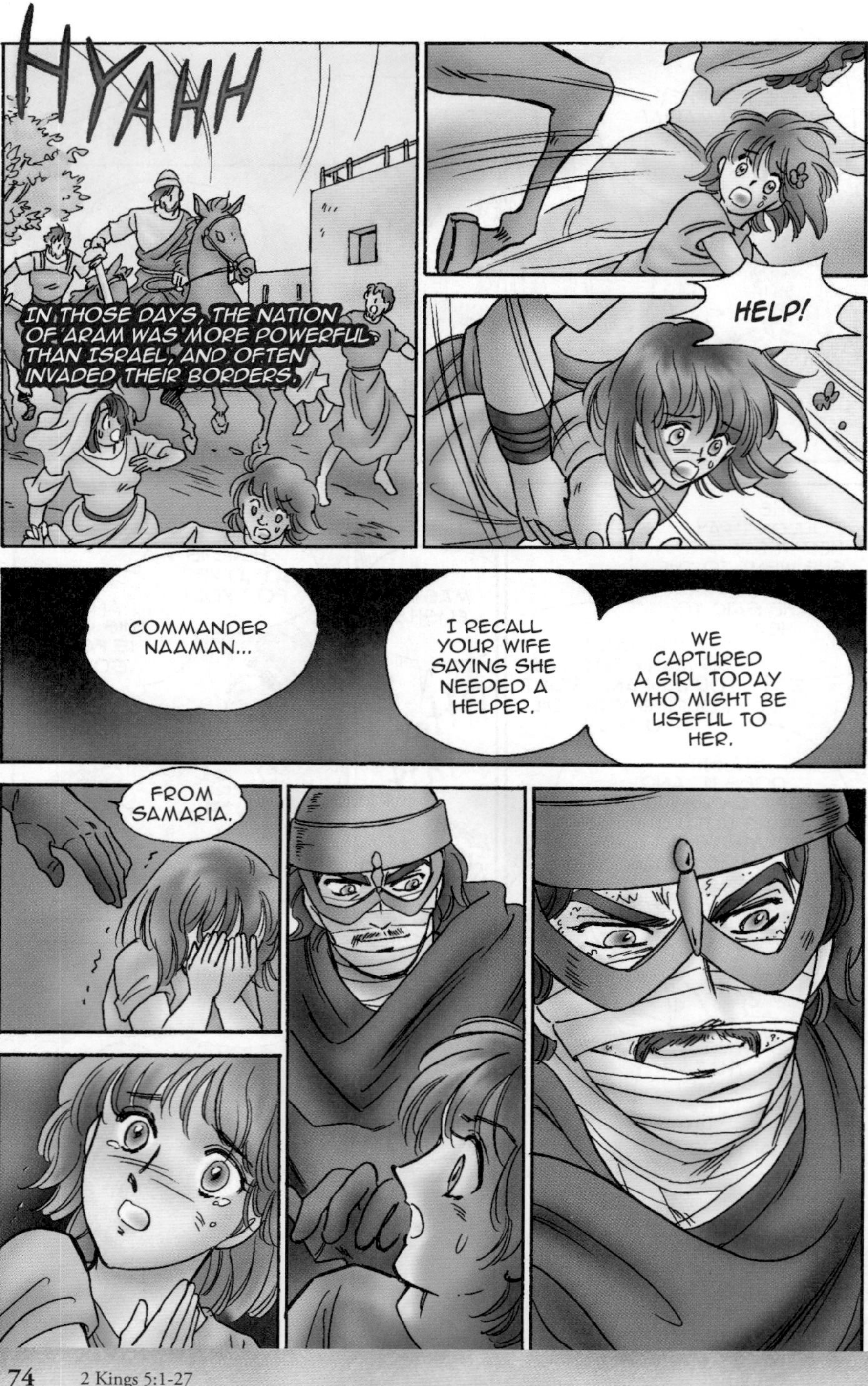
HYAHH
IN THOSE DAYS, THE NATION OF ARAM WAS MORE POWERFUL THAN ISRAEL, AND OFTEN INVADED THEIR BORDERS.
HELP!
COMMANDER NAAMAN...
I RECALL YOUR WIFE SAYING SHE NEEDED A HELPER.
WE CAPTURED A GIRL TODAY WHO MIGHT BE USEFUL TO HER.
FROM SAMARIA.

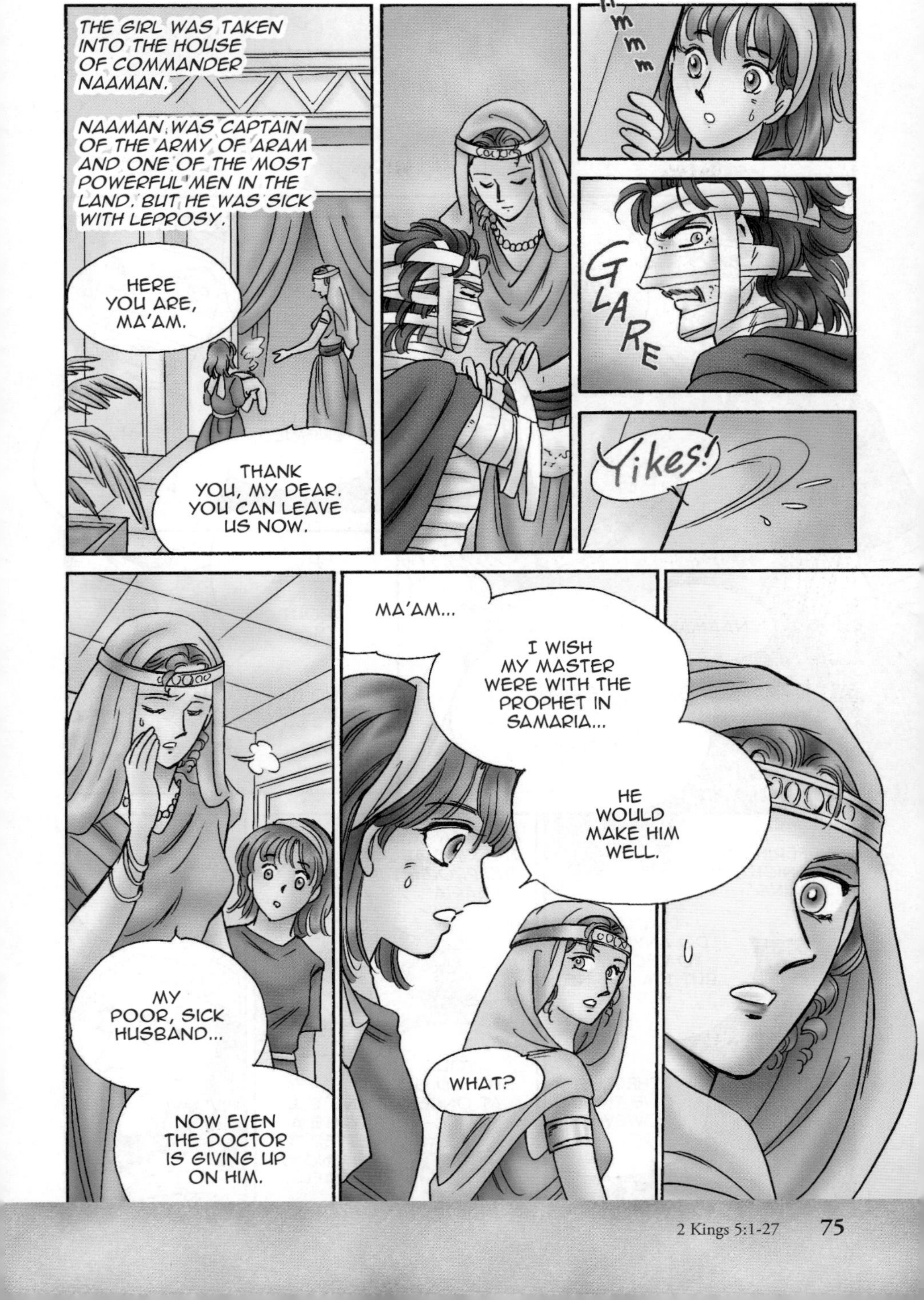
THE GIRL WAS TAKEN INTO THE HOUSE OF COMMANDER NAAMAN.
NAAMAN WAS CAPTAIN OF THE ARMY OF ARAM AND ONE OF THE MOST POWERFUL MEN IN THE LAND. BUT HE WAS SICK WITH LEPROSY.
HERE YOU ARE, MA'AM.
THANK YOU, MY DEAR. YOU CAN LEAVE US NOW.
hmmm
GLARE
Yikes!
MY POOR, SICK HUSBAND...
NOW EVEN THE DOCTOR IS GIVING UP ON HIM.
MA'AM...
I WISH MY MASTER WERE WITH THE PROPHET IN SAMARIA...
HE WOULD MAKE HIM WELL.
WHAT?

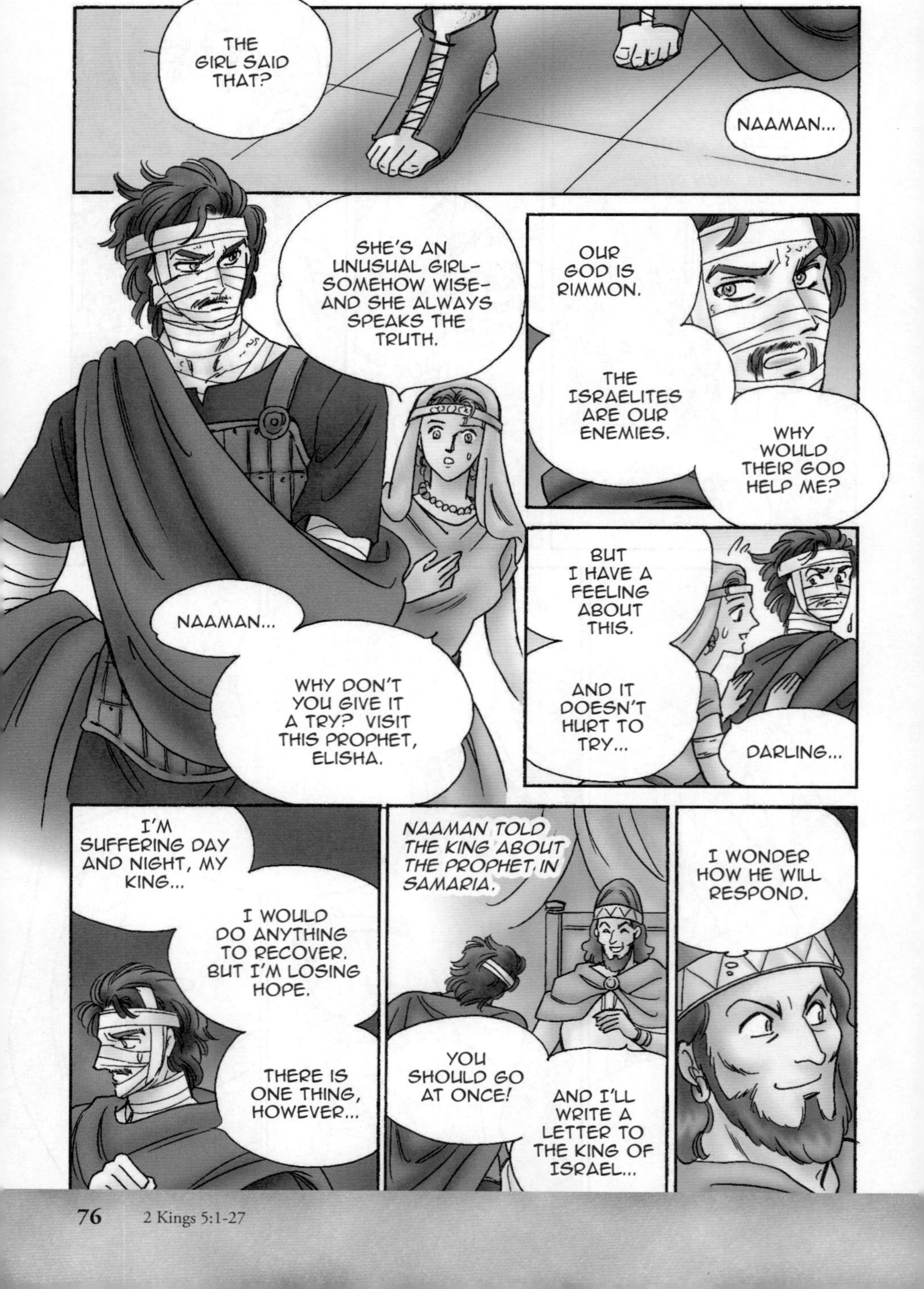
THE GIRL SAID THAT?
NAAMAN...
SHE'S AN UNUSUAL GIRL- SOMEHOW WISE- AND SHE ALWAYS SPEAKS THE TRUTH.
OUR GOD IS RIMMON.
THE ISRAELITES ARE OUR ENEMIES.
WHY WOULD THEIR GOD HELP ME?
NAAMAN...
WHY DON'T YOU GIVE IT A TRY? VISIT THIS PROPHET, ELISHA.
BUT I HAVE A FEELING ABOUT THIS.
AND IT DOESN'T HURT TO TRY...
DARLING...
I'M SUFFERING DAY AND NIGHT, MY KING...
I WOULD DO ANYTHING TO RECOVER. BUT I'M LOSING HOPE.
THERE IS ONE THING, HOWEVER...
NAAMAN TOLD THE KING ABOUT THE PROPHET IN SAMARIA.
YOU SHOULD GO AT ONCE!
AND I'LL WRITE A LETTER TO THE KING OF ISRAEL...
I WONDER HOW HE WILL RESPOND.

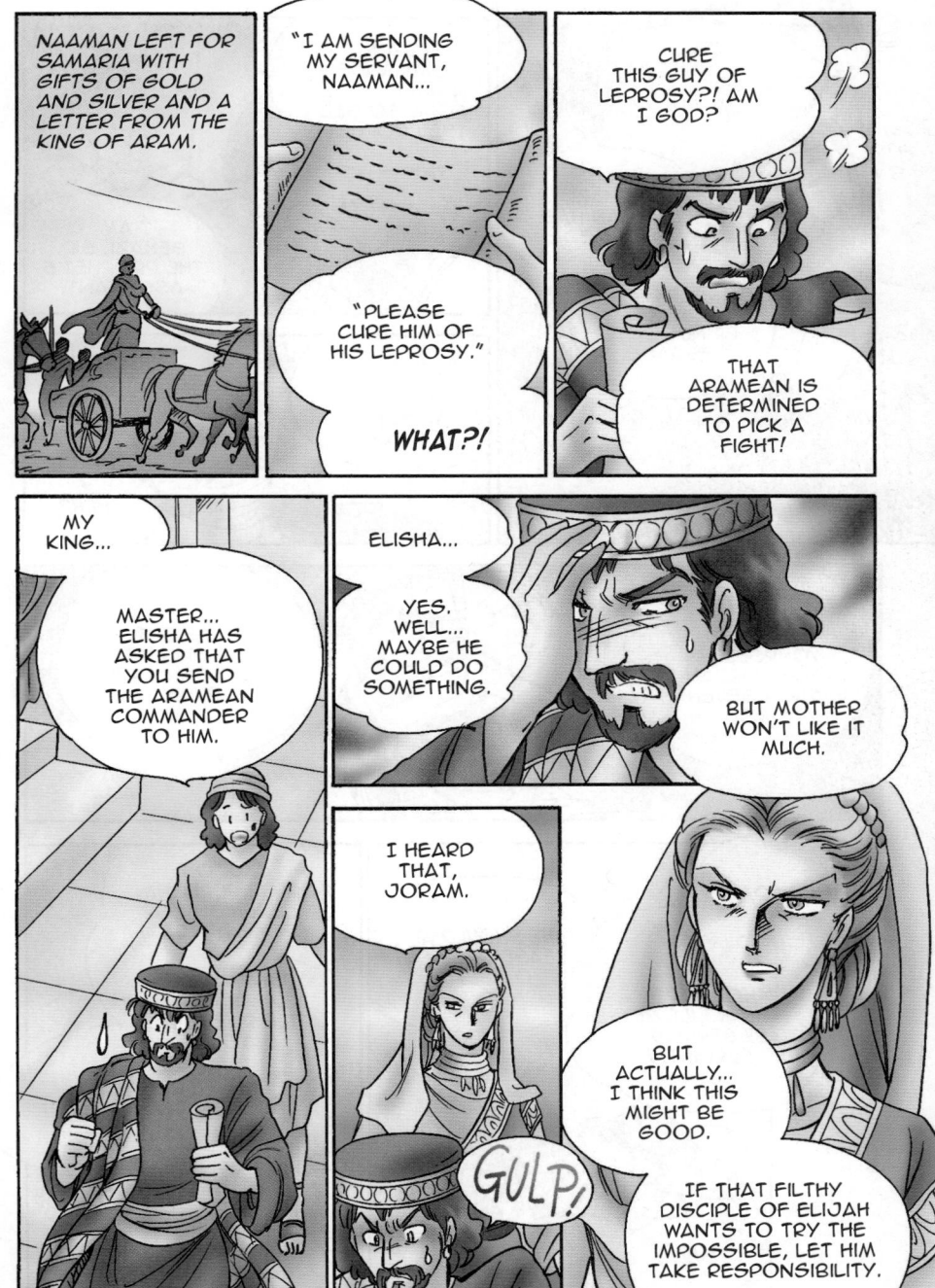

NAAMAN LEFT FOR SAMARIA WITH GIFTS OF GOLD AND SILVER AND A LETTER FROM THE KING OF ARAM.

"I AM SENDING MY SERVANT, NAAMAN...

"PLEASE CURE HIM OF HIS LEPROSY."

WHAT?!

CURE THIS GUY OF LEPROSY?! AM I GOD?

THAT ARAMEAN IS DETERMINED TO PICK A FIGHT!

MY KING...

MASTER... ELISHA HAS ASKED THAT YOU SEND THE ARAMEAN COMMANDER TO HIM.

ELISHA...

YES, WELL... MAYBE HE COULD DO SOMETHING.

BUT MOTHER WON'T LIKE IT MUCH.

I HEARD THAT, JORAM.

GULP!

BUT ACTUALLY... I THINK THIS MIGHT BE GOOD.

IF THAT FILTHY DISCIPLE OF ELIJAH WANTS TO TRY THE IMPOSSIBLE, LET HIM TAKE RESPONSIBILITY.

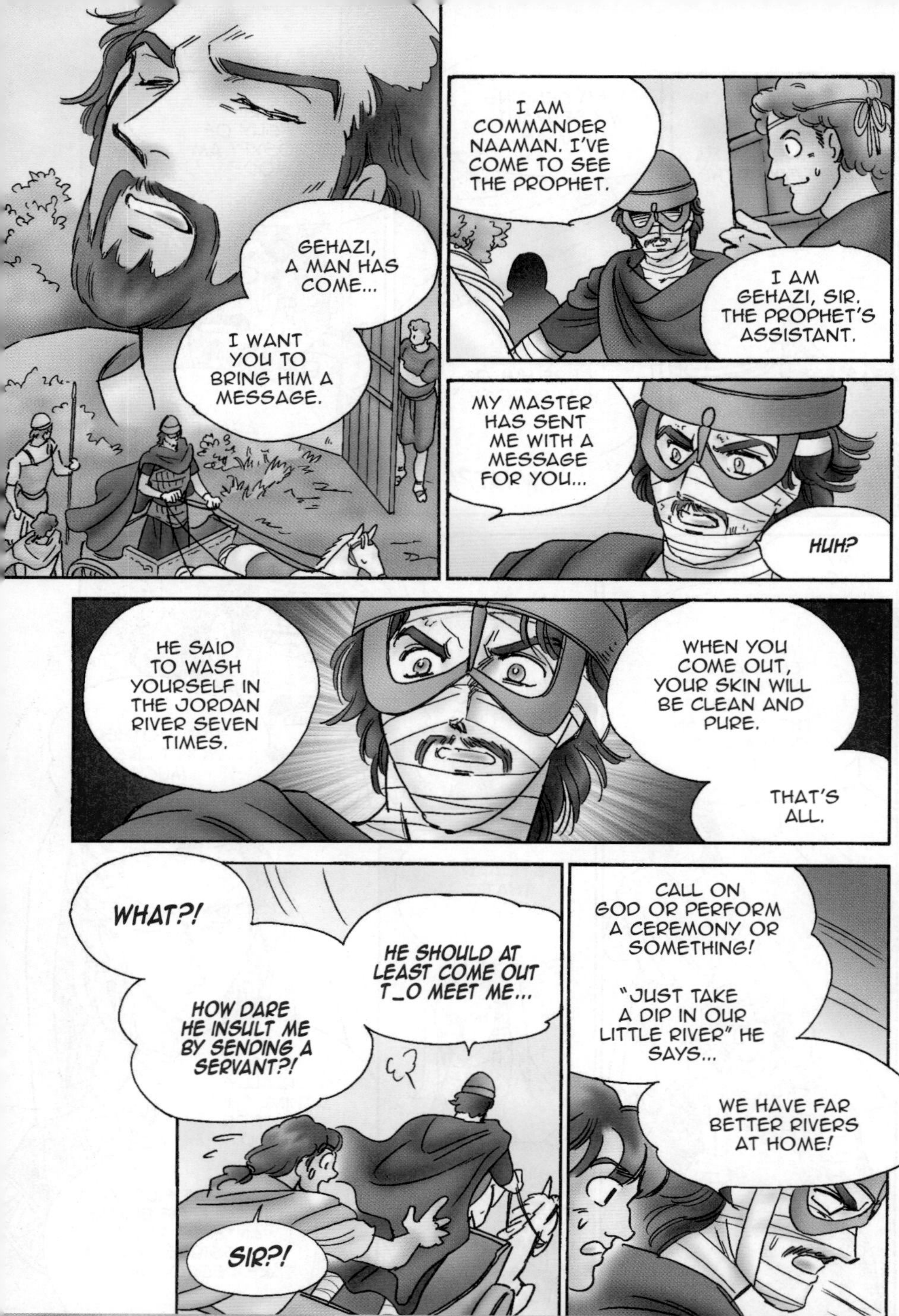
GEHAZI, A MAN HAS COME...
I WANT YOU TO BRING HIM A MESSAGE.
I AM COMMANDER NAAMAN. I'VE COME TO SEE THE PROPHET.
I AM GEHAZI, SIR. THE PROPHET'S ASSISTANT.
MY MASTER HAS SENT ME WITH A MESSAGE FOR YOU...
HUH?
HE SAID TO WASH YOURSELF IN THE JORDAN RIVER SEVEN TIMES.
WHEN YOU COME OUT, YOUR SKIN WILL BE CLEAN AND PURE.
THAT'S ALL.
WHAT?!
HOW DARE HE INSULT ME BY SENDING A SERVANT?!
HE SHOULD AT LEAST COME OUT T_O MEET ME...
SIR?!
CALL ON GOD OR PERFORM A CEREMONY OR SOMETHING!
"JUST TAKE A DIP IN OUR LITTLE RIVER" HE SAYS...
WE HAVE FAR BETTER RIVERS AT HOME!

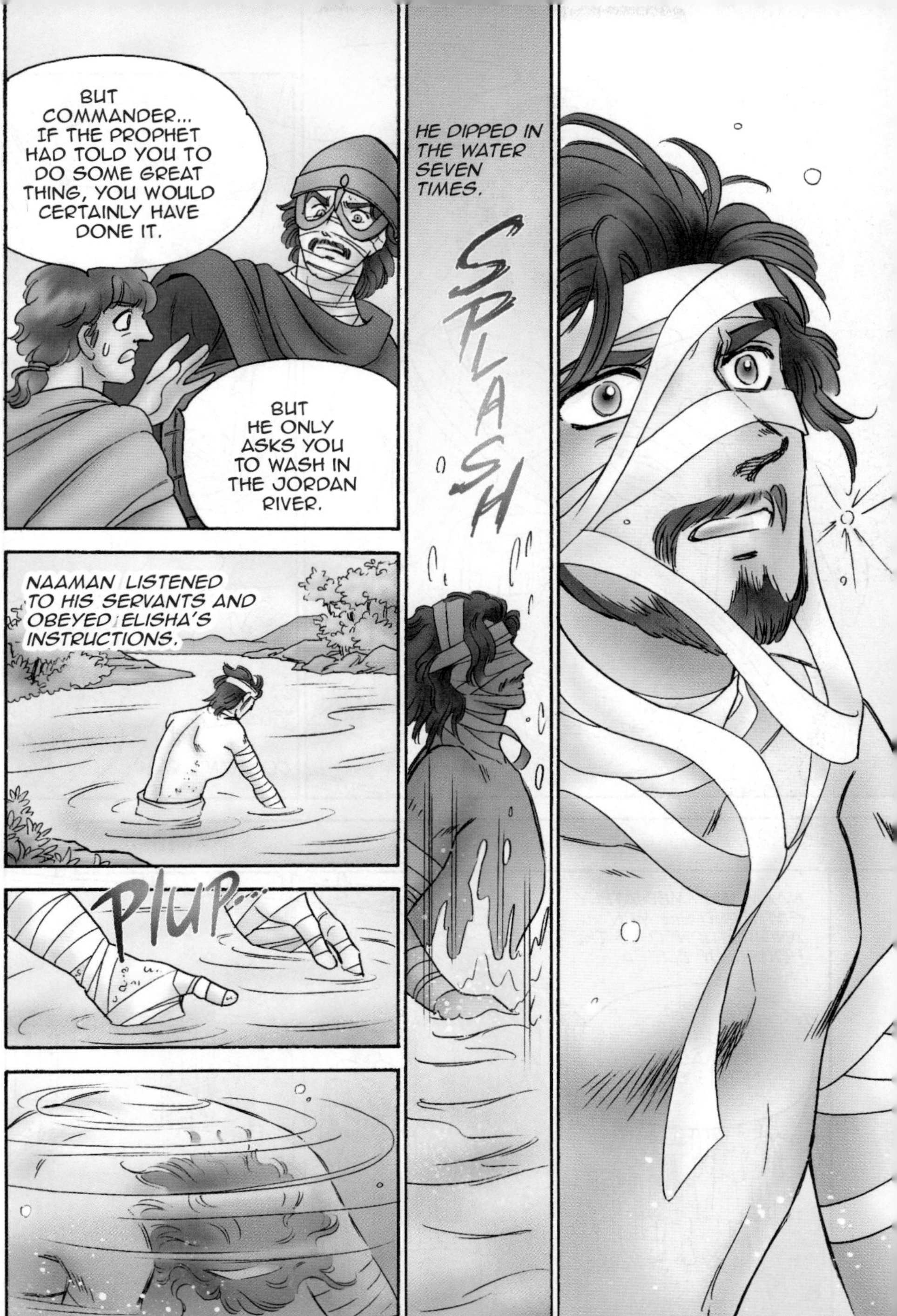
BUT COMMANDER... IF THE PROPHET HAD TOLD YOU TO DO SOME GREAT THING, YOU WOULD CERTAINLY HAVE DONE IT.
BUT HE ONLY ASKS YOU TO WASH IN THE JORDAN RIVER.
NAAMAN LISTENED TO HIS SERVANTS AND OBEYED ELISHA'S INSTRUCTIONS.
PLUP...
HE DIPPED IN THE WATER SEVEN TIMES.
SPLASH

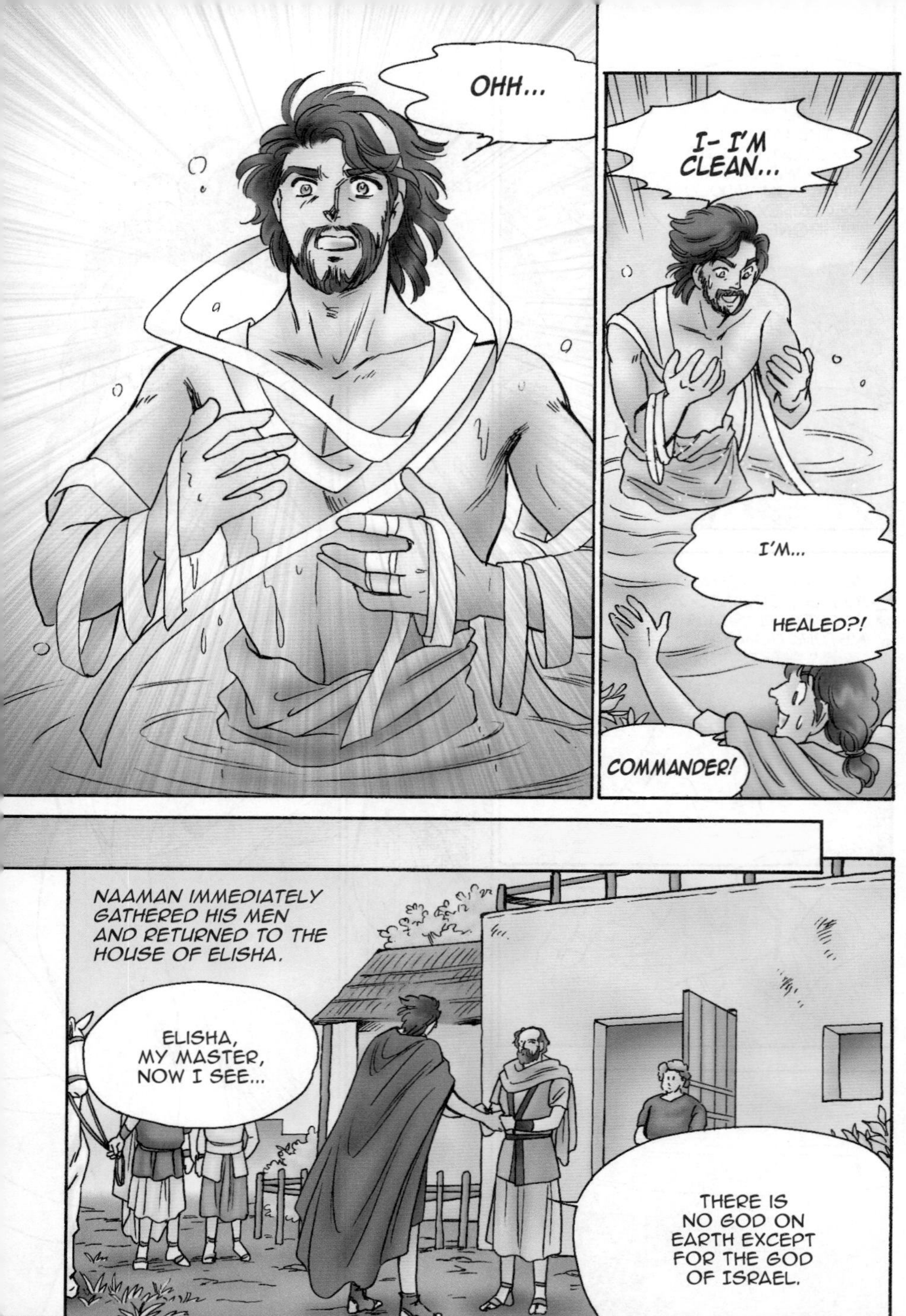
OHH...
I- I'M CLEAN...
I'M...
HEALED?!
COMMANDER!
NAAMAN IMMEDIATELY GATHERED HIS MEN AND RETURNED TO THE HOUSE OF ELISHA.
ELISHA, MY MASTER, NOW I SEE...
THERE IS NO GOD ON EARTH EXCEPT FOR THE GOD OF ISRAEL.

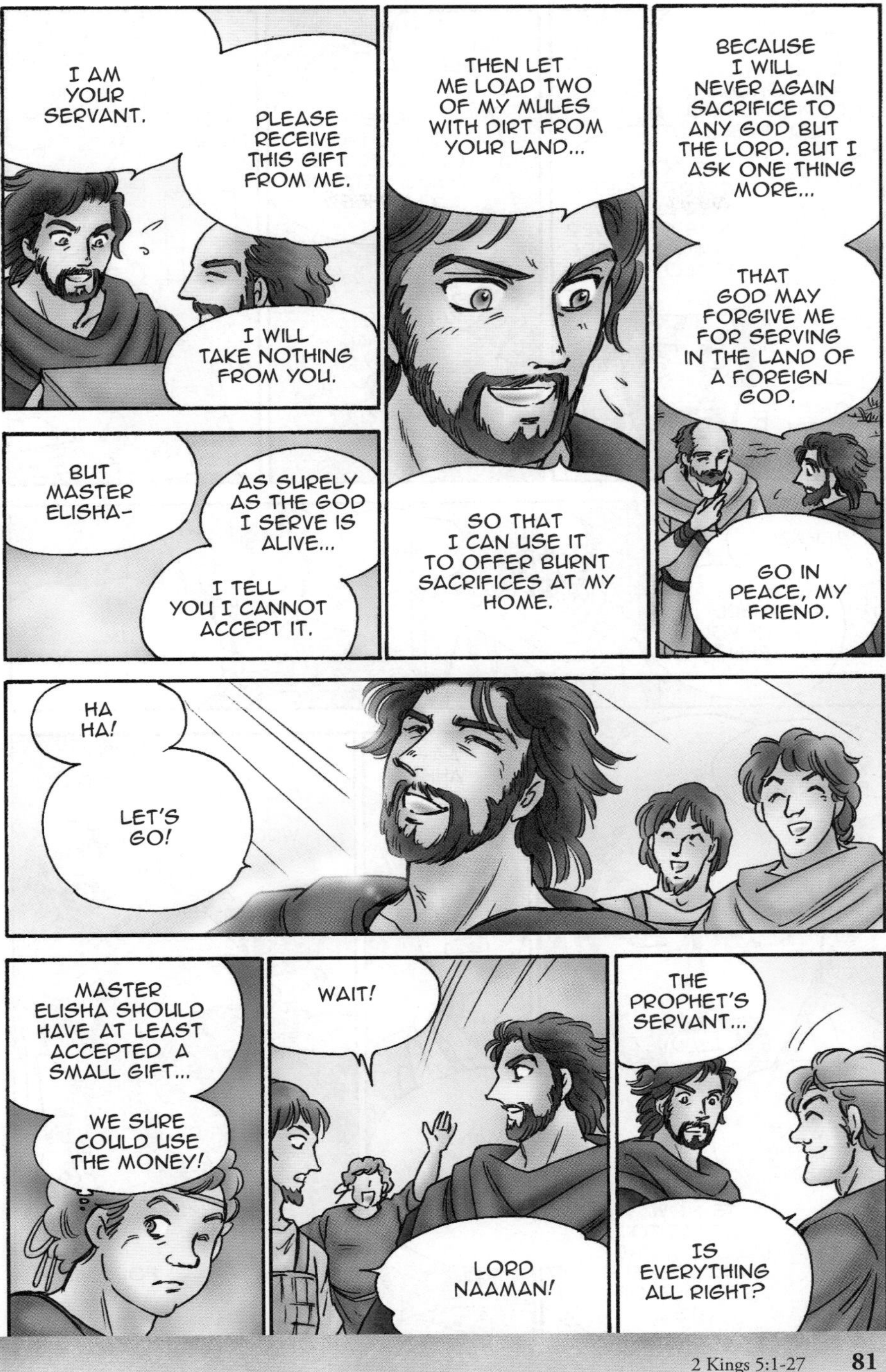
I AM YOUR SERVANT.
PLEASE RECEIVE THIS GIFT FROM ME.
I WILL TAKE NOTHING FROM YOU.
BUT MASTER ELISHA-
AS SURELY AS THE GOD I SERVE IS ALIVE...
I TELL YOU I CANNOT ACCEPT IT.
THEN LET ME LOAD TWO OF MY MULES WITH DIRT FROM YOUR LAND...
SO THAT I CAN USE IT TO OFFER BURNT SACRIFICES AT MY HOME.
BECAUSE I WILL NEVER AGAIN SACRIFICE TO ANY GOD BUT THE LORD. BUT I ASK ONE THING MORE...
THAT GOD MAY FORGIVE ME FOR SERVING IN THE LAND OF A FOREIGN GOD.
GO IN PEACE, MY FRIEND.
HA HA!
LET'S GO!
MASTER ELISHA SHOULD HAVE AT LEAST ACCEPTED A SMALL GIFT...
WE SURE COULD USE THE MONEY!
WAIT!
LORD NAAMAN!
THE PROPHET'S SERVANT...
IS EVERYTHING ALL RIGHT?

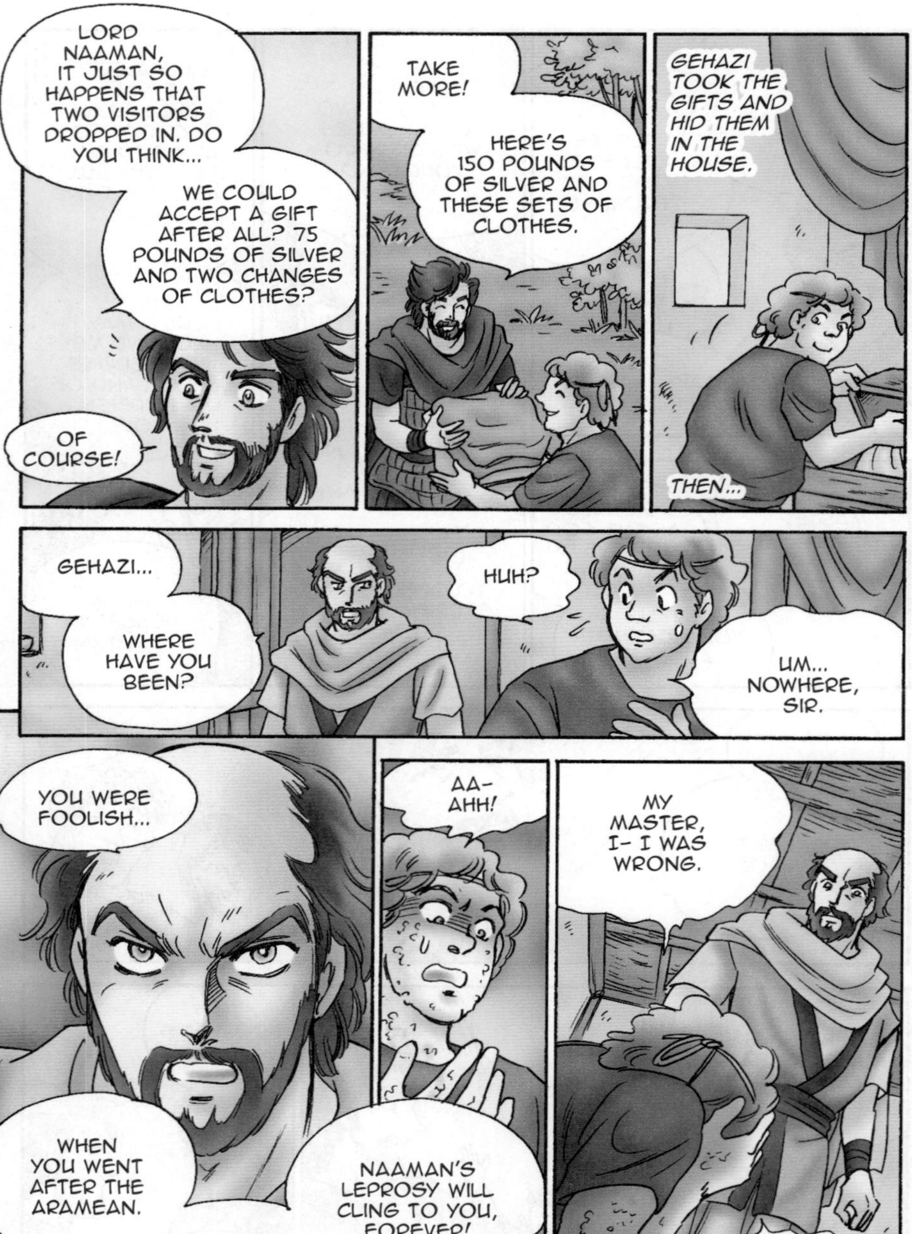
LORD NAAMAN, IT JUST SO HAPPENS THAT TWO VISITORS DROPPED IN. DO YOU THINK...
WE COULD ACCEPT A GIFT AFTER ALL? 75 POUNDS OF SILVER AND TWO CHANGES OF CLOTHES?
OF COURSE!
TAKE MORE!
HERE'S 150 POUNDS OF SILVER AND THESE SETS OF CLOTHES.
GEHAZI TOOK THE GIFTS AND HID THEM IN THE HOUSE.
THEN...
GEHAZI...
WHERE HAVE YOU BEEN?
HUH?
UM... NOWHERE, SIR.
YOU WERE FOOLISH...
WHEN YOU WENT AFTER THE ARAMEAN.
IS NOW A TIME TO RECEIVE MONEY AND CLOTHES? BECAUSE OF THIS...
NAAMAN'S LEPROSY WILL CLING TO YOU, FOREVER!
AA-AHH!
MY MASTER, I- I WAS WRONG.
FORGIVE ME!

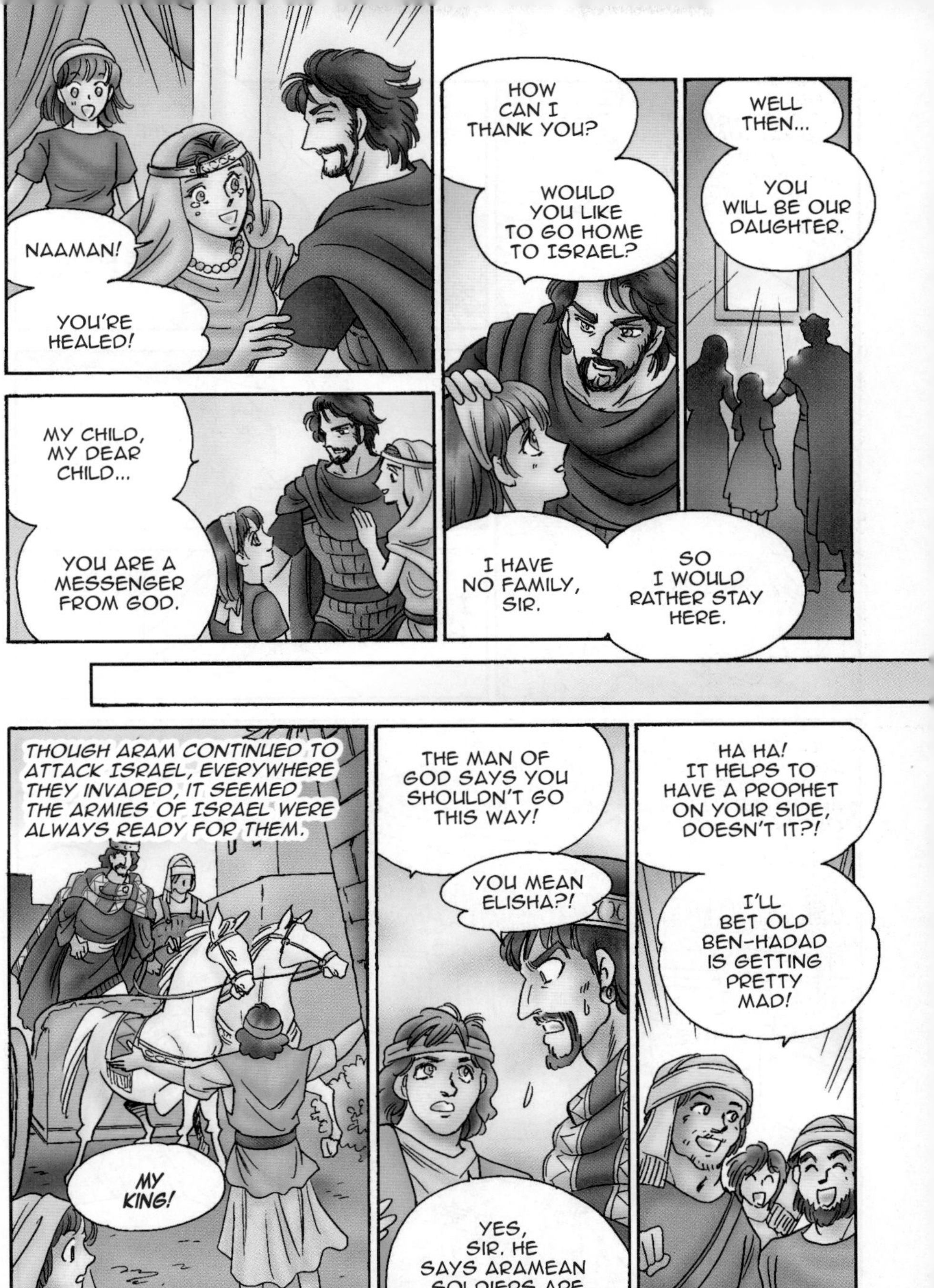
NAAMAN!
YOU'RE HEALED!
HOW CAN I THANK YOU?
WOULD YOU LIKE TO GO HOME TO ISRAEL?
WELL THEN...
YOU WILL BE OUR DAUGHTER.
MY CHILD, MY DEAR CHILD...
YOU ARE A MESSENGER FROM GOD.
I HAVE NO FAMILY, SIR.
SO I WOULD RATHER STAY HERE.
THOUGH ARAM CONTINUED TO ATTACK ISRAEL, EVERYWHERE THEY INVADED, IT SEEMED THE ARMIES OF ISRAEL WERE ALWAYS READY FOR THEM.
MY KING!
THE MAN OF GOD SAYS YOU SHOULDN'T GO THIS WAY!
YOU MEAN ELISHA?!
YES, SIR. HE SAYS ARAMEAN SOLDIERS ARE HIDDEN THERE.
HA HA! IT HELPS TO HAVE A PROPHET ON YOUR SIDE, DOESN'T IT?!
I'LL BET OLD BEN-HADAD IS GETTING PRETTY MAD!

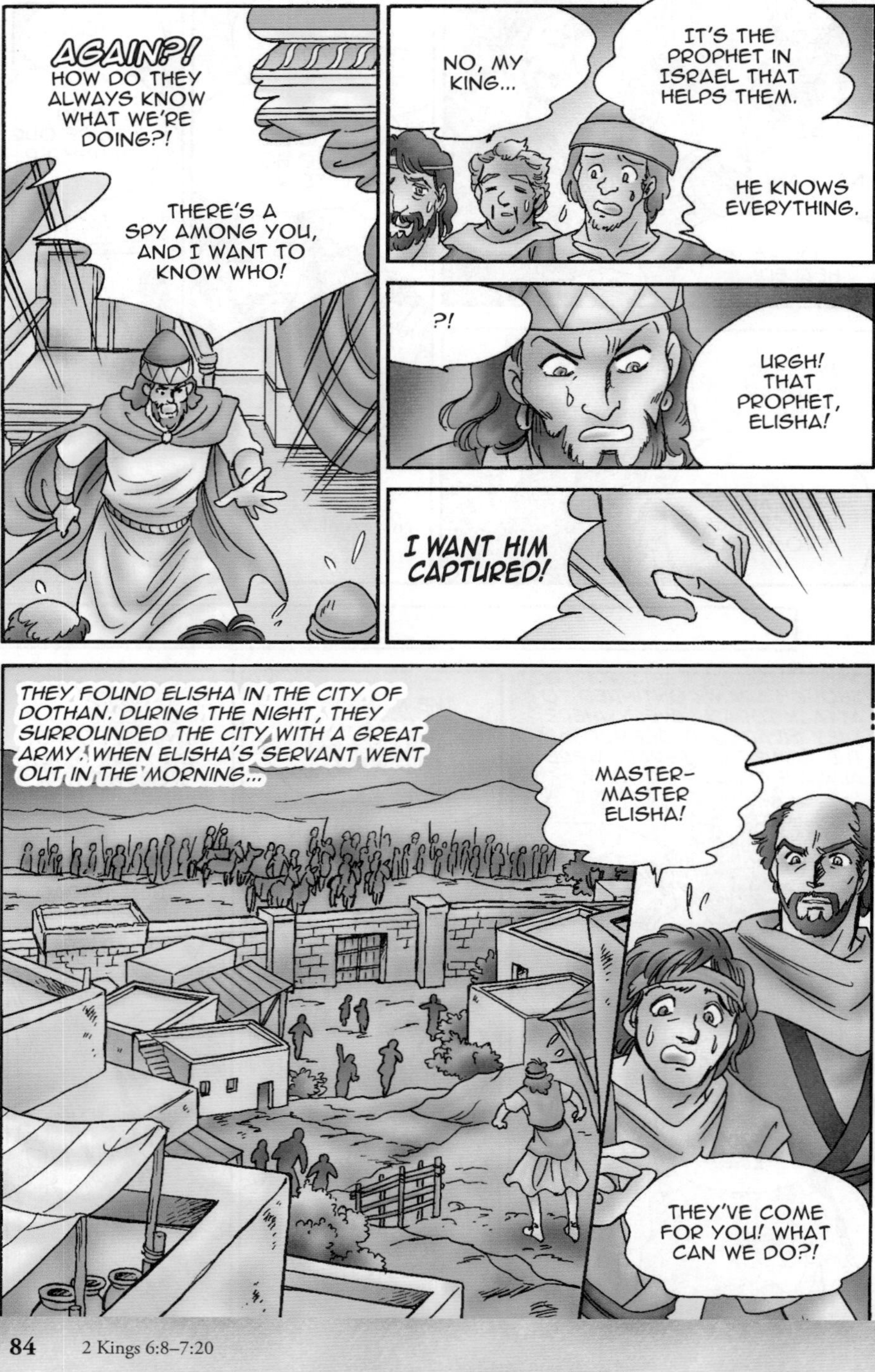
AGAIN?! HOW DO THEY ALWAYS KNOW WHAT WE'RE DOING?!
THERE'S A SPY AMONG YOU, AND I WANT TO KNOW WHO!
NO, MY KING...
IT'S THE PROPHET IN ISRAEL THAT HELPS THEM.
HE KNOWS EVERYTHING.
?!
URGH! THAT PROPHET, ELISHA!
I WANT HIM CAPTURED!
THEY FOUND ELISHA IN THE CITY OF DOTHAN. DURING THE NIGHT, THEY SURROUNDED THE CITY WITH A GREAT ARMY. WHEN ELISHA'S SERVANT WENT OUT IN THE MORNING...
MASTER- MASTER ELISHA!
THEY'VE COME FOR YOU! WHAT CAN WE DO?!

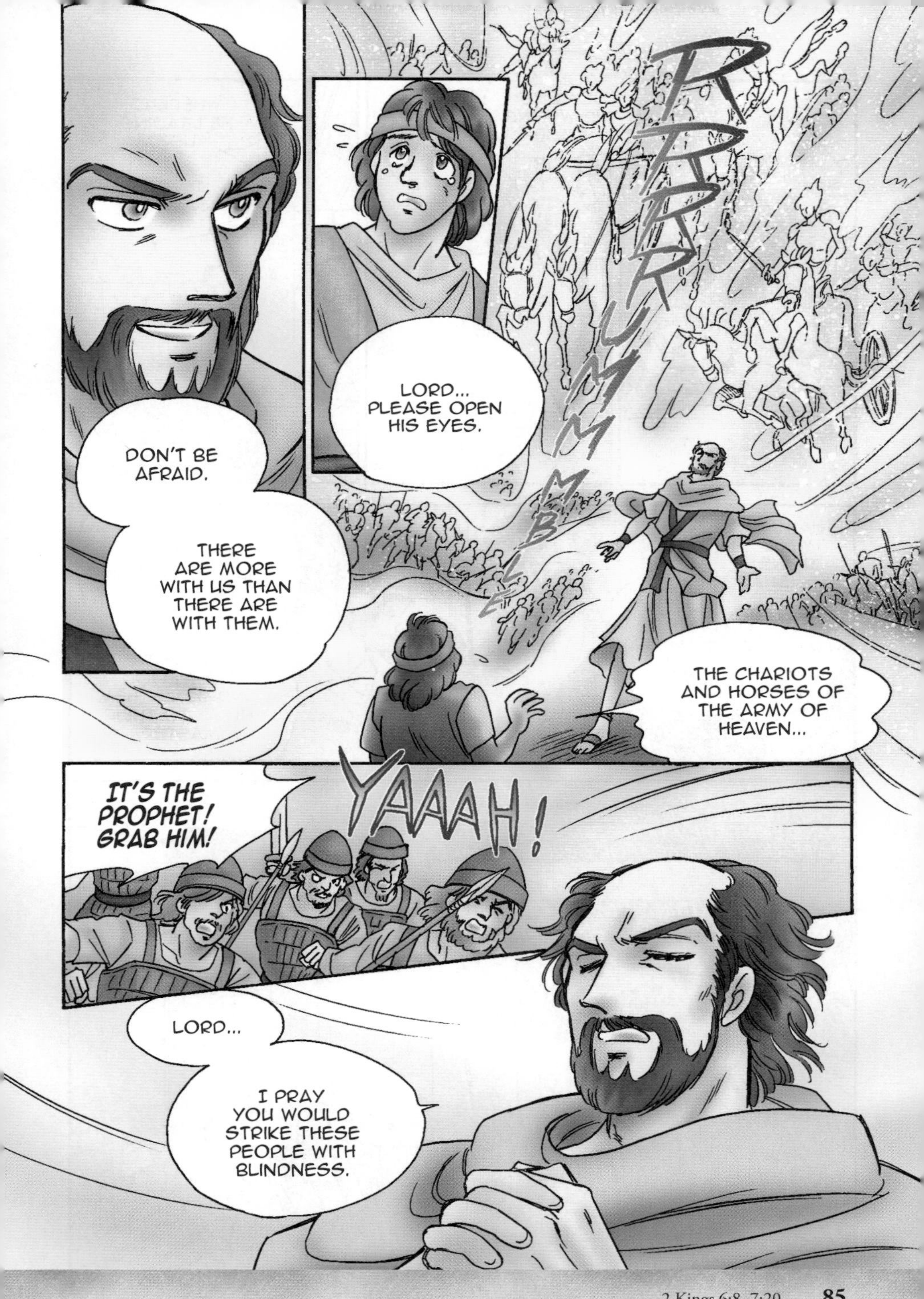
DON'T BE AFRAID.
LORD... PLEASE OPEN HIS EYES.
RRRUMMMMBLE
THERE ARE MORE WITH US THAN THERE ARE WITH THEM.
THE CHARIOTS AND HORSES OF THE ARMY OF HEAVEN...
IT'S THE PROPHET! GRAB HIM!
YAAAH!
LORD...
I PRAY YOU WOULD STRIKE THESE PEOPLE WITH BLINDNESS.

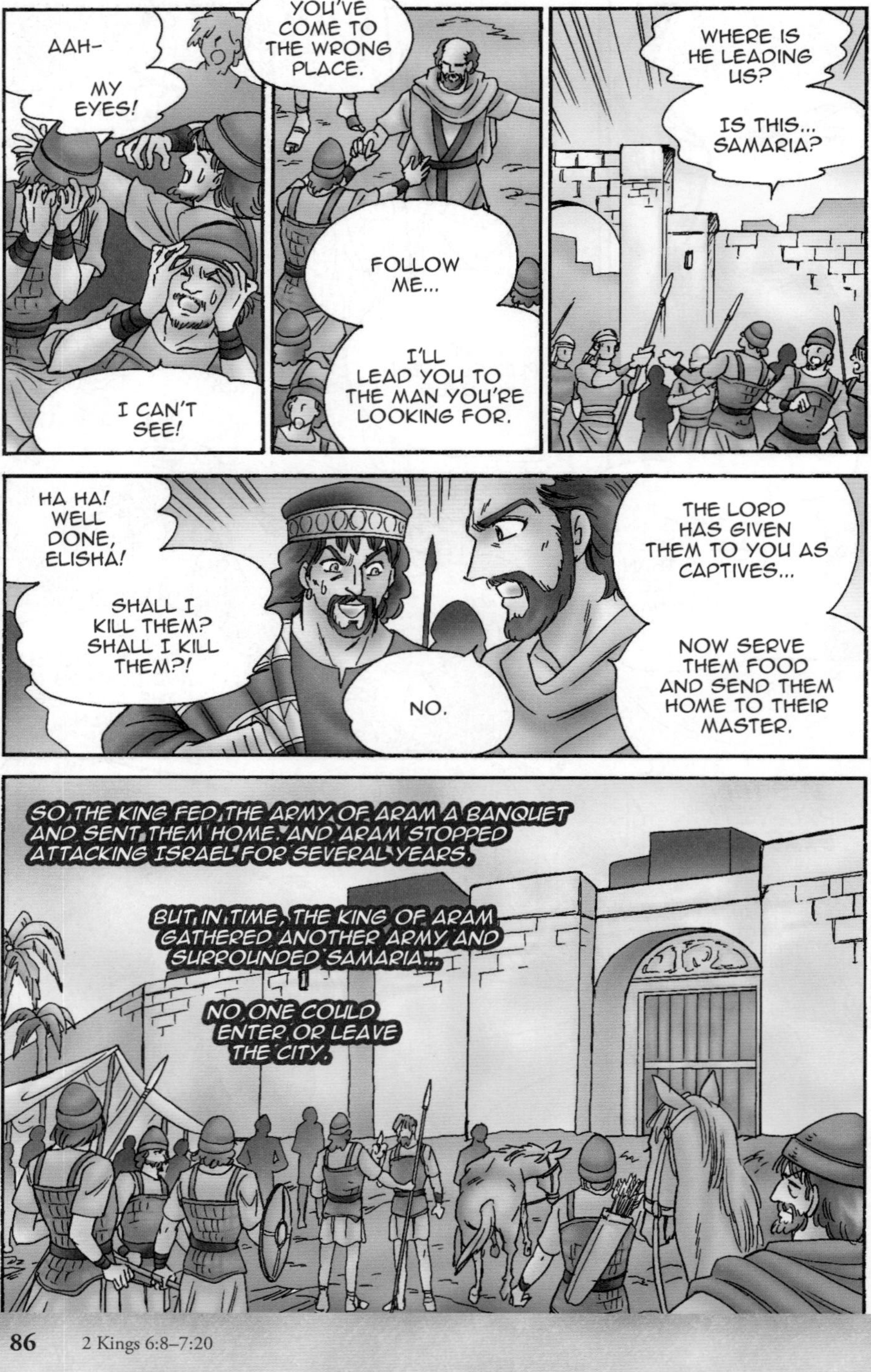
AAH-
MY EYES!
I CAN'T SEE!
YOU'VE COME TO THE WRONG PLACE.
FOLLOW ME...
I'LL LEAD YOU TO THE MAN YOU'RE LOOKING FOR.
WHERE IS HE LEADING US?
IS THIS... SAMARIA?
HA HA! WELL DONE, ELISHA!
SHALL I KILL THEM? SHALL I KILL THEM?!
NO.
THE LORD HAS GIVEN THEM TO YOU AS CAPTIVES...
NOW SERVE THEM FOOD AND SEND THEM HOME TO THEIR MASTER.
SO THE KING FED THE ARMY OF ARAM A BANQUET AND SENT THEM HOME. AND ARAM STOPPED ATTACKING ISRAEL FOR SEVERAL YEARS.
BUT, IN TIME, THE KING OF ARAM GATHERED ANOTHER ARMY AND SURROUNDED SAMARIA...
NO ONE COULD ENTER OR LEAVE THE CITY.

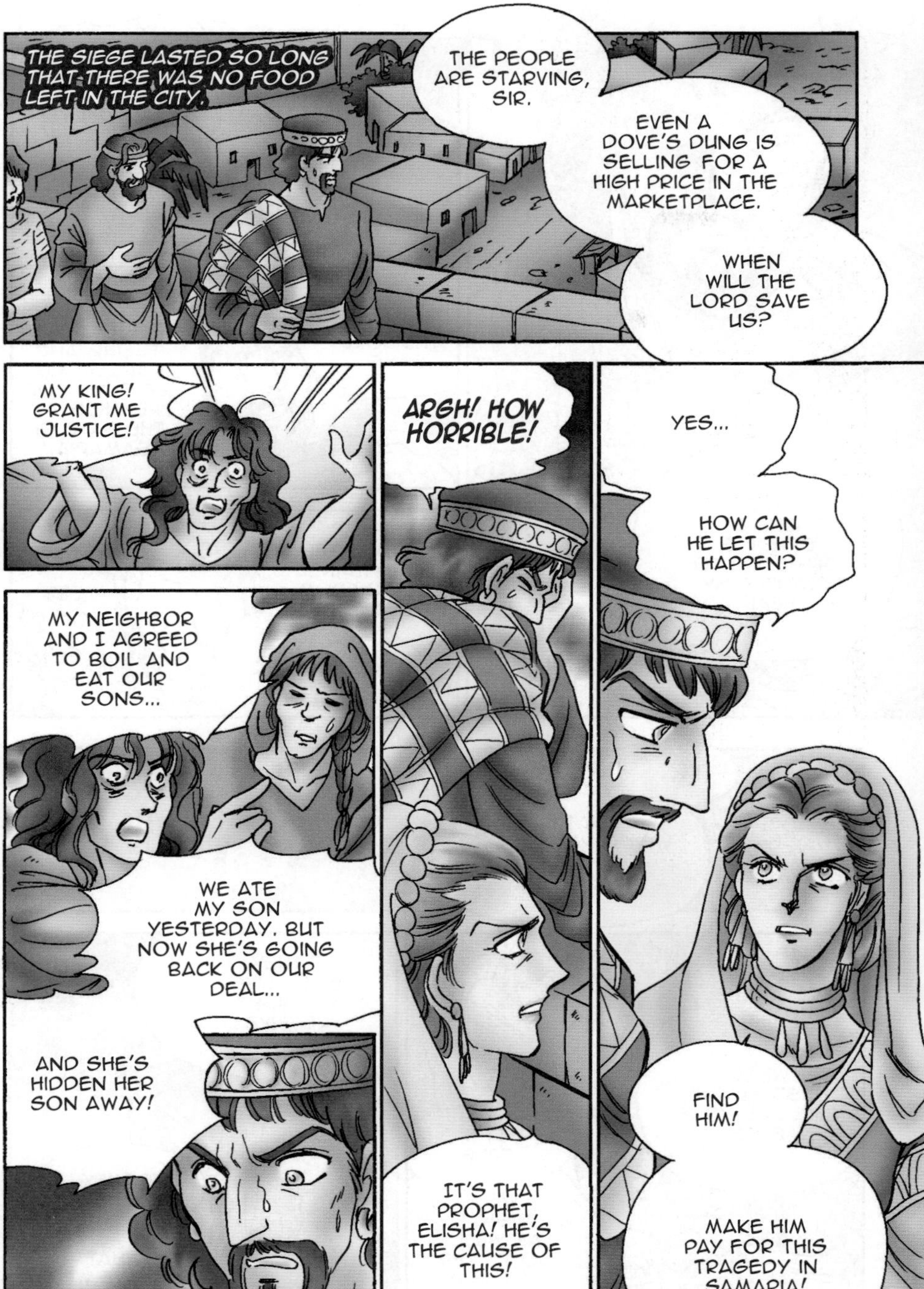
THE SIEGE LASTED SO LONG THAT THERE WAS NO FOOD LEFT IN THE CITY.
THE PEOPLE ARE STARVING, SIR.
EVEN A DOVE'S DUNG IS SELLING FOR A HIGH PRICE IN THE MARKETPLACE.
WHEN WILL THE LORD SAVE US?
MY KING! GRANT ME JUSTICE!
MY NEIGHBOR AND I AGREED TO BOIL AND EAT OUR SONS...
WE ATE MY SON YESTERDAY. BUT NOW SHE'S GOING BACK ON OUR DEAL...
AND SHE'S HIDDEN HER SON AWAY!
ARGH! HOW HORRIBLE!
YES...
HOW CAN HE LET THIS HAPPEN?
IT'S THAT PROPHET, ELISHA! HE'S THE CAUSE OF THIS!
FIND HIM!
MAKE HIM PAY FOR THIS TRAGEDY IN SAMARIA!

OPEN THE DOOR!

OPEN UP BY ORDER OF THE KING!

LISTEN TO WHAT THE LORD SAYS...

"AT THIS TIME TOMORROW, FLOUR AND BARLEY WILL BE SOLD FOR PENNIES AT THE GATE OF SAMARIA."

THE KING'S SENDING SOMEONE TO CUT OFF MY HEAD.

SHUT THAT DOOR AND HOLD IT CLOSED!

WHAT? EVEN IF THE LORD RAINED FOOD FROM HEAVEN...

THAT COULD NEVER HAPPEN!

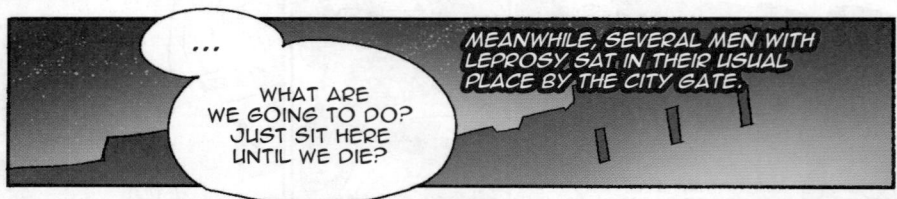

...

WHAT ARE WE GOING TO DO? JUST SIT HERE UNTIL WE DIE?

MEANWHILE, SEVERAL MEN WITH LEPROSY SAT IN THEIR USUAL PLACE BY THE CITY GATE.

IF WE STAY HERE AT THE CITY...

WE'LL JUST STARVE, LIKE EVERYONE ELSE.

IT'S TRUE.

WE MIGHT AS WELL GO TO THE ARAMEAN CAMP.

IF THEY LET US LIVE, WE MIGHT RECEIVE FOOD.

IF THEY KILL US...

WHAT HAVE WE LOST?

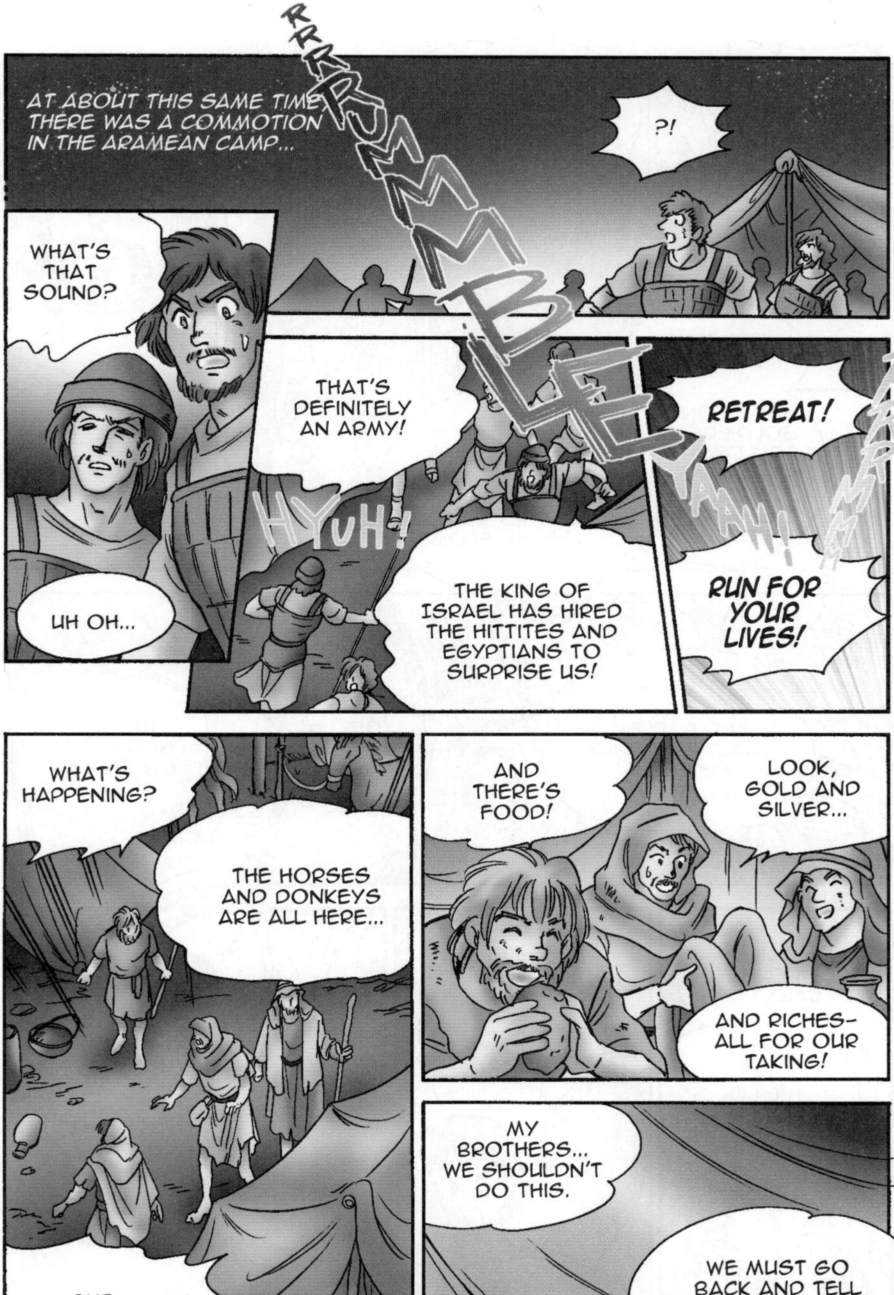
AT ABOUT THIS SAME TIME THERE WAS A COMMOTION IN THE ARAMEAN CAMP...
RRRRUMMMBLE
?!
WHAT'S THAT SOUND?
UH OH...
THAT'S DEFINITELY AN ARMY!
HYUH!
THE KING OF ISRAEL HAS HIRED THE HITTITES AND EGYPTIANS TO SURPRISE US!
RETREAT!
YAAAH!!
RUN FOR YOUR LIVES!
WHAT'S HAPPENING?
THE HORSES AND DONKEYS ARE ALL HERE...
BUT EVERY TENT IS EMPTY!
AND THERE'S FOOD!
LOOK, GOLD AND SILVER...
AND RICHES-ALL FOR OUR TAKING!
MY BROTHERS... WE SHOULDN'T DO THIS.
WE MUST GO BACK AND TELL THE KING AND THE PEOPLE.

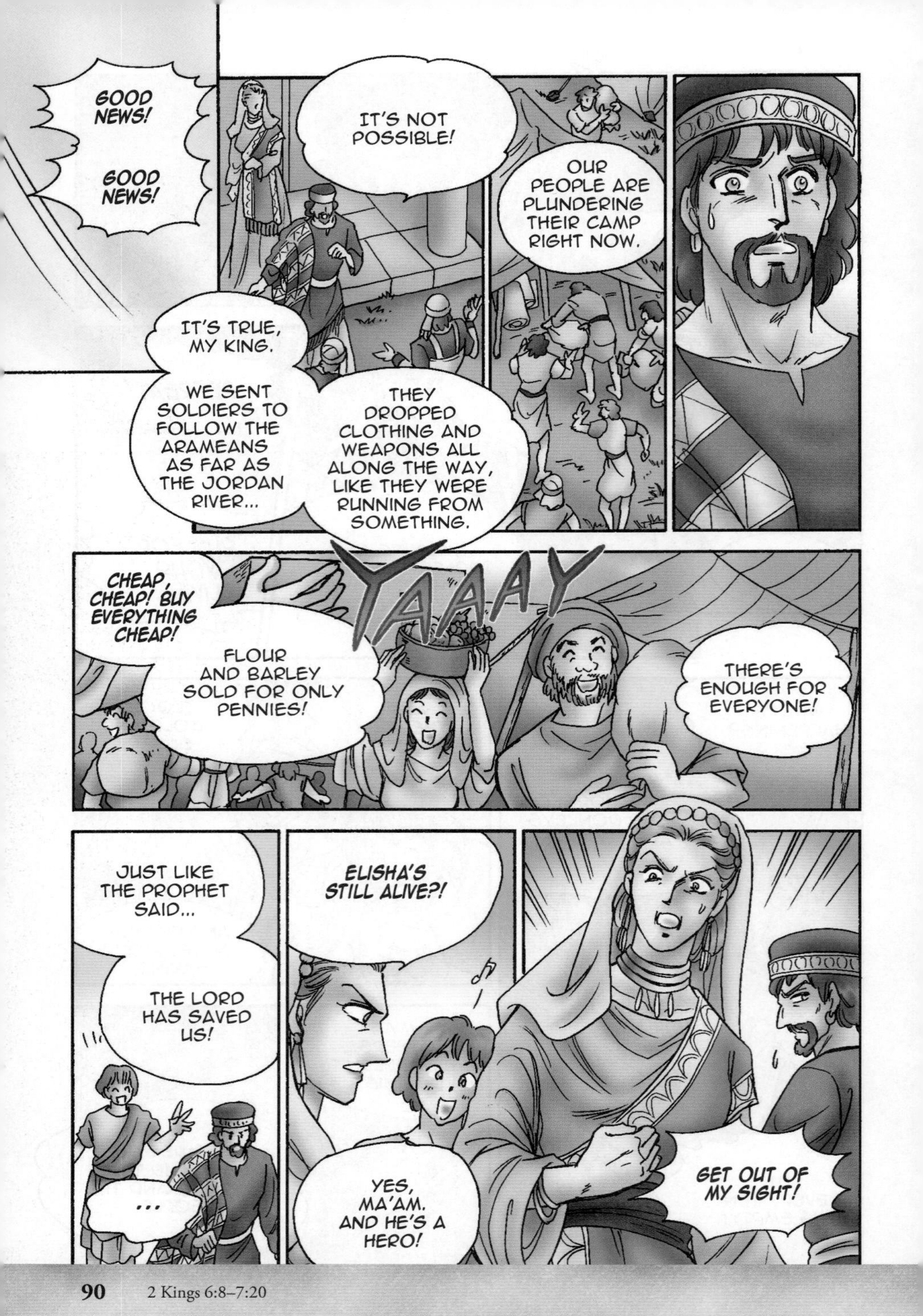
GOOD NEWS!
GOOD NEWS!
IT'S NOT POSSIBLE!
OUR PEOPLE ARE PLUNDERING THEIR CAMP RIGHT NOW.
IT'S TRUE, MY KING.
WE SENT SOLDIERS TO FOLLOW THE ARAMEANS AS FAR AS THE JORDAN RIVER...
THEY DROPPED CLOTHING AND WEAPONS ALL ALONG THE WAY, LIKE THEY WERE RUNNING FROM SOMETHING.
YAAAY
CHEAP, CHEAP! BUY EVERYTHING CHEAP!
FLOUR AND BARLEY SOLD FOR ONLY PENNIES!
THERE'S ENOUGH FOR EVERYONE!
JUST LIKE THE PROPHET SAID...
THE LORD HAS SAVED US!
...
ELISHA'S STILL ALIVE?!
YES, MA'AM. AND HE'S A HERO!
GET OUT OF MY SIGHT!

8. Jehu's Rebellion

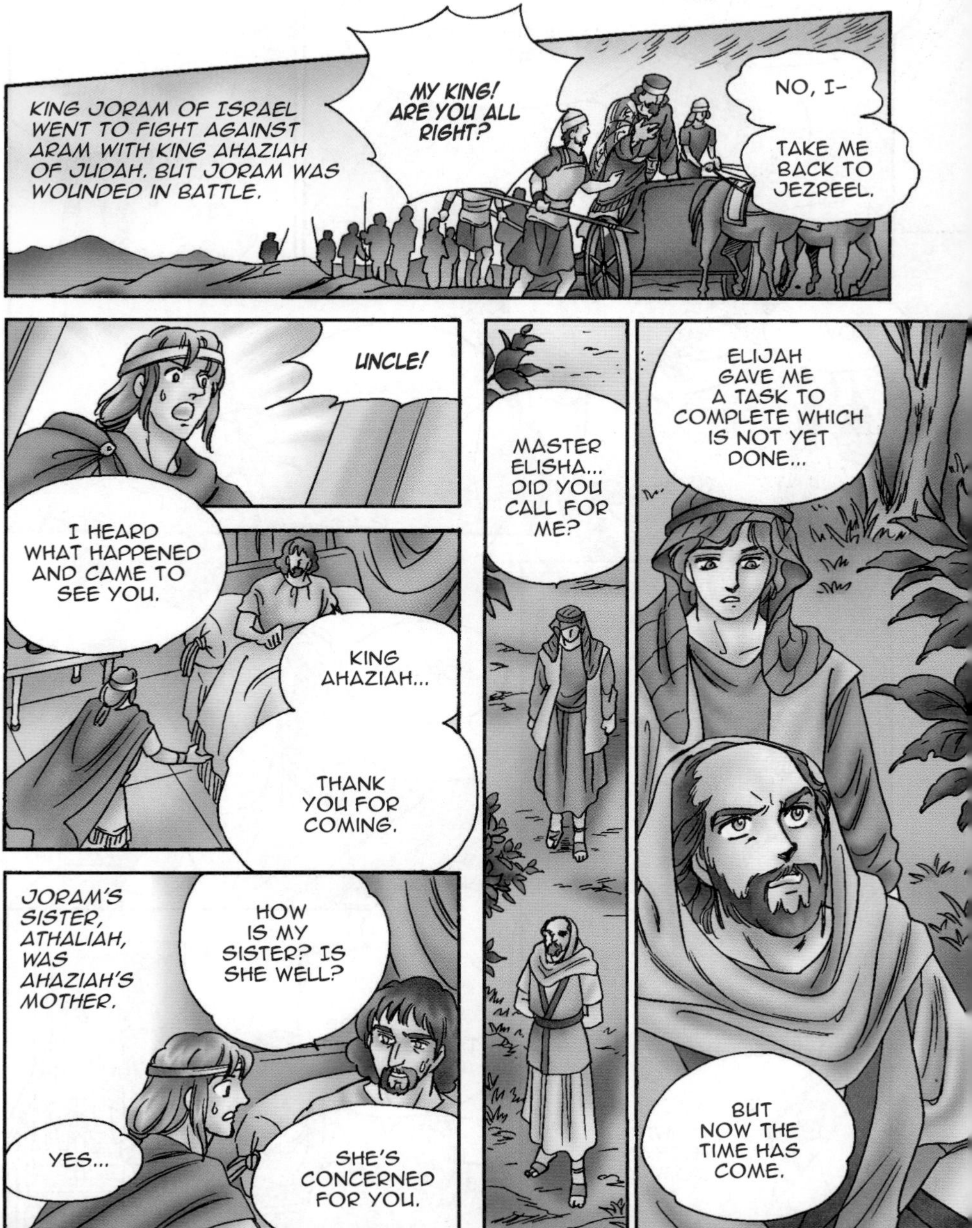
KING JORAM OF ISRAEL WENT TO FIGHT AGAINST ARAM WITH KING AHAZIAH OF JUDAH. BUT JORAM WAS WOUNDED IN BATTLE.
MY KING! ARE YOU ALL RIGHT?
NO, I-
TAKE ME BACK TO JEZREEL.
UNCLE!
I HEARD WHAT HAPPENED AND CAME TO SEE YOU.
KING AHAZIAH...
THANK YOU FOR COMING.
JORAM'S SISTER, ATHALIAH, WAS AHAZIAH'S MOTHER.
HOW IS MY SISTER? IS SHE WELL?
YES...
SHE'S CONCERNED FOR YOU.
MASTER ELISHA... DID YOU CALL FOR ME?
ELIJAH GAVE ME A TASK TO COMPLETE WHICH IS NOT YET DONE...
BUT NOW THE TIME HAS COME.

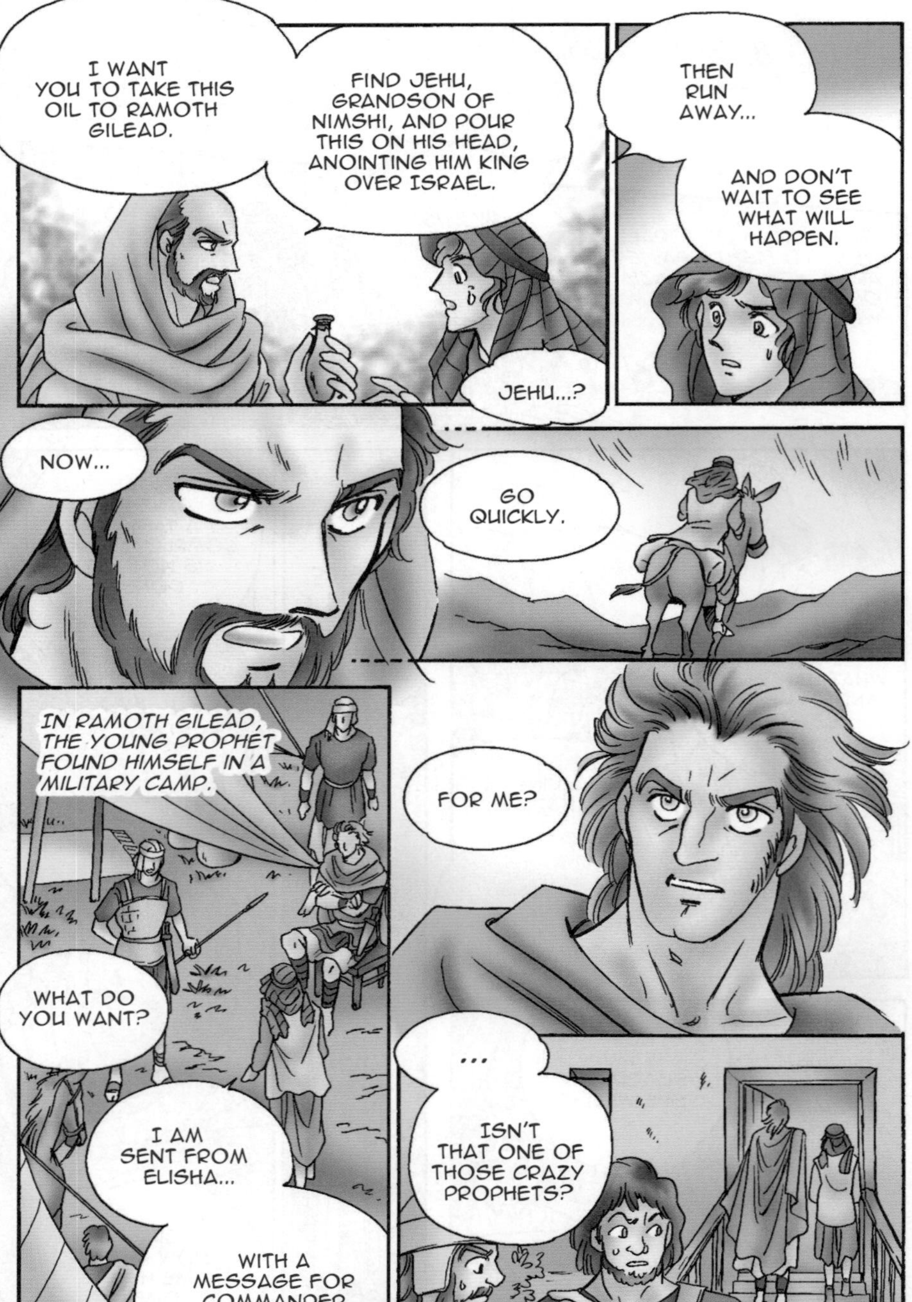
I WANT YOU TO TAKE THIS OIL TO RAMOTH GILEAD.
FIND JEHU, GRANDSON OF NIMSHI, AND POUR THIS ON HIS HEAD, ANOINTING HIM KING OVER ISRAEL.
JEHU...?
THEN RUN AWAY...
AND DON'T WAIT TO SEE WHAT WILL HAPPEN.
NOW...
GO QUICKLY.
IN RAMOTH GILEAD, THE YOUNG PROPHET FOUND HIMSELF IN A MILITARY CAMP.
WHAT DO YOU WANT?
I AM SENT FROM ELISHA...
WITH A MESSAGE FOR COMMANDER JEHU.
FOR ME?
...
ISN'T THAT ONE OF THOSE CRAZY PROPHETS?

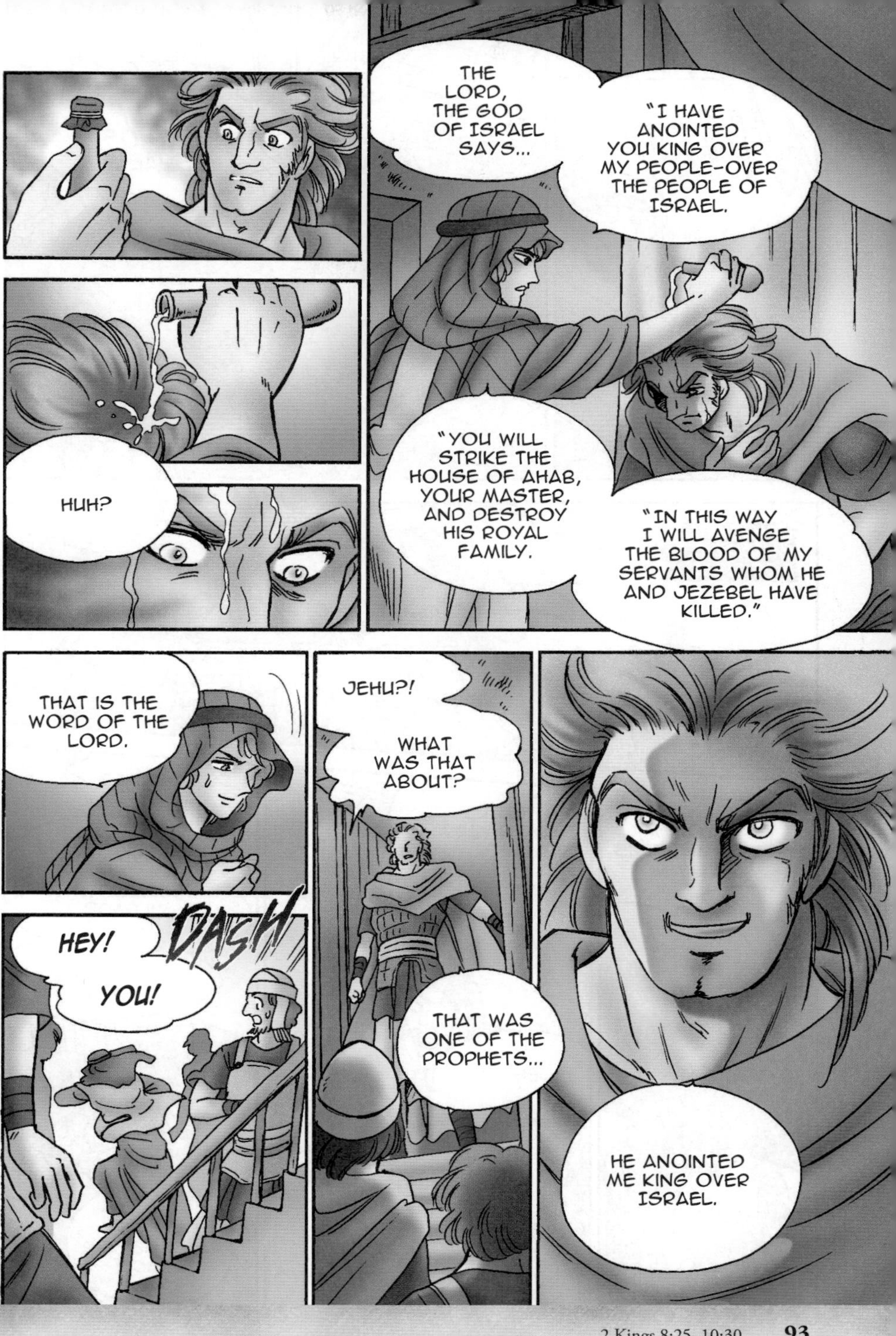
HUH?
THE LORD, THE GOD OF ISRAEL SAYS...
"I HAVE ANOINTED YOU KING OVER MY PEOPLE-OVER THE PEOPLE OF ISRAEL.
"YOU WILL STRIKE THE HOUSE OF AHAB, YOUR MASTER, AND DESTROY HIS ROYAL FAMILY.
"IN THIS WAY I WILL AVENGE THE BLOOD OF MY SERVANTS WHOM HE AND JEZEBEL HAVE KILLED."
THAT IS THE WORD OF THE LORD.
HEY!
YOU!
DASH
JEHU?!
WHAT WAS THAT ABOUT?
THAT WAS ONE OF THE PROPHETS...
HE ANOINTED ME KING OVER ISRAEL.

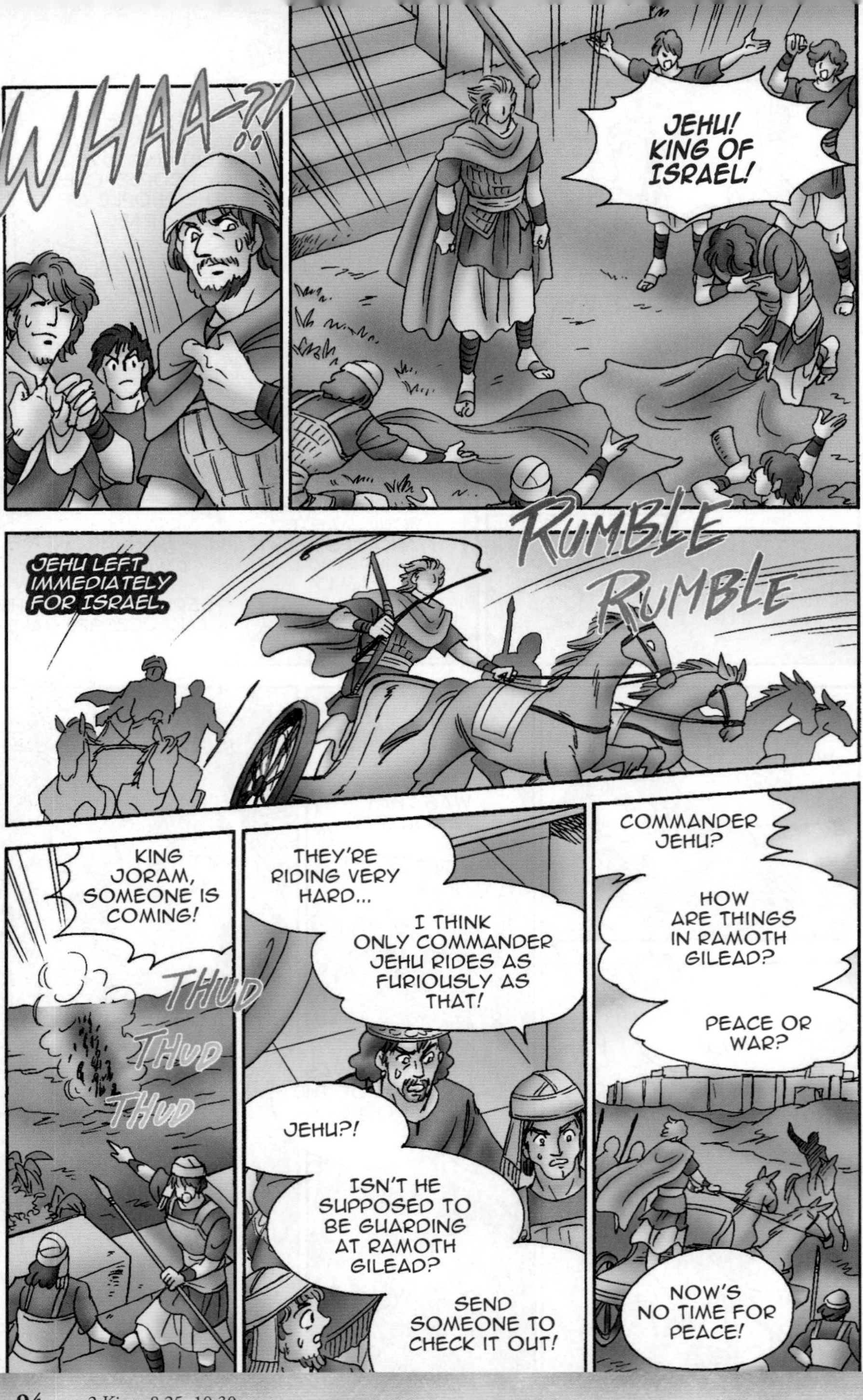
WHAA-?!
JEHU! KING OF ISRAEL!
JEHU LEFT IMMEDIATELY FOR ISRAEL.
RUMBLE RUMBLE
KING JORAM, SOMEONE IS COMING!
THUD THUD THUD
THEY'RE RIDING VERY HARD...
I THINK ONLY COMMANDER JEHU RIDES AS FURIOUSLY AS THAT!
JEHU?!
ISN'T HE SUPPOSED TO BE GUARDING AT RAMOTH GILEAD?
SEND SOMEONE TO CHECK IT OUT!
COMMANDER JEHU?
HOW ARE THINGS IN RAMOTH GILEAD?
PEACE OR WAR?
NOW'S NO TIME FOR PEACE!

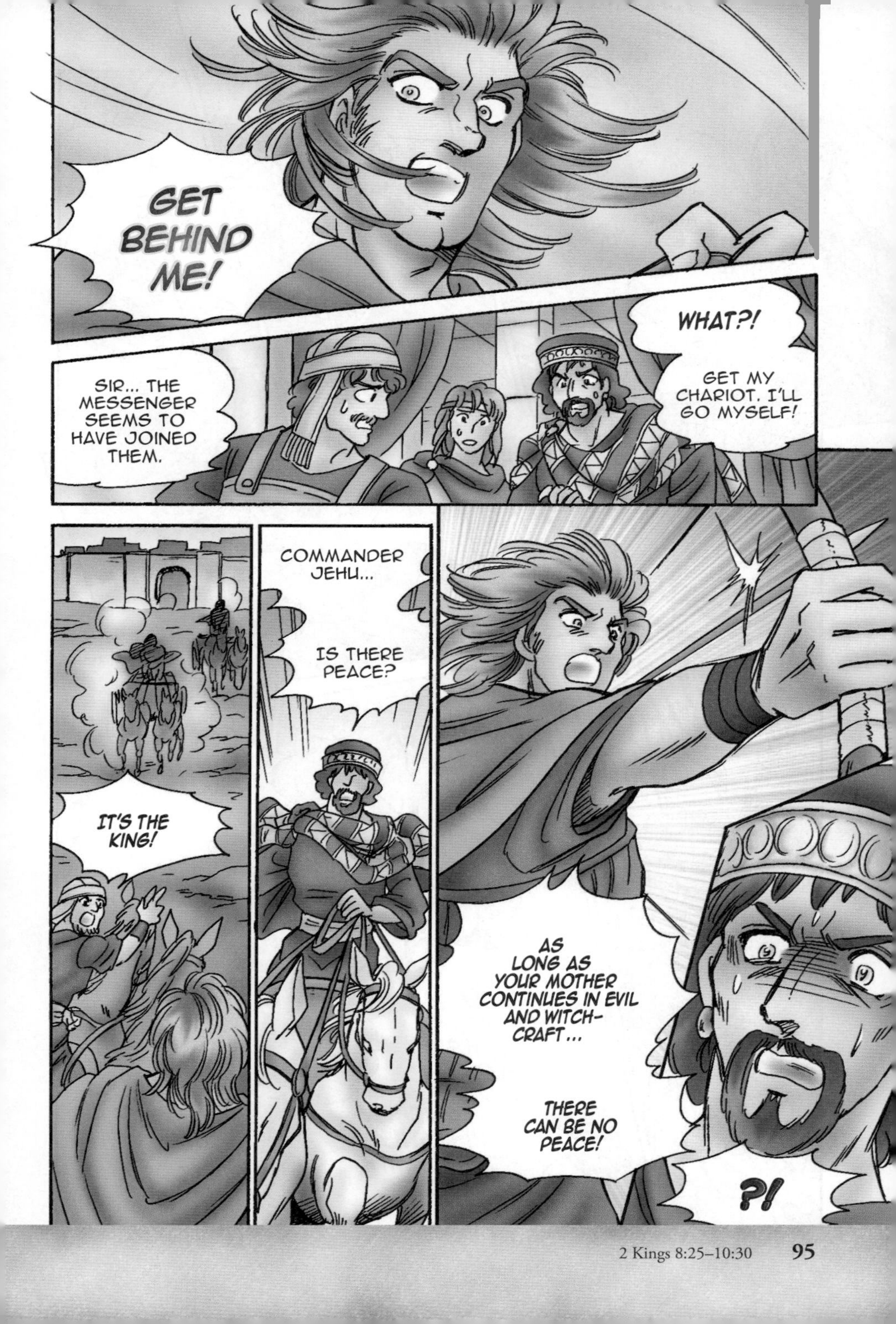
GET BEHIND ME!
WHAT?!
SIR... THE MESSENGER SEEMS TO HAVE JOINED THEM.
GET MY CHARIOT. I'LL GO MYSELF!
IT'S THE KING!
COMMANDER JEHU...
IS THERE PEACE?
AS LONG AS YOUR MOTHER CONTINUES IN EVIL AND WITCH-CRAFT...
THERE CAN BE NO PEACE!
?!

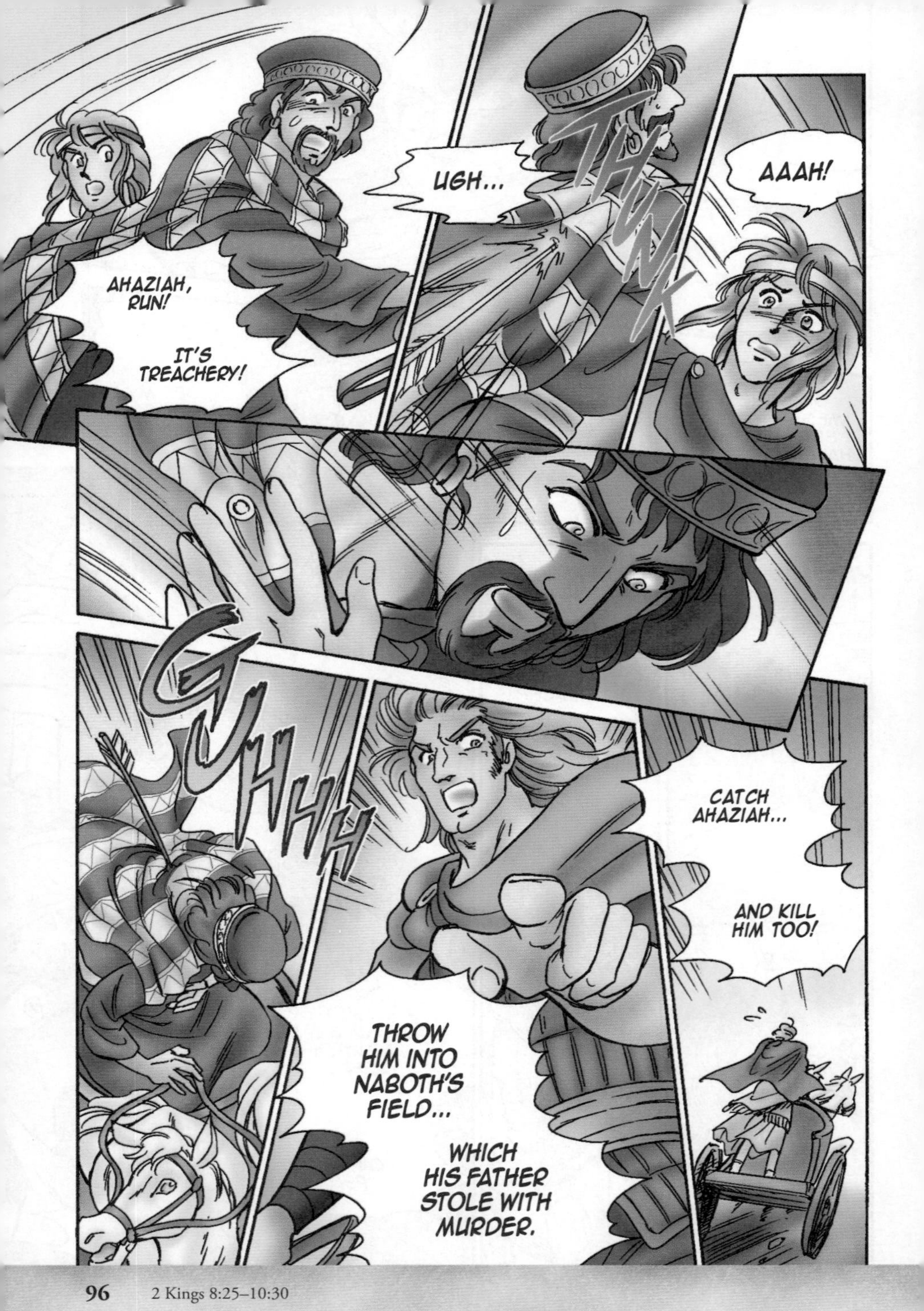
AHAZIAH, RUN!
IT'S TREACHERY!
UGH...
THUNK
AAAH!
GUHHH
CATCH AHAZIAH...
AND KILL HIM TOO!
THROW HIM INTO NABOTH'S FIELD...
WHICH HIS FATHER STOLE WITH MURDER.

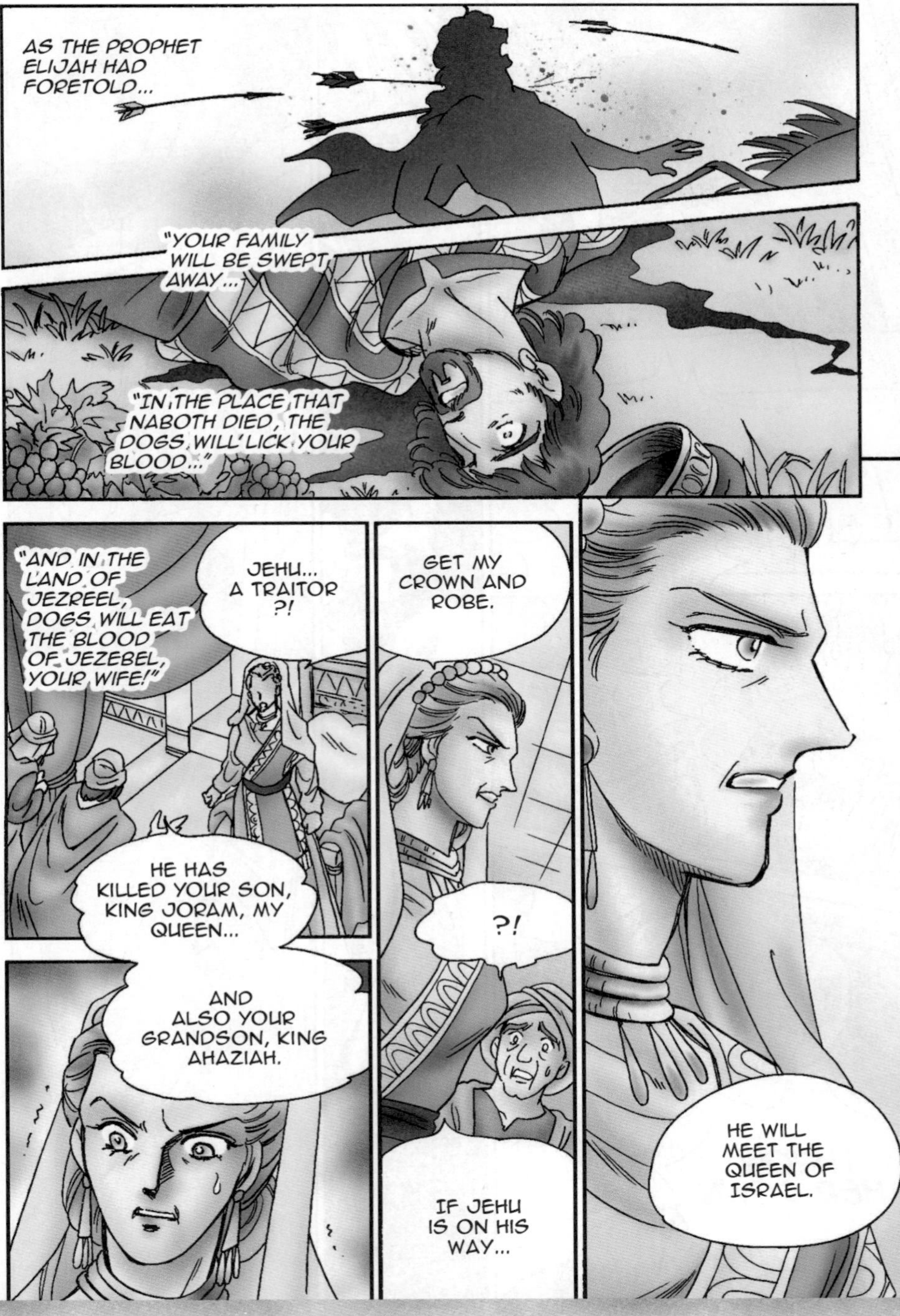
AS THE PROPHET ELIJAH HAD FORETOLD...
"YOUR FAMILY WILL BE SWEPT AWAY...
"IN THE PLACE THAT NABOTH DIED, THE DOGS WILL LICK YOUR BLOOD..."
"AND IN THE LAND OF JEZREEL, DOGS WILL EAT THE BLOOD OF JEZEBEL, YOUR WIFE!"
JEHU... A TRAITOR ?!
HE HAS KILLED YOUR SON, KING JORAM, MY QUEEN...
AND ALSO YOUR GRANDSON, KING AHAZIAH.
GET MY CROWN AND ROBE.
?!
IF JEHU IS ON HIS WAY...
HE WILL MEET THE QUEEN OF ISRAEL.

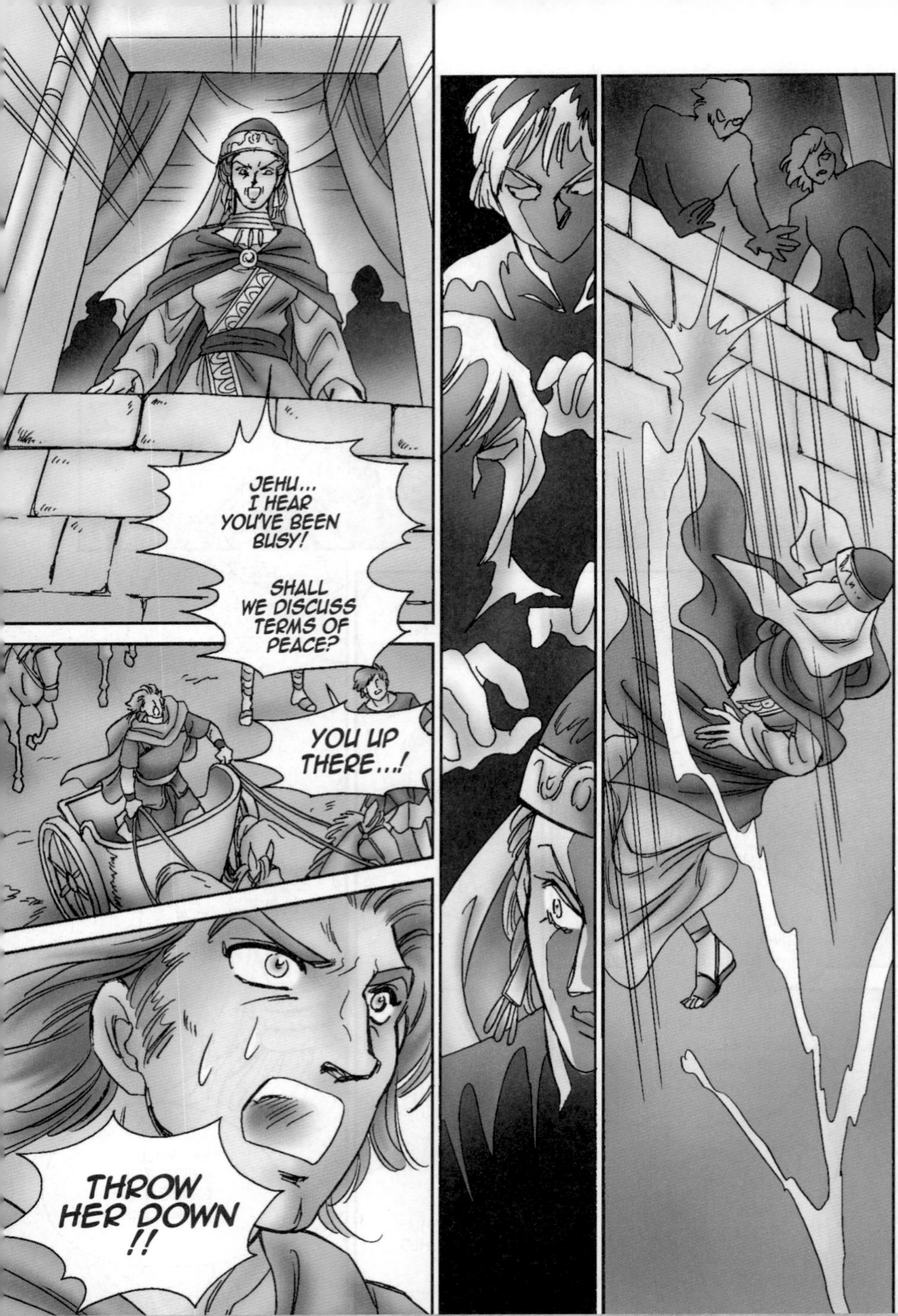
JEHU... I HEAR YOU'VE BEEN BUSY!
SHALL WE DISCUSS TERMS OF PEACE?
YOU UP THERE...!
THROW HER DOWN !!

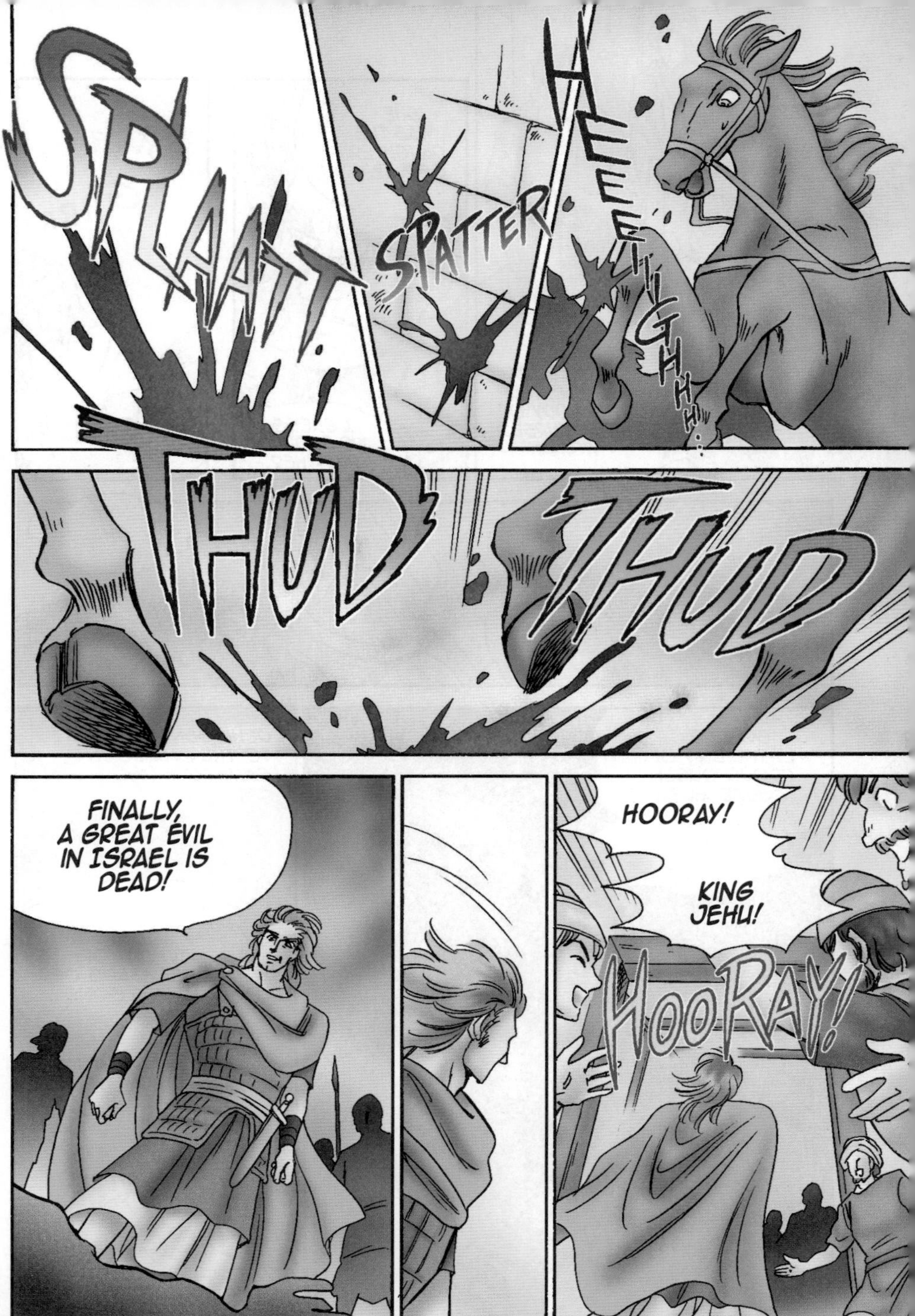
SPLAATT
SPATTER
HEEEIIGHHH...
THUD
THUD
FINALLY, A GREAT EVIL IN ISRAEL IS DEAD!
HOORAY!
KING JEHU!
HOORAY!

HEY!

SOMEBODY GO CLEAN UP THE BODY OF THAT CURSED WOMAN!

SHE WAS THE DAUGHTER OF A KING...

I GUESS WE SHOULD BURY HER.

RRRR

GRRR

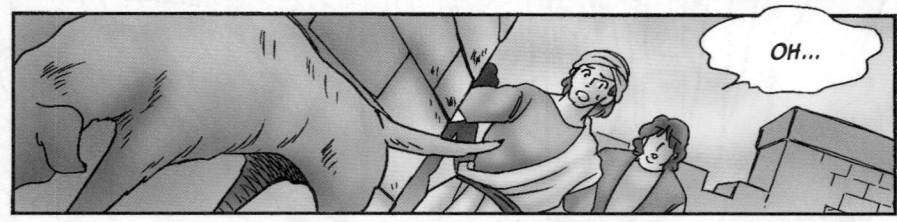

OH...

SO THIS IS THE END OF PROUD QUEEN JEZEBEL?

...

JEHU SENT LETTERS TO THE PALACE IN SAMARIA...

IT SAYS TO CUT OFF THE HEADS OF AHAB'S SONS...

AND BRING THEM THERE!

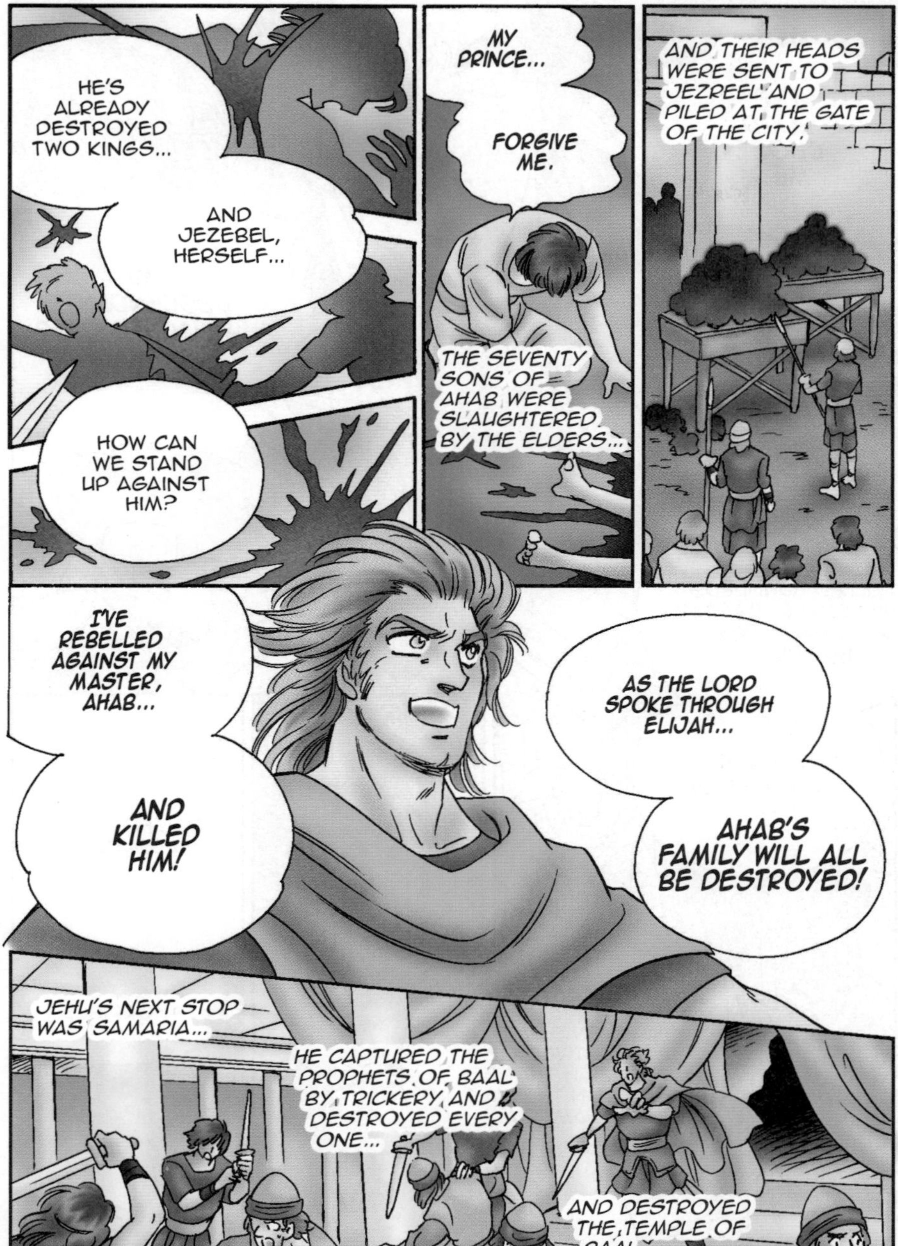
HE'S ALREADY DESTROYED TWO KINGS...
AND JEZEBEL, HERSELF...
HOW CAN WE STAND UP AGAINST HIM?
MY PRINCE...
FORGIVE ME.
THE SEVENTY SONS OF AHAB WERE SLAUGHTERED BY THE ELDERS...
AND THEIR HEADS WERE SENT TO JEZREEL AND PILED AT THE GATE OF THE CITY.
I'VE REBELLED AGAINST MY MASTER, AHAB...
AND KILLED HIM!
AS THE LORD SPOKE THROUGH ELIJAH...
AHAB'S FAMILY WILL ALL BE DESTROYED!
JEHU'S NEXT STOP WAS SAMARIA...
HE CAPTURED THE PROPHETS OF BAAL BY TRICKERY AND DESTROYED EVERY ONE...
AND DESTROYED THE TEMPLE OF BAAL.

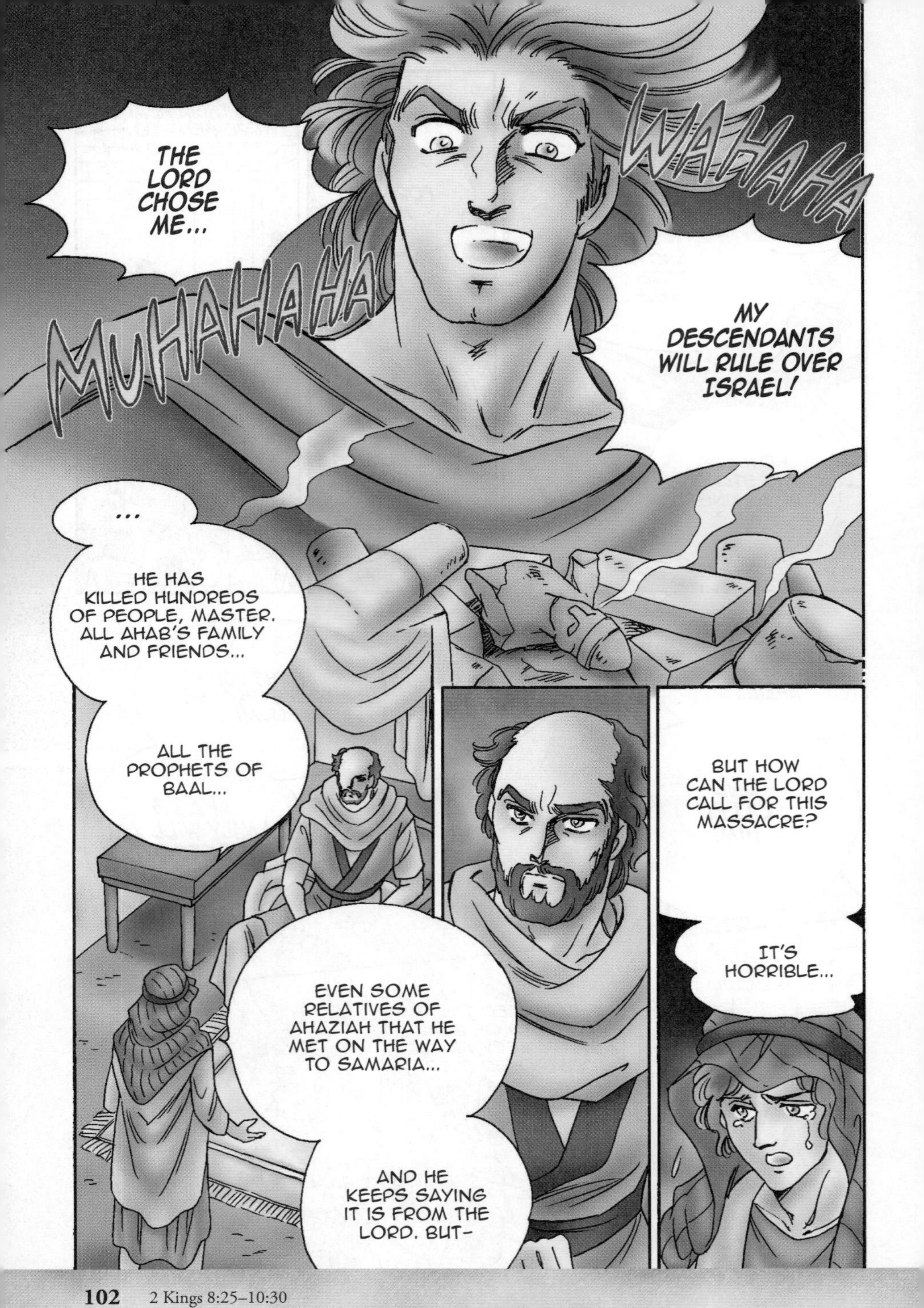
THE LORD CHOSE ME...
WAHAHA
MUHAHAHAHA
MY DESCENDANTS WILL RULE OVER ISRAEL!
...
HE HAS KILLED HUNDREDS OF PEOPLE, MASTER. ALL AHAB'S FAMILY AND FRIENDS...
ALL THE PROPHETS OF BAAL...
EVEN SOME RELATIVES OF AHAZIAH THAT HE MET ON THE WAY TO SAMARIA...
AND HE KEEPS SAYING IT IS FROM THE LORD. BUT-
BUT HOW CAN THE LORD CALL FOR THIS MASSACRE?
IT'S HORRIBLE...

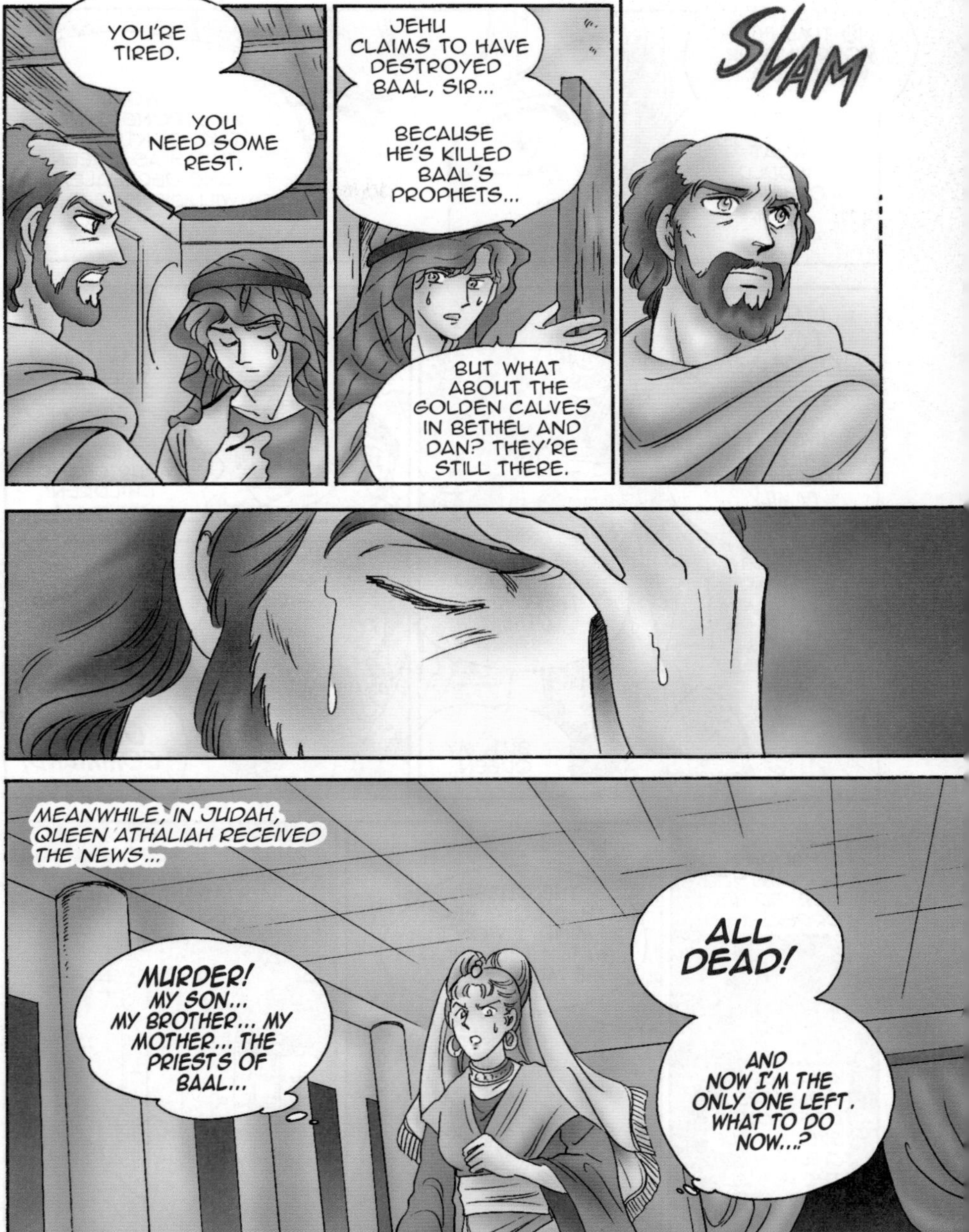
YOU'RE TIRED.
YOU NEED SOME REST.
JEHU CLAIMS TO HAVE DESTROYED BAAL, SIR...
BECAUSE HE'S KILLED BAAL'S PROPHETS...
BUT WHAT ABOUT THE GOLDEN CALVES IN BETHEL AND DAN? THEY'RE STILL THERE.
SLAM
MEANWHILE, IN JUDAH, QUEEN ATHALIAH RECEIVED THE NEWS...
ALL DEAD!
MURDER! MY SON... MY BROTHER... MY MOTHER... THE PRIESTS OF BAAL...
AND NOW I'M THE ONLY ONE LEFT. WHAT TO DO NOW...?

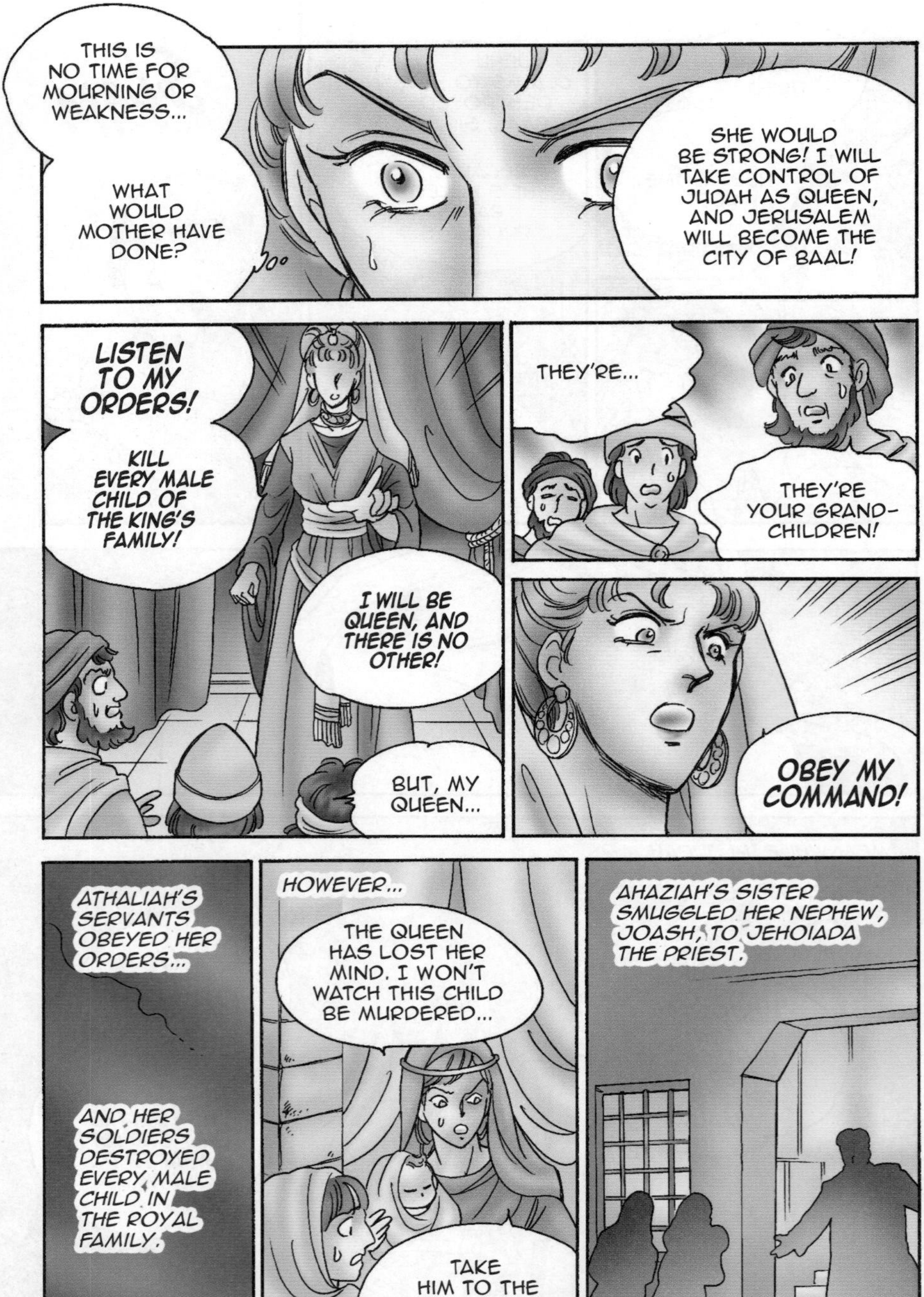
THIS IS NO TIME FOR MOURNING OR WEAKNESS...
WHAT WOULD MOTHER HAVE DONE?
SHE WOULD BE STRONG! I WILL TAKE CONTROL OF JUDAH AS QUEEN, AND JERUSALEM WILL BECOME THE CITY OF BAAL!
LISTEN TO MY ORDERS!
KILL EVERY MALE CHILD OF THE KING'S FAMILY!
I WILL BE QUEEN, AND THERE IS NO OTHER!
BUT, MY QUEEN...
THEY'RE...
THEY'RE YOUR GRAND-CHILDREN!
OBEY MY COMMAND!
ATHALIAH'S SERVANTS OBEYED HER ORDERS...
AND HER SOLDIERS DESTROYED EVERY MALE CHILD IN THE ROYAL FAMILY.
HOWEVER...
THE QUEEN HAS LOST HER MIND. I WON'T WATCH THIS CHILD BE MURDERED...
TAKE HIM TO THE TEMPLE AND HIDE HIM THERE!
AHAZIAH'S SISTER SMUGGLED HER NEPHEW, JOASH, TO JEHOIADA THE PRIEST.

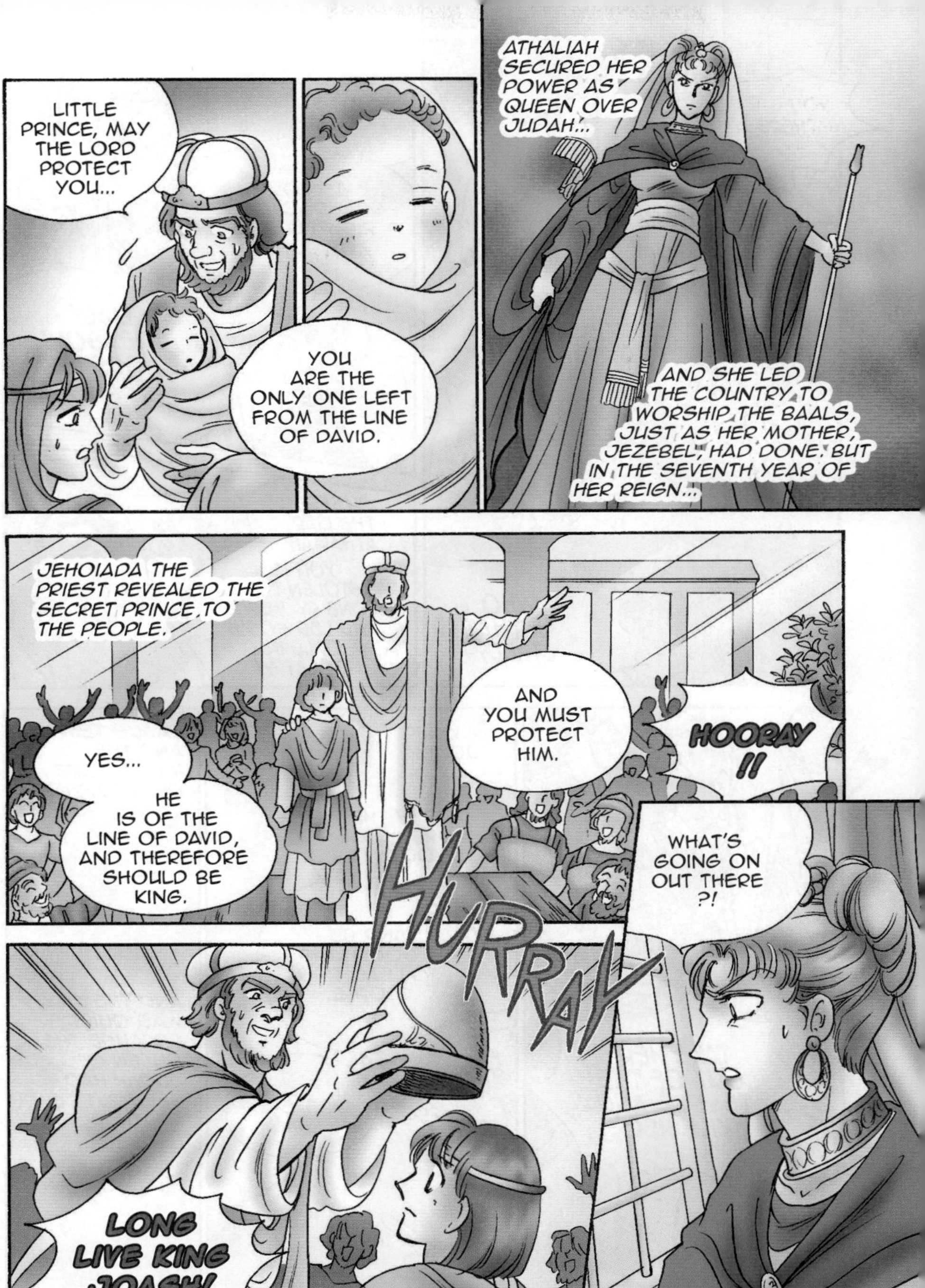
LITTLE PRINCE, MAY THE LORD PROTECT YOU...
YOU ARE THE ONLY ONE LEFT FROM THE LINE OF DAVID.
ATHALIAH SECURED HER POWER AS QUEEN OVER JUDAH...
AND SHE LED THE COUNTRY TO WORSHIP THE BAALS, JUST AS HER MOTHER, JEZEBEL, HAD DONE. BUT IN THE SEVENTH YEAR OF HER REIGN...
JEHOIADA THE PRIEST REVEALED THE SECRET PRINCE TO THE PEOPLE.
YES...
HE IS OF THE LINE OF DAVID, AND THEREFORE SHOULD BE KING.
AND YOU MUST PROTECT HIM.
HOORAY !!
HURRAY
WHAT'S GOING ON OUT THERE ?!
LONG LIVE KING JOASH!

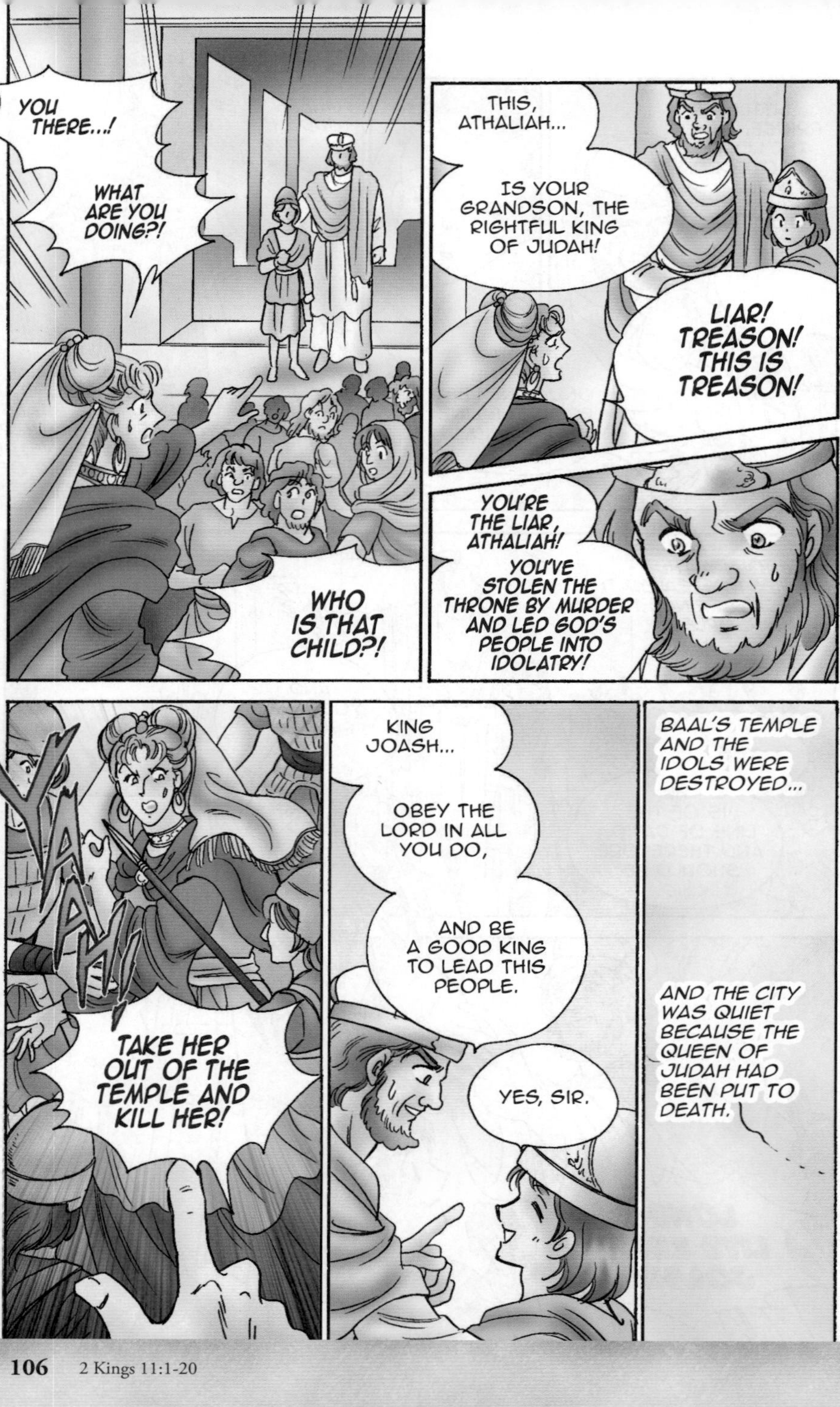
YOU THERE...!
WHAT ARE YOU DOING?!
WHO IS THAT CHILD?!
THIS, ATHALIAH...
IS YOUR GRANDSON, THE RIGHTFUL KING OF JUDAH!
LIAR! TREASON! THIS IS TREASON!
YOU'RE THE LIAR, ATHALIAH!
YOU'VE STOLEN THE THRONE BY MURDER AND LED GOD'S PEOPLE INTO IDOLATRY!
YAAH!
TAKE HER OUT OF THE TEMPLE AND KILL HER!
KING JOASH...
OBEY THE LORD IN ALL YOU DO,
AND BE A GOOD KING TO LEAD THIS PEOPLE.
YES, SIR.
BAAL'S TEMPLE AND THE IDOLS WERE DESTROYED...
AND THE CITY WAS QUIET BECAUSE THE QUEEN OF JUDAH HAD BEEN PUT TO DEATH.

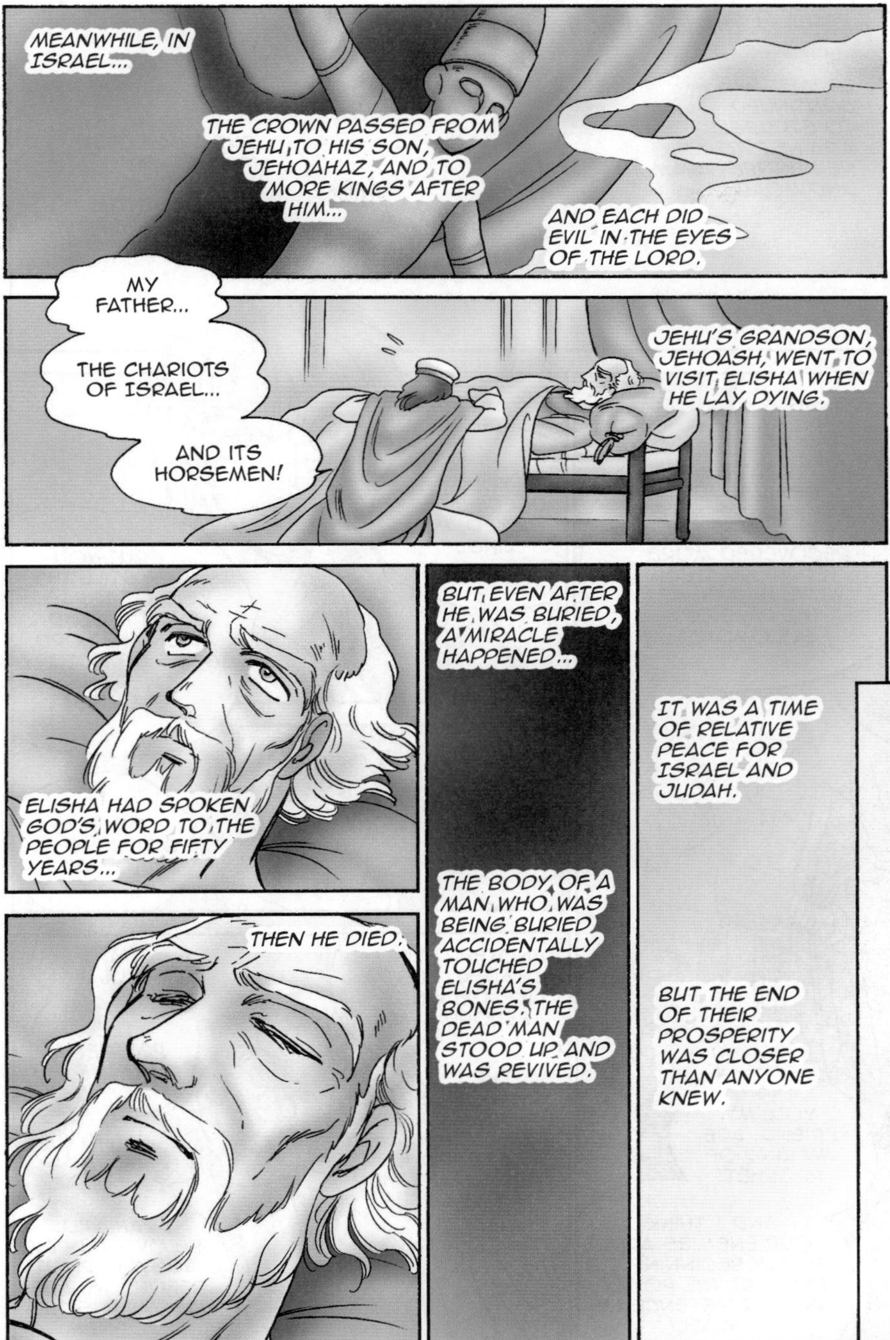
MEANWHILE, IN ISRAEL...
THE CROWN PASSED FROM JEHU TO HIS SON, JEHOAHAZ, AND TO MORE KINGS AFTER HIM...
AND EACH DID EVIL IN THE EYES OF THE LORD.
MY FATHER...
THE CHARIOTS OF ISRAEL...
AND ITS HORSEMEN!
JEHU'S GRANDSON, JEHOASH, WENT TO VISIT ELISHA WHEN HE LAY DYING.
ELISHA HAD SPOKEN GOD'S WORD TO THE PEOPLE FOR FIFTY YEARS...
THEN HE DIED.
BUT EVEN AFTER HE WAS BURIED, A MIRACLE HAPPENED...
THE BODY OF A MAN WHO WAS BEING BURIED ACCIDENTALLY TOUCHED ELISHA'S BONES. THE DEAD MAN STOOD UP AND WAS REVIVED.
IT WAS A TIME OF RELATIVE PEACE FOR ISRAEL AND JUDAH.
BUT THE END OF THEIR PROSPERITY WAS CLOSER THAN ANYONE KNEW.

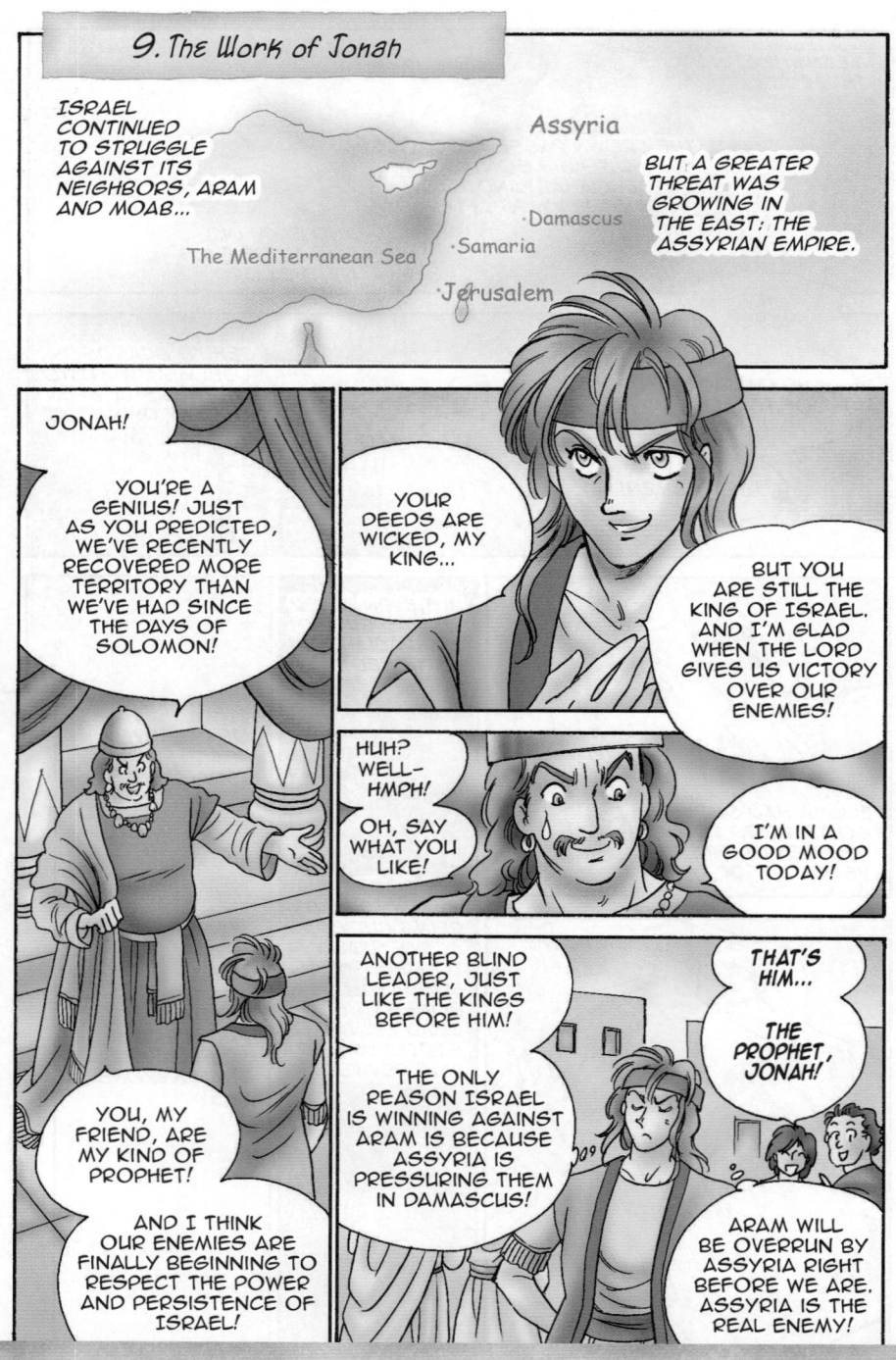

ISRAEL CONTINUED TO STRUGGLE AGAINST ITS NEIGHBORS, ARAM AND MOAB...

Assyria

·Damascus

·Samaria

The Mediterranean Sea

·Jerusalem

BUT A GREATER THREAT WAS GROWING IN THE EAST: THE ASSYRIAN EMPIRE.

JONAH!

YOU'RE A GENIUS! JUST AS YOU PREDICTED, WE'VE RECENTLY RECOVERED MORE TERRITORY THAN WE'VE HAD SINCE THE DAYS OF SOLOMON!

YOUR DEEDS ARE WICKED, MY KING...

BUT YOU ARE STILL THE KING OF ISRAEL. AND I'M GLAD WHEN THE LORD GIVES US VICTORY OVER OUR ENEMIES!

HUH? WELL– HMPH!

OH, SAY WHAT YOU LIKE!

I'M IN A GOOD MOOD TODAY!

YOU, MY FRIEND, ARE MY KIND OF PROPHET!

AND I THINK OUR ENEMIES ARE FINALLY BEGINNING TO RESPECT THE POWER AND PERSISTENCE OF ISRAEL!

ANOTHER BLIND LEADER, JUST LIKE THE KINGS BEFORE HIM!

THE ONLY REASON ISRAEL IS WINNING AGAINST ARAM IS BECAUSE ASSYRIA IS PRESSURING THEM IN DAMASCUS!

THAT'S HIM...

THE PROPHET, JONAH!

ARAM WILL BE OVERRUN BY ASSYRIA RIGHT BEFORE WE ARE. ASSYRIA IS THE REAL ENEMY!

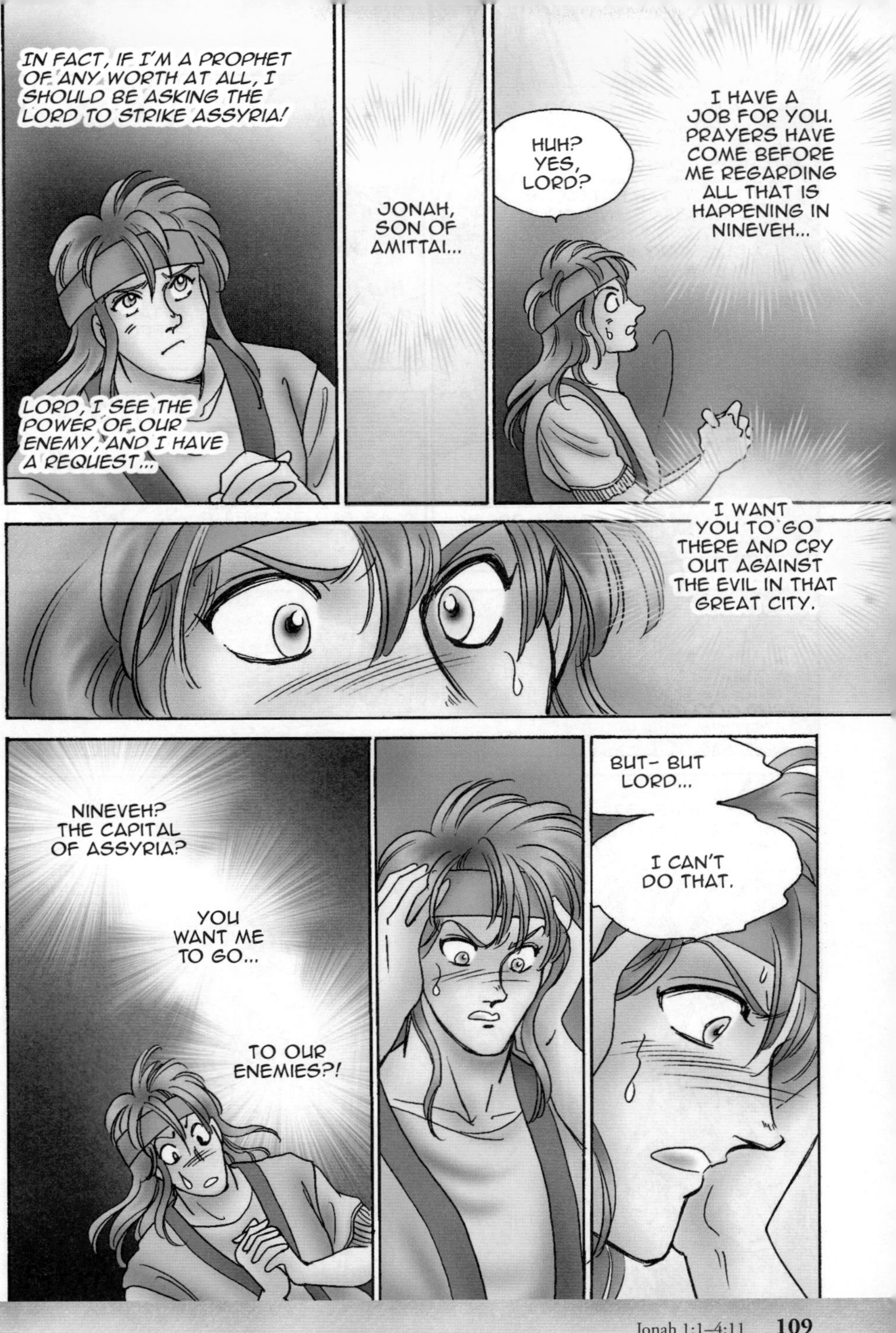
IN FACT, IF I'M A PROPHET OF ANY WORTH AT ALL, I SHOULD BE ASKING THE LORD TO STRIKE ASSYRIA!
LORD, I SEE THE POWER OF OUR ENEMY, AND I HAVE A REQUEST...
JONAH, SON OF AMITTAI...
HUH? YES, LORD?
I HAVE A JOB FOR YOU. PRAYERS HAVE COME BEFORE ME REGARDING ALL THAT IS HAPPENING IN NINEVEH...
I WANT YOU TO GO THERE AND CRY OUT AGAINST THE EVIL IN THAT GREAT CITY.
NINEVEH? THE CAPITAL OF ASSYRIA?
YOU WANT ME TO GO...
TO OUR ENEMIES?!
BUT- BUT LORD...
I CAN'T DO THAT.

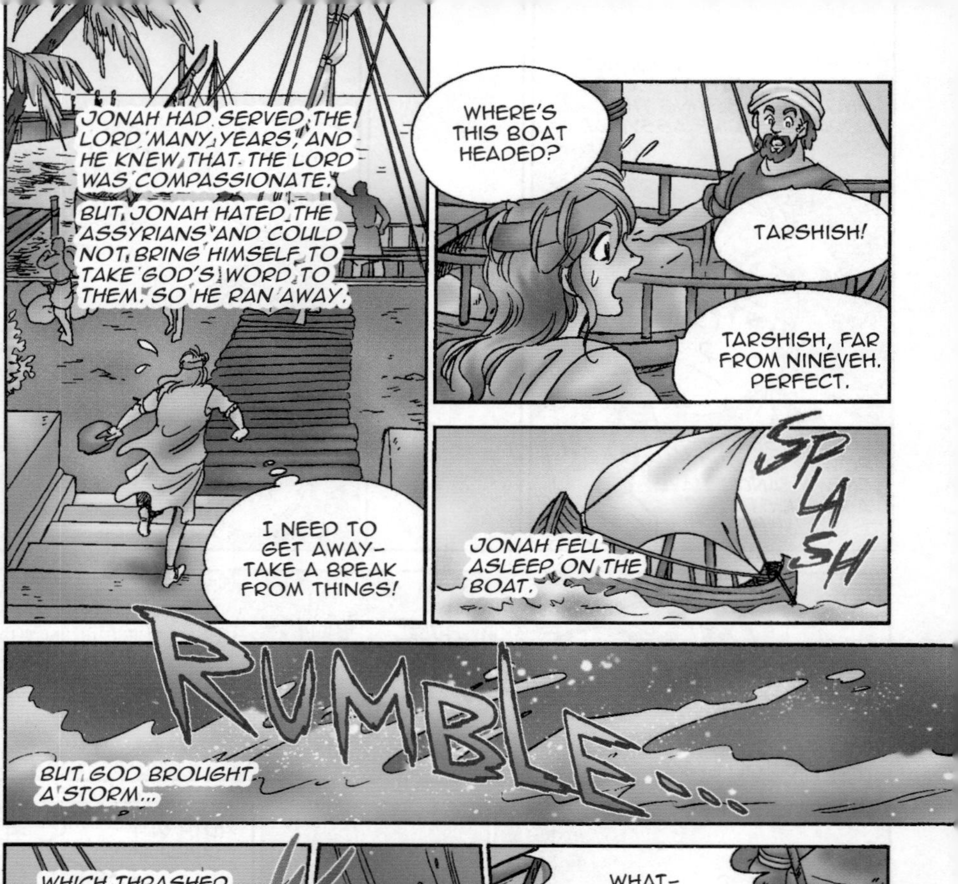
JONAH HAD SERVED THE LORD MANY YEARS, AND HE KNEW THAT THE LORD WAS COMPASSIONATE.
BUT JONAH HATED THE ASSYRIANS AND COULD NOT BRING HIMSELF TO TAKE GOD'S WORD TO THEM. SO HE RAN AWAY.
I NEED TO GET AWAY- TAKE A BREAK FROM THINGS!
WHERE'S THIS BOAT HEADED?
TARSHISH!
TARSHISH, FAR FROM NINEVEH. PERFECT.
SPLASH
JONAH FELL ASLEEP ON THE BOAT.
RUMBLE...
BUT GOD BROUGHT A STORM...
WHICH THRASHED THE BOAT AND THREATENED TO DESTROY IT.
WHOOSH
WE'RE SINKING!
THROW THE CARGO OVERBOARD!
WHAT-
WHAT'RE YOU DOING SLEEPING?!

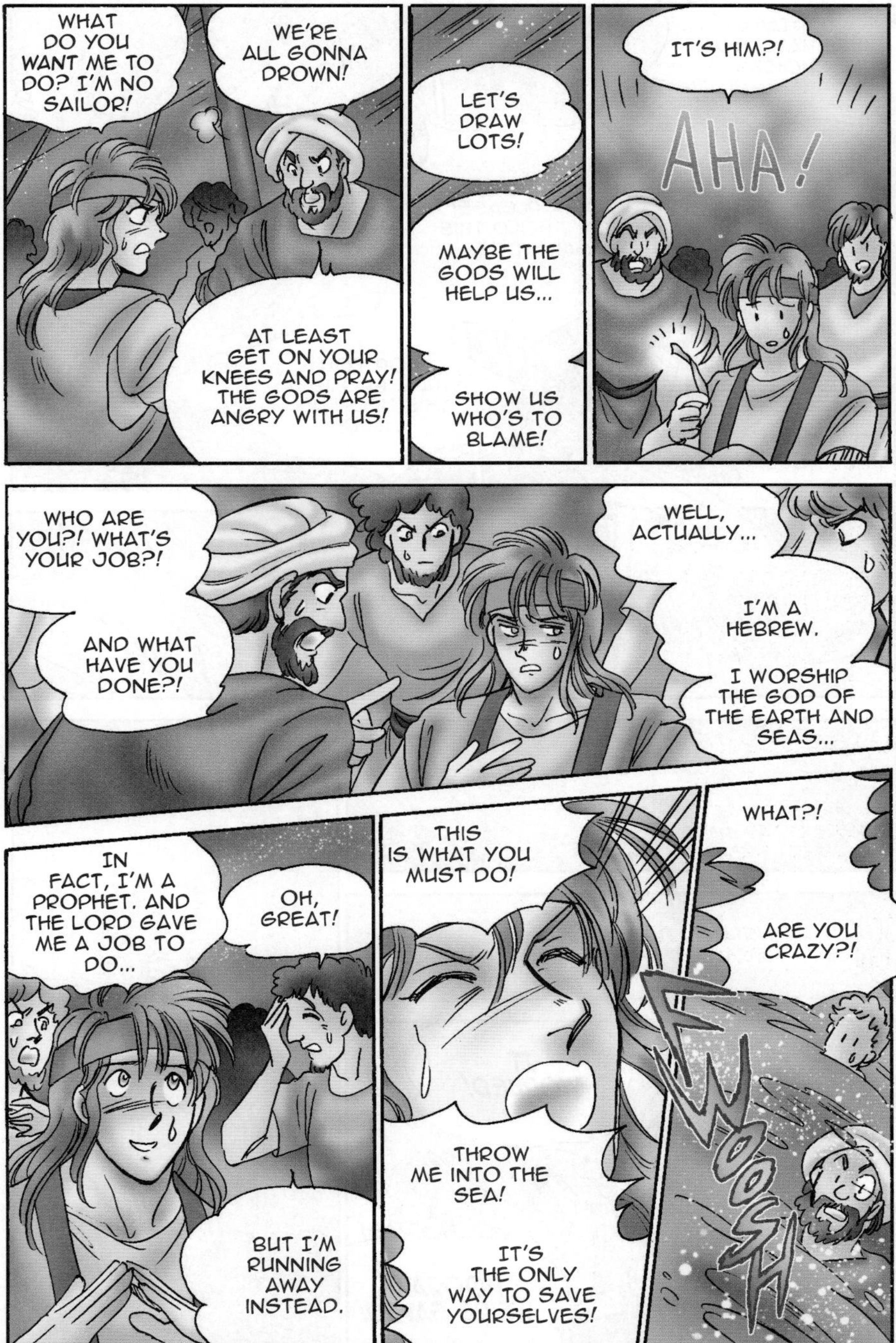
WHAT DO YOU WANT ME TO DO? I'M NO SAILOR!
WE'RE ALL GONNA DROWN!
AT LEAST GET ON YOUR KNEES AND PRAY! THE GODS ARE ANGRY WITH US!
LET'S DRAW LOTS!
MAYBE THE GODS WILL HELP US...
SHOW US WHO'S TO BLAME!
IT'S HIM?!
AHA!
WHO ARE YOU?! WHAT'S YOUR JOB?!
AND WHAT HAVE YOU DONE?!
WELL, ACTUALLY...
I'M A HEBREW.
I WORSHIP THE GOD OF THE EARTH AND SEAS...
IN FACT, I'M A PROPHET. AND THE LORD GAVE ME A JOB TO DO...
OH, GREAT!
BUT I'M RUNNING AWAY INSTEAD.
THIS IS WHAT YOU MUST DO!
THROW ME INTO THE SEA!
IT'S THE ONLY WAY TO SAVE YOURSELVES!
WHAT?!
ARE YOU CRAZY?!
WOOSH

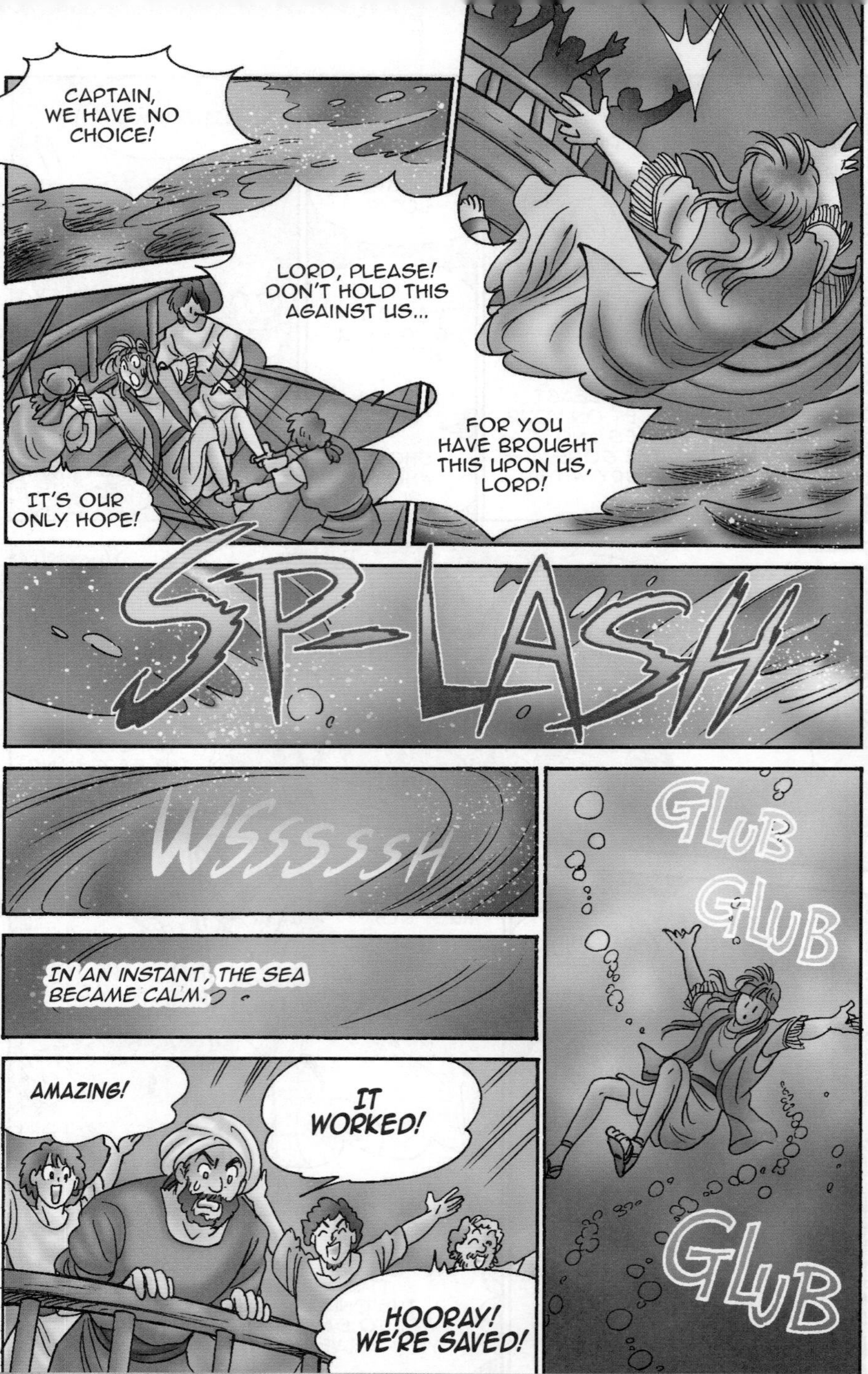
CAPTAIN, WE HAVE NO CHOICE!
LORD, PLEASE! DON'T HOLD THIS AGAINST US...
FOR YOU HAVE BROUGHT THIS UPON US, LORD!
IT'S OUR ONLY HOPE!
SP-LASH
WSSSSSH
IN AN INSTANT, THE SEA BECAME CALM.
AMAZING!
IT WORKED!
HOORAY! WE'RE SAVED!
GLUB
GLUB
GLUB

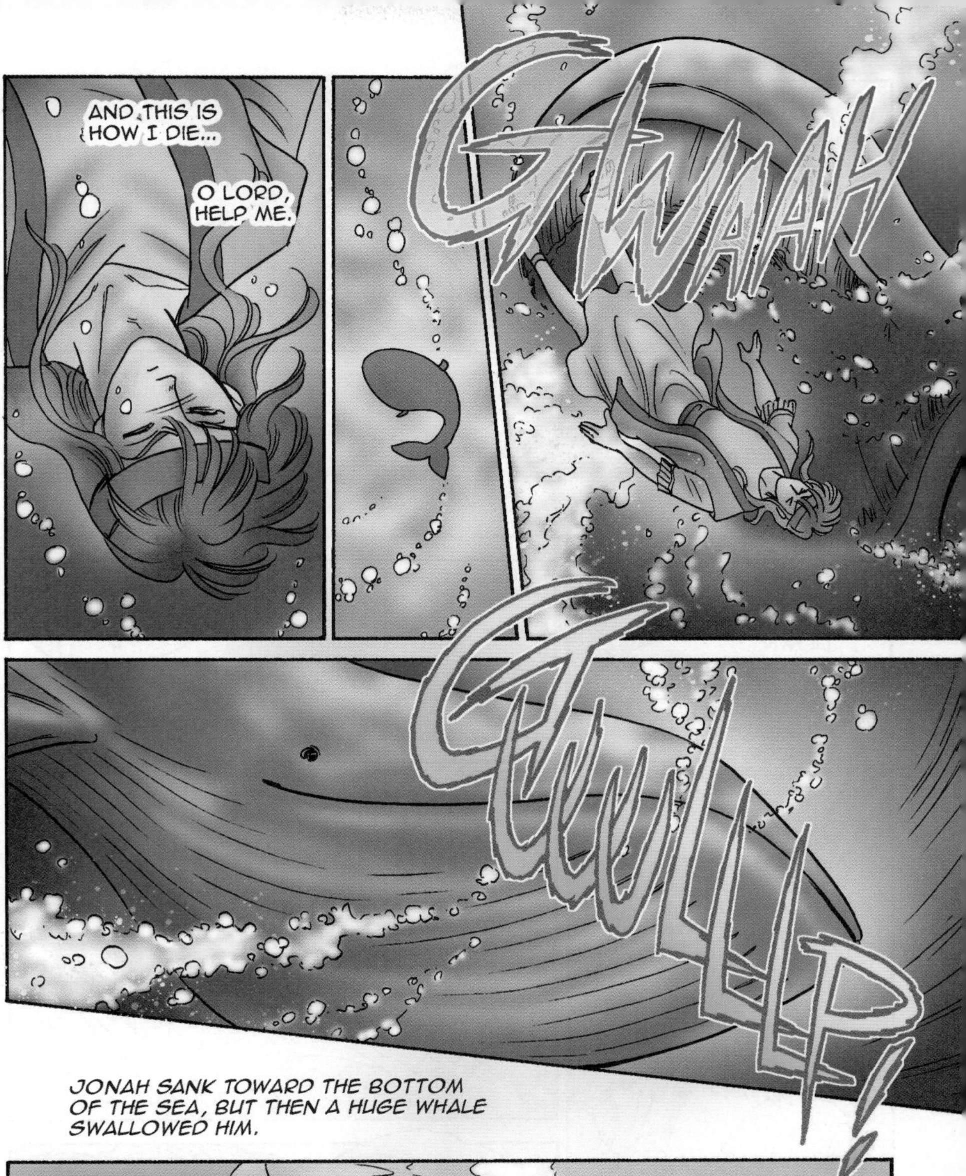
AND THIS IS HOW I DIE...
O LORD, HELP ME.
GWAAH
GULLLP!
JONAH SANK TOWARD THE BOTTOM OF THE SEA, BUT THEN A HUGE WHALE SWALLOWED HIM.
...HUH?

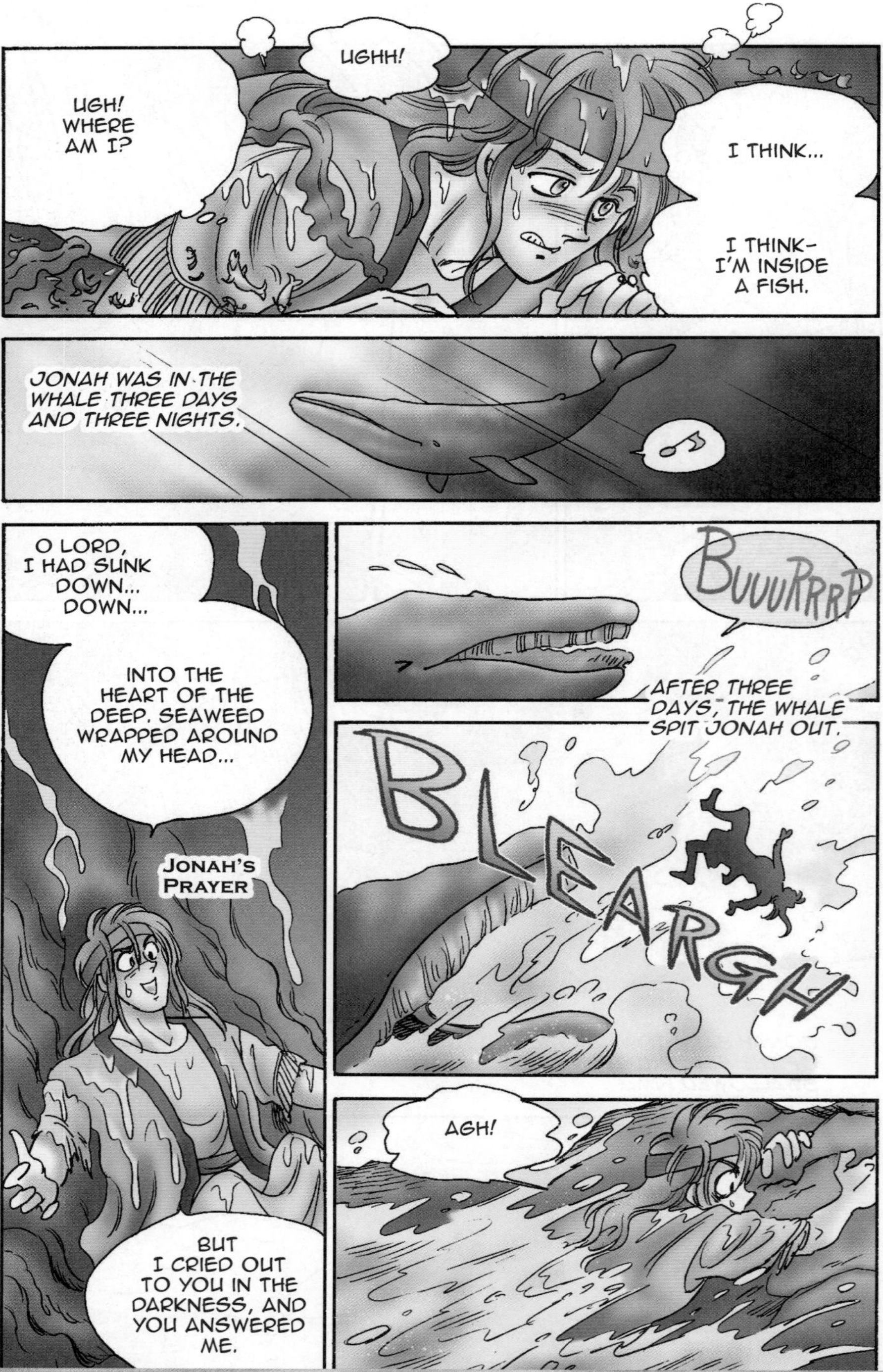
UGH! WHERE AM I?
UGHH!
I THINK...
I THINK- I'M INSIDE A FISH.
JONAH WAS IN THE WHALE THREE DAYS AND THREE NIGHTS.
O LORD, I HAD SUNK DOWN... DOWN...
INTO THE HEART OF THE DEEP. SEAWEED WRAPPED AROUND MY HEAD...
JONAH'S PRAYER
BUT I CRIED OUT TO YOU IN THE DARKNESS, AND YOU ANSWERED ME.
BUUURRRP
AFTER THREE DAYS, THE WHALE SPIT JONAH OUT.
BLEARGH
AGH!

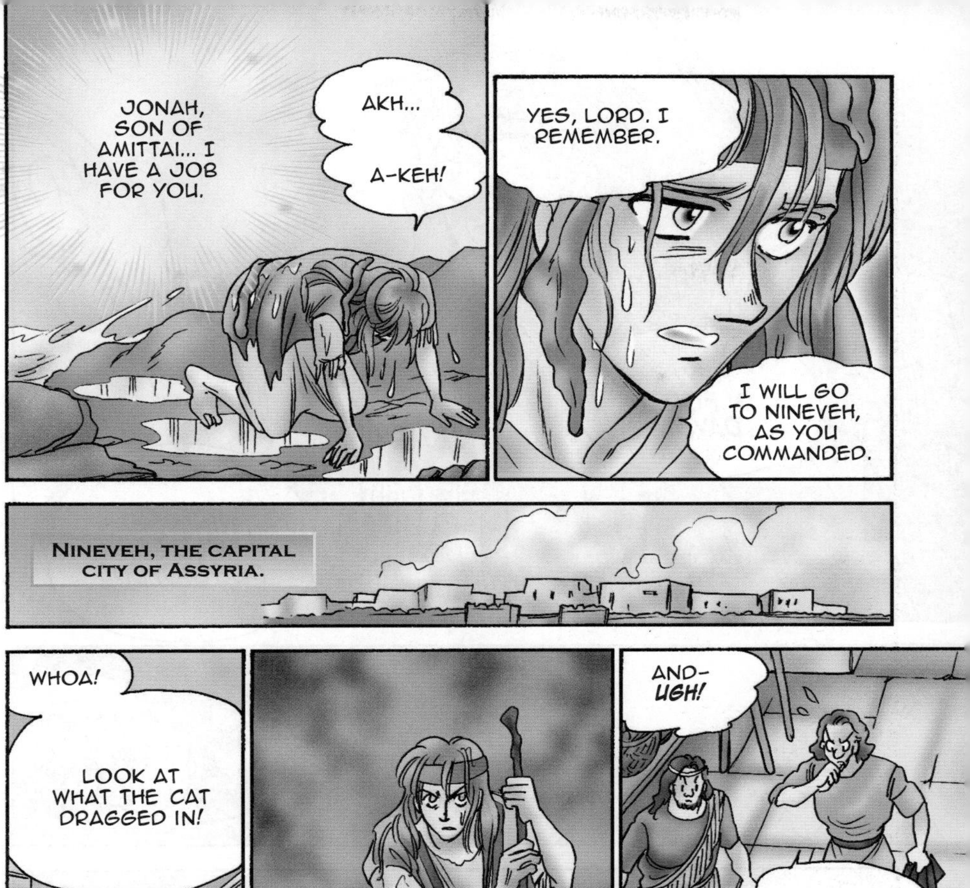
JONAH, SON OF AMITTAI... I HAVE A JOB FOR YOU.
AKH...
A-KEH!
YES, LORD. I REMEMBER.
I WILL GO TO NINEVEH, AS YOU COMMANDED.
NINEVEH, THE CAPITAL CITY OF ASSYRIA.
WHOA!
LOOK AT WHAT THE CAT DRAGGED IN!
DUDE, YOU'RE A MESS!
AND-UGH!
YOU STINK!

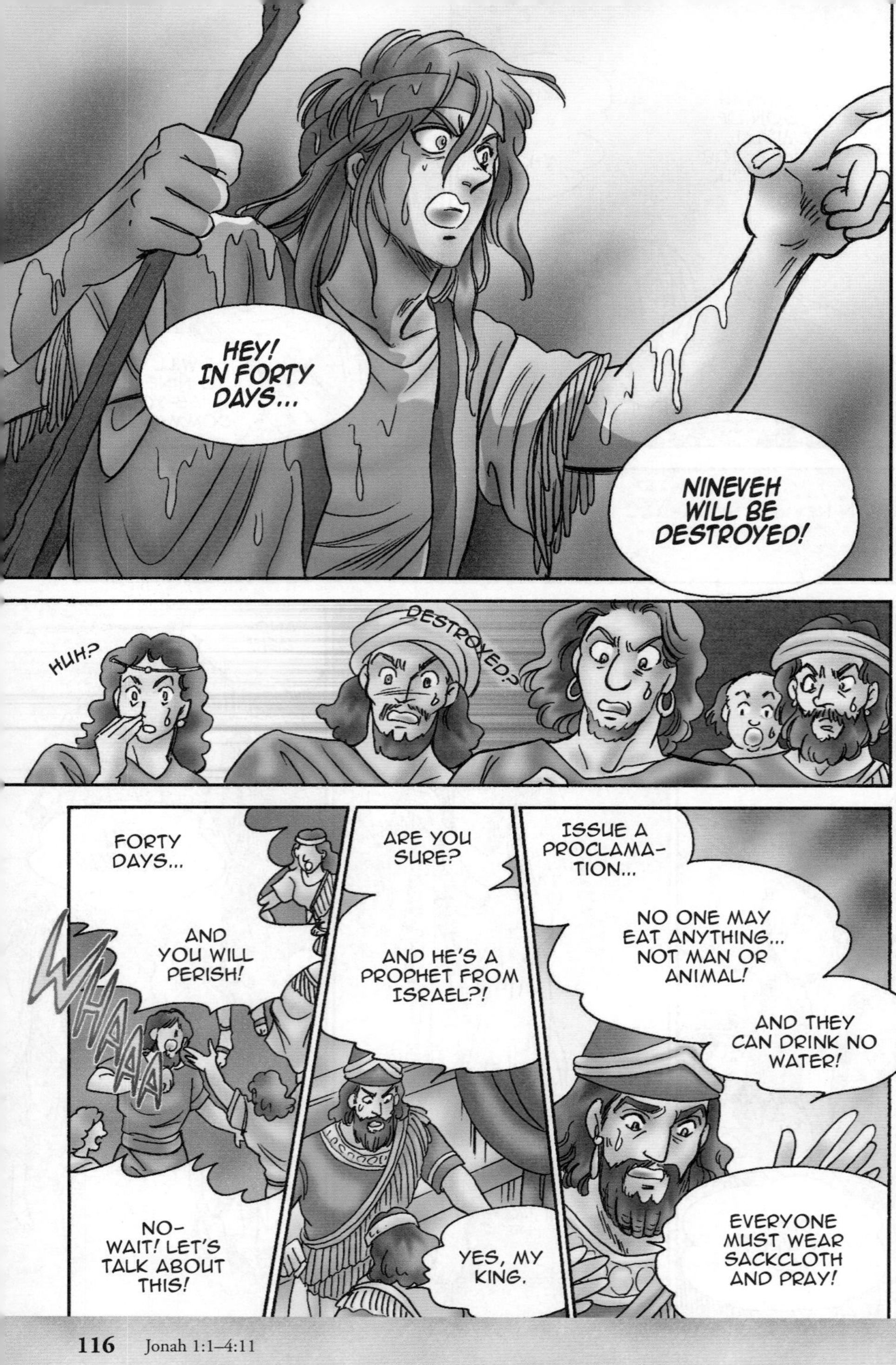
HEY! IN FORTY DAYS...
NINEVEH WILL BE DESTROYED!
HUH?
DESTROYED?
FORTY DAYS...
AND YOU WILL PERISH!
WHAAAA
NO- WAIT! LET'S TALK ABOUT THIS!
ARE YOU SURE?
AND HE'S A PROPHET FROM ISRAEL?!
YES, MY KING.
ISSUE A PROCLAMA-TION...
NO ONE MAY EAT ANYTHING... NOT MAN OR ANIMAL!
AND THEY CAN DRINK NO WATER!
EVERYONE MUST WEAR SACKCLOTH AND PRAY!

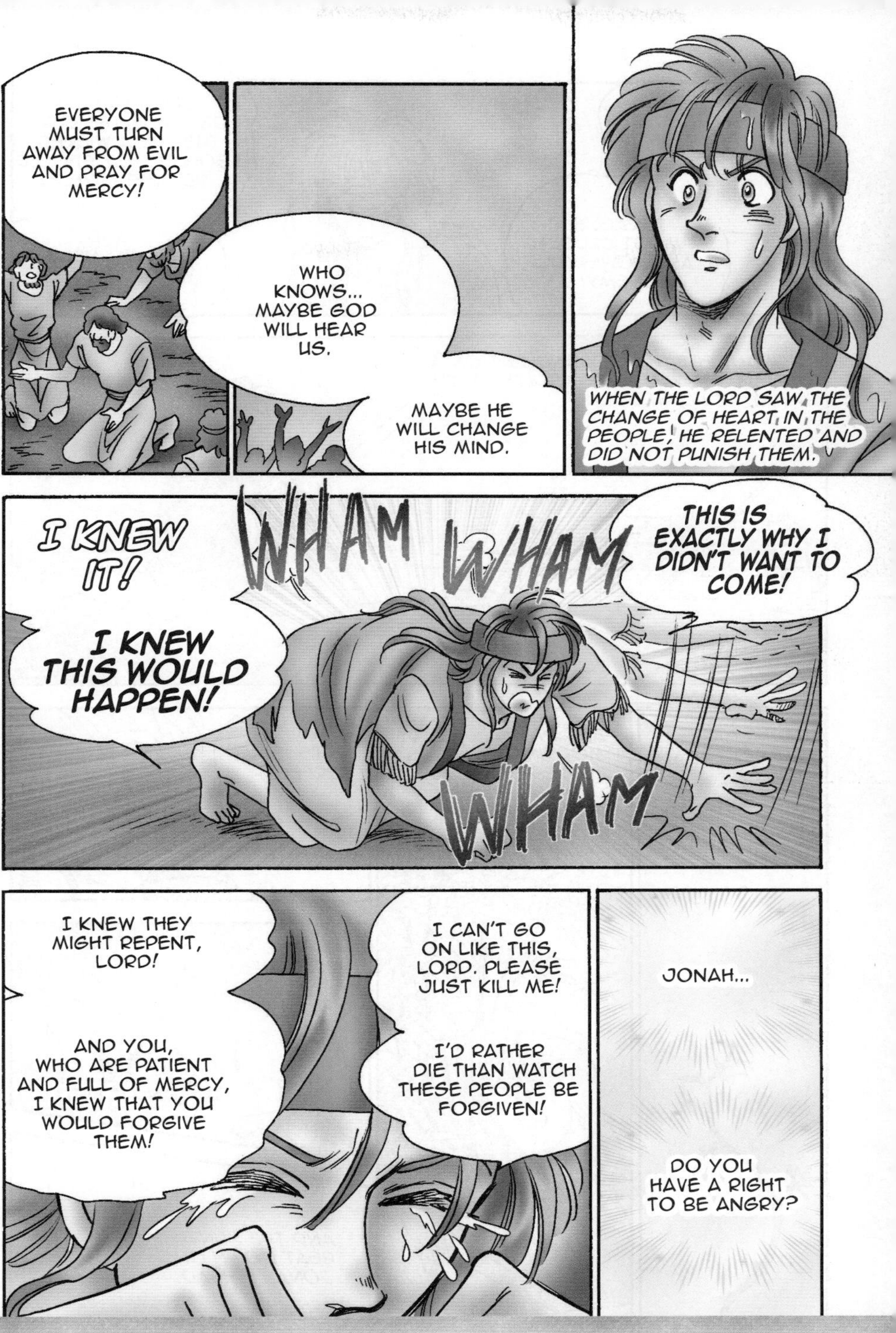
EVERYONE MUST TURN AWAY FROM EVIL AND PRAY FOR MERCY!
WHO KNOWS... MAYBE GOD WILL HEAR US.
MAYBE HE WILL CHANGE HIS MIND.
WHEN THE LORD SAW THE CHANGE OF HEART IN THE PEOPLE, HE RELENTED AND DID NOT PUNISH THEM.
I KNEW IT!
WHAM WHAM
THIS IS EXACTLY WHY I DIDN'T WANT TO COME!
I KNEW THIS WOULD HAPPEN!
WHAM
I KNEW THEY MIGHT REPENT, LORD!
AND YOU, WHO ARE PATIENT AND FULL OF MERCY, I KNEW THAT YOU WOULD FORGIVE THEM!
I CAN'T GO ON LIKE THIS, LORD. PLEASE JUST KILL ME!
I'D RATHER DIE THAN WATCH THESE PEOPLE BE FORGIVEN!
JONAH...
DO YOU HAVE A RIGHT TO BE ANGRY?

NINEVEH, THE CAPITAL OF ASSYRIA...

ISRAEL'S MOST CRUEL AND POWERFUL ENEMY!

IF ONLY THE LORD WOULD DESTROY THE CITY. THEY'RE A WICKED PEOPLE! THEY SHOULD BE DESTROYED!

AND WHAT A HELP THAT WOULD BE TO ISRAEL!

JONAH LEFT THE CITY AND SAT ON A HIGH PLACE WHERE HE COULD WATCH WHAT WOULD HAPPEN.

IN THE NIGHT, A LEAFY PLANT GREW.

AND IN THE MORNING ITS LEAVES SHIELDED JONAH'S HEAD FROM THE SUN!

MM... THIS IS PERFECT.

BUT THE NEXT DAY, A WORM ATE THE PLANT...

AND IT DIED.

AND THE SUN BEAT DOWN ON JONAH'S HEAD.

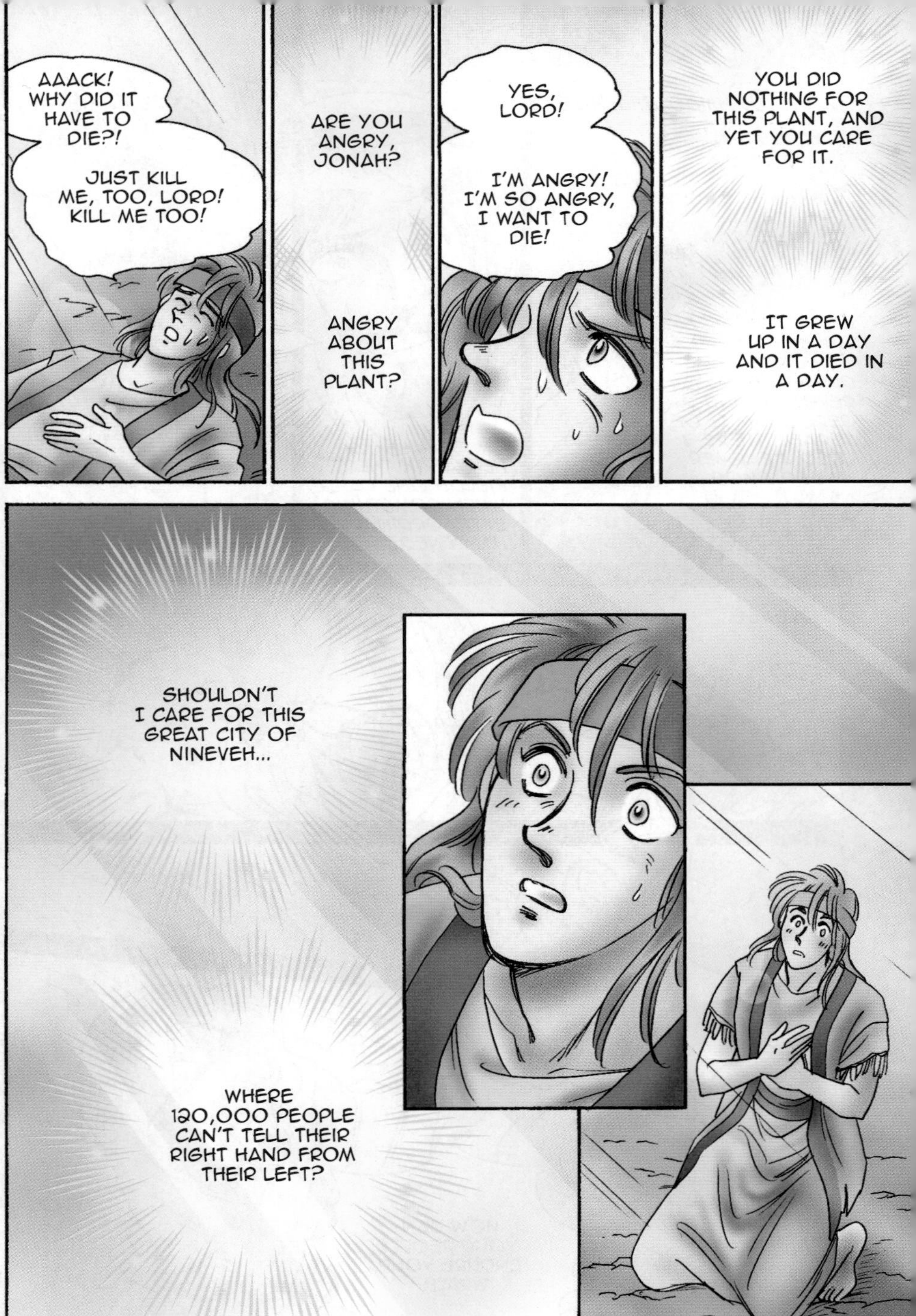
AAACK! WHY DID IT HAVE TO DIE?!
JUST KILL ME, TOO, LORD! KILL ME TOO!
ARE YOU ANGRY, JONAH?
ANGRY ABOUT THIS PLANT?
YES, LORD!
I'M ANGRY! I'M SO ANGRY, I WANT TO DIE!
YOU DID NOTHING FOR THIS PLANT, AND YET YOU CARE FOR IT.
IT GREW UP IN A DAY AND IT DIED IN A DAY.
SHOULDN'T I CARE FOR THIS GREAT CITY OF NINEVEH...
WHERE 120,000 PEOPLE CAN'T TELL THEIR RIGHT HAND FROM THEIR LEFT?

10. Amos and Hosea

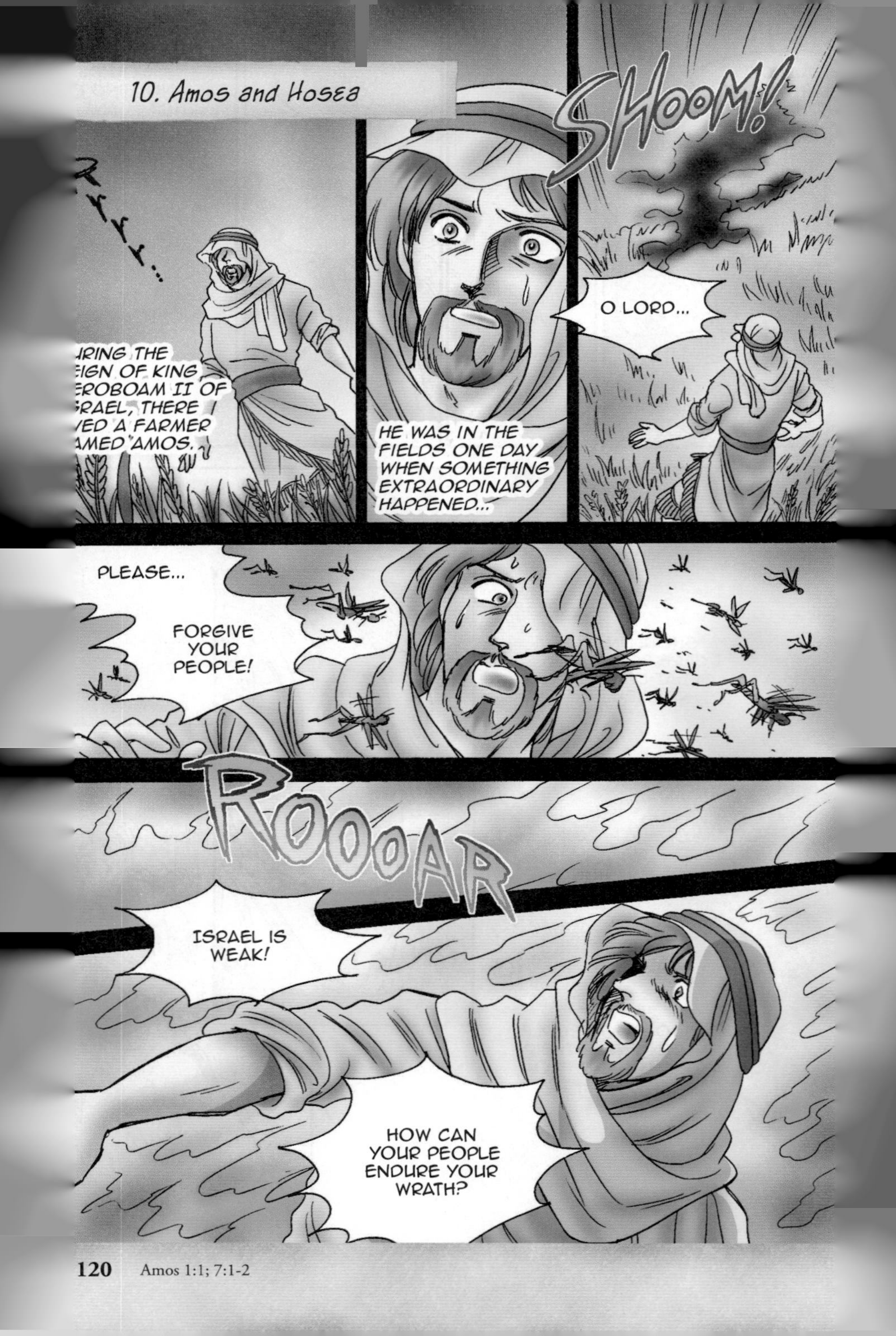

ZZZZ...
URING THE EIGN OF KING EROBOAM II OF SRAEL, THERE VED A FARMER AMED AMOS.
HE WAS IN THE FIELDS ONE DAY WHEN SOMETHING EXTRAORDINARY HAPPENED...
SHOOM!
O LORD...
PLEASE...
FORGIVE YOUR PEOPLE!
ROOOAR
ISRAEL IS WEAK!
HOW CAN YOUR PEOPLE ENDURE YOUR WRATH?

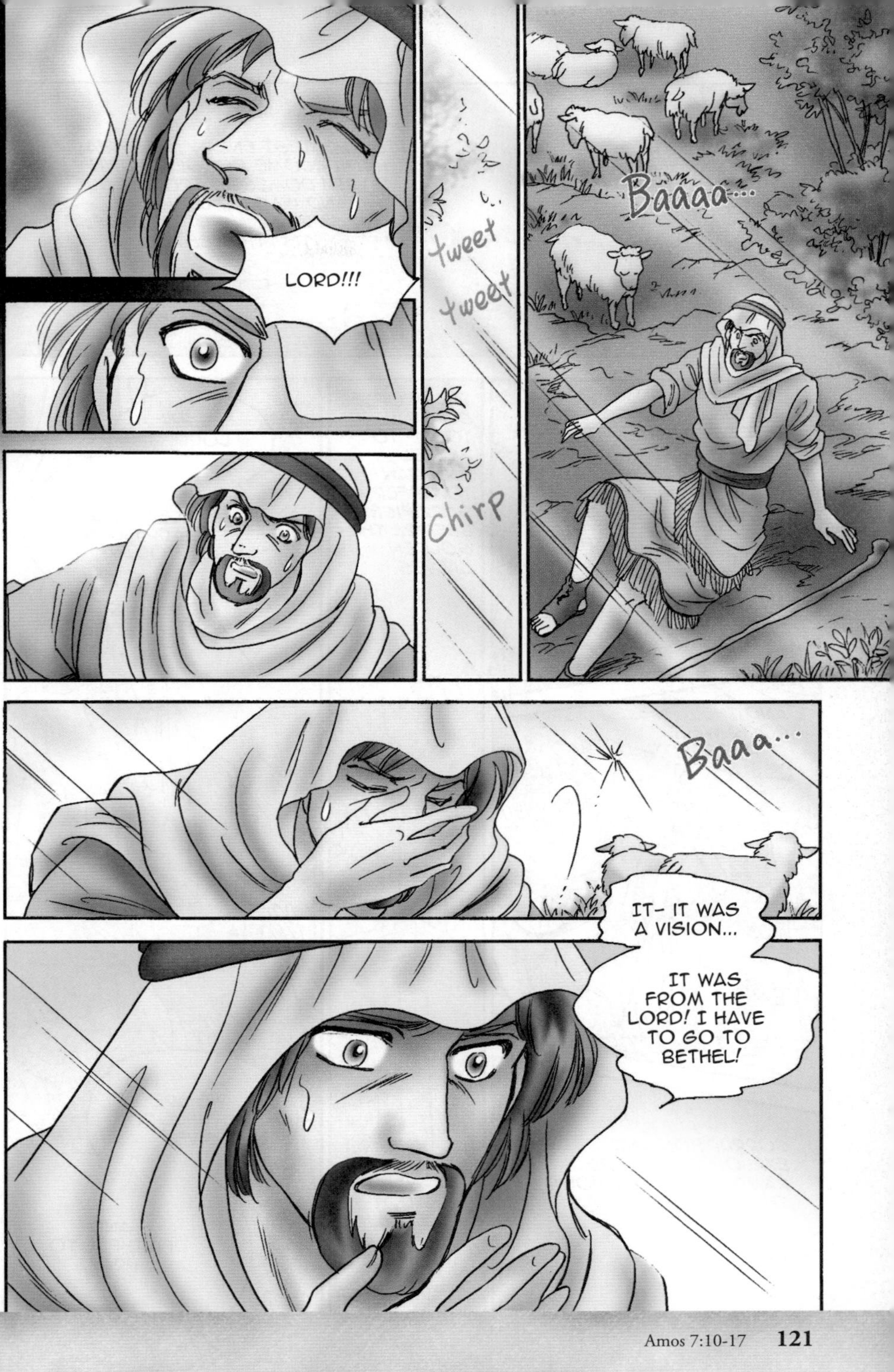
LORD!!!
tweet
tweet
Chirp
Baaaa...
Baaa...
IT- IT WAS A VISION...
IT WAS FROM THE LORD! I HAVE TO GO TO BETHEL!

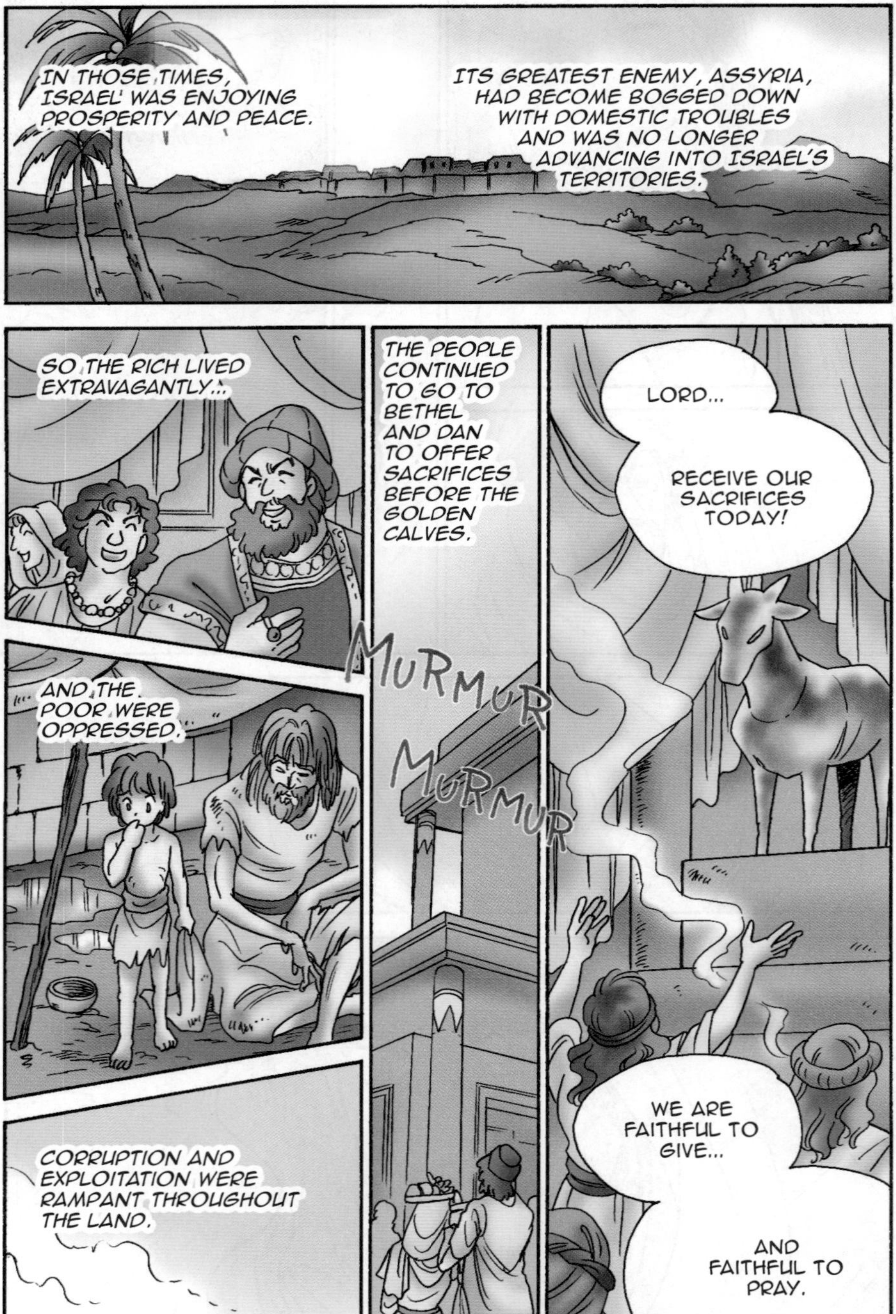
IN THOSE TIMES, ISRAEL WAS ENJOYING PROSPERITY AND PEACE.
ITS GREATEST ENEMY, ASSYRIA, HAD BECOME BOGGED DOWN WITH DOMESTIC TROUBLES AND WAS NO LONGER ADVANCING INTO ISRAEL'S TERRITORIES.
SO THE RICH LIVED EXTRAVAGANTLY...
AND THE POOR WERE OPPRESSED.
CORRUPTION AND EXPLOITATION WERE RAMPANT THROUGHOUT THE LAND.
THE PEOPLE CONTINUED TO GO TO BETHEL AND DAN TO OFFER SACRIFICES BEFORE THE GOLDEN CALVES.
MURMUR
MURMUR
LORD...
RECEIVE OUR SACRIFICES TODAY!
WE ARE FAITHFUL TO GIVE...
AND FAITHFUL TO PRAY.

LET US LIVE IN PROSPERITY, LORD, AND PROTECT OUR ACTIVITIES.

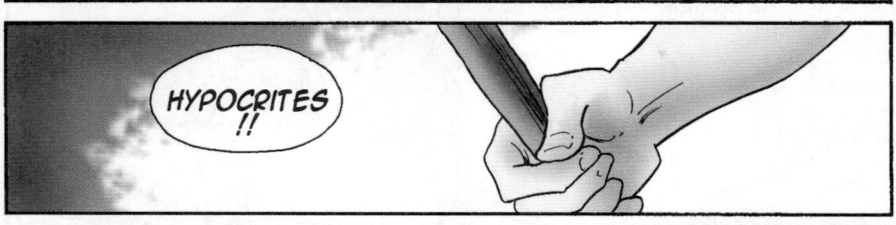

HYPOCRITES!!

I HAVE A WARNING!

YOU PEOPLE OF ISRAEL...

LISTEN TO WHAT THE LORD SAYS...

"I KNOW OF YOUR SINS AND THE DEPTH OF YOUR REBELLIONS.

OH NO... IT'S THAT CRAZY FARMER, AMOS, AGAIN.

"HOW YOU OPPRESS GOOD PEOPLE BY TAKING BRIBES...

"AND DEPRIVE THE POOR OF JUSTICE IN THE COURTS!"

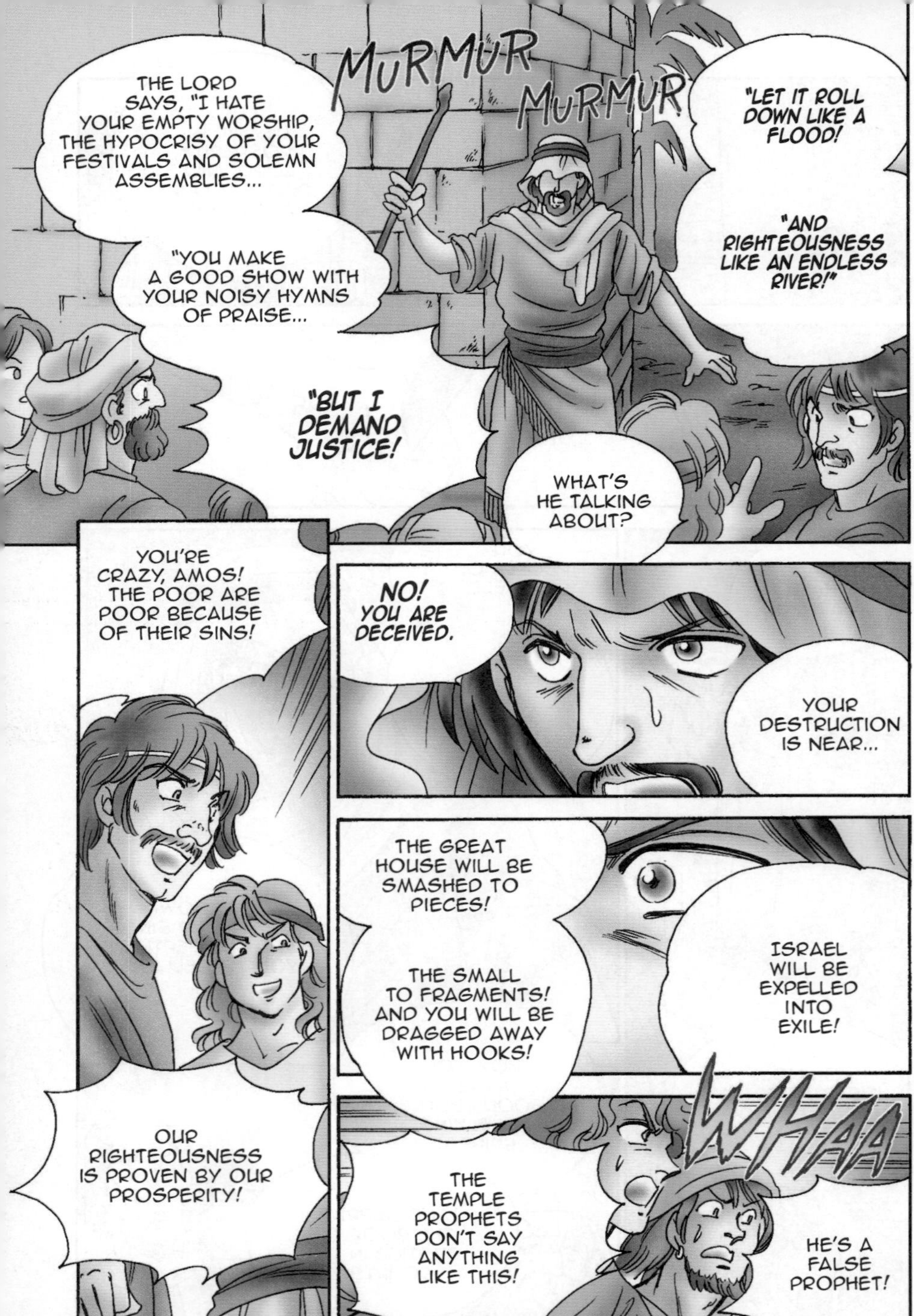
MURMUR
MURMUR
THE LORD SAYS, "I HATE YOUR EMPTY WORSHIP, THE HYPOCRISY OF YOUR FESTIVALS AND SOLEMN ASSEMBLIES...
"YOU MAKE A GOOD SHOW WITH YOUR NOISY HYMNS OF PRAISE...
"BUT I DEMAND JUSTICE!
"LET IT ROLL DOWN LIKE A FLOOD!
"AND RIGHTEOUSNESS LIKE AN ENDLESS RIVER!"
WHAT'S HE TALKING ABOUT?
YOU'RE CRAZY, AMOS! THE POOR ARE POOR BECAUSE OF THEIR SINS!
OUR RIGHTEOUSNESS IS PROVEN BY OUR PROSPERITY!
NO! YOU ARE DECEIVED.
YOUR DESTRUCTION IS NEAR...
THE GREAT HOUSE WILL BE SMASHED TO PIECES!
THE SMALL TO FRAGMENTS! AND YOU WILL BE DRAGGED AWAY WITH HOOKS!
ISRAEL WILL BE EXPELLED INTO EXILE!
WHAA
THE TEMPLE PROPHETS DON'T SAY ANYTHING LIKE THIS!
HE'S A FALSE PROPHET!

YOU'RE A LIAR, AMOS!
GRRR HRRR
WE ARE CHOSEN BY GOD!
YOU LONG FOR THE DAY OF THE LORD...
BUT IT WILL BE DARKNESS! NOT LIGHT!
THERE HE IS!
GRAB HIM!
YOU'RE COMING WITH US!
IF YOU'RE CAUGHT DISTURBING THE PEACE AGAIN...
WE'LL THROW YOU IN PRISON!
AMOS...
WHAT DO YOU SEE?
LORD...
I SEE A PLUMB LINE.

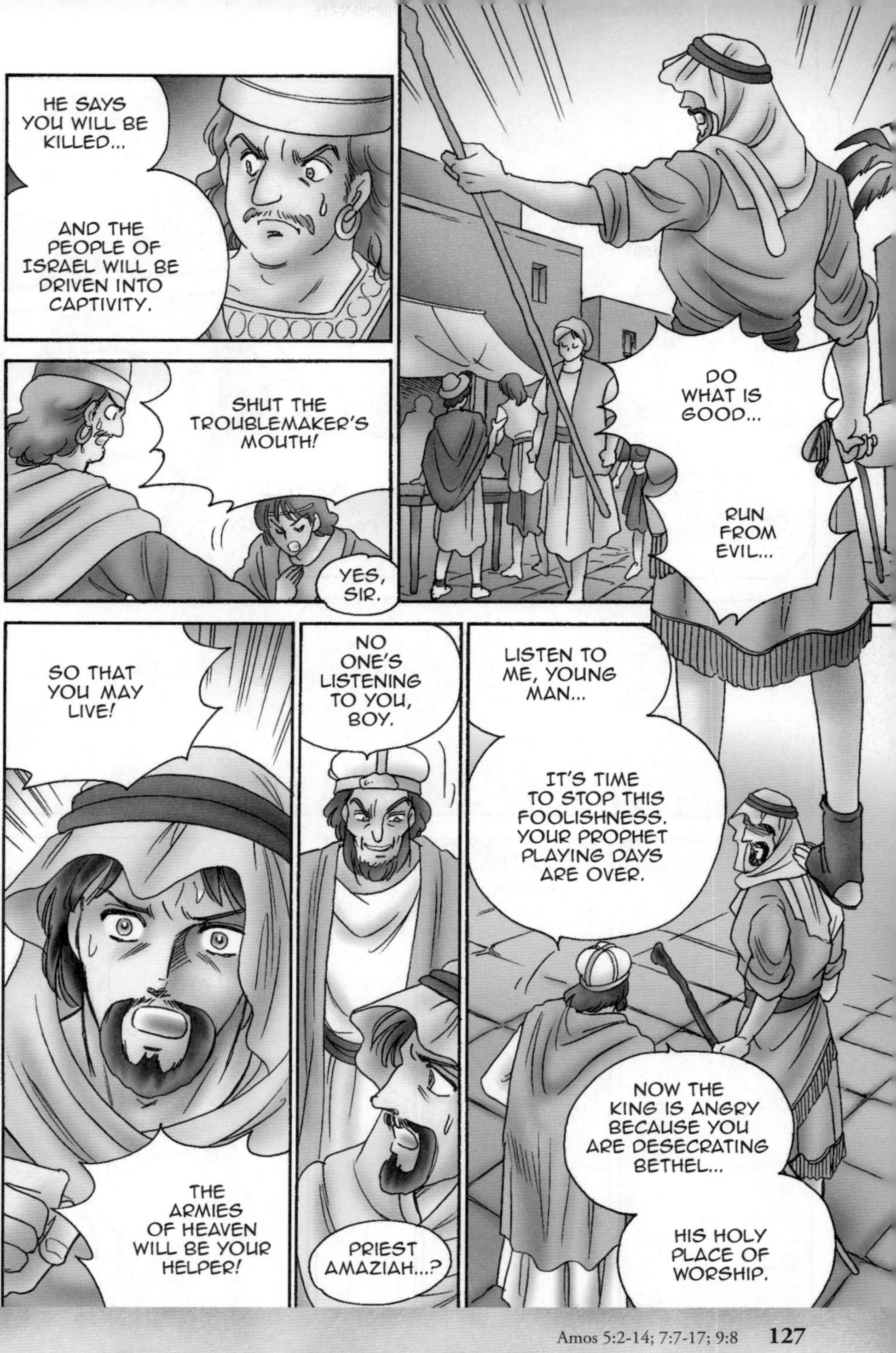
HE SAYS YOU WILL BE KILLED...
AND THE PEOPLE OF ISRAEL WILL BE DRIVEN INTO CAPTIVITY.
SHUT THE TROUBLEMAKER'S MOUTH!
YES, SIR.
DO WHAT IS GOOD...
RUN FROM EVIL...
SO THAT YOU MAY LIVE!
THE ARMIES OF HEAVEN WILL BE YOUR HELPER!
NO ONE'S LISTENING TO YOU, BOY.
PRIEST AMAZIAH...?
LISTEN TO ME, YOUNG MAN...
IT'S TIME TO STOP THIS FOOLISHNESS. YOUR PROPHET PLAYING DAYS ARE OVER.
NOW THE KING IS ANGRY BECAUSE YOU ARE DESECRATING BETHEL...
HIS HOLY PLACE OF WORSHIP.

I HAVE NOT CLAIMED TO BE A PROPHET...
AND I'M NOT THE FOLLOWER OF A PROPHET...
I'M NOTHING MORE THAN A FARMER OF FIGS AND SHEEP.
BUT THE LORD TOLD ME TO SPEAK THESE WORDS TO ISRAEL.
THEN GO BACK TO JUDAH AND SPEAK YOUR WORDS THERE!
YOU TELL ME TO STOP PROPHESYING?!
BUT THE LORD SAYS, "THERE WILL BE CRYING IN THE PUBLIC SQUARES..."
"AND MOURNING ON EVERY STREET."
YOU WHO TWIST JUSTICE...
YOU WHO TRAMPLE THE POOR...
YOU WHO HATE HONEST JUDGES!
OLD MAN...
WHY ARE YOU ALWAYS SAYING SCARY THINGS?

NO- NO MY CHILD. GOD CALLS US BACK TO HIMSELF. HE SAYS TO HIS PEOPLE...

WILL GOD DESTROY ISRAEL...

BECAUSE HE HATES US?

"COME BACK. COME BACK TO ME AND LIVE."

SO I CAN'T STOP SPEAKING.

GOD'S WORD IS HOPE FOR OUR PEOPLE. IT'S OUR ONLY HOPE!

OH- SORRY.

THUMP

PLEASE EXCUSE ME.

...

WAIT- I RECOGNIZE THAT MAN...

HE'S A PROPHET.

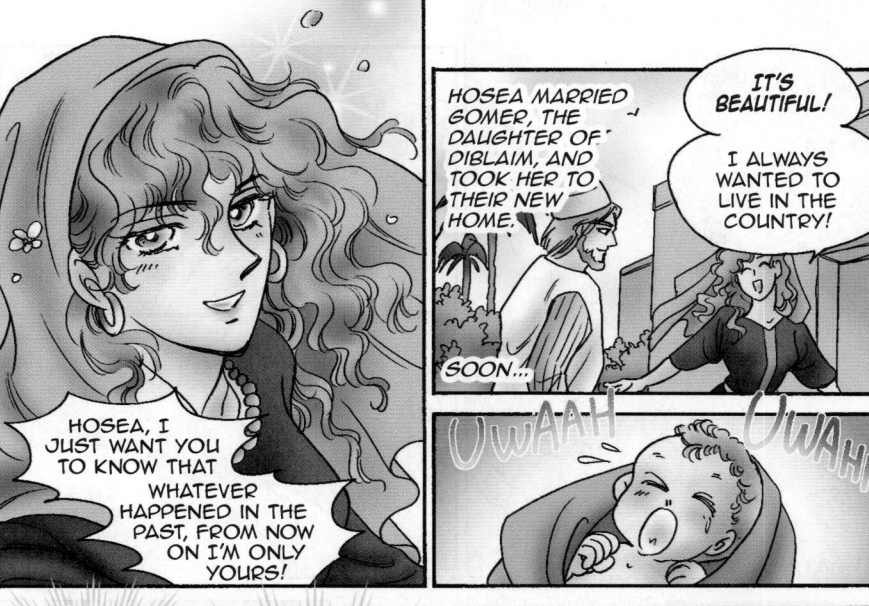

HOSEA MARRIED GOMER, THE DAUGHTER OF DIBLAIM, AND TOOK HER TO THEIR NEW HOME.

IT'S BEAUTIFUL!

I ALWAYS WANTED TO LIVE IN THE COUNTRY!

SOON...

HOSEA, I JUST WANT YOU TO KNOW THAT WHATEVER HAPPENED IN THE PAST, FROM NOW ON I'M ONLY YOURS!

UWAAH

UWAHH

NAME HIM JEZREEL, HOSEA.

BECAUSE SOON I WILL PUNISH THE HOUSE OF JEHU FOR THE BLOODSHED IN THE JEZREEL VALLEY.

IT'S QUITE SOMETHING TO BE MARRIED TO A PROPHET ...

YOU'RE SURE AN AMAZING HUSBAND!

I GUESS I'M LUCKY...

JEZREEL...

AND I WILL OVERTHROW HIS DYNASTY.

EVEN THOUGH YOU'RE VERY DIFFERENT FROM ME.

sigh...

AND IT CAN GET BORING OUT HERE.

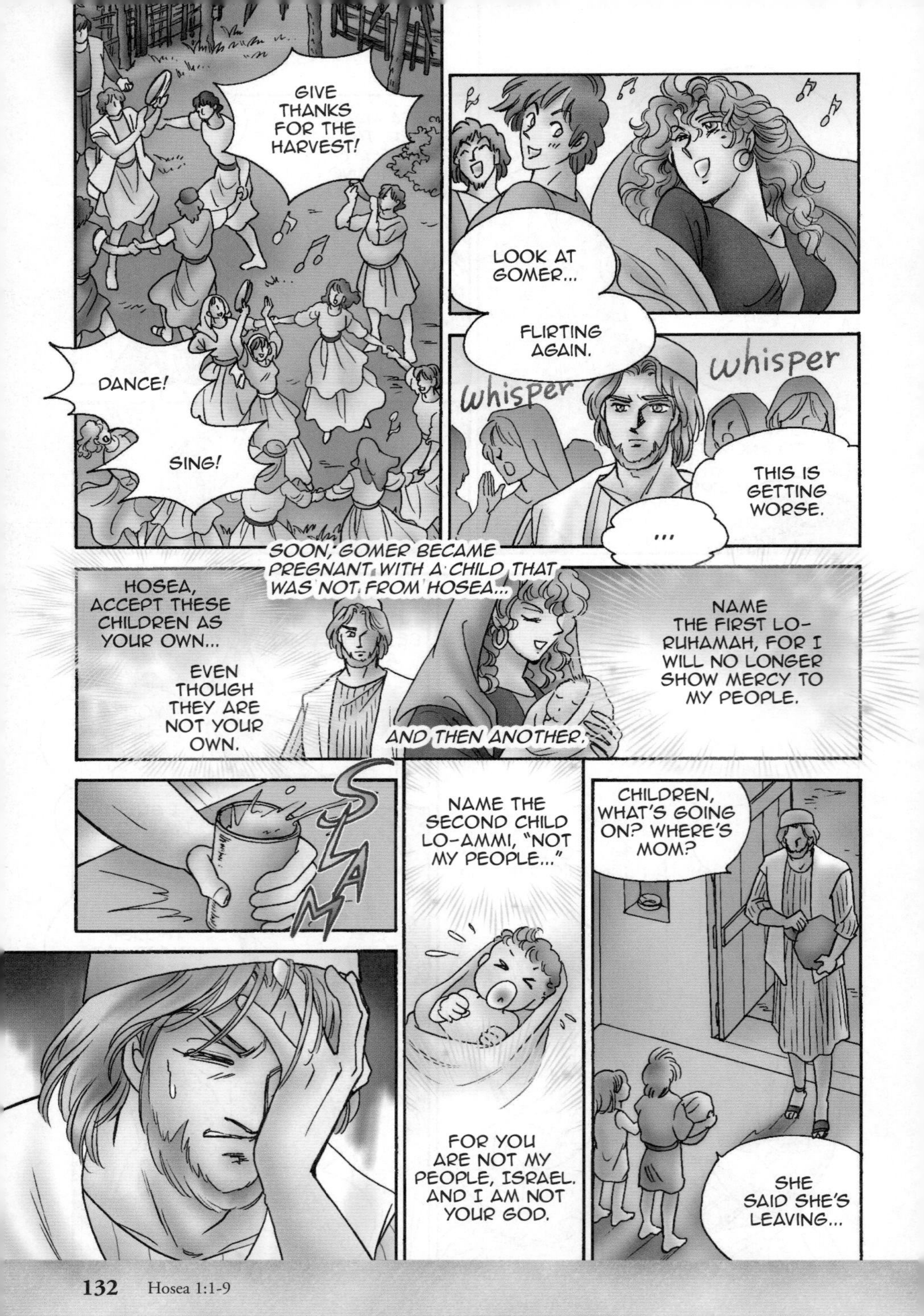
GIVE THANKS FOR THE HARVEST!
DANCE!
SING!
LOOK AT GOMER...
FLIRTING AGAIN.
whisper
whisper
THIS IS GETTING WORSE.
...
SOON, GOMER BECAME PREGNANT WITH A CHILD THAT WAS NOT FROM HOSEA...
HOSEA, ACCEPT THESE CHILDREN AS YOUR OWN...
EVEN THOUGH THEY ARE NOT YOUR OWN.
NAME THE FIRST LO-RUHAMAH, FOR I WILL NO LONGER SHOW MERCY TO MY PEOPLE.
AND THEN ANOTHER.
SLAM
NAME THE SECOND CHILD LO-AMMI, "NOT MY PEOPLE..."
FOR YOU ARE NOT MY PEOPLE, ISRAEL. AND I AM NOT YOUR GOD.
CHILDREN, WHAT'S GOING ON? WHERE'S MOM?
SHE SAID SHE'S LEAVING...

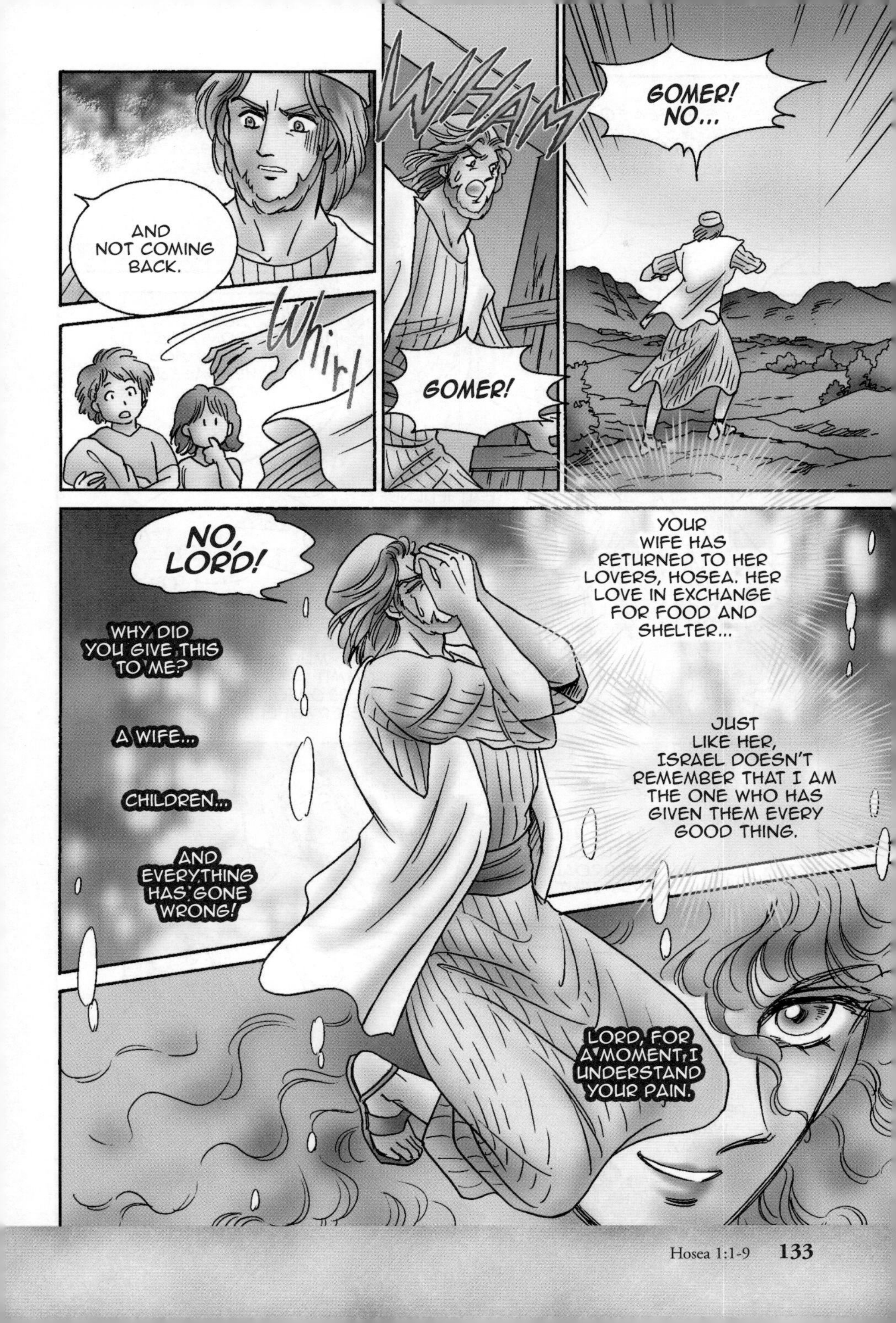
AND NOT COMING BACK.
Whirl
WHAM
GOMER!
GOMER! NO...
NO, LORD!
WHY DID YOU GIVE THIS TO ME?
A WIFE...
CHILDREN...
AND EVERYTHING HAS GONE WRONG!
YOUR WIFE HAS RETURNED TO HER LOVERS, HOSEA. HER LOVE IN EXCHANGE FOR FOOD AND SHELTER...
JUST LIKE HER, ISRAEL DOESN'T REMEMBER THAT I AM THE ONE WHO HAS GIVEN THEM EVERY GOOD THING.
LORD, FOR A MOMENT, I UNDERSTAND YOUR PAIN.

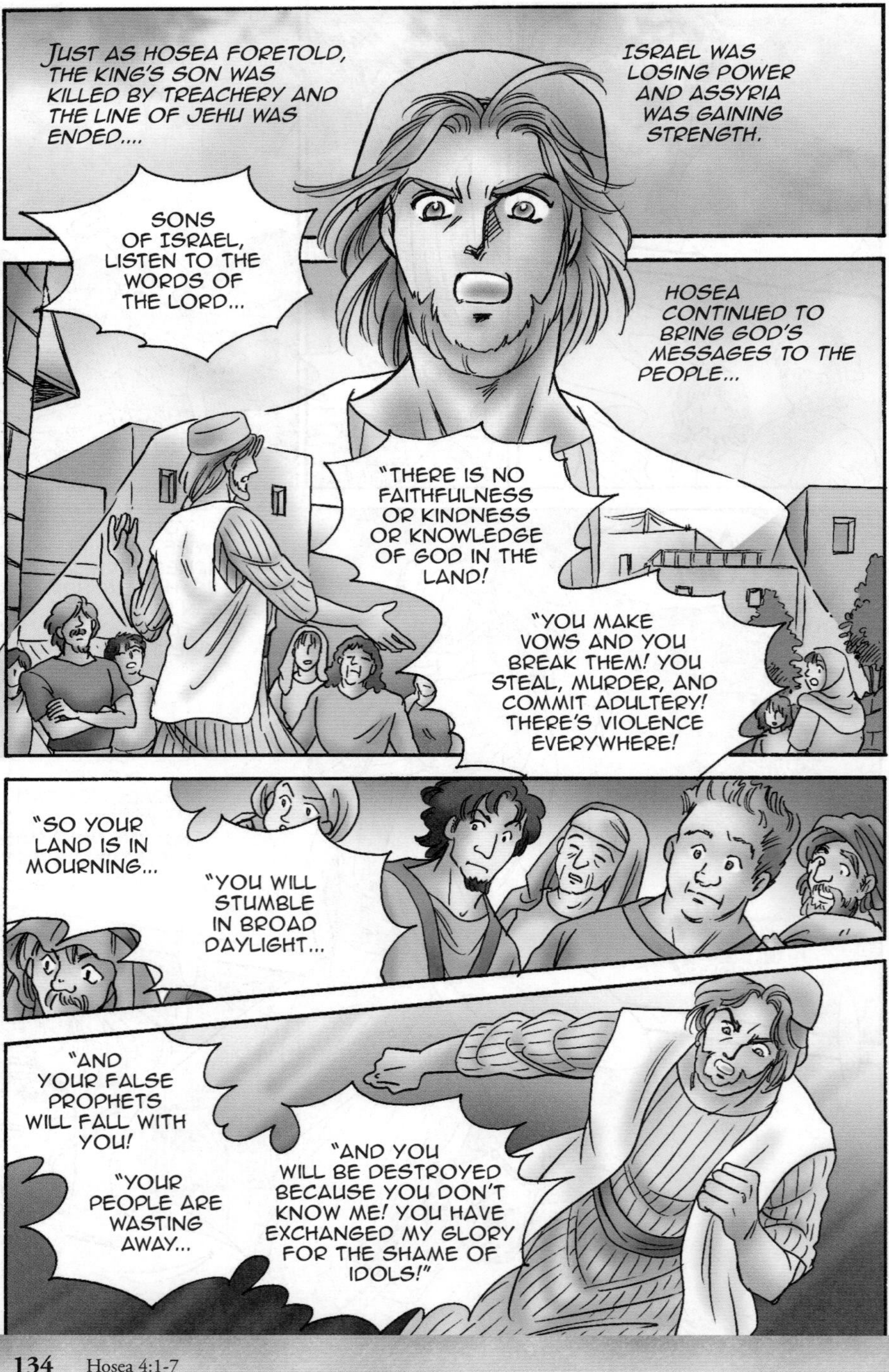
JUST AS HOSEA FORETOLD, THE KING'S SON WAS KILLED BY TREACHERY AND THE LINE OF JEHU WAS ENDED....
ISRAEL WAS LOSING POWER AND ASSYRIA WAS GAINING STRENGTH.
SONS OF ISRAEL, LISTEN TO THE WORDS OF THE LORD...
HOSEA CONTINUED TO BRING GOD'S MESSAGES TO THE PEOPLE...
"THERE IS NO FAITHFULNESS OR KINDNESS OR KNOWLEDGE OF GOD IN THE LAND!
"YOU MAKE VOWS AND YOU BREAK THEM! YOU STEAL, MURDER, AND COMMIT ADULTERY! THERE'S VIOLENCE EVERYWHERE!
"SO YOUR LAND IS IN MOURNING...
"YOU WILL STUMBLE IN BROAD DAYLIGHT...
"AND YOUR FALSE PROPHETS WILL FALL WITH YOU!
"YOUR PEOPLE ARE WASTING AWAY...
"AND YOU WILL BE DESTROYED BECAUSE YOU DON'T KNOW ME! YOU HAVE EXCHANGED MY GLORY FOR THE SHAME OF IDOLS!"

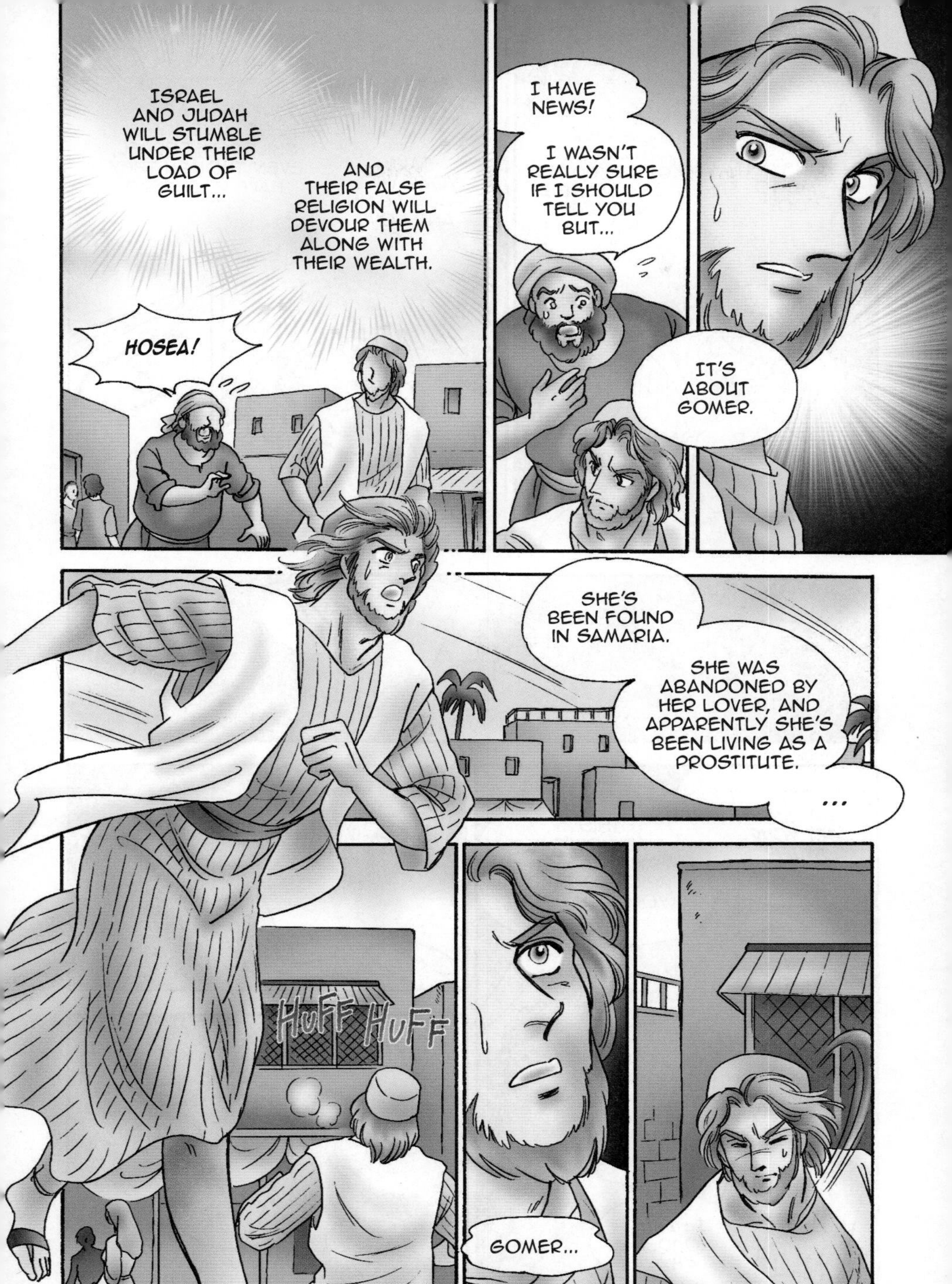
ISRAEL AND JUDAH WILL STUMBLE UNDER THEIR LOAD OF GUILT...
AND THEIR FALSE RELIGION WILL DEVOUR THEM ALONG WITH THEIR WEALTH.
HOSEA!
I HAVE NEWS!
I WASN'T REALLY SURE IF I SHOULD TELL YOU BUT...
IT'S ABOUT GOMER.
SHE'S BEEN FOUND IN SAMARIA.
SHE WAS ABANDONED BY HER LOVER, AND APPARENTLY SHE'S BEEN LIVING AS A PROSTITUTE.
...
HUFF HUFF
GOMER...

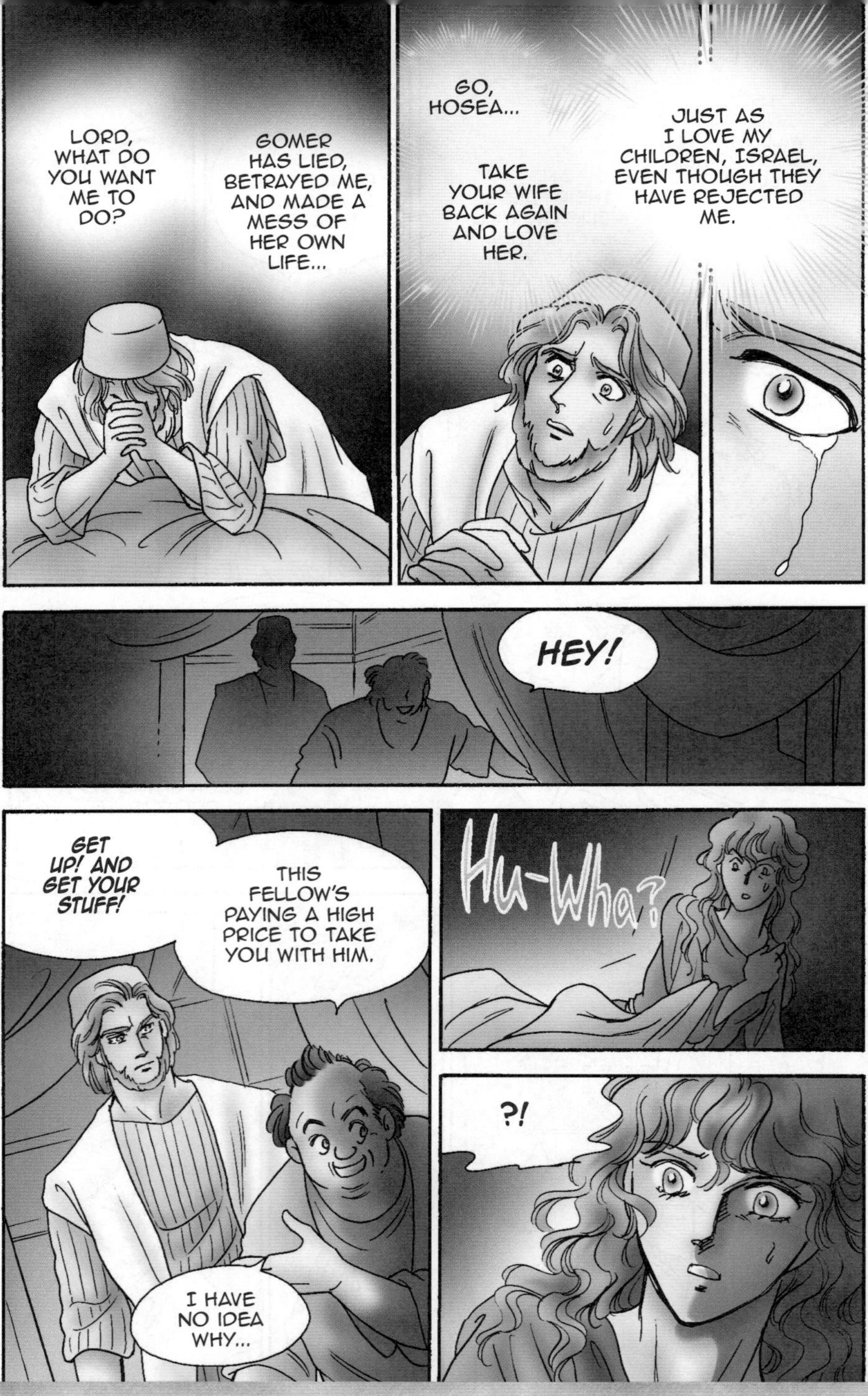

LORD, WHAT DO YOU WANT ME TO DO?
GOMER HAS LIED, BETRAYED ME, AND MADE A MESS OF HER OWN LIFE...
GO, HOSEA...
TAKE YOUR WIFE BACK AGAIN AND LOVE HER.
JUST AS I LOVE MY CHILDREN, ISRAEL, EVEN THOUGH THEY HAVE REJECTED ME.
HEY!
GET UP! AND GET YOUR STUFF!
THIS FELLOW'S PAYING A HIGH PRICE TO TAKE YOU WITH HIM.
I HAVE NO IDEA WHY...
Hu-Wha?
?!

GOMER, I LOVE YOU.

COME BACK WITH ME...

HOSEA...?

AND BE MY WIFE AGAIN.

YES, HOSEA. I WILL.

THE LORD SAYS...

"FOR MANY DAYS, ISRAEL WILL BE WITHOUT KING OR PRINCE...

"WITHOUT SACRIFICES OR PILLARS, PRIESTS, OR IDOLS, BUT THEN MY PEOPLE WILL RETURN TO ME.

"THEY WILL DEVOTE THEMSELVES AND I WILL RECEIVE THEM...

"FOR I CANNOT GIVE THEM UP. I CANNOT LET THEM GO."

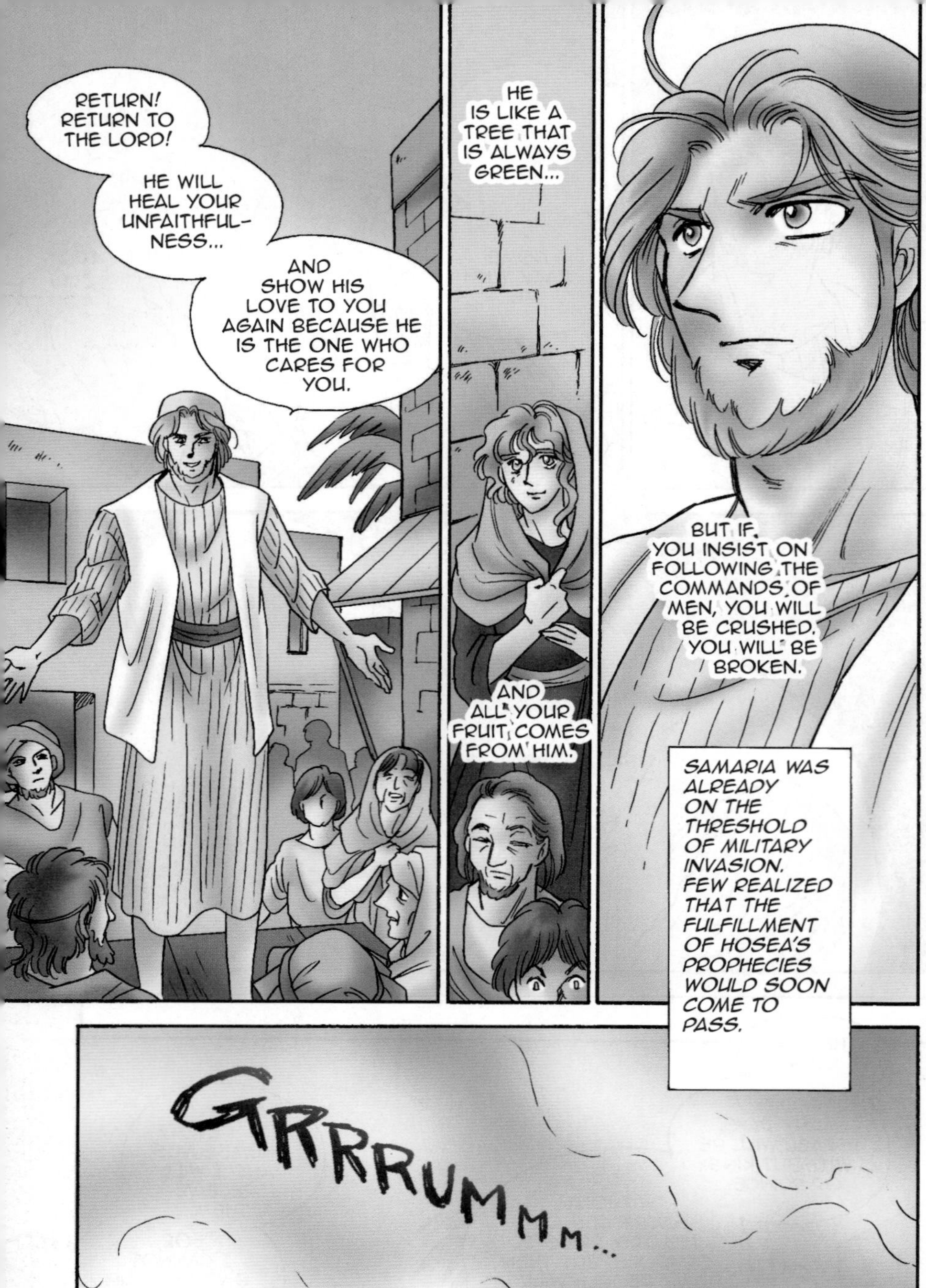
RETURN! RETURN TO THE LORD!
HE WILL HEAL YOUR UNFAITHFUL-NESS...
AND SHOW HIS LOVE TO YOU AGAIN BECAUSE HE IS THE ONE WHO CARES FOR YOU.
HE IS LIKE A TREE THAT IS ALWAYS GREEN...
AND ALL YOUR FRUIT COMES FROM HIM.
BUT IF YOU INSIST ON FOLLOWING THE COMMANDS OF MEN, YOU WILL BE CRUSHED. YOU WILL BE BROKEN.
SAMARIA WAS ALREADY ON THE THRESHOLD OF MILITARY INVASION. FEW REALIZED THAT THE FULFILLMENT OF HOSEA'S PROPHECIES WOULD SOON COME TO PASS.
GRRRUMMM...

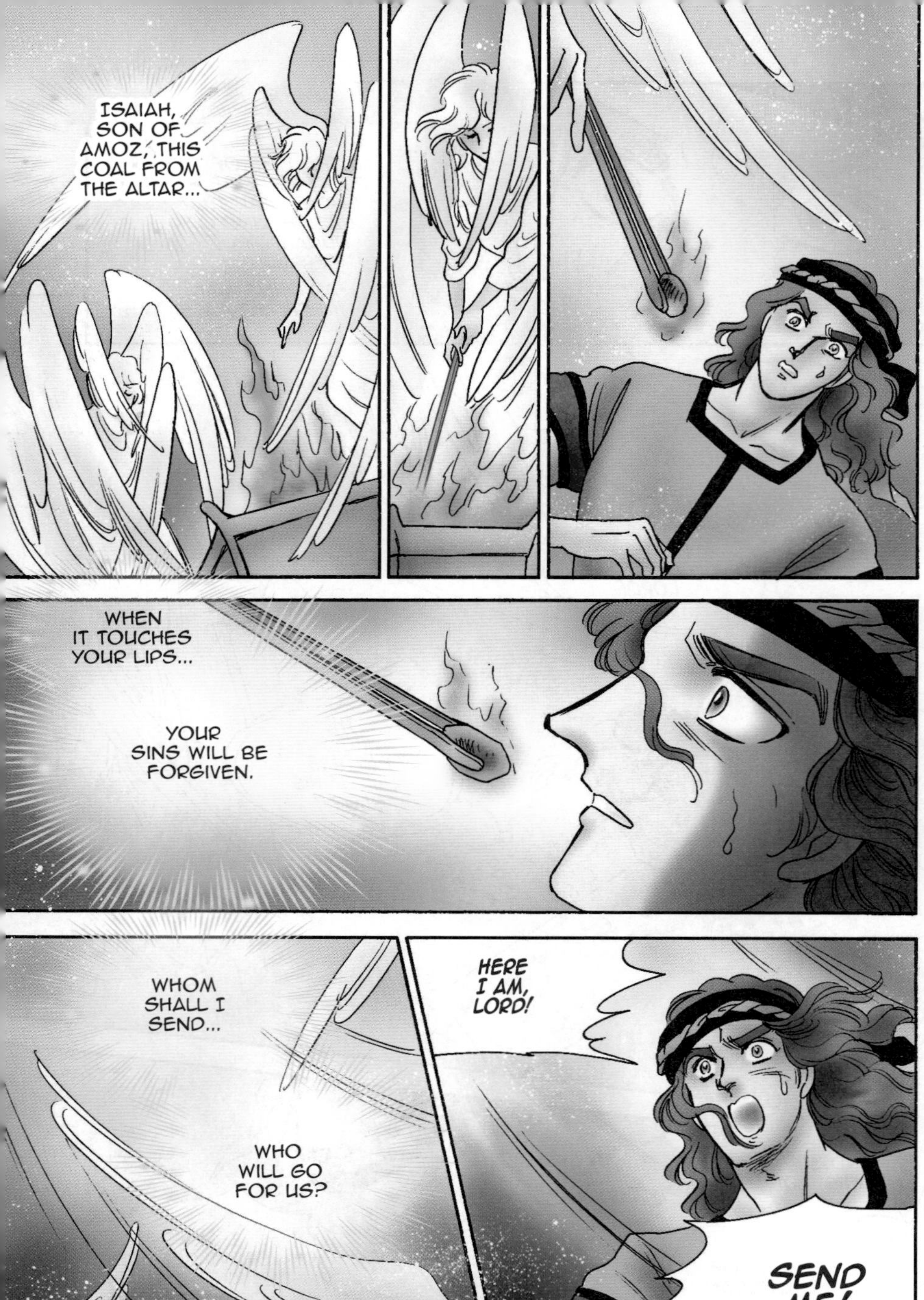
ISAIAH, SON OF AMOZ, THIS COAL FROM THE ALTAR...
WHEN IT TOUCHES YOUR LIPS...
YOUR SINS WILL BE FORGIVEN.
WHOM SHALL I SEND...
WHO WILL GO FOR US?
HERE I AM, LORD!
SEND ME!

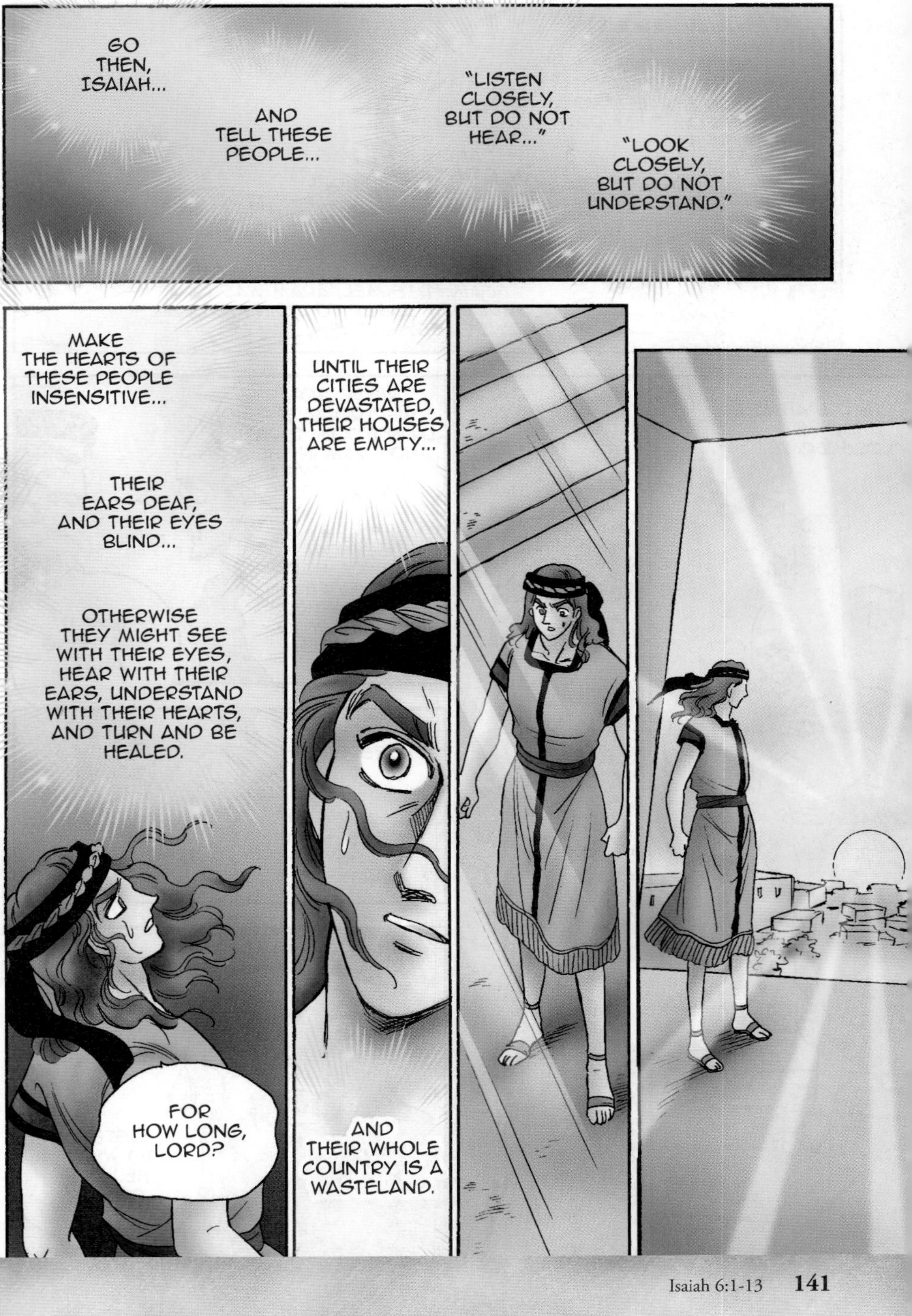
GO THEN, ISAIAH...
AND TELL THESE PEOPLE...
"LISTEN CLOSELY, BUT DO NOT HEAR..."
"LOOK CLOSELY, BUT DO NOT UNDERSTAND."
MAKE THE HEARTS OF THESE PEOPLE INSENSITIVE...
THEIR EARS DEAF, AND THEIR EYES BLIND...
OTHERWISE THEY MIGHT SEE WITH THEIR EYES, HEAR WITH THEIR EARS, UNDERSTAND WITH THEIR HEARTS, AND TURN AND BE HEALED.
FOR HOW LONG, LORD?
UNTIL THEIR CITIES ARE DEVASTATED, THEIR HOUSES ARE EMPTY...
AND THEIR WHOLE COUNTRY IS A WASTELAND.

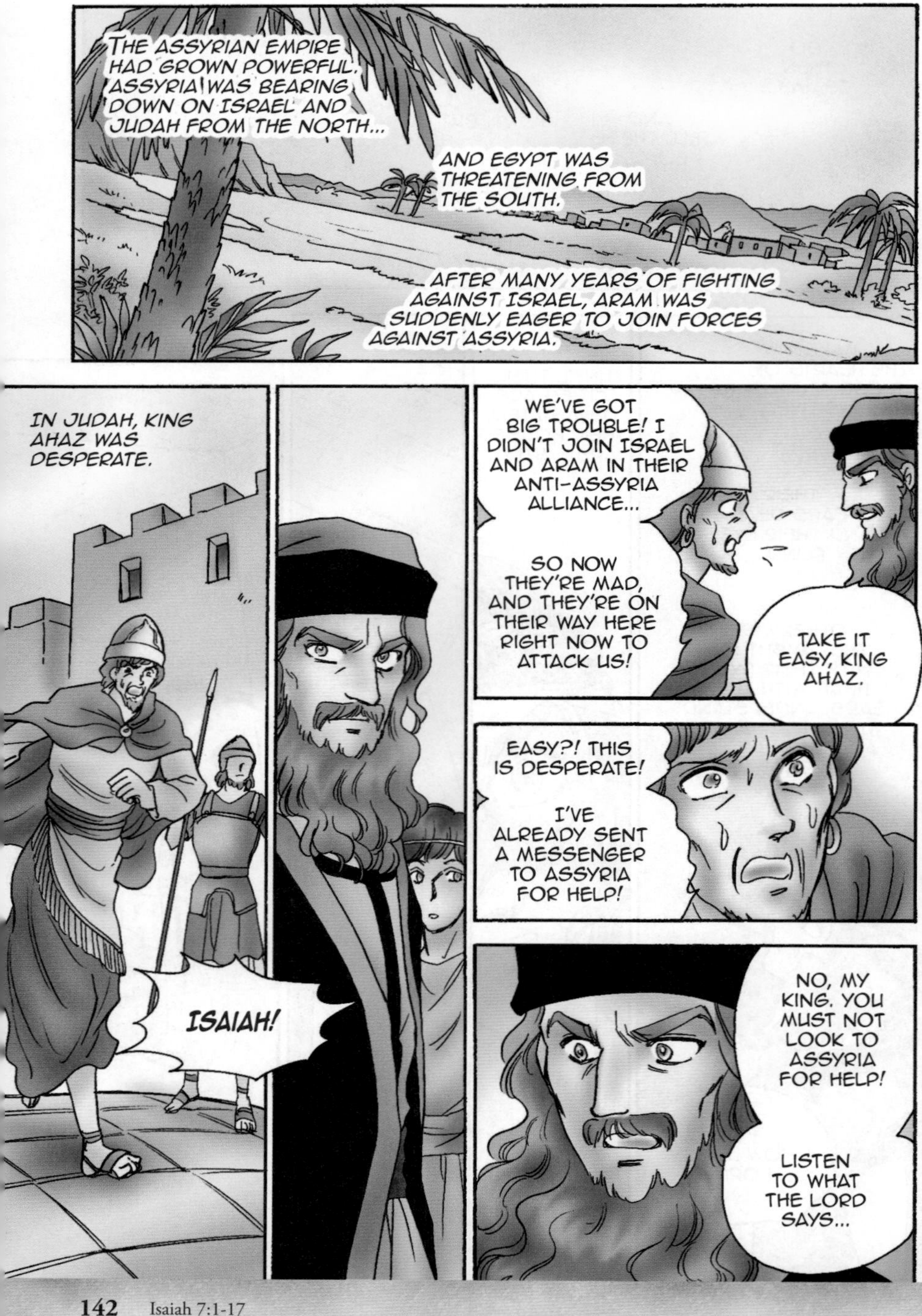

THE ASSYRIAN EMPIRE HAD GROWN POWERFUL. ASSYRIA WAS BEARING DOWN ON ISRAEL AND JUDAH FROM THE NORTH...
AND EGYPT WAS THREATENING FROM THE SOUTH.
AFTER MANY YEARS OF FIGHTING AGAINST ISRAEL, ARAM WAS SUDDENLY EAGER TO JOIN FORCES AGAINST ASSYRIA.
IN JUDAH, KING AHAZ WAS DESPERATE.
ISAIAH!
WE'VE GOT BIG TROUBLE! I DIDN'T JOIN ISRAEL AND ARAM IN THEIR ANTI-ASSYRIA ALLIANCE...
SO NOW THEY'RE MAD, AND THEY'RE ON THEIR WAY HERE RIGHT NOW TO ATTACK US!
TAKE IT EASY, KING AHAZ.
EASY?! THIS IS DESPERATE!
I'VE ALREADY SENT A MESSENGER TO ASSYRIA FOR HELP!
NO, MY KING. YOU MUST NOT LOOK TO ASSYRIA FOR HELP!
LISTEN TO WHAT THE LORD SAYS...

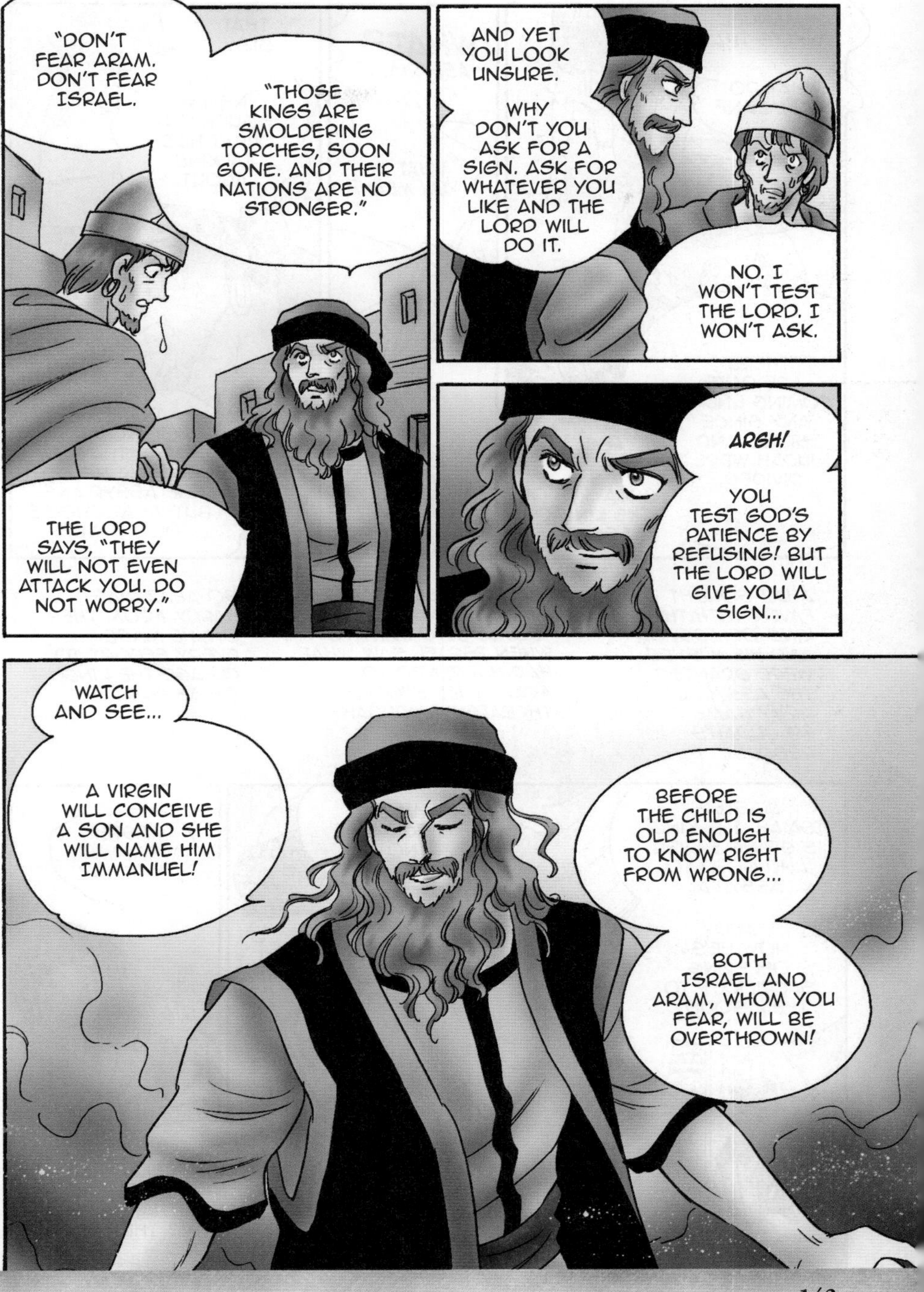
"DON'T FEAR ARAM. DON'T FEAR ISRAEL.
"THOSE KINGS ARE SMOLDERING TORCHES, SOON GONE. AND THEIR NATIONS ARE NO STRONGER."
THE LORD SAYS, "THEY WILL NOT EVEN ATTACK YOU. DO NOT WORRY."
AND YET YOU LOOK UNSURE.
WHY DON'T YOU ASK FOR A SIGN. ASK FOR WHATEVER YOU LIKE AND THE LORD WILL DO IT.
NO. I WON'T TEST THE LORD. I WON'T ASK.
ARGH!
YOU TEST GOD'S PATIENCE BY REFUSING! BUT THE LORD WILL GIVE YOU A SIGN...
WATCH AND SEE...
A VIRGIN WILL CONCEIVE A SON AND SHE WILL NAME HIM IMMANUEL!
BEFORE THE CHILD IS OLD ENOUGH TO KNOW RIGHT FROM WRONG...
BOTH ISRAEL AND ARAM, WHOM YOU FEAR, WILL BE OVERTHROWN!

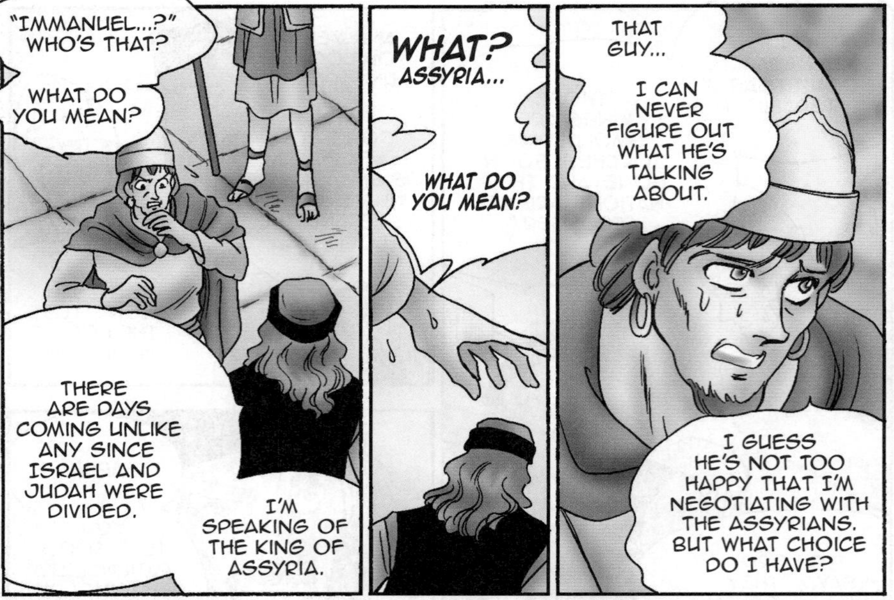

"IMMANUEL...?" WHO'S THAT?
WHAT DO YOU MEAN?
THERE ARE DAYS COMING UNLIKE ANY SINCE ISRAEL AND JUDAH WERE DIVIDED.
I'M SPEAKING OF THE KING OF ASSYRIA.
WHAT? ASSYRIA...
WHAT DO YOU MEAN?
THAT GUY...
I CAN NEVER FIGURE OUT WHAT HE'S TALKING ABOUT.
I GUESS HE'S NOT TOO HAPPY THAT I'M NEGOTIATING WITH THE ASSYRIANS. BUT WHAT CHOICE DO I HAVE?

AHAZ SOUGHT FAVOR WITH THE KING OF ASSYRIA AND HIS WISHES WERE GRANTED; THE ASSYRIAN ARMY CAME TO JUDAH'S RESCUE...

THEY INVADED ARAM, KILLED ITS KING, AND SENT ITS PEOPLE INTO CAPTIVITY. WHEN ISRAEL SAW WHAT HAD HAPPENED TO ARAM, THEY STOPPED THREATENING JUDAH.

SO AHAZ WAS HAPPY. FROM THEN ON, HE MADE EVERY EFFORT TO PLEASE THE KING OF ASSYRIA.

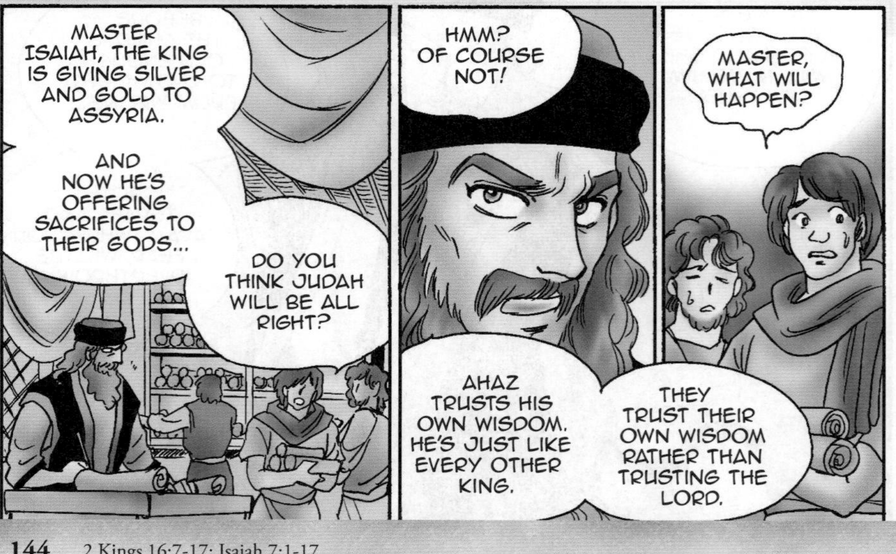

MASTER ISAIAH, THE KING IS GIVING SILVER AND GOLD TO ASSYRIA.
AND NOW HE'S OFFERING SACRIFICES TO THEIR GODS...
DO YOU THINK JUDAH WILL BE ALL RIGHT?
HMM? OF COURSE NOT!
AHAZ TRUSTS HIS OWN WISDOM. HE'S JUST LIKE EVERY OTHER KING.
MASTER, WHAT WILL HAPPEN?
THEY TRUST THEIR OWN WISDOM RATHER THAN TRUSTING THE LORD.

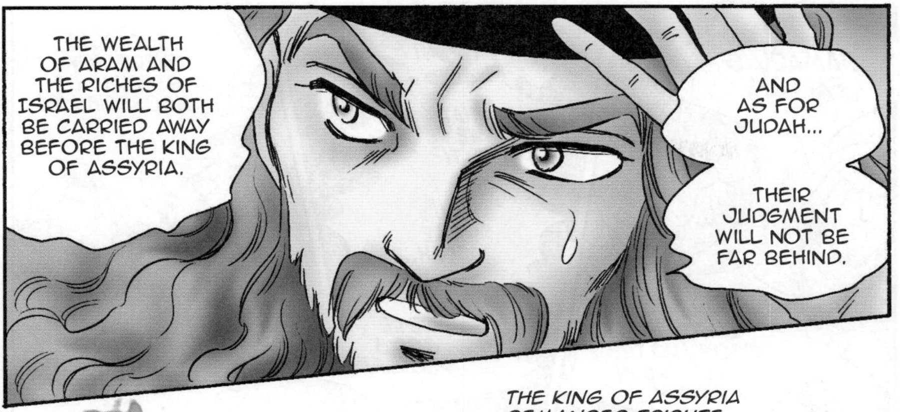
THE WEALTH OF ARAM AND THE RICHES OF ISRAEL WILL BOTH BE CARRIED AWAY BEFORE THE KING OF ASSYRIA.
AND AS FOR JUDAH...
THEIR JUDGMENT WILL NOT BE FAR BEHIND.

THE KING OF ASSYRIA DEMANDED TRIBUTE FROM ISRAEL, BUT WHEN ISRAEL RESISTED...

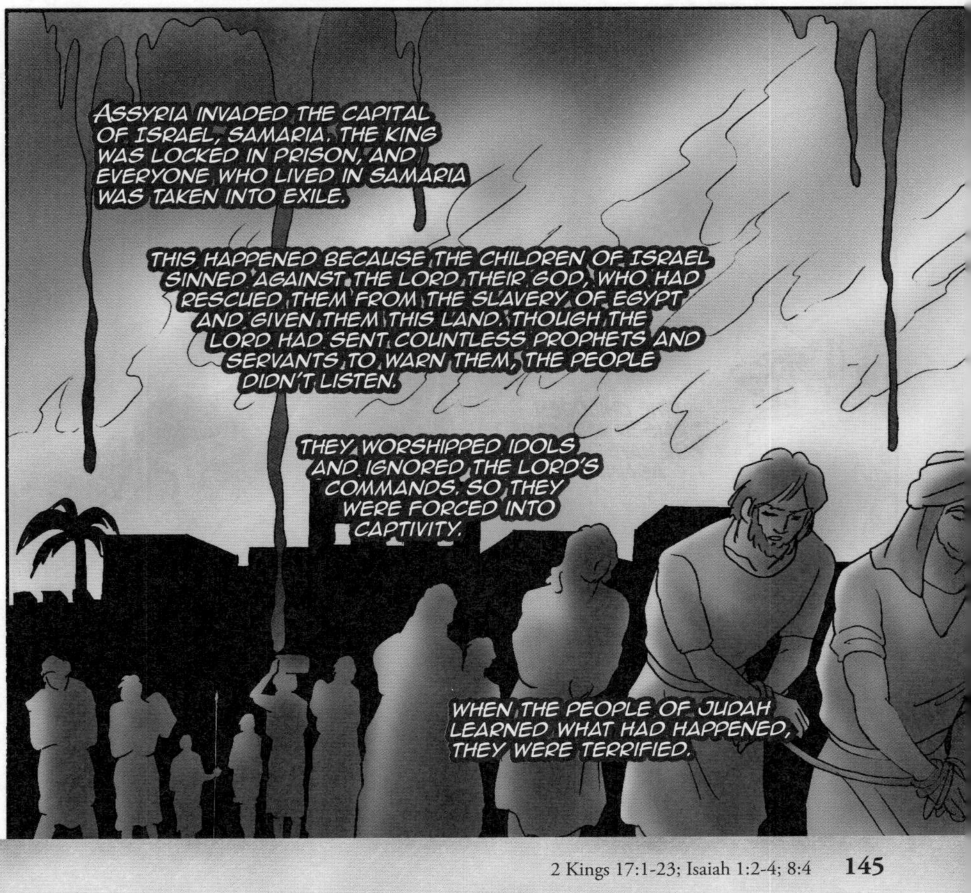
ASSYRIA INVADED THE CAPITAL OF ISRAEL, SAMARIA. THE KING WAS LOCKED IN PRISON, AND EVERYONE WHO LIVED IN SAMARIA WAS TAKEN INTO EXILE.
THIS HAPPENED BECAUSE THE CHILDREN OF ISRAEL SINNED AGAINST THE LORD THEIR GOD, WHO HAD RESCUED THEM FROM THE SLAVERY OF EGYPT AND GIVEN THEM THIS LAND. THOUGH THE LORD HAD SENT COUNTLESS PROPHETS AND SERVANTS TO WARN THEM, THE PEOPLE DIDN'T LISTEN.
THEY WORSHIPPED IDOLS AND IGNORED THE LORD'S COMMANDS. SO THEY WERE FORCED INTO CAPTIVITY.
WHEN THE PEOPLE OF JUDAH LEARNED WHAT HAD HAPPENED, THEY WERE TERRIFIED.

SAMARIA'S FALLEN!

THE KING IS IN PRISON AND THE PEOPLE ARE IN CHAINS!

WHAT IF WE'RE NEXT!?

NO! WE'RE JUDAH...

WE'RE GOD'S PEOPLE!

ISRAEL IS OVERTHROWN BECAUSE OF DISOBEDIENCE!

BUT WE'RE NOT LIKE THEM!

LISTEN, O HEAVENS! PAY ATTENTION, EARTH!

ISAIAH CONTINUED TO WARN THE PEOPLE OF JUDAH...

THE LORD SAYS...

"THE CHILDREN I RAISED AND CARED FOR HAVE REBELLED AGAINST ME!

"EVEN AN OX KNOWS ITS OWNER, BUT MY PEOPLE DON'T RECOGNIZE THAT I CARE FOR THEM!"

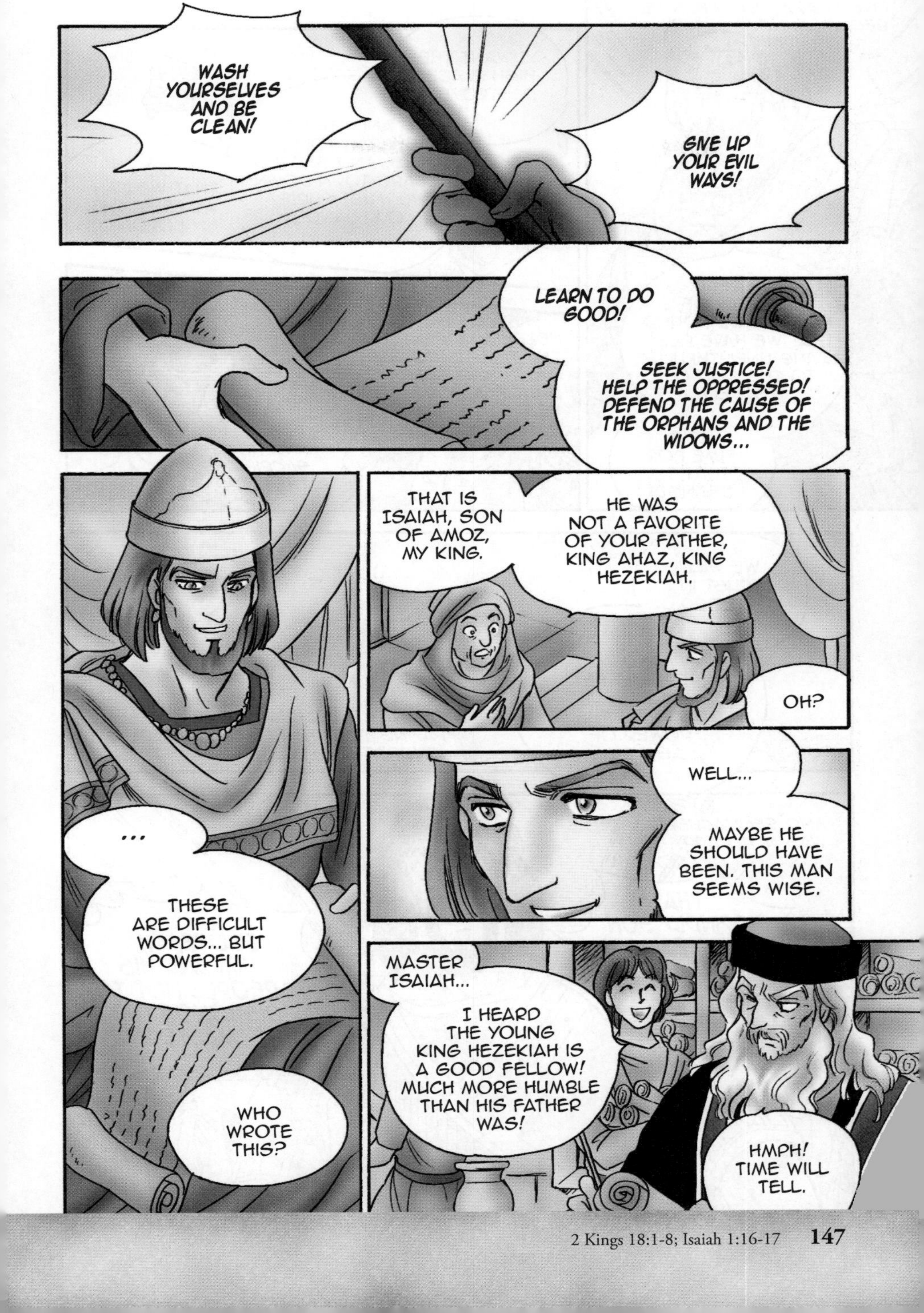
WASH YOURSELVES AND BE CLEAN!
GIVE UP YOUR EVIL WAYS!
LEARN TO DO GOOD!
SEEK JUSTICE! HELP THE OPPRESSED! DEFEND THE CAUSE OF THE ORPHANS AND THE WIDOWS...
...
THESE ARE DIFFICULT WORDS... BUT POWERFUL.
WHO WROTE THIS?
THAT IS ISAIAH, SON OF AMOZ, MY KING.
HE WAS NOT A FAVORITE OF YOUR FATHER, KING AHAZ, KING HEZEKIAH.
OH?
WELL...
MAYBE HE SHOULD HAVE BEEN. THIS MAN SEEMS WISE.
MASTER ISAIAH...
I HEARD THE YOUNG KING HEZEKIAH IS A GOOD FELLOW! MUCH MORE HUMBLE THAN HIS FATHER WAS!
HMPH! TIME WILL TELL.

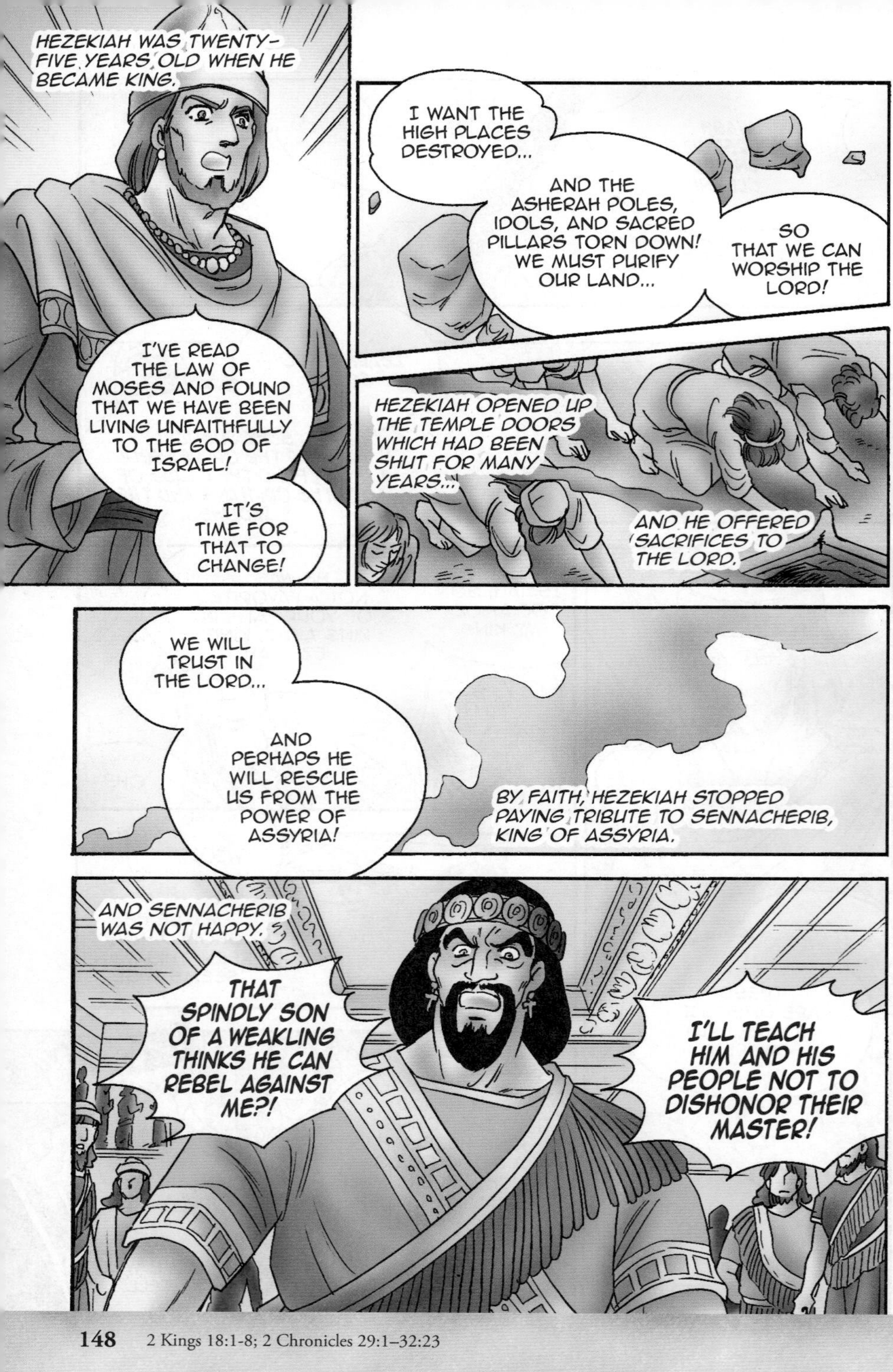
HEZEKIAH WAS TWENTY-FIVE YEARS OLD WHEN HE BECAME KING.
I'VE READ THE LAW OF MOSES AND FOUND THAT WE HAVE BEEN LIVING UNFAITHFULLY TO THE GOD OF ISRAEL!
IT'S TIME FOR THAT TO CHANGE!
I WANT THE HIGH PLACES DESTROYED...
AND THE ASHERAH POLES, IDOLS, AND SACRED PILLARS TORN DOWN! WE MUST PURIFY OUR LAND...
SO THAT WE CAN WORSHIP THE LORD!
HEZEKIAH OPENED UP THE TEMPLE DOORS WHICH HAD BEEN SHUT FOR MANY YEARS...
AND HE OFFERED SACRIFICES TO THE LORD.
WE WILL TRUST IN THE LORD...
AND PERHAPS HE WILL RESCUE US FROM THE POWER OF ASSYRIA!
BY FAITH, HEZEKIAH STOPPED PAYING TRIBUTE TO SENNACHERIB, KING OF ASSYRIA.
AND SENNACHERIB WAS NOT HAPPY.
THAT SPINDLY SON OF A WEAKLING THINKS HE CAN REBEL AGAINST ME?!
I'LL TEACH HIM AND HIS PEOPLE NOT TO DISHONOR THEIR MASTER!

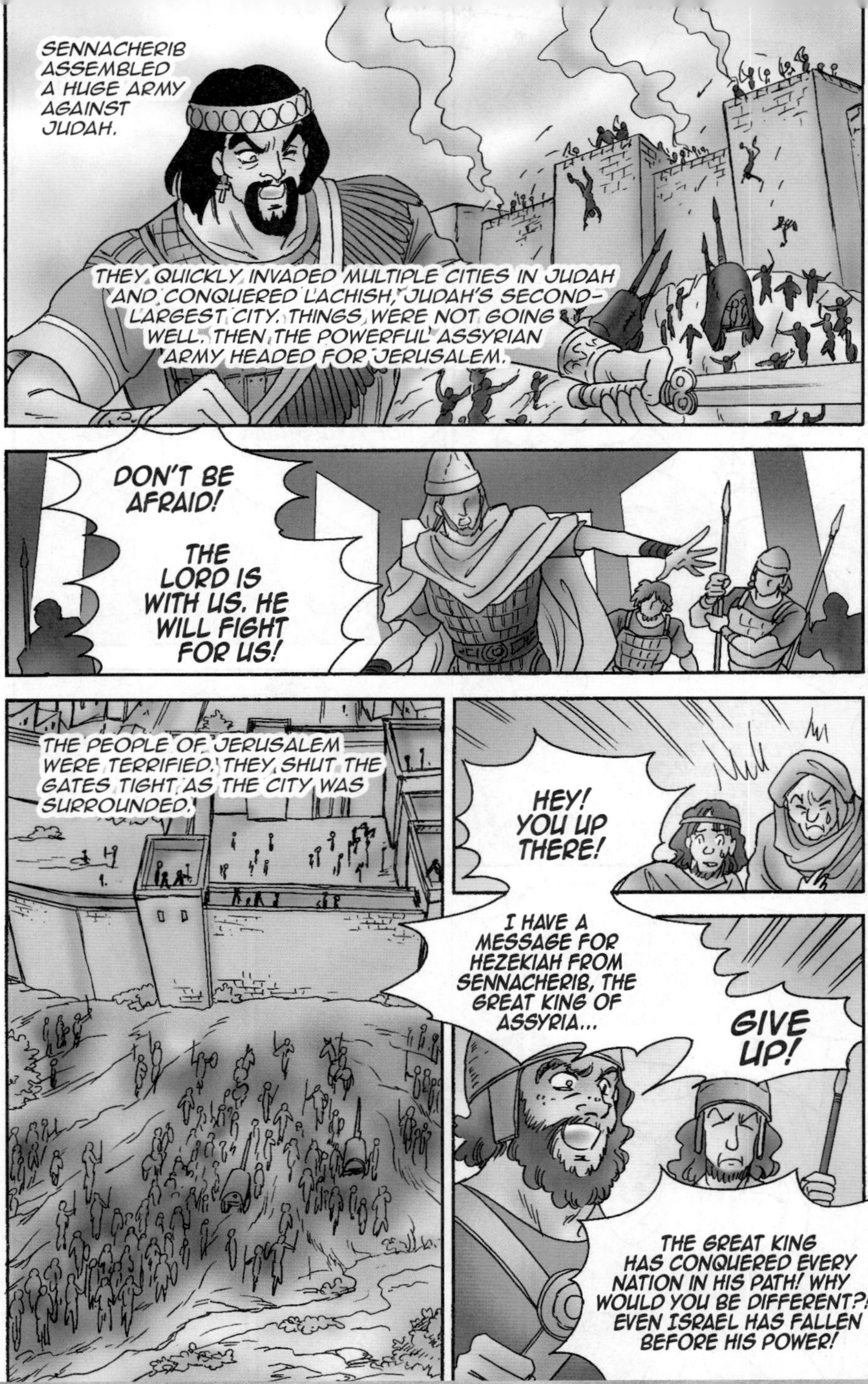
SENNACHERIB ASSEMBLED A HUGE ARMY AGAINST JUDAH.
THEY QUICKLY INVADED MULTIPLE CITIES IN JUDAH AND CONQUERED LACHISH, JUDAH'S SECOND-LARGEST CITY. THINGS WERE NOT GOING WELL. THEN THE POWERFUL ASSYRIAN ARMY HEADED FOR JERUSALEM.
DON'T BE AFRAID!
THE LORD IS WITH US. HE WILL FIGHT FOR US!
THE PEOPLE OF JERUSALEM WERE TERRIFIED. THEY SHUT THE GATES TIGHT AS THE CITY WAS SURROUNDED.
HEY! YOU UP THERE!
I HAVE A MESSAGE FOR HEZEKIAH FROM SENNACHERIB, THE GREAT KING OF ASSYRIA...
GIVE UP!
THE GREAT KING HAS CONQUERED EVERY NATION IN HIS PATH! WHY WOULD YOU BE DIFFERENT?! EVEN ISRAEL HAS FALLEN BEFORE HIS POWER!

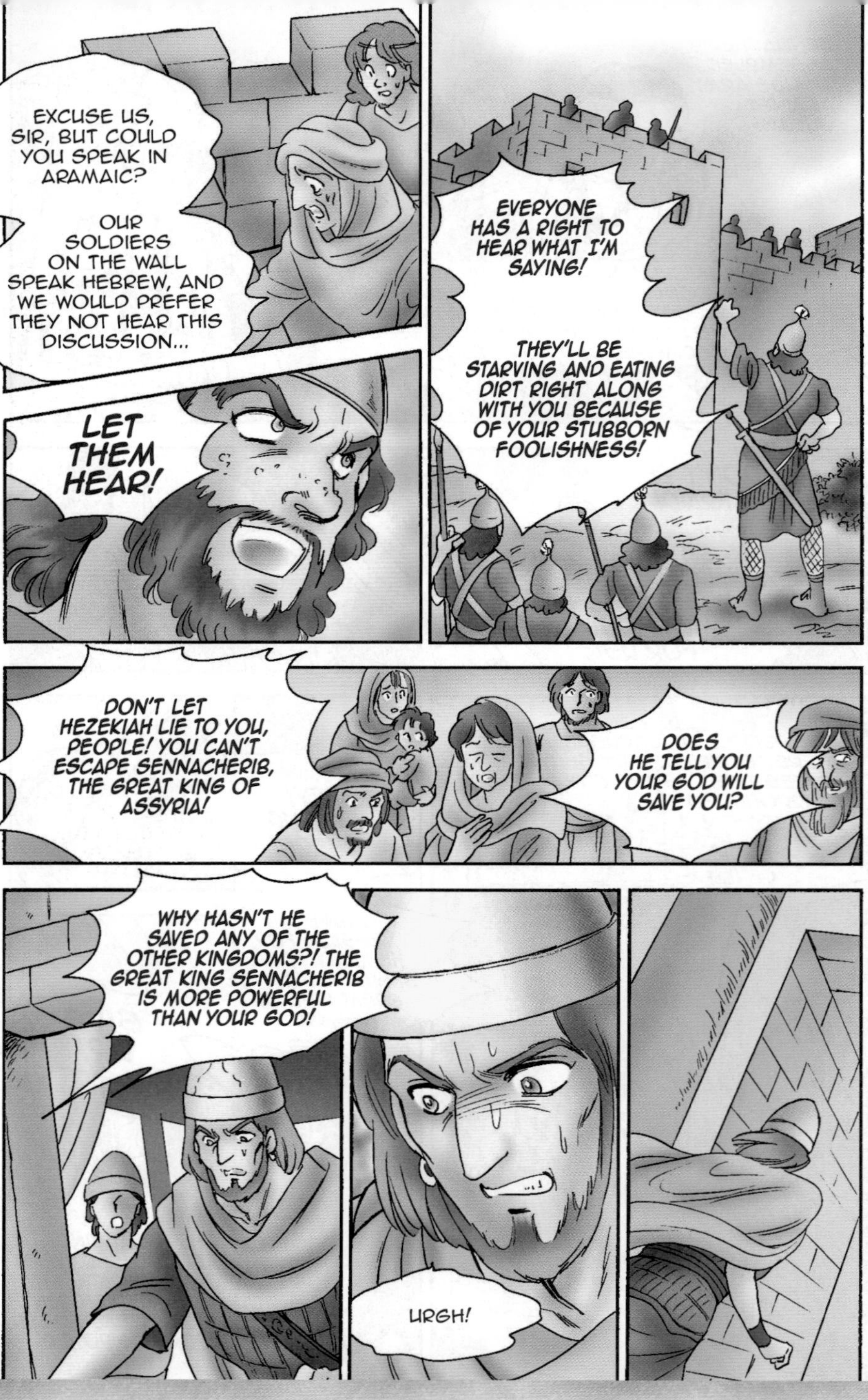
EXCUSE US, SIR, BUT COULD YOU SPEAK IN ARAMAIC?
OUR SOLDIERS ON THE WALL SPEAK HEBREW, AND WE WOULD PREFER THEY NOT HEAR THIS DISCUSSION...
LET THEM HEAR!
EVERYONE HAS A RIGHT TO HEAR WHAT I'M SAYING!
THEY'LL BE STARVING AND EATING DIRT RIGHT ALONG WITH YOU BECAUSE OF YOUR STUBBORN FOOLISHNESS!
DON'T LET HEZEKIAH LIE TO YOU, PEOPLE! YOU CAN'T ESCAPE SENNACHERIB, THE GREAT KING OF ASSYRIA!
DOES HE TELL YOU YOUR GOD WILL SAVE YOU?
WHY HASN'T HE SAVED ANY OF THE OTHER KINGDOMS?! THE GREAT KING SENNACHERIB IS MORE POWERFUL THAN YOUR GOD!
URGH!

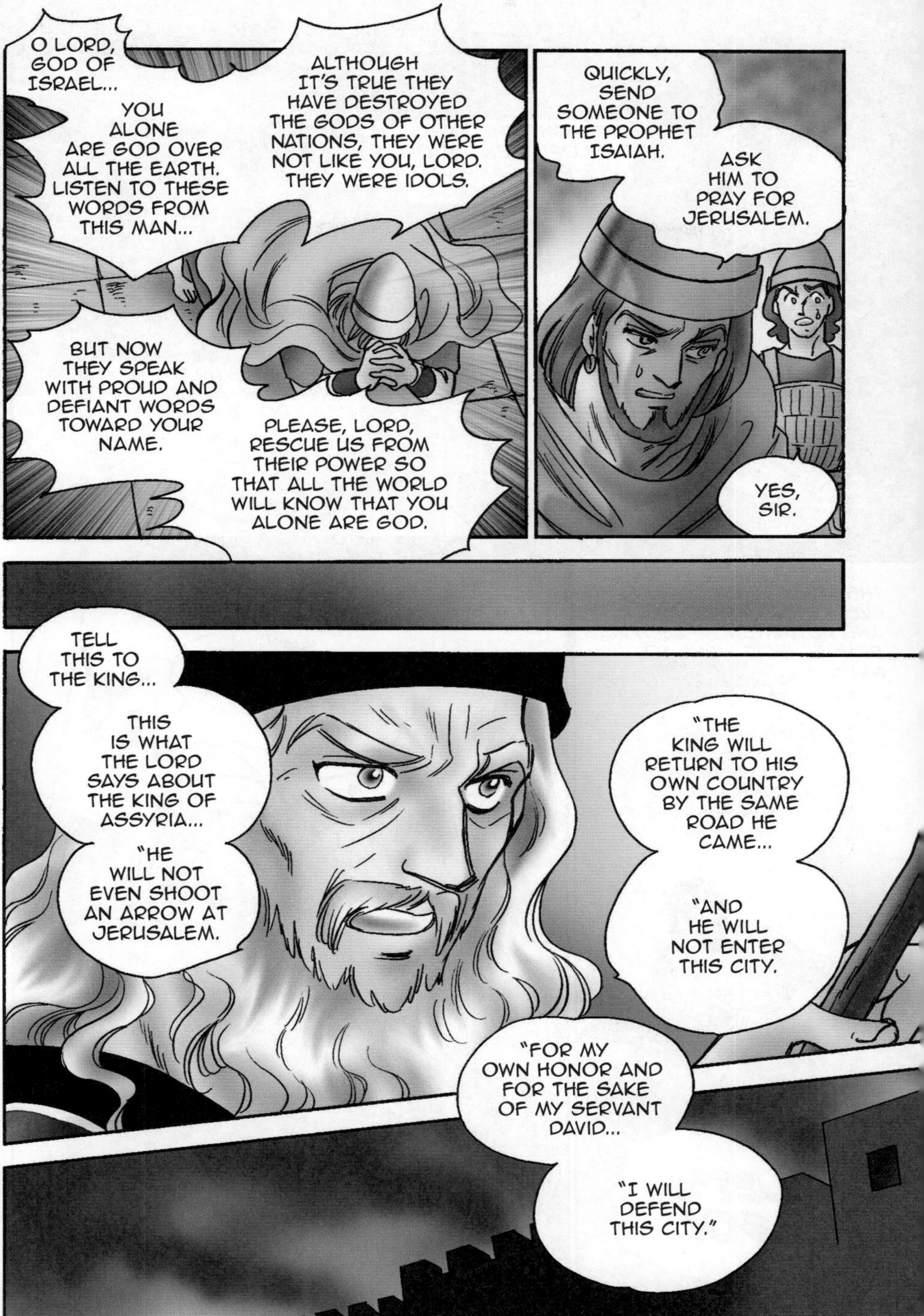
O LORD, GOD OF ISRAEL...
YOU ALONE ARE GOD OVER ALL THE EARTH. LISTEN TO THESE WORDS FROM THIS MAN...
ALTHOUGH IT'S TRUE THEY HAVE DESTROYED THE GODS OF OTHER NATIONS, THEY WERE NOT LIKE YOU, LORD. THEY WERE IDOLS.
BUT NOW THEY SPEAK WITH PROUD AND DEFIANT WORDS TOWARD YOUR NAME.
PLEASE, LORD, RESCUE US FROM THEIR POWER SO THAT ALL THE WORLD WILL KNOW THAT YOU ALONE ARE GOD.
QUICKLY, SEND SOMEONE TO THE PROPHET ISAIAH.
ASK HIM TO PRAY FOR JERUSALEM.
YES, SIR.
TELL THIS TO THE KING...
THIS IS WHAT THE LORD SAYS ABOUT THE KING OF ASSYRIA...
"HE WILL NOT EVEN SHOOT AN ARROW AT JERUSALEM.
"THE KING WILL RETURN TO HIS OWN COUNTRY BY THE SAME ROAD HE CAME...
"AND HE WILL NOT ENTER THIS CITY.
"FOR MY OWN HONOR AND FOR THE SAKE OF MY SERVANT DAVID...
"I WILL DEFEND THIS CITY."

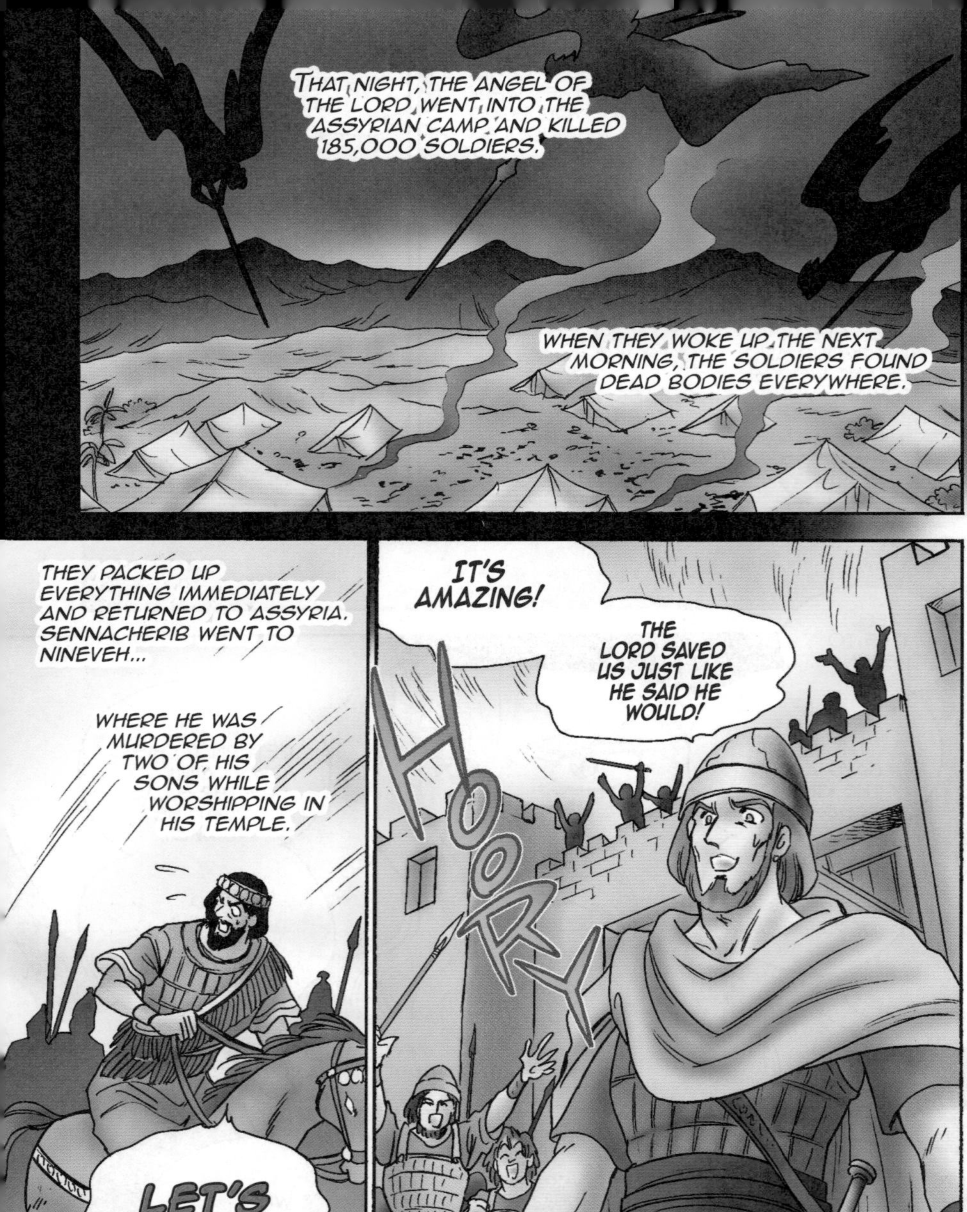
THAT NIGHT, THE ANGEL OF THE LORD WENT INTO THE ASSYRIAN CAMP AND KILLED 185,000 SOLDIERS.
WHEN THEY WOKE UP THE NEXT MORNING, THE SOLDIERS FOUND DEAD BODIES EVERYWHERE.
THEY PACKED UP EVERYTHING IMMEDIATELY AND RETURNED TO ASSYRIA. SENNACHERIB WENT TO NINEVEH...
WHERE HE WAS MURDERED BY TWO OF HIS SONS WHILE WORSHIPPING IN HIS TEMPLE.
LET'S GO!
IT'S AMAZING!
THE LORD SAVED US JUST LIKE HE SAID HE WOULD!
HOORY

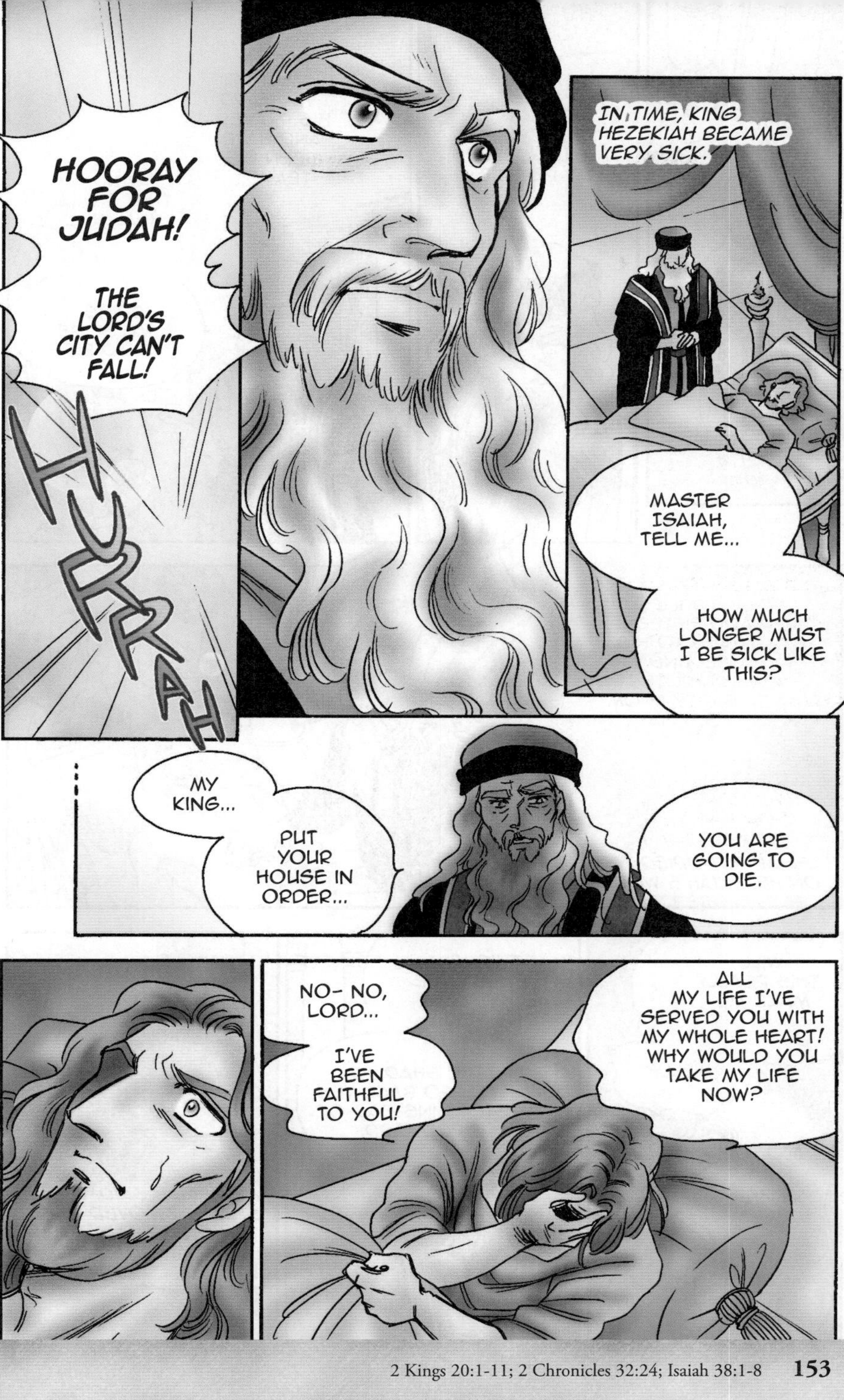
HOORAY FOR JUDAH!
THE LORD'S CITY CAN'T FALL!
HURRAH
IN TIME, KING HEZEKIAH BECAME VERY SICK.
MASTER ISAIAH, TELL ME...
HOW MUCH LONGER MUST I BE SICK LIKE THIS?
MY KING...
PUT YOUR HOUSE IN ORDER...
YOU ARE GOING TO DIE.
NO- NO, LORD...
I'VE BEEN FAITHFUL TO YOU!
ALL MY LIFE I'VE SERVED YOU WITH MY WHOLE HEART! WHY WOULD YOU TAKE MY LIFE NOW?

2 Kings 20:1-11; 2 Chronicles 32:24; Isaiah 38:1-8

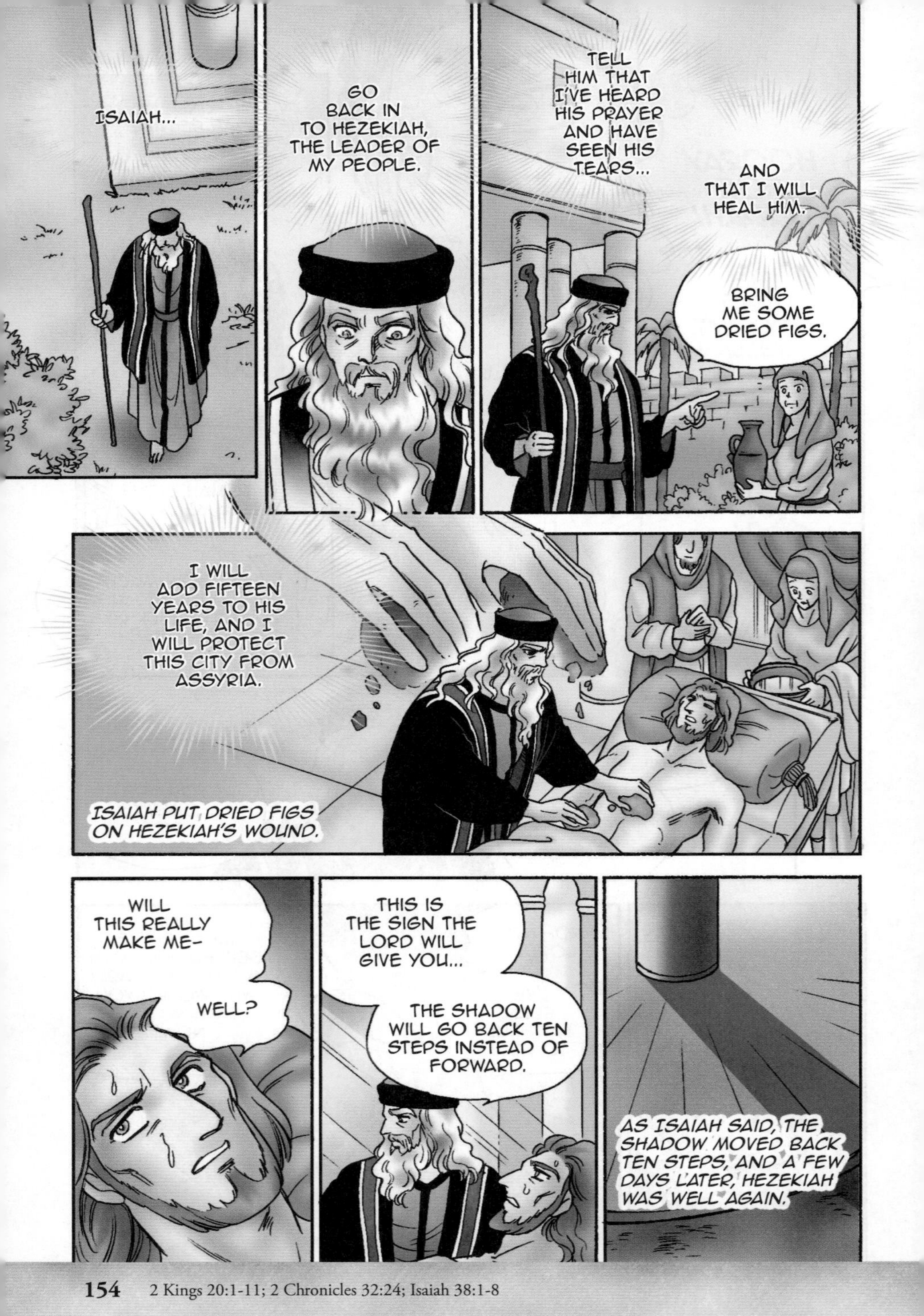

ISAIAH...
GO BACK IN TO HEZEKIAH, THE LEADER OF MY PEOPLE.
TELL HIM THAT I'VE HEARD HIS PRAYER AND HAVE SEEN HIS TEARS...
AND THAT I WILL HEAL HIM.
BRING ME SOME DRIED FIGS.
I WILL ADD FIFTEEN YEARS TO HIS LIFE, AND I WILL PROTECT THIS CITY FROM ASSYRIA.
ISAIAH PUT DRIED FIGS ON HEZEKIAH'S WOUND.
WILL THIS REALLY MAKE ME-
WELL?
THIS IS THE SIGN THE LORD WILL GIVE YOU...
THE SHADOW WILL GO BACK TEN STEPS INSTEAD OF FORWARD.
AS ISAIAH SAID, THE SHADOW MOVED BACK TEN STEPS, AND A FEW DAYS LATER, HEZEKIAH WAS WELL AGAIN.

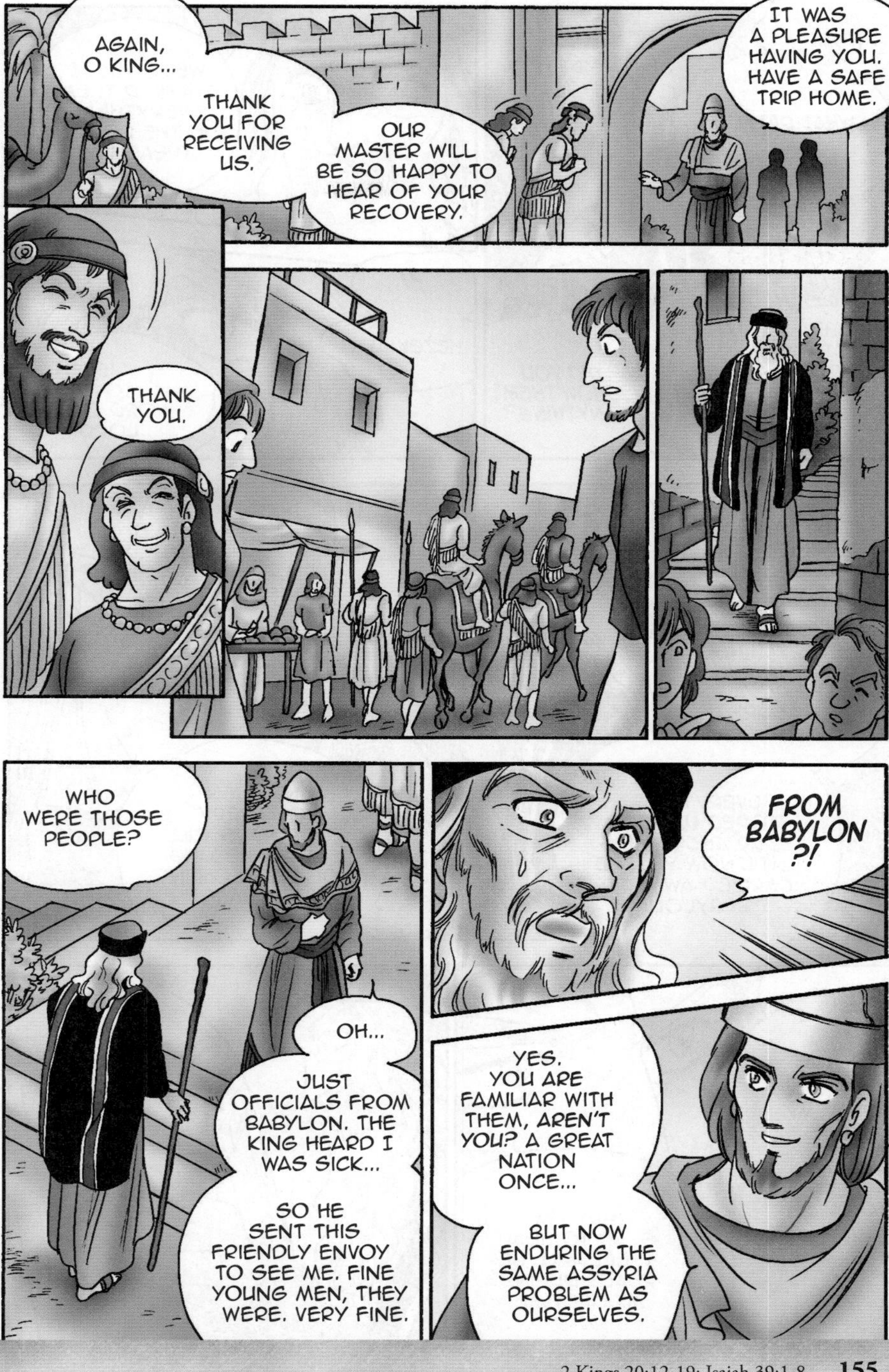
AGAIN, O KING...
THANK YOU FOR RECEIVING US.
OUR MASTER WILL BE SO HAPPY TO HEAR OF YOUR RECOVERY.
IT WAS A PLEASURE HAVING YOU. HAVE A SAFE TRIP HOME.
THANK YOU.
WHO WERE THOSE PEOPLE?
OH...
JUST OFFICIALS FROM BABYLON. THE KING HEARD I WAS SICK...
SO HE SENT THIS FRIENDLY ENVOY TO SEE ME. FINE YOUNG MEN, THEY WERE. VERY FINE.
FROM BABYLON ?!
YES. YOU ARE FAMILIAR WITH THEM, AREN'T YOU? A GREAT NATION ONCE...
BUT NOW ENDURING THE SAME ASSYRIA PROBLEM AS OURSELVES.

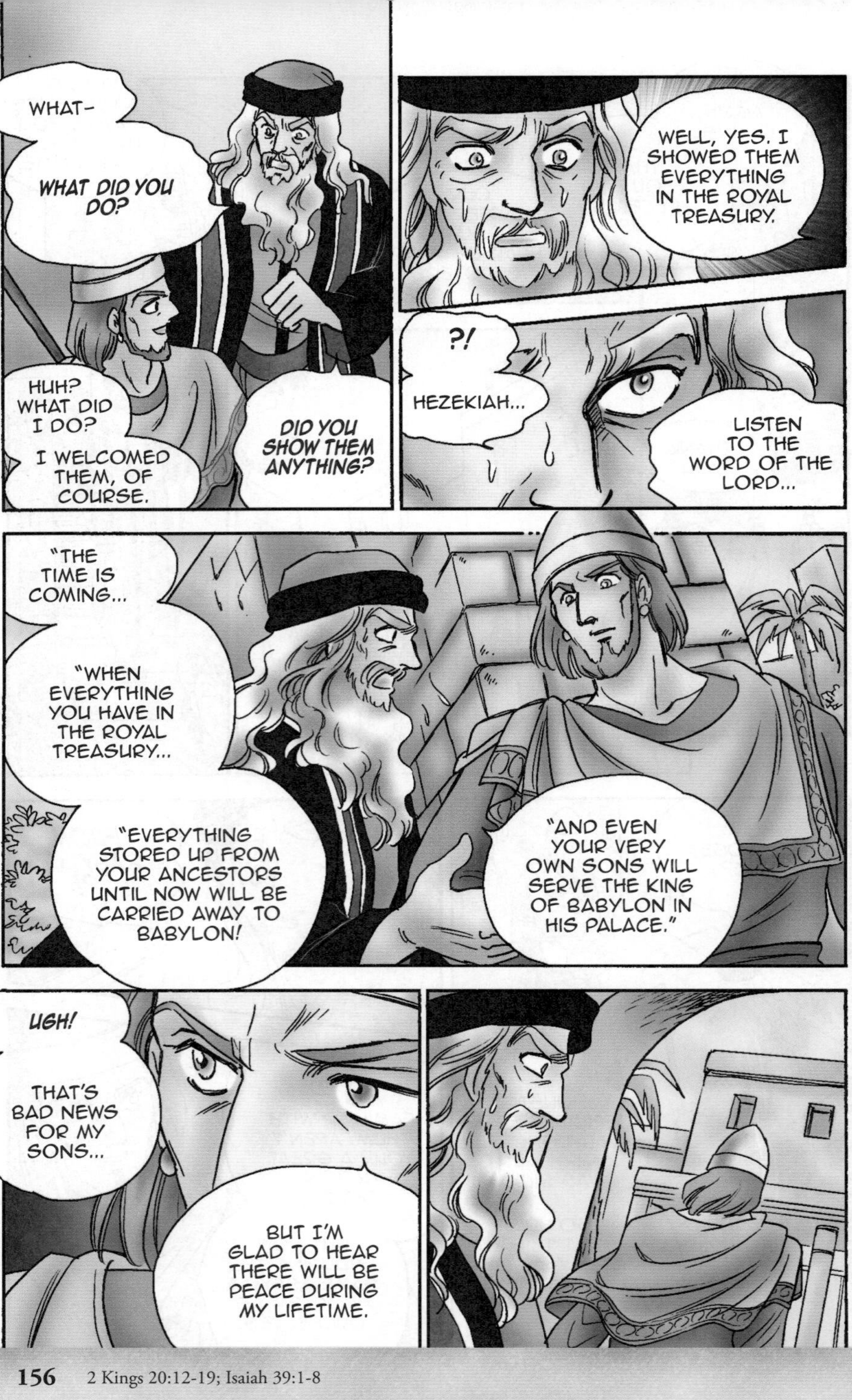
WHAT-
WHAT DID YOU DO?
HUH? WHAT DID I DO?
I WELCOMED THEM, OF COURSE.
DID YOU SHOW THEM ANYTHING?
WELL, YES. I SHOWED THEM EVERYTHING IN THE ROYAL TREASURY.
?!
HEZEKIAH...
LISTEN TO THE WORD OF THE LORD...
"THE TIME IS COMING...
"WHEN EVERYTHING YOU HAVE IN THE ROYAL TREASURY...
"EVERYTHING STORED UP FROM YOUR ANCESTORS UNTIL NOW WILL BE CARRIED AWAY TO BABYLON!
"AND EVEN YOUR VERY OWN SONS WILL SERVE THE KING OF BABYLON IN HIS PALACE."
UGH!
THAT'S BAD NEWS FOR MY SONS...
BUT I'M GLAD TO HEAR THERE WILL BE PEACE DURING MY LIFETIME.

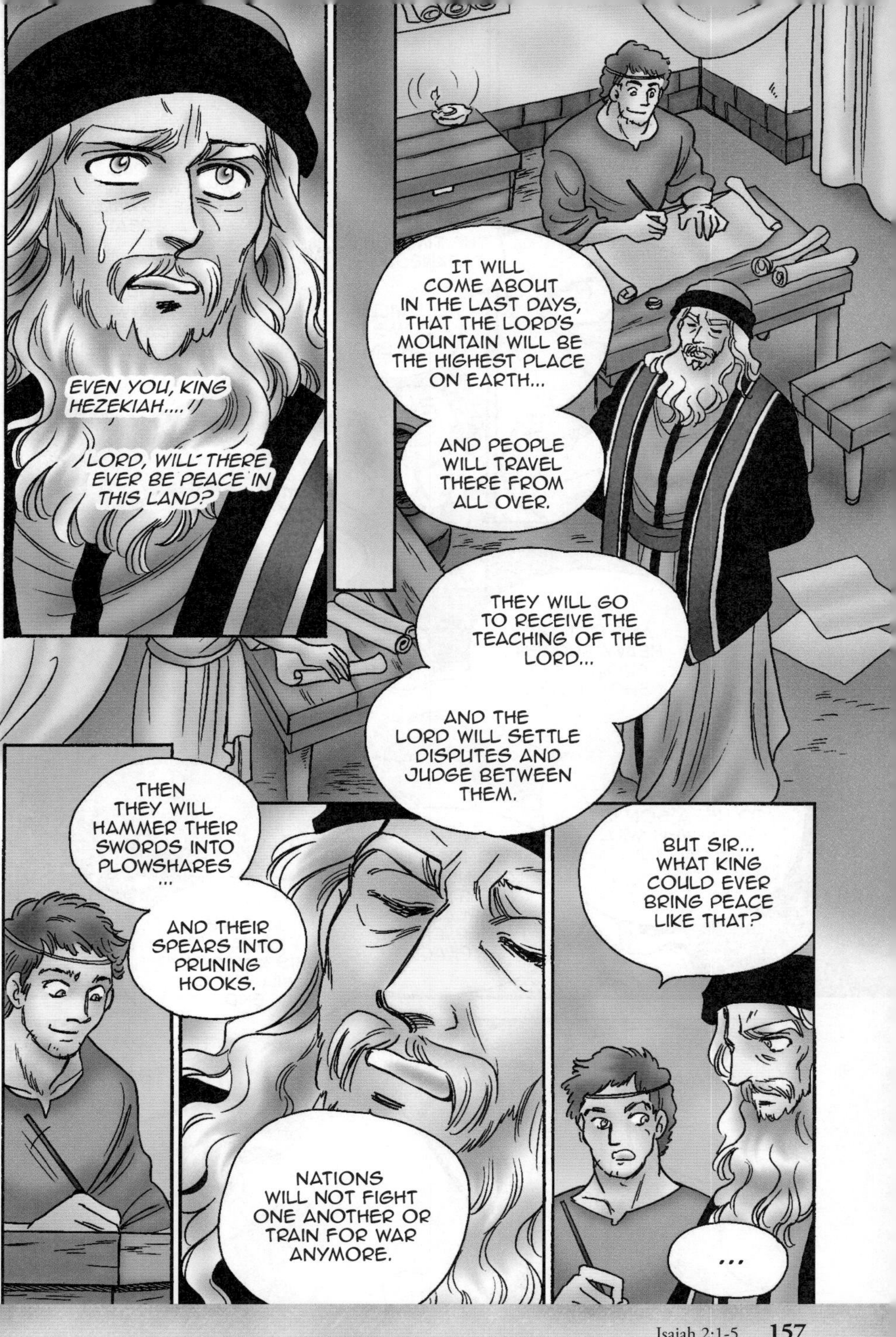
EVEN YOU, KING HEZEKIAH....
LORD, WILL THERE EVER BE PEACE IN THIS LAND?
IT WILL COME ABOUT IN THE LAST DAYS, THAT THE LORD'S MOUNTAIN WILL BE THE HIGHEST PLACE ON EARTH...
AND PEOPLE WILL TRAVEL THERE FROM ALL OVER.
THEY WILL GO TO RECEIVE THE TEACHING OF THE LORD...
AND THE LORD WILL SETTLE DISPUTES AND JUDGE BETWEEN THEM.
THEN THEY WILL HAMMER THEIR SWORDS INTO PLOWSHARES ...
AND THEIR SPEARS INTO PRUNING HOOKS.
NATIONS WILL NOT FIGHT ONE ANOTHER OR TRAIN FOR WAR ANYMORE.
BUT SIR... WHAT KING COULD EVER BRING PEACE LIKE THAT?
...

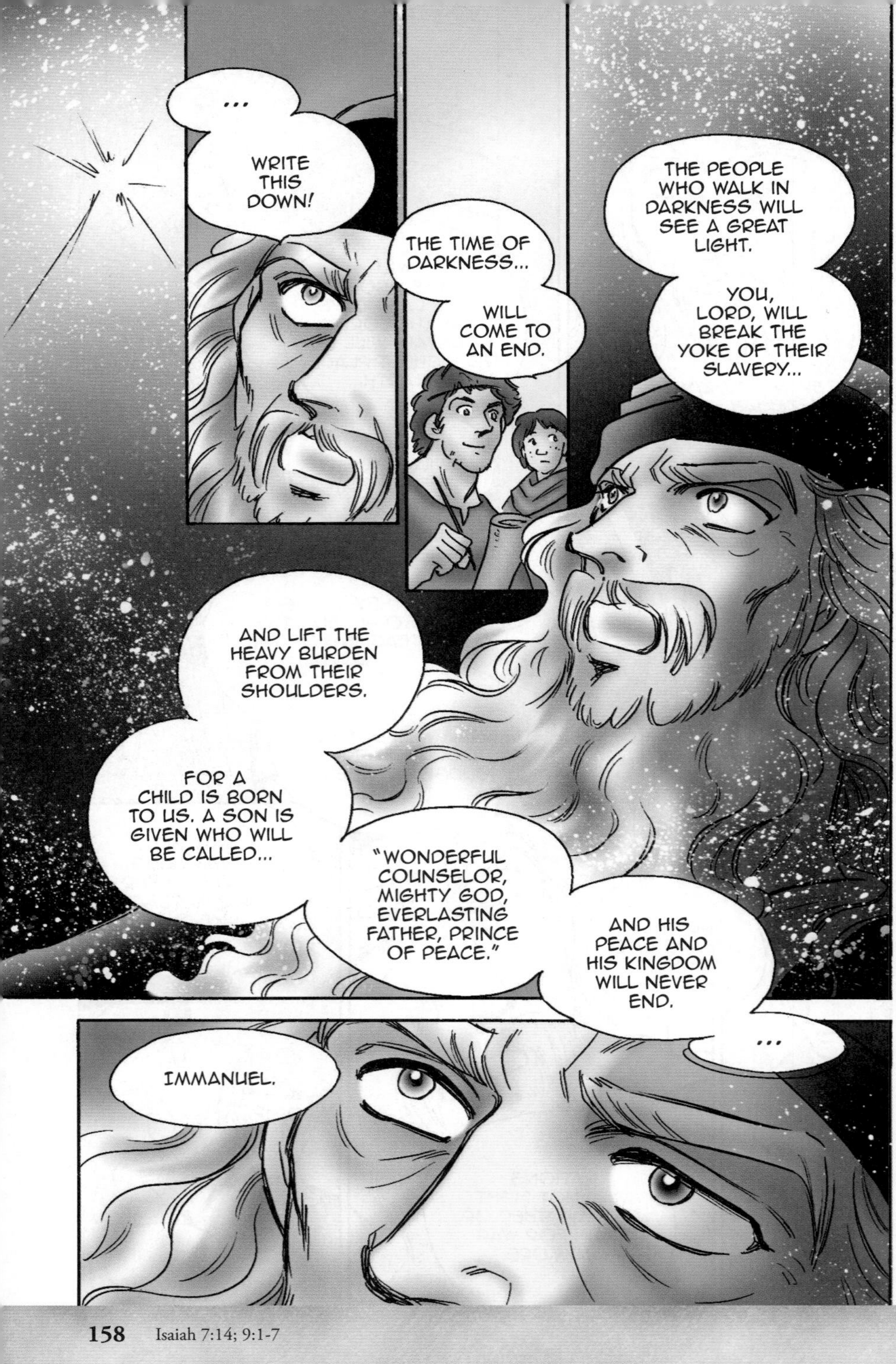
...
WRITE THIS DOWN!
THE TIME OF DARKNESS...
WILL COME TO AN END.
THE PEOPLE WHO WALK IN DARKNESS WILL SEE A GREAT LIGHT.
YOU, LORD, WILL BREAK THE YOKE OF THEIR SLAVERY...
AND LIFT THE HEAVY BURDEN FROM THEIR SHOULDERS.
FOR A CHILD IS BORN TO US. A SON IS GIVEN WHO WILL BE CALLED...
"WONDERFUL COUNSELOR, MIGHTY GOD, EVERLASTING FATHER, PRINCE OF PEACE."
AND HIS PEACE AND HIS KINGDOM WILL NEVER END.
...
IMMANUEL.

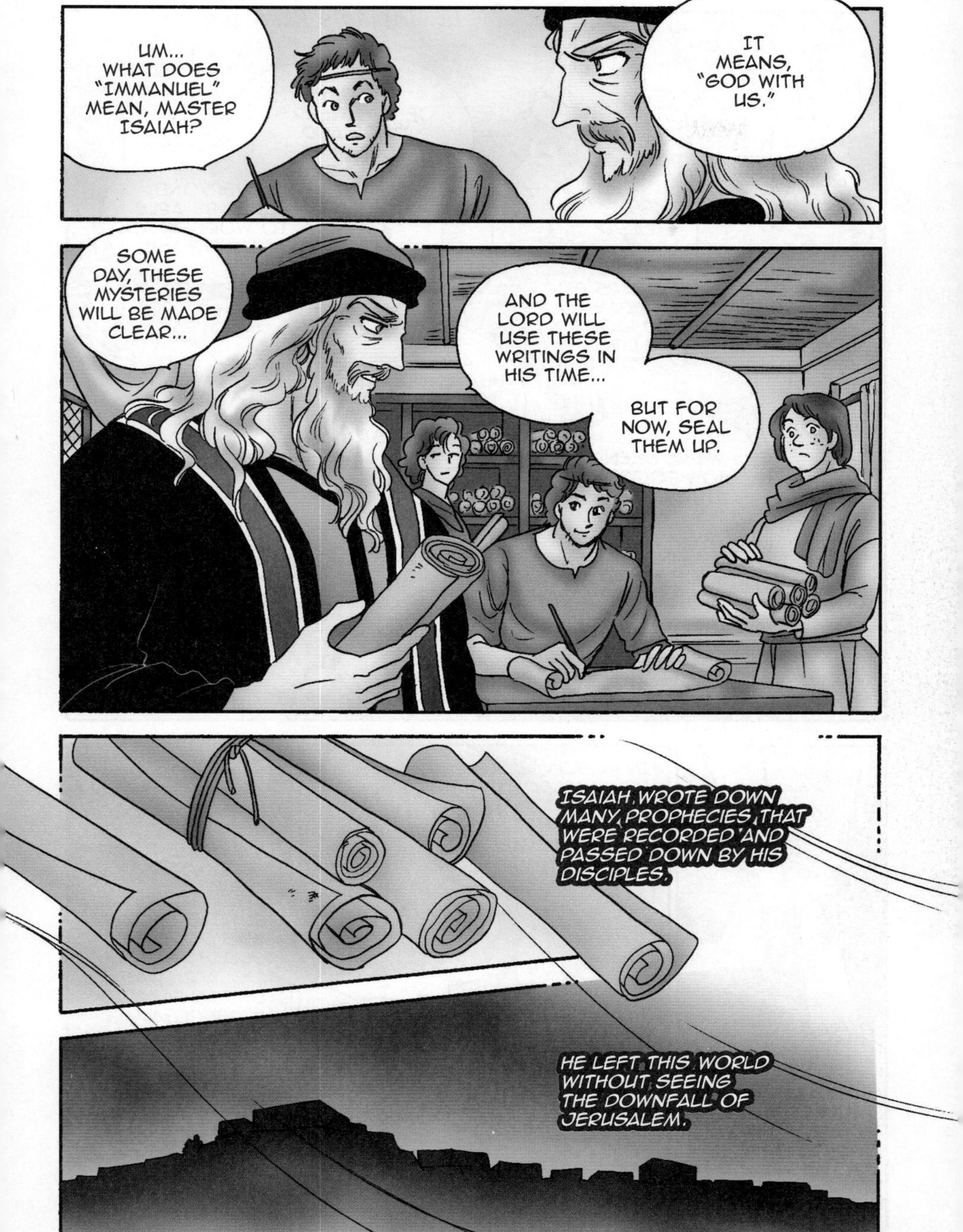
UM... WHAT DOES "IMMANUEL" MEAN, MASTER ISAIAH?
IT MEANS, "GOD WITH US."
SOME DAY, THESE MYSTERIES WILL BE MADE CLEAR...
AND THE LORD WILL USE THESE WRITINGS IN HIS TIME...
BUT FOR NOW, SEAL THEM UP.
ISAIAH WROTE DOWN MANY PROPHECIES THAT WERE RECORDED AND PASSED DOWN BY HIS DISCIPLES.
HE LEFT THIS WORLD WITHOUT SEEING THE DOWNFALL OF JERUSALEM.

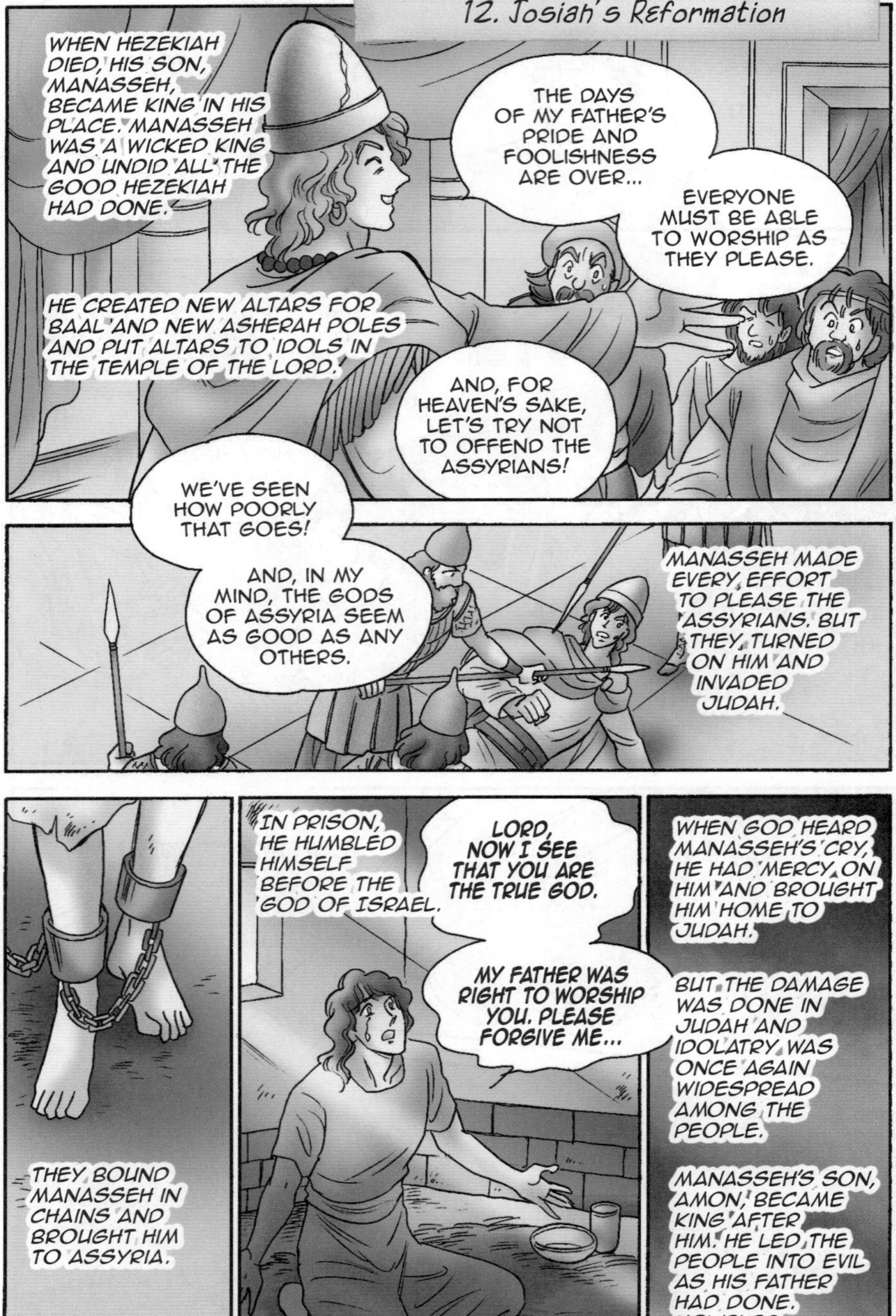
WHEN HEZEKIAH DIED, HIS SON, MANASSEH, BECAME KING IN HIS PLACE. MANASSEH WAS A WICKED KING AND UNDID ALL THE GOOD HEZEKIAH HAD DONE.
THE DAYS OF MY FATHER'S PRIDE AND FOOLISHNESS ARE OVER...
EVERYONE MUST BE ABLE TO WORSHIP AS THEY PLEASE.
HE CREATED NEW ALTARS FOR BAAL AND NEW ASHERAH POLES AND PUT ALTARS TO IDOLS IN THE TEMPLE OF THE LORD.
AND, FOR HEAVEN'S SAKE, LET'S TRY NOT TO OFFEND THE ASSYRIANS!
WE'VE SEEN HOW POORLY THAT GOES!
AND, IN MY MIND, THE GODS OF ASSYRIA SEEM AS GOOD AS ANY OTHERS.
MANASSEH MADE EVERY EFFORT TO PLEASE THE ASSYRIANS. BUT THEY TURNED ON HIM AND INVADED JUDAH.
THEY BOUND MANASSEH IN CHAINS AND BROUGHT HIM TO ASSYRIA.
IN PRISON, HE HUMBLED HIMSELF BEFORE THE GOD OF ISRAEL.
LORD, NOW I SEE THAT YOU ARE THE TRUE GOD.
MY FATHER WAS RIGHT TO WORSHIP YOU. PLEASE FORGIVE ME...
WHEN GOD HEARD MANASSEH'S CRY, HE HAD MERCY ON HIM AND BROUGHT HIM HOME TO JUDAH.
BUT THE DAMAGE WAS DONE IN JUDAH AND IDOLATRY WAS ONCE AGAIN WIDESPREAD AMONG THE PEOPLE.
MANASSEH'S SON, AMON, BECAME KING AFTER HIM. HE LED THE PEOPLE INTO EVIL AS HIS FATHER HAD DONE. HOWEVER...

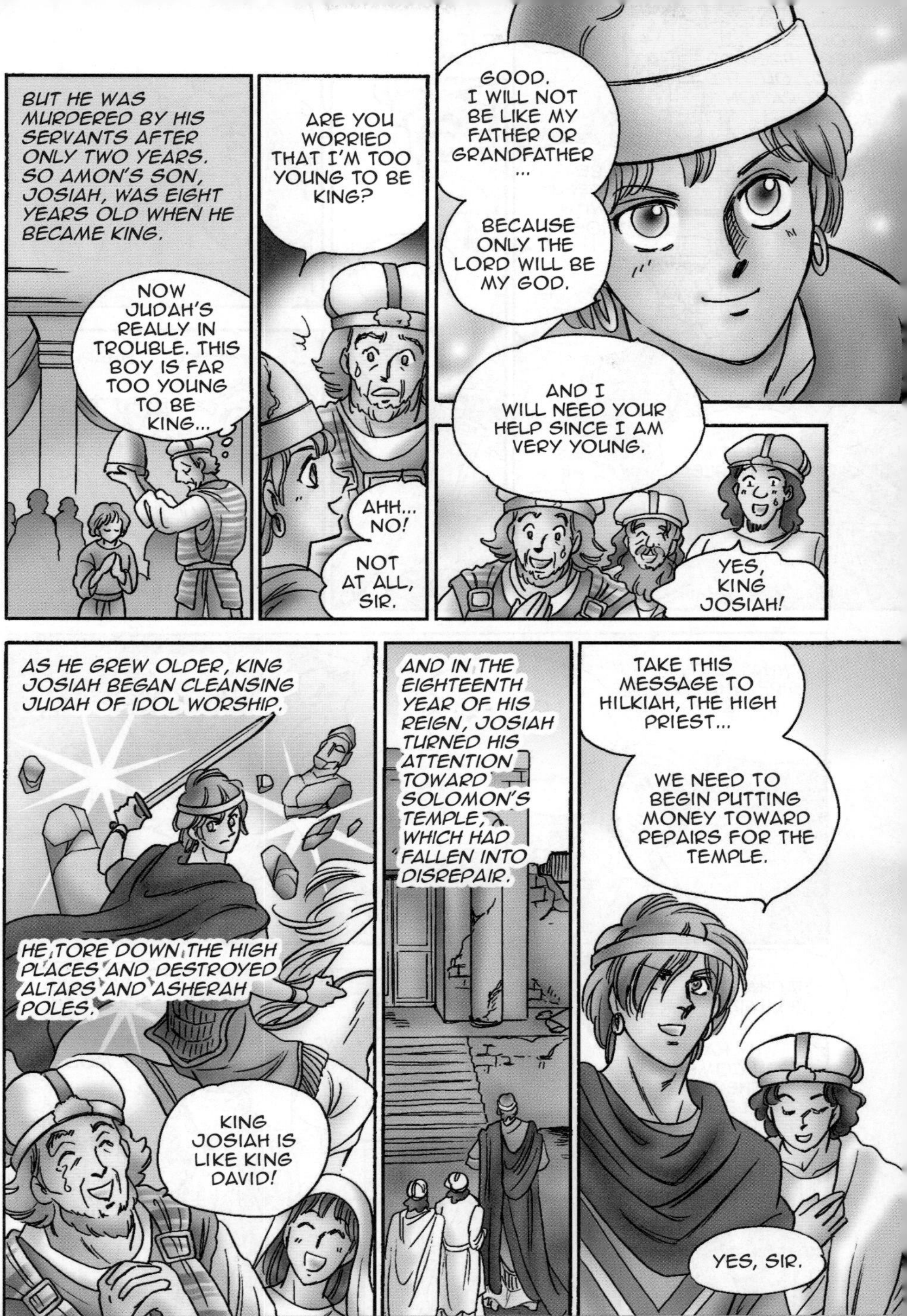
BUT HE WAS MURDERED BY HIS SERVANTS AFTER ONLY TWO YEARS. SO AMON'S SON, JOSIAH, WAS EIGHT YEARS OLD WHEN HE BECAME KING.
NOW JUDAH'S REALLY IN TROUBLE. THIS BOY IS FAR TOO YOUNG TO BE KING...
ARE YOU WORRIED THAT I'M TOO YOUNG TO BE KING?
AHH... NO!
NOT AT ALL, SIR.
GOOD. I WILL NOT BE LIKE MY FATHER OR GRANDFATHER ...
BECAUSE ONLY THE LORD WILL BE MY GOD.
AND I WILL NEED YOUR HELP SINCE I AM VERY YOUNG.
YES, KING JOSIAH!
AS HE GREW OLDER, KING JOSIAH BEGAN CLEANSING JUDAH OF IDOL WORSHIP.
HE TORE DOWN THE HIGH PLACES AND DESTROYED ALTARS AND ASHERAH POLES.
KING JOSIAH IS LIKE KING DAVID!
AND IN THE EIGHTEENTH YEAR OF HIS REIGN, JOSIAH TURNED HIS ATTENTION TOWARD SOLOMON'S TEMPLE, WHICH HAD FALLEN INTO DISREPAIR.
TAKE THIS MESSAGE TO HILKIAH, THE HIGH PRIEST...
WE NEED TO BEGIN PUTTING MONEY TOWARD REPAIRS FOR THE TEMPLE.
YES, SIR.

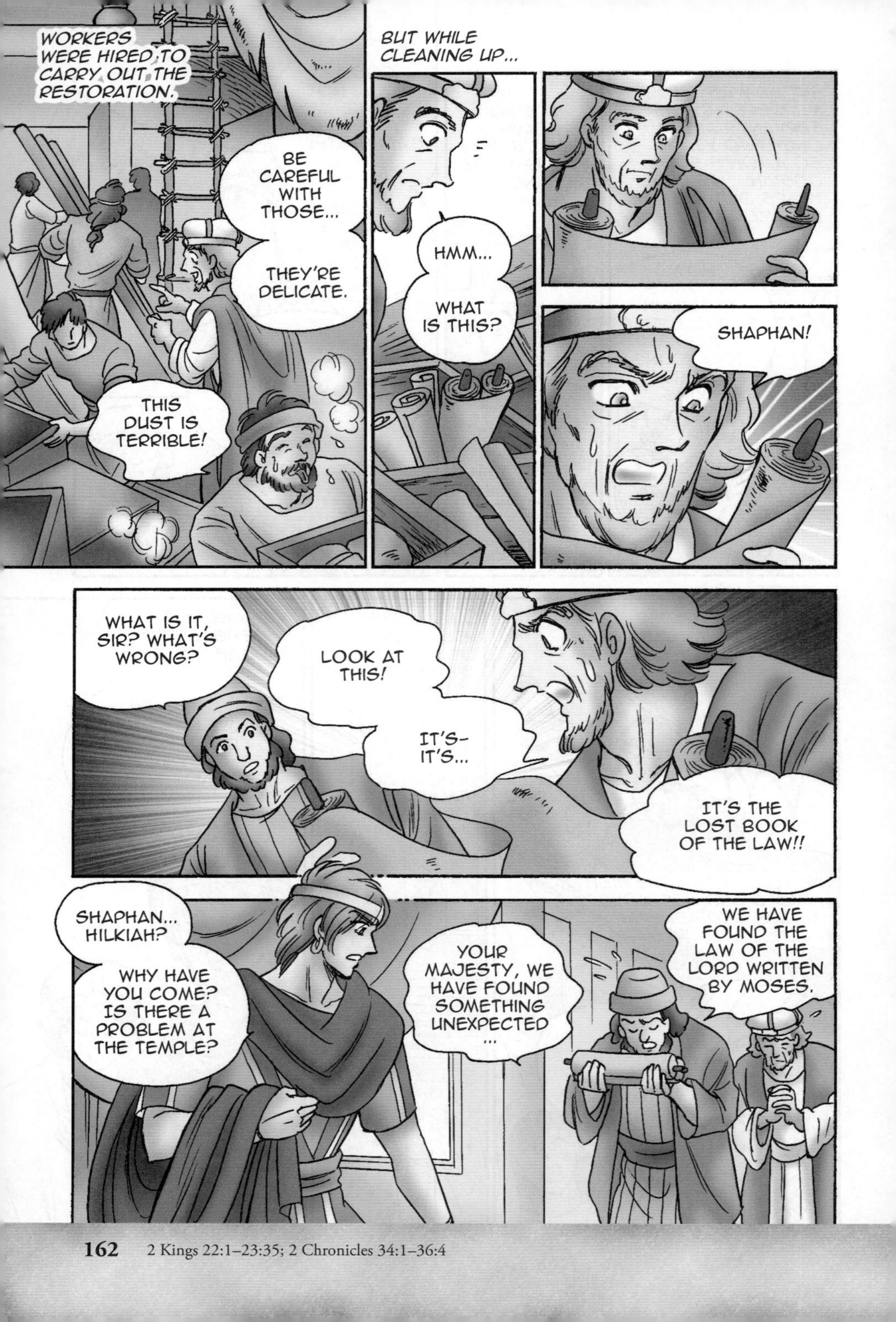
WORKERS WERE HIRED TO CARRY OUT THE RESTORATION.
BE CAREFUL WITH THOSE...
THEY'RE DELICATE.
THIS DUST IS TERRIBLE!
BUT WHILE CLEANING UP...
HMM...
WHAT IS THIS?
SHAPHAN!
WHAT IS IT, SIR? WHAT'S WRONG?
LOOK AT THIS!
IT'S- IT'S...
IT'S THE LOST BOOK OF THE LAW!!
SHAPHAN... HILKIAH?
WHY HAVE YOU COME? IS THERE A PROBLEM AT THE TEMPLE?
YOUR MAJESTY, WE HAVE FOUND SOMETHING UNEXPECTED ...
WE HAVE FOUND THE LAW OF THE LORD WRITTEN BY MOSES.

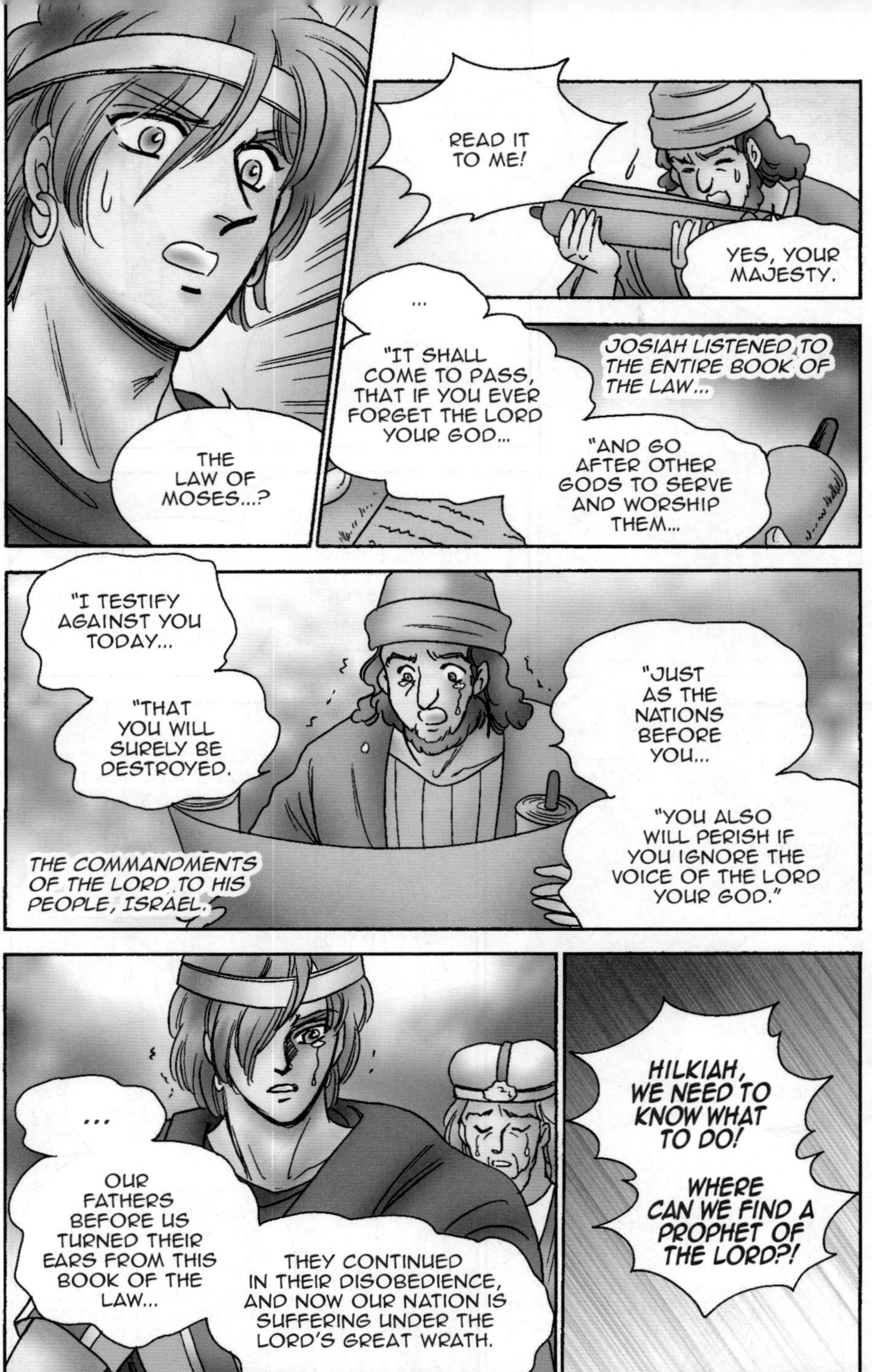
THE LAW OF MOSES...?
READ IT TO ME!
YES, YOUR MAJESTY.
...
"IT SHALL COME TO PASS, THAT IF YOU EVER FORGET THE LORD YOUR GOD...
JOSIAH LISTENED TO THE ENTIRE BOOK OF THE LAW...
"AND GO AFTER OTHER GODS TO SERVE AND WORSHIP THEM...
"I TESTIFY AGAINST YOU TODAY...
"THAT YOU WILL SURELY BE DESTROYED.
"JUST AS THE NATIONS BEFORE YOU...
"YOU ALSO WILL PERISH IF YOU IGNORE THE VOICE OF THE LORD YOUR GOD."
THE COMMANDMENTS OF THE LORD TO HIS PEOPLE, ISRAEL.
...
OUR FATHERS BEFORE US TURNED THEIR EARS FROM THIS BOOK OF THE LAW...
THEY CONTINUED IN THEIR DISOBEDIENCE, AND NOW OUR NATION IS SUFFERING UNDER THE LORD'S GREAT WRATH.
HILKIAH, WE NEED TO KNOW WHAT TO DO!
WHERE CAN WE FIND A PROPHET OF THE LORD?!

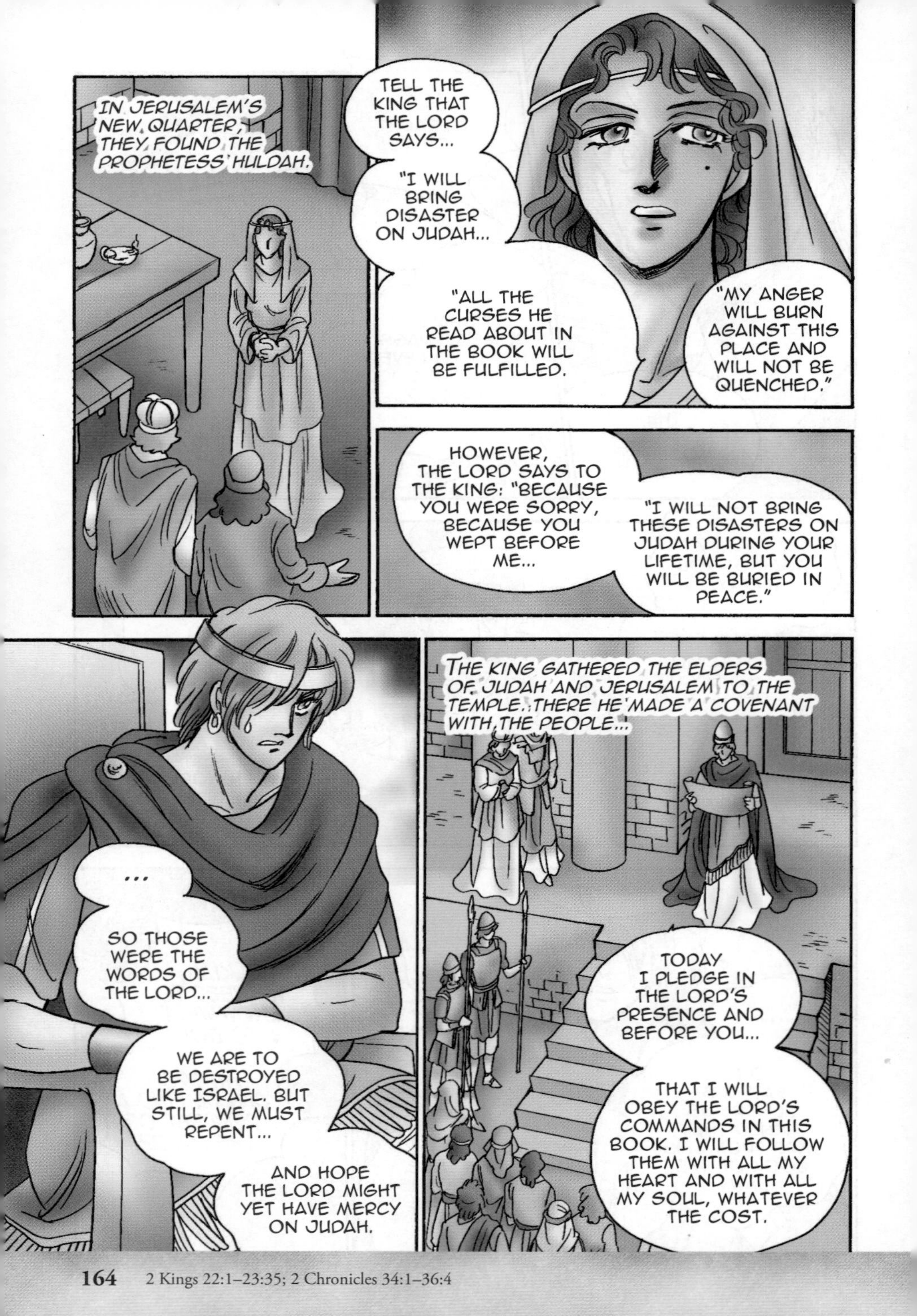
IN JERUSALEM'S NEW QUARTER, THEY FOUND THE PROPHETESS HULDAH.
TELL THE KING THAT THE LORD SAYS...
"I WILL BRING DISASTER ON JUDAH...
"ALL THE CURSES HE READ ABOUT IN THE BOOK WILL BE FULFILLED.
"MY ANGER WILL BURN AGAINST THIS PLACE AND WILL NOT BE QUENCHED."
HOWEVER, THE LORD SAYS TO THE KING: "BECAUSE YOU WERE SORRY, BECAUSE YOU WEPT BEFORE ME...
"I WILL NOT BRING THESE DISASTERS ON JUDAH DURING YOUR LIFETIME, BUT YOU WILL BE BURIED IN PEACE."
...
SO THOSE WERE THE WORDS OF THE LORD...
WE ARE TO BE DESTROYED LIKE ISRAEL. BUT STILL, WE MUST REPENT...
AND HOPE THE LORD MIGHT YET HAVE MERCY ON JUDAH.
THE KING GATHERED THE ELDERS OF JUDAH AND JERUSALEM TO THE TEMPLE. THERE HE MADE A COVENANT WITH THE PEOPLE...
TODAY I PLEDGE IN THE LORD'S PRESENCE AND BEFORE YOU...
THAT I WILL OBEY THE LORD'S COMMANDS IN THIS BOOK. I WILL FOLLOW THEM WITH ALL MY HEART AND WITH ALL MY SOUL, WHATEVER THE COST.

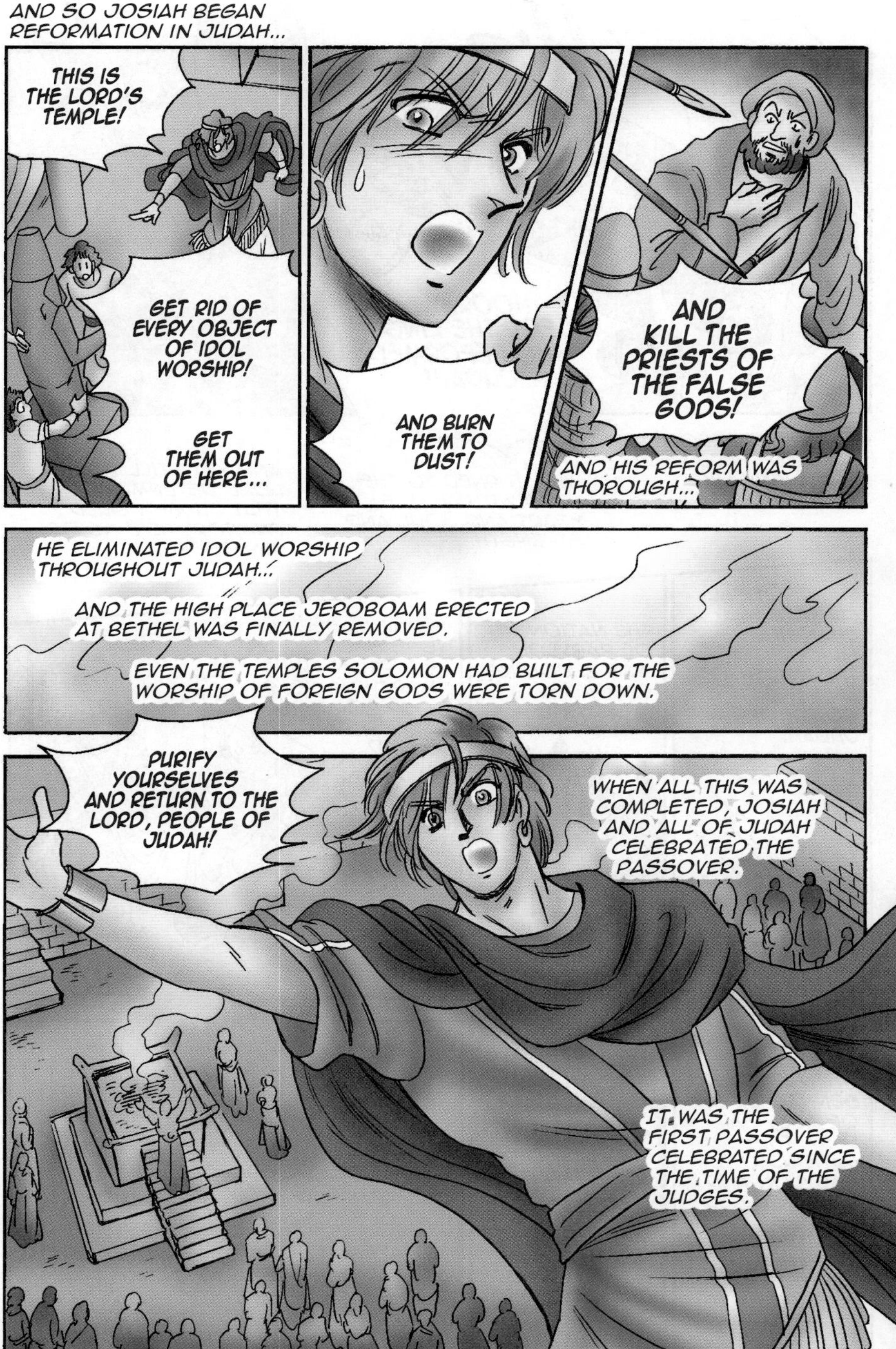
AND SO JOSIAH BEGAN REFORMATION IN JUDAH...
THIS IS THE LORD'S TEMPLE!
GET RID OF EVERY OBJECT OF IDOL WORSHIP!
GET THEM OUT OF HERE...
AND BURN THEM TO DUST!
AND KILL THE PRIESTS OF THE FALSE GODS!
AND HIS REFORM WAS THOROUGH...
HE ELIMINATED IDOL WORSHIP THROUGHOUT JUDAH...
AND THE HIGH PLACE JEROBOAM ERECTED AT BETHEL WAS FINALLY REMOVED.
EVEN THE TEMPLES SOLOMON HAD BUILT FOR THE WORSHIP OF FOREIGN GODS WERE TORN DOWN.
PURIFY YOURSELVES AND RETURN TO THE LORD, PEOPLE OF JUDAH!
WHEN ALL THIS WAS COMPLETED, JOSIAH AND ALL OF JUDAH CELEBRATED THE PASSOVER.
IT WAS THE FIRST PASSOVER CELEBRATED SINCE THE TIME OF THE JUDGES.

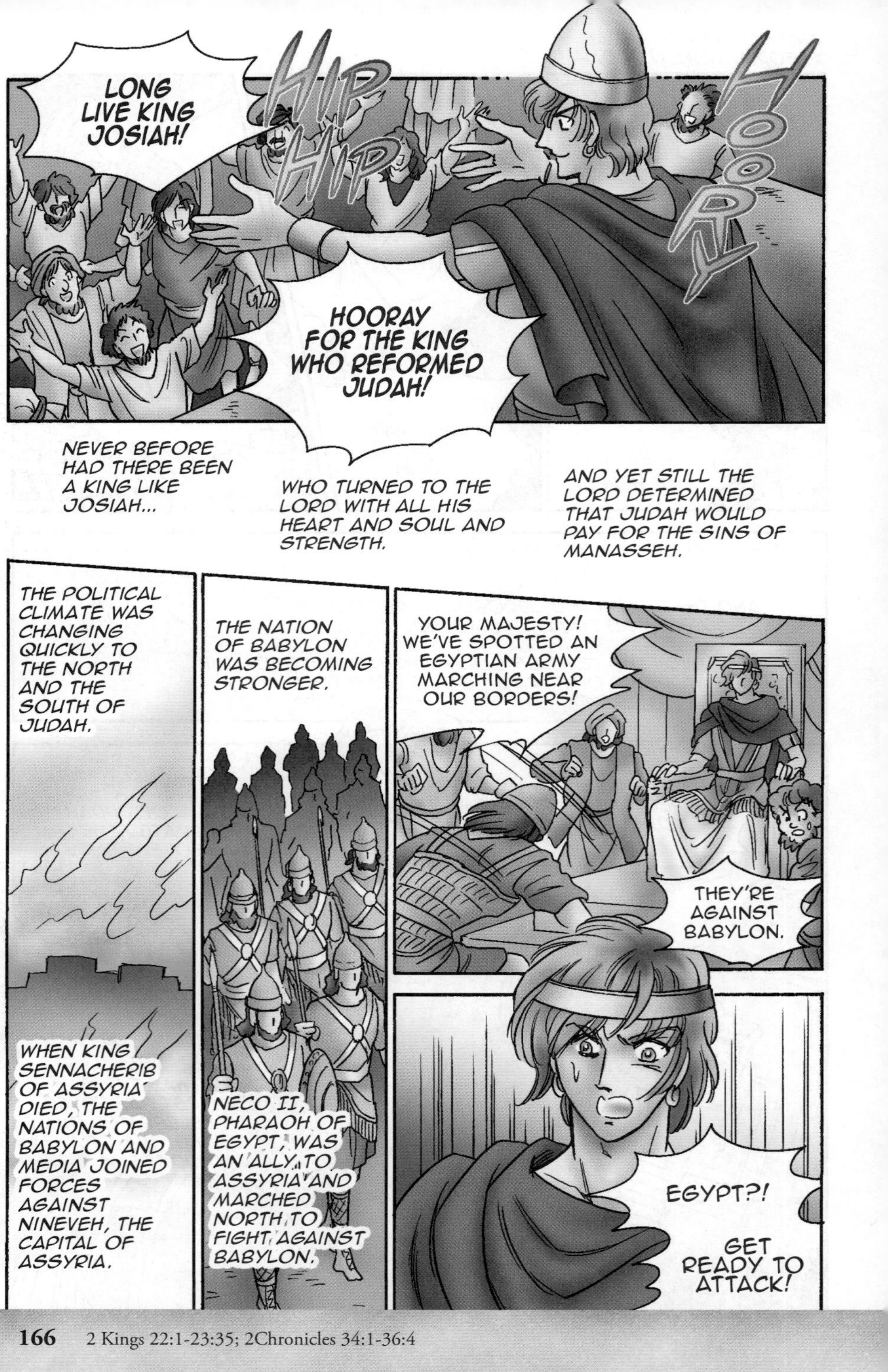
LONG LIVE KING JOSIAH!
HIP HIP
HOORAY
HOORAY FOR THE KING WHO REFORMED JUDAH!
NEVER BEFORE HAD THERE BEEN A KING LIKE JOSIAH...
WHO TURNED TO THE LORD WITH ALL HIS HEART AND SOUL AND STRENGTH.
AND YET STILL THE LORD DETERMINED THAT JUDAH WOULD PAY FOR THE SINS OF MANASSEH.
THE POLITICAL CLIMATE WAS CHANGING QUICKLY TO THE NORTH AND THE SOUTH OF JUDAH.
WHEN KING SENNACHERIB OF ASSYRIA DIED, THE NATIONS OF BABYLON AND MEDIA JOINED FORCES AGAINST NINEVEH, THE CAPITAL OF ASSYRIA.
THE NATION OF BABYLON WAS BECOMING STRONGER.
NECO II, PHARAOH OF EGYPT, WAS AN ALLY TO ASSYRIA AND MARCHED NORTH TO FIGHT AGAINST BABYLON.
YOUR MAJESTY! WE'VE SPOTTED AN EGYPTIAN ARMY MARCHING NEAR OUR BORDERS!
THEY'RE AGAINST BABYLON.
EGYPT?!
GET READY TO ATTACK!

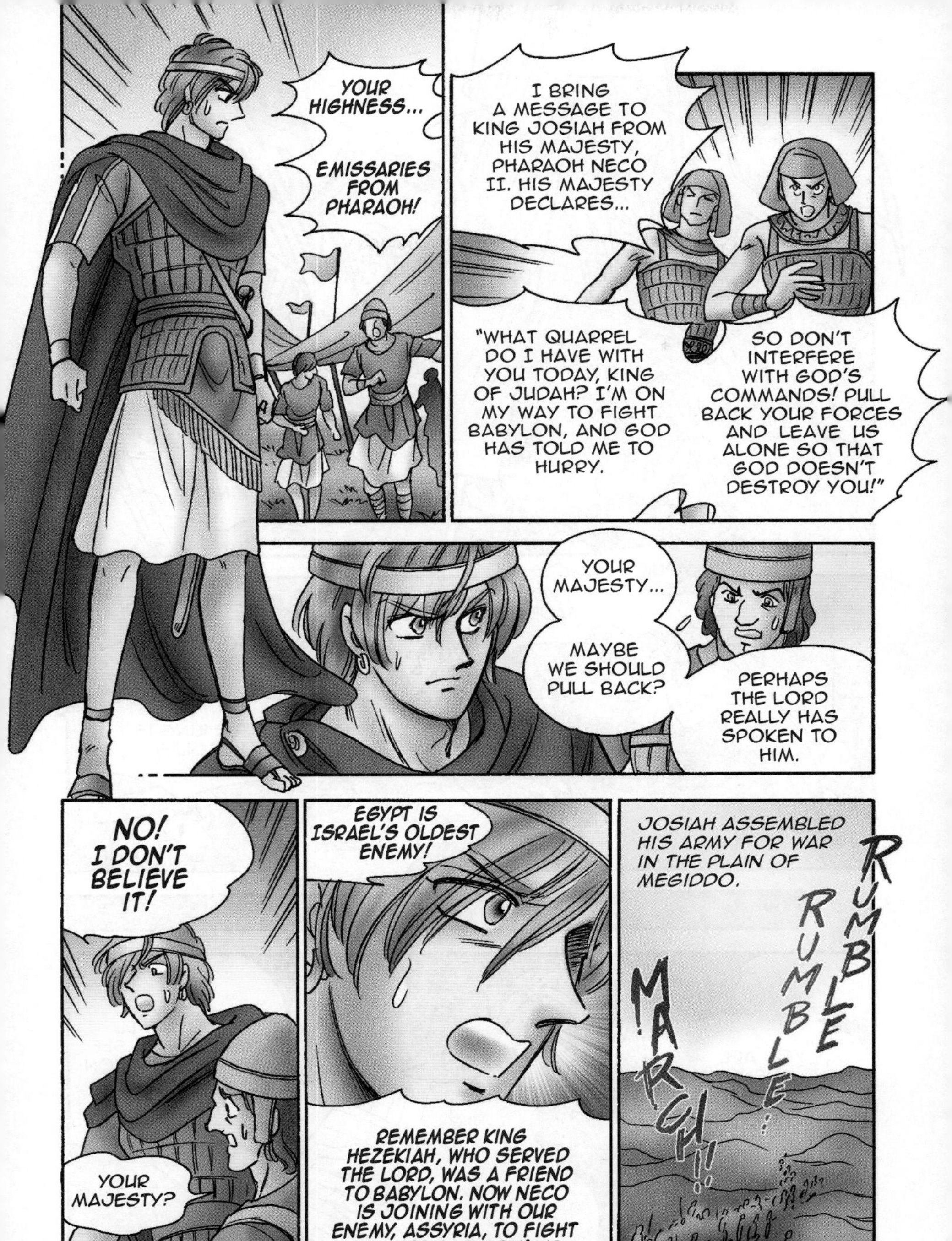
YOUR HIGHNESS...
EMISSARIES FROM PHARAOH!
I BRING A MESSAGE TO KING JOSIAH FROM HIS MAJESTY, PHARAOH NECO II. HIS MAJESTY DECLARES...
"WHAT QUARREL DO I HAVE WITH YOU TODAY, KING OF JUDAH? I'M ON MY WAY TO FIGHT BABYLON, AND GOD HAS TOLD ME TO HURRY.
SO DON'T INTERFERE WITH GOD'S COMMANDS! PULL BACK YOUR FORCES AND LEAVE US ALONE SO THAT GOD DOESN'T DESTROY YOU!"
YOUR MAJESTY...
MAYBE WE SHOULD PULL BACK?
PERHAPS THE LORD REALLY HAS SPOKEN TO HIM.
NO! I DON'T BELIEVE IT!
YOUR MAJESTY?
EGYPT IS ISRAEL'S OLDEST ENEMY!
REMEMBER KING HEZEKIAH, WHO SERVED THE LORD, WAS A FRIEND TO BABYLON. NOW NECO IS JOINING WITH OUR ENEMY, ASSYRIA, TO FIGHT AGAINST BABYLON! WE WON'T LET HIM PASS!
JOSIAH ASSEMBLED HIS ARMY FOR WAR IN THE PLAIN OF MEGIDDO.
RUMBLE
RUMBLE...
MARCH!!

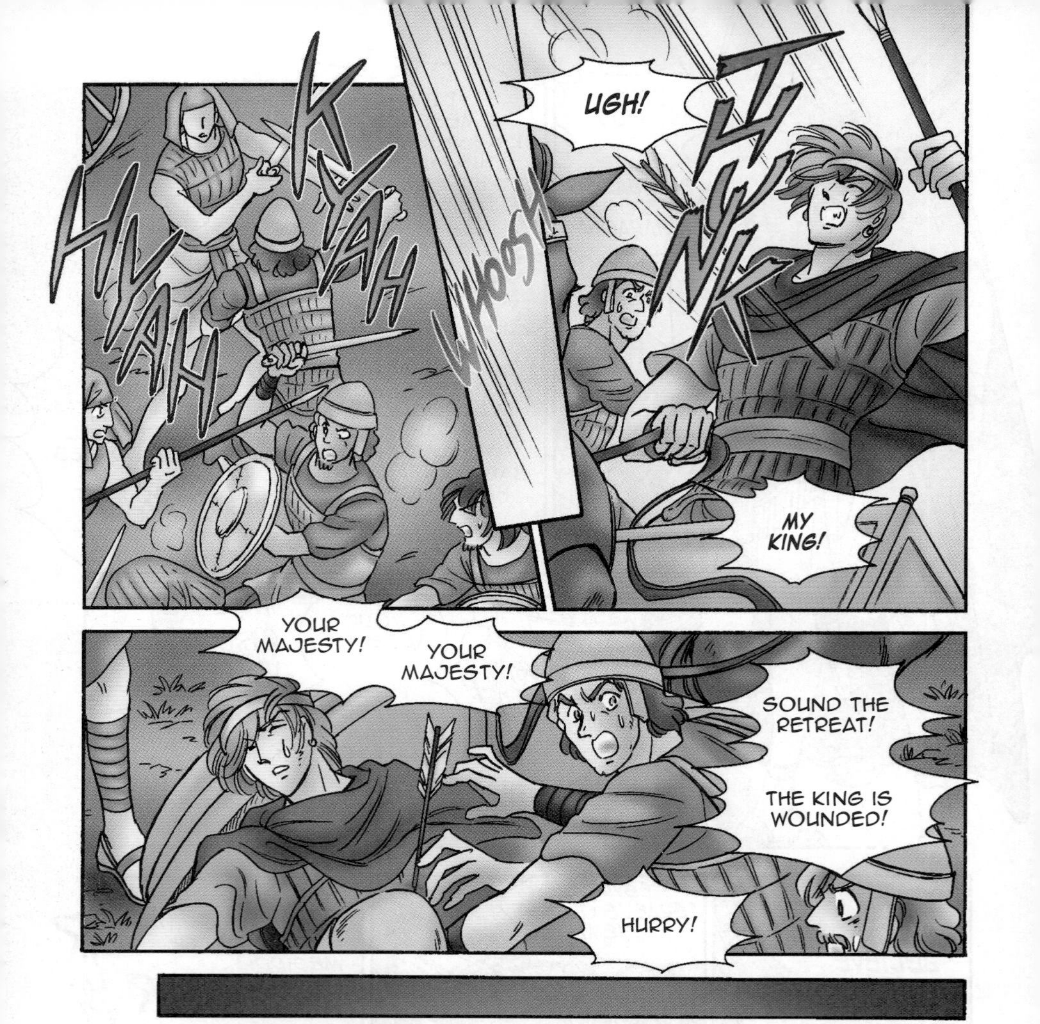
HYAH
KYAH
YAH
WHOOSH
THUNK
UGH!
MY KING!
YOUR MAJESTY!
YOUR MAJESTY!
SOUND THE RETREAT!
THE KING IS WOUNDED!
HURRY!
...
YOU ARE THE LORD. MAY YOUR WILL BE DONE.
AS YOU SAID, I WILL NOT LIVE TO SEE THE DESTRUCTION OF JUDAH.

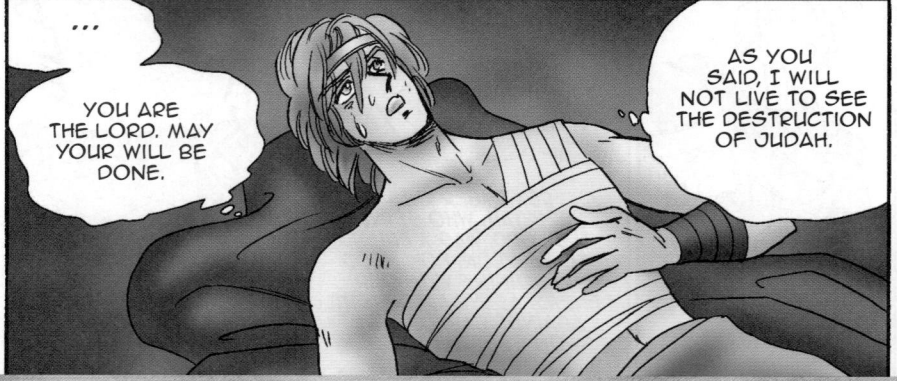

YOU HAVE HAD MERCY ON MY LIFE...

AND ON OTHERS BEFORE ME.

BRING YOUR MERCY AGAIN, LORD. FOR YOUR NAME...

FOR YOUR PEOPLE...

JOSIAH WAS TAKEN BACK TO JERUSALEM WHERE HE DIED.

ALL OF JUDAH MOURNED THE LOSS OF THEIR NOBLE KING, AND JOSIAH'S SON JEHOAHAZ BECAME KING IN HIS PLACE.

BUT PHARAOH NECO II WAS ANGRY ABOUT JUDAH'S ATTACK AT MEGIDDO.

IN RETALIATION, EGYPT RETURNED AND DEPOSED JEHOAHAZ.

JEHOAHAZ WAS TAKEN BACK TO EGYPT, WHERE HE DIED. NECO II MADE HIS BROTHER JEHOIAKIM KING IN HIS PLACE.

SHORTLY AFTER THIS, EGYPT, AND ASSYRIA WERE SOUNDLY DEFEATED IN BATTLE BY BABYLON.

BABYLON HAD BECOME THE MOST POWERFUL KINGDOM IN THE LAND.

BABYLON WAS LED BY AN IMMENSELY POWERFUL LEADER NAMED NEBUCHADNEZZAR II.

THE KING OF BABYLON ENTERED JUDAH AND MADE JEHOIAKIM SUBMIT TO HIS AUTHORITY.

NEBUCHADNEZZAR II

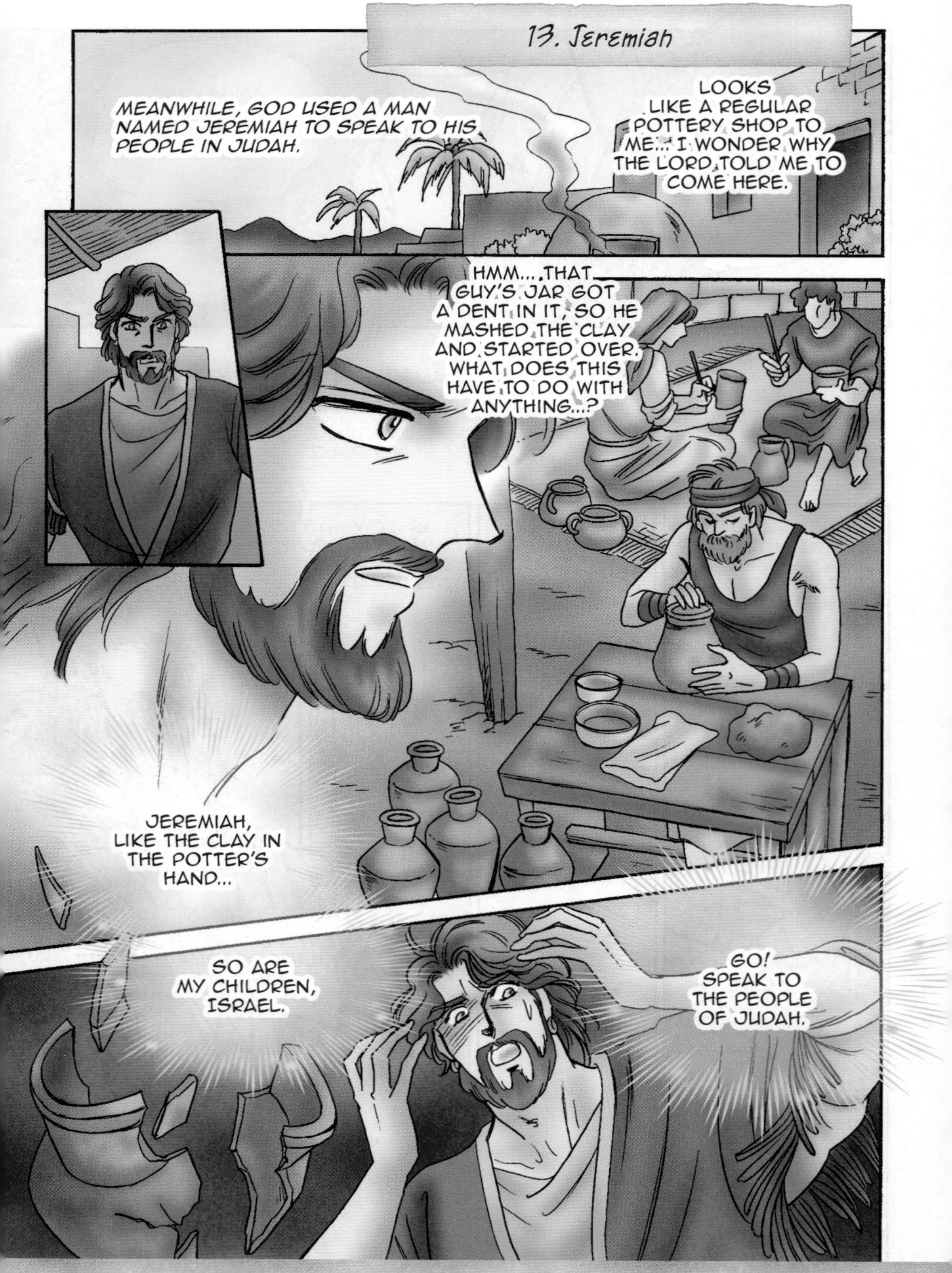
13. Jeremiah
MEANWHILE, GOD USED A MAN NAMED JEREMIAH TO SPEAK TO HIS PEOPLE IN JUDAH.
LOOKS LIKE A REGULAR POTTERY SHOP TO ME... I WONDER WHY THE LORD TOLD ME TO COME HERE.
HMM... THAT GUY'S JAR GOT A DENT IN IT, SO HE MASHED THE CLAY AND STARTED OVER. WHAT DOES THIS HAVE TO DO WITH ANYTHING...?
JEREMIAH, LIKE THE CLAY IN THE POTTER'S HAND...
SO ARE MY CHILDREN, ISRAEL.
GO! SPEAK TO THE PEOPLE OF JUDAH.

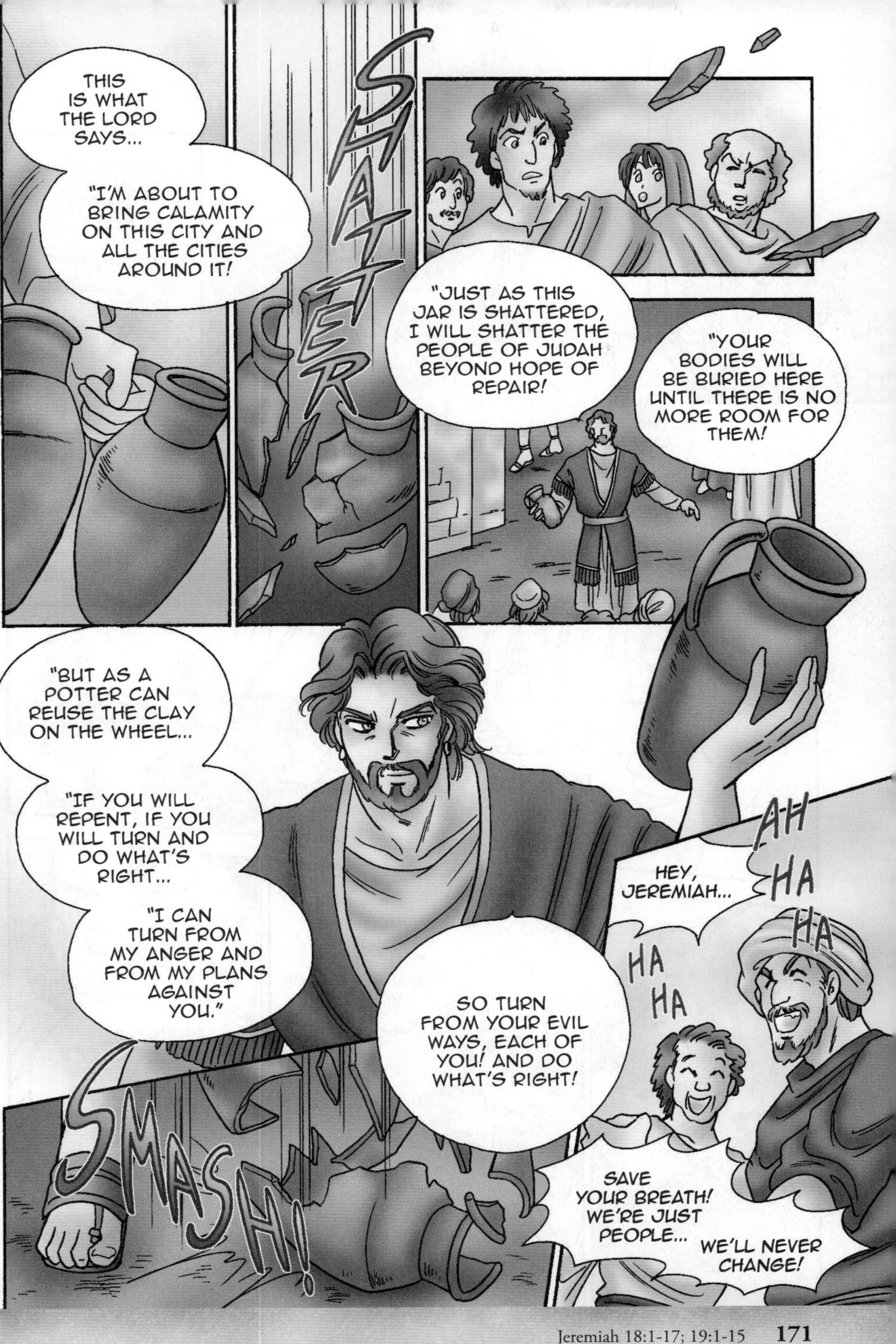
THIS IS WHAT THE LORD SAYS...
"I'M ABOUT TO BRING CALAMITY ON THIS CITY AND ALL THE CITIES AROUND IT!
SHATTER!
"JUST AS THIS JAR IS SHATTERED, I WILL SHATTER THE PEOPLE OF JUDAH BEYOND HOPE OF REPAIR!
"YOUR BODIES WILL BE BURIED HERE UNTIL THERE IS NO MORE ROOM FOR THEM!
"BUT AS A POTTER CAN REUSE THE CLAY ON THE WHEEL...
"IF YOU WILL REPENT, IF YOU WILL TURN AND DO WHAT'S RIGHT...
"I CAN TURN FROM MY ANGER AND FROM MY PLANS AGAINST YOU."
SMASH!
SO TURN FROM YOUR EVIL WAYS, EACH OF YOU! AND DO WHAT'S RIGHT!
HEY, JEREMIAH...
AH HA HA
HA HA
SAVE YOUR BREATH! WE'RE JUST PEOPLE...
WE'LL NEVER CHANGE!

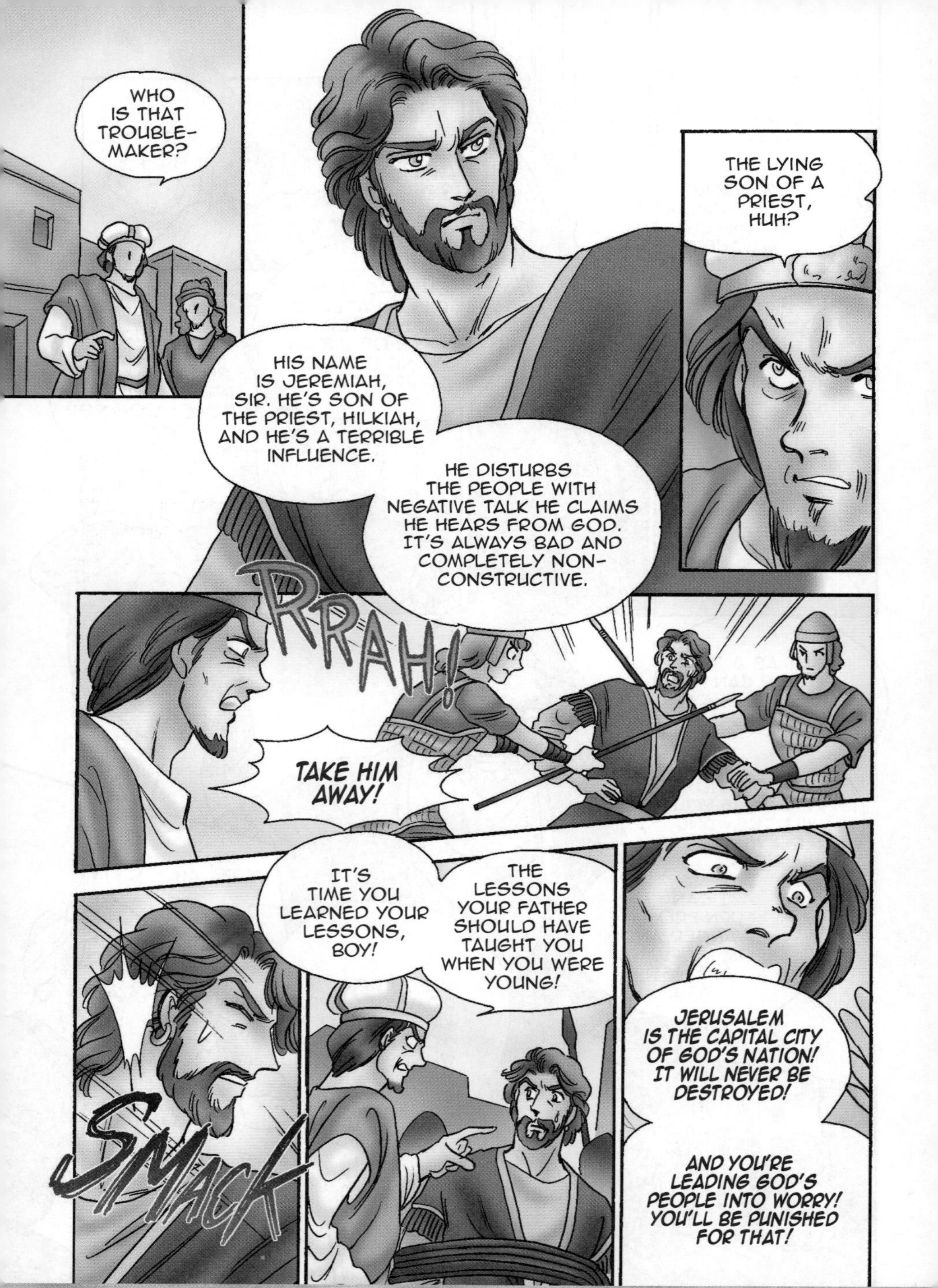
WHO IS THAT TROUBLE-MAKER?
THE LYING SON OF A PRIEST, HUH?
HIS NAME IS JEREMIAH, SIR. HE'S SON OF THE PRIEST, HILKIAH, AND HE'S A TERRIBLE INFLUENCE.
HE DISTURBS THE PEOPLE WITH NEGATIVE TALK HE CLAIMS HE HEARS FROM GOD. IT'S ALWAYS BAD AND COMPLETELY NON-CONSTRUCTIVE.
RRAH!
TAKE HIM AWAY!
IT'S TIME YOU LEARNED YOUR LESSONS, BOY!
THE LESSONS YOUR FATHER SHOULD HAVE TAUGHT YOU WHEN YOU WERE YOUNG!
SMACK
JERUSALEM IS THE CAPITAL CITY OF GOD'S NATION! IT WILL NEVER BE DESTROYED!
AND YOU'RE LEADING GOD'S PEOPLE INTO WORRY! YOU'LL BE PUNISHED FOR THAT!

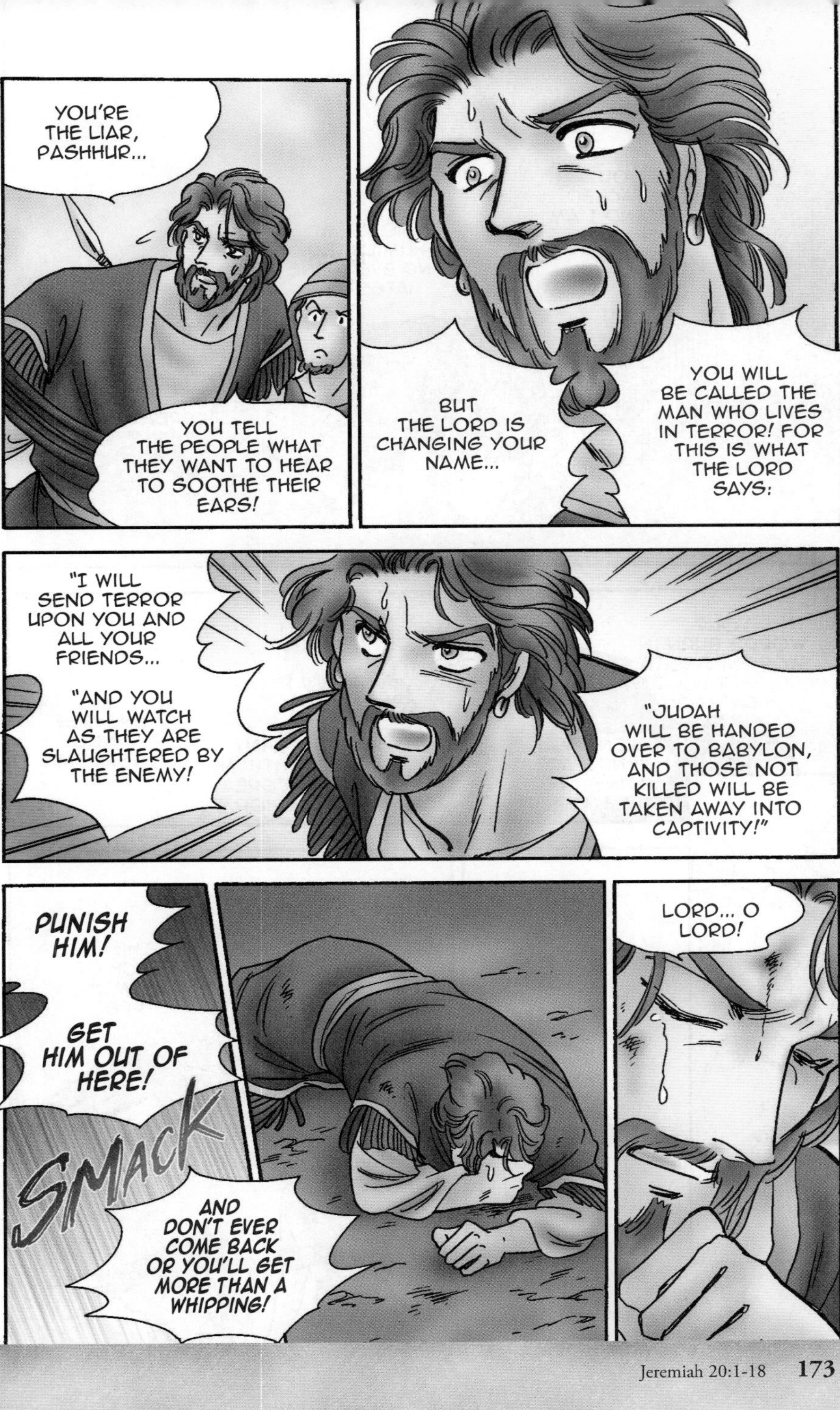
YOU'RE THE LIAR, PASHHUR...
YOU TELL THE PEOPLE WHAT THEY WANT TO HEAR TO SOOTHE THEIR EARS!
BUT THE LORD IS CHANGING YOUR NAME...
YOU WILL BE CALLED THE MAN WHO LIVES IN TERROR! FOR THIS IS WHAT THE LORD SAYS:
"I WILL SEND TERROR UPON YOU AND ALL YOUR FRIENDS...
"AND YOU WILL WATCH AS THEY ARE SLAUGHTERED BY THE ENEMY!
"JUDAH WILL BE HANDED OVER TO BABYLON, AND THOSE NOT KILLED WILL BE TAKEN AWAY INTO CAPTIVITY!"
PUNISH HIM!
GET HIM OUT OF HERE!
SMACK
AND DON'T EVER COME BACK OR YOU'LL GET MORE THAN A WHIPPING!
LORD... O LORD!

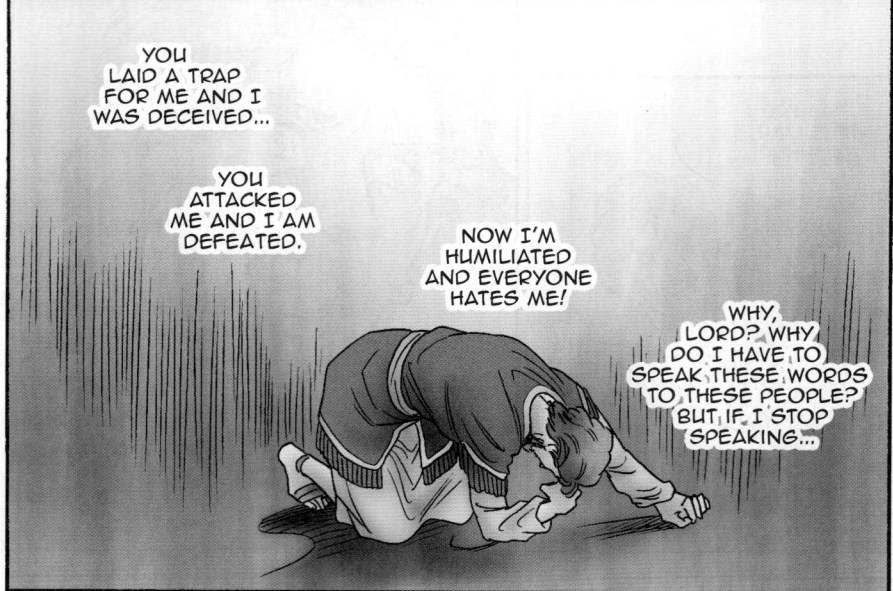

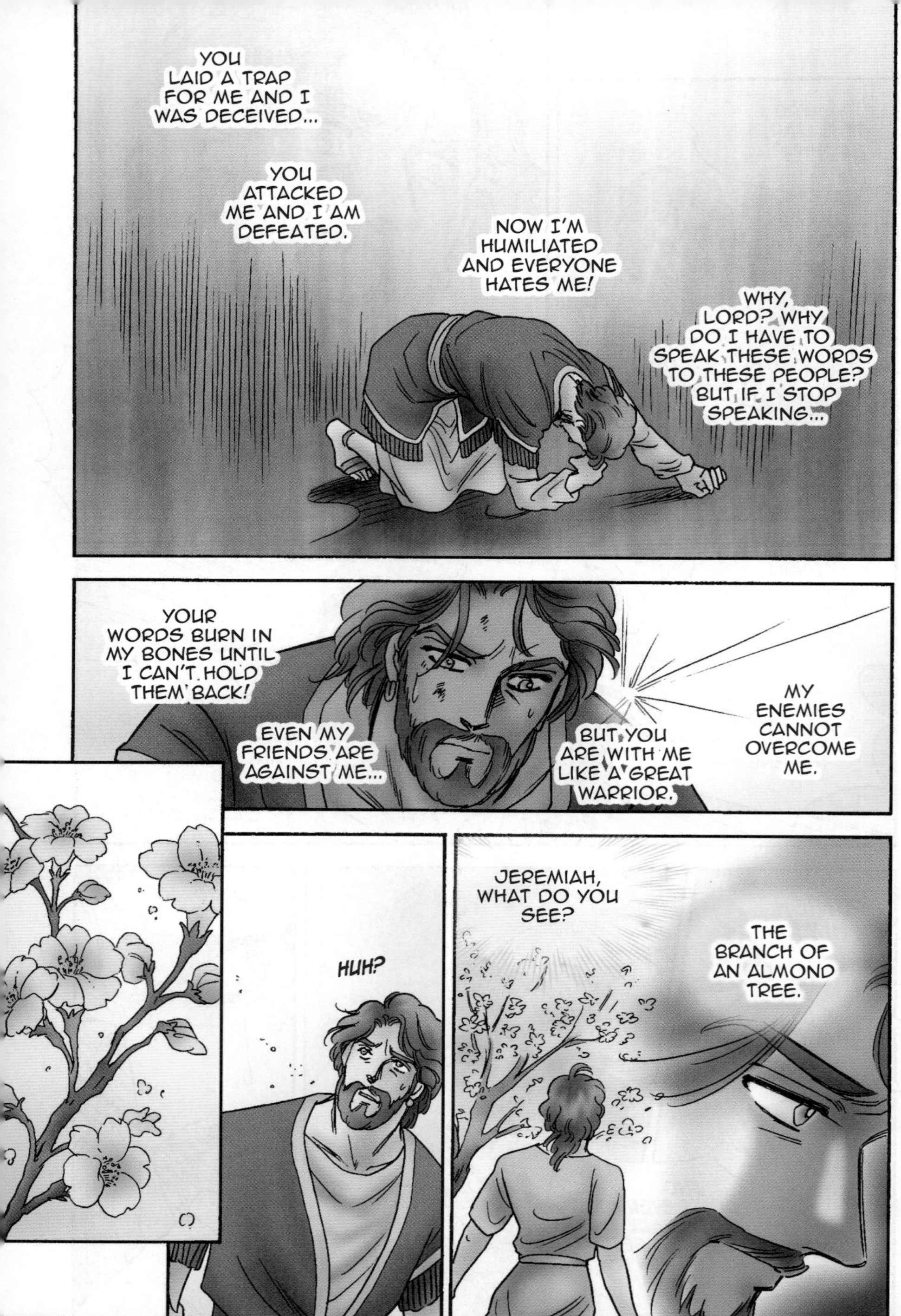
YOU LAID A TRAP FOR ME AND I WAS DECEIVED...
YOU ATTACKED ME AND I AM DEFEATED.
NOW I'M HUMILIATED AND EVERYONE HATES ME!
WHY, LORD? WHY DO I HAVE TO SPEAK THESE WORDS TO THESE PEOPLE? BUT IF I STOP SPEAKING...
YOUR WORDS BURN IN MY BONES UNTIL I CAN'T HOLD THEM BACK!
EVEN MY FRIENDS ARE AGAINST ME...
BUT YOU ARE WITH ME LIKE A GREAT WARRIOR.
MY ENEMIES CANNOT OVERCOME ME.
HUH?
JEREMIAH, WHAT DO YOU SEE?
THE BRANCH OF AN ALMOND TREE.

YES, JEREMIAH. YOU HAVE SEEN CORRECTLY. AND I AM WATCHING OVER MY WORD, SO THAT EVERYTHING WILL HAPPEN JUST AS I TELL YOU.

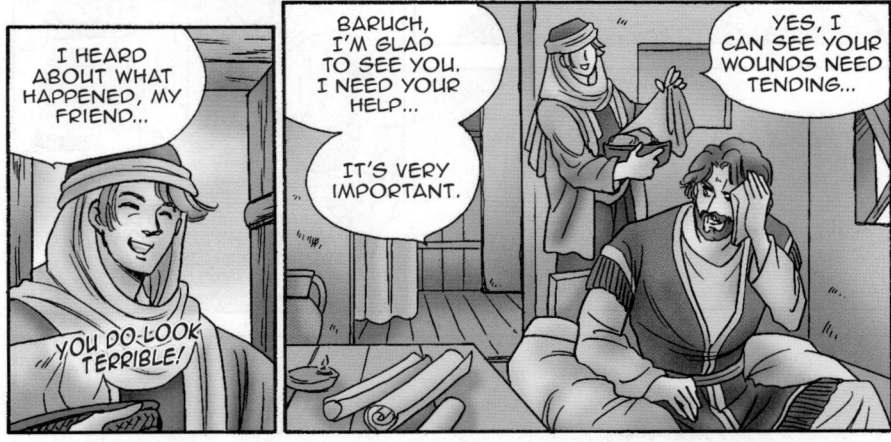

I HEARD ABOUT WHAT HAPPENED, MY FRIEND...

BARUCH, I'M GLAD TO SEE YOU. I NEED YOUR HELP...

IT'S VERY IMPORTANT.

YES, I CAN SEE YOUR WOUNDS NEED TENDING...

YOU DO LOOK TERRIBLE!

I ALWAYS SAY IT WOULD BE GOOD FOR YOU TO HAVE A WIFE, JEREMIAH. SHE'D CERTAINLY CARE FOR YOU BETTER THAN I WILL.

RIGHT. BUT YOU KNOW THE LORD'S TOLD ME NOT TO MARRY.

I SHOULDN'T TEASE YOU AFTER A BEATING...

SORRY.

HE'S SAID YOU CAN'T MARRY WHILE YOU'RE HERE... BUT MAYBE YOU COULD MOVE!

BARUCH, THIS IS IMPORTANT. THEY'RE NOT GOING TO LET ME BACK INTO THE TEMPLE, BUT I HAVE MORE WORDS FROM THE LORD...

AND THEY MUST BE SPOKEN THERE.

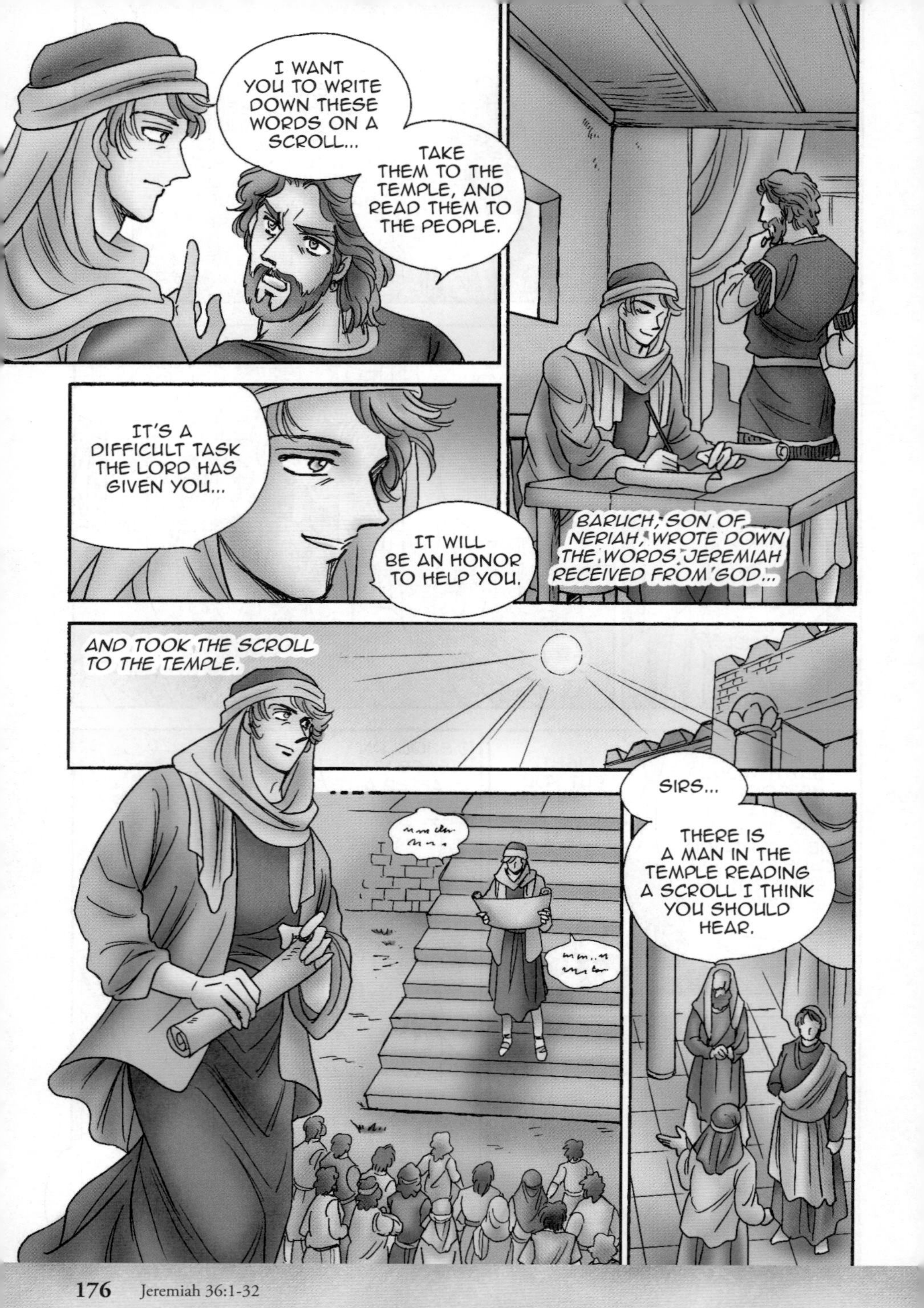

I WANT YOU TO WRITE DOWN THESE WORDS ON A SCROLL...
TAKE THEM TO THE TEMPLE, AND READ THEM TO THE PEOPLE.
IT'S A DIFFICULT TASK THE LORD HAS GIVEN YOU...
IT WILL BE AN HONOR TO HELP YOU.
BARUCH, SON OF NERIAH, WROTE DOWN THE WORDS JEREMIAH RECEIVED FROM GOD...
AND TOOK THE SCROLL TO THE TEMPLE.
SIRS...
THERE IS A MAN IN THE TEMPLE READING A SCROLL I THINK YOU SHOULD HEAR.

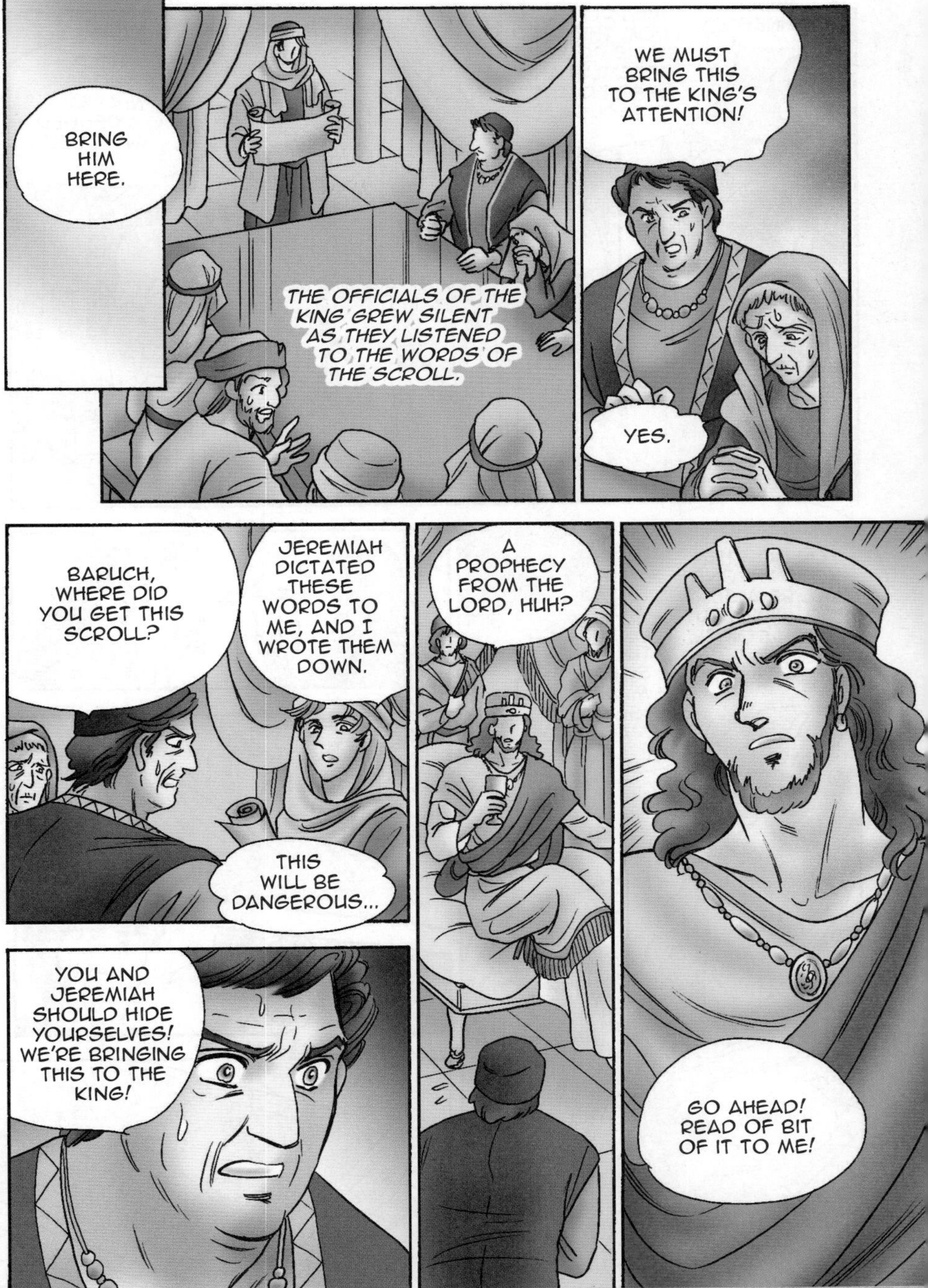
BRING HIM HERE.
THE OFFICIALS OF THE KING GREW SILENT AS THEY LISTENED TO THE WORDS OF THE SCROLL.
WE MUST BRING THIS TO THE KING'S ATTENTION!
YES.
BARUCH, WHERE DID YOU GET THIS SCROLL?
JEREMIAH DICTATED THESE WORDS TO ME, AND I WROTE THEM DOWN.
THIS WILL BE DANGEROUS...
YOU AND JEREMIAH SHOULD HIDE YOURSELVES! WE'RE BRINGING THIS TO THE KING!
A PROPHECY FROM THE LORD, HUH?
GO AHEAD! READ OF BIT OF IT TO ME!

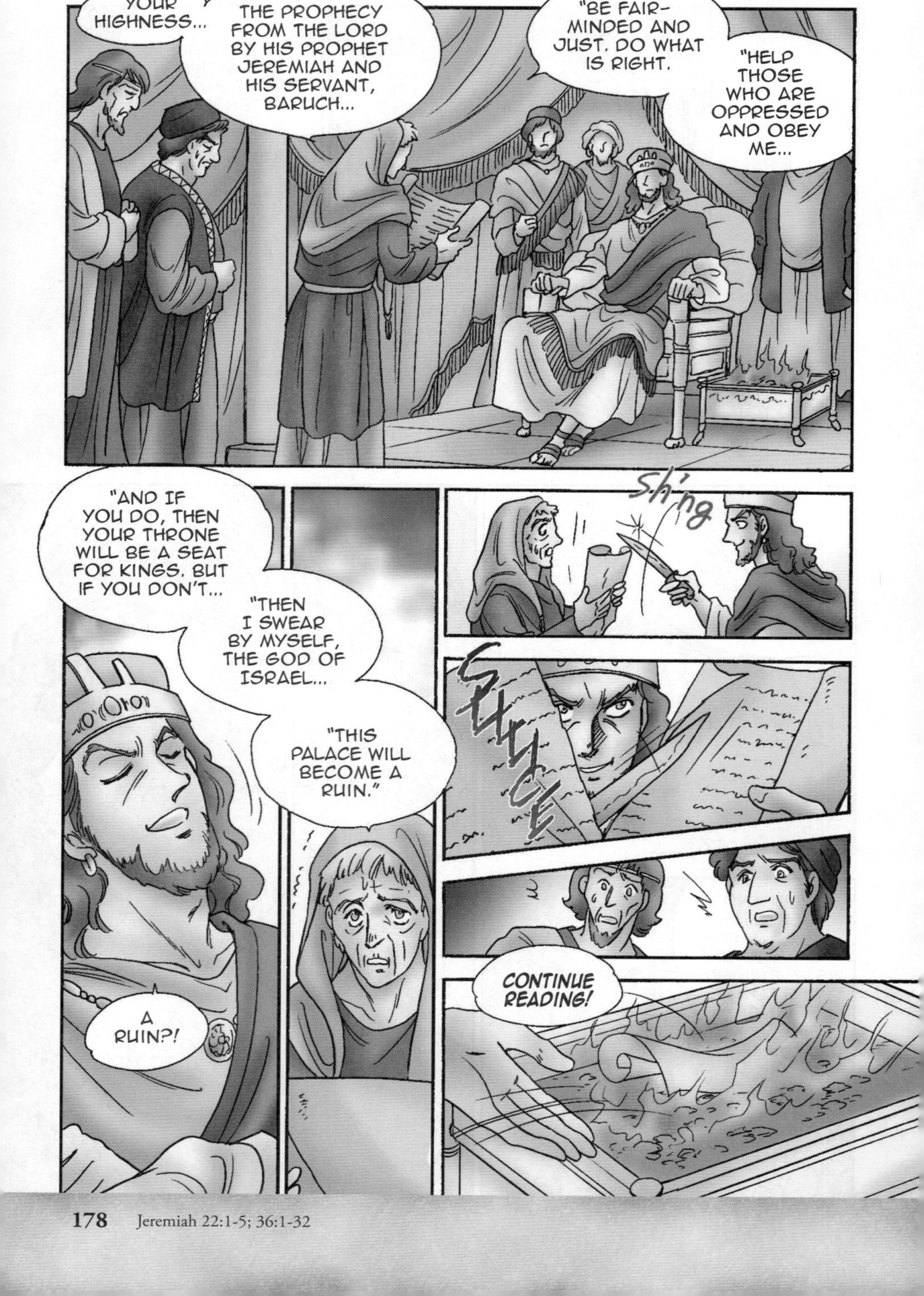
YOUR HIGHNESS...
THE PROPHECY FROM THE LORD BY HIS PROPHET JEREMIAH AND HIS SERVANT, BARUCH...
"BE FAIR-MINDED AND JUST. DO WHAT IS RIGHT.
"HELP THOSE WHO ARE OPPRESSED AND OBEY ME...
"AND IF YOU DO, THEN YOUR THRONE WILL BE A SEAT FOR KINGS. BUT IF YOU DON'T...
"THEN I SWEAR BY MYSELF, THE GOD OF ISRAEL...
"THIS PALACE WILL BECOME A RUIN."
A RUIN?!
Shing
SLICE
CONTINUE READING!

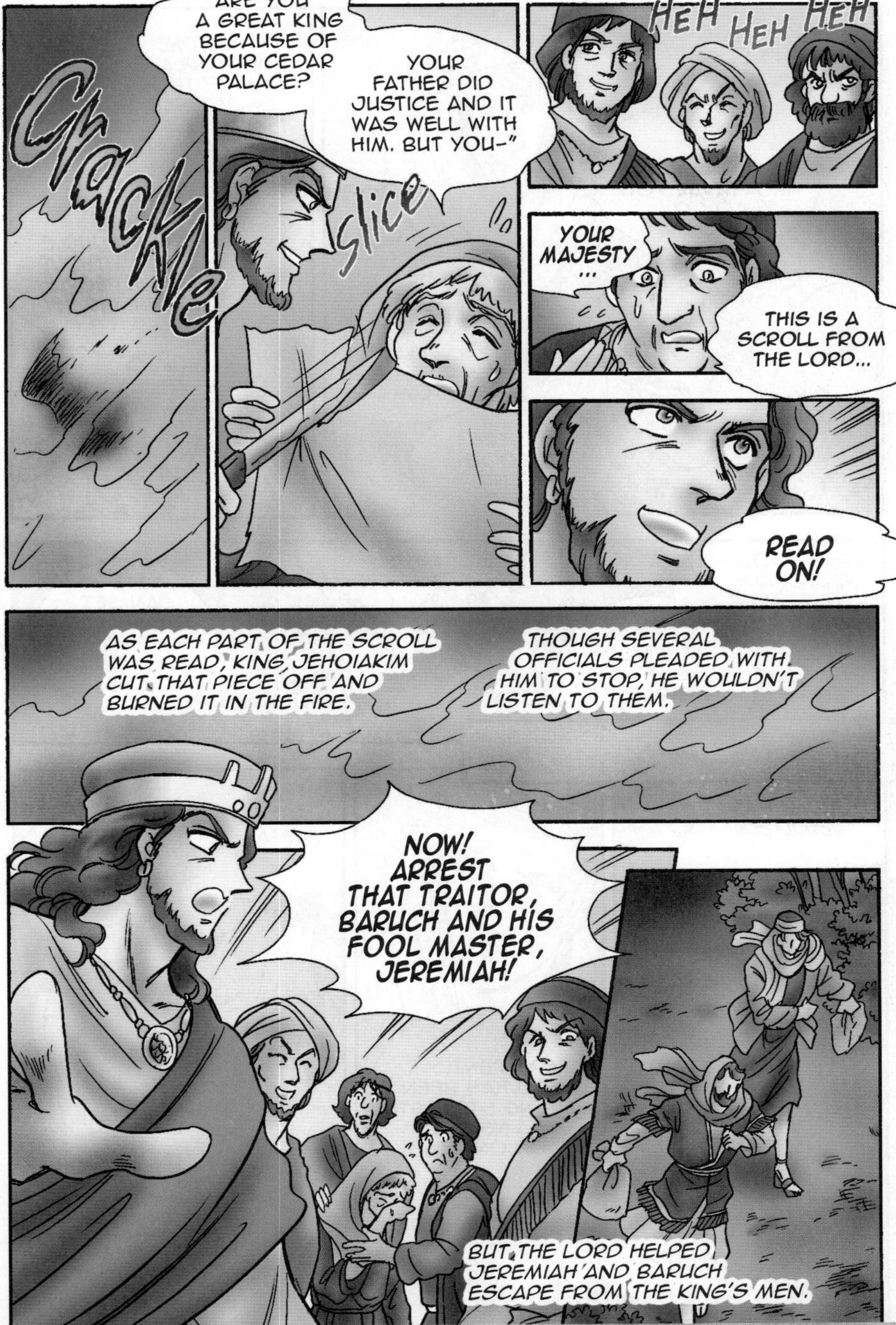
"ARE YOU A GREAT KING BECAUSE OF YOUR CEDAR PALACE?
YOUR FATHER DID JUSTICE AND IT WAS WELL WITH HIM. BUT YOU-"
Crackle
slice
HEH HEH HEH
YOUR MAJESTY ...
THIS IS A SCROLL FROM THE LORD...
READ ON!
AS EACH PART OF THE SCROLL WAS READ, KING JEHOIAKIM CUT THAT PIECE OFF AND BURNED IT IN THE FIRE.
THOUGH SEVERAL OFFICIALS PLEADED WITH HIM TO STOP, HE WOULDN'T LISTEN TO THEM.
NOW! ARREST THAT TRAITOR, BARUCH AND HIS FOOL MASTER, JEREMIAH!
BUT THE LORD HELPED JEREMIAH AND BARUCH ESCAPE FROM THE KING'S MEN.

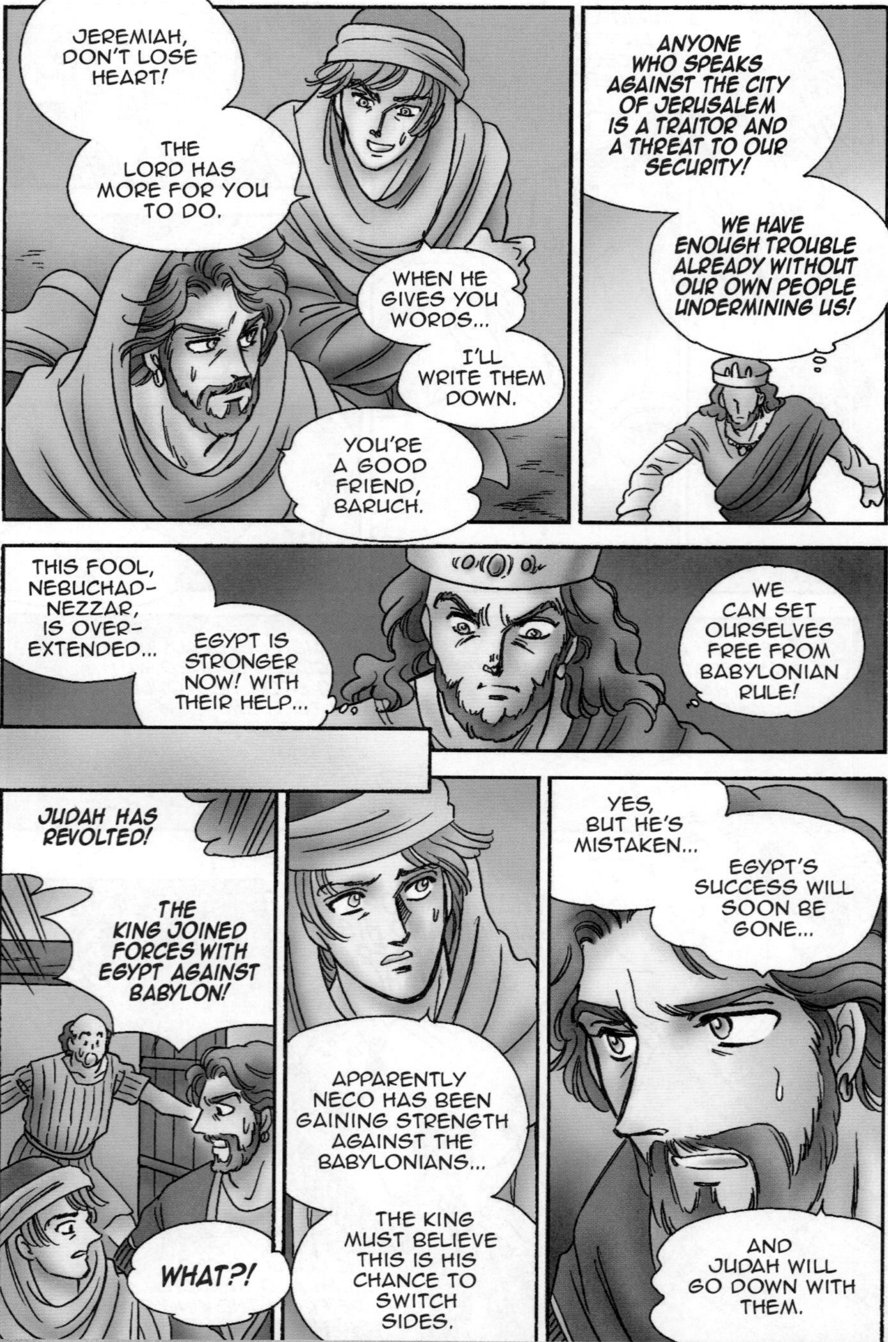
JEREMIAH, DON'T LOSE HEART!
THE LORD HAS MORE FOR YOU TO DO.
WHEN HE GIVES YOU WORDS...
I'LL WRITE THEM DOWN.
YOU'RE A GOOD FRIEND, BARUCH.
ANYONE WHO SPEAKS AGAINST THE CITY OF JERUSALEM IS A TRAITOR AND A THREAT TO OUR SECURITY!
WE HAVE ENOUGH TROUBLE ALREADY WITHOUT OUR OWN PEOPLE UNDERMINING US!
THIS FOOL, NEBUCHAD-NEZZAR, IS OVER-EXTENDED...
EGYPT IS STRONGER NOW! WITH THEIR HELP...
WE CAN SET OURSELVES FREE FROM BABYLONIAN RULE!
JUDAH HAS REVOLTED!
THE KING JOINED FORCES WITH EGYPT AGAINST BABYLON!
WHAT?!
APPARENTLY NECO HAS BEEN GAINING STRENGTH AGAINST THE BABYLONIANS...
THE KING MUST BELIEVE THIS IS HIS CHANCE TO SWITCH SIDES.
YES, BUT HE'S MISTAKEN...
EGYPT'S SUCCESS WILL SOON BE GONE...
AND JUDAH WILL GO DOWN WITH THEM.

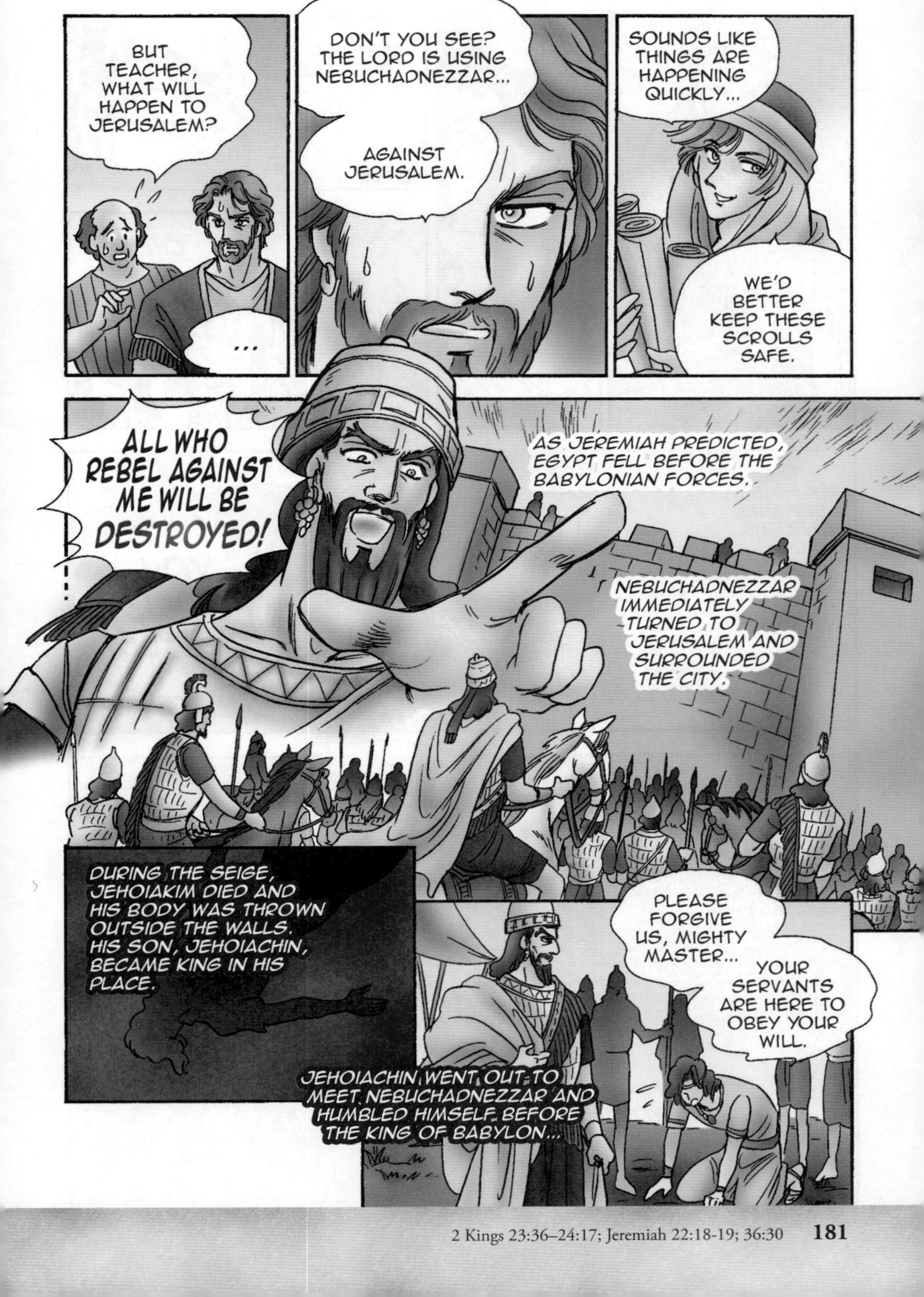

BUT TEACHER, WHAT WILL HAPPEN TO JERUSALEM?
...
DON'T YOU SEE? THE LORD IS USING NEBUCHADNEZZAR...
AGAINST JERUSALEM.
SOUNDS LIKE THINGS ARE HAPPENING QUICKLY...
WE'D BETTER KEEP THESE SCROLLS SAFE.
ALL WHO REBEL AGAINST ME WILL BE DESTROYED!
AS JEREMIAH PREDICTED, EGYPT FELL BEFORE THE BABYLONIAN FORCES.
NEBUCHADNEZZAR IMMEDIATELY TURNED TO JERUSALEM AND SURROUNDED THE CITY.
DURING THE SEIGE, JEHOIAKIM DIED AND HIS BODY WAS THROWN OUTSIDE THE WALLS. HIS SON, JEHOIACHIN, BECAME KING IN HIS PLACE.
PLEASE FORGIVE US, MIGHTY MASTER...
YOUR SERVANTS ARE HERE TO OBEY YOUR WILL.
JEHOIACHIN WENT OUT TO MEET NEBUCHADNEZZAR AND HUMBLED HIMSELF BEFORE THE KING OF BABYLON...

AHH!

I WON'T TRUST THE SON OF A TRAITOR.

CHAIN HIM!

SLINK

TAP TAP

TAKE HIS MOTHER, SERVANTS, OFFICIALS...

EVERYONE FROM THE PALACE...

AND BRING THEM TO BABYLON!

YOU FOOLISH REBELS!

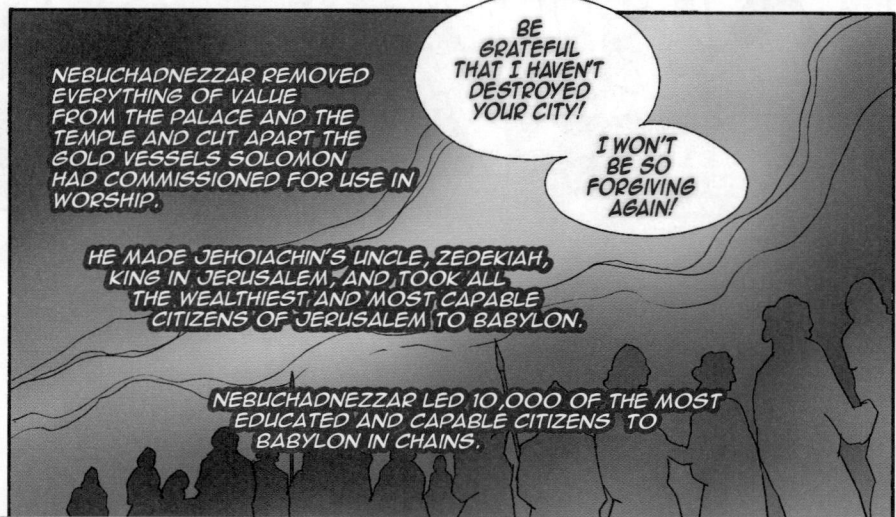

NEBUCHADNEZZAR REMOVED EVERYTHING OF VALUE FROM THE PALACE AND THE TEMPLE AND CUT APART THE GOLD VESSELS SOLOMON HAD COMMISSIONED FOR USE IN WORSHIP.

BE GRATEFUL THAT I HAVEN'T DESTROYED YOUR CITY!

I WON'T BE SO FORGIVING AGAIN!

HE MADE JEHOIACHIN'S UNCLE, ZEDEKIAH, KING IN JERUSALEM, AND TOOK ALL THE WEALTHIEST AND MOST CAPABLE CITIZENS OF JERUSALEM TO BABYLON.

NEBUCHADNEZZAR LED 10,000 OF THE MOST EDUCATED AND CAPABLE CITIZENS TO BABYLON IN CHAINS.

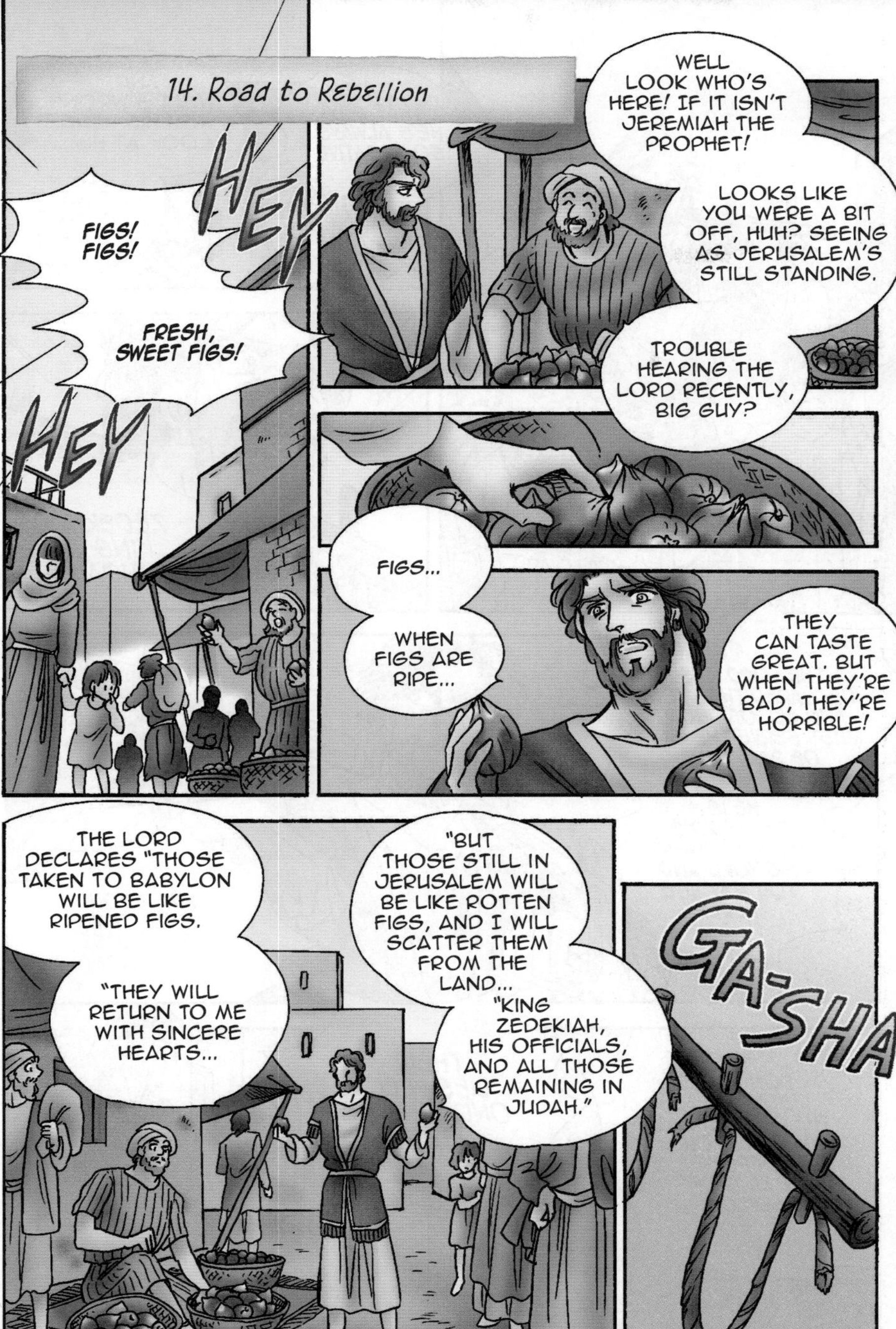
14. Road to Rebellion
HEY
FIGS! FIGS!
FRESH, SWEET FIGS!
HEY
WELL LOOK WHO'S HERE! IF IT ISN'T JEREMIAH THE PROPHET!
LOOKS LIKE YOU WERE A BIT OFF, HUH? SEEING AS JERUSALEM'S STILL STANDING.
TROUBLE HEARING THE LORD RECENTLY, BIG GUY?
FIGS...
WHEN FIGS ARE RIPE...
THEY CAN TASTE GREAT. BUT WHEN THEY'RE BAD, THEY'RE HORRIBLE!
THE LORD DECLARES "THOSE TAKEN TO BABYLON WILL BE LIKE RIPENED FIGS.
"THEY WILL RETURN TO ME WITH SINCERE HEARTS...
"BUT THOSE STILL IN JERUSALEM WILL BE LIKE ROTTEN FIGS, AND I WILL SCATTER THEM FROM THE LAND...
"KING ZEDEKIAH, HIS OFFICIALS, AND ALL THOSE REMAINING IN JUDAH."
GA-SHA

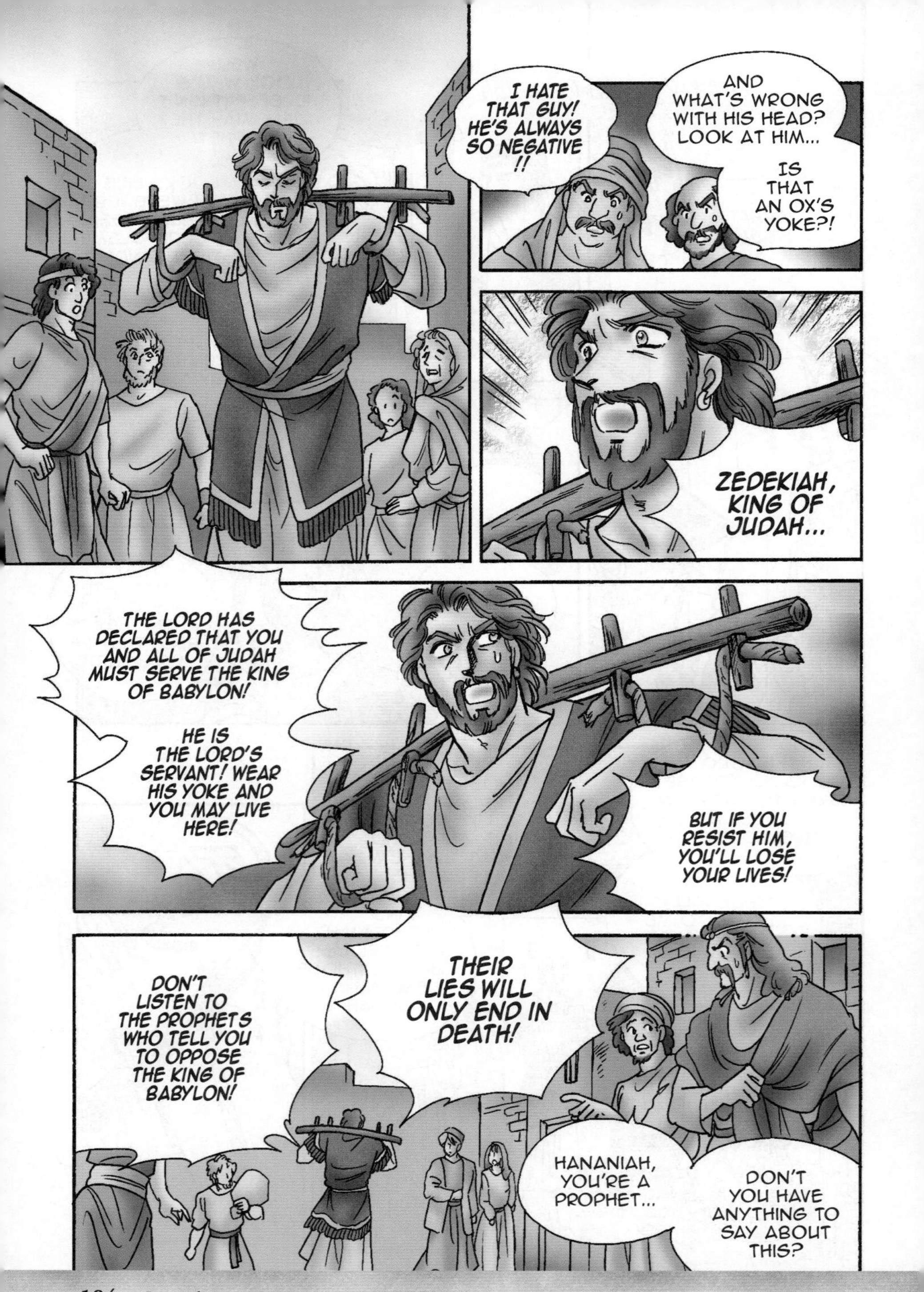
I HATE THAT GUY! HE'S ALWAYS SO NEGATIVE !!
AND WHAT'S WRONG WITH HIS HEAD? LOOK AT HIM...
IS THAT AN OX'S YOKE?!
ZEDEKIAH, KING OF JUDAH...
THE LORD HAS DECLARED THAT YOU AND ALL OF JUDAH MUST SERVE THE KING OF BABYLON!
HE IS THE LORD'S SERVANT! WEAR HIS YOKE AND YOU MAY LIVE HERE!
BUT IF YOU RESIST HIM, YOU'LL LOSE YOUR LIVES!
DON'T LISTEN TO THE PROPHETS WHO TELL YOU TO OPPOSE THE KING OF BABYLON!
THEIR LIES WILL ONLY END IN DEATH!
HANANIAH, YOU'RE A PROPHET...
DON'T YOU HAVE ANYTHING TO SAY ABOUT THIS?

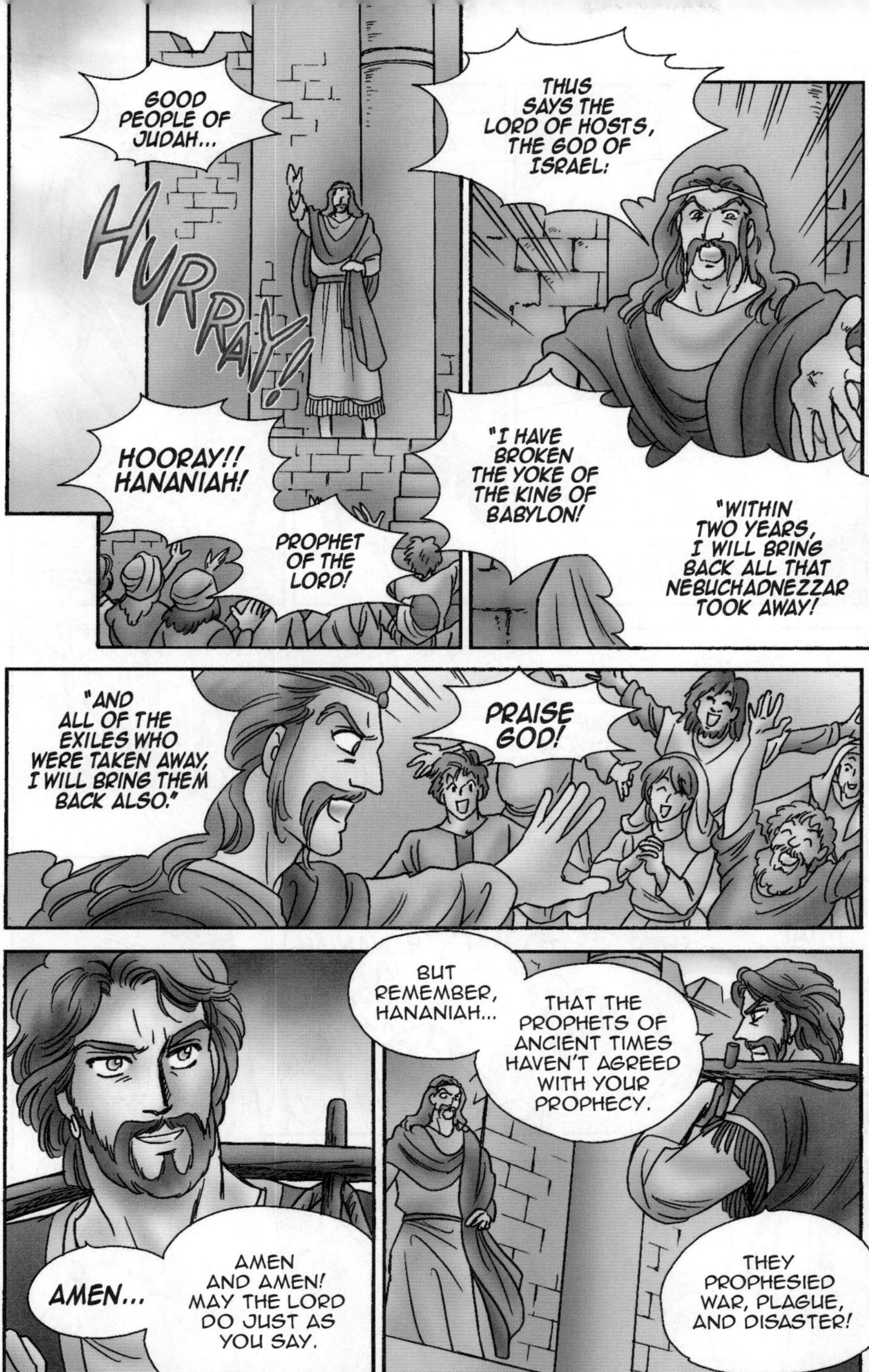
GOOD PEOPLE OF JUDAH...
HURRAY!
HOORAY!! HANANIAH!
PROPHET OF THE LORD!
THUS SAYS THE LORD OF HOSTS, THE GOD OF ISRAEL:
"I HAVE BROKEN THE YOKE OF THE KING OF BABYLON!
"WITHIN TWO YEARS, I WILL BRING BACK ALL THAT NEBUCHADNEZZAR TOOK AWAY!
"AND ALL OF THE EXILES WHO WERE TAKEN AWAY, I WILL BRING THEM BACK ALSO."
PRAISE GOD!
AMEN...
AMEN AND AMEN! MAY THE LORD DO JUST AS YOU SAY.
BUT REMEMBER, HANANIAH...
THAT THE PROPHETS OF ANCIENT TIMES HAVEN'T AGREED WITH YOUR PROPHECY.
THEY PROPHESIED WAR, PLAGUE, AND DISASTER!

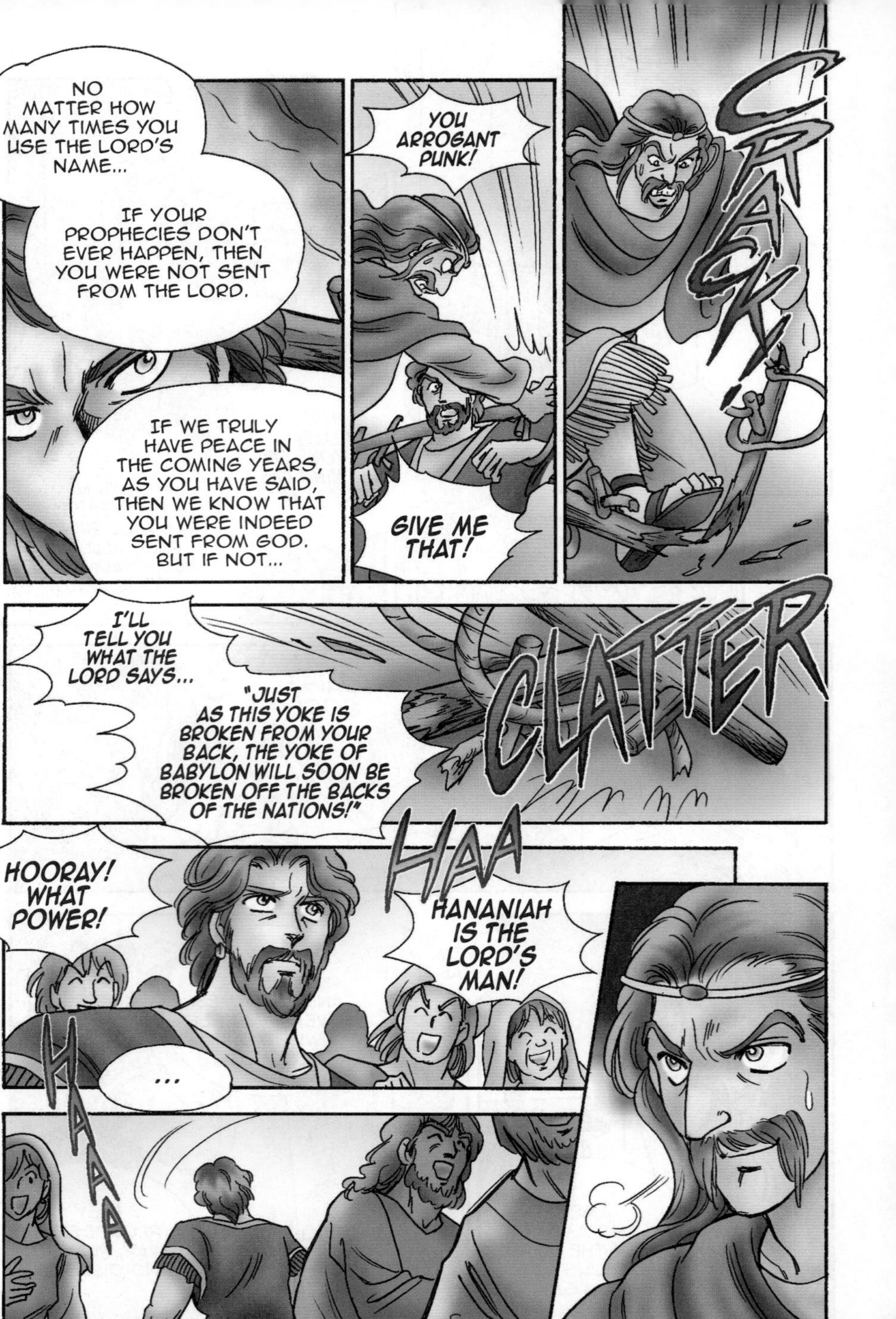
NO MATTER HOW MANY TIMES YOU USE THE LORD'S NAME...
IF YOUR PROPHECIES DON'T EVER HAPPEN, THEN YOU WERE NOT SENT FROM THE LORD.
IF WE TRULY HAVE PEACE IN THE COMING YEARS, AS YOU HAVE SAID, THEN WE KNOW THAT YOU WERE INDEED SENT FROM GOD. BUT IF NOT...
YOU ARROGANT PUNK!
GIVE ME THAT!
CRACK!
I'LL TELL YOU WHAT THE LORD SAYS...
"JUST AS THIS YOKE IS BROKEN FROM YOUR BACK, THE YOKE OF BABYLON WILL SOON BE BROKEN OFF THE BACKS OF THE NATIONS!"
CLATTER
HAA
HOORAY! WHAT POWER!
HANANIAH IS THE LORD'S MAN!
...
HAAAA

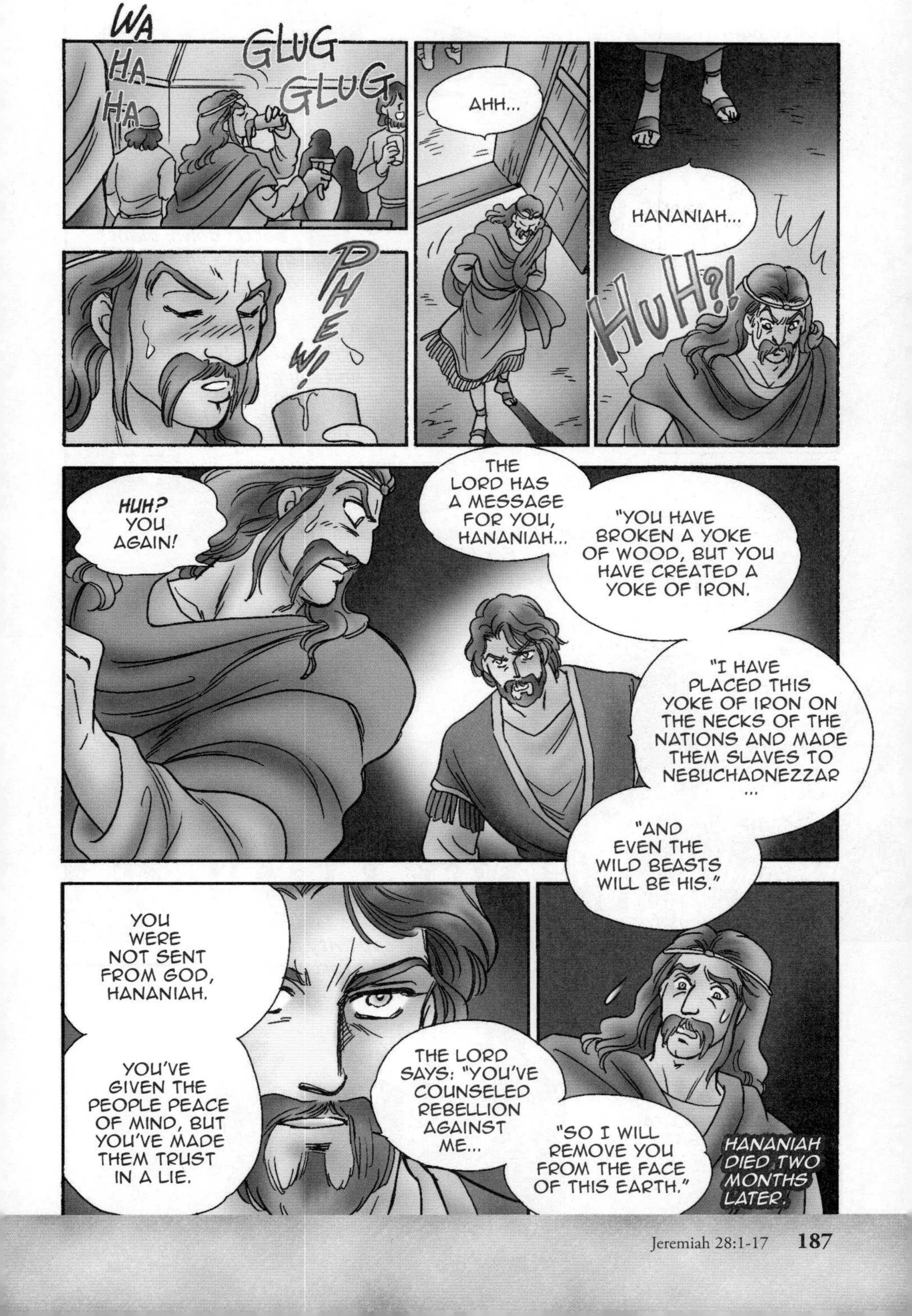
WA HA HA
GLUG GLUG
AHH...
HANANIAH...
PHEW!
HUH?!
HUH? YOU AGAIN!
THE LORD HAS A MESSAGE FOR YOU, HANANIAH...
"YOU HAVE BROKEN A YOKE OF WOOD, BUT YOU HAVE CREATED A YOKE OF IRON.
"I HAVE PLACED THIS YOKE OF IRON ON THE NECKS OF THE NATIONS AND MADE THEM SLAVES TO NEBUCHADNEZZAR ...
"AND EVEN THE WILD BEASTS WILL BE HIS."
YOU WERE NOT SENT FROM GOD, HANANIAH.
YOU'VE GIVEN THE PEOPLE PEACE OF MIND, BUT YOU'VE MADE THEM TRUST IN A LIE.
THE LORD SAYS: "YOU'VE COUNSELED REBELLION AGAINST ME...
"SO I WILL REMOVE YOU FROM THE FACE OF THIS EARTH."
HANANIAH DIED TWO MONTHS LATER.

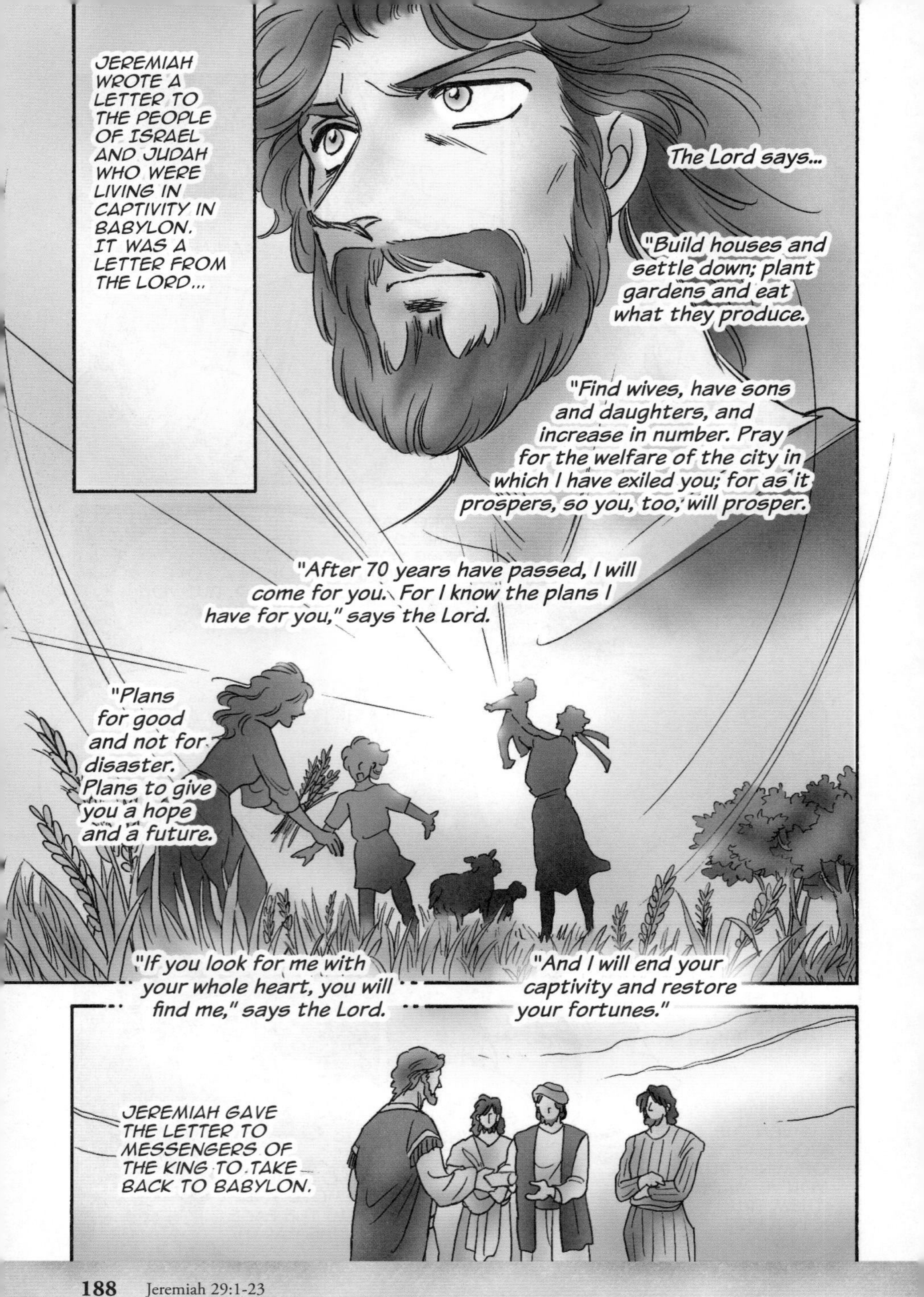

JEREMIAH WROTE A LETTER TO THE PEOPLE OF ISRAEL AND JUDAH WHO WERE LIVING IN CAPTIVITY IN BABYLON. IT WAS A LETTER FROM THE LORD...
The Lord says...
"Build houses and settle down; plant gardens and eat what they produce.
"Find wives, have sons and daughters, and increase in number. Pray for the welfare of the city in which I have exiled you; for as it prospers, so you, too, will prosper.
"After 70 years have passed, I will come for you. For I know the plans I have for you," says the Lord.
"Plans for good and not for disaster. Plans to give you a hope and a future.
"If you look for me with your whole heart, you will find me," says the Lord.
"And I will end your captivity and restore your fortunes."
JEREMIAH GAVE THE LETTER TO MESSENGERS OF THE KING TO TAKE BACK TO BABYLON.

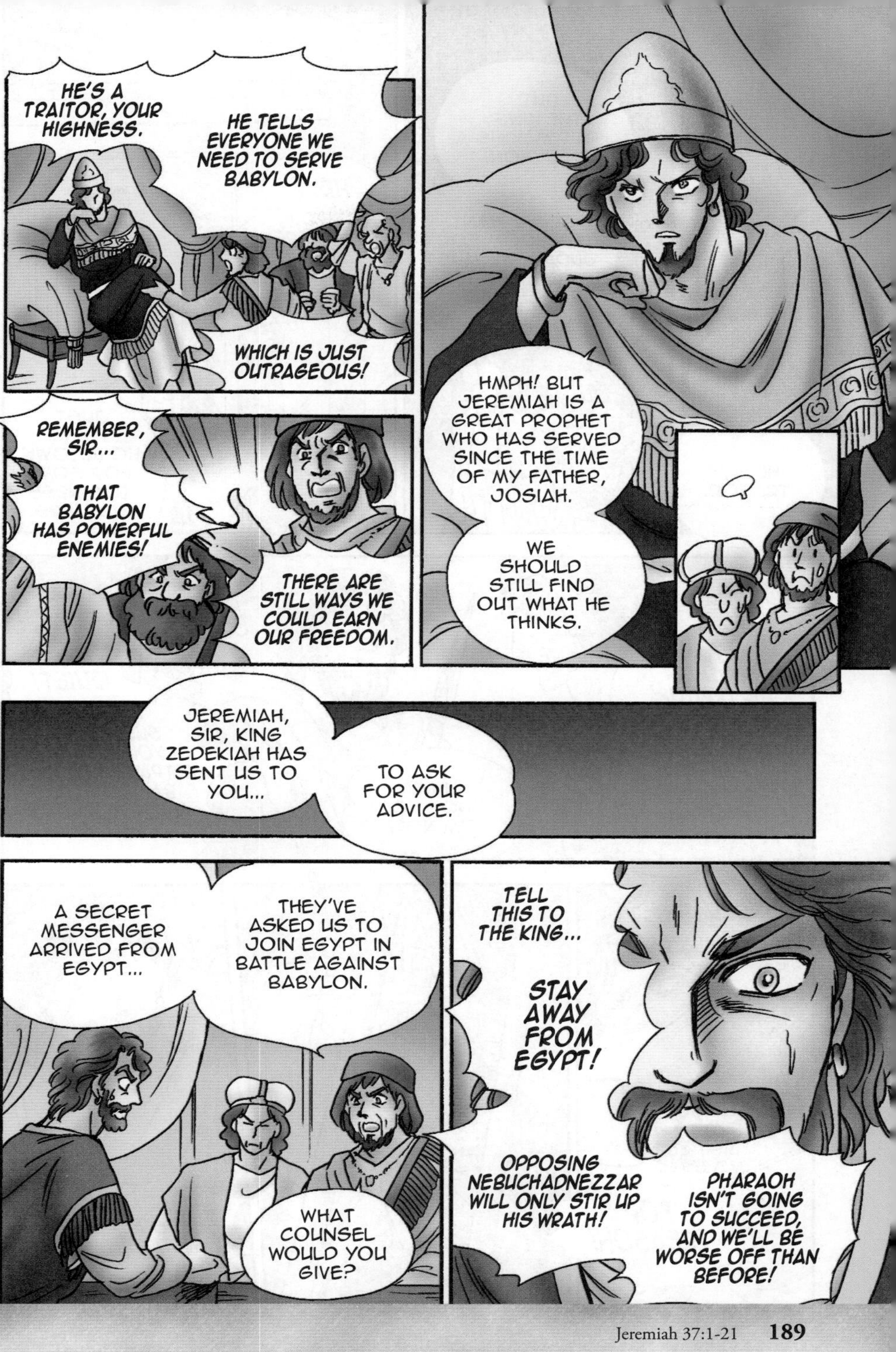
HE'S A TRAITOR, YOUR HIGHNESS.
HE TELLS EVERYONE WE NEED TO SERVE BABYLON.
WHICH IS JUST OUTRAGEOUS!
REMEMBER, SIR...
THAT BABYLON HAS POWERFUL ENEMIES!
THERE ARE STILL WAYS WE COULD EARN OUR FREEDOM.
HMPH! BUT JEREMIAH IS A GREAT PROPHET WHO HAS SERVED SINCE THE TIME OF MY FATHER, JOSIAH.
WE SHOULD STILL FIND OUT WHAT HE THINKS.
JEREMIAH, SIR, KING ZEDEKIAH HAS SENT US TO YOU...
TO ASK FOR YOUR ADVICE.
A SECRET MESSENGER ARRIVED FROM EGYPT...
THEY'VE ASKED US TO JOIN EGYPT IN BATTLE AGAINST BABYLON.
WHAT COUNSEL WOULD YOU GIVE?
TELL THIS TO THE KING...
STAY AWAY FROM EGYPT!
OPPOSING NEBUCHADNEZZAR WILL ONLY STIR UP HIS WRATH!
PHARAOH ISN'T GOING TO SUCCEED, AND WE'LL BE WORSE OFF THAN BEFORE!

SEVERAL DAYS LATER...

BUT THE KING ISN'T MAKING A DECISION.

IF WE WANT FREEDOM FOR JUDAH, WE MUST INCREASE THE PRESSURE.

AS I'VE SAID...

HE'S A TRAITOR.

HEY!

WHERE ARE YOU GOING?

ME? UH–

JUST TO MY HOMETOWN. FOR SOME BUSINESS MATTERS.

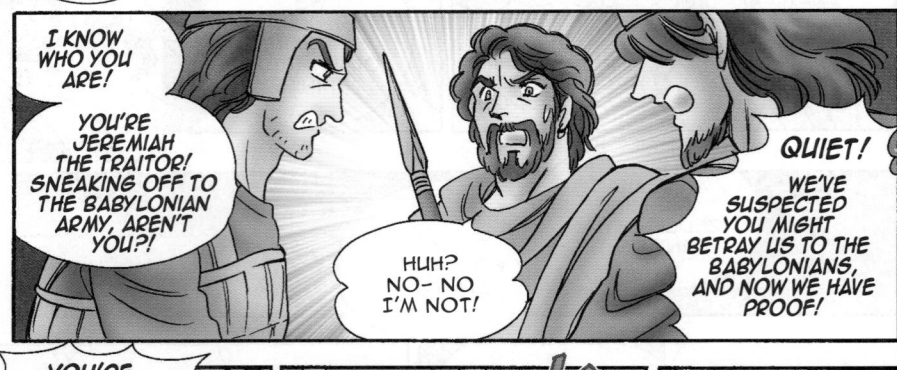

I KNOW WHO YOU ARE!

YOU'RE JEREMIAH THE TRAITOR! SNEAKING OFF TO THE BABYLONIAN ARMY, AREN'T YOU?!

HUH? NO– NO I'M NOT!

QUIET!

WE'VE SUSPECTED YOU MIGHT BETRAY US TO THE BABYLONIANS, AND NOW WE HAVE PROOF!

YOU'RE UNDER ARREST...

CLANK

SMACK

FOR TREASON!

NO– IT'S A MISTAKE!

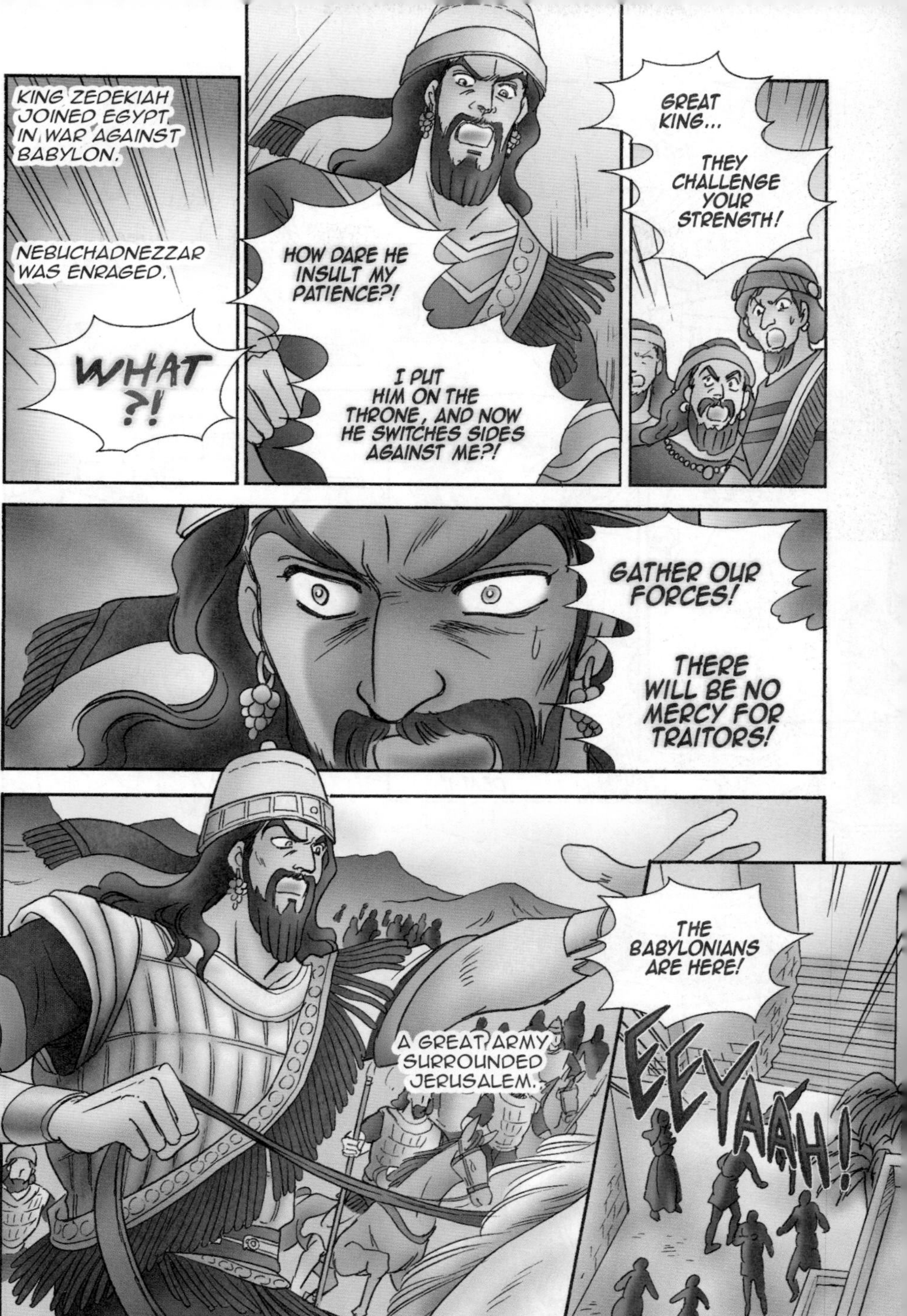

KING ZEDEKIAH JOINED EGYPT IN WAR AGAINST BABYLON.
NEBUCHADNEZZAR WAS ENRAGED.
WHAT ?!
HOW DARE HE INSULT MY PATIENCE?!
I PUT HIM ON THE THRONE, AND NOW HE SWITCHES SIDES AGAINST ME?!
GREAT KING...
THEY CHALLENGE YOUR STRENGTH!
GATHER OUR FORCES!
THERE WILL BE NO MERCY FOR TRAITORS!
THE BABYLONIANS ARE HERE!
A GREAT ARMY SURROUNDED JERUSALEM.
EEYAAH!

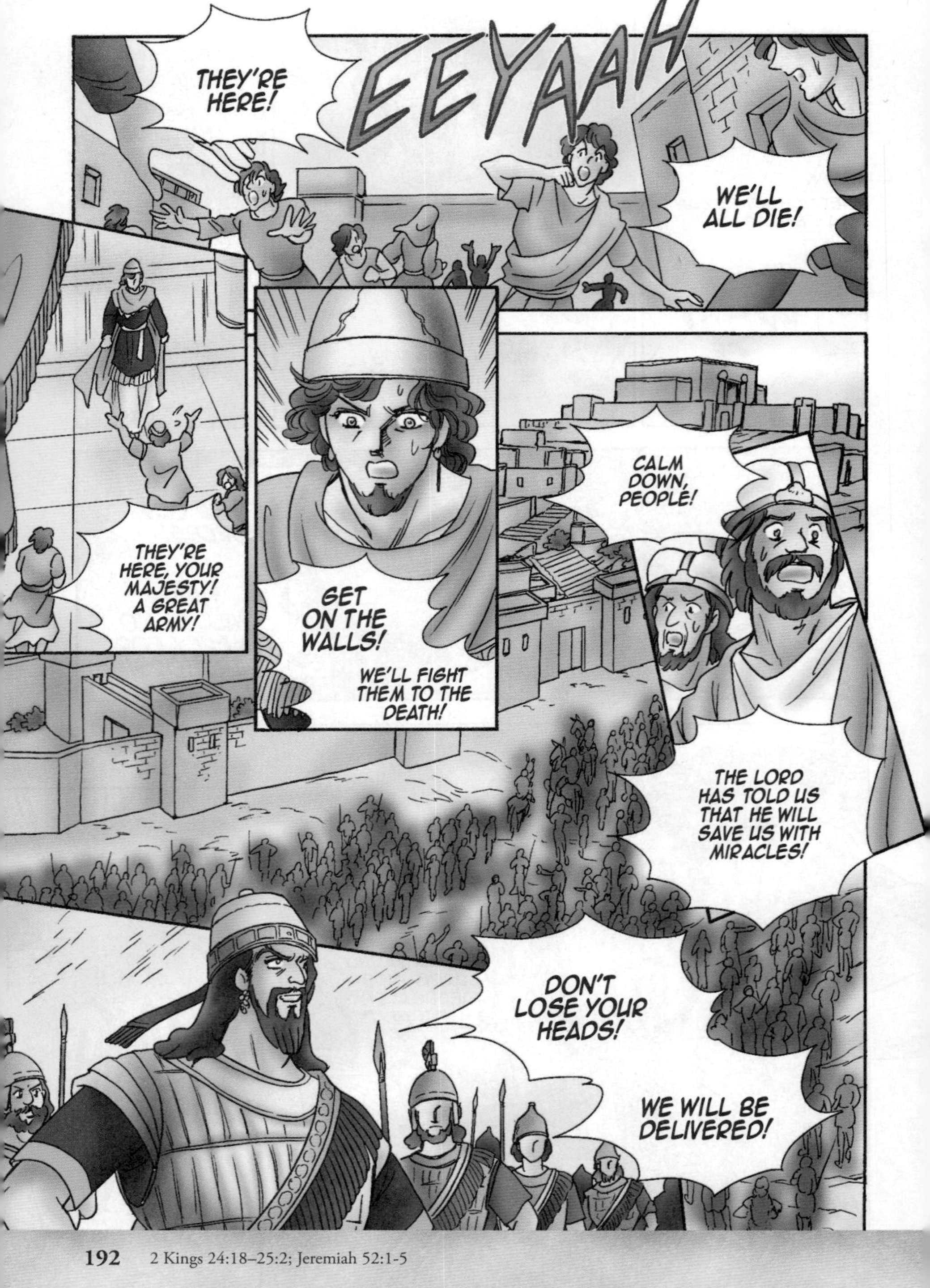
THEY'RE HERE!
EEYAAH
WE'LL ALL DIE!
THEY'RE HERE, YOUR MAJESTY! A GREAT ARMY!
GET ON THE WALLS!
WE'LL FIGHT THEM TO THE DEATH!
CALM DOWN, PEOPLE!
THE LORD HAS TOLD US THAT HE WILL SAVE US WITH MIRACLES!
DON'T LOSE YOUR HEADS!
WE WILL BE DELIVERED!

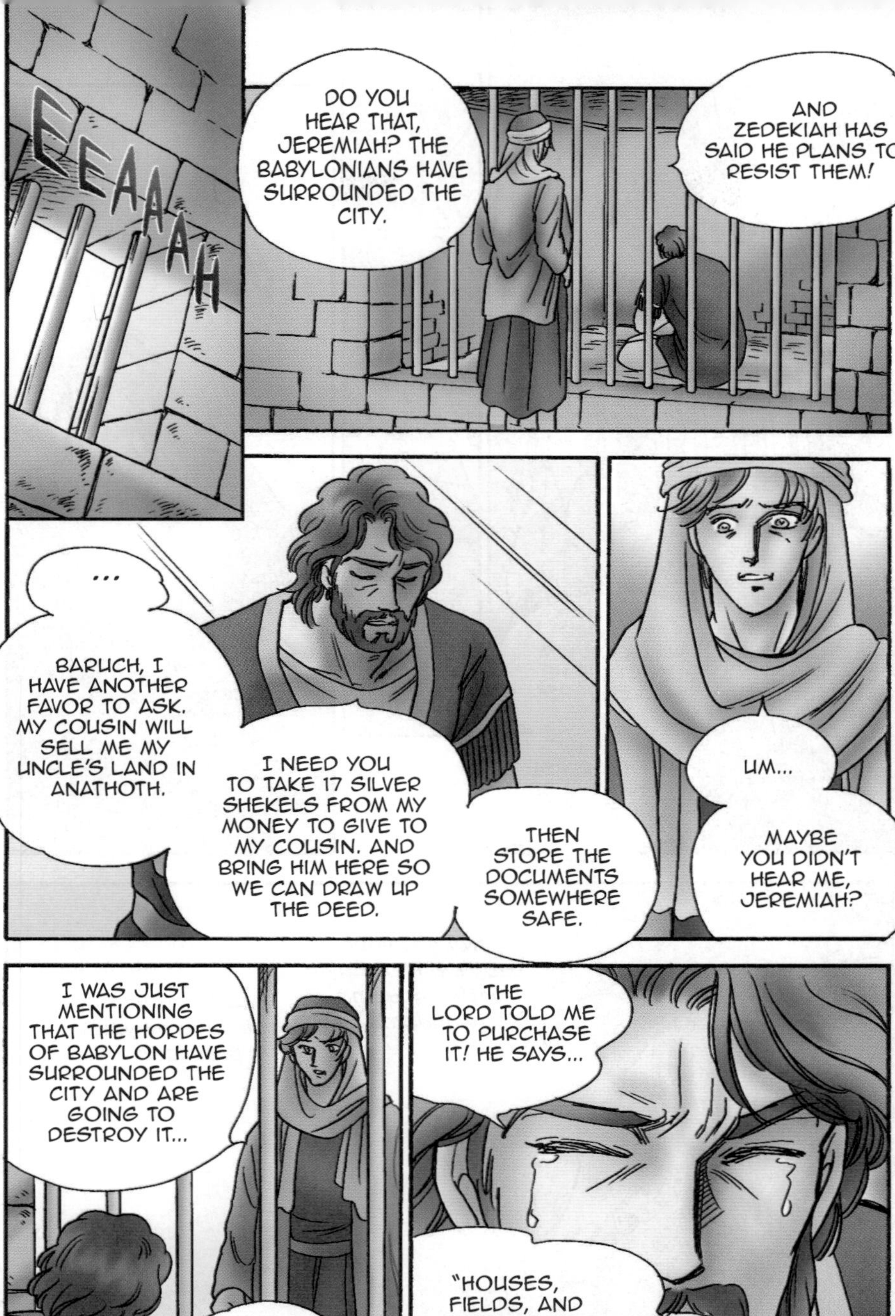
EEAAAAH
DO YOU HEAR THAT, JEREMIAH? THE BABYLONIANS HAVE SURROUNDED THE CITY.
AND ZEDEKIAH HAS SAID HE PLANS TO RESIST THEM!
...
BARUCH, I HAVE ANOTHER FAVOR TO ASK. MY COUSIN WILL SELL ME MY UNCLE'S LAND IN ANATHOTH.
I NEED YOU TO TAKE 17 SILVER SHEKELS FROM MY MONEY TO GIVE TO MY COUSIN. AND BRING HIM HERE SO WE CAN DRAW UP THE DEED.
THEN STORE THE DOCUMENTS SOMEWHERE SAFE.
UM...
MAYBE YOU DIDN'T HEAR ME, JEREMIAH?
I WAS JUST MENTIONING THAT THE HORDES OF BABYLON HAVE SURROUNDED THE CITY AND ARE GOING TO DESTROY IT...
YES, BARUCH....
THE LORD TOLD ME TO PURCHASE IT! HE SAYS...
"HOUSES, FIELDS, AND VINEYARDS WILL ONCE AGAIN BE BOUGHT IN THIS LAND!"

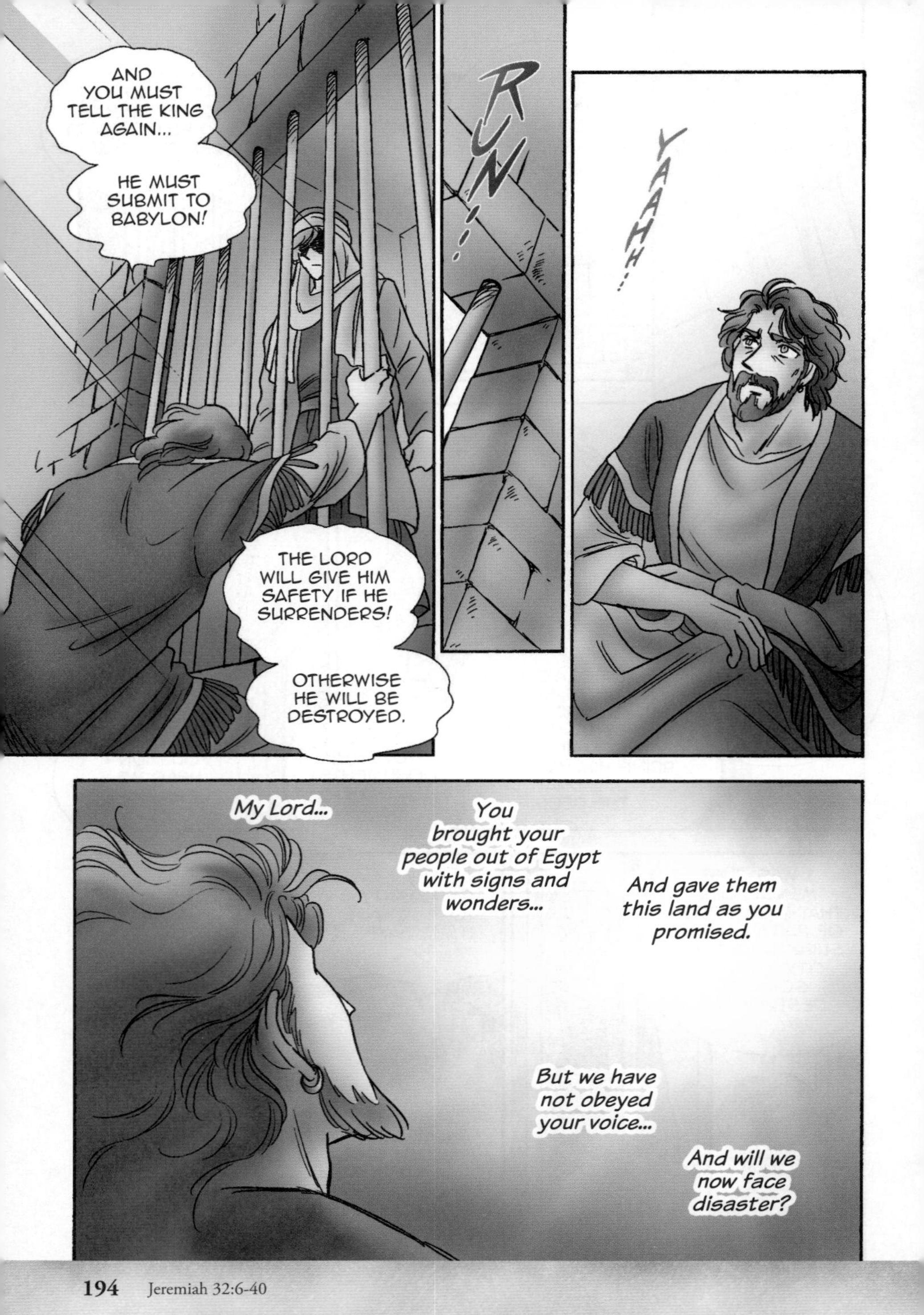
AND YOU MUST TELL THE KING AGAIN...
HE MUST SUBMIT TO BABYLON!
THE LORD WILL GIVE HIM SAFETY IF HE SURRENDERS!
OTHERWISE HE WILL BE DESTROYED.
RUN...!
YAAHH!
My Lord...
You brought your people out of Egypt with signs and wonders...
And gave them this land as you promised.
But we have not obeyed your voice...
And will we now face disaster?

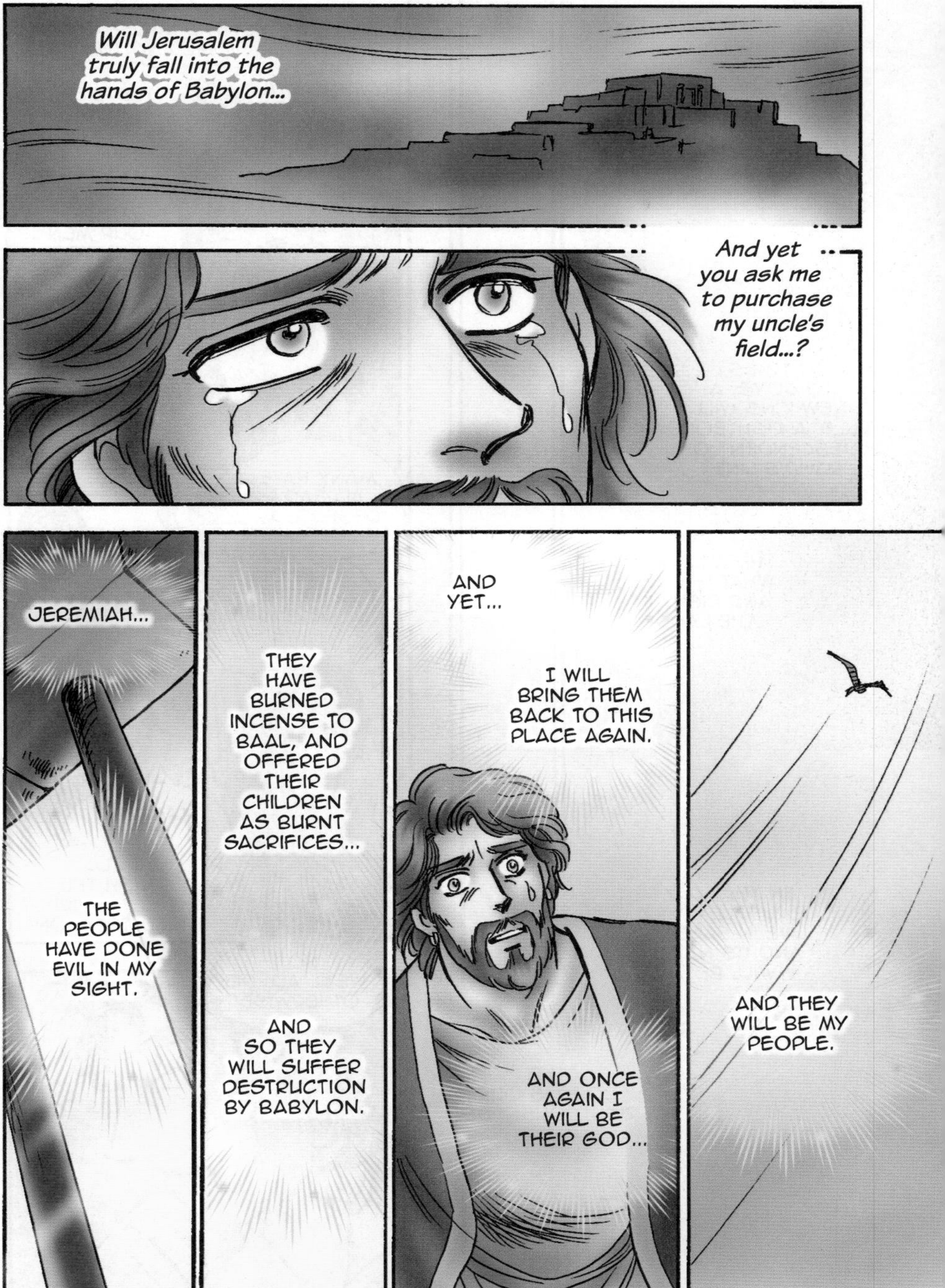
Will Jerusalem truly fall into the hands of Babylon...
And yet you ask me to purchase my uncle's field...?
JEREMIAH...
THE PEOPLE HAVE DONE EVIL IN MY SIGHT.
THEY HAVE BURNED INCENSE TO BAAL, AND OFFERED THEIR CHILDREN AS BURNT SACRIFICES...
AND SO THEY WILL SUFFER DESTRUCTION BY BABYLON.
AND YET...
I WILL BRING THEM BACK TO THIS PLACE AGAIN.
AND ONCE AGAIN I WILL BE THEIR GOD...
AND THEY WILL BE MY PEOPLE.

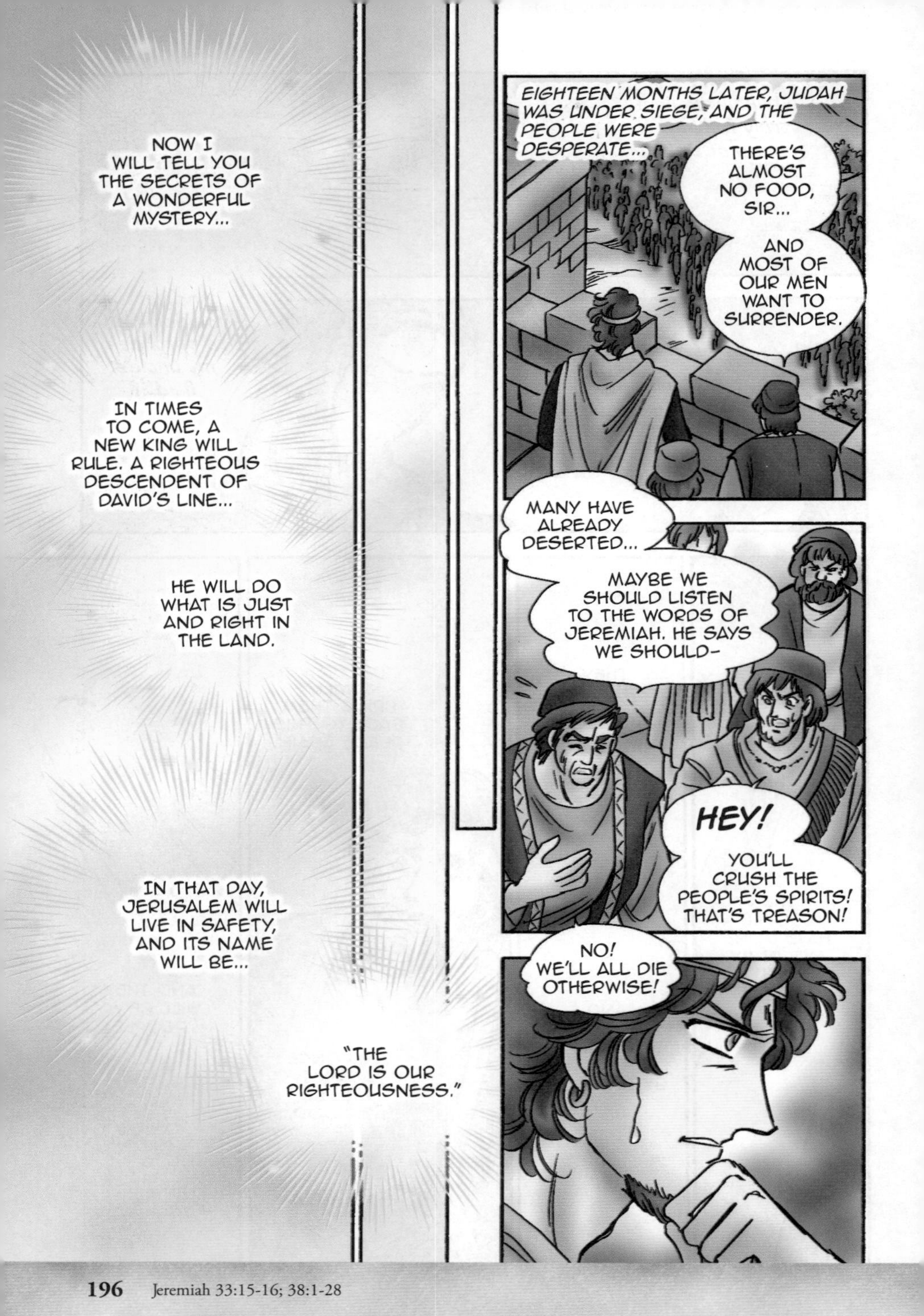
NOW I WILL TELL YOU THE SECRETS OF A WONDERFUL MYSTERY...
IN TIMES TO COME, A NEW KING WILL RULE. A RIGHTEOUS DESCENDENT OF DAVID'S LINE...
HE WILL DO WHAT IS JUST AND RIGHT IN THE LAND.
IN THAT DAY, JERUSALEM WILL LIVE IN SAFETY, AND ITS NAME WILL BE...
"THE LORD IS OUR RIGHTEOUSNESS."
EIGHTEEN MONTHS LATER, JUDAH WAS UNDER SIEGE, AND THE PEOPLE WERE DESPERATE...
THERE'S ALMOST NO FOOD, SIR...
AND MOST OF OUR MEN WANT TO SURRENDER.
MANY HAVE ALREADY DESERTED...
MAYBE WE SHOULD LISTEN TO THE WORDS OF JEREMIAH. HE SAYS WE SHOULD-
HEY!
YOU'LL CRUSH THE PEOPLE'S SPIRITS! THAT'S TREASON!
NO! WE'LL ALL DIE OTHERWISE!

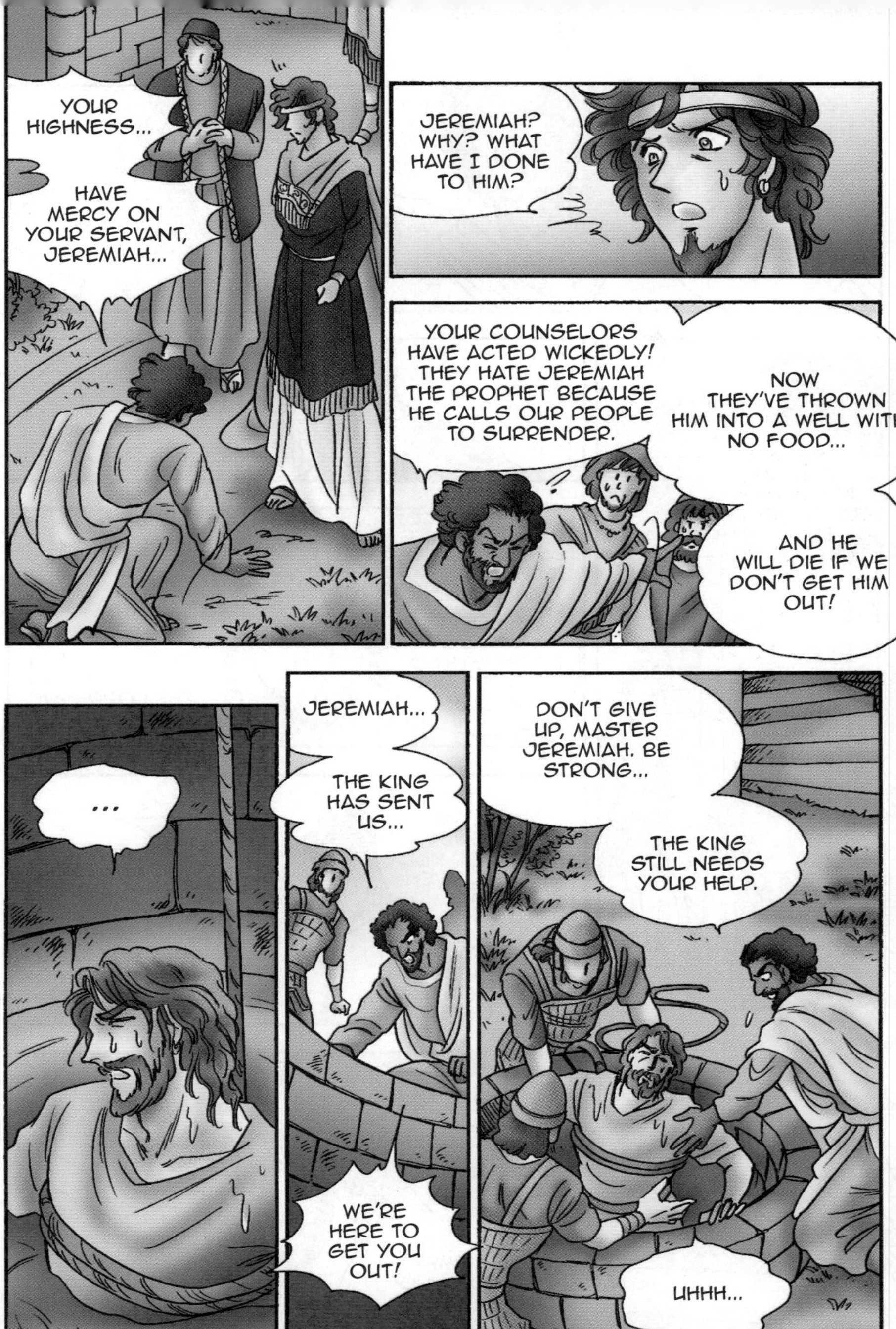
YOUR HIGHNESS...
HAVE MERCY ON YOUR SERVANT, JEREMIAH...
JEREMIAH? WHY? WHAT HAVE I DONE TO HIM?
YOUR COUNSELORS HAVE ACTED WICKEDLY! THEY HATE JEREMIAH THE PROPHET BECAUSE HE CALLS OUR PEOPLE TO SURRENDER.
NOW THEY'VE THROWN HIM INTO A WELL WITH NO FOOD...
AND HE WILL DIE IF WE DON'T GET HIM OUT!
...
JEREMIAH...
THE KING HAS SENT US...
WE'RE HERE TO GET YOU OUT!
DON'T GIVE UP, MASTER JEREMIAH. BE STRONG...
THE KING STILL NEEDS YOUR HELP.
UHHH...

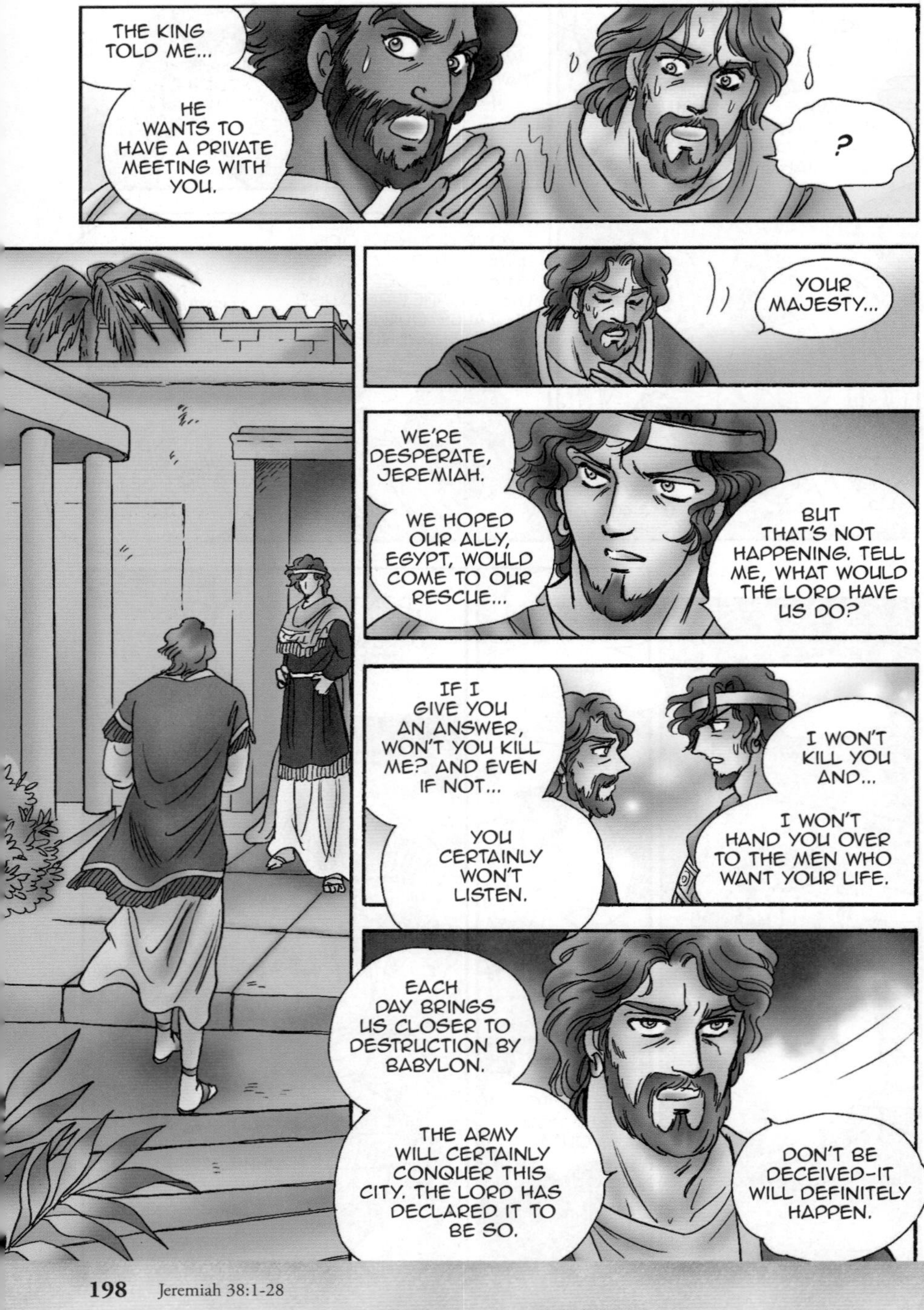
THE KING TOLD ME...
HE WANTS TO HAVE A PRIVATE MEETING WITH YOU.
?
YOUR MAJESTY...
WE'RE DESPERATE, JEREMIAH.
WE HOPED OUR ALLY, EGYPT, WOULD COME TO OUR RESCUE...
BUT THAT'S NOT HAPPENING. TELL ME, WHAT WOULD THE LORD HAVE US DO?
IF I GIVE YOU AN ANSWER, WON'T YOU KILL ME? AND EVEN IF NOT...
YOU CERTAINLY WON'T LISTEN.
I WON'T KILL YOU AND...
I WON'T HAND YOU OVER TO THE MEN WHO WANT YOUR LIFE.
EACH DAY BRINGS US CLOSER TO DESTRUCTION BY BABYLON.
THE ARMY WILL CERTAINLY CONQUER THIS CITY. THE LORD HAS DECLARED IT TO BE SO.
DON'T BE DECEIVED–IT WILL DEFINITELY HAPPEN.

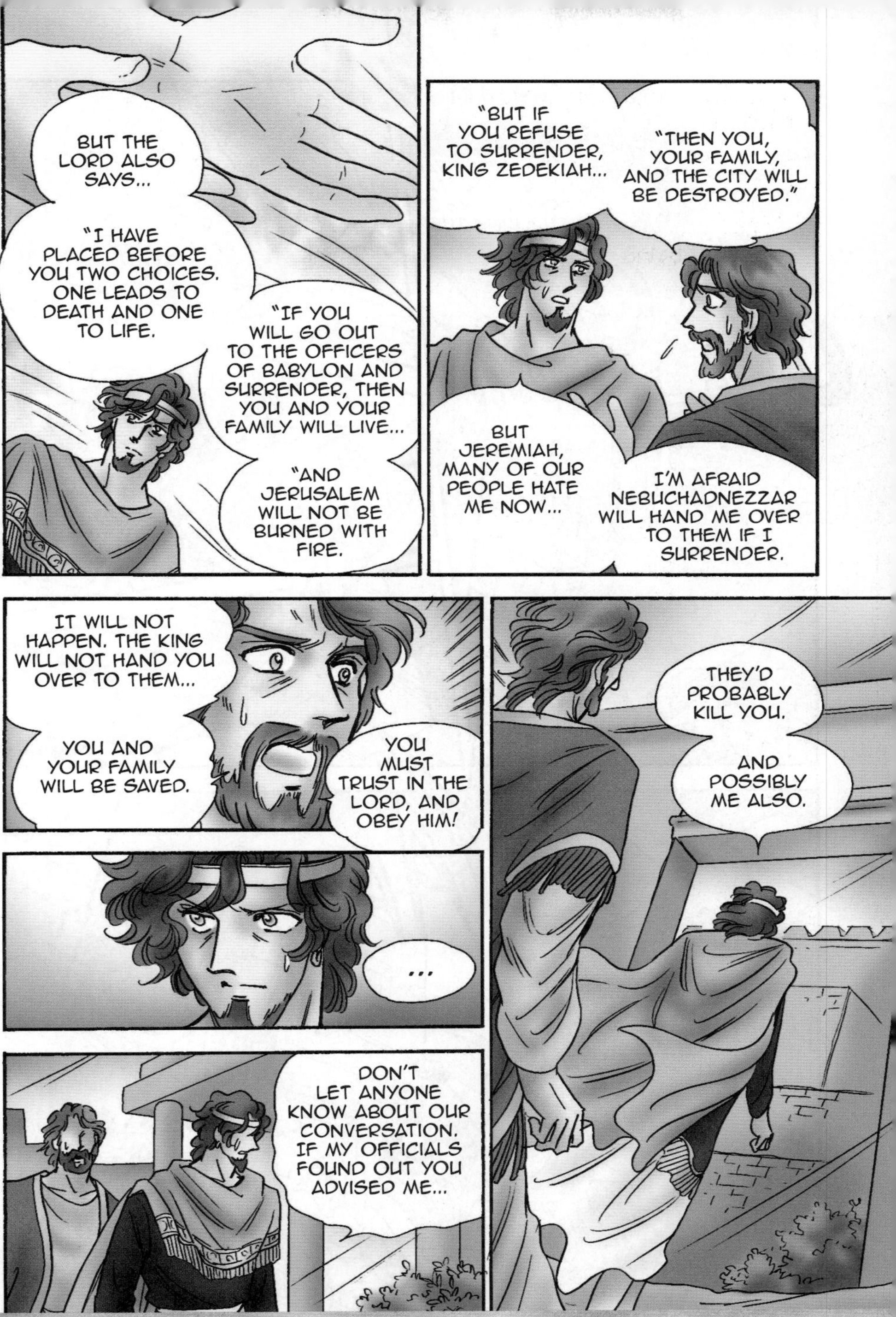
BUT THE LORD ALSO SAYS...
"I HAVE PLACED BEFORE YOU TWO CHOICES. ONE LEADS TO DEATH AND ONE TO LIFE.
"IF YOU WILL GO OUT TO THE OFFICERS OF BABYLON AND SURRENDER, THEN YOU AND YOUR FAMILY WILL LIVE...
"AND JERUSALEM WILL NOT BE BURNED WITH FIRE.
"BUT IF YOU REFUSE TO SURRENDER, KING ZEDEKIAH...
"THEN YOU, YOUR FAMILY, AND THE CITY WILL BE DESTROYED."
BUT JEREMIAH, MANY OF OUR PEOPLE HATE ME NOW...
I'M AFRAID NEBUCHADNEZZAR WILL HAND ME OVER TO THEM IF I SURRENDER.
IT WILL NOT HAPPEN. THE KING WILL NOT HAND YOU OVER TO THEM...
YOU AND YOUR FAMILY WILL BE SAVED.
YOU MUST TRUST IN THE LORD, AND OBEY HIM!
...
DON'T LET ANYONE KNOW ABOUT OUR CONVERSATION. IF MY OFFICIALS FOUND OUT YOU ADVISED ME...
THEY'D PROBABLY KILL YOU.
AND POSSIBLY ME ALSO.

15. The Fall of Jerusalem

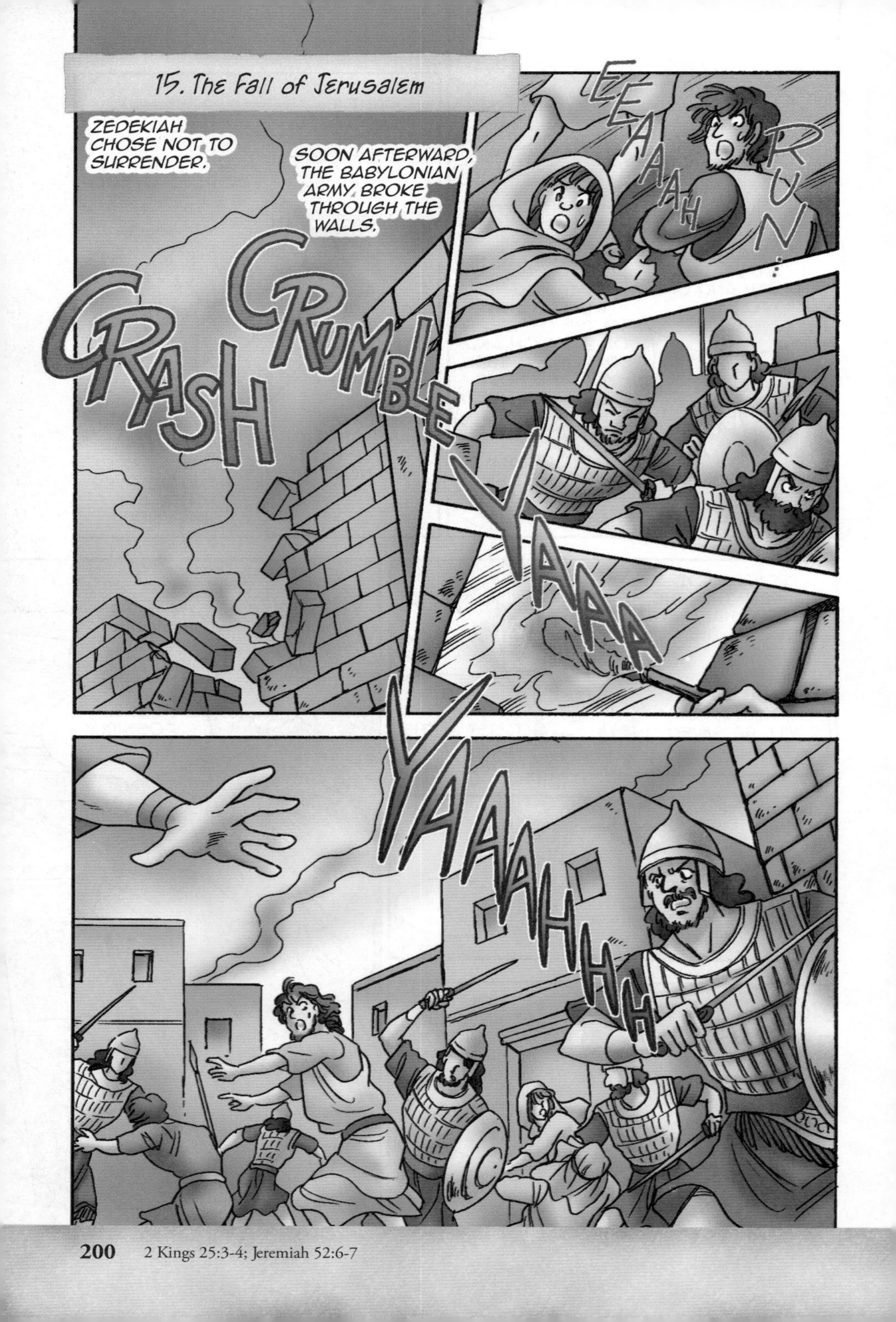
ZEDEKIAH CHOSE NOT TO SURRENDER.
SOON AFTERWARD, THE BABYLONIAN ARMY BROKE THROUGH THE WALLS.
EEAAAAH
RUN!
CRASH
CRUMBLE
YAAAA
YAAAAHHHH

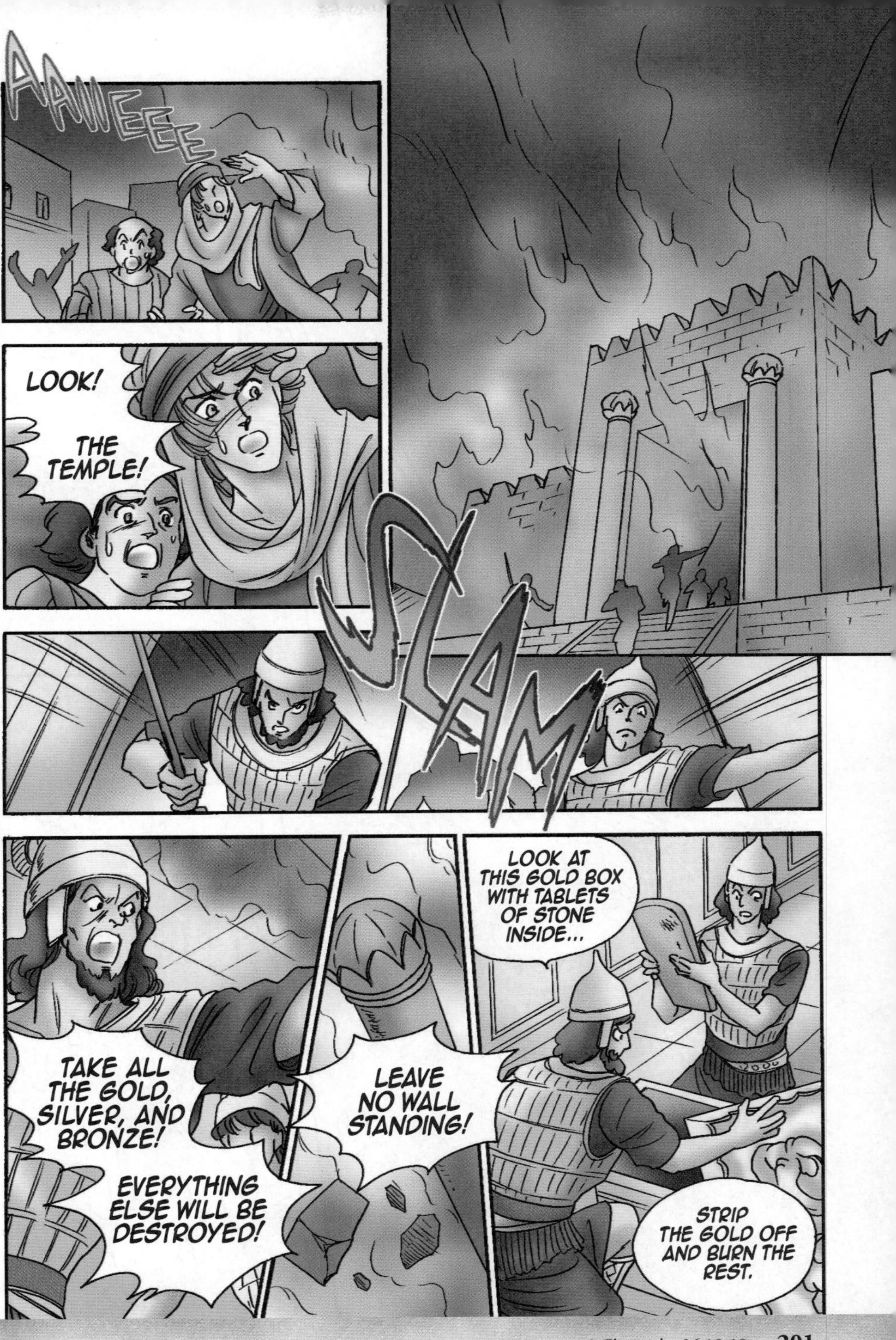
AAIIEEEE
LOOK!
THE TEMPLE!
SLAM
TAKE ALL THE GOLD, SILVER, AND BRONZE!
EVERYTHING ELSE WILL BE DESTROYED!
LEAVE NO WALL STANDING!
LOOK AT THIS GOLD BOX WITH TABLETS OF STONE INSIDE...
STRIP THE GOLD OFF AND BURN THE REST.

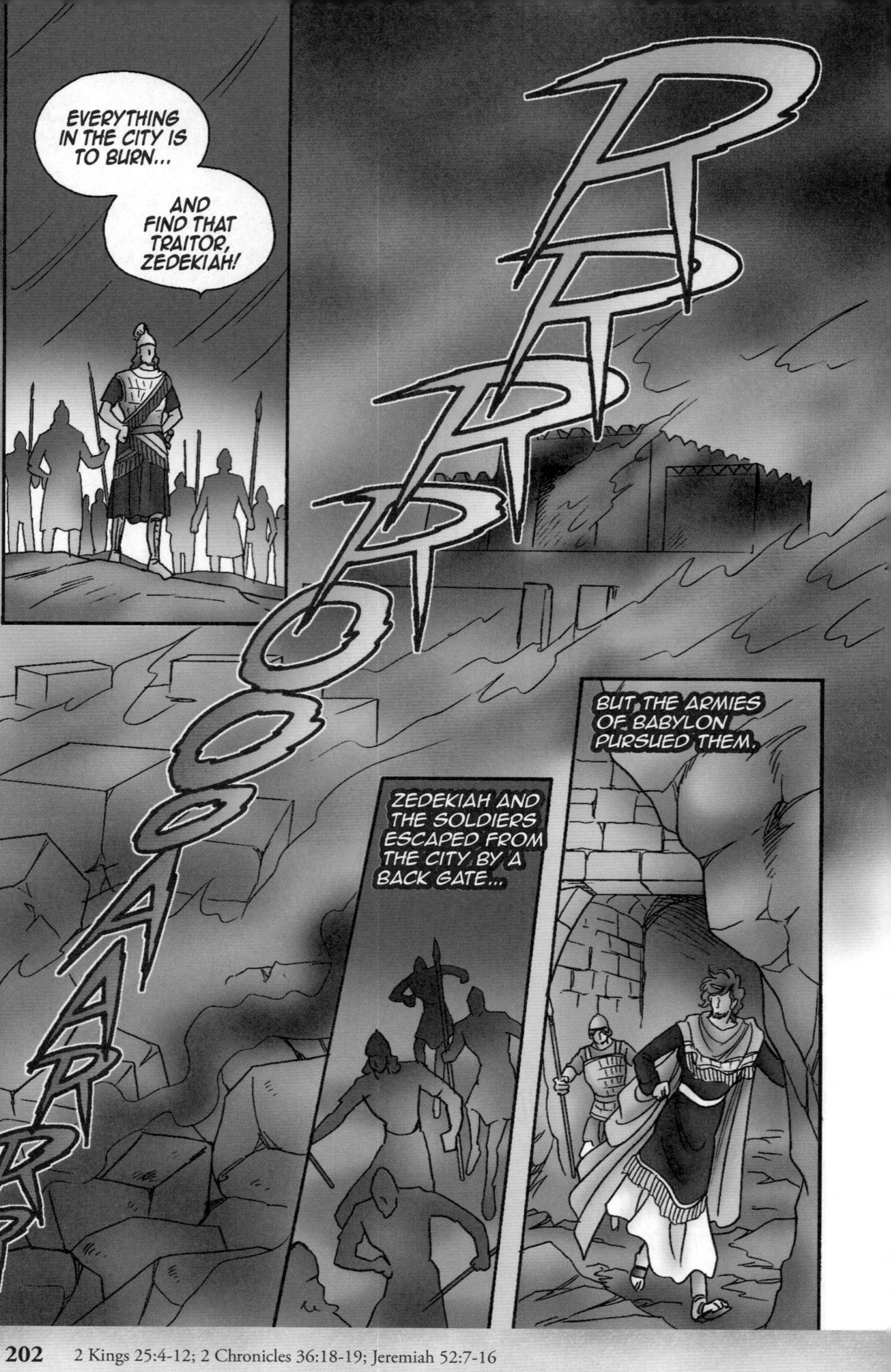
EVERYTHING IN THE CITY IS TO BURN...
AND FIND THAT TRAITOR, ZEDEKIAH!
ZEDEKIAH AND THE SOLDIERS ESCAPED FROM THE CITY BY A BACK GATE...
BUT THE ARMIES OF BABYLON PURSUED THEM.

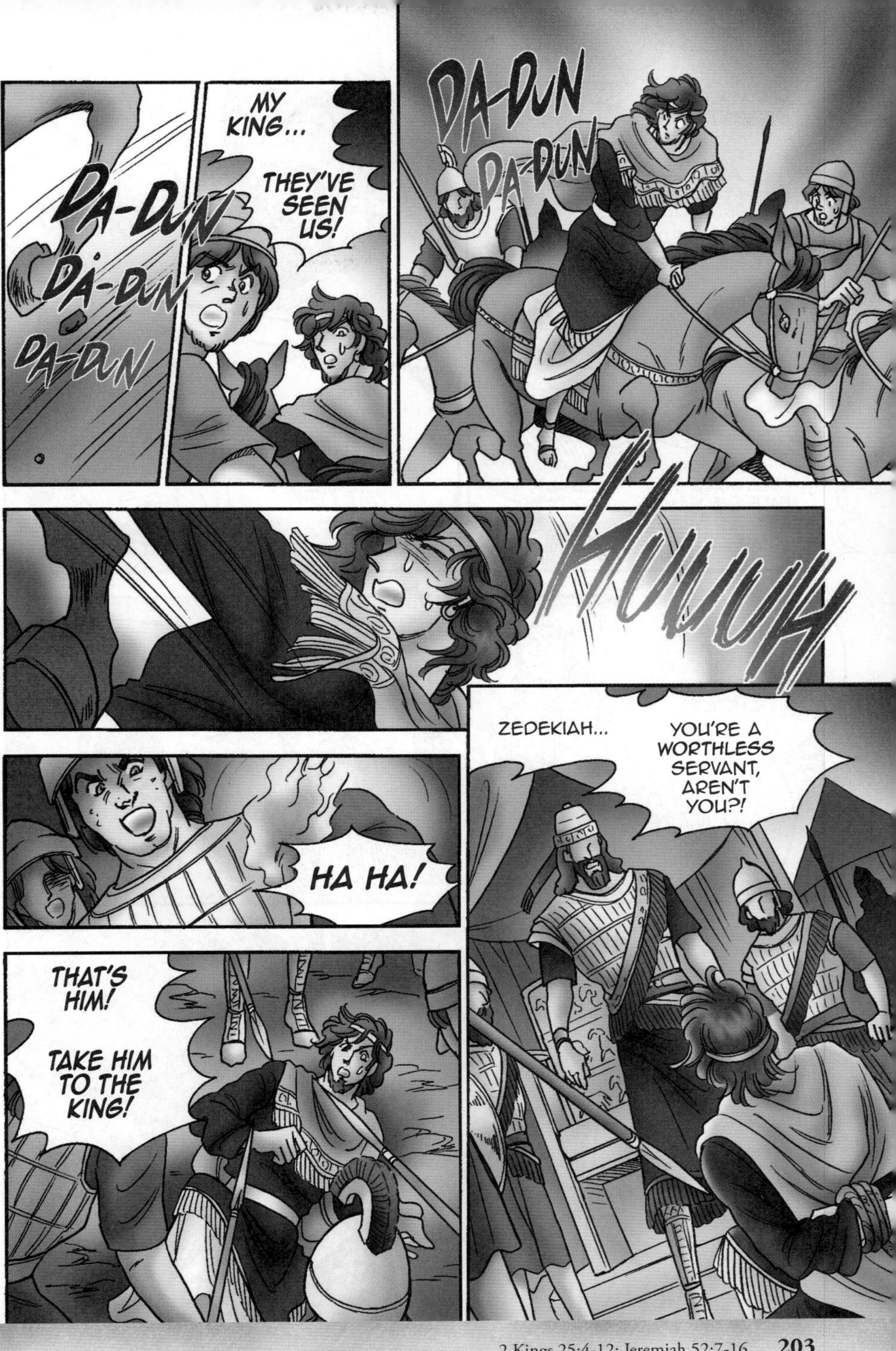
DA-DUN
DA-DUN
DA-DUN
MY KING...
THEY'VE SEEN US!
DA-DUN
DA-DUN
HUUUUH
HA HA!
THAT'S HIM!
TAKE HIM TO THE KING!
ZEDEKIAH...
YOU'RE A WORTHLESS SERVANT, AREN'T YOU?!

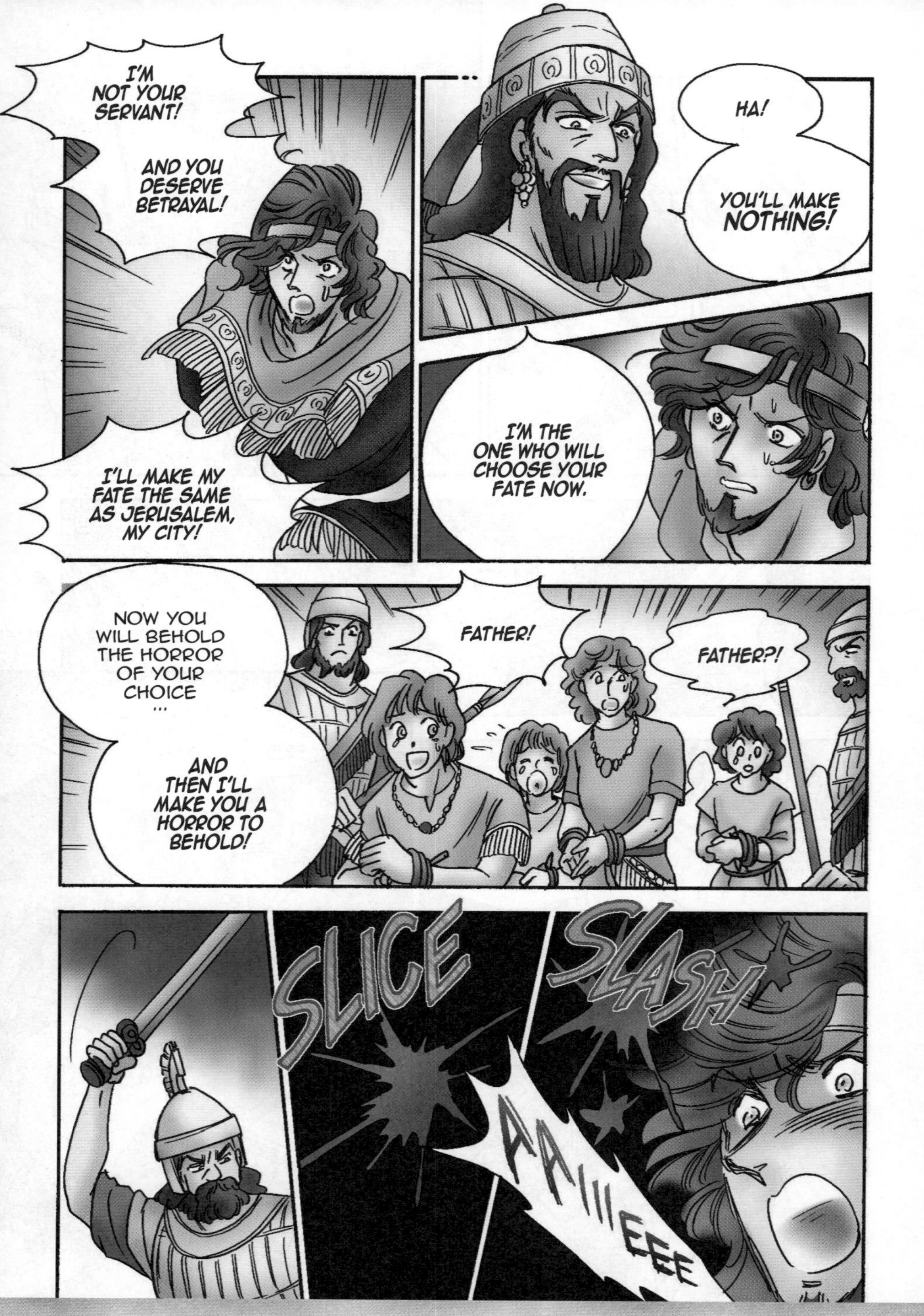
I'M NOT YOUR SERVANT!
AND YOU DESERVE BETRAYAL!
I'LL MAKE MY FATE THE SAME AS JERUSALEM, MY CITY!
...
HA!
YOU'LL MAKE NOTHING!
I'M THE ONE WHO WILL CHOOSE YOUR FATE NOW.
NOW YOU WILL BEHOLD THE HORROR OF YOUR CHOICE ...
AND THEN I'LL MAKE YOU A HORROR TO BEHOLD!
FATHER!
FATHER?!
SLICE
SLASH
AAIIIEEE

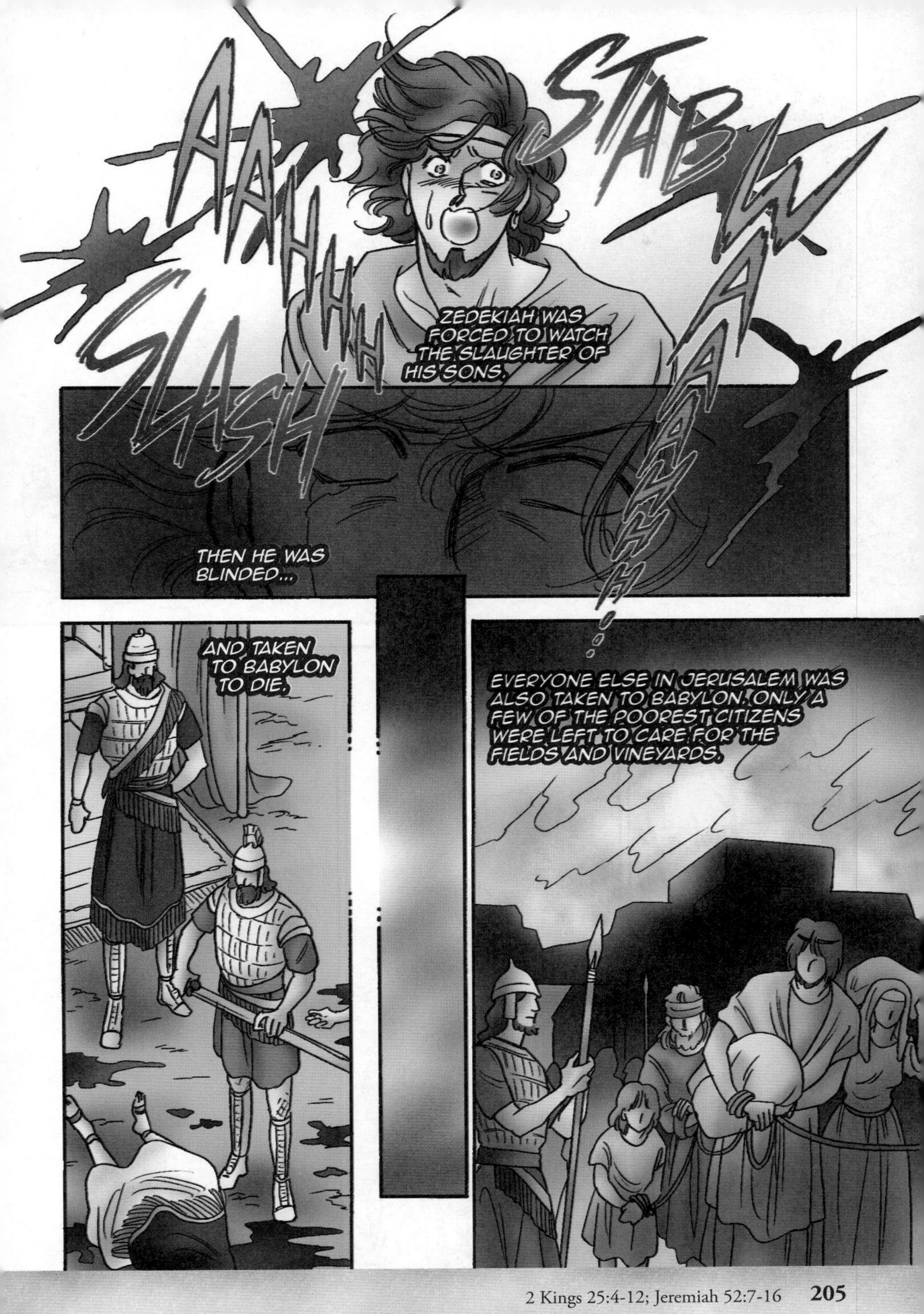
AAHHHHH
STAB
SLASH
ZEDEKIAH WAS FORCED TO WATCH THE SLAUGHTER OF HIS SONS.
AAAAHHHH...
THEN HE WAS BLINDED...
AND TAKEN TO BABYLON TO DIE.
EVERYONE ELSE IN JERUSALEM WAS ALSO TAKEN TO BABYLON. ONLY A FEW OF THE POOREST CITIZENS WERE LEFT TO CARE FOR THE FIELDS AND VINEYARDS.

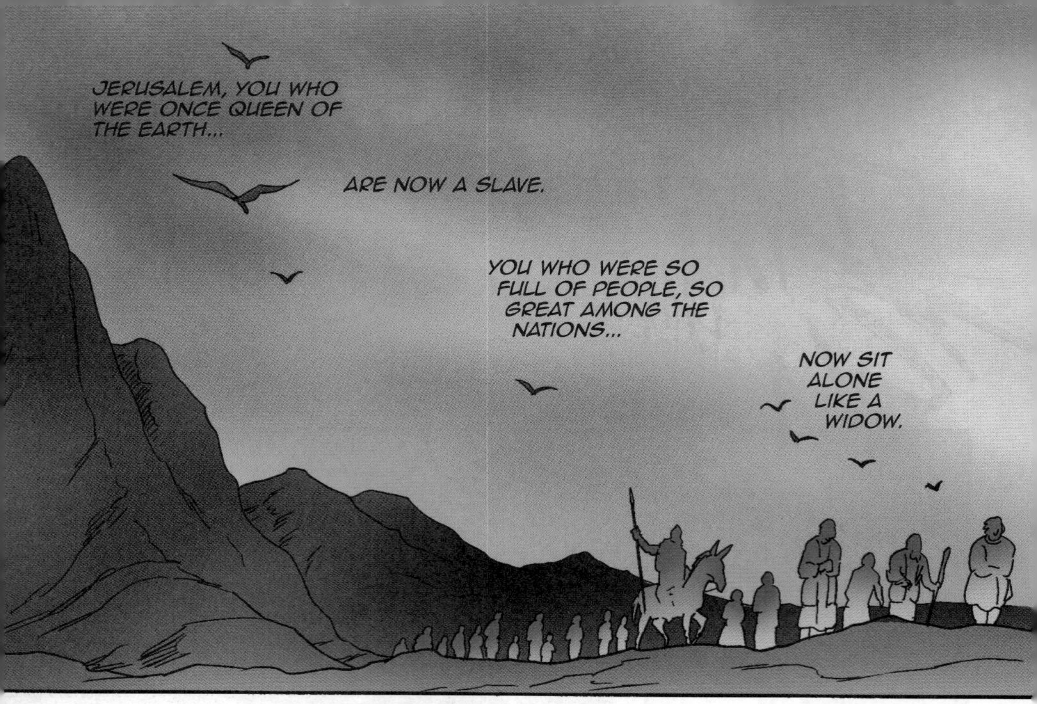
JERUSALEM, YOU WHO WERE ONCE QUEEN OF THE EARTH...
ARE NOW A SLAVE.
YOU WHO WERE SO FULL OF PEOPLE, SO GREAT AMONG THE NATIONS...
NOW SIT ALONE LIKE A WIDOW.

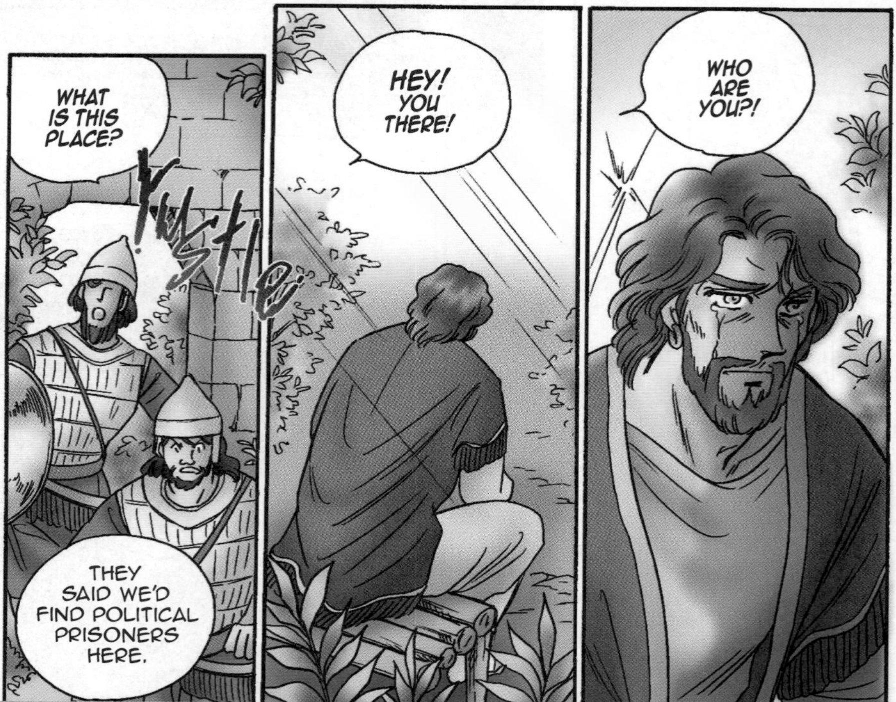
WHAT IS THIS PLACE?
RUSTLE
THEY SAID WE'D FIND POLITICAL PRISONERS HERE.
HEY! YOU THERE!
WHO ARE YOU?!

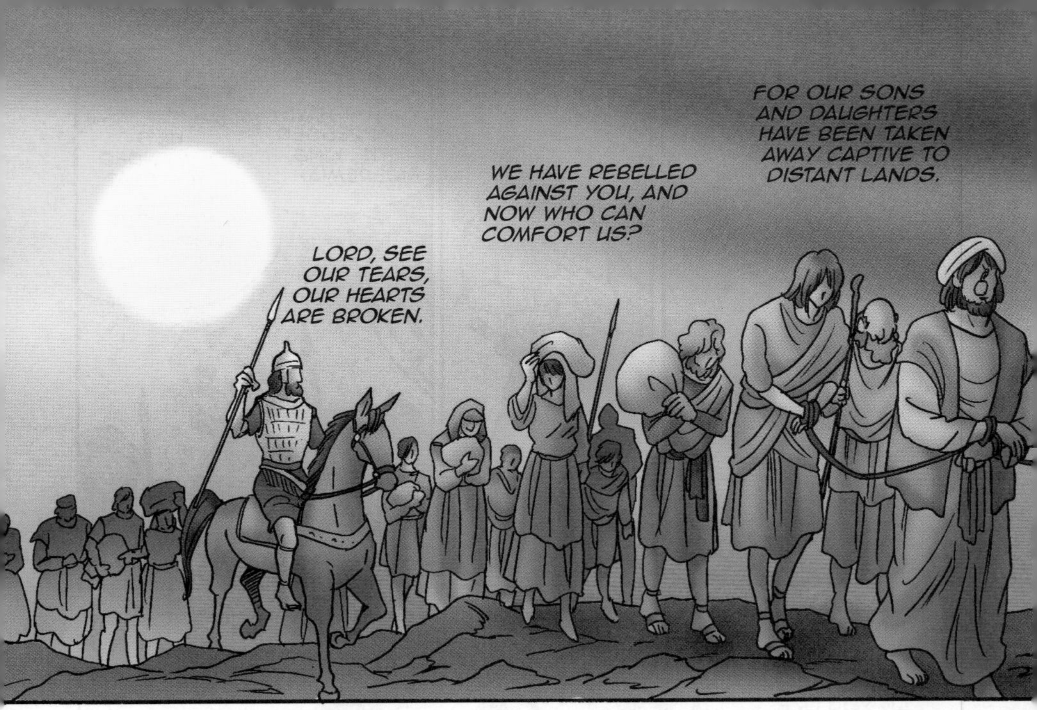
LORD, SEE OUR TEARS, OUR HEARTS ARE BROKEN.
WE HAVE REBELLED AGAINST YOU, AND NOW WHO CAN COMFORT US?
FOR OUR SONS AND DAUGHTERS HAVE BEEN TAKEN AWAY CAPTIVE TO DISTANT LANDS.

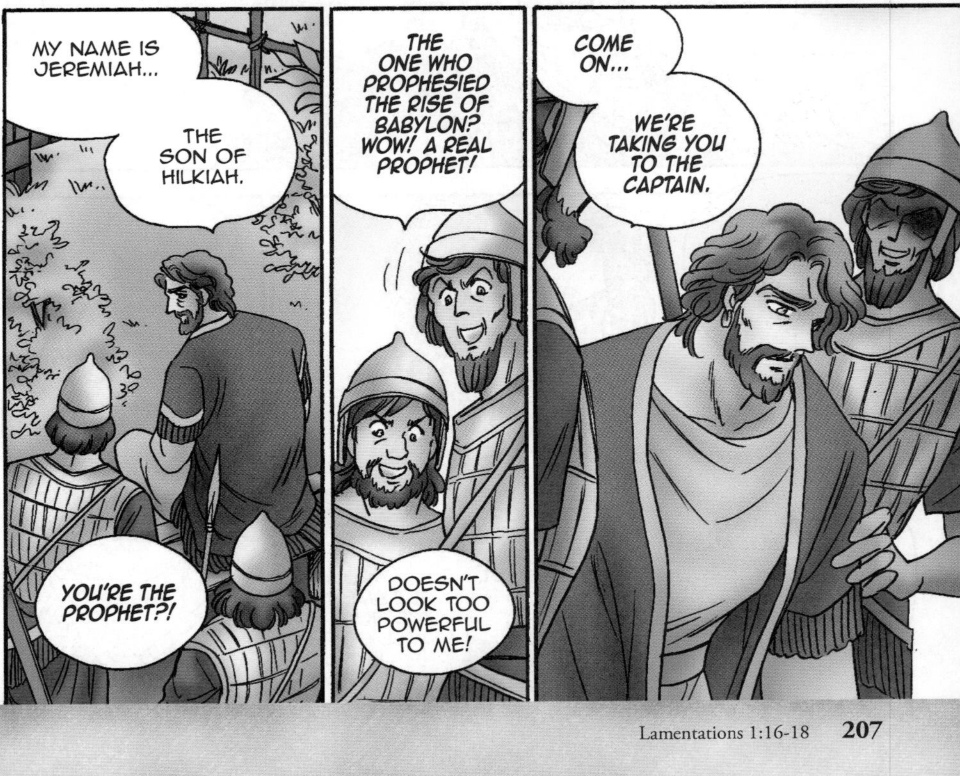
MY NAME IS JEREMIAH...
THE SON OF HILKIAH.
YOU'RE THE PROPHET?!
THE ONE WHO PROPHESIED THE RISE OF BABYLON? WOW! A REAL PROPHET!
DOESN'T LOOK TOO POWERFUL TO ME!
COME ON...
WE'RE TAKING YOU TO THE CAPTAIN.

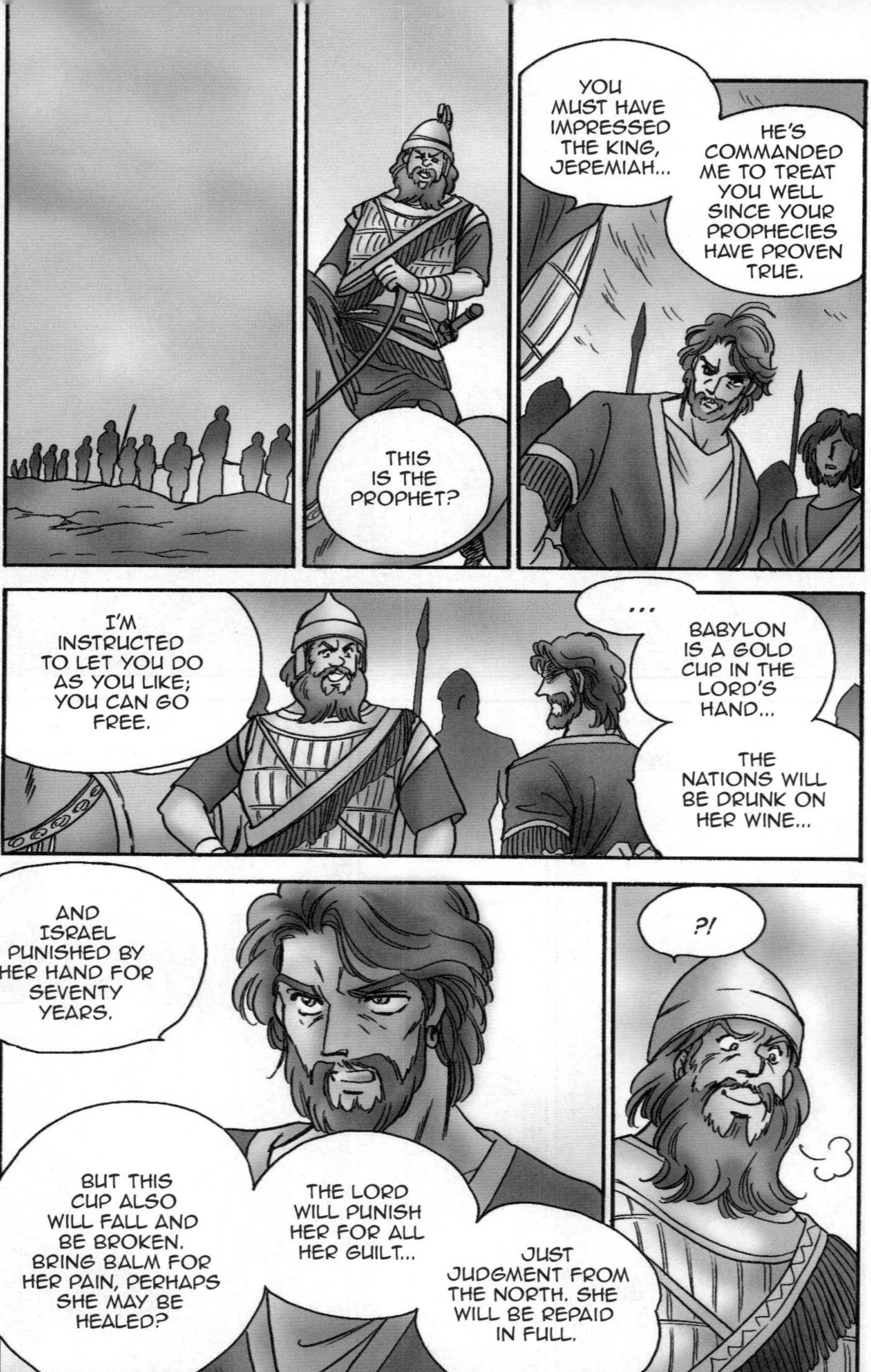
THIS IS THE PROPHET?
YOU MUST HAVE IMPRESSED THE KING, JEREMIAH...
HE'S COMMANDED ME TO TREAT YOU WELL SINCE YOUR PROPHECIES HAVE PROVEN TRUE.
I'M INSTRUCTED TO LET YOU DO AS YOU LIKE; YOU CAN GO FREE.
...
BABYLON IS A GOLD CUP IN THE LORD'S HAND...
THE NATIONS WILL BE DRUNK ON HER WINE...
AND ISRAEL PUNISHED BY HER HAND FOR SEVENTY YEARS.
?!
BUT THIS CUP ALSO WILL FALL AND BE BROKEN. BRING BALM FOR HER PAIN, PERHAPS SHE MAY BE HEALED?
THE LORD WILL PUNISH HER FOR ALL HER GUILT...
JUST JUDGMENT FROM THE NORTH. SHE WILL BE REPAID IN FULL.

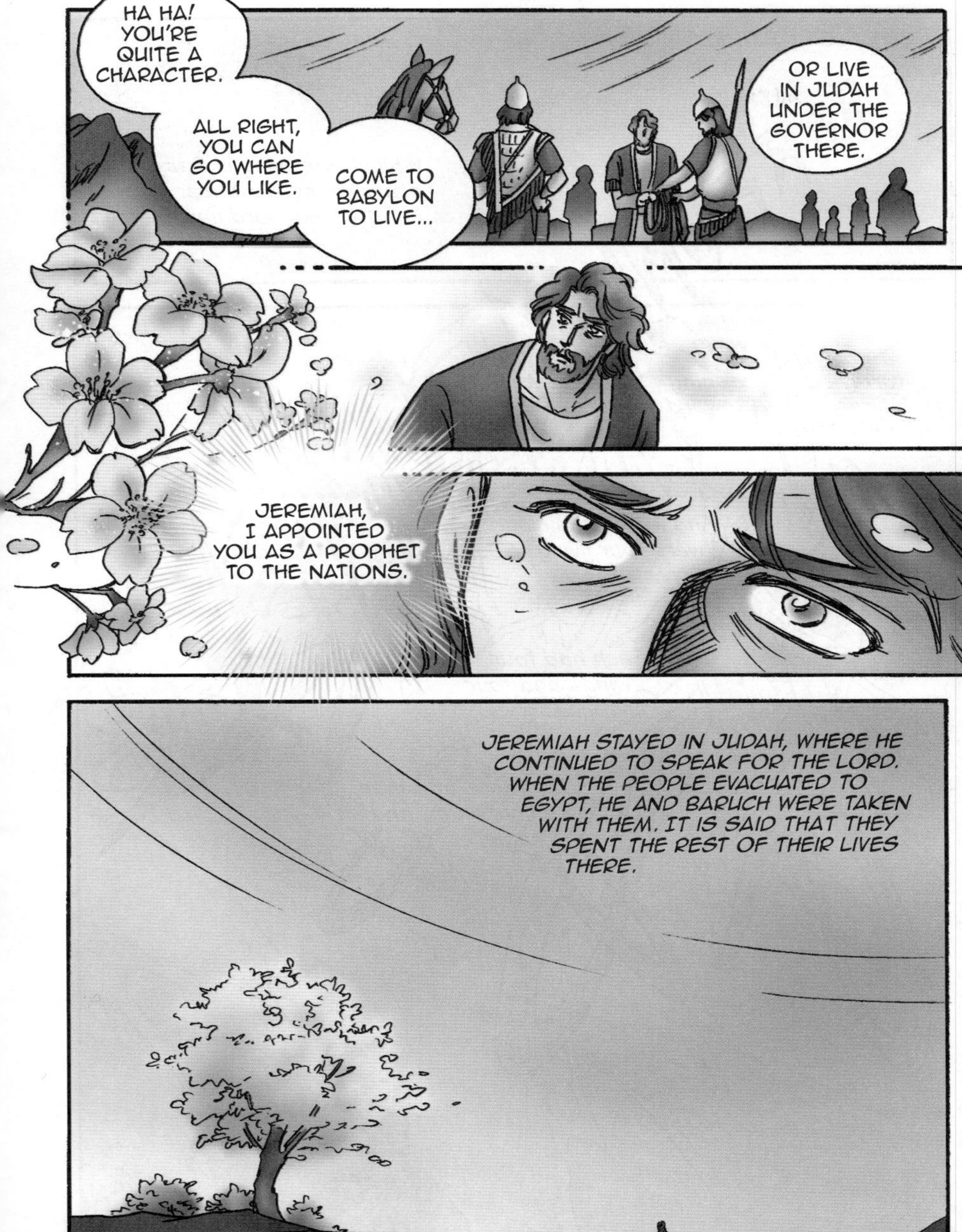
HA HA! YOU'RE QUITE A CHARACTER.
ALL RIGHT, YOU CAN GO WHERE YOU LIKE.
COME TO BABYLON TO LIVE...
OR LIVE IN JUDAH UNDER THE GOVERNOR THERE.
JEREMIAH, I APPOINTED YOU AS A PROPHET TO THE NATIONS.
JEREMIAH STAYED IN JUDAH, WHERE HE CONTINUED TO SPEAK FOR THE LORD. WHEN THE PEOPLE EVACUATED TO EGYPT, HE AND BARUCH WERE TAKEN WITH THEM. IT IS SAID THAT THEY SPENT THE REST OF THEIR LIVES THERE.

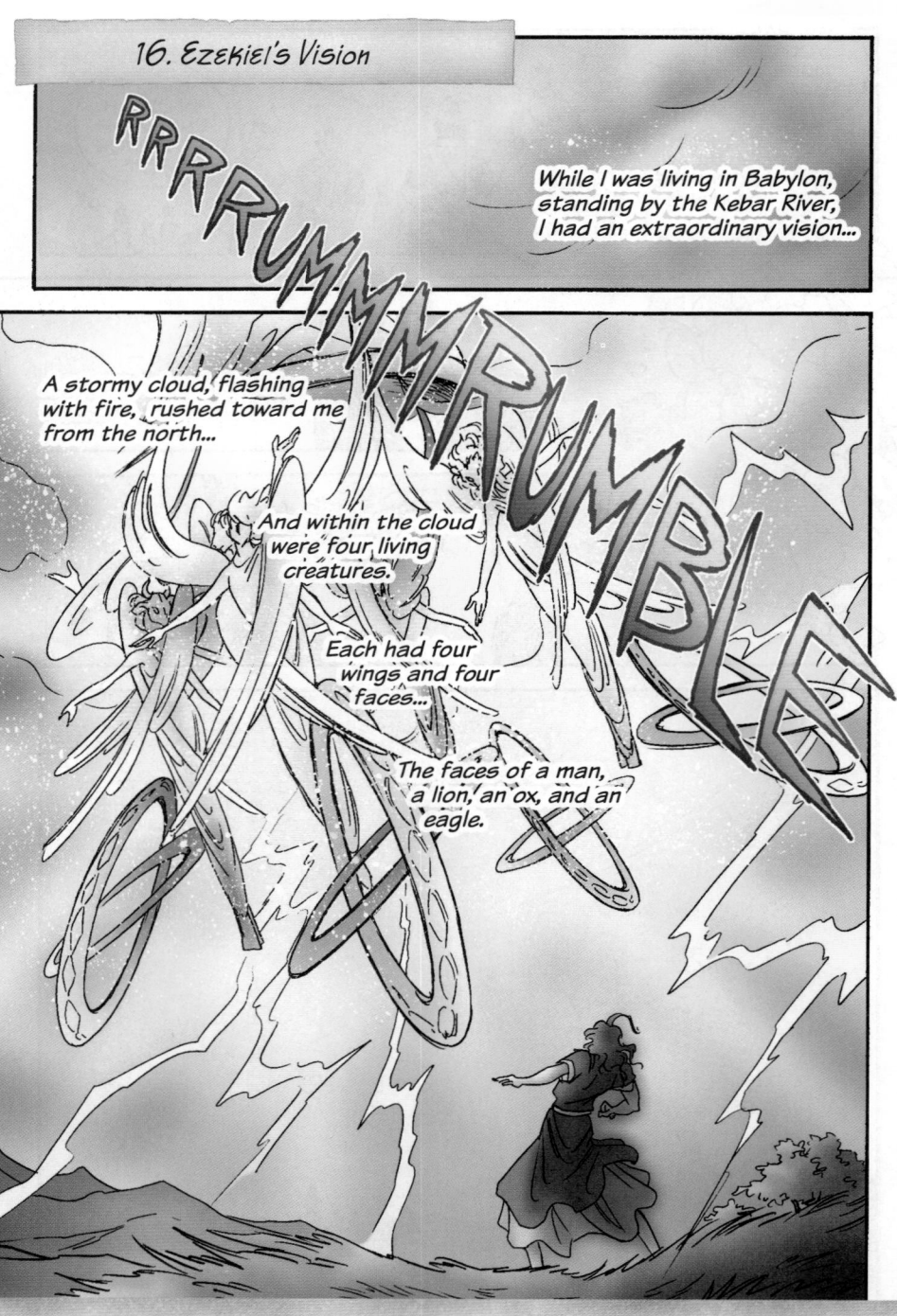

16. Ezekiel's Vision

While I was living in Babylon, standing by the Kebar River, I had an extraordinary vision...

A stormy cloud, flashing with fire, rushed toward me from the north...

And within the cloud were four living creatures.

Each had four wings and four faces...

The faces of a man, a lion, an ox, and an eagle.

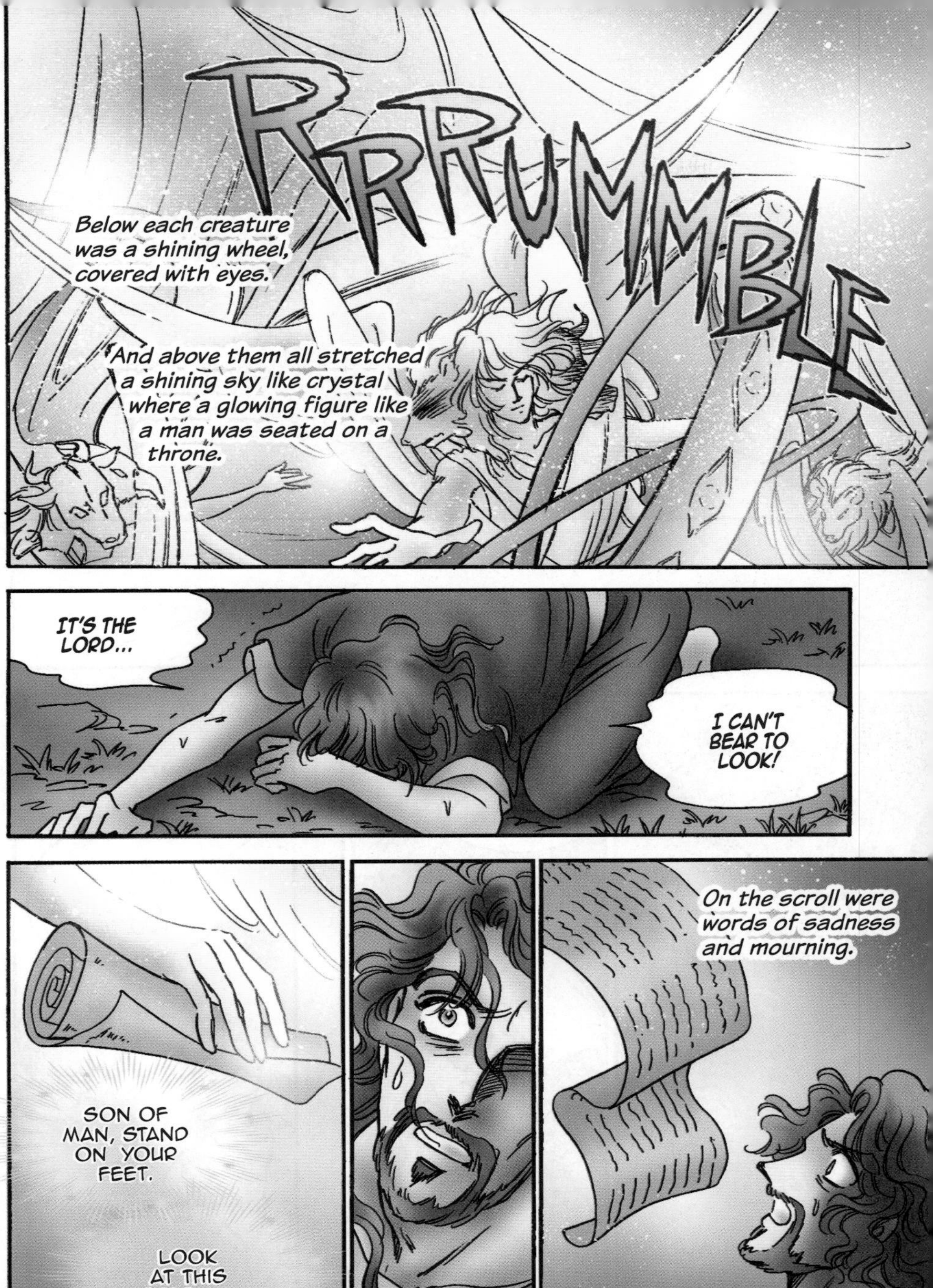
RRRUMMBLE
Below each creature was a shining wheel, covered with eyes.
And above them all stretched a shining sky like crystal where a glowing figure like a man was seated on a throne.
IT'S THE LORD...
I CAN'T BEAR TO LOOK!
SON OF MAN, STAND ON YOUR FEET.
LOOK AT THIS SCROLL...
On the scroll were words of sadness and mourning.

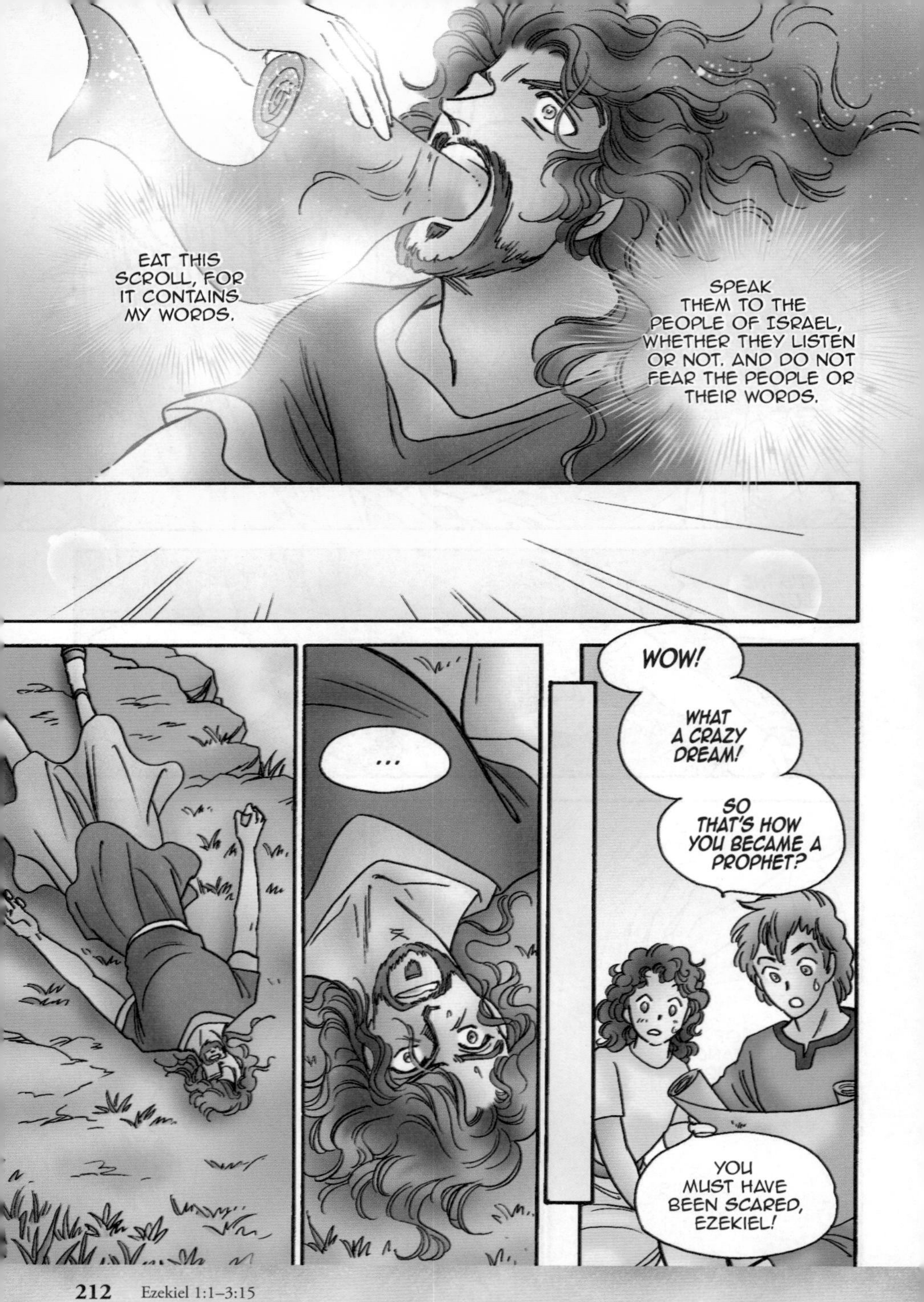
EAT THIS SCROLL, FOR IT CONTAINS MY WORDS.
SPEAK THEM TO THE PEOPLE OF ISRAEL, WHETHER THEY LISTEN OR NOT. AND DO NOT FEAR THE PEOPLE OR THEIR WORDS.
...
WOW!
WHAT A CRAZY DREAM!
SO THAT'S HOW YOU BECAME A PROPHET?
YOU MUST HAVE BEEN SCARED, EZEKIEL!

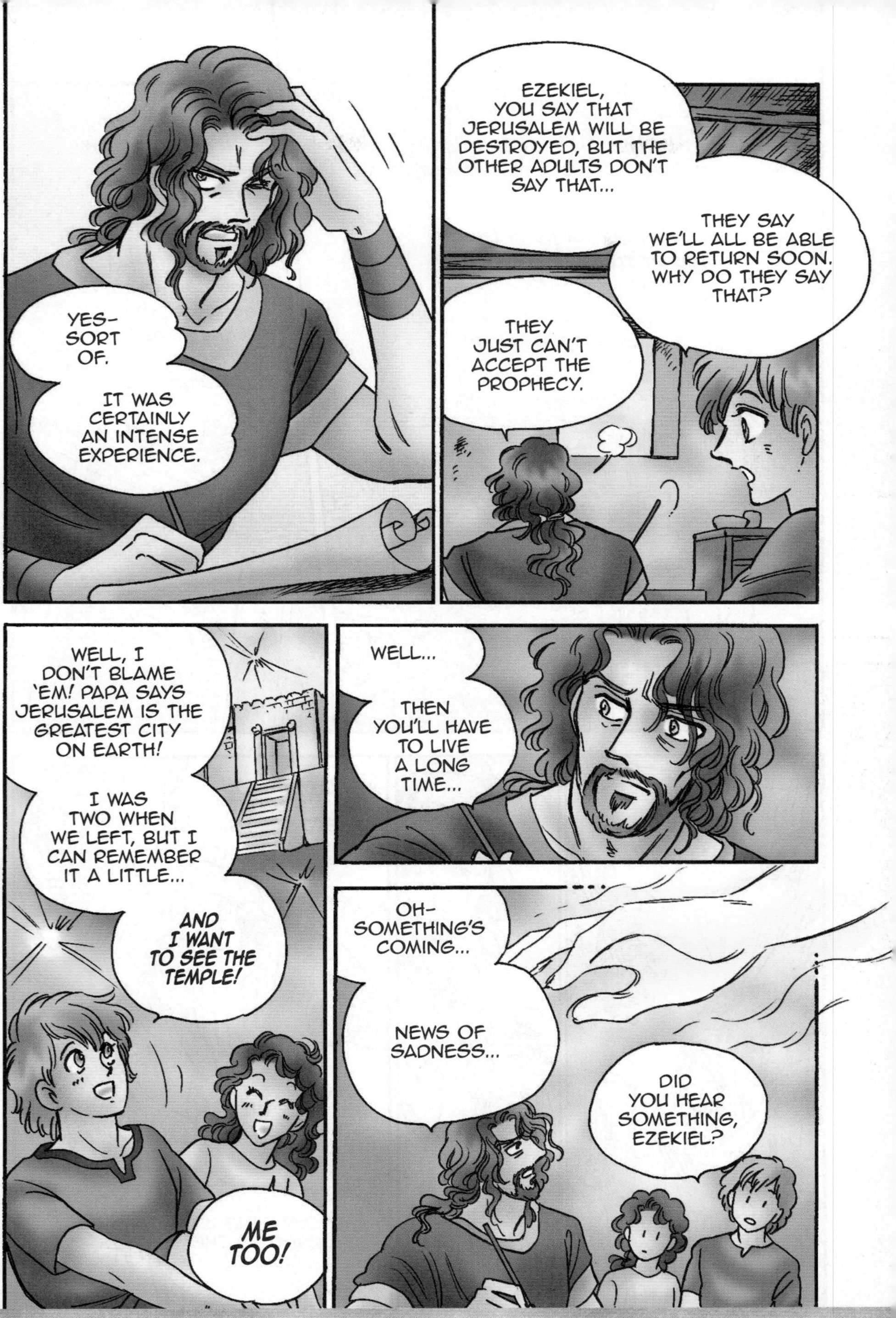
YES-SORT OF.
IT WAS CERTAINLY AN INTENSE EXPERIENCE.
EZEKIEL, YOU SAY THAT JERUSALEM WILL BE DESTROYED, BUT THE OTHER ADULTS DON'T SAY THAT...
THEY SAY WE'LL ALL BE ABLE TO RETURN SOON. WHY DO THEY SAY THAT?
THEY JUST CAN'T ACCEPT THE PROPHECY.
WELL, I DON'T BLAME 'EM! PAPA SAYS JERUSALEM IS THE GREATEST CITY ON EARTH!
I WAS TWO WHEN WE LEFT, BUT I CAN REMEMBER IT A LITTLE...
AND I WANT TO SEE THE TEMPLE!
ME TOO!
WELL...
THEN YOU'LL HAVE TO LIVE A LONG TIME...
OH-SOMETHING'S COMING...
NEWS OF SADNESS...
DID YOU HEAR SOMETHING, EZEKIEL?

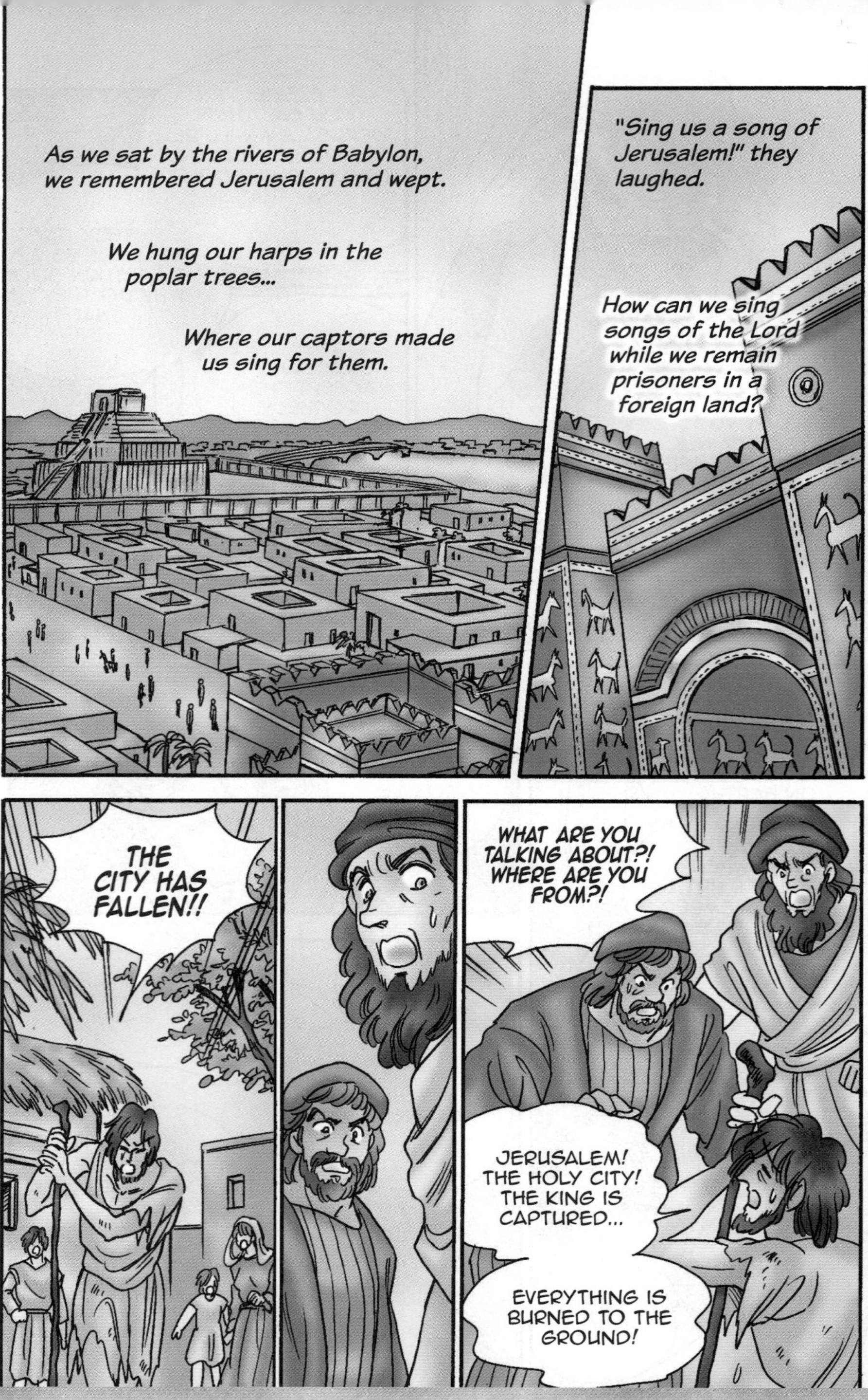
As we sat by the rivers of Babylon, we remembered Jerusalem and wept.
We hung our harps in the poplar trees...
Where our captors made us sing for them.
"Sing us a song of Jerusalem!" they laughed.
How can we sing songs of the Lord while we remain prisoners in a foreign land?
THE CITY HAS FALLEN!!
WHAT ARE YOU TALKING ABOUT?! WHERE ARE YOU FROM?!
JERUSALEM! THE HOLY CITY! THE KING IS CAPTURED...
EVERYTHING IS BURNED TO THE GROUND!

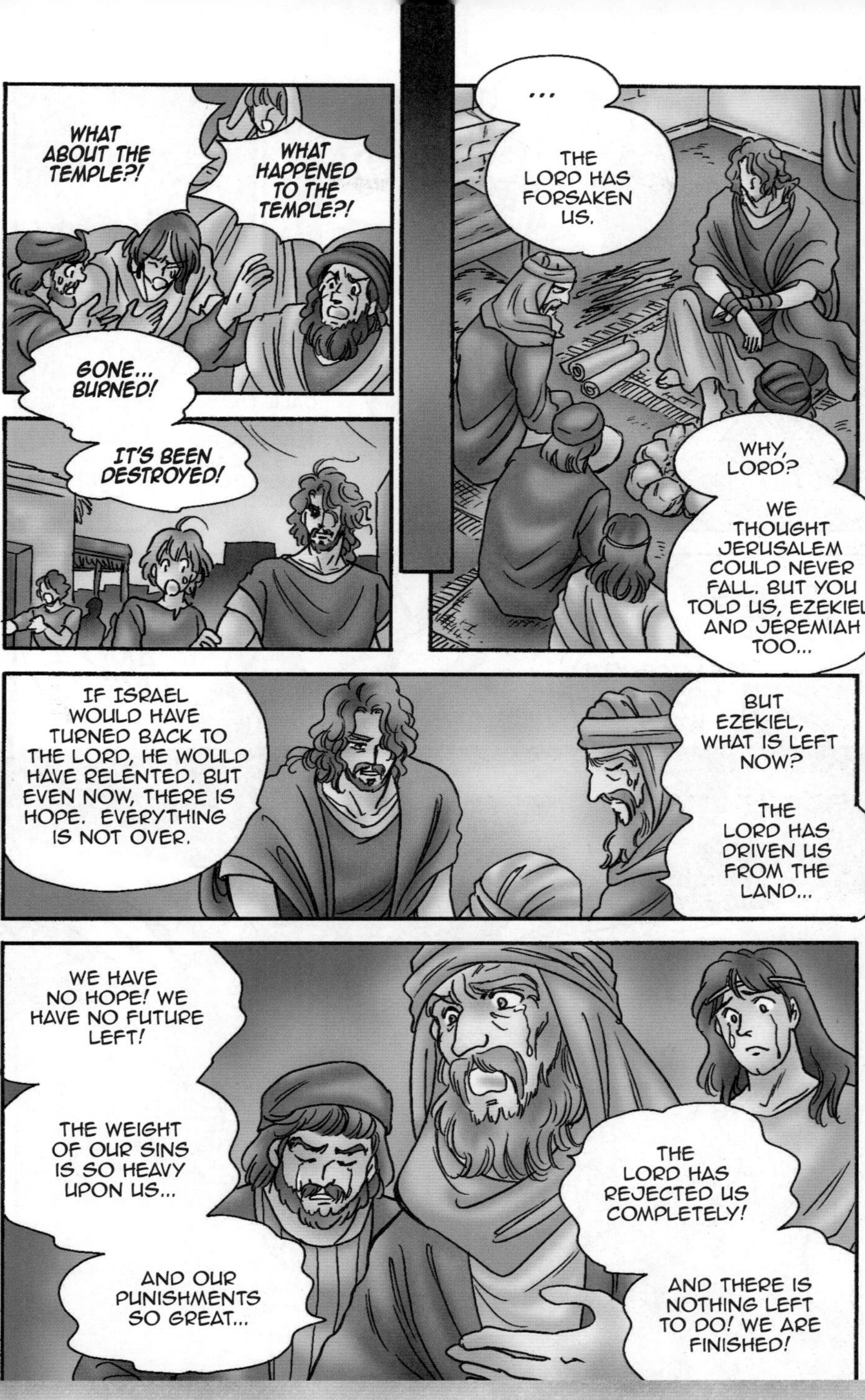
WHAT ABOUT THE TEMPLE?!
WHAT HAPPENED TO THE TEMPLE?!
GONE... BURNED!
IT'S BEEN DESTROYED!
...
THE LORD HAS FORSAKEN US.
WHY, LORD?
WE THOUGHT JERUSALEM COULD NEVER FALL. BUT YOU TOLD US, EZEKIEL. AND JEREMIAH TOO...
IF ISRAEL WOULD HAVE TURNED BACK TO THE LORD, HE WOULD HAVE RELENTED. BUT EVEN NOW, THERE IS HOPE. EVERYTHING IS NOT OVER.
BUT EZEKIEL, WHAT IS LEFT NOW?
THE LORD HAS DRIVEN US FROM THE LAND...
WE HAVE NO HOPE! WE HAVE NO FUTURE LEFT!
THE WEIGHT OF OUR SINS IS SO HEAVY UPON US...
AND OUR PUNISHMENTS SO GREAT...
THE LORD HAS REJECTED US COMPLETELY!
AND THERE IS NOTHING LEFT TO DO! WE ARE FINISHED!

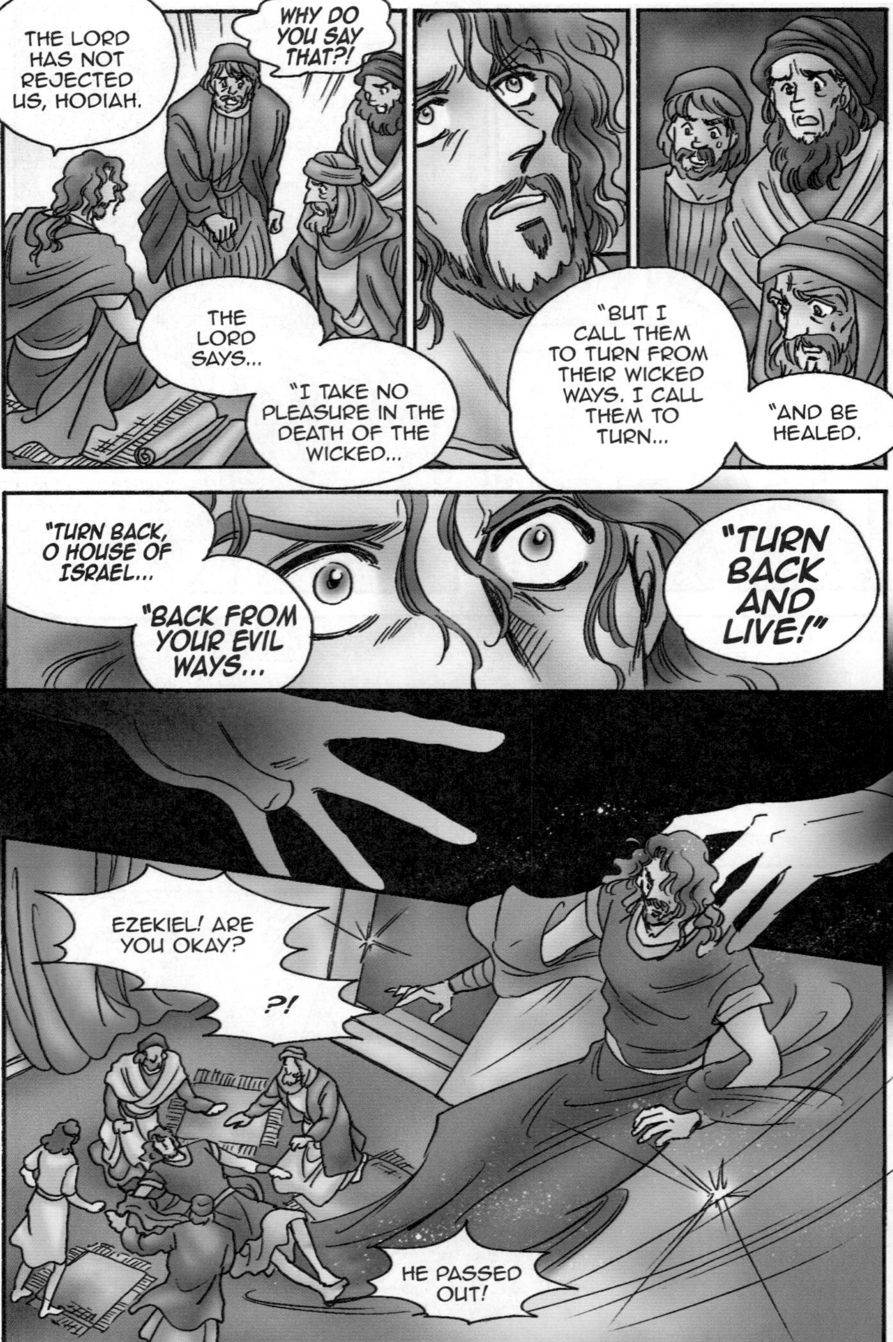
THE LORD HAS NOT REJECTED US, HODIAH.
WHY DO YOU SAY THAT?!
THE LORD SAYS...
"I TAKE NO PLEASURE IN THE DEATH OF THE WICKED...
"BUT I CALL THEM TO TURN FROM THEIR WICKED WAYS. I CALL THEM TO TURN...
"AND BE HEALED.
"TURN BACK, O HOUSE OF ISRAEL...
"BACK FROM YOUR EVIL WAYS...
"TURN BACK AND LIVE!"
EZEKIEL! ARE YOU OKAY?
?!
HE PASSED OUT!

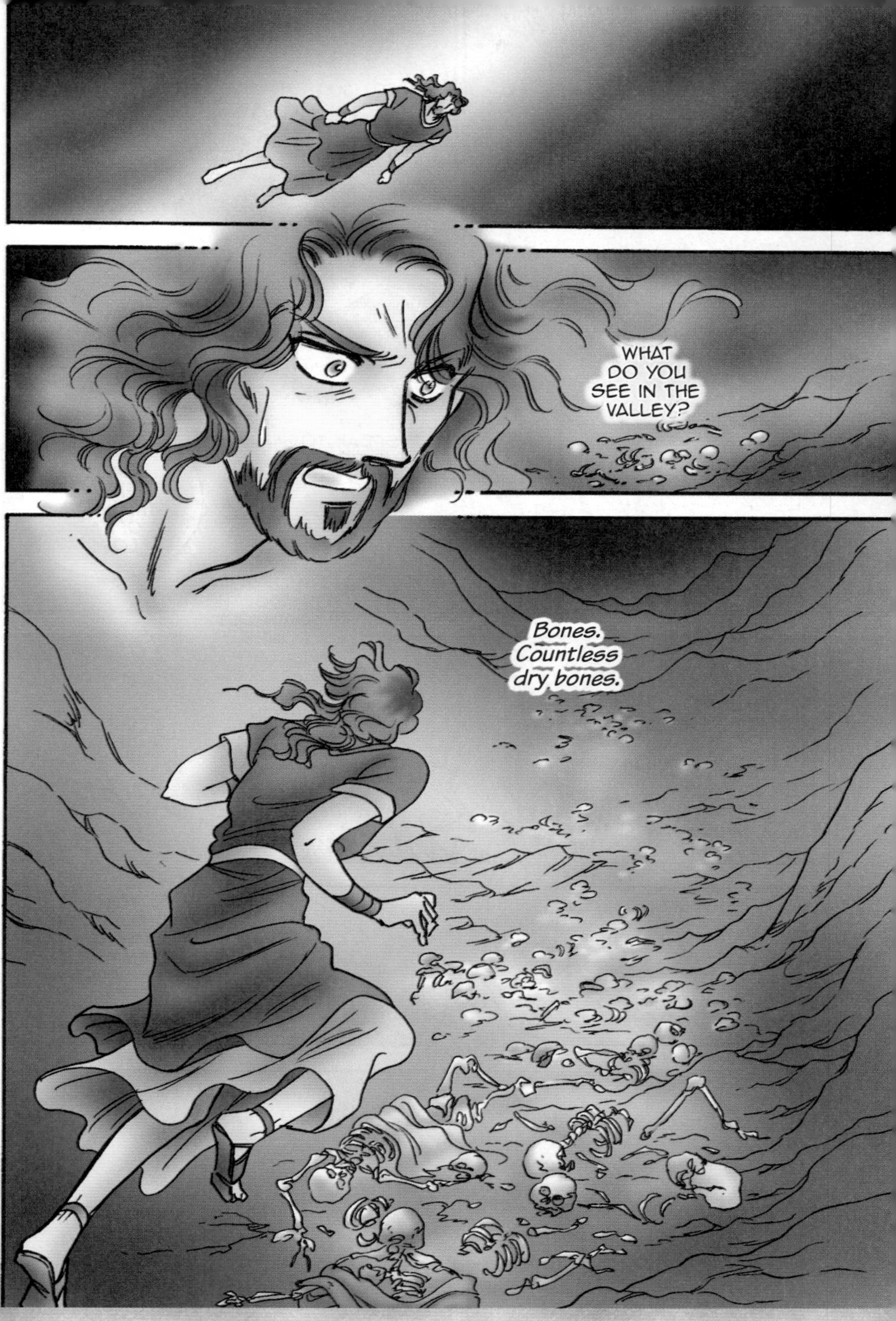
WHAT DO YOU SEE IN THE VALLEY?
Bones. Countless dry bones.

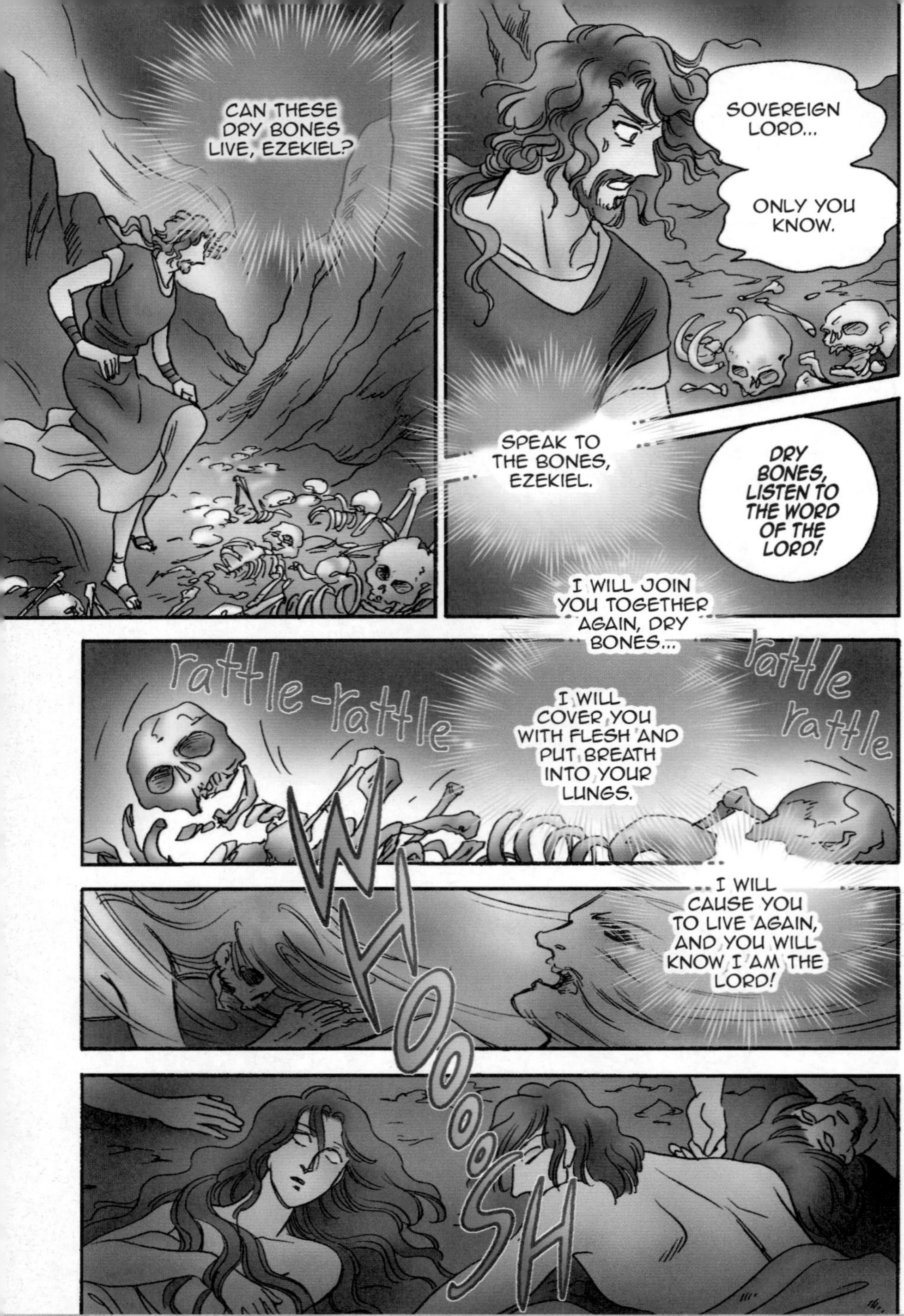
CAN THESE DRY BONES LIVE, EZEKIEL?
SOVEREIGN LORD...
ONLY YOU KNOW.
SPEAK TO THE BONES, EZEKIEL.
DRY BONES, LISTEN TO THE WORD OF THE LORD!
I WILL JOIN YOU TOGETHER AGAIN, DRY BONES...
rattle-rattle
rattle rattle
I WILL COVER YOU WITH FLESH AND PUT BREATH INTO YOUR LUNGS.
...I WILL CAUSE YOU TO LIVE AGAIN, AND YOU WILL KNOW I AM THE LORD!
WHOOoooSH

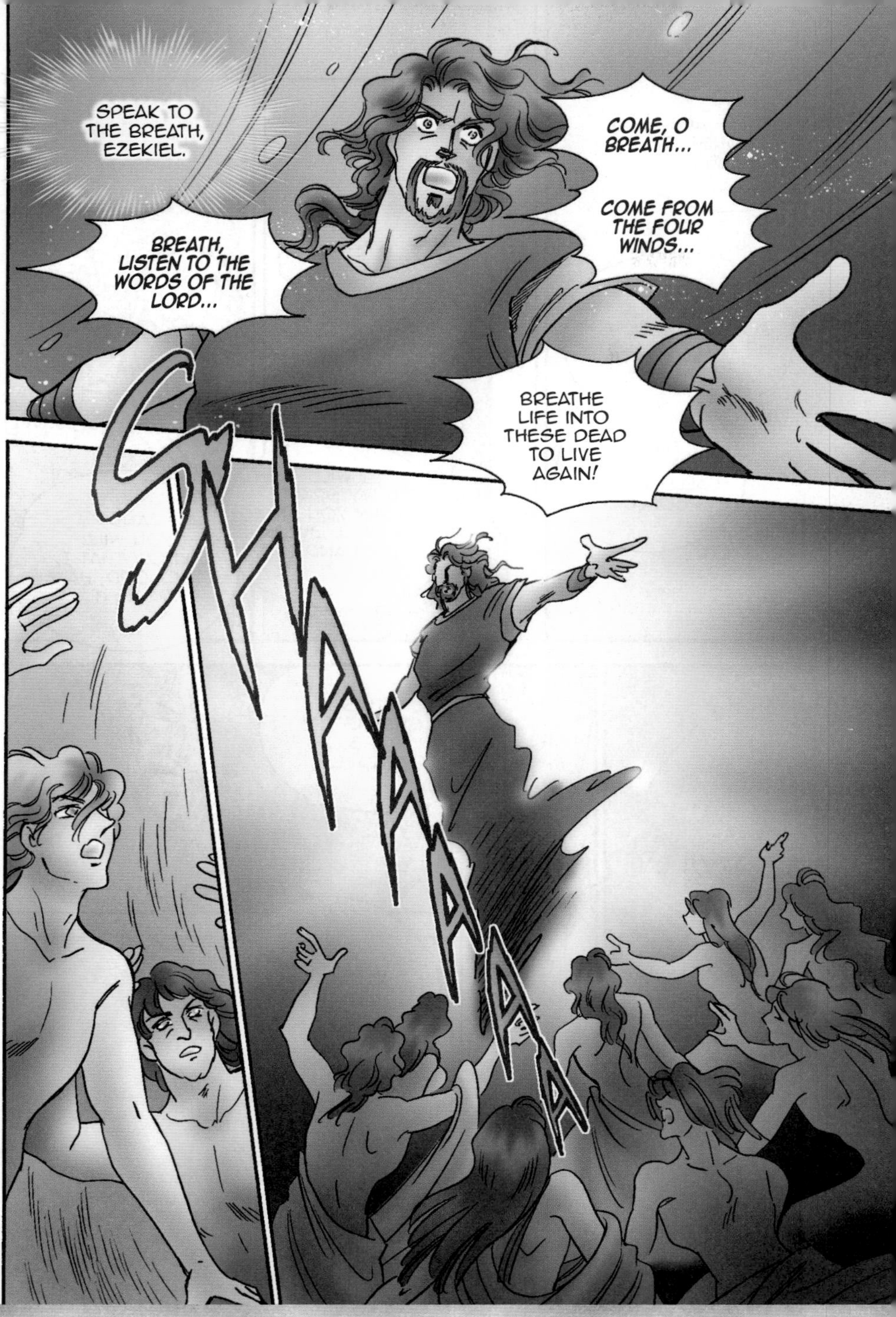
SPEAK TO THE BREATH, EZEKIEL.
BREATH, LISTEN TO THE WORDS OF THE LORD...
COME, O BREATH...
COME FROM THE FOUR WINDS...
BREATHE LIFE INTO THESE DEAD TO LIVE AGAIN!
SHAAAAAAA

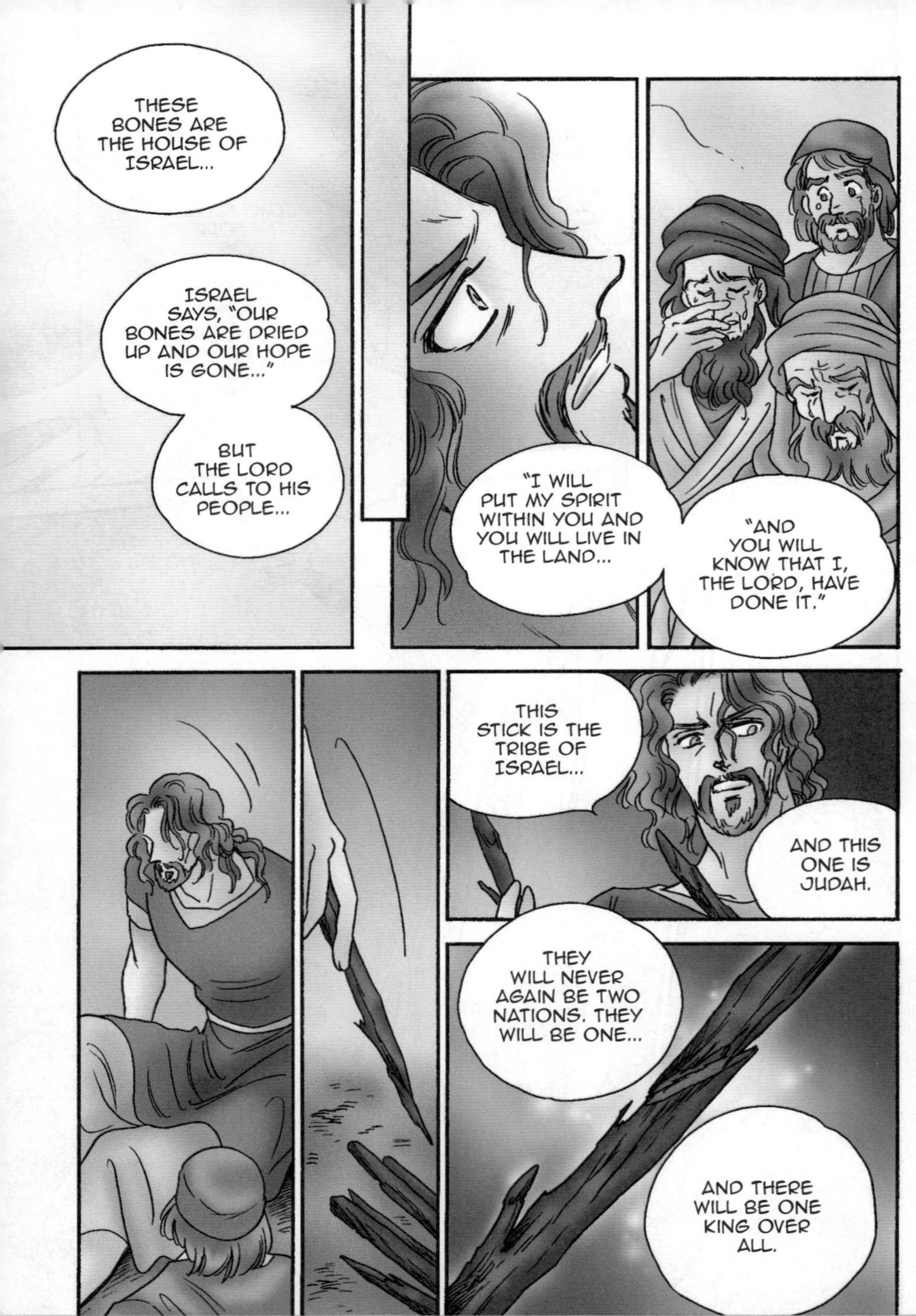
THESE BONES ARE THE HOUSE OF ISRAEL...
ISRAEL SAYS, "OUR BONES ARE DRIED UP AND OUR HOPE IS GONE..."
BUT THE LORD CALLS TO HIS PEOPLE...
"I WILL PUT MY SPIRIT WITHIN YOU AND YOU WILL LIVE IN THE LAND...
"AND YOU WILL KNOW THAT I, THE LORD, HAVE DONE IT."
THIS STICK IS THE TRIBE OF ISRAEL...
AND THIS ONE IS JUDAH.
THEY WILL NEVER AGAIN BE TWO NATIONS. THEY WILL BE ONE...
AND THERE WILL BE ONE KING OVER ALL.

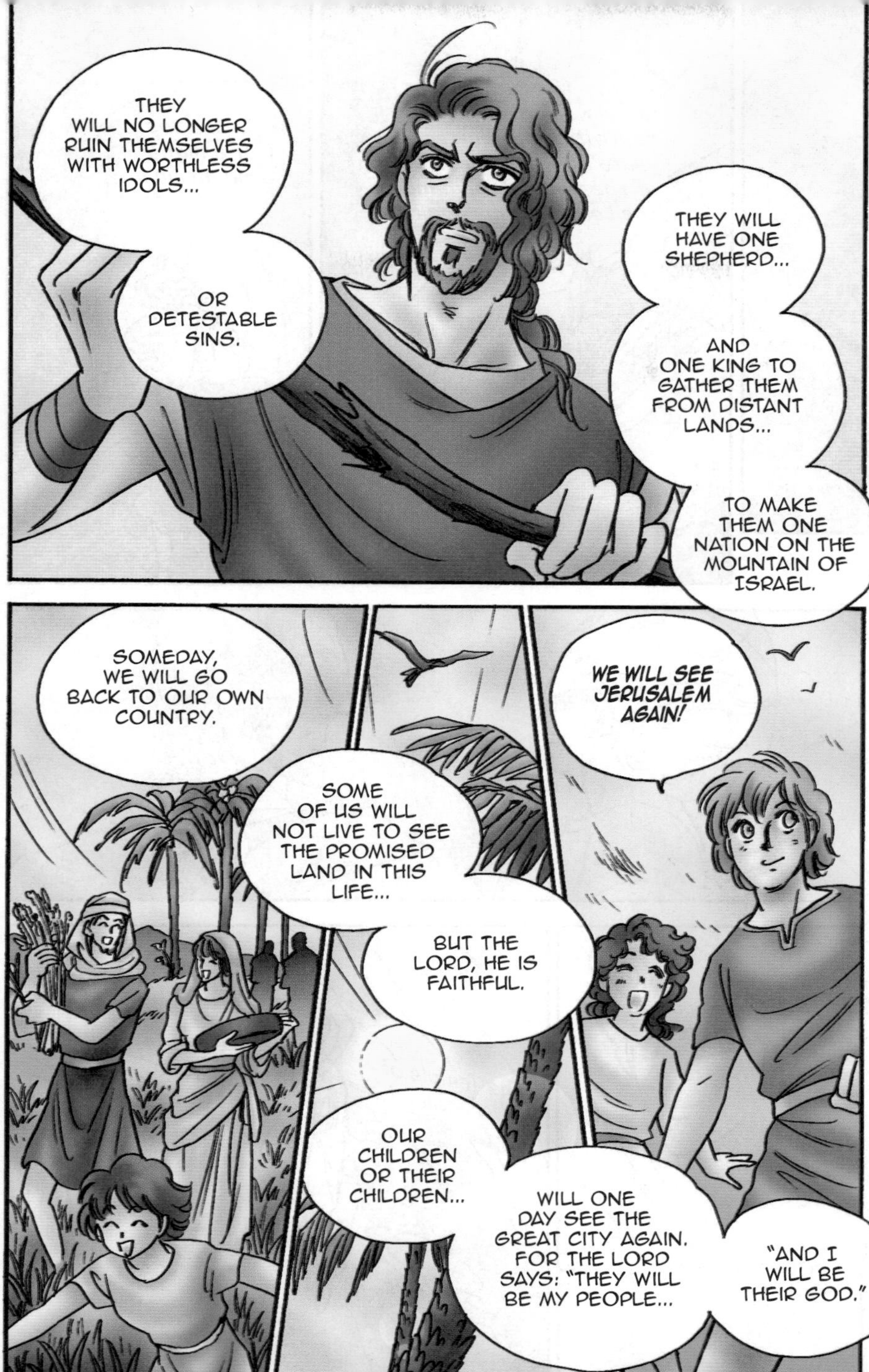
THEY WILL NO LONGER RUIN THEMSELVES WITH WORTHLESS IDOLS...
OR DETESTABLE SINS.
THEY WILL HAVE ONE SHEPHERD...
AND ONE KING TO GATHER THEM FROM DISTANT LANDS...
TO MAKE THEM ONE NATION ON THE MOUNTAIN OF ISRAEL.
SOMEDAY, WE WILL GO BACK TO OUR OWN COUNTRY.
SOME OF US WILL NOT LIVE TO SEE THE PROMISED LAND IN THIS LIFE...
BUT THE LORD, HE IS FAITHFUL.
OUR CHILDREN OR THEIR CHILDREN...
WILL ONE DAY SEE THE GREAT CITY AGAIN. FOR THE LORD SAYS: "THEY WILL BE MY PEOPLE...
"AND I WILL BE THEIR GOD."
WE WILL SEE JERUSALEM AGAIN!

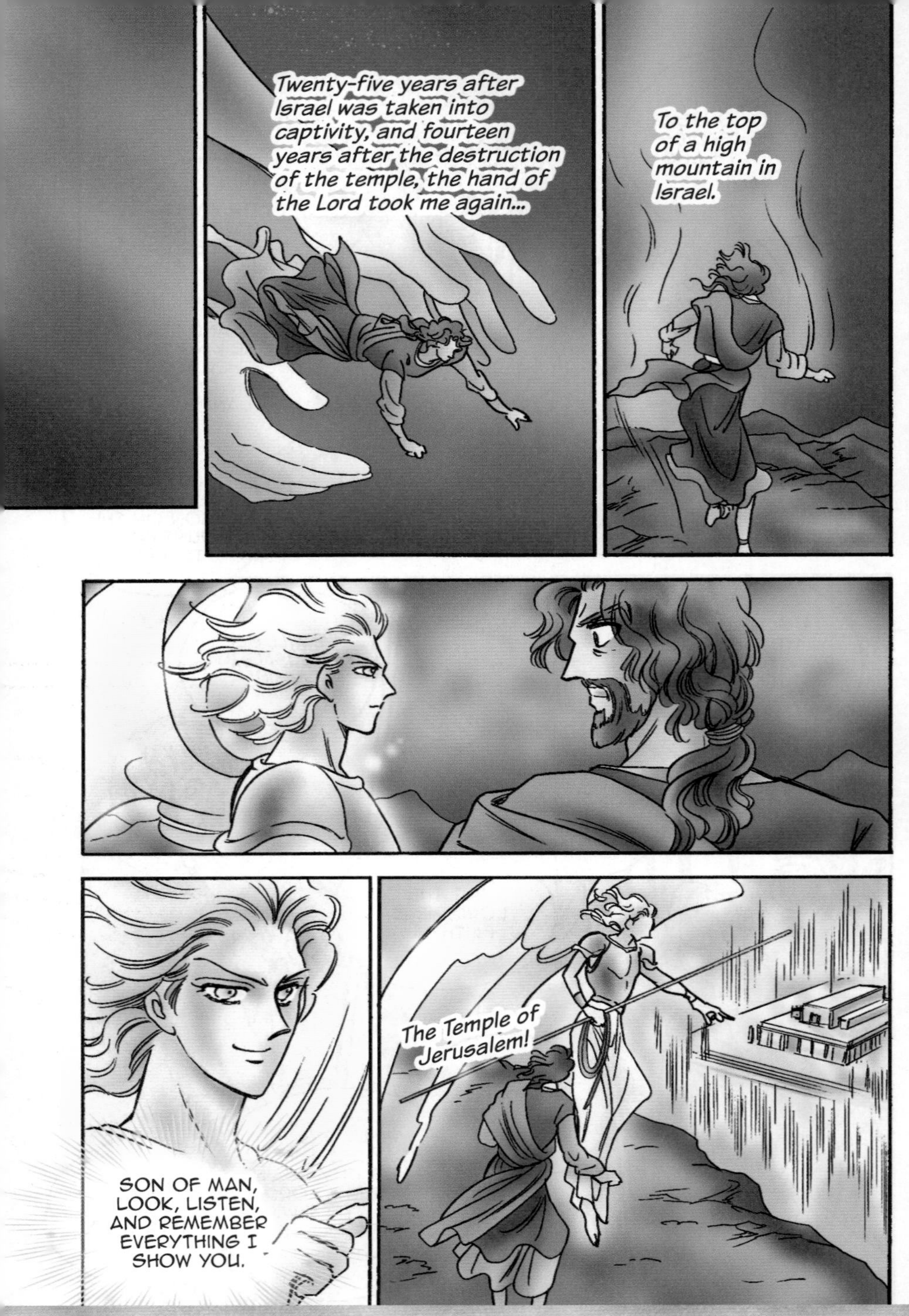
Twenty-five years after Israel was taken into captivity, and fourteen years after the destruction of the temple, the hand of the Lord took me again...
To the top of a high mountain in Israel.
SON OF MAN, LOOK, LISTEN, AND REMEMBER EVERYTHING I SHOW YOU.
The Temple of Jerusalem!

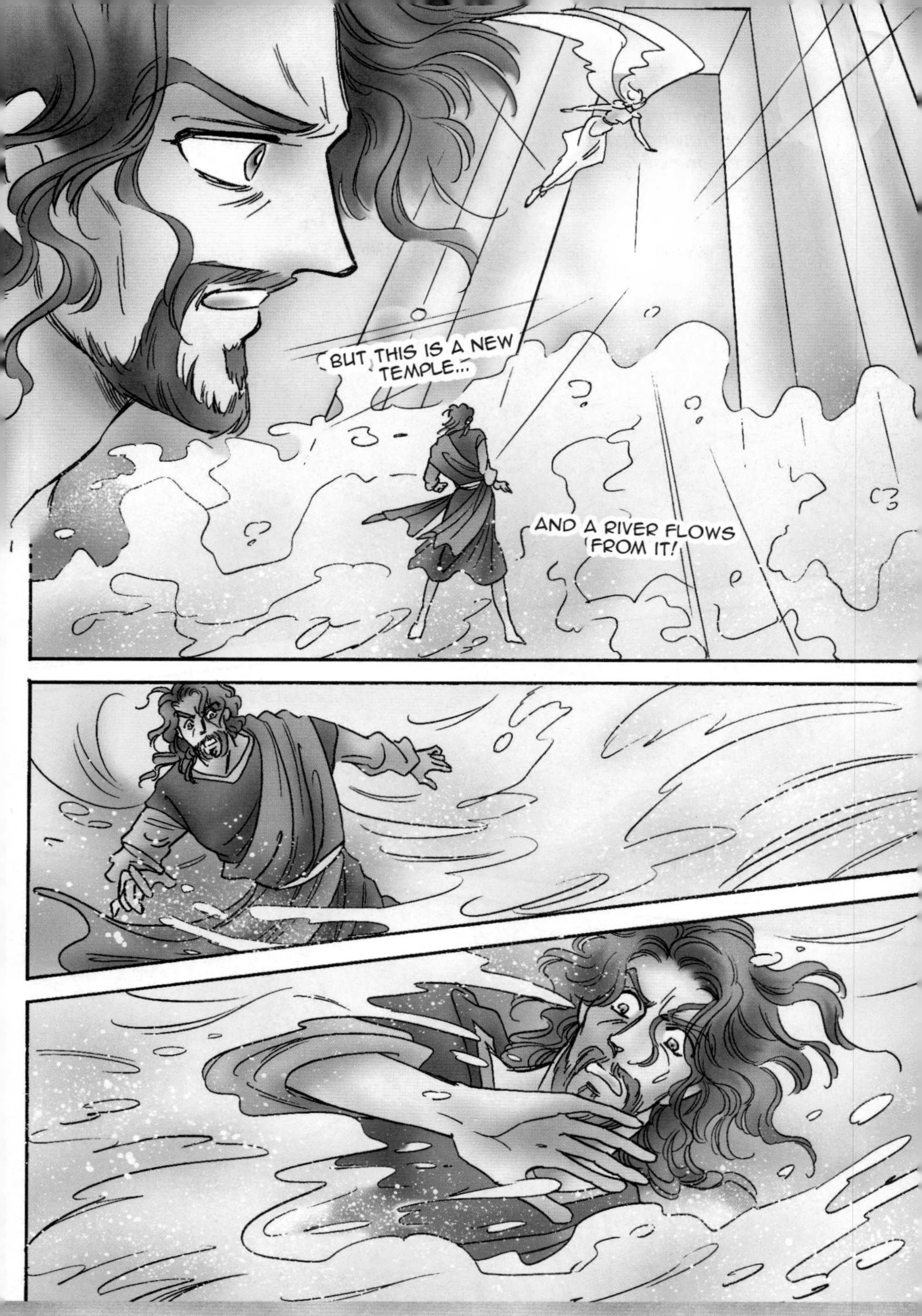
BUT THIS IS A NEW TEMPLE...
AND A RIVER FLOWS FROM IT!

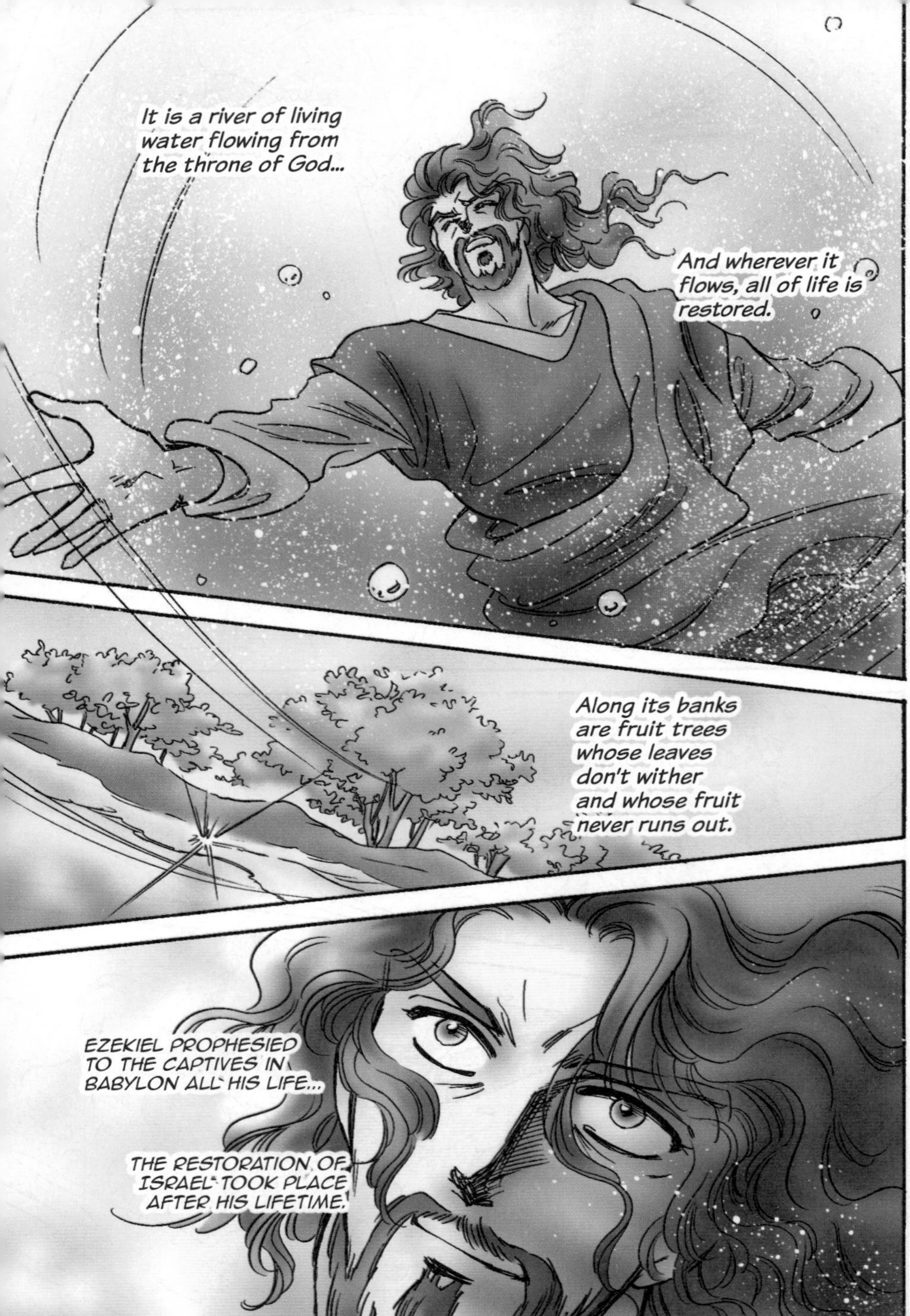
It is a river of living water flowing from the throne of God...
And wherever it flows, all of life is restored.
Along its banks are fruit trees whose leaves don't wither and whose fruit never runs out.
EZEKIEL PROPHESIED TO THE CAPTIVES IN BABYLON ALL HIS LIFE...
THE RESTORATION OF ISRAEL TOOK PLACE AFTER HIS LIFETIME.

SHAAA

IN BABYLON, KING NEBUCHADNEZZAR'S WISE MEN WERE TERRIFIED. THE KING DEMANDED THEY TELL HIM THE MEANING OF HIS DREAM, AS WELL AS WHAT HE HAD DREAMED. WHEN NO ONE COULD DO SO, HE COMMANDED THEY ALL BE TORN LIMB FROM LIMB. ONE OF THE KING'S WISE MEN WAS A YOUNG MAN FROM JUDAH NAMED DANIEL.

SO YOU'VE COME TO TELL ME MY DREAM? YOU KNOW THE OTHER WISE MEN FAILED TO DO THIS. YOU MUST ALSO KNOW THAT IF YOU FAIL...

YOU TOO WILL CERTAINLY DIE!

YES, YOUR HIGHNESS. I WILL TELL YOU YOUR DREAM AND ITS MEANING.

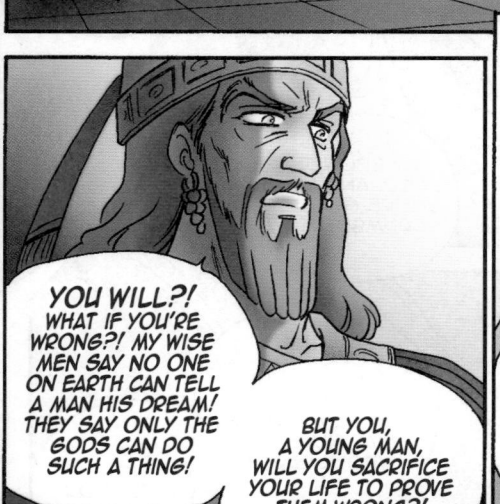

YOU WILL?! WHAT IF YOU'RE WRONG?! MY WISE MEN SAY NO ONE ON EARTH CAN TELL A MAN HIS DREAM! THEY SAY ONLY THE GODS CAN DO SUCH A THING!

BUT YOU, A YOUNG MAN, WILL YOU SACRIFICE YOUR LIFE TO PROVE THEM WRONG?!

YOUR SERVANTS ARE RIGHT, YOUR MAJESTY, TO SAY THAT NO MAN CAN TELL YOU YOUR DREAM. BUT THERE IS A GOD IN HEAVEN WHO REVEALS MYSTERIES...

AND HE HAS REVEALED TO ME BOTH YOUR DREAM AND ITS MEANING.

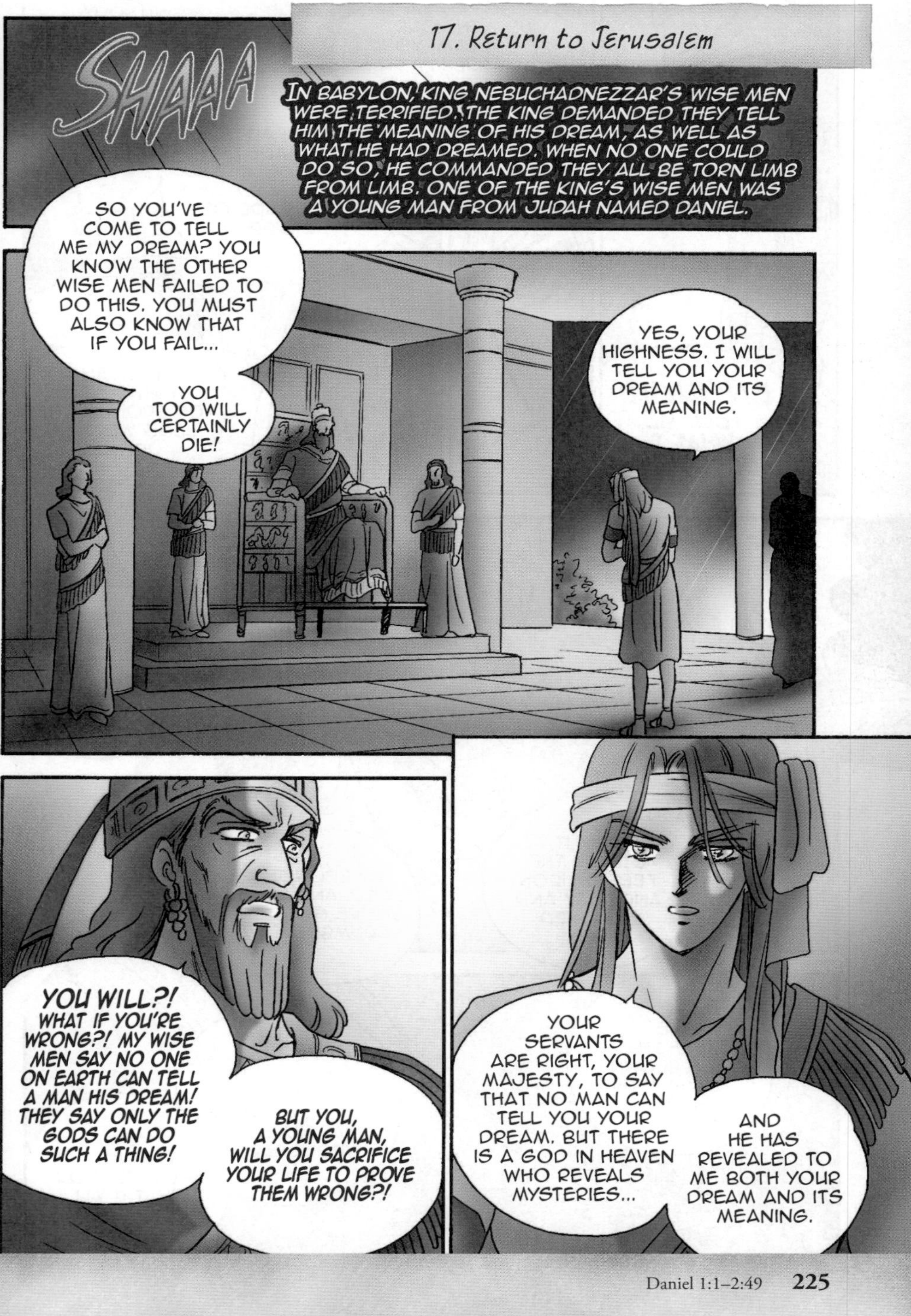

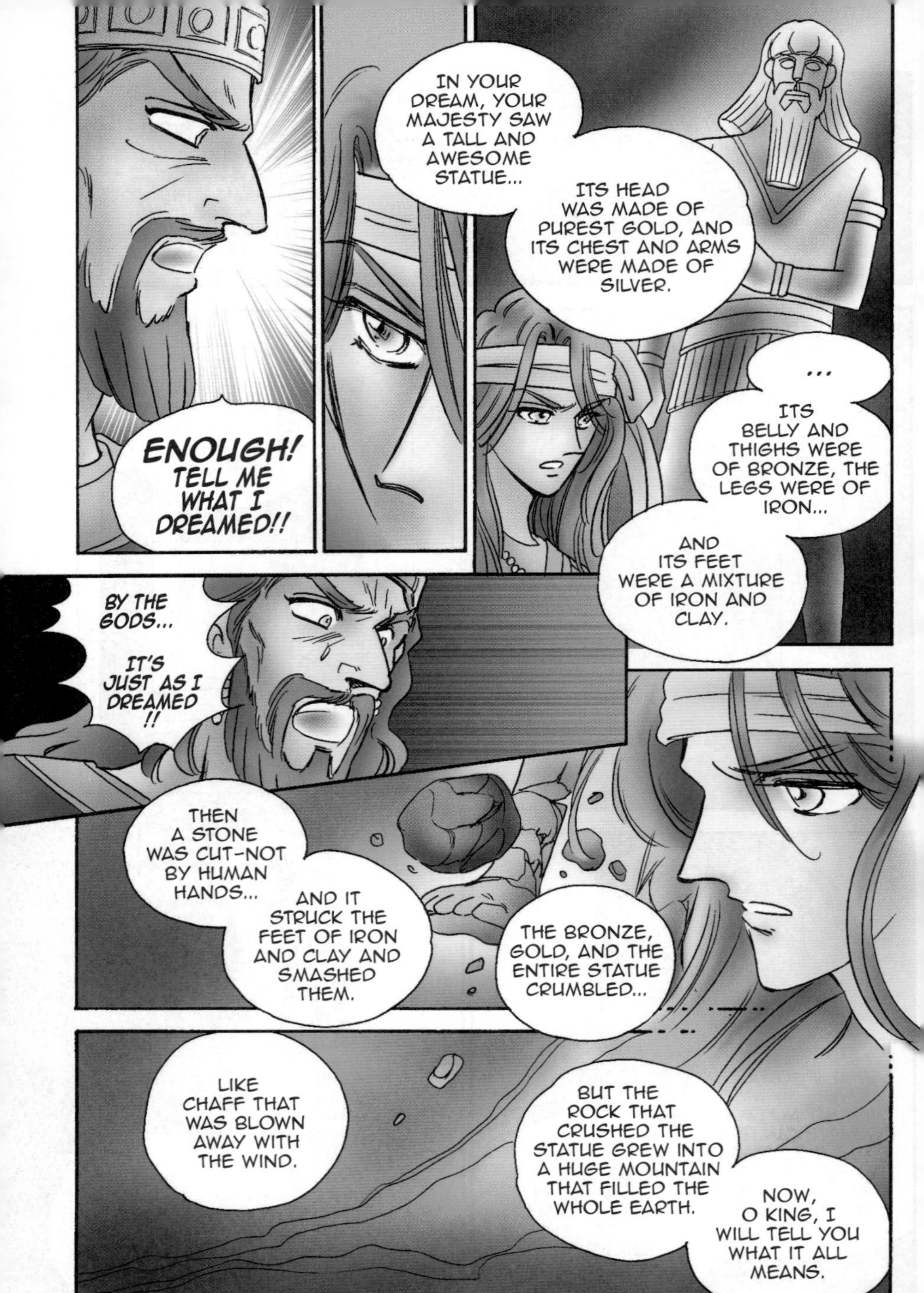
ENOUGH! TELL ME WHAT I DREAMED!!
IN YOUR DREAM, YOUR MAJESTY SAW A TALL AND AWESOME STATUE...
ITS HEAD WAS MADE OF PUREST GOLD, AND ITS CHEST AND ARMS WERE MADE OF SILVER.
...
ITS BELLY AND THIGHS WERE OF BRONZE, THE LEGS WERE OF IRON...
AND ITS FEET WERE A MIXTURE OF IRON AND CLAY.
BY THE GODS...
IT'S JUST AS I DREAMED!!
THEN A STONE WAS CUT–NOT BY HUMAN HANDS...
AND IT STRUCK THE FEET OF IRON AND CLAY AND SMASHED THEM.
THE BRONZE, GOLD, AND THE ENTIRE STATUE CRUMBLED...
LIKE CHAFF THAT WAS BLOWN AWAY WITH THE WIND.
BUT THE ROCK THAT CRUSHED THE STATUE GREW INTO A HUGE MOUNTAIN THAT FILLED THE WHOLE EARTH.
NOW, O KING, I WILL TELL YOU WHAT IT ALL MEANS.

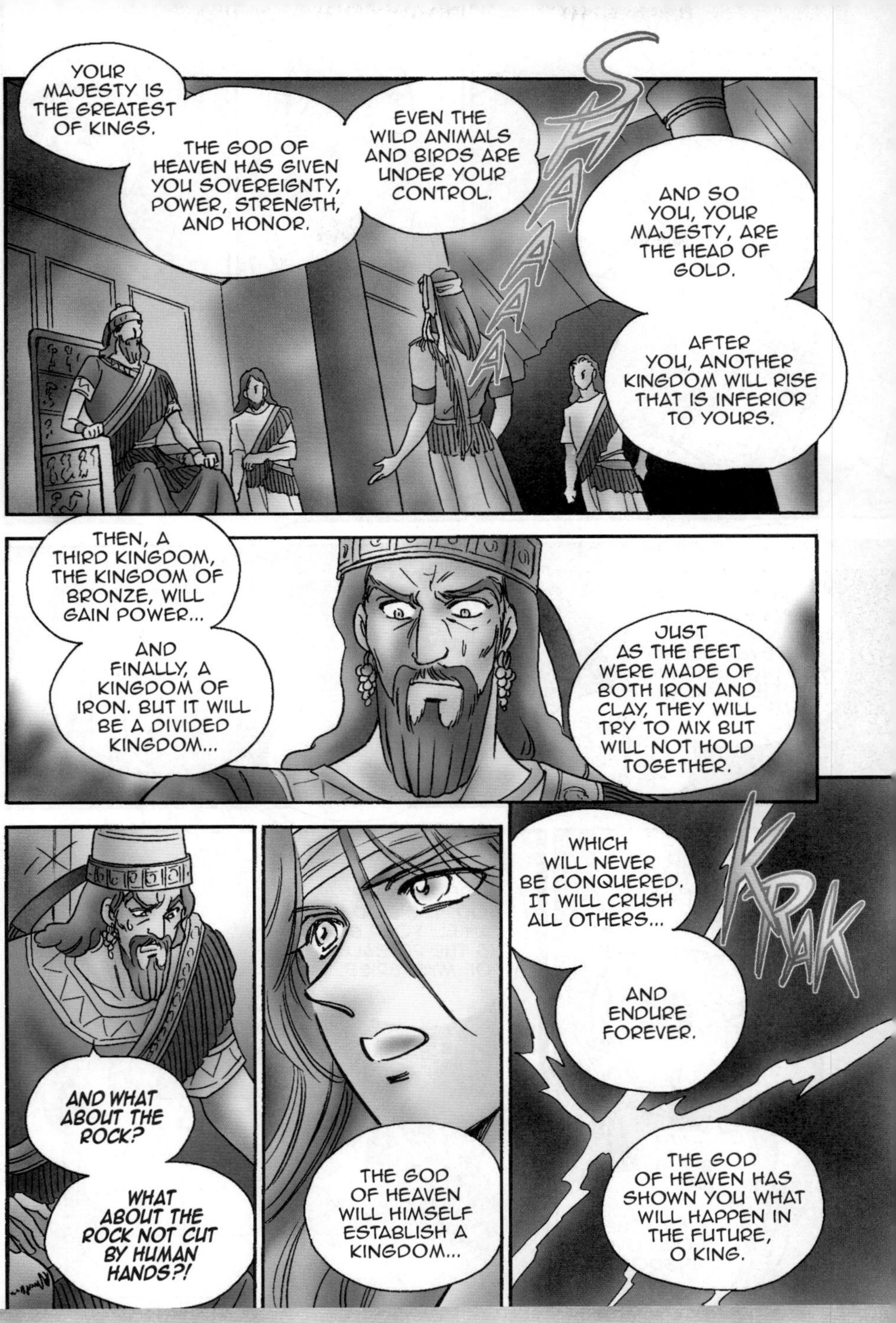
YOUR MAJESTY IS THE GREATEST OF KINGS.
THE GOD OF HEAVEN HAS GIVEN YOU SOVEREIGNTY, POWER, STRENGTH, AND HONOR.
EVEN THE WILD ANIMALS AND BIRDS ARE UNDER YOUR CONTROL.
SHAAAAA
AND SO YOU, YOUR MAJESTY, ARE THE HEAD OF GOLD.
AFTER YOU, ANOTHER KINGDOM WILL RISE THAT IS INFERIOR TO YOURS.
THEN, A THIRD KINGDOM, THE KINGDOM OF BRONZE, WILL GAIN POWER...
AND FINALLY, A KINGDOM OF IRON. BUT IT WILL BE A DIVIDED KINGDOM...
JUST AS THE FEET WERE MADE OF BOTH IRON AND CLAY, THEY WILL TRY TO MIX BUT WILL NOT HOLD TOGETHER.
AND WHAT ABOUT THE ROCK?
WHAT ABOUT THE ROCK NOT CUT BY HUMAN HANDS?!
THE GOD OF HEAVEN WILL HIMSELF ESTABLISH A KINGDOM...
WHICH WILL NEVER BE CONQUERED. IT WILL CRUSH ALL OTHERS...
KRAK
AND ENDURE FOREVER.
THE GOD OF HEAVEN HAS SHOWN YOU WHAT WILL HAPPEN IN THE FUTURE, O KING.

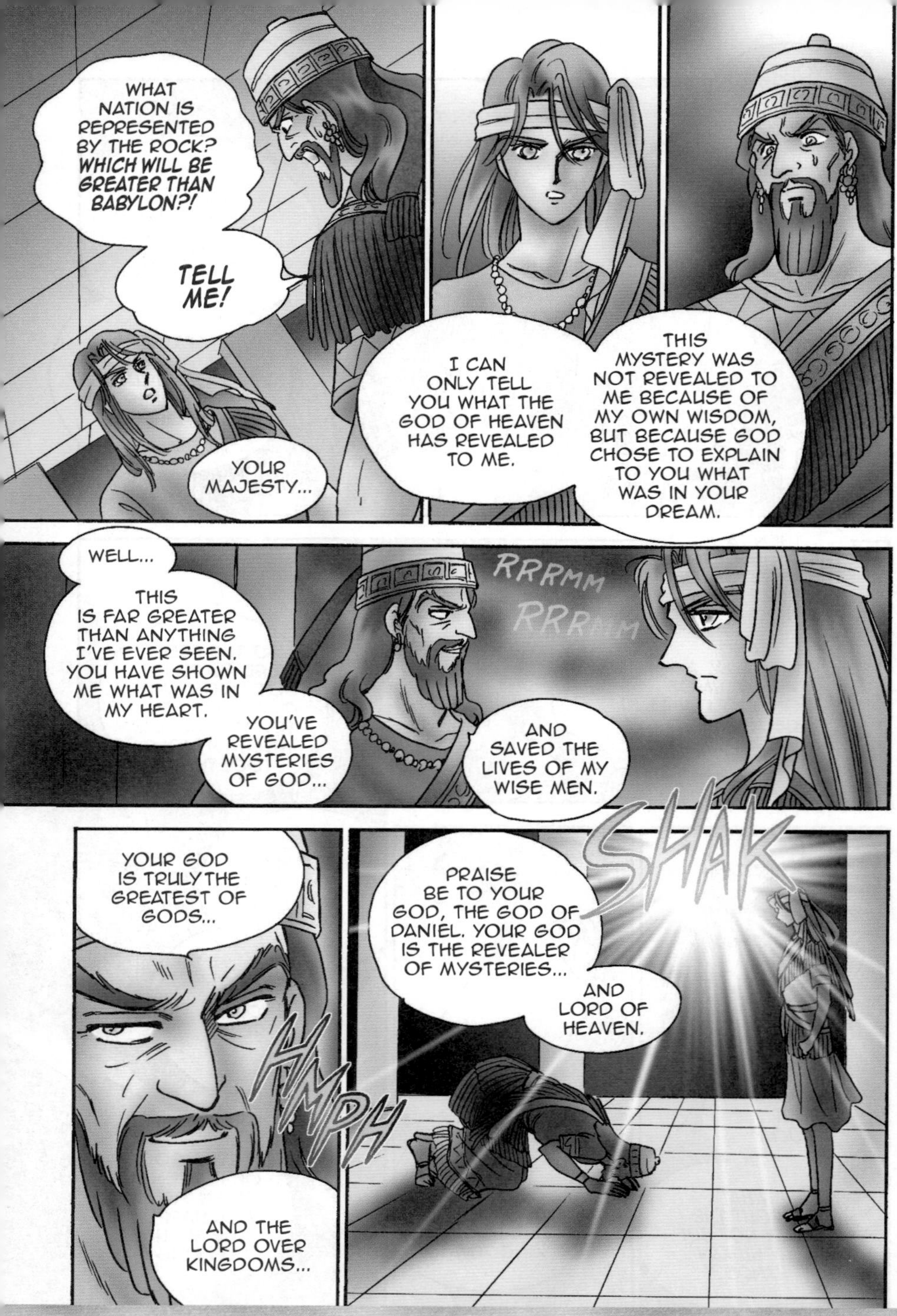
WHAT NATION IS REPRESENTED BY THE ROCK? WHICH WILL BE GREATER THAN BABYLON?!
TELL ME!
YOUR MAJESTY...
I CAN ONLY TELL YOU WHAT THE GOD OF HEAVEN HAS REVEALED TO ME.
THIS MYSTERY WAS NOT REVEALED TO ME BECAUSE OF MY OWN WISDOM, BUT BECAUSE GOD CHOSE TO EXPLAIN TO YOU WHAT WAS IN YOUR DREAM.
WELL...
THIS IS FAR GREATER THAN ANYTHING I'VE EVER SEEN. YOU HAVE SHOWN ME WHAT WAS IN MY HEART.
RRRMM
RRRMM
YOU'VE REVEALED MYSTERIES OF GOD...
AND SAVED THE LIVES OF MY WISE MEN.
YOUR GOD IS TRULY THE GREATEST OF GODS...
HMPH
AND THE LORD OVER KINGDOMS...
SHAK
PRAISE BE TO YOUR GOD, THE GOD OF DANIEL. YOUR GOD IS THE REVEALER OF MYSTERIES...
AND LORD OF HEAVEN.

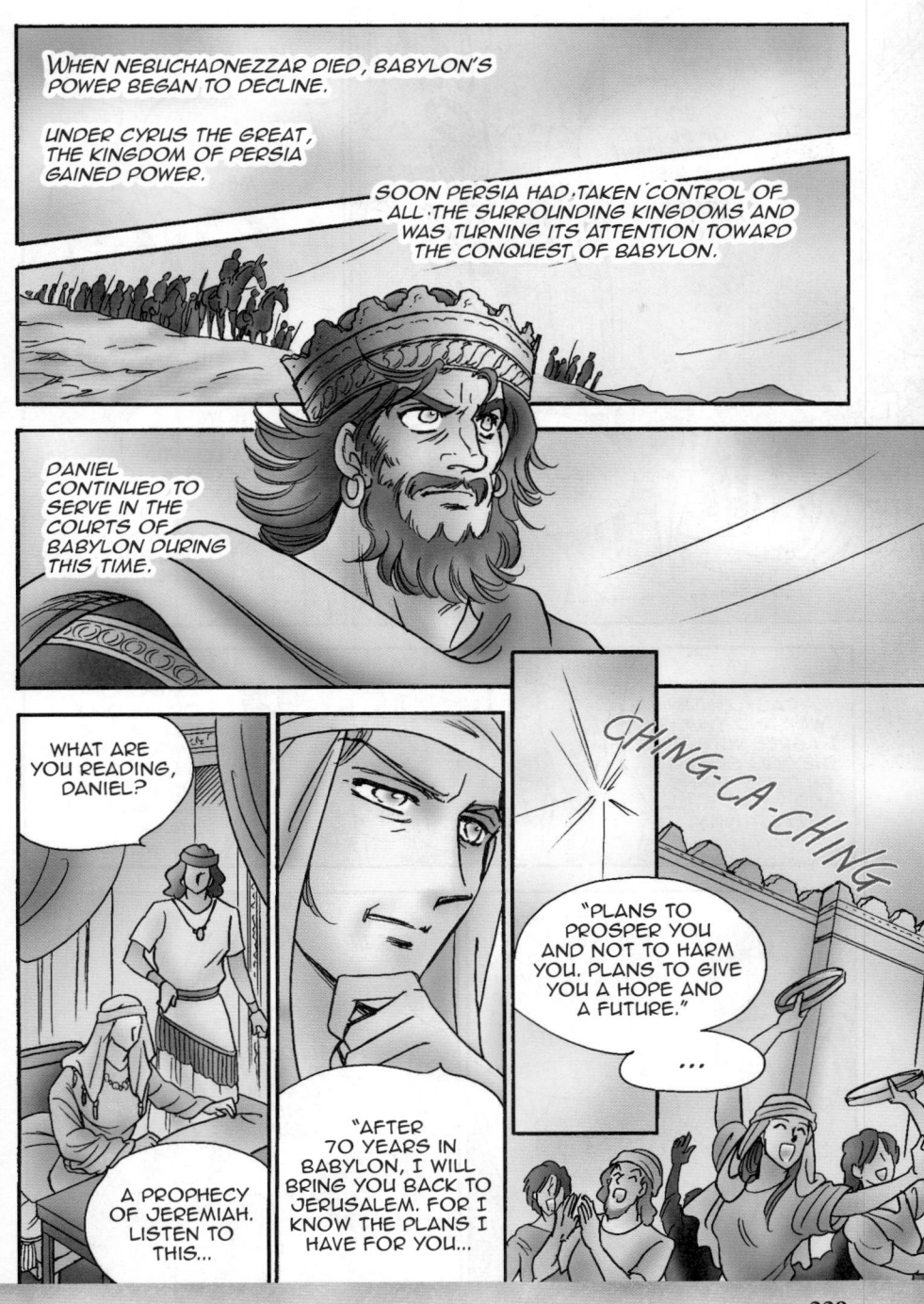

WHEN NEBUCHADNEZZAR DIED, BABYLON'S POWER BEGAN TO DECLINE.

UNDER CYRUS THE GREAT, THE KINGDOM OF PERSIA GAINED POWER.

SOON PERSIA HAD TAKEN CONTROL OF ALL THE SURROUNDING KINGDOMS AND WAS TURNING ITS ATTENTION TOWARD THE CONQUEST OF BABYLON.

DANIEL CONTINUED TO SERVE IN THE COURTS OF BABYLON DURING THIS TIME.

WHAT ARE YOU READING, DANIEL?

CHING-CA-CHING

"PLANS TO PROSPER YOU AND NOT TO HARM YOU. PLANS TO GIVE YOU A HOPE AND A FUTURE."

...

A PROPHECY OF JEREMIAH. LISTEN TO THIS...

"AFTER 70 YEARS IN BABYLON, I WILL BRING YOU BACK TO JERUSALEM. FOR I KNOW THE PLANS I HAVE FOR YOU...

WHO WILL PROTECT US FROM CYRUS THE GREAT?

BABYLON HAS BECOME A PEACEFUL HOME FOR MOST OF US! IT DOESN'T SEEM LIKE KING BELSHAZZAR, WILL PROTECT US!

GOD HAS CHOSEN KING CYRUS TO FREE ISRAEL.

THE PROPHET ISAIAH SAID GOD WOULD USE CYRUS TO RETURN US TO ISRAEL AND REBUILD JERUSALEM.

HUH?!

AND JEREMIAH SAID 70 YEARS IN EXILE! THAT TIME IS ALMOST UP!

HEY! THAT'S TRUE!

THAT MEANS WE COULD BE RESTORED SOON!

BUT IF THERE'S A WAR... WHAT IF WE ALL DIE?

PERHAPS THINGS WILL END MORE PEACEFULLY THAN WE EXPECT. CERTAINLY THE LORD KNOWS THE PLANS HE HAS FOR BABYLON...

AND FOR ISRAEL AS WELL.

I HEAR YOUR CONCERN. BUT WE MUST TRUST THAT THE LORD WILL BE FAITHFUL TO DO AS HE SAYS.

I CAN ENCOURAGE YOU WITH THIS, HOWEVER. KING CYRUS ISN'T ONLY A MILITARY KING, HE'S ALSO A WISE AND TOLERANT LEADER.

EVERYONE IS UNHAPPY WITH KING BELSHAZZAR. THOUGH WAR IS CLOSE AT HAND, HE CELEBRATES WITH FRIENDS.

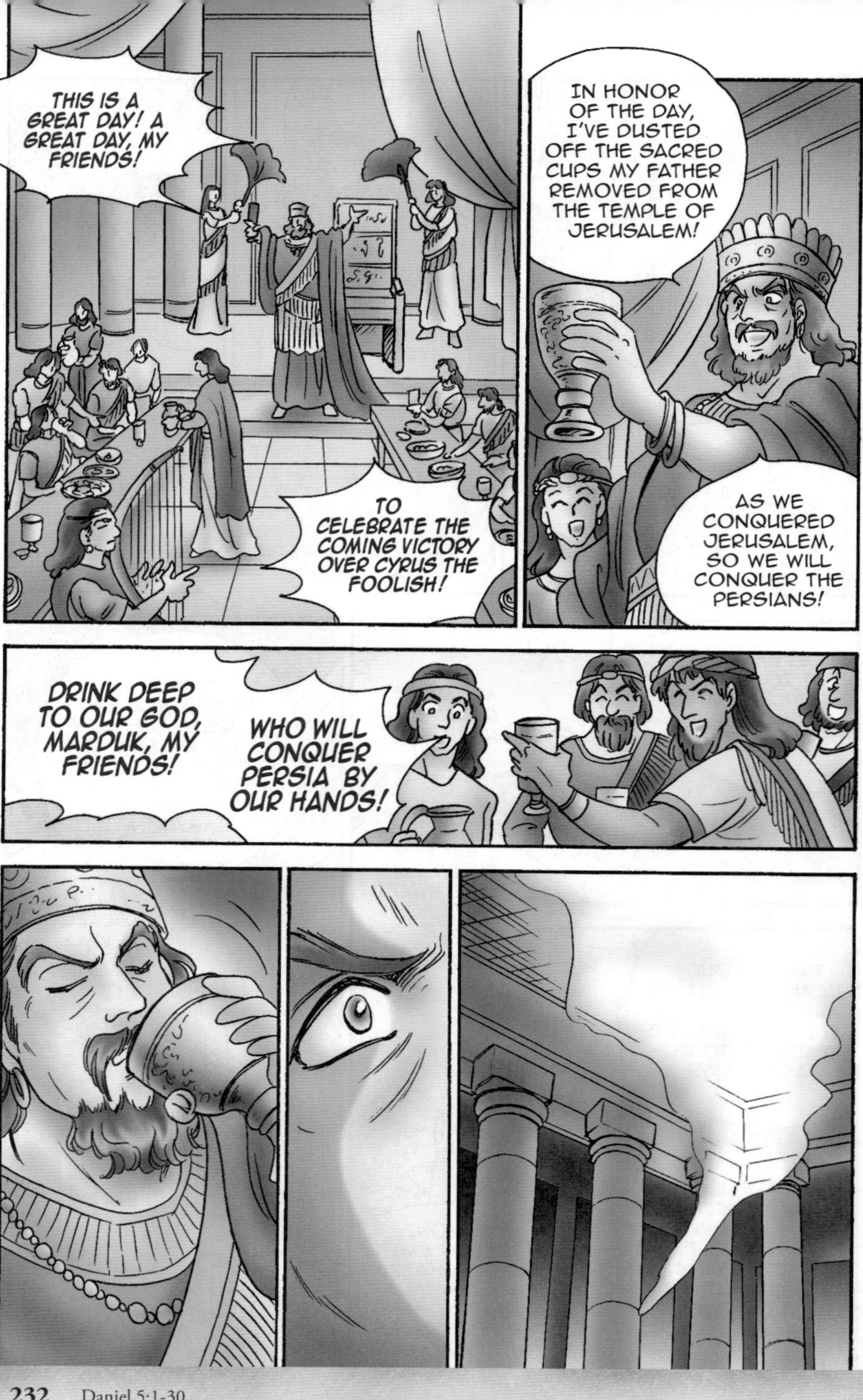
THIS IS A GREAT DAY! A GREAT DAY, MY FRIENDS!
TO CELEBRATE THE COMING VICTORY OVER CYRUS THE FOOLISH!
IN HONOR OF THE DAY, I'VE DUSTED OFF THE SACRED CUPS MY FATHER REMOVED FROM THE TEMPLE OF JERUSALEM!
AS WE CONQUERED JERUSALEM, SO WE WILL CONQUER THE PERSIANS!
DRINK DEEP TO OUR GOD, MARDUK, MY FRIENDS!
WHO WILL CONQUER PERSIA BY OUR HANDS!

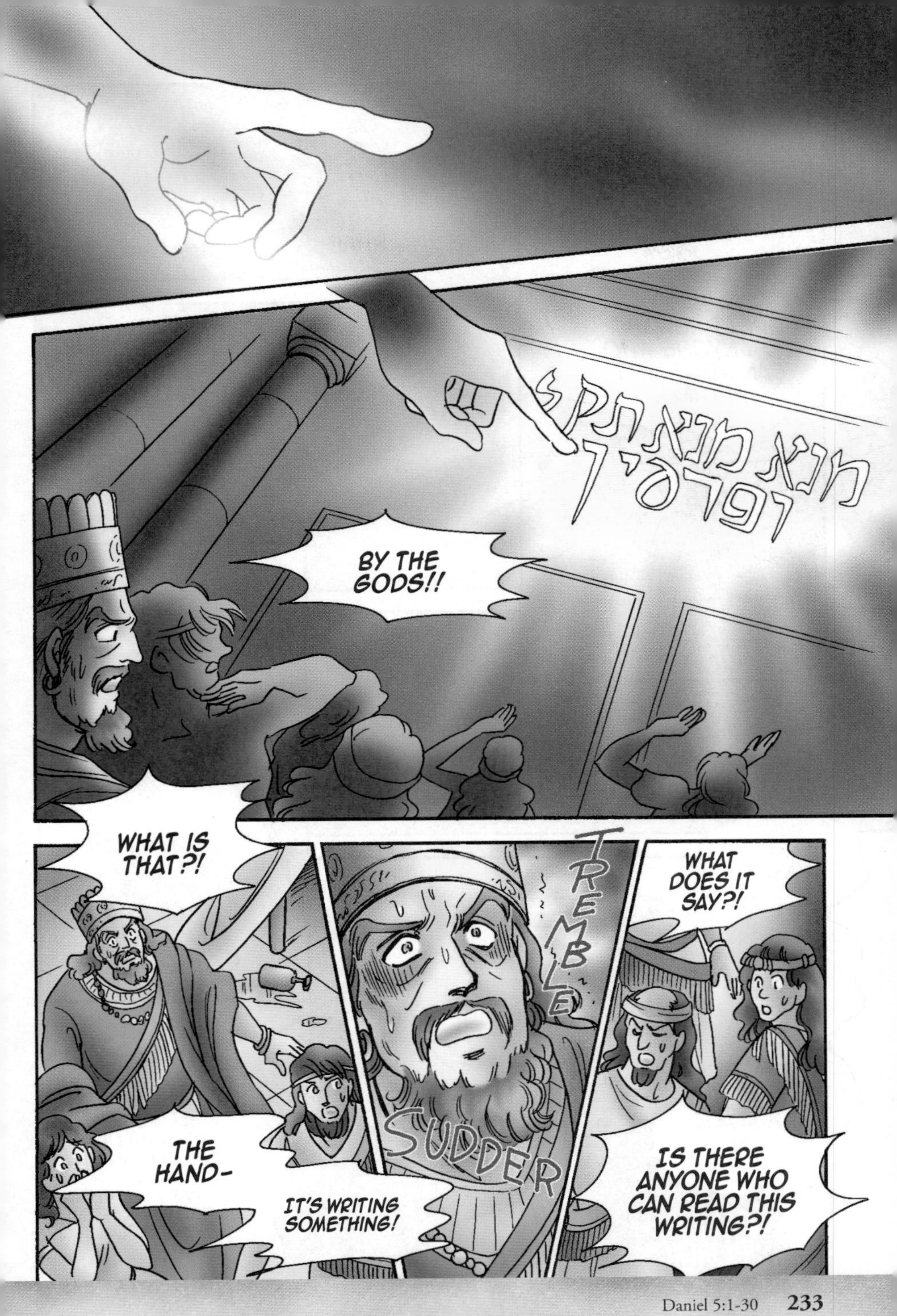

מנא מנא תקל
ופרסין
BY THE GODS!!
WHAT IS THAT?!
TREMBLE
WHAT DOES IT SAY?!
THE HAND-
IT'S WRITING SOMETHING!
SUDDER
IS THERE ANYONE WHO CAN READ THIS WRITING?!

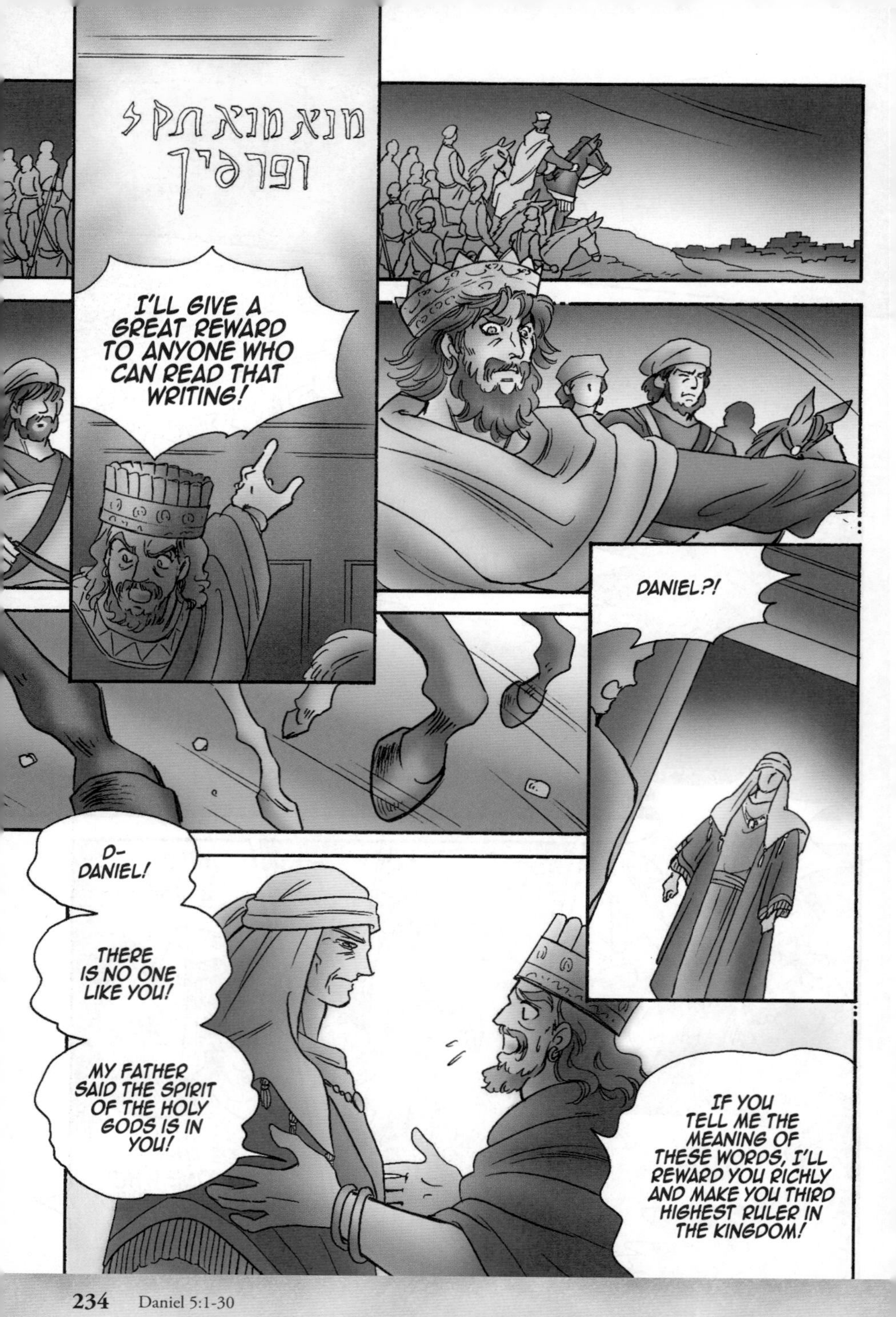
מנא מנא תקל
ופרסין
I'LL GIVE A GREAT REWARD TO ANYONE WHO CAN READ THAT WRITING!
DANIEL?!
D- DANIEL!
THERE IS NO ONE LIKE YOU!
MY FATHER SAID THE SPIRIT OF THE HOLY GODS IS IN YOU!
IF YOU TELL ME THE MEANING OF THESE WORDS, I'LL REWARD YOU RICHLY AND MAKE YOU THIRD HIGHEST RULER IN THE KINGDOM!

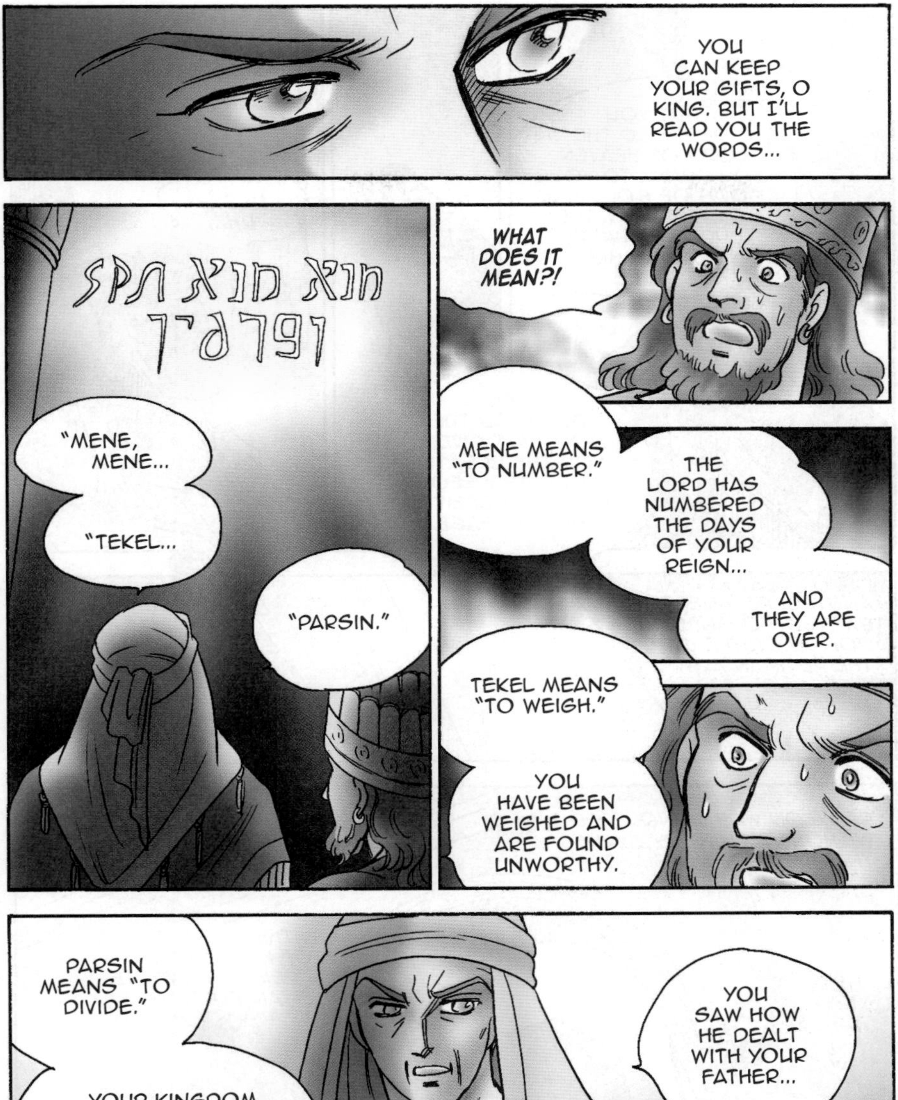
YOU CAN KEEP YOUR GIFTS, O KING. BUT I'LL READ YOU THE WORDS...
"MENE, MENE...
"TEKEL...
"PARSIN."
WHAT DOES IT MEAN?!
MENE MEANS "TO NUMBER."
THE LORD HAS NUMBERED THE DAYS OF YOUR REIGN...
AND THEY ARE OVER.
TEKEL MEANS "TO WEIGH."
YOU HAVE BEEN WEIGHED AND ARE FOUND UNWORTHY.
PARSIN MEANS "TO DIVIDE."
YOUR KINGDOM HAS BEEN DIVIDED. IT WILL BE GIVEN TO THE MEDES AND PERSIANS BECAUSE YOU, KING BELSHAZZAR, HAVE NOT HUMBLED YOURSELF BEFORE THE LORD, THE GOD OF HEAVEN.
YOU SAW HOW HE DEALT WITH YOUR FATHER...
HOW HE RAISED HIM UP AND BROUGHT HIM LOW. AND YET YOU DID NOT BOW BEFORE THE LORD.

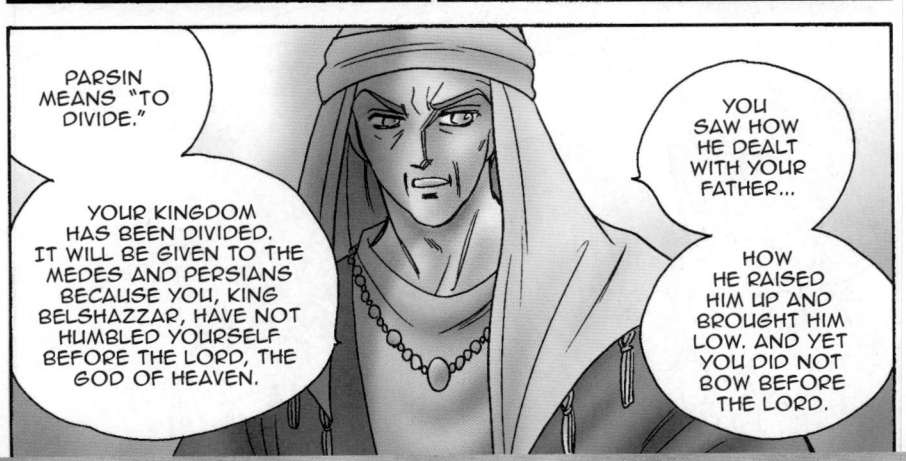

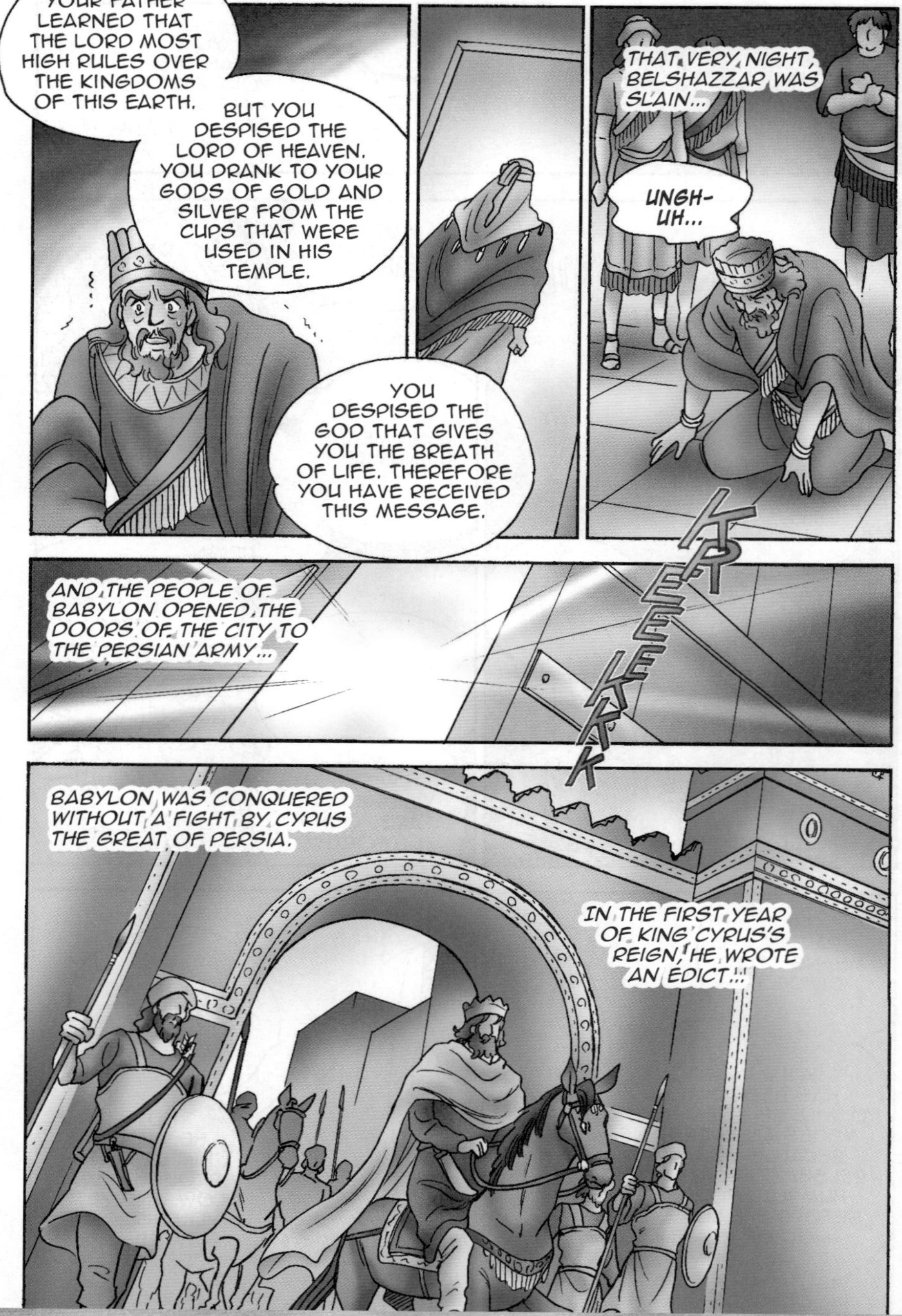
YOUR FATHER LEARNED THAT THE LORD MOST HIGH RULES OVER THE KINGDOMS OF THIS EARTH.
BUT YOU DESPISED THE LORD OF HEAVEN. YOU DRANK TO YOUR GODS OF GOLD AND SILVER FROM THE CUPS THAT WERE USED IN HIS TEMPLE.
YOU DESPISED THE GOD THAT GIVES YOU THE BREATH OF LIFE. THEREFORE YOU HAVE RECEIVED THIS MESSAGE.
THAT VERY NIGHT, BELSHAZZAR WAS SLAIN...
UNGH-UH...
KREEEEKKKK
AND THE PEOPLE OF BABYLON OPENED THE DOORS OF THE CITY TO THE PERSIAN ARMY...
BABYLON WAS CONQUERED WITHOUT A FIGHT BY CYRUS THE GREAT OF PERSIA.
IN THE FIRST YEAR OF KING CYRUS'S REIGN, HE WROTE AN EDICT...

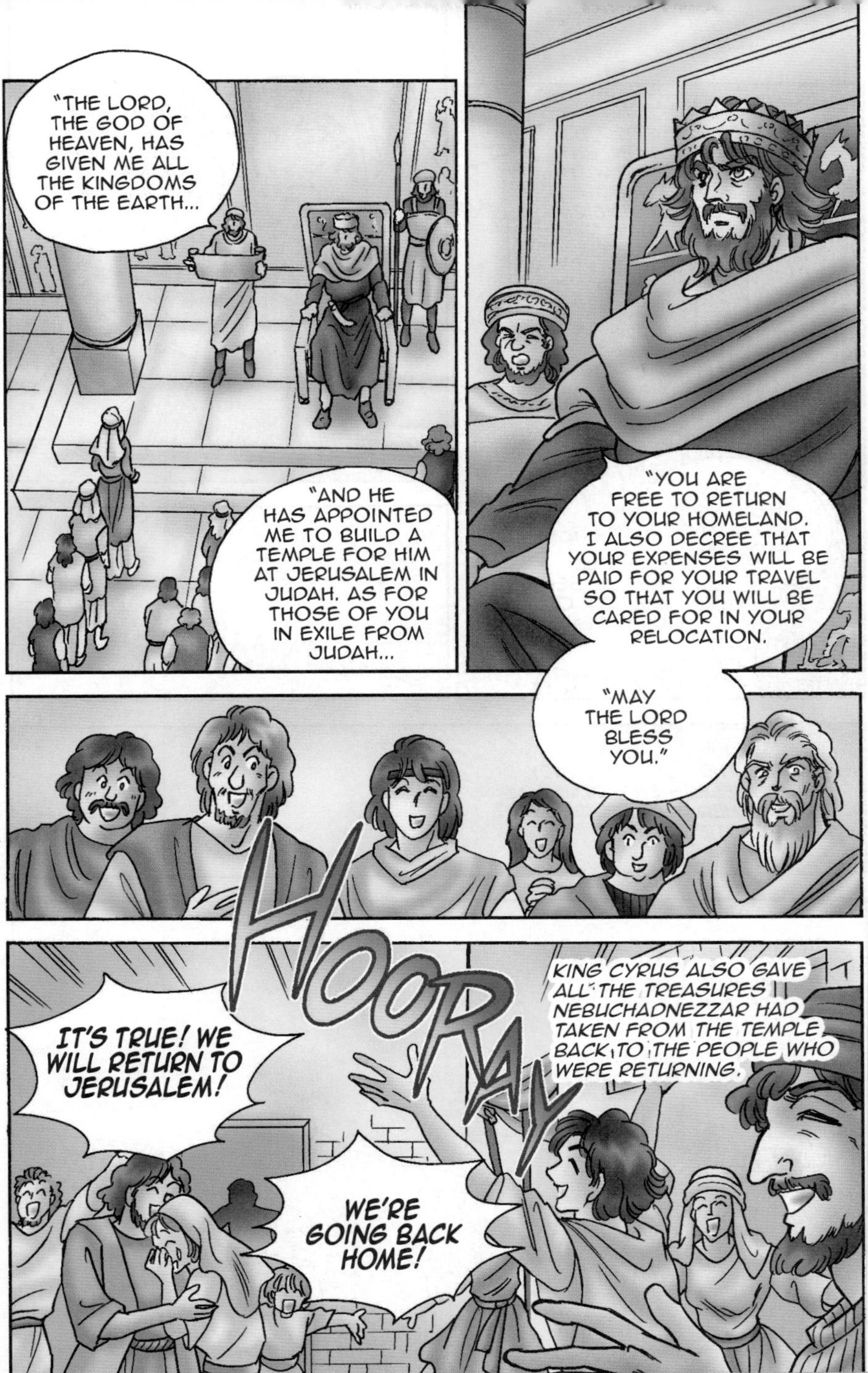
"THE LORD, THE GOD OF HEAVEN, HAS GIVEN ME ALL THE KINGDOMS OF THE EARTH...
"AND HE HAS APPOINTED ME TO BUILD A TEMPLE FOR HIM AT JERUSALEM IN JUDAH. AS FOR THOSE OF YOU IN EXILE FROM JUDAH...
"YOU ARE FREE TO RETURN TO YOUR HOMELAND. I ALSO DECREE THAT YOUR EXPENSES WILL BE PAID FOR YOUR TRAVEL SO THAT YOU WILL BE CARED FOR IN YOUR RELOCATION.
"MAY THE LORD BLESS YOU."
HOORAY
IT'S TRUE! WE WILL RETURN TO JERUSALEM!
KING CYRUS ALSO GAVE ALL THE TREASURES NEBUCHADNEZZAR HAD TAKEN FROM THE TEMPLE BACK TO THE PEOPLE WHO WERE RETURNING.
WE'RE GOING BACK HOME!

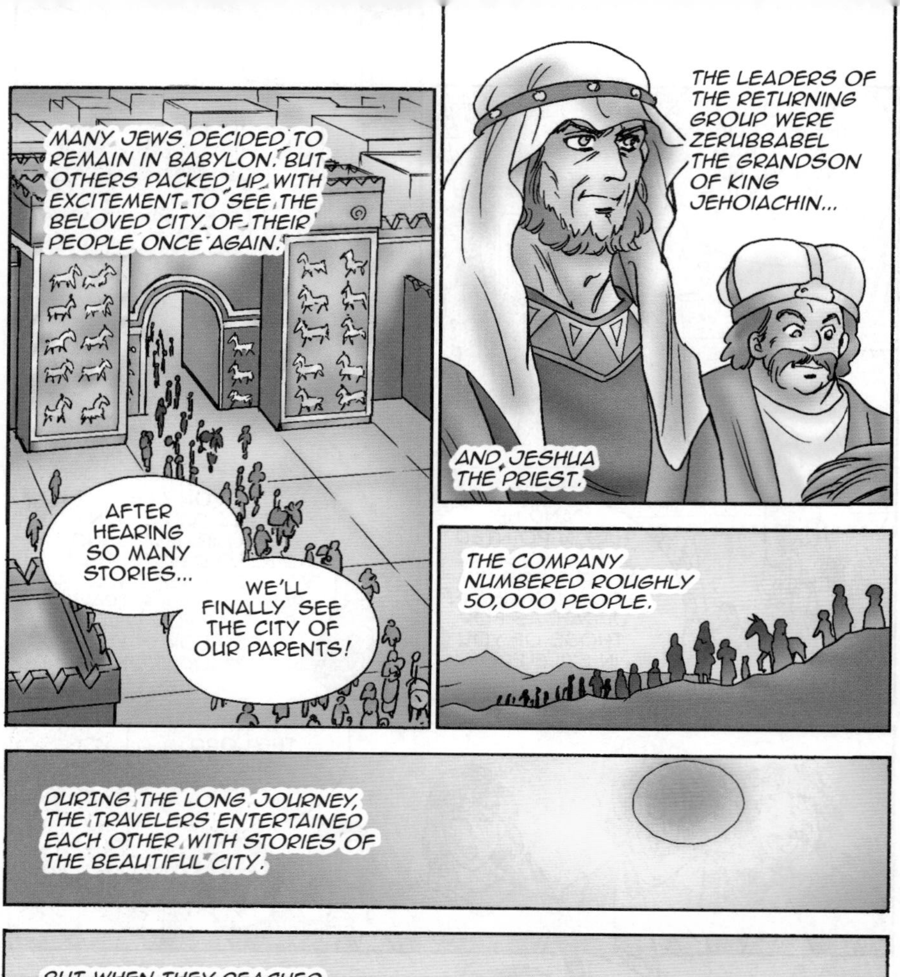
MANY JEWS DECIDED TO REMAIN IN BABYLON. BUT OTHERS PACKED UP WITH EXCITEMENT TO SEE THE BELOVED CITY OF THEIR PEOPLE ONCE AGAIN.
AFTER HEARING SO MANY STORIES...
WE'LL FINALLY SEE THE CITY OF OUR PARENTS!
THE LEADERS OF THE RETURNING GROUP WERE ZERUBBABEL THE GRANDSON OF KING JEHOIACHIN...
AND JESHUA THE PRIEST.
THE COMPANY NUMBERED ROUGHLY 50,000 PEOPLE.
DURING THE LONG JOURNEY, THE TRAVELERS ENTERTAINED EACH OTHER WITH STORIES OF THE BEAUTIFUL CITY.
BUT WHEN THEY REACHED JERUSALEM, WHAT THEY FOUND WAS A DESOLATE CITY OF RUINS.

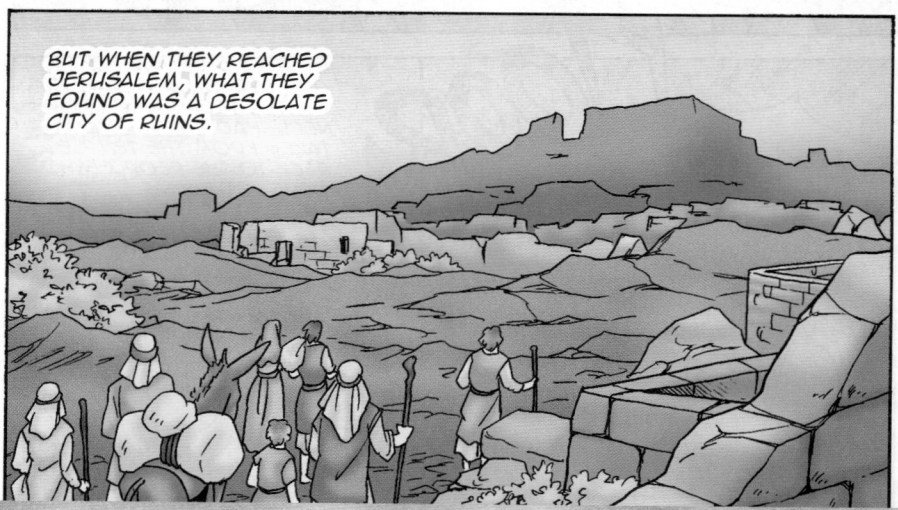

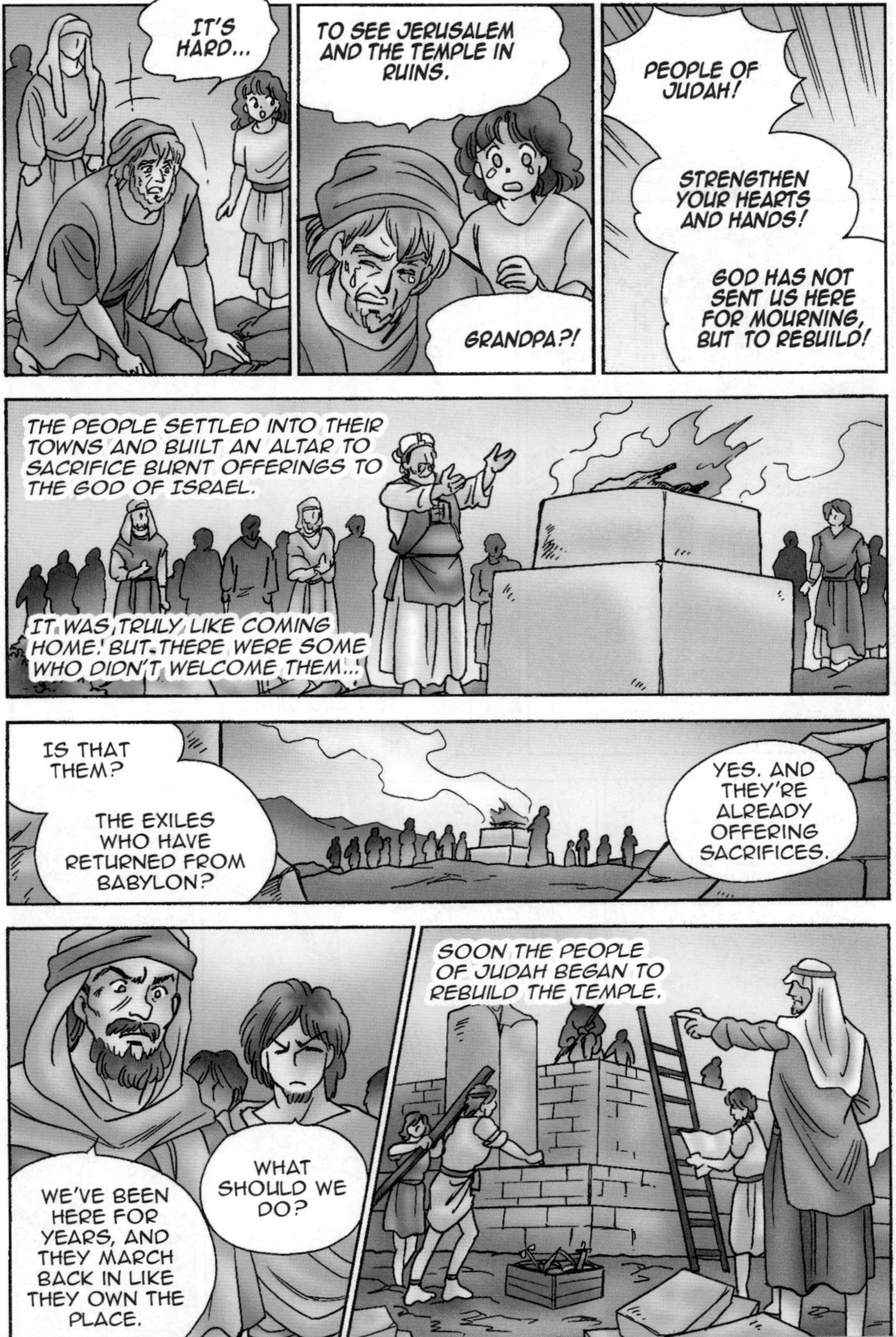
IT'S HARD...
TO SEE JERUSALEM AND THE TEMPLE IN RUINS.
GRANDPA?!
PEOPLE OF JUDAH!
STRENGTHEN YOUR HEARTS AND HANDS!
GOD HAS NOT SENT US HERE FOR MOURNING, BUT TO REBUILD!
THE PEOPLE SETTLED INTO THEIR TOWNS AND BUILT AN ALTAR TO SACRIFICE BURNT OFFERINGS TO THE GOD OF ISRAEL.
IT WAS TRULY LIKE COMING HOME! BUT THERE WERE SOME WHO DIDN'T WELCOME THEM...
IS THAT THEM?
THE EXILES WHO HAVE RETURNED FROM BABYLON?
YES. AND THEY'RE ALREADY OFFERING SACRIFICES.
WE'VE BEEN HERE FOR YEARS, AND THEY MARCH BACK IN LIKE THEY OWN THE PLACE.
WHAT SHOULD WE DO?
SOON THE PEOPLE OF JUDAH BEGAN TO REBUILD THE TEMPLE.

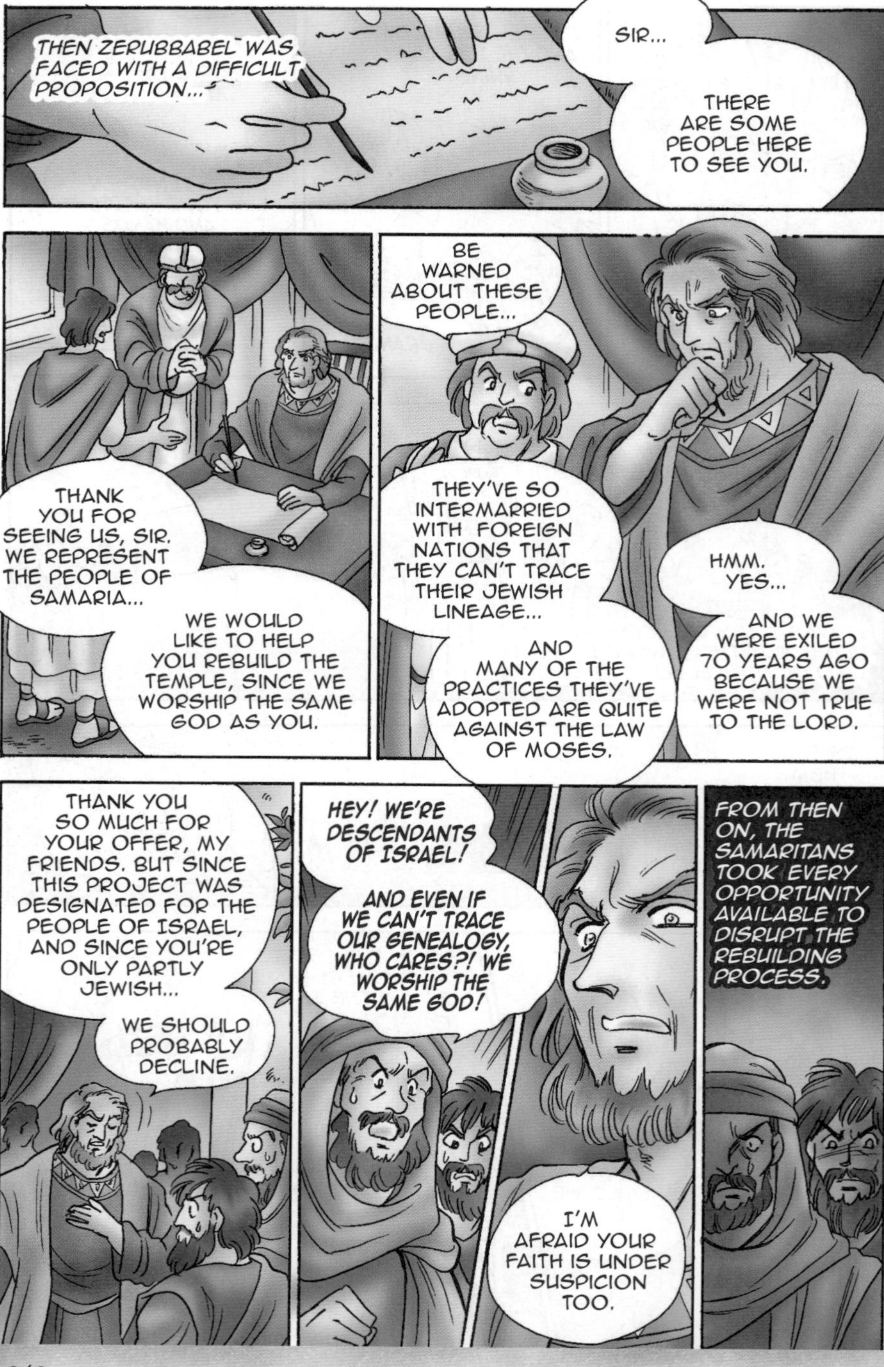
THEN ZERUBBABEL WAS FACED WITH A DIFFICULT PROPOSITION...
SIR...
THERE ARE SOME PEOPLE HERE TO SEE YOU.
THANK YOU FOR SEEING US, SIR. WE REPRESENT THE PEOPLE OF SAMARIA...
WE WOULD LIKE TO HELP YOU REBUILD THE TEMPLE, SINCE WE WORSHIP THE SAME GOD AS YOU.
BE WARNED ABOUT THESE PEOPLE...
THEY'VE SO INTERMARRIED WITH FOREIGN NATIONS THAT THEY CAN'T TRACE THEIR JEWISH LINEAGE...
AND MANY OF THE PRACTICES THEY'VE ADOPTED ARE QUITE AGAINST THE LAW OF MOSES.
HMM. YES...
AND WE WERE EXILED 70 YEARS AGO BECAUSE WE WERE NOT TRUE TO THE LORD.
THANK YOU SO MUCH FOR YOUR OFFER, MY FRIENDS. BUT SINCE THIS PROJECT WAS DESIGNATED FOR THE PEOPLE OF ISRAEL, AND SINCE YOU'RE ONLY PARTLY JEWISH...
WE SHOULD PROBABLY DECLINE.
HEY! WE'RE DESCENDANTS OF ISRAEL!
AND EVEN IF WE CAN'T TRACE OUR GENEALOGY, WHO CARES?! WE WORSHIP THE SAME GOD!
I'M AFRAID YOUR FAITH IS UNDER SUSPICION TOO.
FROM THEN ON, THE SAMARITANS TOOK EVERY OPPORTUNITY AVAILABLE TO DISRUPT THE REBUILDING PROCESS.

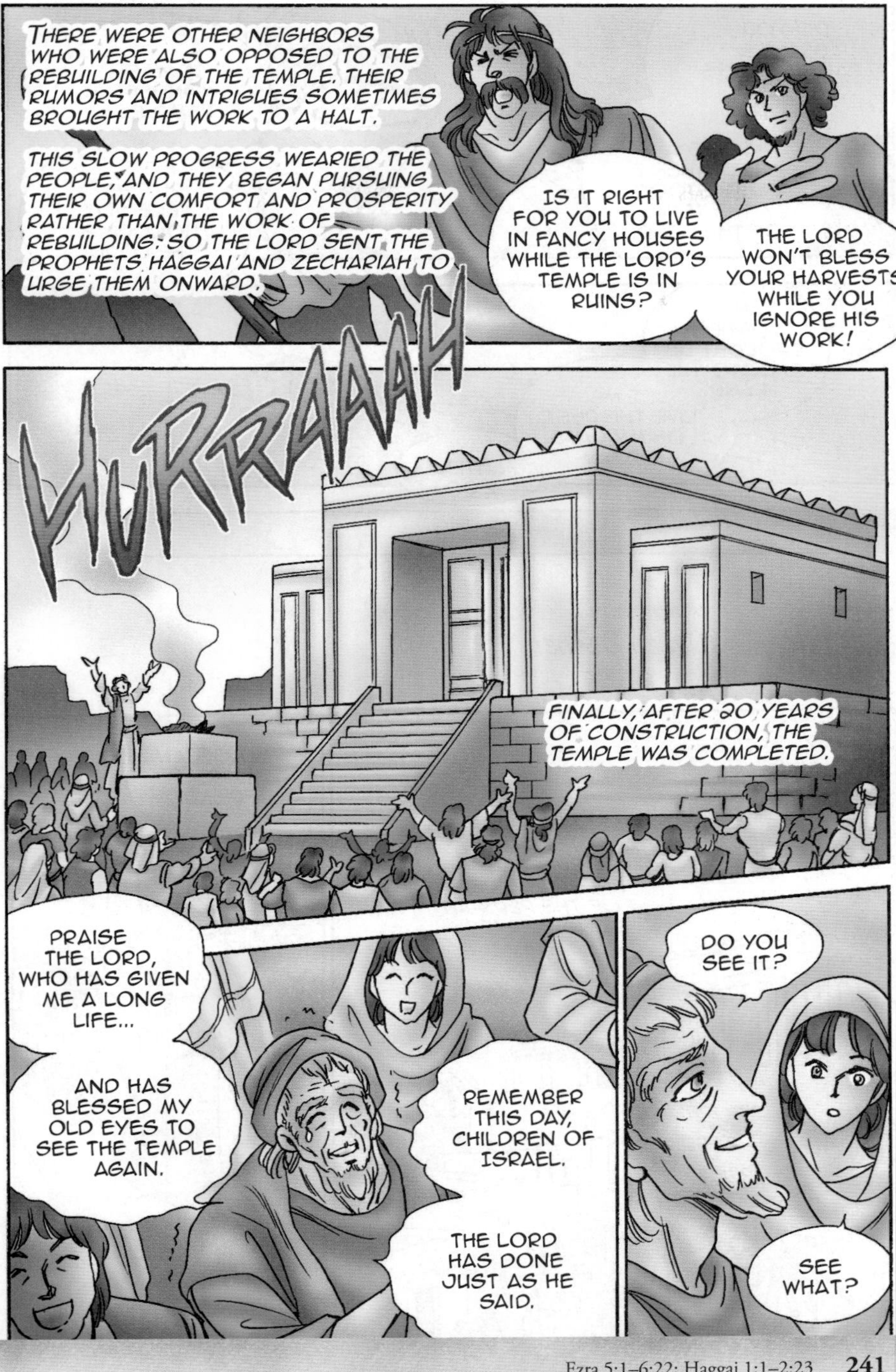
THERE WERE OTHER NEIGHBORS WHO WERE ALSO OPPOSED TO THE REBUILDING OF THE TEMPLE. THEIR RUMORS AND INTRIGUES SOMETIMES BROUGHT THE WORK TO A HALT.
THIS SLOW PROGRESS WEARIED THE PEOPLE, AND THEY BEGAN PURSUING THEIR OWN COMFORT AND PROSPERITY RATHER THAN THE WORK OF REBUILDING. SO THE LORD SENT THE PROPHETS HAGGAI AND ZECHARIAH TO URGE THEM ONWARD.
IS IT RIGHT FOR YOU TO LIVE IN FANCY HOUSES WHILE THE LORD'S TEMPLE IS IN RUINS?
THE LORD WON'T BLESS YOUR HARVESTS WHILE YOU IGNORE HIS WORK!
HURRAAAH
FINALLY, AFTER 20 YEARS OF CONSTRUCTION, THE TEMPLE WAS COMPLETED.
PRAISE THE LORD, WHO HAS GIVEN ME A LONG LIFE...
AND HAS BLESSED MY OLD EYES TO SEE THE TEMPLE AGAIN.
REMEMBER THIS DAY, CHILDREN OF ISRAEL.
THE LORD HAS DONE JUST AS HE SAID.
DO YOU SEE IT?
SEE WHAT?

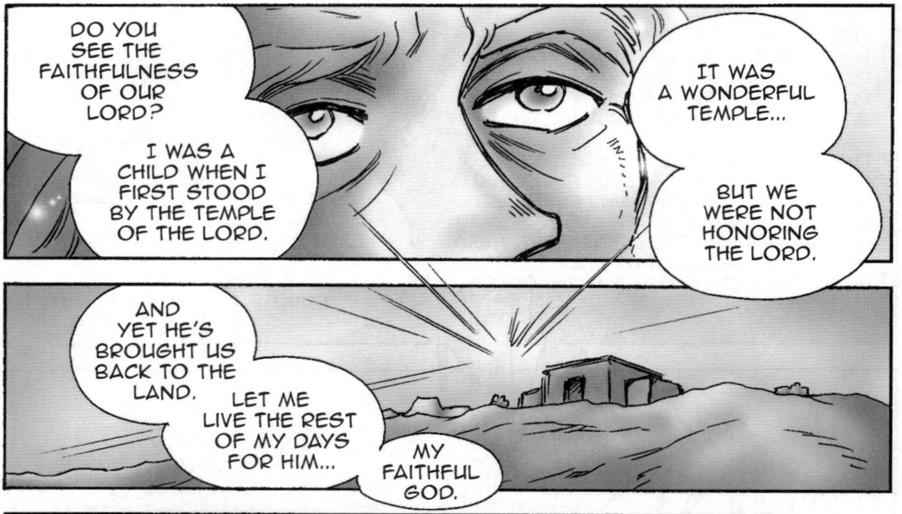
DO YOU SEE THE FAITHFULNESS OF OUR LORD?
I WAS A CHILD WHEN I FIRST STOOD BY THE TEMPLE OF THE LORD.
IT WAS A WONDERFUL TEMPLE...
BUT WE WERE NOT HONORING THE LORD.
AND YET HE'S BROUGHT US BACK TO THE LAND.
LET ME LIVE THE REST OF MY DAYS FOR HIM...
MY FAITHFUL GOD.

18. Queen Esther

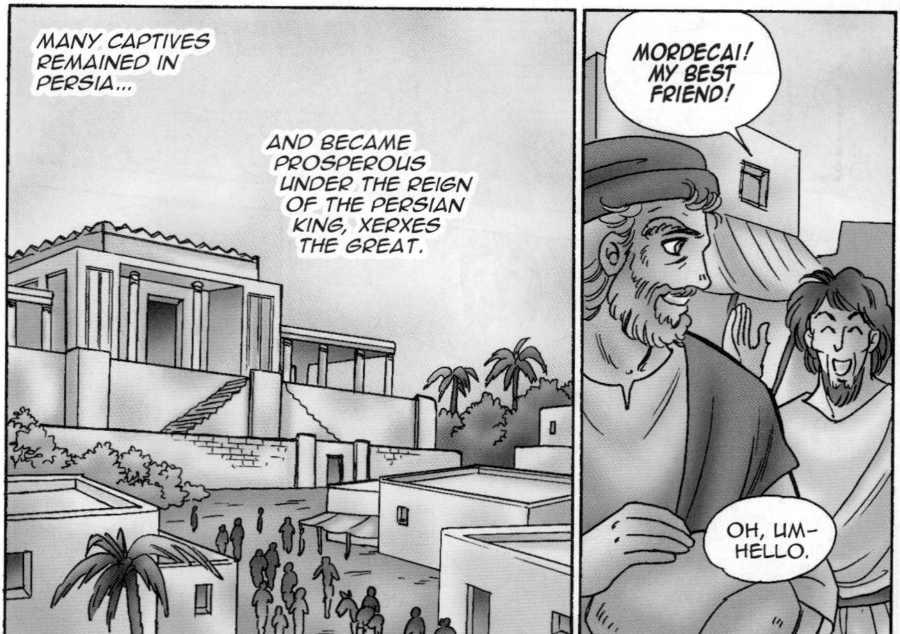
MANY CAPTIVES REMAINED IN PERSIA...
AND BECAME PROSPEROUS UNDER THE REIGN OF THE PERSIAN KING, XERXES THE GREAT.
MORDECAI! MY BEST FRIEND!
OH, UM- HELLO.

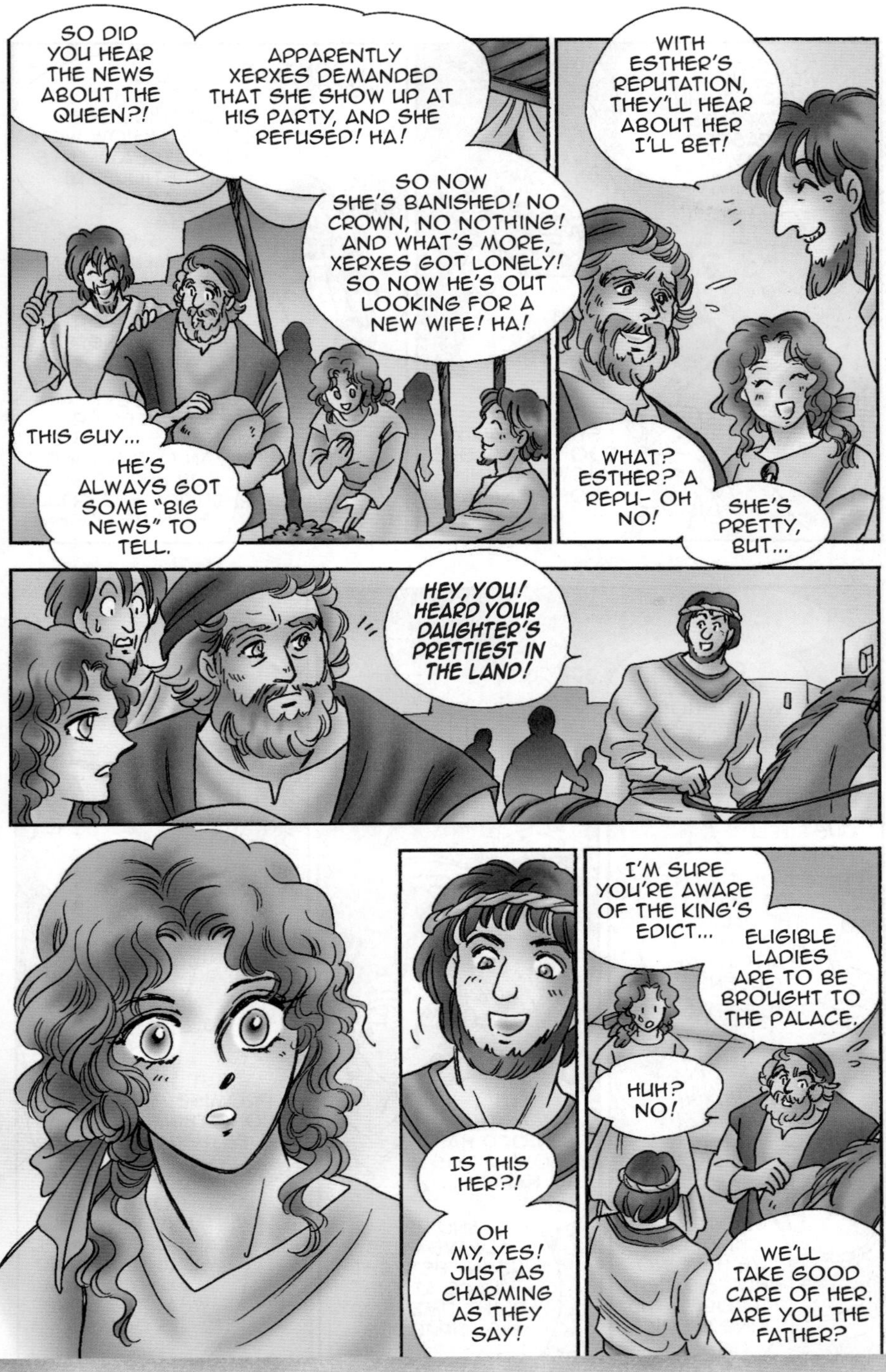
SO DID YOU HEAR THE NEWS ABOUT THE QUEEN?!
APPARENTLY XERXES DEMANDED THAT SHE SHOW UP AT HIS PARTY, AND SHE REFUSED! HA!
SO NOW SHE'S BANISHED! NO CROWN, NO NOTHING! AND WHAT'S MORE, XERXES GOT LONELY! SO NOW HE'S OUT LOOKING FOR A NEW WIFE! HA!
THIS GUY...
HE'S ALWAYS GOT SOME "BIG NEWS" TO TELL.
WITH ESTHER'S REPUTATION, THEY'LL HEAR ABOUT HER I'LL BET!
WHAT? ESTHER? A REPU- OH NO!
SHE'S PRETTY, BUT...
HEY, YOU! HEARD YOUR DAUGHTER'S PRETTIEST IN THE LAND!
IS THIS HER?!
OH MY, YES! JUST AS CHARMING AS THEY SAY!
I'M SURE YOU'RE AWARE OF THE KING'S EDICT...
ELIGIBLE LADIES ARE TO BE BROUGHT TO THE PALACE.
HUH? NO!
WE'LL TAKE GOOD CARE OF HER. ARE YOU THE FATHER?

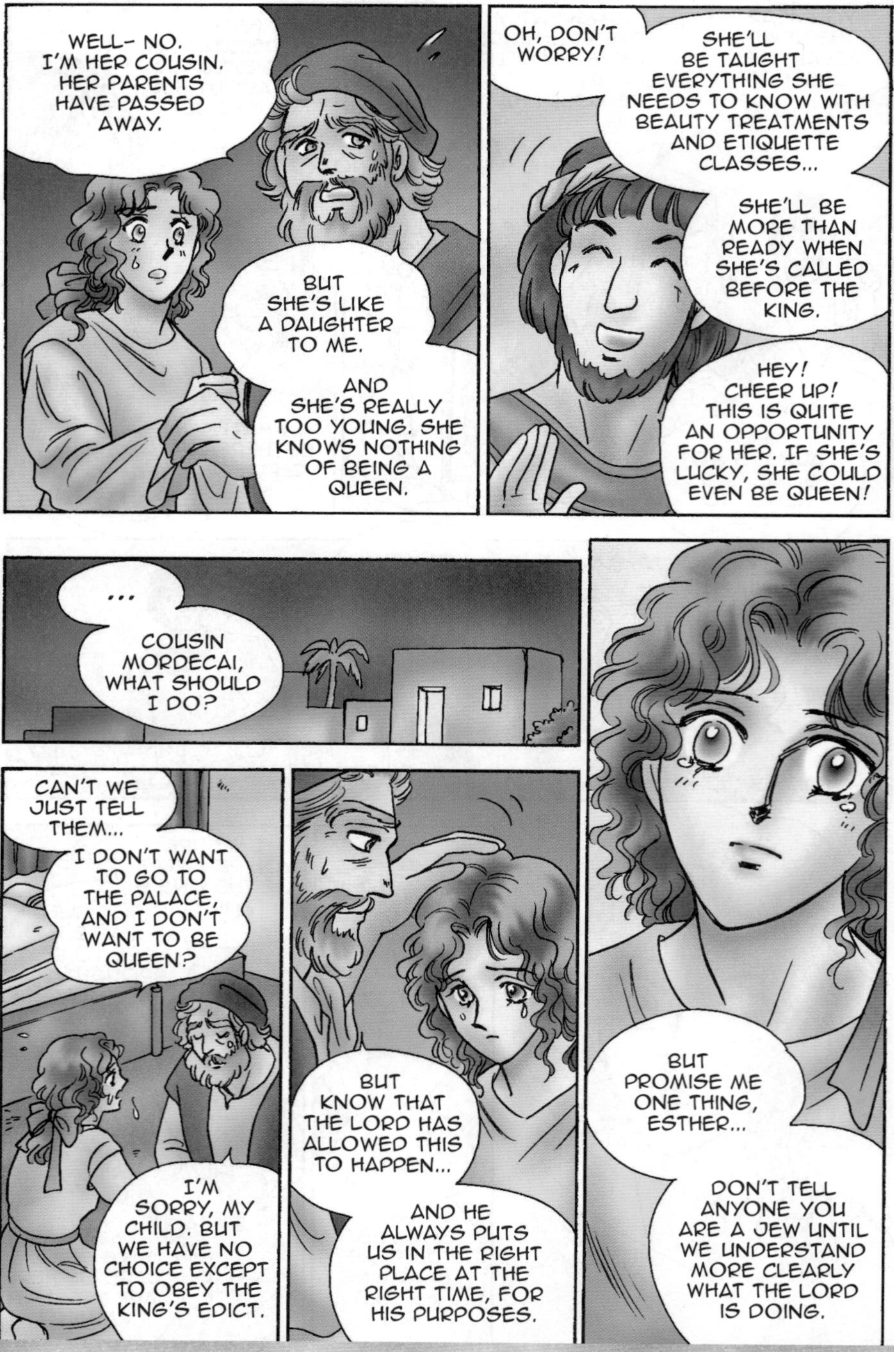
WELL- NO. I'M HER COUSIN. HER PARENTS HAVE PASSED AWAY.
BUT SHE'S LIKE A DAUGHTER TO ME.
AND SHE'S REALLY TOO YOUNG. SHE KNOWS NOTHING OF BEING A QUEEN.
OH, DON'T WORRY!
SHE'LL BE TAUGHT EVERYTHING SHE NEEDS TO KNOW WITH BEAUTY TREATMENTS AND ETIQUETTE CLASSES...
SHE'LL BE MORE THAN READY WHEN SHE'S CALLED BEFORE THE KING.
HEY! CHEER UP! THIS IS QUITE AN OPPORTUNITY FOR HER. IF SHE'S LUCKY, SHE COULD EVEN BE QUEEN!
...
COUSIN MORDECAI, WHAT SHOULD I DO?
CAN'T WE JUST TELL THEM...
I DON'T WANT TO GO TO THE PALACE, AND I DON'T WANT TO BE QUEEN?
I'M SORRY, MY CHILD. BUT WE HAVE NO CHOICE EXCEPT TO OBEY THE KING'S EDICT.
BUT KNOW THAT THE LORD HAS ALLOWED THIS TO HAPPEN...
AND HE ALWAYS PUTS US IN THE RIGHT PLACE AT THE RIGHT TIME, FOR HIS PURPOSES.
BUT PROMISE ME ONE THING, ESTHER...
DON'T TELL ANYONE YOU ARE A JEW UNTIL WE UNDERSTAND MORE CLEARLY WHAT THE LORD IS DOING.

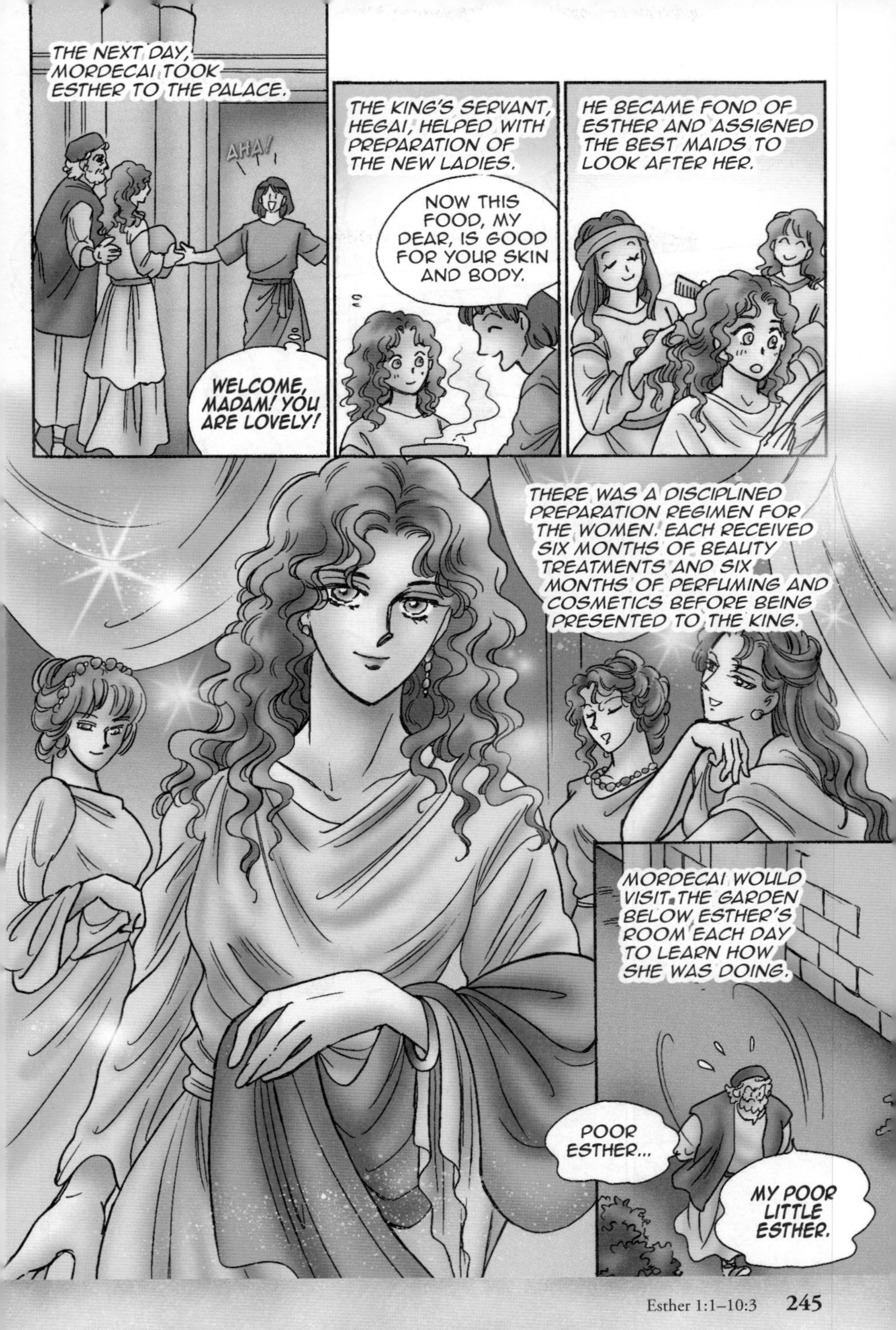
THE NEXT DAY, MORDECAI TOOK ESTHER TO THE PALACE.
AHA!
WELCOME, MADAM! YOU ARE LOVELY!
THE KING'S SERVANT, HEGAI, HELPED WITH PREPARATION OF THE NEW LADIES.
NOW THIS FOOD, MY DEAR, IS GOOD FOR YOUR SKIN AND BODY.
HE BECAME FOND OF ESTHER AND ASSIGNED THE BEST MAIDS TO LOOK AFTER HER.
THERE WAS A DISCIPLINED PREPARATION REGIMEN FOR THE WOMEN. EACH RECEIVED SIX MONTHS OF BEAUTY TREATMENTS AND SIX MONTHS OF PERFUMING AND COSMETICS BEFORE BEING PRESENTED TO THE KING.
MORDECAI WOULD VISIT THE GARDEN BELOW ESTHER'S ROOM EACH DAY TO LEARN HOW SHE WAS DOING.
POOR ESTHER...
MY POOR LITTLE ESTHER.

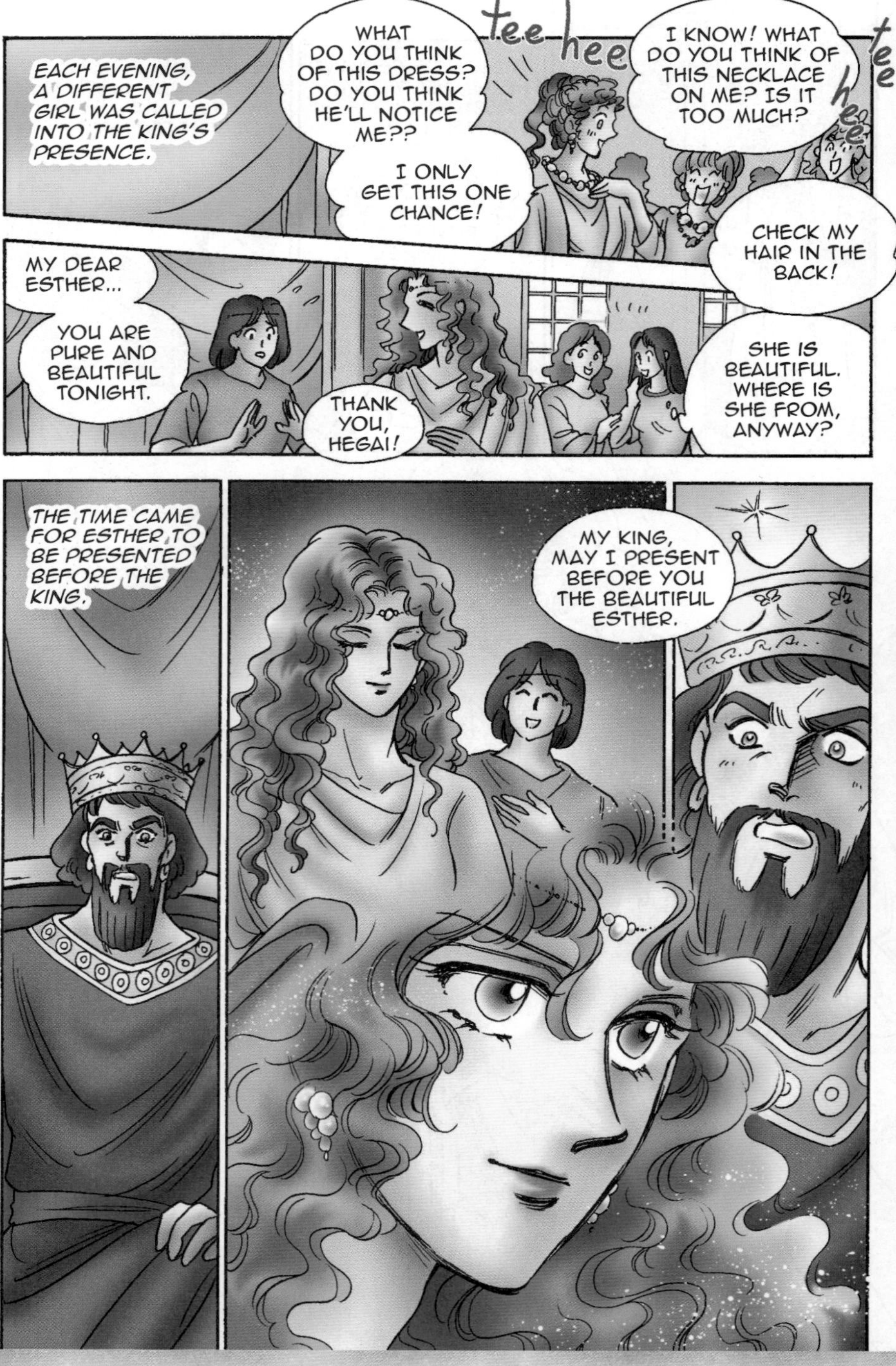
EACH EVENING, A DIFFERENT GIRL WAS CALLED INTO THE KING'S PRESENCE.
WHAT DO YOU THINK OF THIS DRESS? DO YOU THINK HE'LL NOTICE ME??
I ONLY GET THIS ONE CHANCE!
tee hee
I KNOW! WHAT DO YOU THINK OF THIS NECKLACE ON ME? IS IT TOO MUCH?
tee hee
CHECK MY HAIR IN THE BACK!
MY DEAR ESTHER...
YOU ARE PURE AND BEAUTIFUL TONIGHT.
THANK YOU, HEGAI!
SHE IS BEAUTIFUL. WHERE IS SHE FROM, ANYWAY?
THE TIME CAME FOR ESTHER TO BE PRESENTED BEFORE THE KING.
MY KING, MAY I PRESENT BEFORE YOU THE BEAUTIFUL ESTHER.

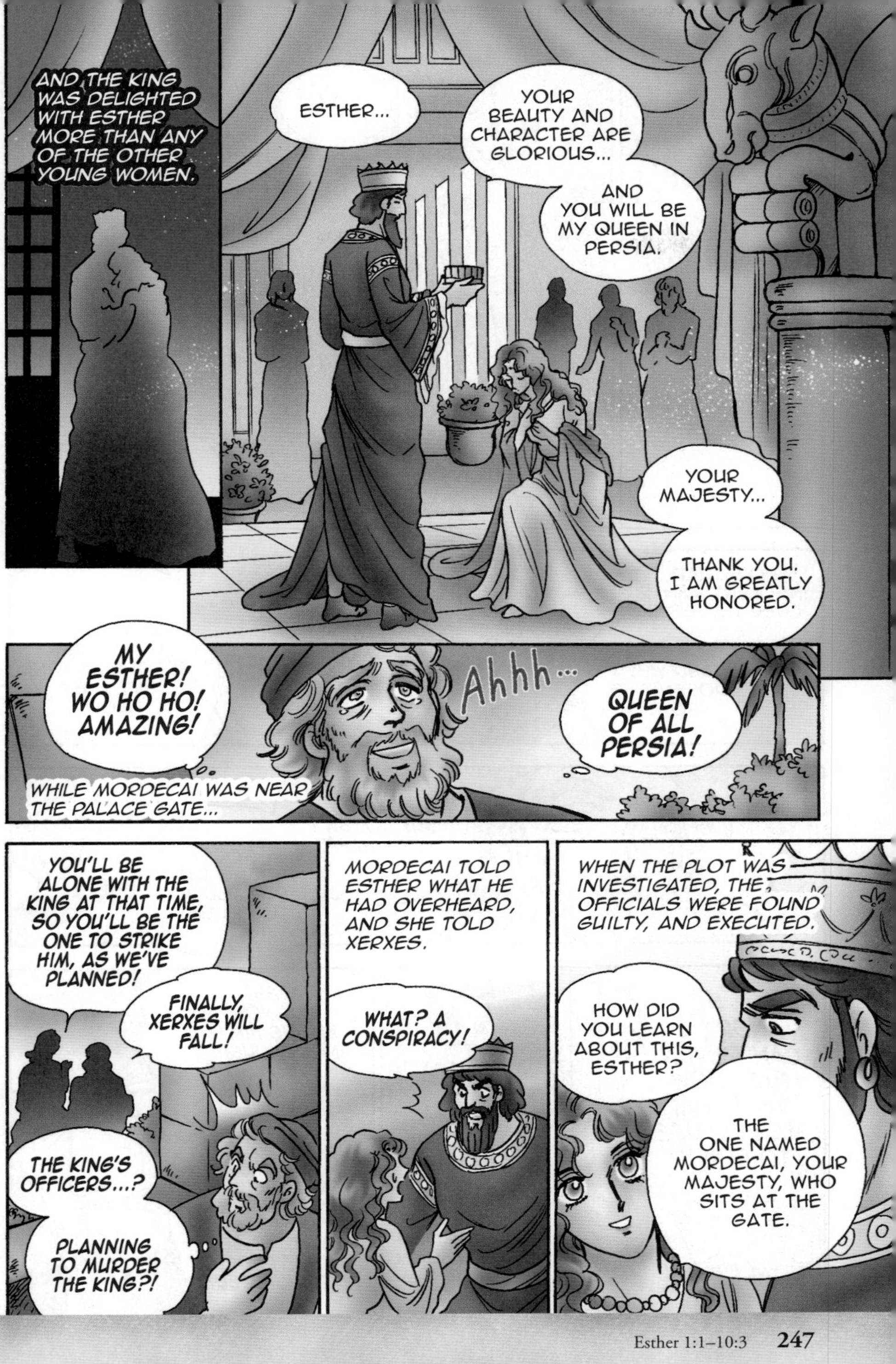
AND THE KING WAS DELIGHTED WITH ESTHER MORE THAN ANY OF THE OTHER YOUNG WOMEN.
ESTHER...
YOUR BEAUTY AND CHARACTER ARE GLORIOUS...
AND YOU WILL BE MY QUEEN IN PERSIA.
YOUR MAJESTY...
THANK YOU. I AM GREATLY HONORED.
MY ESTHER! WO HO HO! AMAZING!
Ahhh...
QUEEN OF ALL PERSIA!
WHILE MORDECAI WAS NEAR THE PALACE GATE...
YOU'LL BE ALONE WITH THE KING AT THAT TIME, SO YOU'LL BE THE ONE TO STRIKE HIM, AS WE'VE PLANNED!
FINALLY, XERXES WILL FALL!
THE KING'S OFFICERS...?
PLANNING TO MURDER THE KING?!
MORDECAI TOLD ESTHER WHAT HE HAD OVERHEARD, AND SHE TOLD XERXES.
WHAT? A CONSPIRACY!
WHEN THE PLOT WAS INVESTIGATED, THE OFFICIALS WERE FOUND GUILTY, AND EXECUTED.
HOW DID YOU LEARN ABOUT THIS, ESTHER?
THE ONE NAMED MORDECAI, YOUR MAJESTY, WHO SITS AT THE GATE.

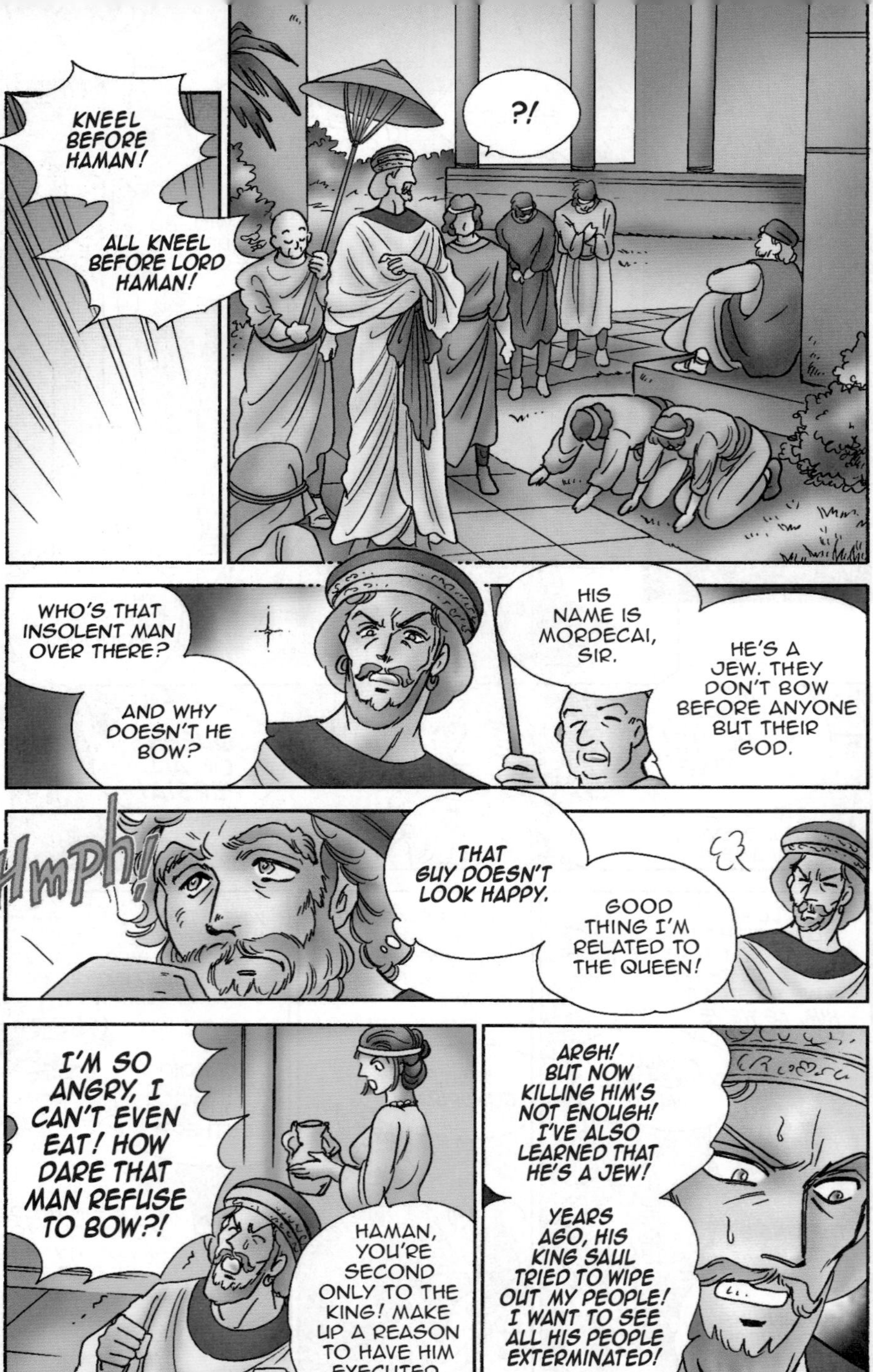
KNEEL BEFORE HAMAN!
ALL KNEEL BEFORE LORD HAMAN!
?!
WHO'S THAT INSOLENT MAN OVER THERE?
AND WHY DOESN'T HE BOW?
HIS NAME IS MORDECAI, SIR.
HE'S A JEW. THEY DON'T BOW BEFORE ANYONE BUT THEIR GOD.
HMPH!
THAT GUY DOESN'T LOOK HAPPY.
GOOD THING I'M RELATED TO THE QUEEN!
I'M SO ANGRY, I CAN'T EVEN EAT! HOW DARE THAT MAN REFUSE TO BOW?!
HAMAN, YOU'RE SECOND ONLY TO THE KING! MAKE UP A REASON TO HAVE HIM EXECUTED.
ARGH! BUT NOW KILLING HIM'S NOT ENOUGH! I'VE ALSO LEARNED THAT HE'S A JEW!
YEARS AGO, HIS KING SAUL TRIED TO WIPE OUT MY PEOPLE! I WANT TO SEE ALL HIS PEOPLE EXTERMINATED!

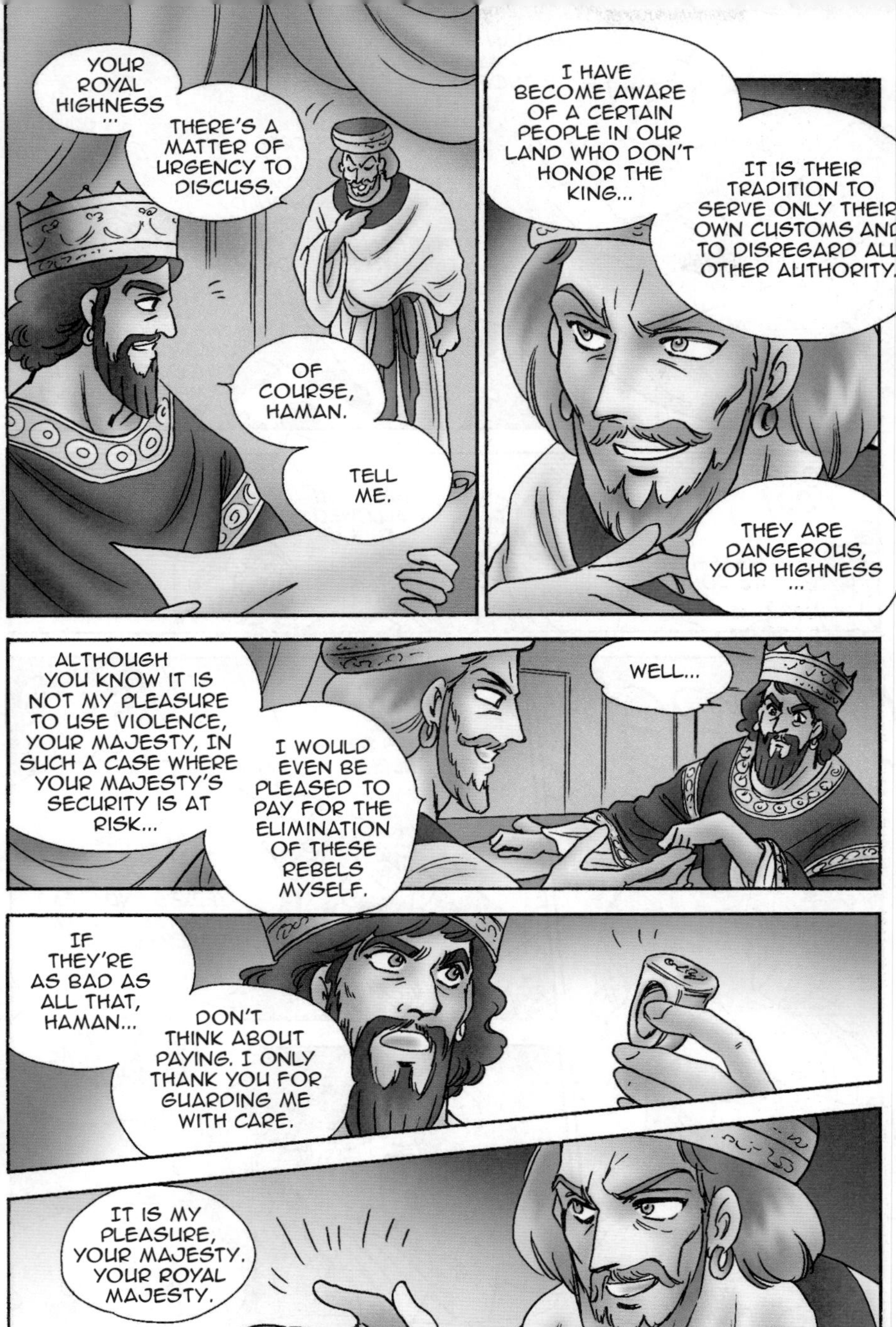
YOUR ROYAL HIGHNESS ...
THERE'S A MATTER OF URGENCY TO DISCUSS.
OF COURSE, HAMAN.
TELL ME.
I HAVE BECOME AWARE OF A CERTAIN PEOPLE IN OUR LAND WHO DON'T HONOR THE KING...
IT IS THEIR TRADITION TO SERVE ONLY THEIR OWN CUSTOMS AND TO DISREGARD ALL OTHER AUTHORITY.
THEY ARE DANGEROUS, YOUR HIGHNESS ...
ALTHOUGH YOU KNOW IT IS NOT MY PLEASURE TO USE VIOLENCE, YOUR MAJESTY, IN SUCH A CASE WHERE YOUR MAJESTY'S SECURITY IS AT RISK...
I WOULD EVEN BE PLEASED TO PAY FOR THE ELIMINATION OF THESE REBELS MYSELF.
WELL...
IF THEY'RE AS BAD AS ALL THAT, HAMAN...
DON'T THINK ABOUT PAYING. I ONLY THANK YOU FOR GUARDING ME WITH CARE.
IT IS MY PLEASURE, YOUR MAJESTY. YOUR ROYAL MAJESTY.

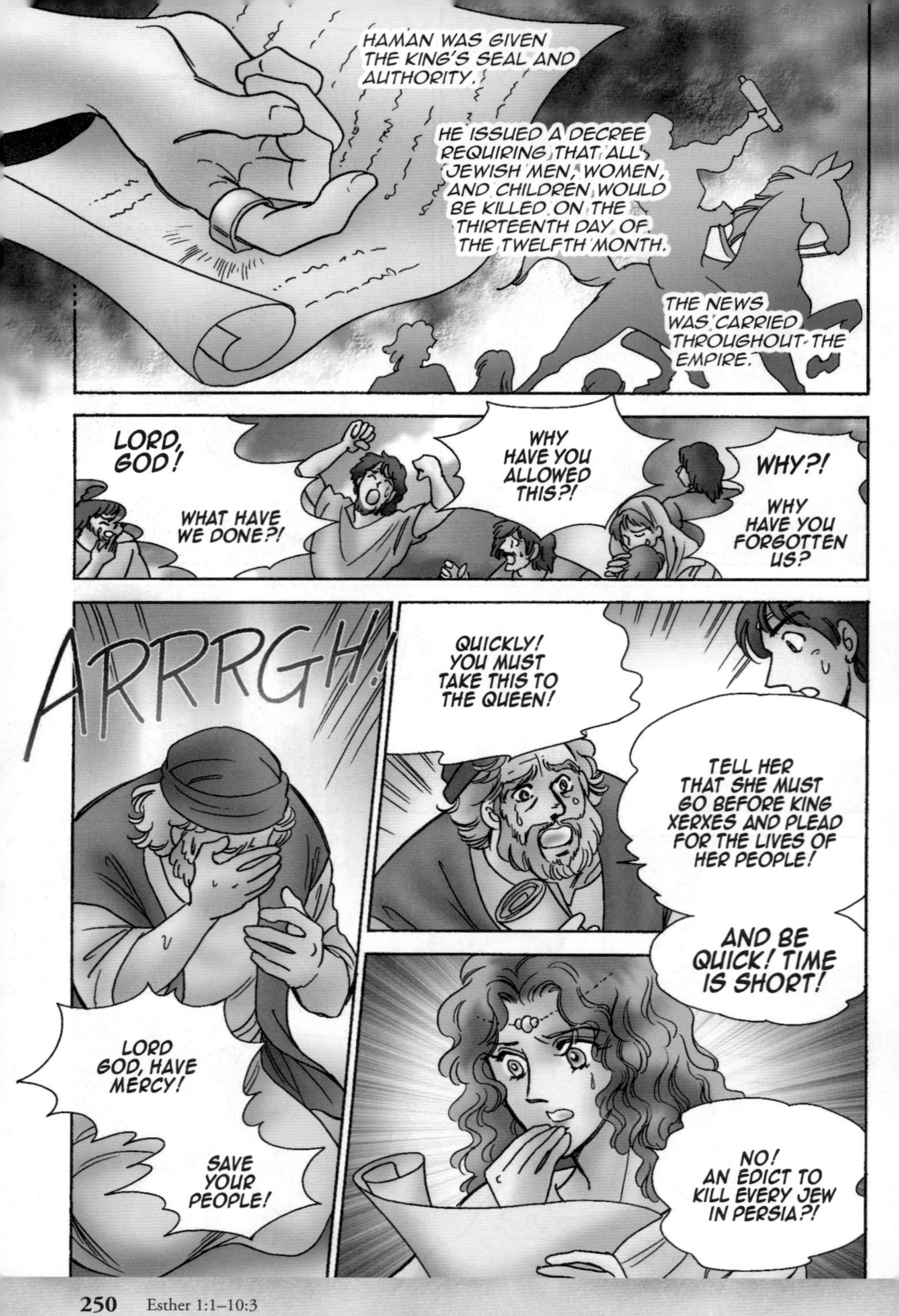

HAMAN WAS GIVEN THE KING'S SEAL AND AUTHORITY.
HE ISSUED A DECREE REQUIRING THAT ALL JEWISH MEN, WOMEN, AND CHILDREN WOULD BE KILLED ON THE THIRTEENTH DAY OF THE TWELFTH MONTH.
THE NEWS WAS CARRIED THROUGHOUT THE EMPIRE.
LORD, GOD!
WHAT HAVE WE DONE?!
WHY HAVE YOU ALLOWED THIS?!
WHY?!
WHY HAVE YOU FORGOTTEN US?
ARRRGH!
LORD GOD, HAVE MERCY!
SAVE YOUR PEOPLE!
QUICKLY! YOU MUST TAKE THIS TO THE QUEEN!
TELL HER THAT SHE MUST GO BEFORE KING XERXES AND PLEAD FOR THE LIVES OF HER PEOPLE!
AND BE QUICK! TIME IS SHORT!
NO! AN EDICT TO KILL EVERY JEW IN PERSIA?!

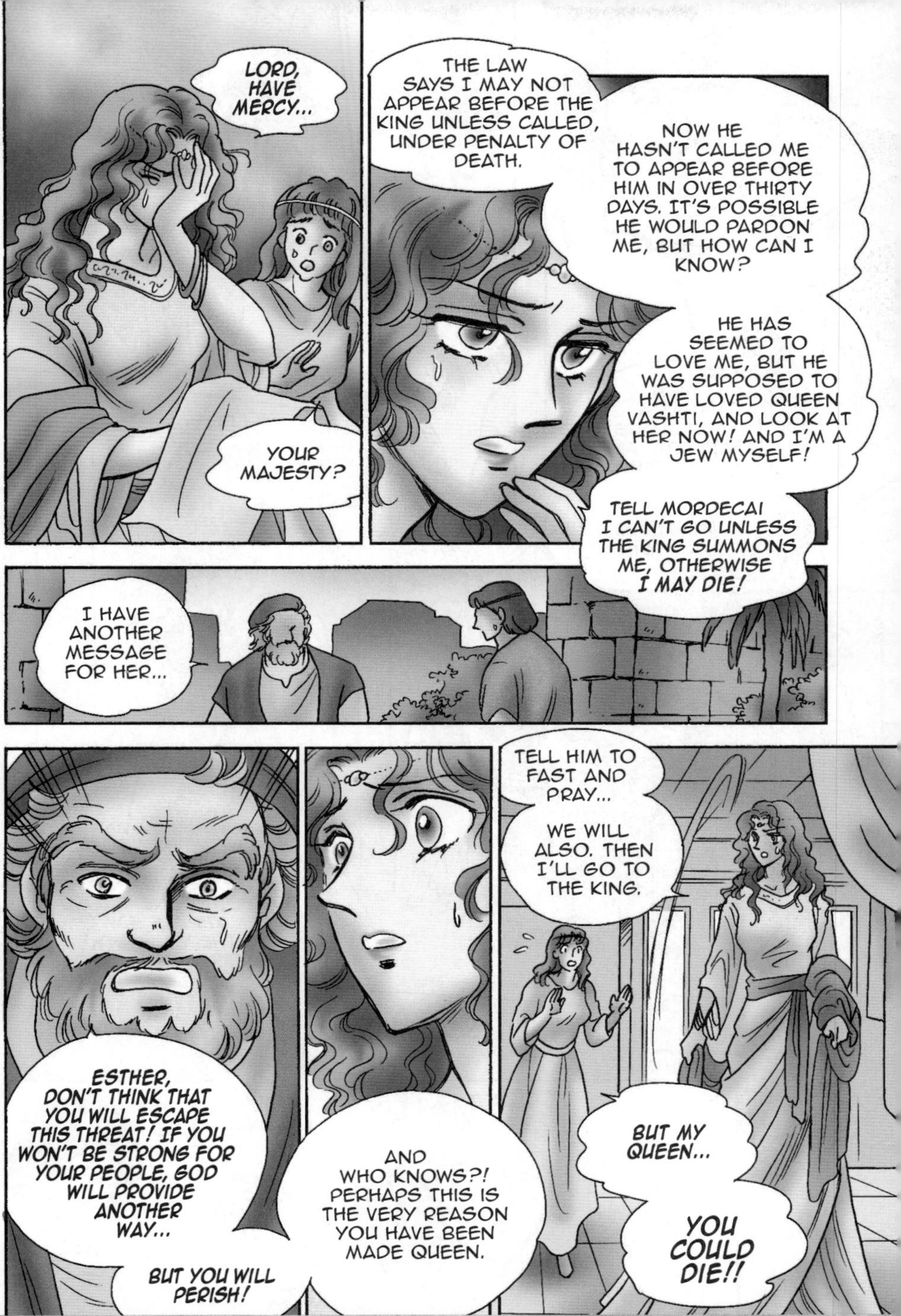
LORD, HAVE MERCY...
YOUR MAJESTY?
THE LAW SAYS I MAY NOT APPEAR BEFORE THE KING UNLESS CALLED, UNDER PENALTY OF DEATH.
NOW HE HASN'T CALLED ME TO APPEAR BEFORE HIM IN OVER THIRTY DAYS. IT'S POSSIBLE HE WOULD PARDON ME, BUT HOW CAN I KNOW?
HE HAS SEEMED TO LOVE ME, BUT HE WAS SUPPOSED TO HAVE LOVED QUEEN VASHTI, AND LOOK AT HER NOW! AND I'M A JEW MYSELF!
TELL MORDECAI I CAN'T GO UNLESS THE KING SUMMONS ME, OTHERWISE I MAY DIE!
I HAVE ANOTHER MESSAGE FOR HER...
ESTHER, DON'T THINK THAT YOU WILL ESCAPE THIS THREAT! IF YOU WON'T BE STRONG FOR YOUR PEOPLE, GOD WILL PROVIDE ANOTHER WAY...
BUT YOU WILL PERISH!
AND WHO KNOWS?! PERHAPS THIS IS THE VERY REASON YOU HAVE BEEN MADE QUEEN.
TELL HIM TO FAST AND PRAY...
WE WILL ALSO. THEN I'LL GO TO THE KING.
BUT MY QUEEN...
YOU COULD DIE!!

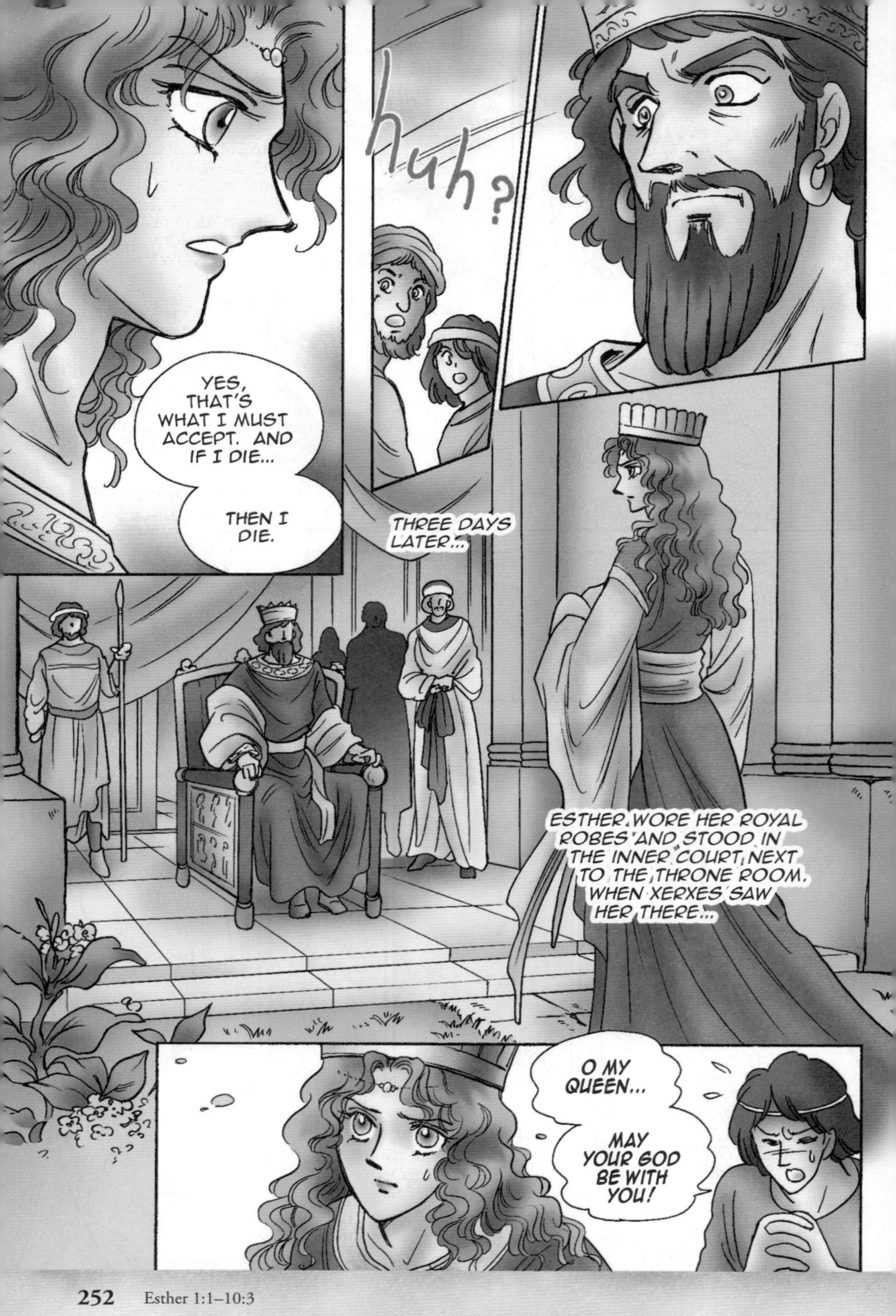
huh?
YES, THAT'S WHAT I MUST ACCEPT. AND IF I DIE...
THEN I DIE.
THREE DAYS LATER...
ESTHER WORE HER ROYAL ROBES AND STOOD IN THE INNER COURT NEXT TO THE THRONE ROOM. WHEN XERXES SAW HER THERE...
O MY QUEEN...
MAY YOUR GOD BE WITH YOU!

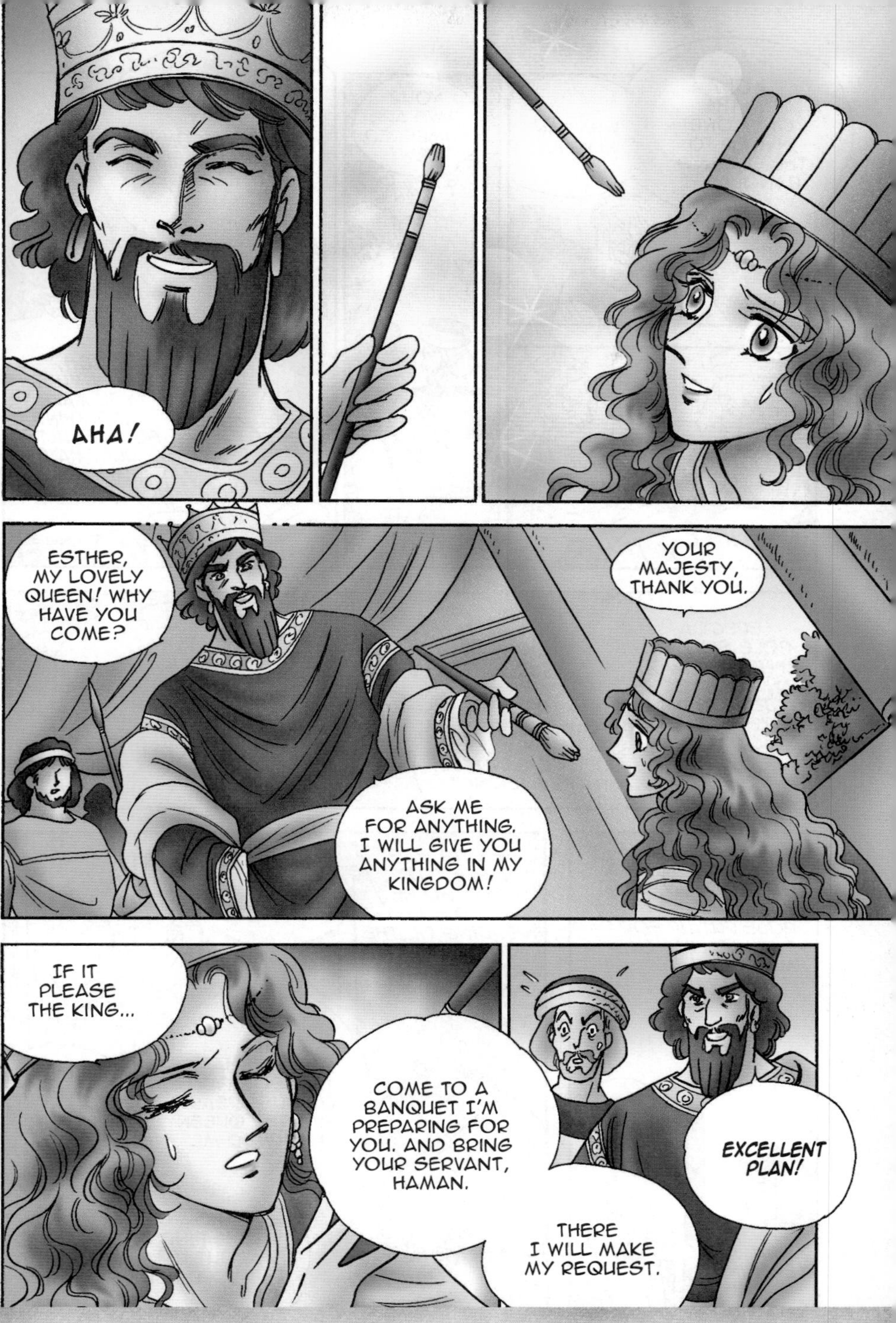
AHA!
ESTHER, MY LOVELY QUEEN! WHY HAVE YOU COME?
YOUR MAJESTY, THANK YOU.
ASK ME FOR ANYTHING. I WILL GIVE YOU ANYTHING IN MY KINGDOM!
IF IT PLEASE THE KING...
COME TO A BANQUET I'M PREPARING FOR YOU. AND BRING YOUR SERVANT, HAMAN.
THERE I WILL MAKE MY REQUEST.
EXCELLENT PLAN!

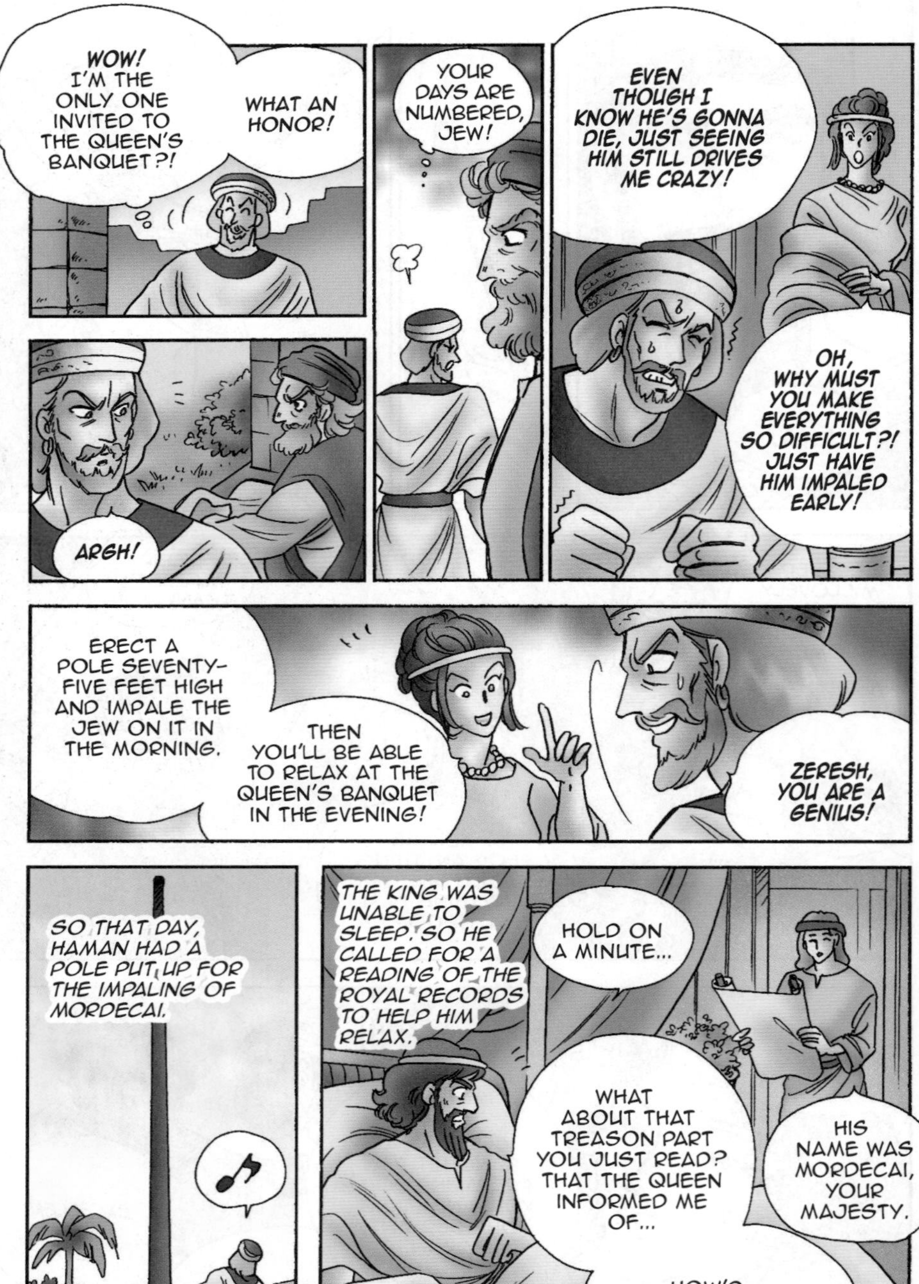
WOW! I'M THE ONLY ONE INVITED TO THE QUEEN'S BANQUET?!
WHAT AN HONOR!
YOUR DAYS ARE NUMBERED, JEW!
EVEN THOUGH I KNOW HE'S GONNA DIE, JUST SEEING HIM STILL DRIVES ME CRAZY!
ARGH!
OH, WHY MUST YOU MAKE EVERYTHING SO DIFFICULT?! JUST HAVE HIM IMPALED EARLY!
ERECT A POLE SEVENTY-FIVE FEET HIGH AND IMPALE THE JEW ON IT IN THE MORNING.
THEN YOU'LL BE ABLE TO RELAX AT THE QUEEN'S BANQUET IN THE EVENING!
ZERESH, YOU ARE A GENIUS!
SO THAT DAY, HAMAN HAD A POLE PUT UP FOR THE IMPALING OF MORDECAI.
THAT SAME EVENING...
THE KING WAS UNABLE TO SLEEP. SO HE CALLED FOR A READING OF THE ROYAL RECORDS TO HELP HIM RELAX.
HOLD ON A MINUTE...
WHAT ABOUT THAT TREASON PART YOU JUST READ? THAT THE QUEEN INFORMED ME OF...
HOW'D SHE FIND OUT ABOUT IT? WHO TOLD HER?
HIS NAME WAS MORDECAI, YOUR MAJESTY.

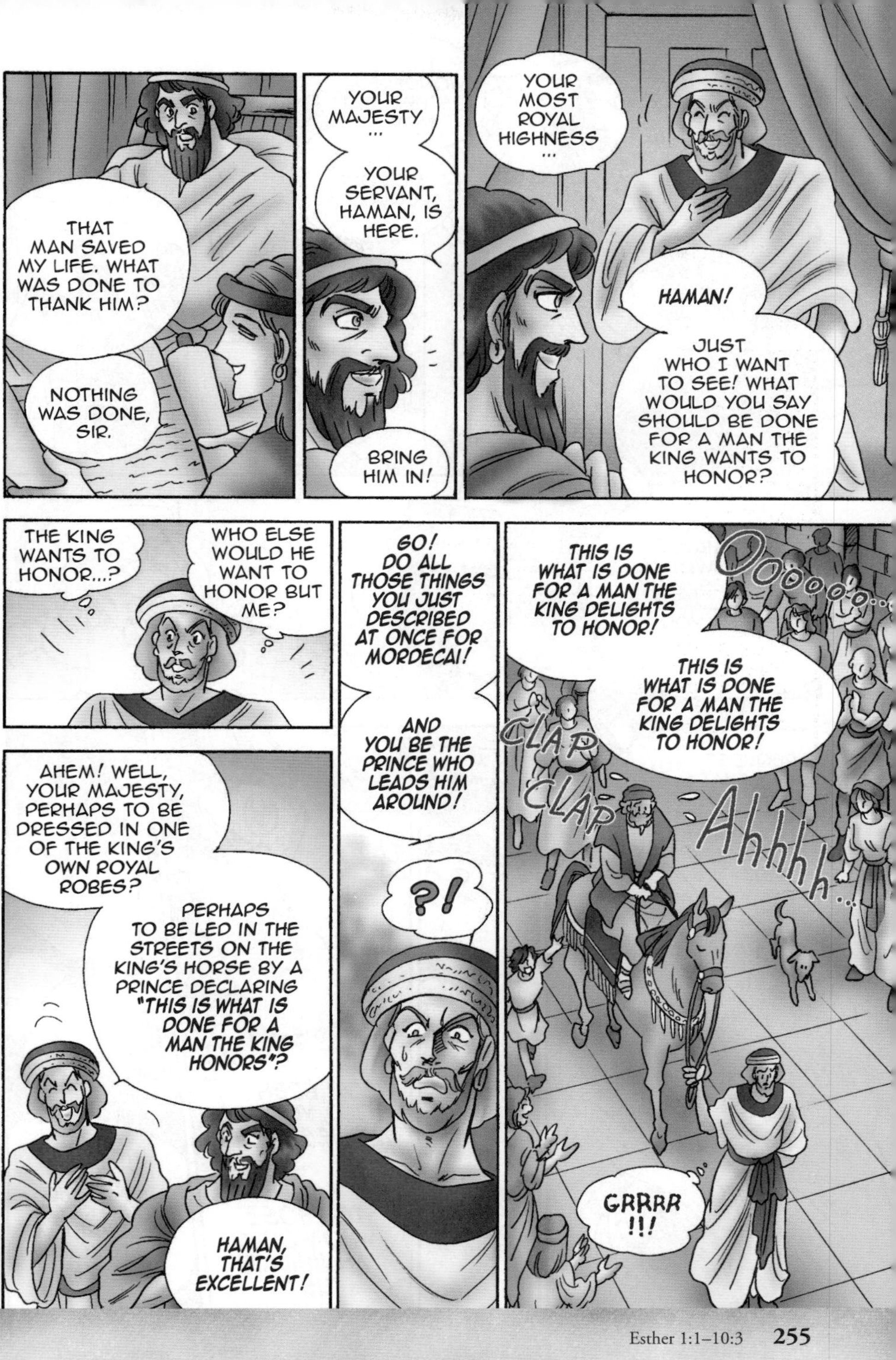
THAT MAN SAVED MY LIFE. WHAT WAS DONE TO THANK HIM?
NOTHING WAS DONE, SIR.
YOUR MAJESTY ...
YOUR SERVANT, HAMAN, IS HERE.
BRING HIM IN!
YOUR MOST ROYAL HIGHNESS ...
HAMAN!
JUST WHO I WANT TO SEE! WHAT WOULD YOU SAY SHOULD BE DONE FOR A MAN THE KING WANTS TO HONOR?
THE KING WANTS TO HONOR...?
WHO ELSE WOULD HE WANT TO HONOR BUT ME?
AHEM! WELL, YOUR MAJESTY, PERHAPS TO BE DRESSED IN ONE OF THE KING'S OWN ROYAL ROBES?
PERHAPS TO BE LED IN THE STREETS ON THE KING'S HORSE BY A PRINCE DECLARING "THIS IS WHAT IS DONE FOR A MAN THE KING HONORS"?
HAMAN, THAT'S EXCELLENT!
GO! DO ALL THOSE THINGS YOU JUST DESCRIBED AT ONCE FOR MORDECAI!
AND YOU BE THE PRINCE WHO LEADS HIM AROUND!
?!
THIS IS WHAT IS DONE FOR A MAN THE KING DELIGHTS TO HONOR!
Oooooo...
THIS IS WHAT IS DONE FOR A MAN THE KING DELIGHTS TO HONOR!
CLAP
CLAP
CLAP
Ahhhhh...
GRRRR !!!

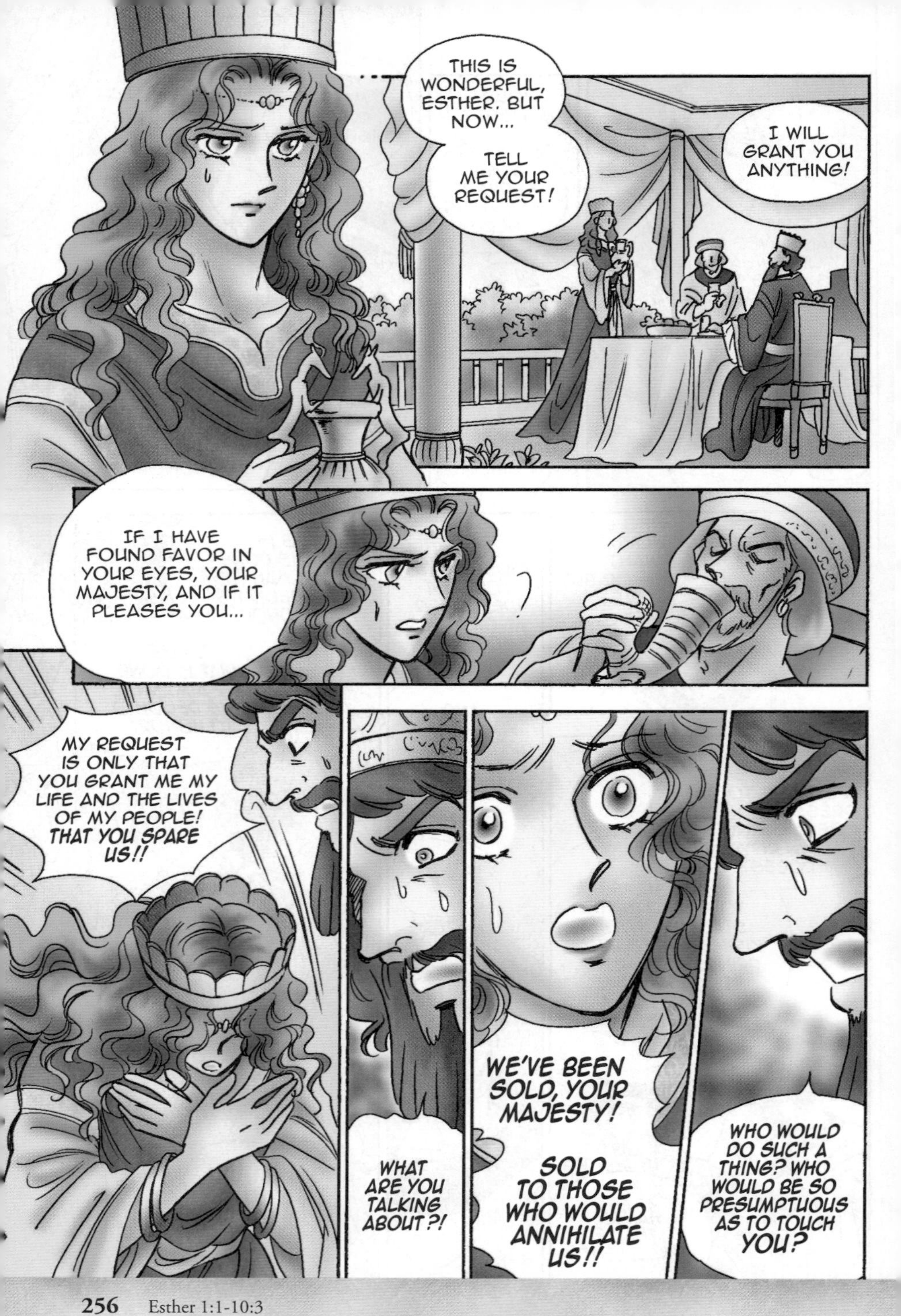
THIS IS WONDERFUL, ESTHER. BUT NOW...
TELL ME YOUR REQUEST!
I WILL GRANT YOU ANYTHING!
IF I HAVE FOUND FAVOR IN YOUR EYES, YOUR MAJESTY, AND IF IT PLEASES YOU...
MY REQUEST IS ONLY THAT YOU GRANT ME MY LIFE AND THE LIVES OF MY PEOPLE! THAT YOU SPARE US!!
WHAT ARE YOU TALKING ABOUT?!
WE'VE BEEN SOLD, YOUR MAJESTY!
SOLD TO THOSE WHO WOULD ANNIHILATE US!!
WHO WOULD DO SUCH A THING? WHO WOULD BE SO PRESUMPTUOUS AS TO TOUCH YOU?

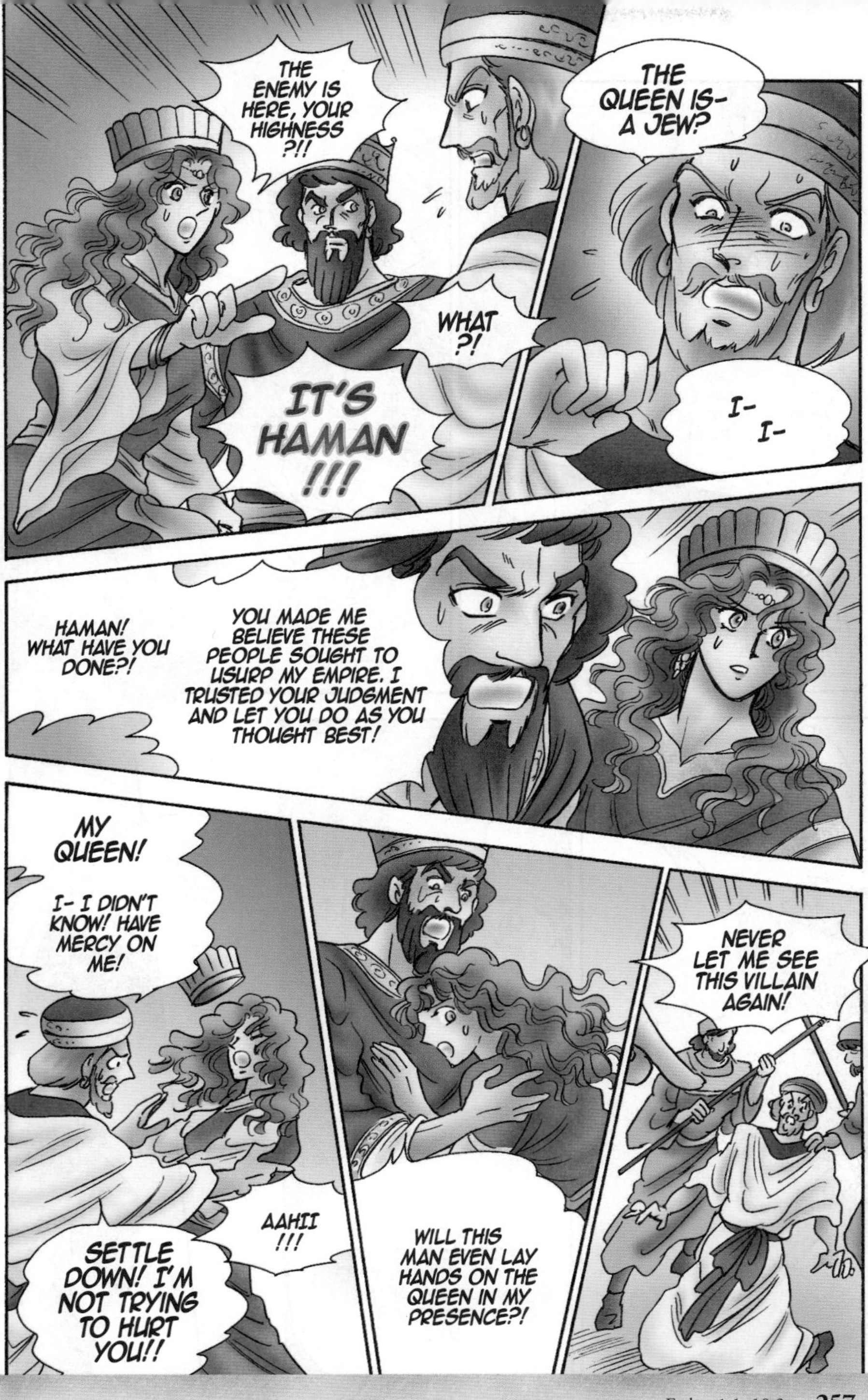
THE ENEMY IS HERE, YOUR HIGHNESS ?!!
IT'S HAMAN !!!
WHAT ?!
THE QUEEN IS- A JEW?
I- I-
HAMAN! WHAT HAVE YOU DONE?!
YOU MADE ME BELIEVE THESE PEOPLE SOUGHT TO USURP MY EMPIRE. I TRUSTED YOUR JUDGMENT AND LET YOU DO AS YOU THOUGHT BEST!
MY QUEEN!
I- I DIDN'T KNOW! HAVE MERCY ON ME!
AAHII !!!
SETTLE DOWN! I'M NOT TRYING TO HURT YOU!!
WILL THIS MAN EVEN LAY HANDS ON THE QUEEN IN MY PRESENCE?!
NEVER LET ME SEE THIS VILLAIN AGAIN!

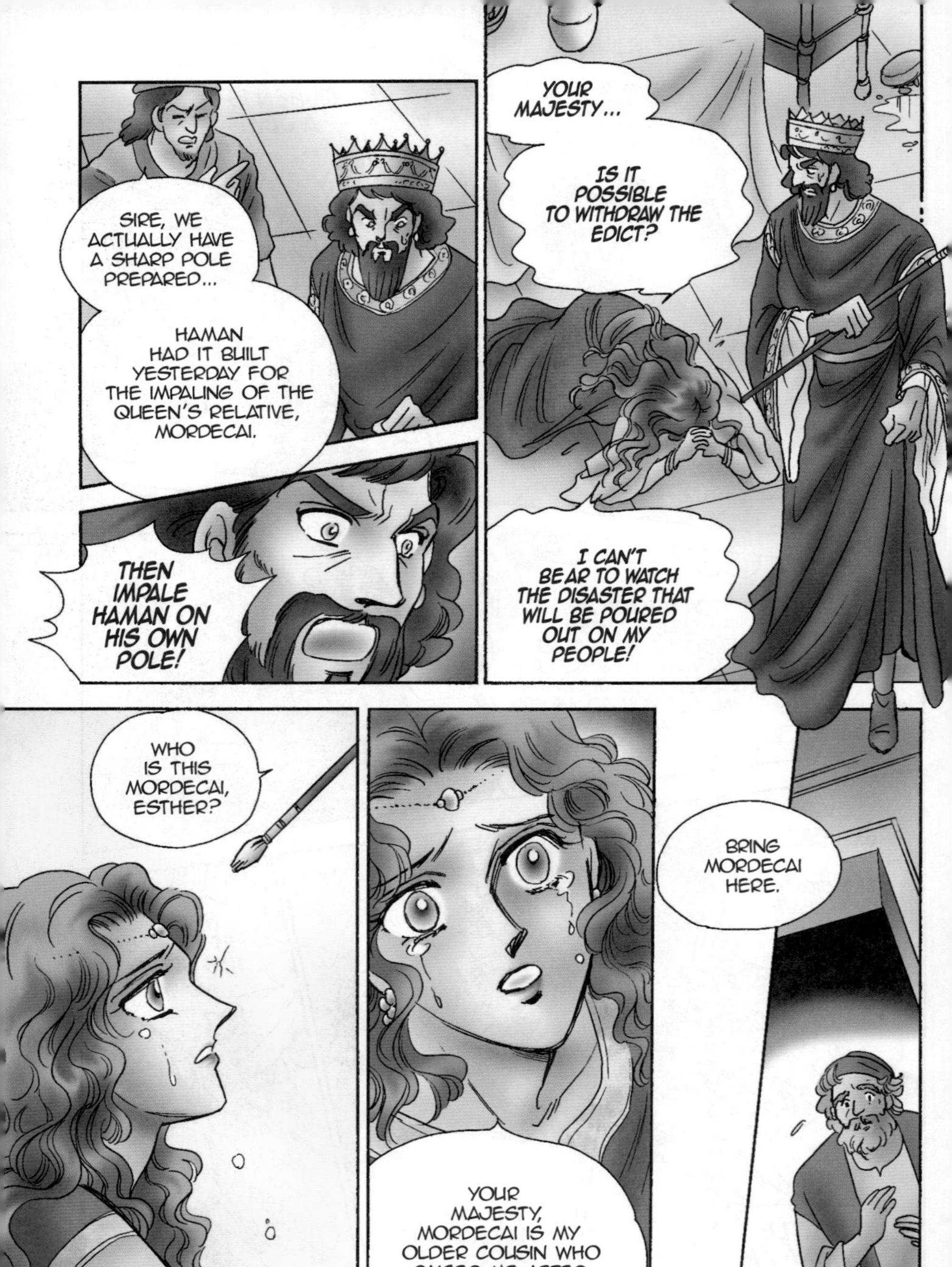
SIRE, WE ACTUALLY HAVE A SHARP POLE PREPARED...
HAMAN HAD IT BUILT YESTERDAY FOR THE IMPALING OF THE QUEEN'S RELATIVE, MORDECAI.
THEN IMPALE HAMAN ON HIS OWN POLE!
YOUR MAJESTY...
IS IT POSSIBLE TO WITHDRAW THE EDICT?
I CAN'T BEAR TO WATCH THE DISASTER THAT WILL BE POURED OUT ON MY PEOPLE!
WHO IS THIS MORDECAI, ESTHER?
YOUR MAJESTY, MORDECAI IS MY OLDER COUSIN WHO RAISED ME AFTER MY PARENTS DIED.
BRING MORDECAI HERE.

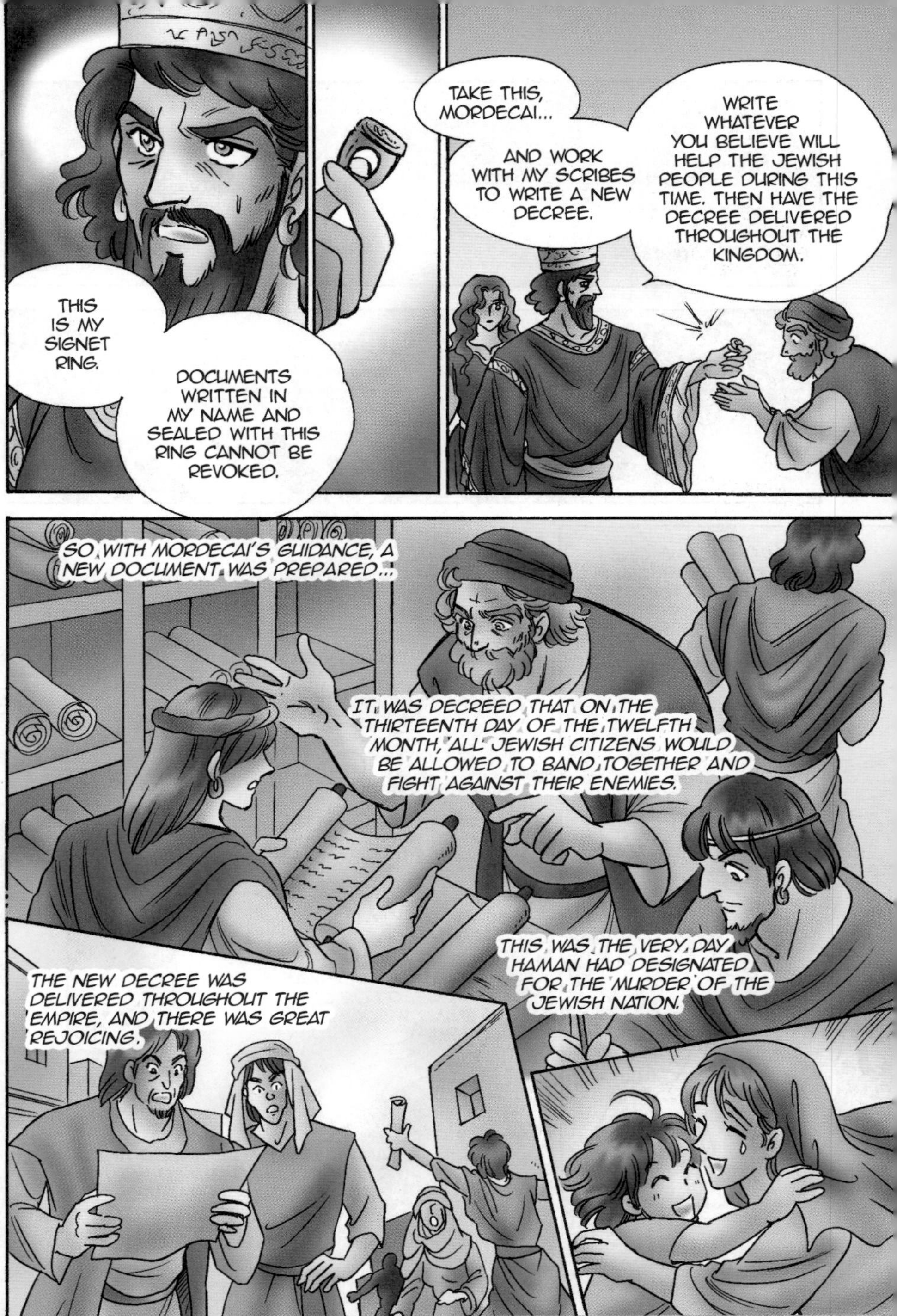
THIS IS MY SIGNET RING.
DOCUMENTS WRITTEN IN MY NAME AND SEALED WITH THIS RING CANNOT BE REVOKED.
TAKE THIS, MORDECAI...
AND WORK WITH MY SCRIBES TO WRITE A NEW DECREE.
WRITE WHATEVER YOU BELIEVE WILL HELP THE JEWISH PEOPLE DURING THIS TIME. THEN HAVE THE DECREE DELIVERED THROUGHOUT THE KINGDOM.
SO WITH MORDECAI'S GUIDANCE, A NEW DOCUMENT WAS PREPARED...
IT WAS DECREED THAT ON THE THIRTEENTH DAY OF THE TWELFTH MONTH, ALL JEWISH CITIZENS WOULD BE ALLOWED TO BAND TOGETHER AND FIGHT AGAINST THEIR ENEMIES.
THIS WAS THE VERY DAY HAMAN HAD DESIGNATED FOR THE MURDER OF THE JEWISH NATION.
THE NEW DECREE WAS DELIVERED THROUGHOUT THE EMPIRE, AND THERE WAS GREAT REJOICING.

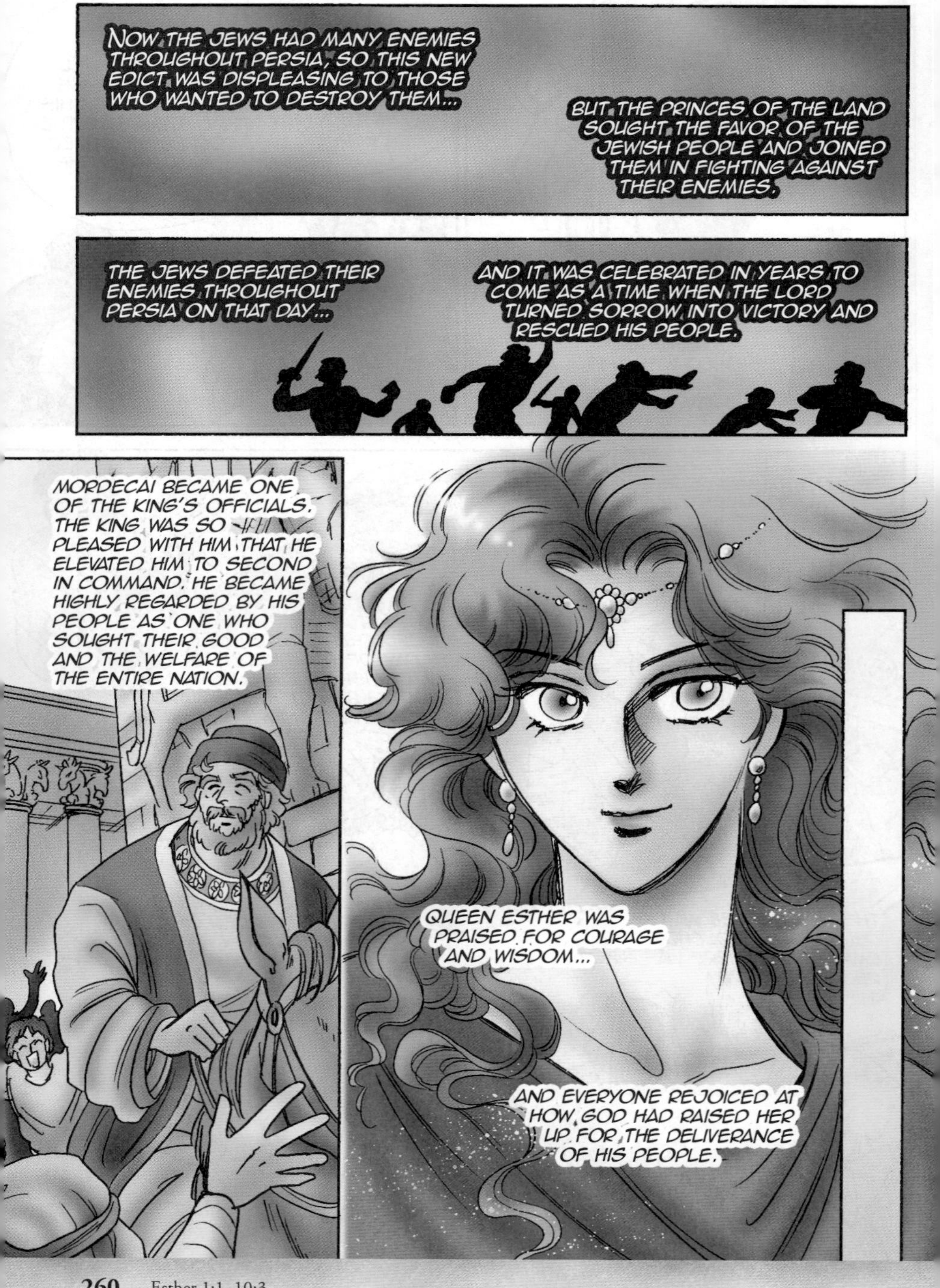
NOW THE JEWS HAD MANY ENEMIES THROUGHOUT PERSIA, SO THIS NEW EDICT WAS DISPLEASING TO THOSE WHO WANTED TO DESTROY THEM...
BUT THE PRINCES OF THE LAND SOUGHT THE FAVOR OF THE JEWISH PEOPLE AND JOINED THEM IN FIGHTING AGAINST THEIR ENEMIES.
THE JEWS DEFEATED THEIR ENEMIES THROUGHOUT PERSIA ON THAT DAY...
AND IT WAS CELEBRATED IN YEARS TO COME AS A TIME WHEN THE LORD TURNED SORROW INTO VICTORY AND RESCUED HIS PEOPLE.
MORDECAI BECAME ONE OF THE KING'S OFFICIALS. THE KING WAS SO PLEASED WITH HIM THAT HE ELEVATED HIM TO SECOND IN COMMAND. HE BECAME HIGHLY REGARDED BY HIS PEOPLE AS ONE WHO SOUGHT THEIR GOOD AND THE WELFARE OF THE ENTIRE NATION.
QUEEN ESTHER WAS PRAISED FOR COURAGE AND WISDOM...
AND EVERYONE REJOICED AT HOW GOD HAD RAISED HER UP FOR THE DELIVERANCE OF HIS PEOPLE.

19. The Last Prophet

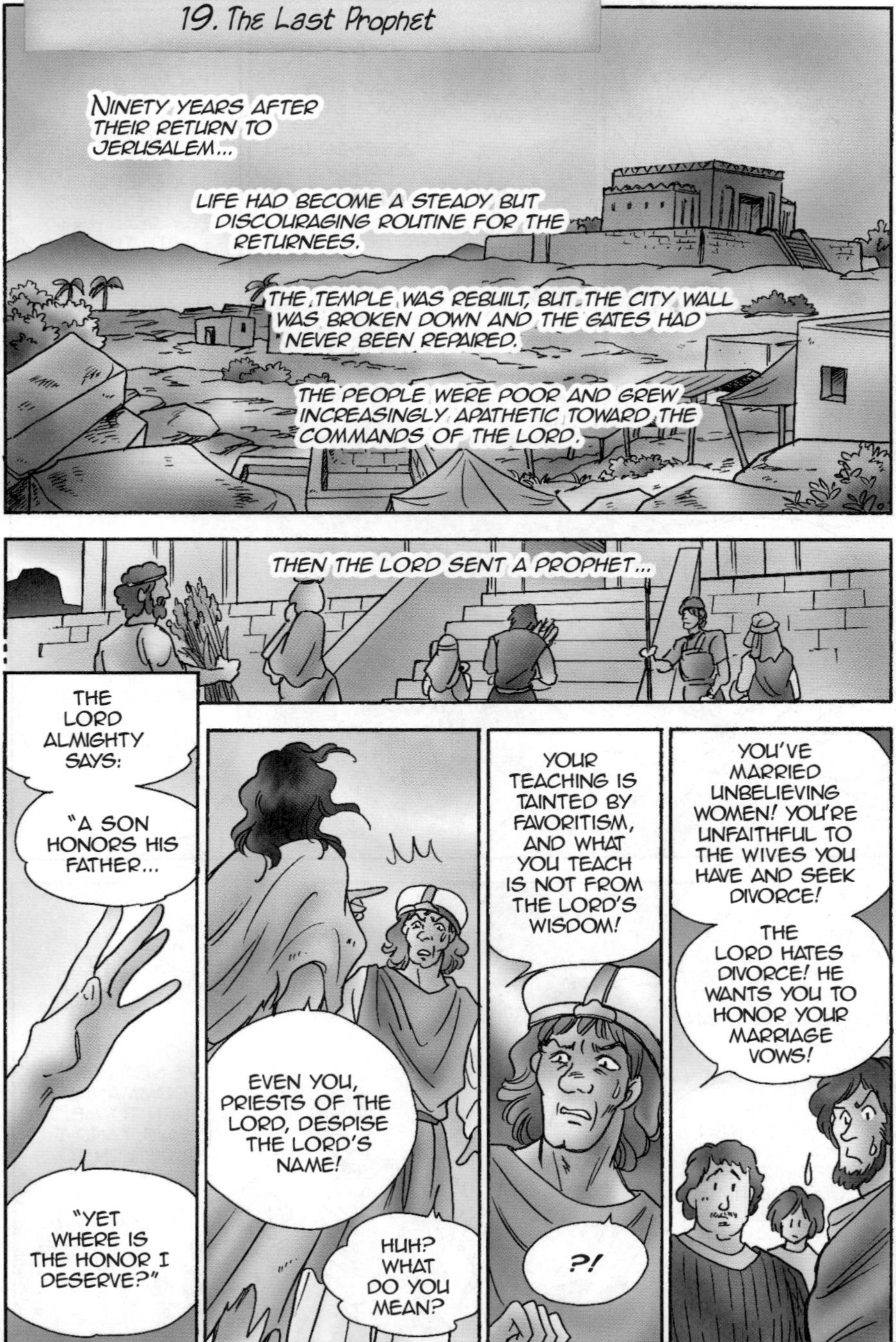
NINETY YEARS AFTER THEIR RETURN TO JERUSALEM...
LIFE HAD BECOME A STEADY BUT DISCOURAGING ROUTINE FOR THE RETURNEES.
THE TEMPLE WAS REBUILT, BUT THE CITY WALL WAS BROKEN DOWN AND THE GATES HAD NEVER BEEN REPAIRED.
THE PEOPLE WERE POOR AND GREW INCREASINGLY APATHETIC TOWARD THE COMMANDS OF THE LORD.
THEN THE LORD SENT A PROPHET...
THE LORD ALMIGHTY SAYS:
"A SON HONORS HIS FATHER...
"YET WHERE IS THE HONOR I DESERVE?"
EVEN YOU, PRIESTS OF THE LORD, DESPISE THE LORD'S NAME!
HUH? WHAT DO YOU MEAN?
YOUR TEACHING IS TAINTED BY FAVORITISM, AND WHAT YOU TEACH IS NOT FROM THE LORD'S WISDOM!
?!
YOU'VE MARRIED UNBELIEVING WOMEN! YOU'RE UNFAITHFUL TO THE WIVES YOU HAVE AND SEEK DIVORCE!
THE LORD HATES DIVORCE! HE WANTS YOU TO HONOR YOUR MARRIAGE VOWS!

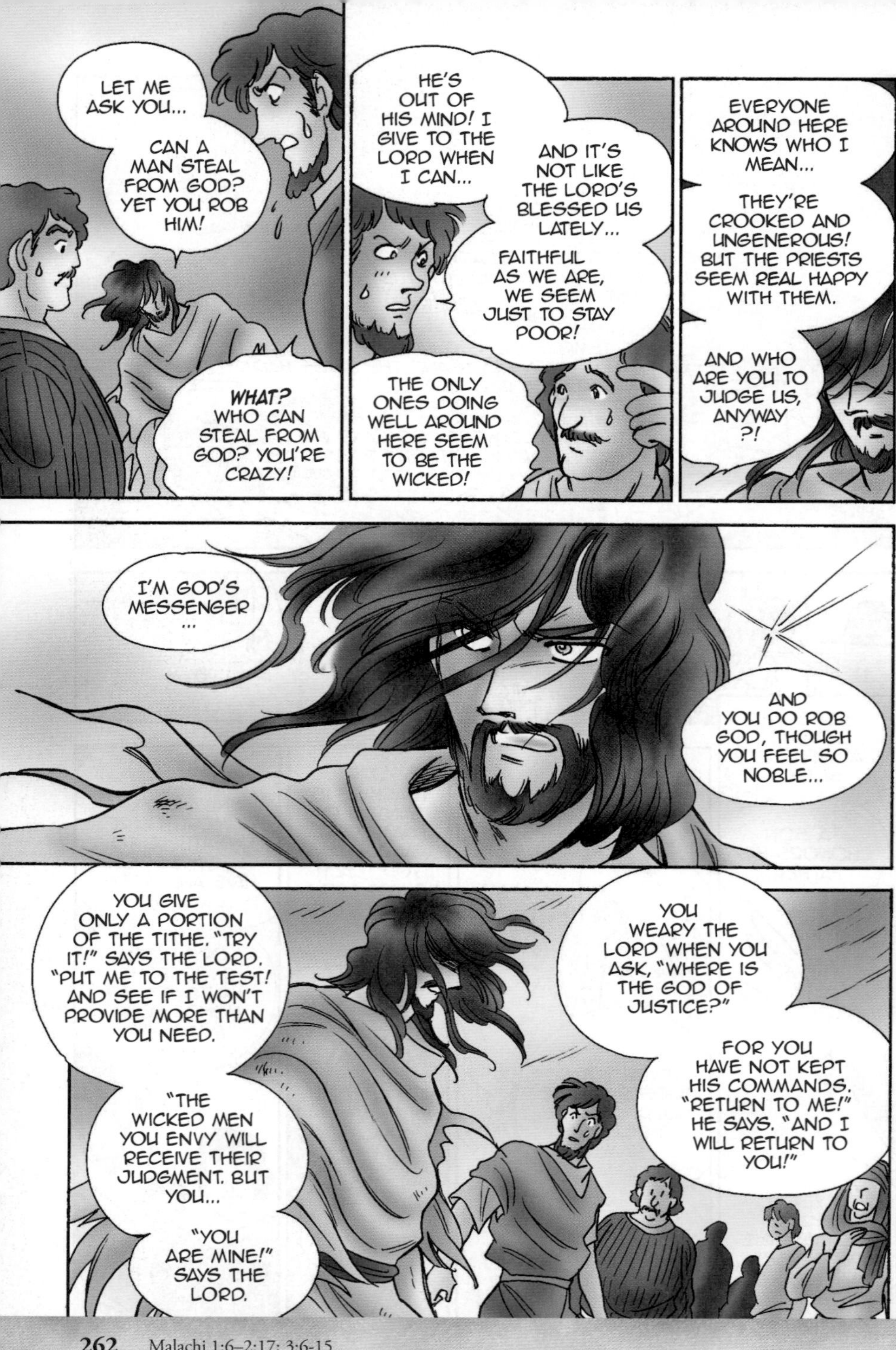
LET ME ASK YOU...
CAN A MAN STEAL FROM GOD? YET YOU ROB HIM!
WHAT? WHO CAN STEAL FROM GOD? YOU'RE CRAZY!
HE'S OUT OF HIS MIND! I GIVE TO THE LORD WHEN I CAN...
AND IT'S NOT LIKE THE LORD'S BLESSED US LATELY...
FAITHFUL AS WE ARE, WE SEEM JUST TO STAY POOR!
THE ONLY ONES DOING WELL AROUND HERE SEEM TO BE THE WICKED!
EVERYONE AROUND HERE KNOWS WHO I MEAN...
THEY'RE CROOKED AND UNGENEROUS! BUT THE PRIESTS SEEM REAL HAPPY WITH THEM.
AND WHO ARE YOU TO JUDGE US, ANYWAY?!
I'M GOD'S MESSENGER...
AND YOU DO ROB GOD, THOUGH YOU FEEL SO NOBLE...
YOU GIVE ONLY A PORTION OF THE TITHE. "TRY IT!" SAYS THE LORD. "PUT ME TO THE TEST! AND SEE IF I WON'T PROVIDE MORE THAN YOU NEED.
"THE WICKED MEN YOU ENVY WILL RECEIVE THEIR JUDGMENT. BUT YOU...
"YOU ARE MINE!" SAYS THE LORD.
YOU WEARY THE LORD WHEN YOU ASK, "WHERE IS THE GOD OF JUSTICE?"
FOR YOU HAVE NOT KEPT HIS COMMANDS. "RETURN TO ME!" HE SAYS. "AND I WILL RETURN TO YOU!"

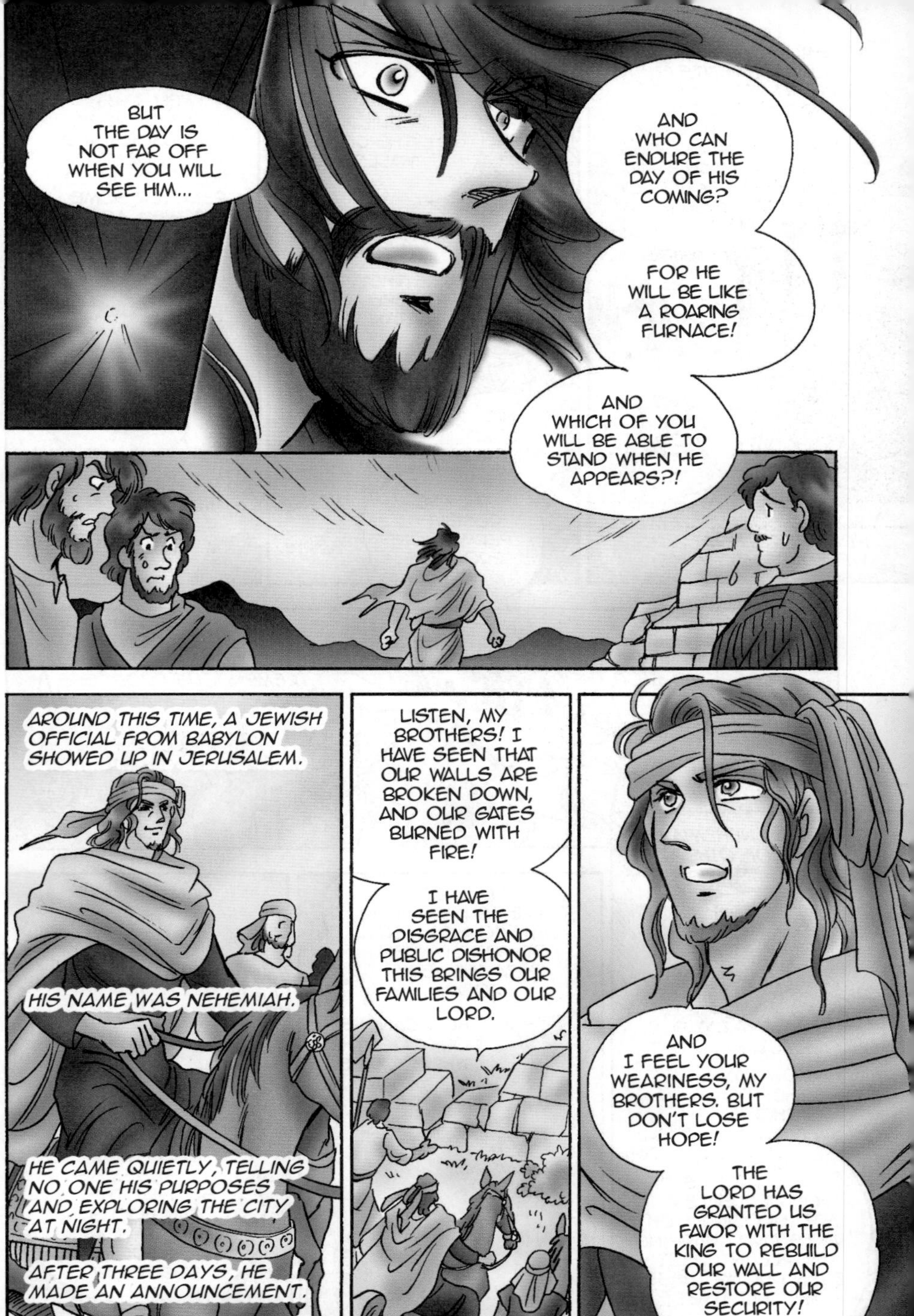
BUT THE DAY IS NOT FAR OFF WHEN YOU WILL SEE HIM...
AND WHO CAN ENDURE THE DAY OF HIS COMING?
FOR HE WILL BE LIKE A ROARING FURNACE!
AND WHICH OF YOU WILL BE ABLE TO STAND WHEN HE APPEARS?!
AROUND THIS TIME, A JEWISH OFFICIAL FROM BABYLON SHOWED UP IN JERUSALEM.
HIS NAME WAS NEHEMIAH.
HE CAME QUIETLY, TELLING NO ONE HIS PURPOSES AND EXPLORING THE CITY AT NIGHT.
AFTER THREE DAYS, HE MADE AN ANNOUNCEMENT.
LISTEN, MY BROTHERS! I HAVE SEEN THAT OUR WALLS ARE BROKEN DOWN, AND OUR GATES BURNED WITH FIRE!
I HAVE SEEN THE DISGRACE AND PUBLIC DISHONOR THIS BRINGS OUR FAMILIES AND OUR LORD.
AND I FEEL YOUR WEARINESS, MY BROTHERS. BUT DON'T LOSE HOPE!
THE LORD HAS GRANTED US FAVOR WITH THE KING TO REBUILD OUR WALL AND RESTORE OUR SECURITY!

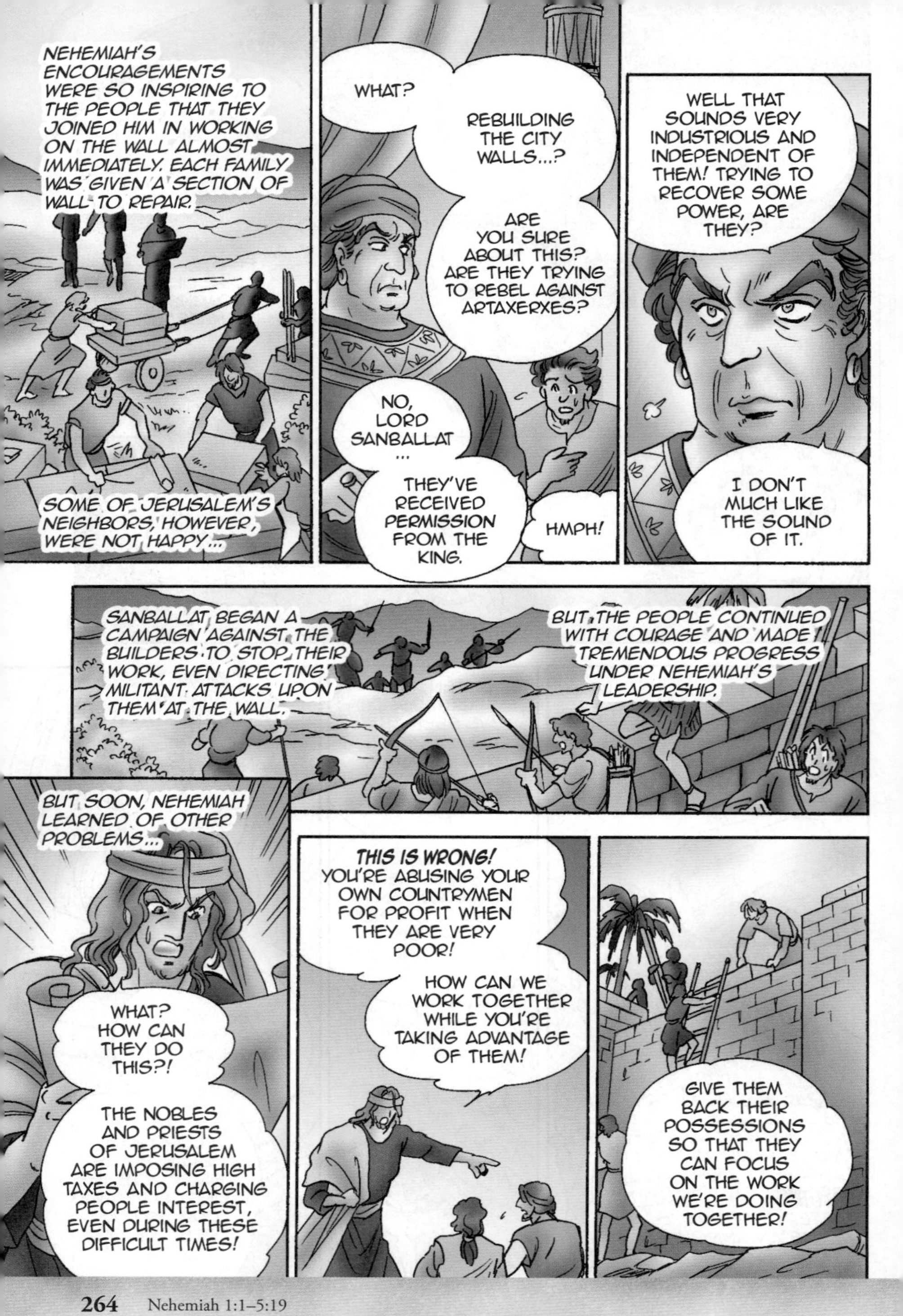

NEHEMIAH'S ENCOURAGEMENTS WERE SO INSPIRING TO THE PEOPLE THAT THEY JOINED HIM IN WORKING ON THE WALL ALMOST IMMEDIATELY. EACH FAMILY WAS GIVEN A SECTION OF WALL TO REPAIR.
SOME OF JERUSALEM'S NEIGHBORS, HOWEVER, WERE NOT HAPPY...
WHAT?
REBUILDING THE CITY WALLS...?
ARE YOU SURE ABOUT THIS? ARE THEY TRYING TO REBEL AGAINST ARTAXERXES?
NO, LORD SANBALLAT ...
THEY'VE RECEIVED PERMISSION FROM THE KING.
HMPH!
WELL THAT SOUNDS VERY INDUSTRIOUS AND INDEPENDENT OF THEM! TRYING TO RECOVER SOME POWER, ARE THEY?
I DON'T MUCH LIKE THE SOUND OF IT.
SANBALLAT BEGAN A CAMPAIGN AGAINST THE BUILDERS TO STOP THEIR WORK, EVEN DIRECTING MILITANT ATTACKS UPON THEM AT THE WALL.
BUT THE PEOPLE CONTINUED WITH COURAGE AND MADE TREMENDOUS PROGRESS UNDER NEHEMIAH'S LEADERSHIP.
BUT SOON, NEHEMIAH LEARNED OF OTHER PROBLEMS...
WHAT? HOW CAN THEY DO THIS?!
THE NOBLES AND PRIESTS OF JERUSALEM ARE IMPOSING HIGH TAXES AND CHARGING PEOPLE INTEREST, EVEN DURING THESE DIFFICULT TIMES!
THIS IS WRONG! YOU'RE ABUSING YOUR OWN COUNTRYMEN FOR PROFIT WHEN THEY ARE VERY POOR!
HOW CAN WE WORK TOGETHER WHILE YOU'RE TAKING ADVANTAGE OF THEM!
GIVE THEM BACK THEIR POSSESSIONS SO THAT THEY CAN FOCUS ON THE WORK WE'RE DOING TOGETHER!

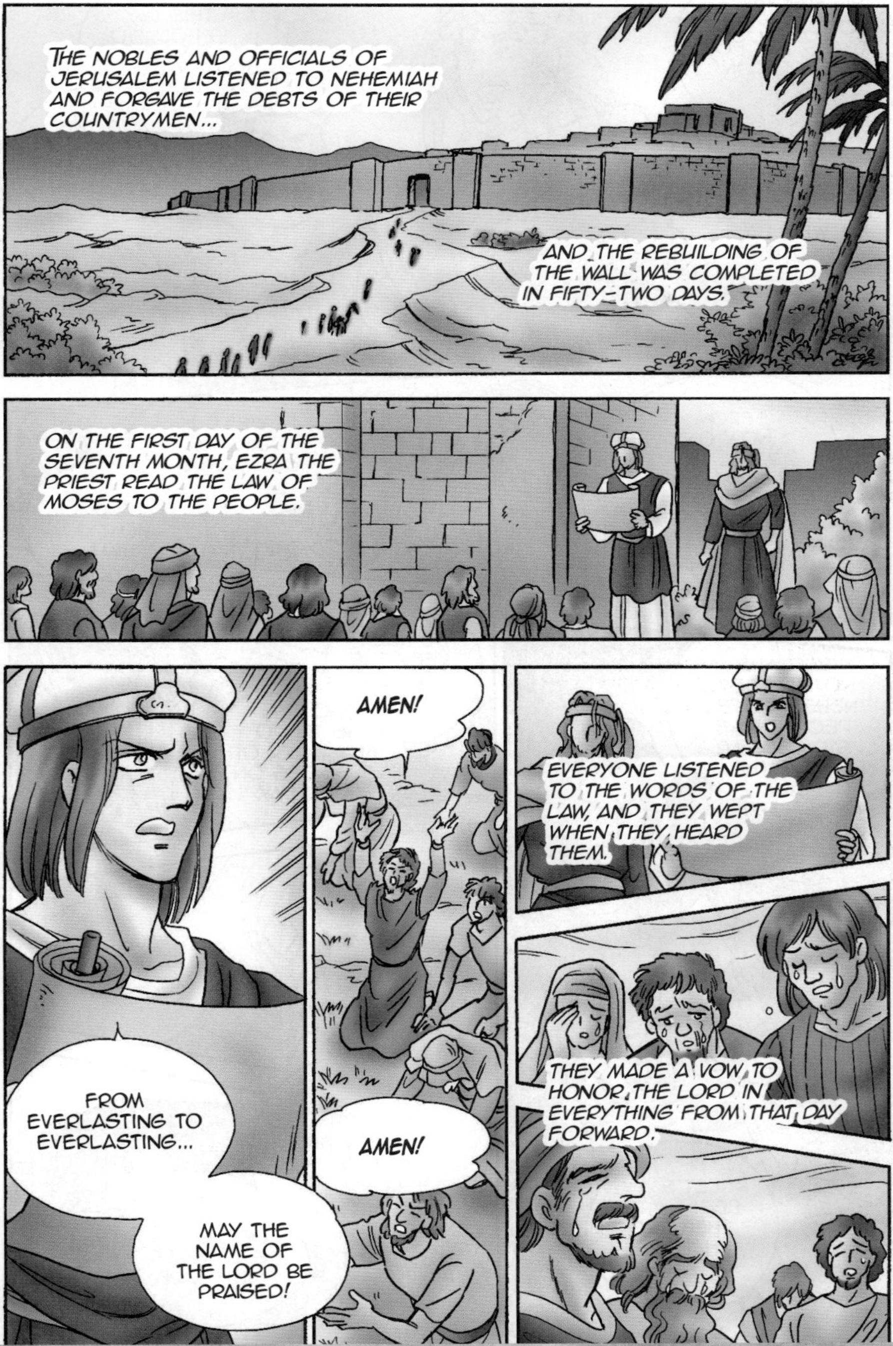
THE NOBLES AND OFFICIALS OF JERUSALEM LISTENED TO NEHEMIAH AND FORGAVE THE DEBTS OF THEIR COUNTRYMEN...
AND THE REBUILDING OF THE WALL WAS COMPLETED IN FIFTY-TWO DAYS.
ON THE FIRST DAY OF THE SEVENTH MONTH, EZRA THE PRIEST READ THE LAW OF MOSES TO THE PEOPLE.
FROM EVERLASTING TO EVERLASTING...
MAY THE NAME OF THE LORD BE PRAISED!
AMEN!
AMEN!
EVERYONE LISTENED TO THE WORDS OF THE LAW, AND THEY WEPT WHEN THEY HEARD THEM.
THEY MADE A VOW TO HONOR THE LORD IN EVERYTHING FROM THAT DAY FORWARD.

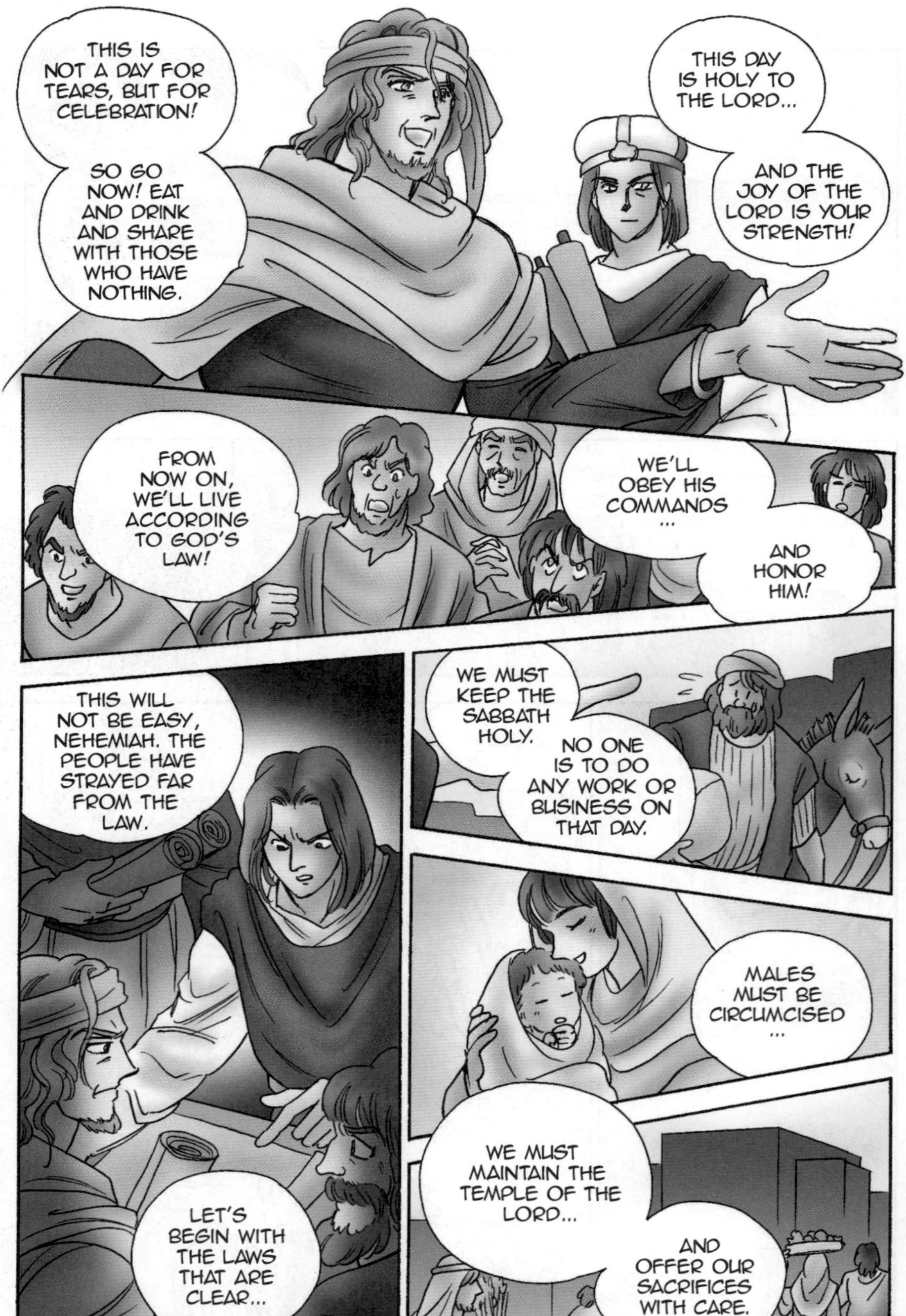
THIS IS NOT A DAY FOR TEARS, BUT FOR CELEBRATION!
SO GO NOW! EAT AND DRINK AND SHARE WITH THOSE WHO HAVE NOTHING.
THIS DAY IS HOLY TO THE LORD...
AND THE JOY OF THE LORD IS YOUR STRENGTH!
FROM NOW ON, WE'LL LIVE ACCORDING TO GOD'S LAW!
WE'LL OBEY HIS COMMANDS ...
AND HONOR HIM!
THIS WILL NOT BE EASY, NEHEMIAH. THE PEOPLE HAVE STRAYED FAR FROM THE LAW.
LET'S BEGIN WITH THE LAWS THAT ARE CLEAR...
WE MUST KEEP THE SABBATH HOLY.
NO ONE IS TO DO ANY WORK OR BUSINESS ON THAT DAY.
MALES MUST BE CIRCUMCISED ...
WE MUST MAINTAIN THE TEMPLE OF THE LORD...
AND OFFER OUR SACRIFICES WITH CARE.

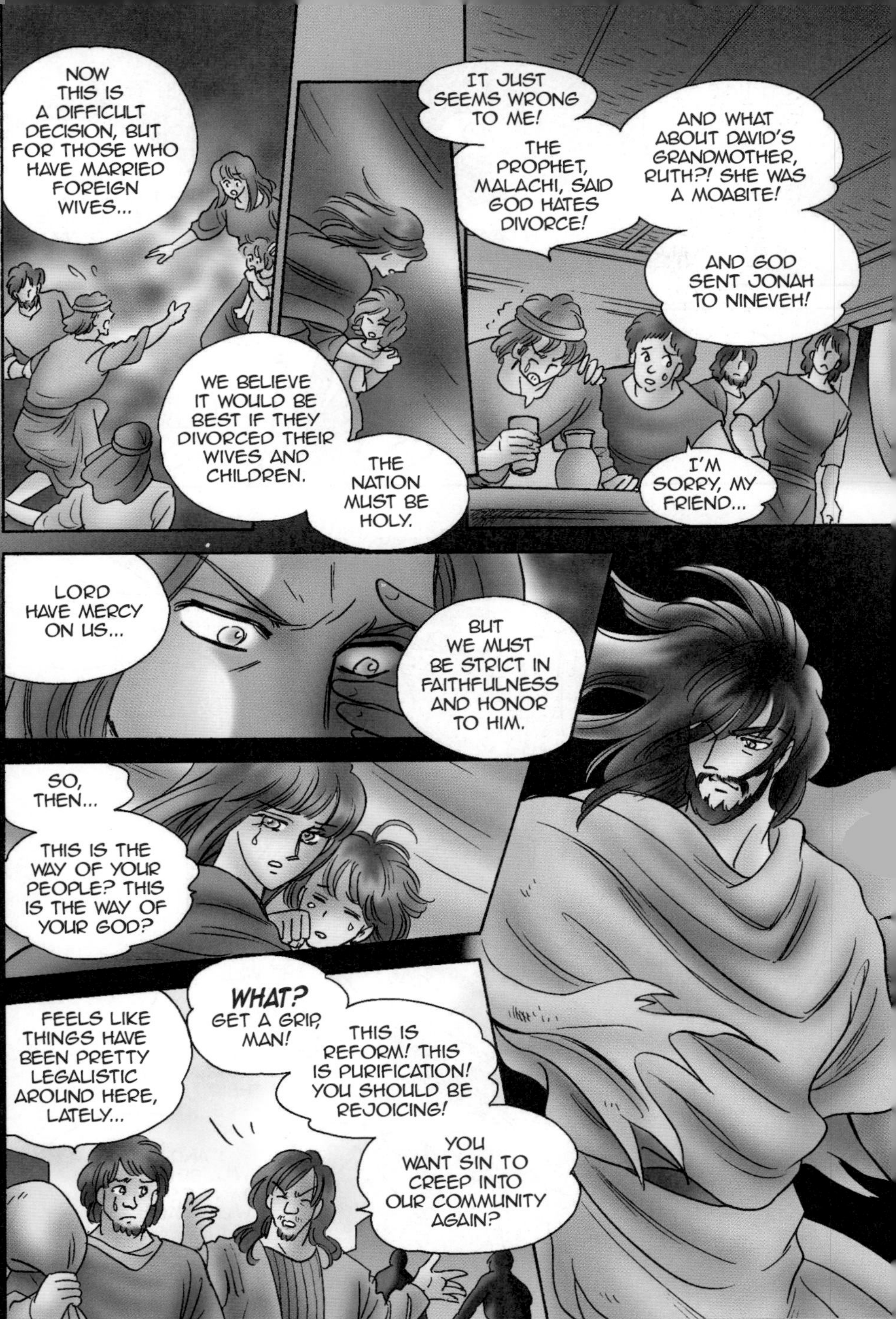
NOW THIS IS A DIFFICULT DECISION, BUT FOR THOSE WHO HAVE MARRIED FOREIGN WIVES...
WE BELIEVE IT WOULD BE BEST IF THEY DIVORCED THEIR WIVES AND CHILDREN.
THE NATION MUST BE HOLY.
IT JUST SEEMS WRONG TO ME!
THE PROPHET, MALACHI, SAID GOD HATES DIVORCE!
AND WHAT ABOUT DAVID'S GRANDMOTHER, RUTH?! SHE WAS A MOABITE!
AND GOD SENT JONAH TO NINEVEH!
I'M SORRY, MY FRIEND...
LORD HAVE MERCY ON US...
BUT WE MUST BE STRICT IN FAITHFULNESS AND HONOR TO HIM.
SO, THEN...
THIS IS THE WAY OF YOUR PEOPLE? THIS IS THE WAY OF YOUR GOD?
FEELS LIKE THINGS HAVE BEEN PRETTY LEGALISTIC AROUND HERE, LATELY...
WHAT? GET A GRIP, MAN!
THIS IS REFORM! THIS IS PURIFICATION! YOU SHOULD BE REJOICING!
YOU WANT SIN TO CREEP INTO OUR COMMUNITY AGAIN?

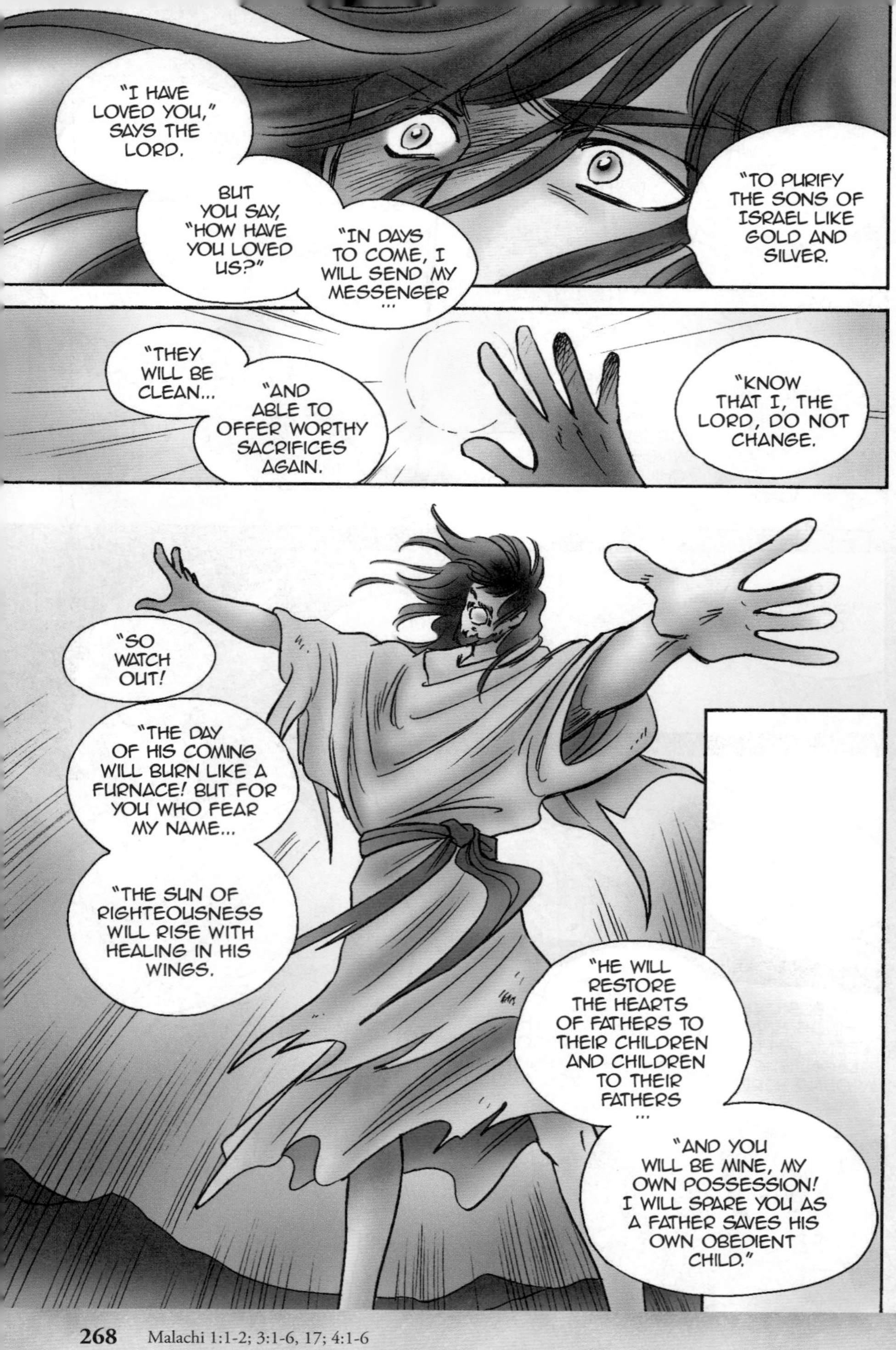
"I HAVE LOVED YOU," SAYS THE LORD.
BUT YOU SAY, "HOW HAVE YOU LOVED US?"
"IN DAYS TO COME, I WILL SEND MY MESSENGER ...
"TO PURIFY THE SONS OF ISRAEL LIKE GOLD AND SILVER.
"THEY WILL BE CLEAN...
"AND ABLE TO OFFER WORTHY SACRIFICES AGAIN.
"KNOW THAT I, THE LORD, DO NOT CHANGE.
"SO WATCH OUT!
"THE DAY OF HIS COMING WILL BURN LIKE A FURNACE! BUT FOR YOU WHO FEAR MY NAME...
"THE SUN OF RIGHTEOUSNESS WILL RISE WITH HEALING IN HIS WINGS.
"HE WILL RESTORE THE HEARTS OF FATHERS TO THEIR CHILDREN AND CHILDREN TO THEIR FATHERS ...
"AND YOU WILL BE MINE, MY OWN POSSESSION! I WILL SPARE YOU AS A FATHER SAVES HIS OWN OBEDIENT CHILD."

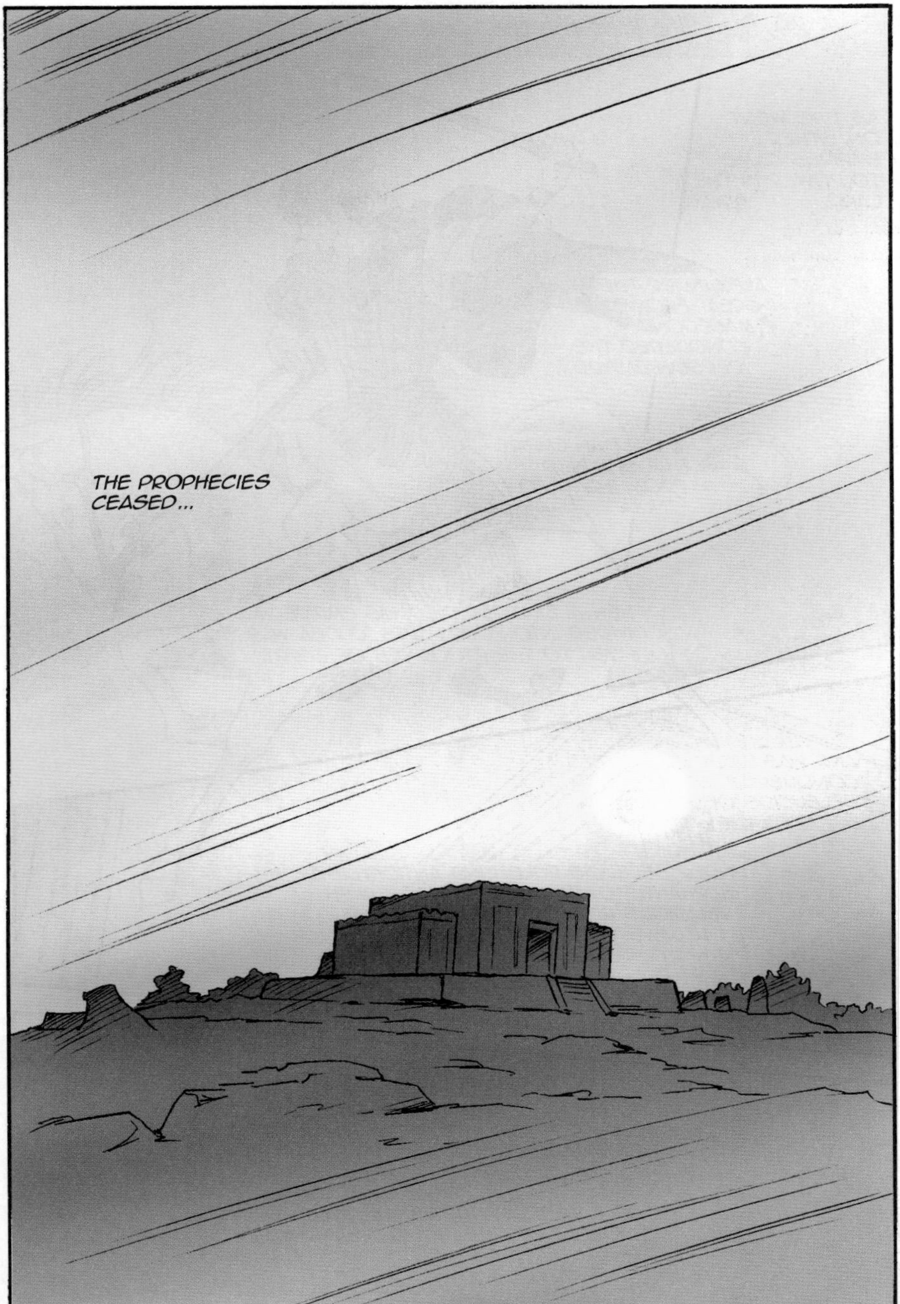
THE PROPHECIES CEASED...

20. They Who Wait for the Lord

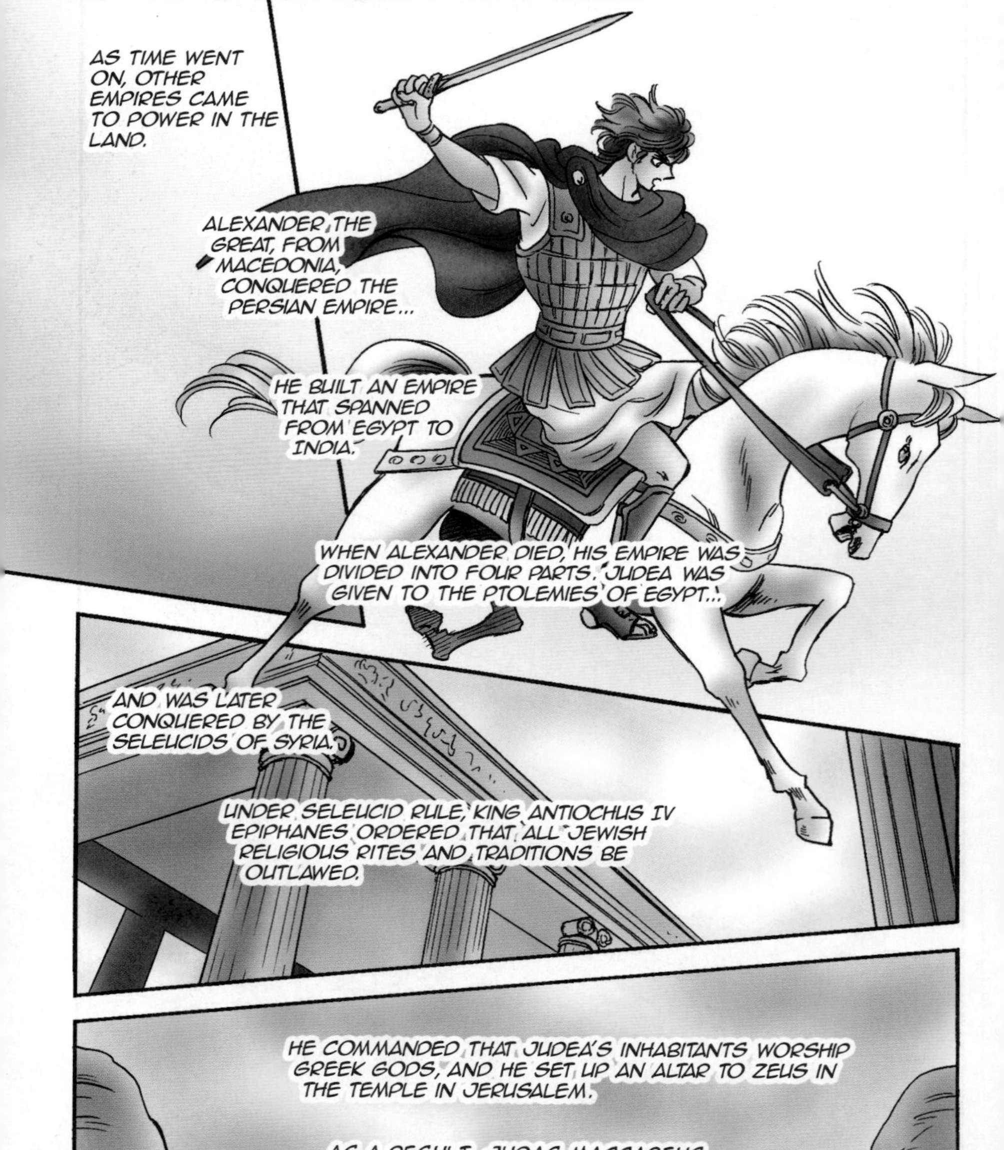
AS TIME WENT ON, OTHER EMPIRES CAME TO POWER IN THE LAND.
ALEXANDER THE GREAT, FROM MACEDONIA, CONQUERED THE PERSIAN EMPIRE...
HE BUILT AN EMPIRE THAT SPANNED FROM EGYPT TO INDIA.
WHEN ALEXANDER DIED, HIS EMPIRE WAS DIVIDED INTO FOUR PARTS. JUDEA WAS GIVEN TO THE PTOLEMIES OF EGYPT...
AND WAS LATER CONQUERED BY THE SELEUCIDS OF SYRIA.
UNDER SELEUCID RULE, KING ANTIOCHUS IV EPIPHANES ORDERED THAT ALL JEWISH RELIGIOUS RITES AND TRADITIONS BE OUTLAWED.
HE COMMANDED THAT JUDEA'S INHABITANTS WORSHIP GREEK GODS, AND HE SET UP AN ALTAR TO ZEUS IN THE TEMPLE IN JERUSALEM.
AS A RESULT, JUDAS MACCABEUS, LEADER OF THE HASMONEAN FAMILY, INITIATED A FIE
RCE REVOLT.
NOTE: The rest of this book is based on the Old Testament as well as general history.

I HAVE TOLD YOU BEFORE, MY CHILDREN, THAT THE WORLD IS A DARK AND CONFUSING PLACE.

YES, RABBI.

VERY GOOD. SO LET'S LOOK TOGETHER...

THE TEACHINGS FROM THE LORD GIVE US WISDOM FOR OUR LIVES AND EACH DAY.

CAN WE READ GENESIS?

YEAH! AND SAMSON!

WE WILL BEGIN WITH GENESIS...

THEN EXODUS.

AND ABOUT KING DAVID...

NOW, IN THE BEGINNING...

AFTER GOD CREATED THE HEAVENS AND THE EARTH...

WHO KNOWS WHAT HE SAID...?

I KNOW! I KNOW!

"IT IS VERY GOOD."

WAIT TILL I CALL ON YOU, ELI...

BUT THAT'S CORRECT.

AND IT WAS VERY GOOD. IT WAS A BEAUTIFUL PLACE. AND GOD WALKED WITH MAN IN HIS GARDEN.

BUT IT DID NOT STAY THAT WAY, DID IT?

BECAUSE OUR ANCESTORS DISOBEYED GOD AND WERE SENT FROM THE GARDEN. BUT GOD DIDN'T GIVE UP ON MEN, DID HE?

271

HE PREPARED A PLAN TO BRING US BACK TO HIMSELF. HE FIRST CHOSE OUR FATHER, ABRAHAM, TO BECOME THE FATHER OF A NEW NATION.

THEN HE GAVE HIS BLESSINGS AND TEACHINGS TO ABRAHAM'S DESCENDANTS, ISAAC AND JACOB.

THEY BECAME A GREAT PEOPLE IN EGYPT, BUT BECAME SLAVES TO THE RULERS OF THE LAND.

SO THE LORD RAISED UP A LEADER, MOSES, AND BROUGHT THEM OUT OF EGYPT WITH MIGHTY ACTS OF POWER.

HE TOOK THEM TO A HOME OF THEIR OWN, IN CANAAN. BUT THE PEOPLE WERE DISOBEDIENT...

AND THEIR SINS CREATED MANY PROBLEMS FOR THEM.

THE LORD GAVE US A WONDERFUL KING IN DAVID...

AND HIS SON SOLOMON BROUGHT PEACE TO ISRAEL.

BUT THE KINGS WHO CAME AFTER THEM REJECTED THE LORD AND OFTEN SERVED OTHER GODS.

THEY WOULD NOT LISTEN TO GOD'S MESSENGERS OR HIS LAW.

SO WE WERE INVADED AND JERUSALEM AND THE TEMPLE OF THE LORD WERE BURNED, AND OUR PEOPLE WERE TAKEN AWAY AS CAPTIVES TO BABYLON.

THOUGH IT SEEMED WE HAD LOST EVERYTHING, THE LORD HAD NOT FORGOTTEN HIS PEOPLE.

HIS PROPHETS TOLD US THAT WE STILL HAD A HOPE AND A FUTURE...

AND AFTER 70 YEARS OF CAPTIVITY, THE LORD BROUGHT US BACK TO THE LAND.

SNIFF

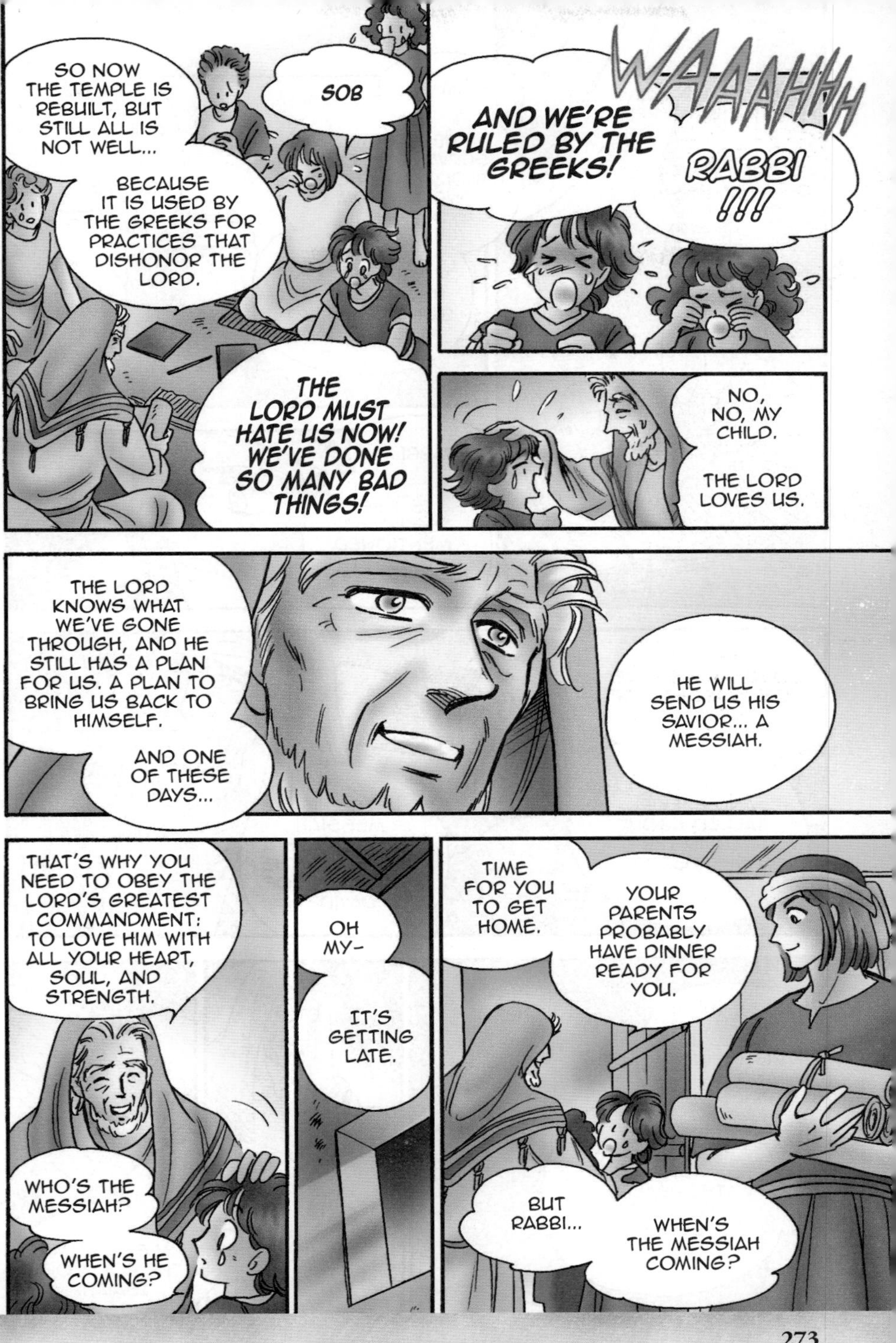
SO NOW THE TEMPLE IS REBUILT, BUT STILL ALL IS NOT WELL...
SOB
BECAUSE IT IS USED BY THE GREEKS FOR PRACTICES THAT DISHONOR THE LORD.
THE LORD MUST HATE US NOW! WE'VE DONE SO MANY BAD THINGS!
AND WE'RE RULED BY THE GREEKS!
WAAAAHHH
RABBI !!!
NO, NO, MY CHILD.
THE LORD LOVES US.
THE LORD KNOWS WHAT WE'VE GONE THROUGH, AND HE STILL HAS A PLAN FOR US. A PLAN TO BRING US BACK TO HIMSELF.
AND ONE OF THESE DAYS...
HE WILL SEND US HIS SAVIOR... A MESSIAH.
THAT'S WHY YOU NEED TO OBEY THE LORD'S GREATEST COMMANDMENT: TO LOVE HIM WITH ALL YOUR HEART, SOUL, AND STRENGTH.
WHO'S THE MESSIAH?
WHEN'S HE COMING?
OH MY-
IT'S GETTING LATE.
TIME FOR YOU TO GET HOME.
YOUR PARENTS PROBABLY HAVE DINNER READY FOR YOU.
BUT RABBI...
WHEN'S THE MESSIAH COMING?

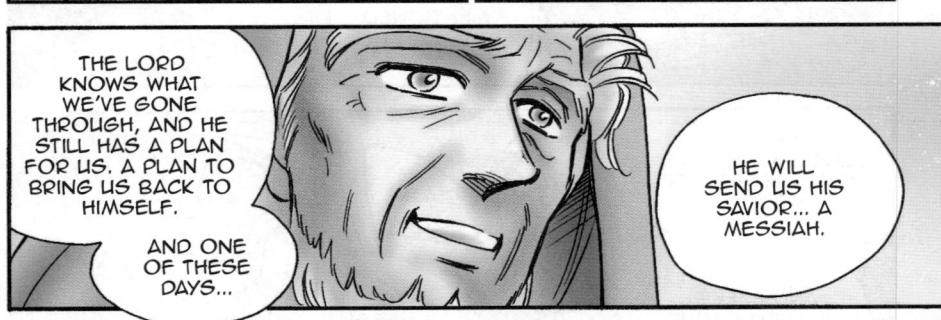

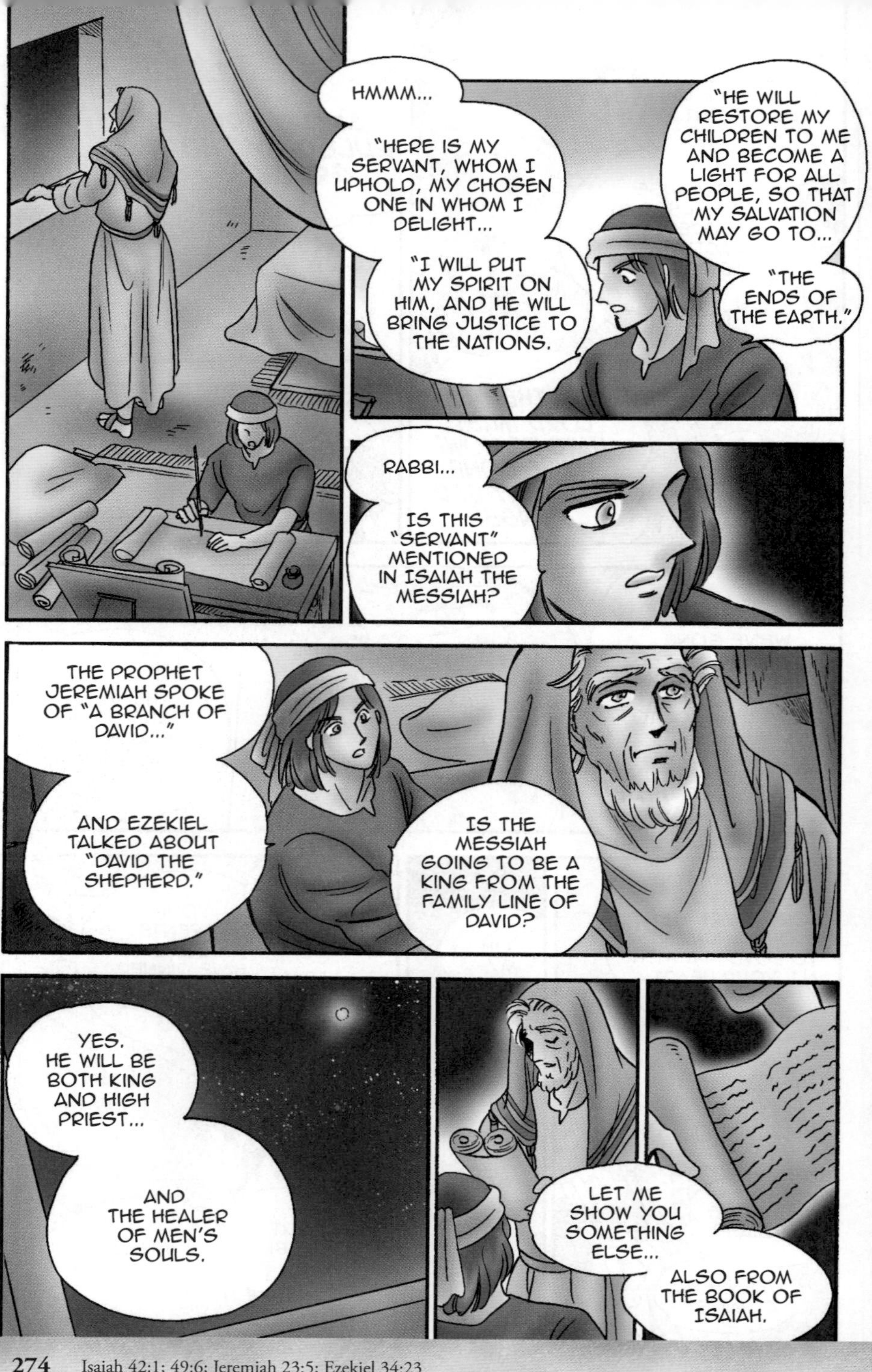
HMMM...
"HERE IS MY SERVANT, WHOM I UPHOLD, MY CHOSEN ONE IN WHOM I DELIGHT...
"I WILL PUT MY SPIRIT ON HIM, AND HE WILL BRING JUSTICE TO THE NATIONS.
"HE WILL RESTORE MY CHILDREN TO ME AND BECOME A LIGHT FOR ALL PEOPLE, SO THAT MY SALVATION MAY GO TO...
"THE ENDS OF THE EARTH."
RABBI...
IS THIS "SERVANT" MENTIONED IN ISAIAH THE MESSIAH?
THE PROPHET JEREMIAH SPOKE OF "A BRANCH OF DAVID..."
AND EZEKIEL TALKED ABOUT "DAVID THE SHEPHERD."
IS THE MESSIAH GOING TO BE A KING FROM THE FAMILY LINE OF DAVID?
YES. HE WILL BE BOTH KING AND HIGH PRIEST...
AND THE HEALER OF MEN'S SOULS.
LET ME SHOW YOU SOMETHING ELSE...
ALSO FROM THE BOOK OF ISAIAH.

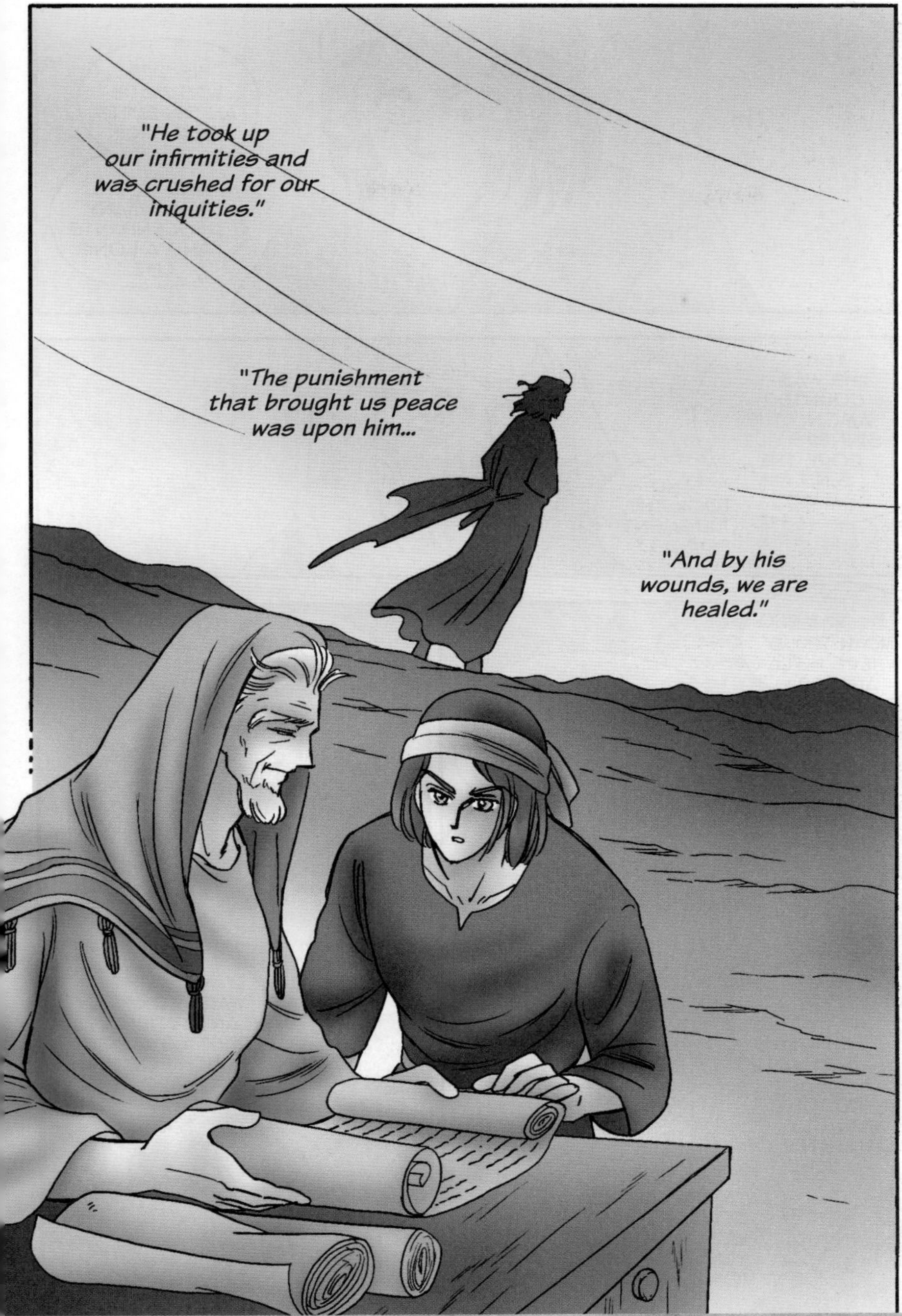
"He took up our infirmities and was crushed for our iniquities."
"The punishment that brought us peace was upon him...
"And by his wounds, we are healed."

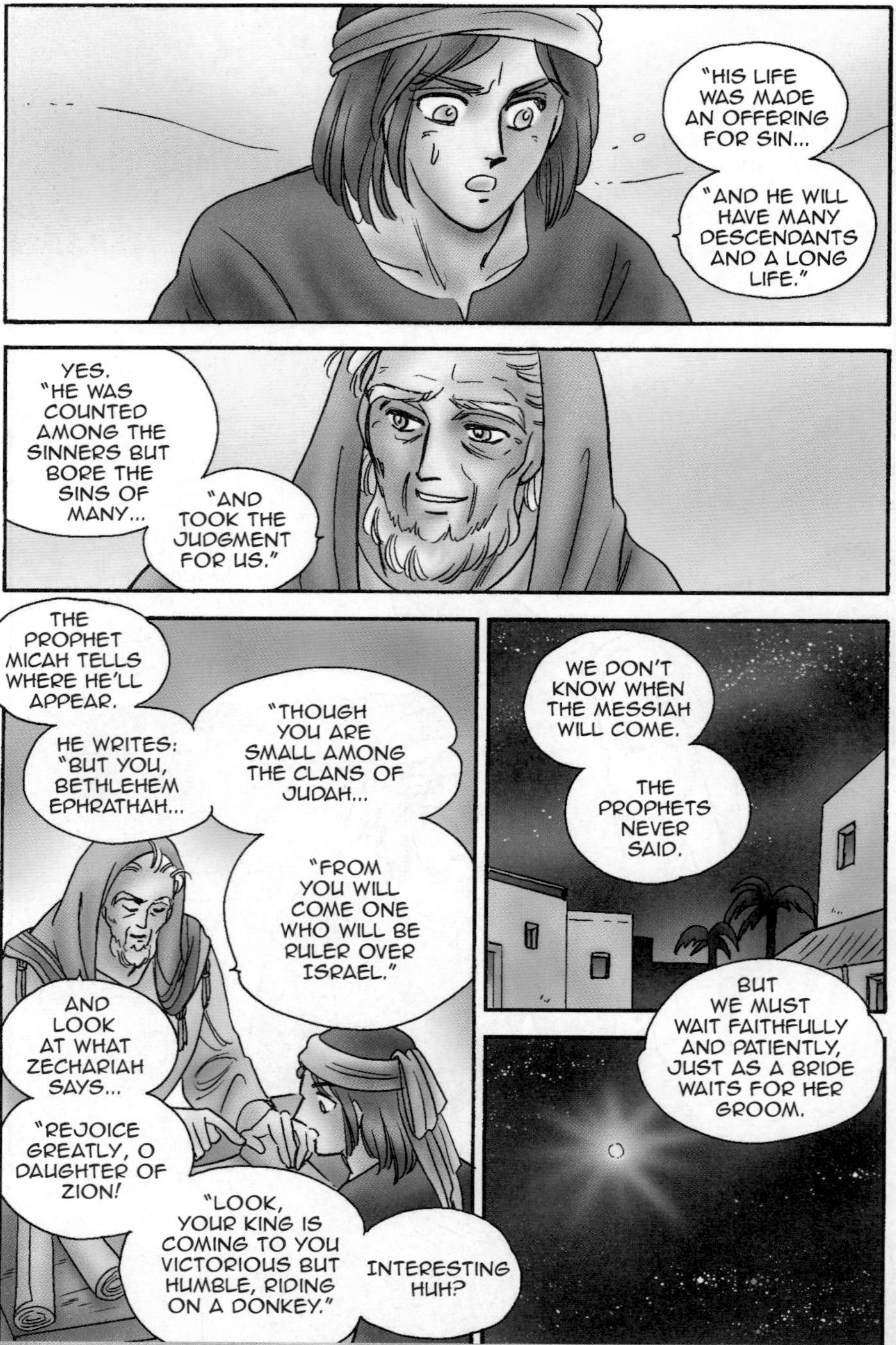
"HIS LIFE WAS MADE AN OFFERING FOR SIN...
"AND HE WILL HAVE MANY DESCENDANTS AND A LONG LIFE."
YES. "HE WAS COUNTED AMONG THE SINNERS BUT BORE THE SINS OF MANY...
"AND TOOK THE JUDGMENT FOR US."
THE PROPHET MICAH TELLS WHERE HE'LL APPEAR.
HE WRITES: "BUT YOU, BETHLEHEM EPHRATHAH...
"THOUGH YOU ARE SMALL AMONG THE CLANS OF JUDAH...
"FROM YOU WILL COME ONE WHO WILL BE RULER OVER ISRAEL."
AND LOOK AT WHAT ZECHARIAH SAYS...
"REJOICE GREATLY, O DAUGHTER OF ZION!
"LOOK, YOUR KING IS COMING TO YOU VICTORIOUS BUT HUMBLE, RIDING ON A DONKEY."
INTERESTING HUH?
WE DON'T KNOW WHEN THE MESSIAH WILL COME.
THE PROPHETS NEVER SAID.
BUT WE MUST WAIT FAITHFULLY AND PATIENTLY, JUST AS A BRIDE WAITS FOR HER GROOM.

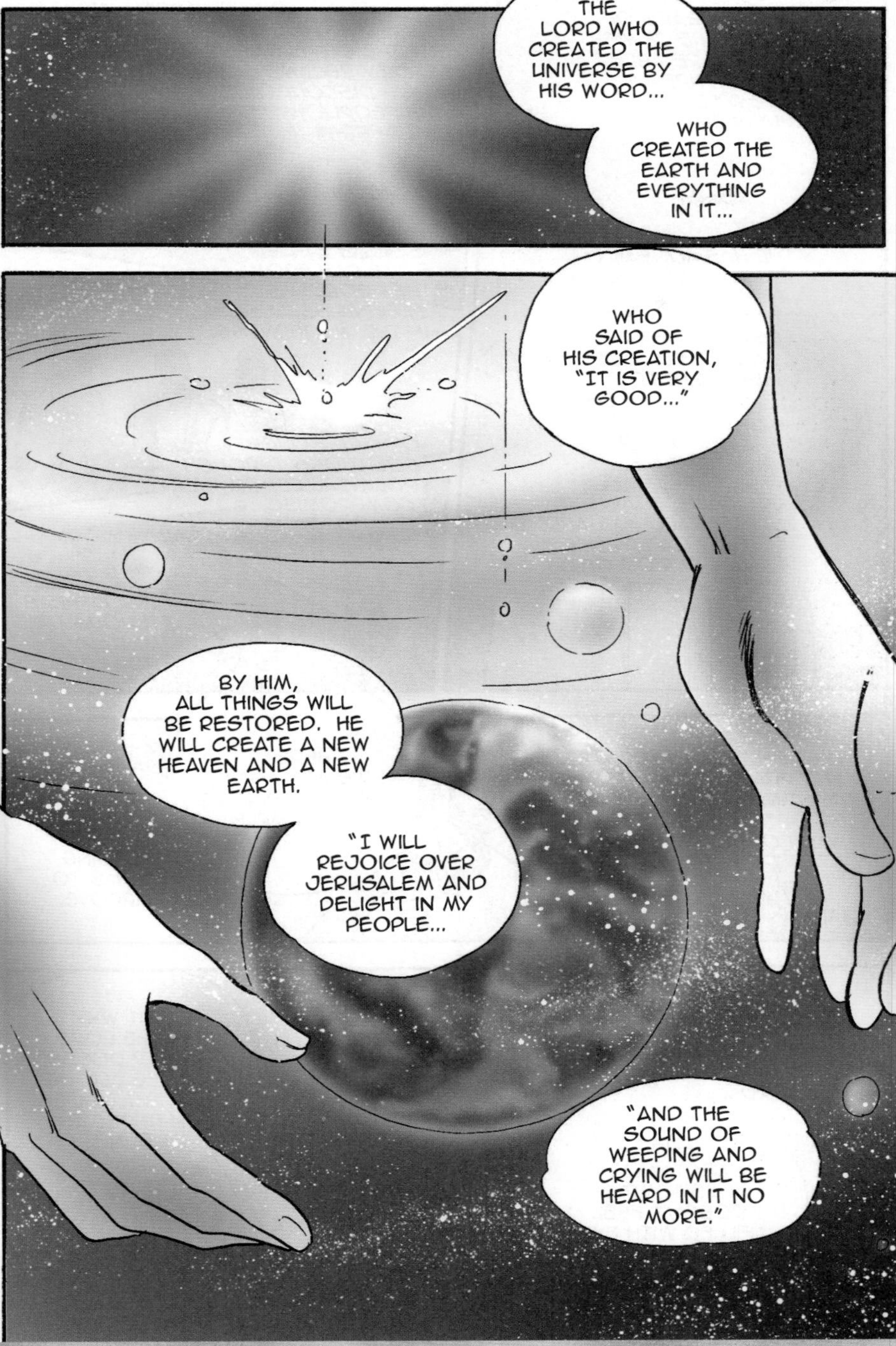
THE LORD WHO CREATED THE UNIVERSE BY HIS WORD...
WHO CREATED THE EARTH AND EVERYTHING IN IT...
WHO SAID OF HIS CREATION, "IT IS VERY GOOD..."
BY HIM, ALL THINGS WILL BE RESTORED. HE WILL CREATE A NEW HEAVEN AND A NEW EARTH.
"I WILL REJOICE OVER JERUSALEM AND DELIGHT IN MY PEOPLE...
"AND THE SOUND OF WEEPING AND CRYING WILL BE HEARD IN IT NO MORE."

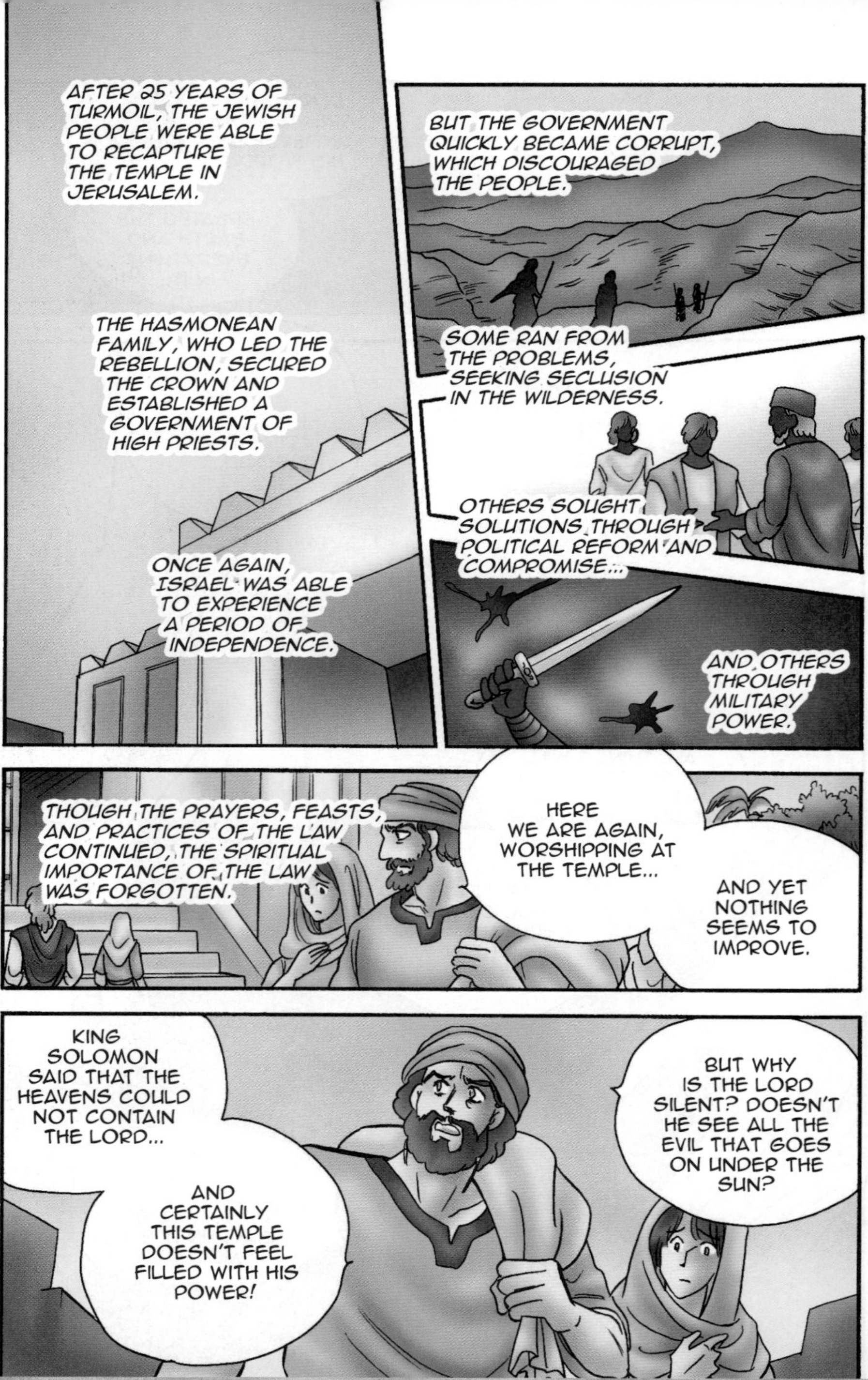
AFTER 25 YEARS OF TURMOIL, THE JEWISH PEOPLE WERE ABLE TO RECAPTURE THE TEMPLE IN JERUSALEM.
THE HASMONEAN FAMILY, WHO LED THE REBELLION, SECURED THE CROWN AND ESTABLISHED A GOVERNMENT OF HIGH PRIESTS.
ONCE AGAIN, ISRAEL WAS ABLE TO EXPERIENCE A PERIOD OF INDEPENDENCE.
BUT THE GOVERNMENT QUICKLY BECAME CORRUPT, WHICH DISCOURAGED THE PEOPLE.
SOME RAN FROM THE PROBLEMS, SEEKING SECLUSION IN THE WILDERNESS.
OTHERS SOUGHT SOLUTIONS THROUGH POLITICAL REFORM AND COMPROMISE...
AND OTHERS THROUGH MILITARY POWER.
THOUGH THE PRAYERS, FEASTS, AND PRACTICES OF THE LAW CONTINUED, THE SPIRITUAL IMPORTANCE OF THE LAW WAS FORGOTTEN.
HERE WE ARE AGAIN, WORSHIPPING AT THE TEMPLE...
AND YET NOTHING SEEMS TO IMPROVE.
KING SOLOMON SAID THAT THE HEAVENS COULD NOT CONTAIN THE LORD...
AND CERTAINLY THIS TEMPLE DOESN'T FEEL FILLED WITH HIS POWER!
BUT WHY IS THE LORD SILENT? DOESN'T HE SEE ALL THE EVIL THAT GOES ON UNDER THE SUN?

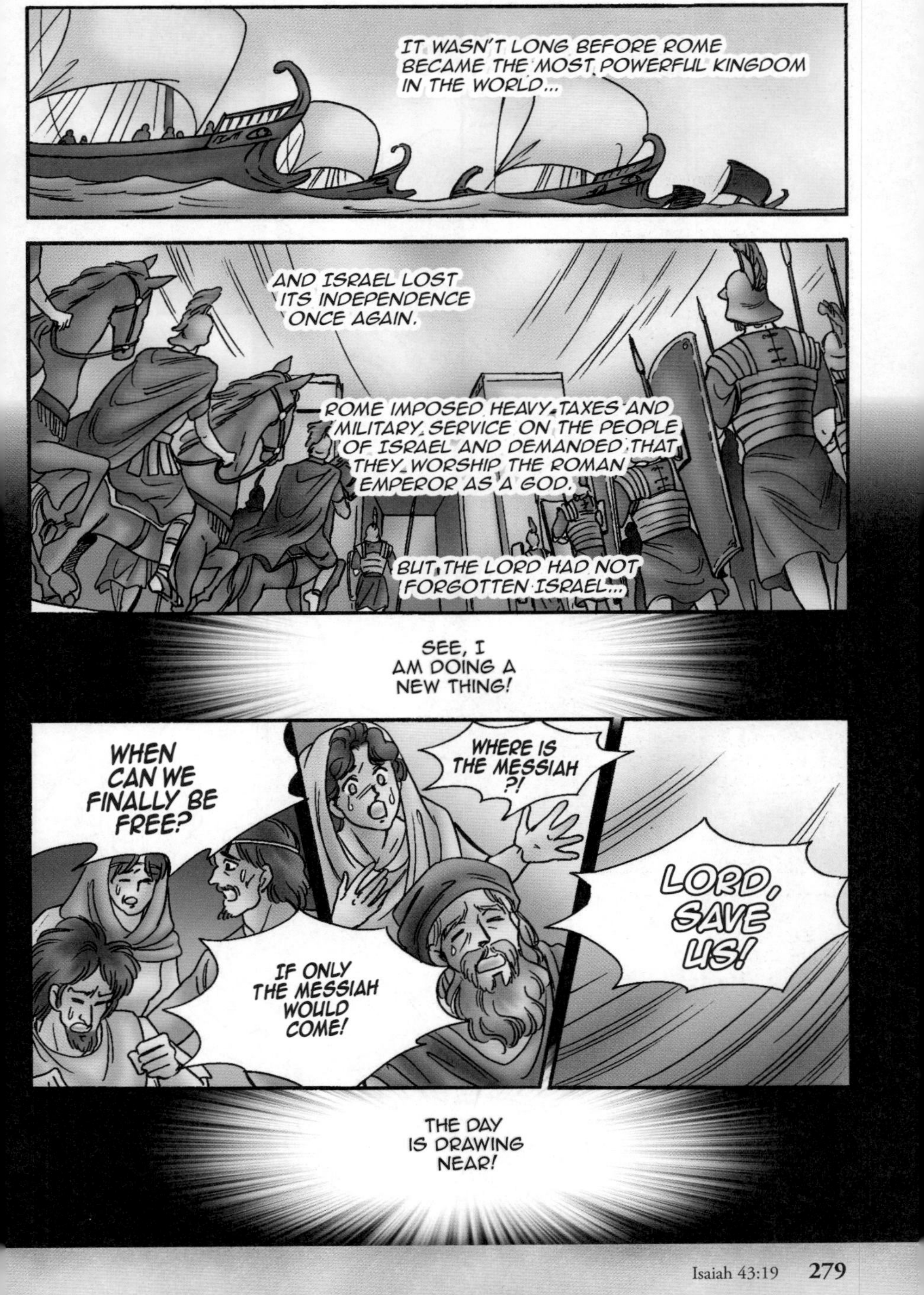
IT WASN'T LONG BEFORE ROME BECAME THE MOST POWERFUL KINGDOM IN THE WORLD...
AND ISRAEL LOST ITS INDEPENDENCE ONCE AGAIN.
ROME IMPOSED HEAVY TAXES AND MILITARY SERVICE ON THE PEOPLE OF ISRAEL AND DEMANDED THAT THEY WORSHIP THE ROMAN EMPEROR AS A GOD.
BUT THE LORD HAD NOT FORGOTTEN ISRAEL...
SEE, I AM DOING A NEW THING!
WHEN CAN WE FINALLY BE FREE?
WHERE IS THE MESSIAH ?!
LORD, SAVE US!
IF ONLY THE MESSIAH WOULD COME!
THE DAY IS DRAWING NEAR!

Isaiah 43:19

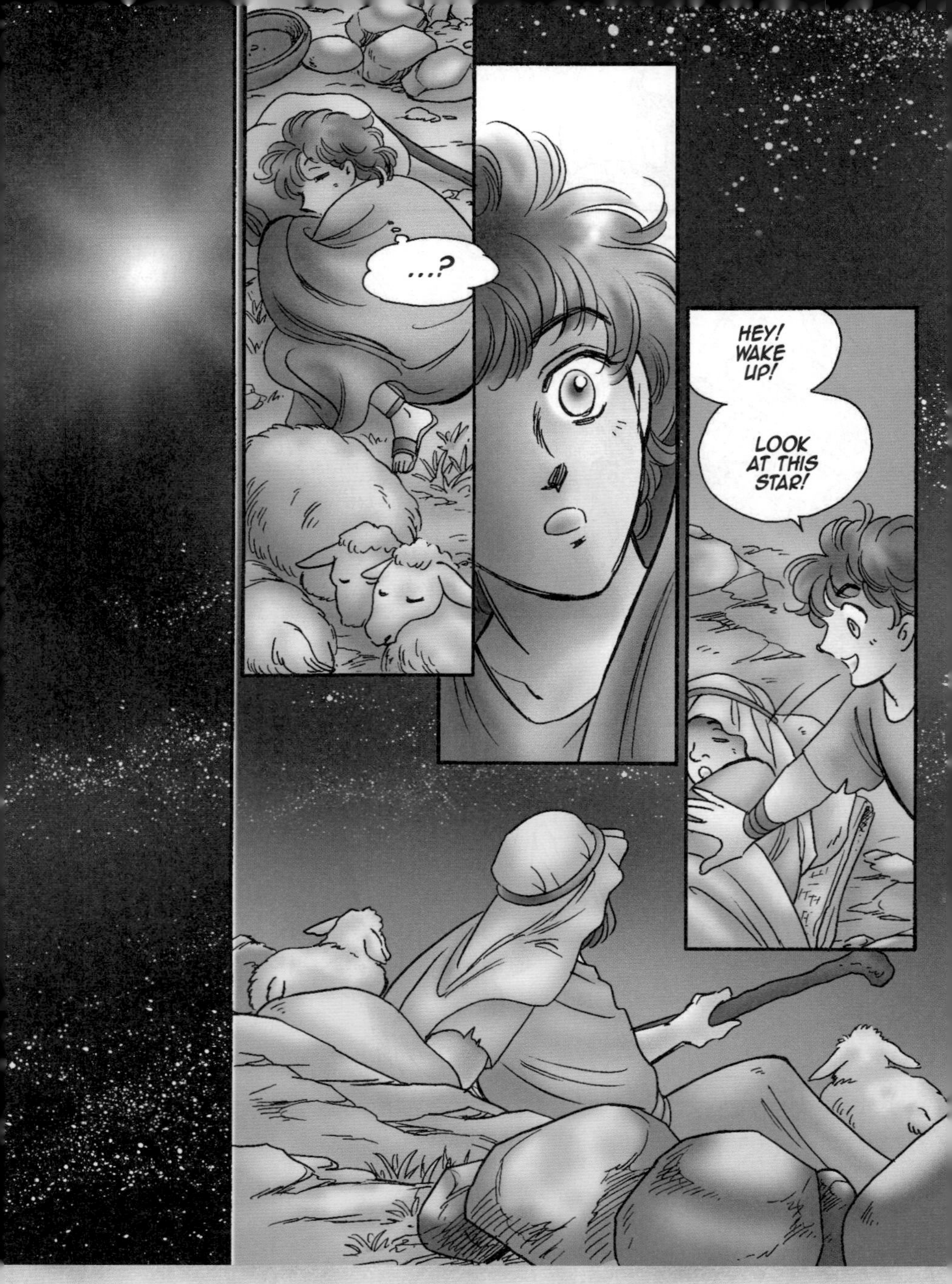
...?
HEY! WAKE UP!
LOOK AT THIS STAR!

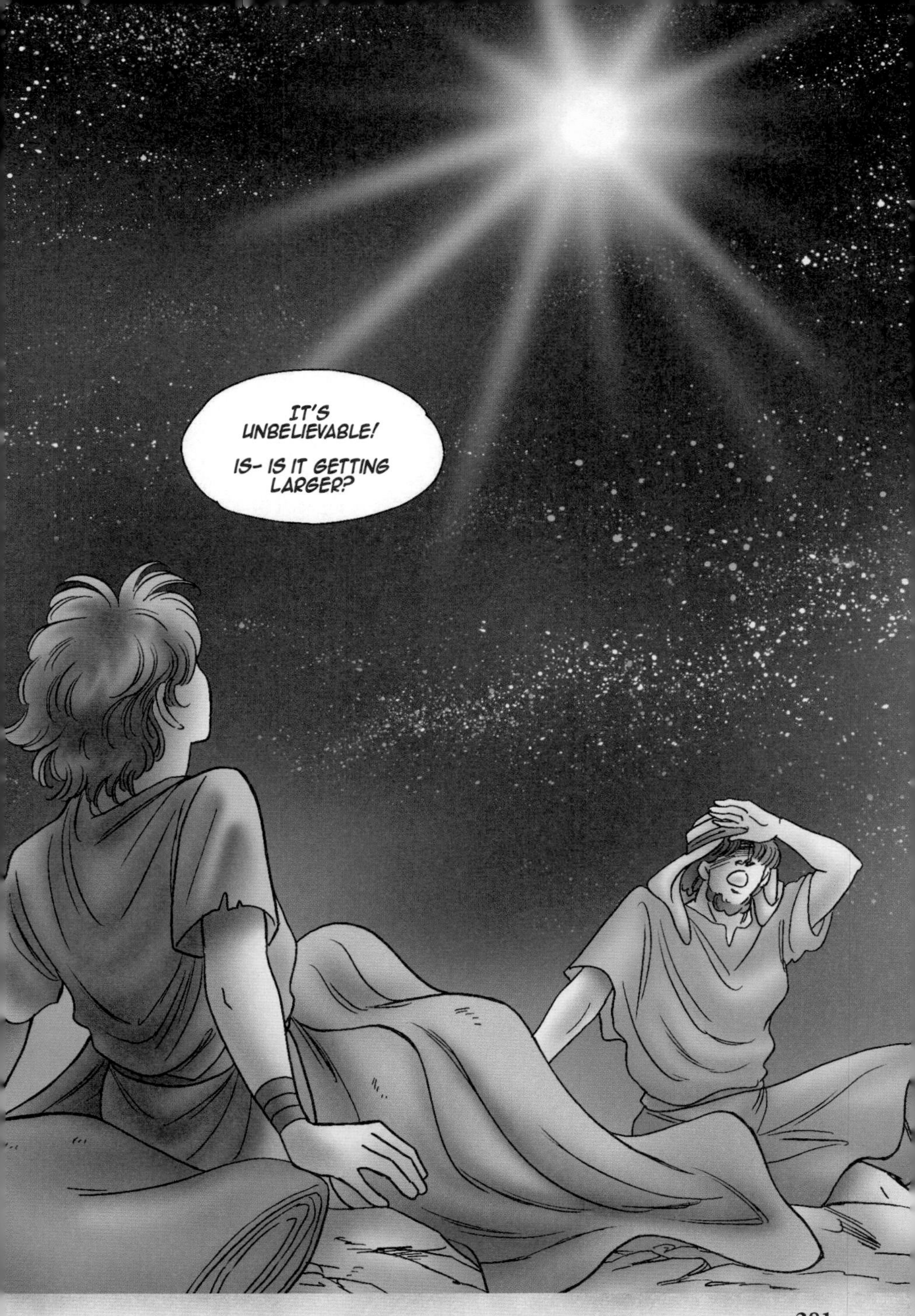
IT'S UNBELIEVABLE!
IS- IS IT GETTING LARGER?

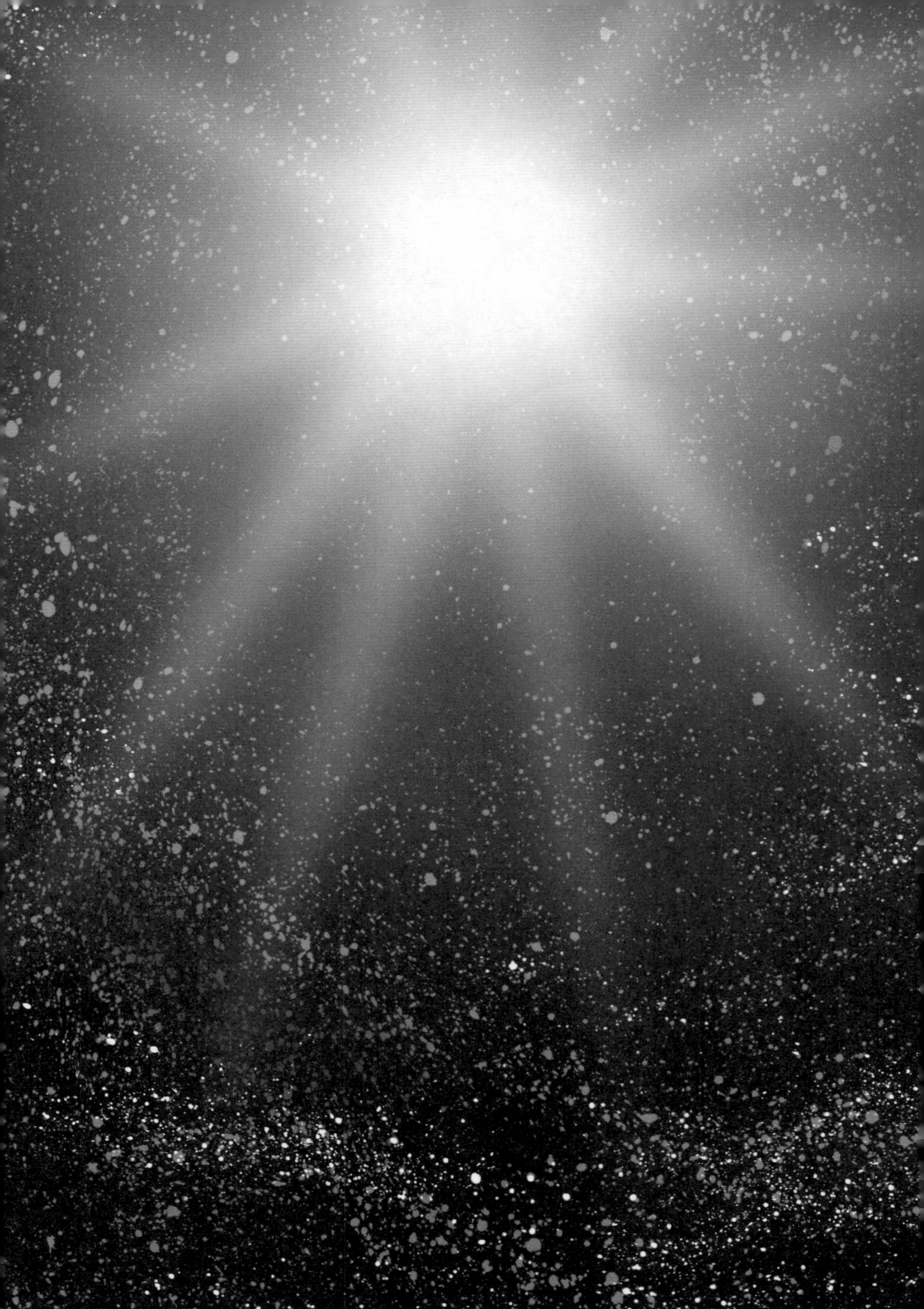

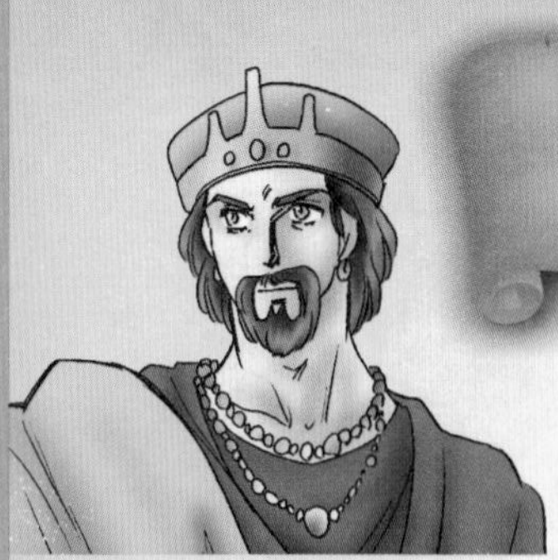

SIMPLIFIED CHRONOLOGY OF THE AGE OF THE PROPHETS

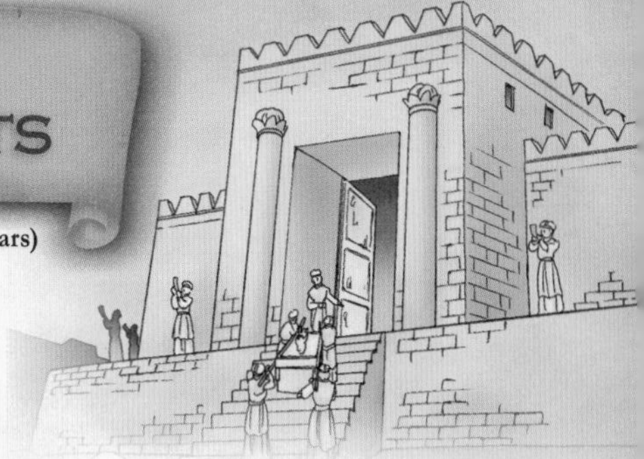

Obedient kings — Disobedient kings — Length of reign (years)

KINGDOM OF ISRAEL (UNITED MONARCHY)

SOLOMON (Ruled 40 years)

PROPHETS

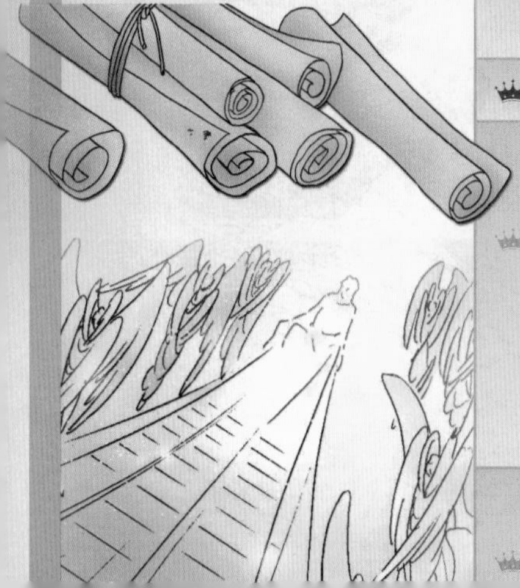

SOUTHERN KINGDOM OF JUDAH

REHOBOAM (17)

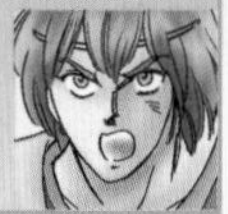

ABIJAM (3)

ASA (41)

His heart was with God throughout his life.

JEHOSHAPHAT

NORTHERN KINGDOM OF ISRAEL

JEROBOAM (22)

He made gold calves.

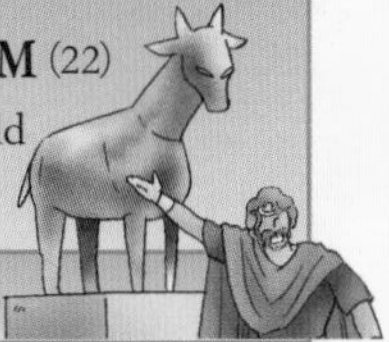

NADAB (2)

BAASHA (24)

He destroyed the house of Jeroboam

ELAH (2)

ZIMRI (7 days)

OMRI (12) The capital was relocated to Samaria.

AHAB (22)

JEZEBEL

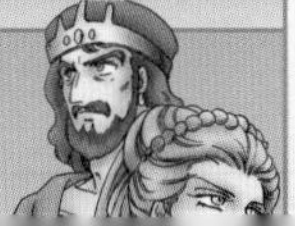

PROPHETS

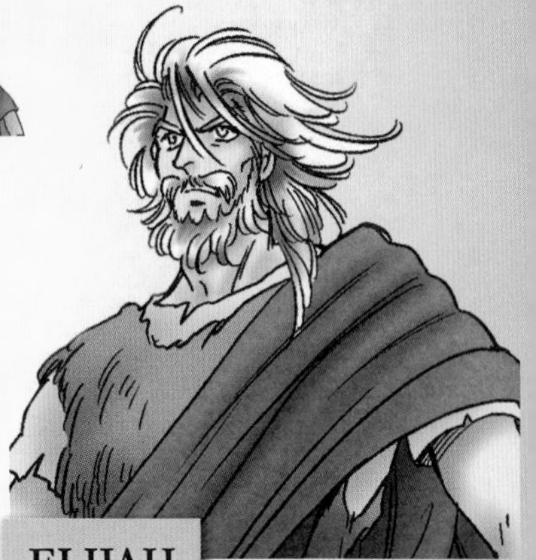

ELIJAH

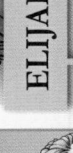

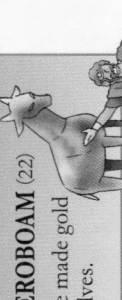

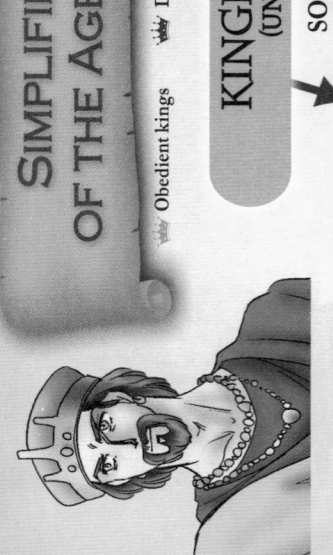

800 BC

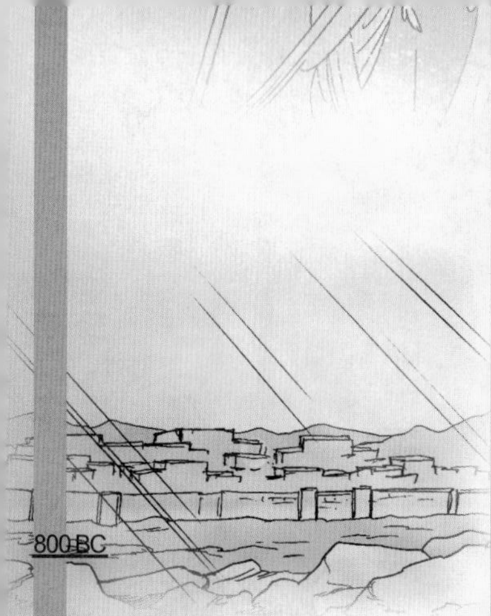

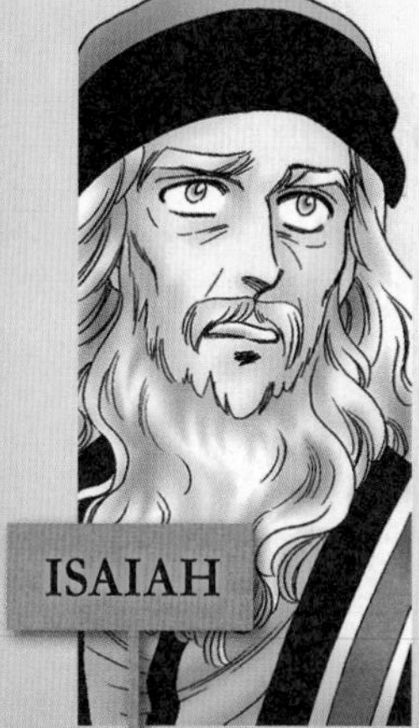

ISAIAH

He took a daughter of King Ahab named Athaliah as his wife.

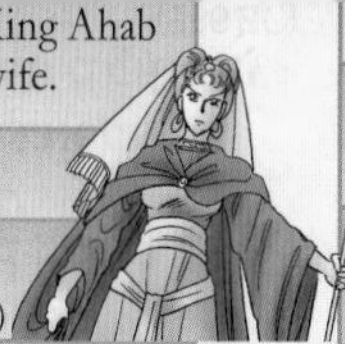

AHAZIAH (1)

THE MOTHER OF AHAZIAH
ATHALIAH (6)

JOASH (40)

He was crowned at age 7. Damages to the Temple were repaired under his authority.

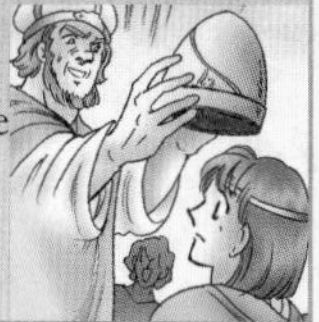

AMAZIAH (29)

UZZIAH (AZARIAH) (52)

Years of prosperity and peace continued during his reign. He got a serious skin disease at the end of his life.

JORAM (12)

JEHU (28)

He destroyed the house of Ahab.

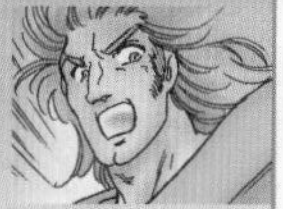

JEHOAHAZ (17)

JEHOASH (16)

JEROBOAM II (41)

Recovered territories of Israel as Jonah prophesied.

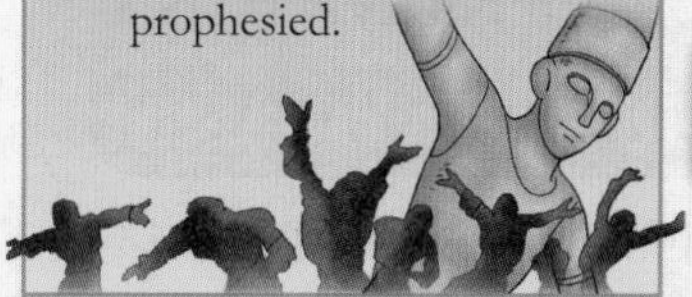

ZECHARIAH (6 mos)

SHALLUM (1 mo)

MENAHEM (10)

PEKAHIAH (2)

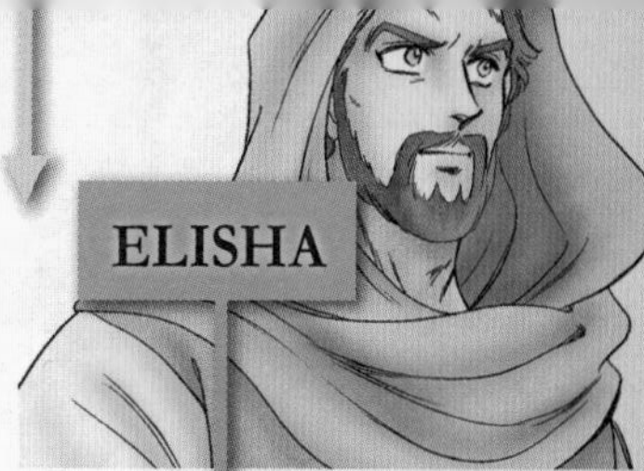

ELISHA

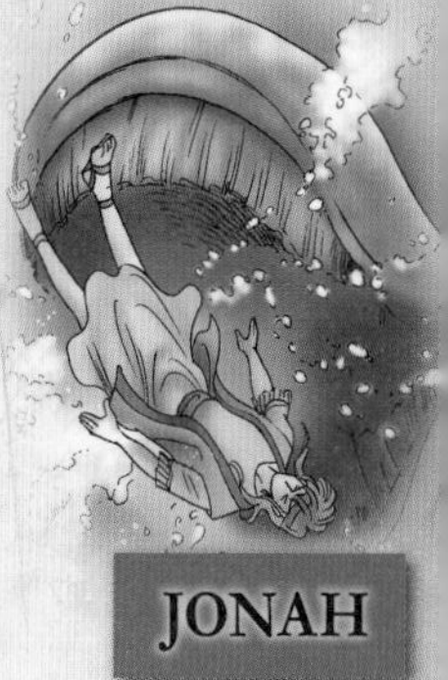

JONAH

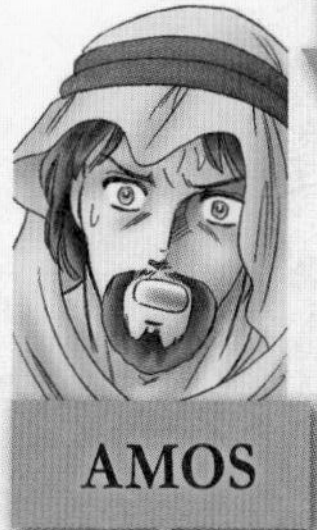

AMOS

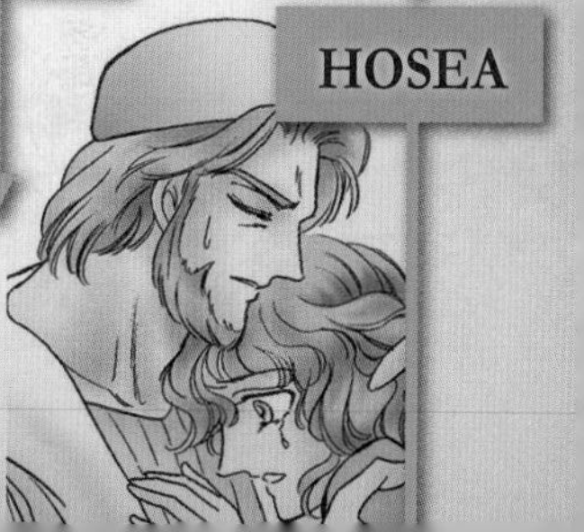

HOSEA

PEKAH (20)
Some citizens who got attacked by the king of Assyria were led away.

HOSHEA (9)

<The fall of Samaria>
<Forced immigration to Assyria>
(722 BC)

ASSYRIAN EMPIRE

SHALMANESER
SARGON II
SENNACHERIB

<The fall of Nineveh>
(612 BC)

NEO-ASSYRIAN EMPIRE

<The rise of Nebuchadnezzar>

EZEKIEL

DANIEL

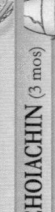

JOTHAM (16)

AHAZ (16)

HEZEKIAH (29)
15 years were added to his life by the grace of God.

MANASSEH (55)
He finally came to repent to God after he vigorously worshipped idols.

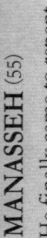
AMON (2)

JOSIAH (31)
The last glory of the kingdom of Judah.
He led a reformation.

JEHOAHAZ (3 mos) He was led away to Egypt.

JEHOIAKIM (11)

JEHOIACHIN (3 mos)

ZEDEKIAH (11)

<The fall of Jerusalem and Babylonian captivity>
(586 BC)

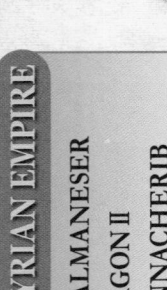

MICAH

JEREMIAH

700 BC

600 BC

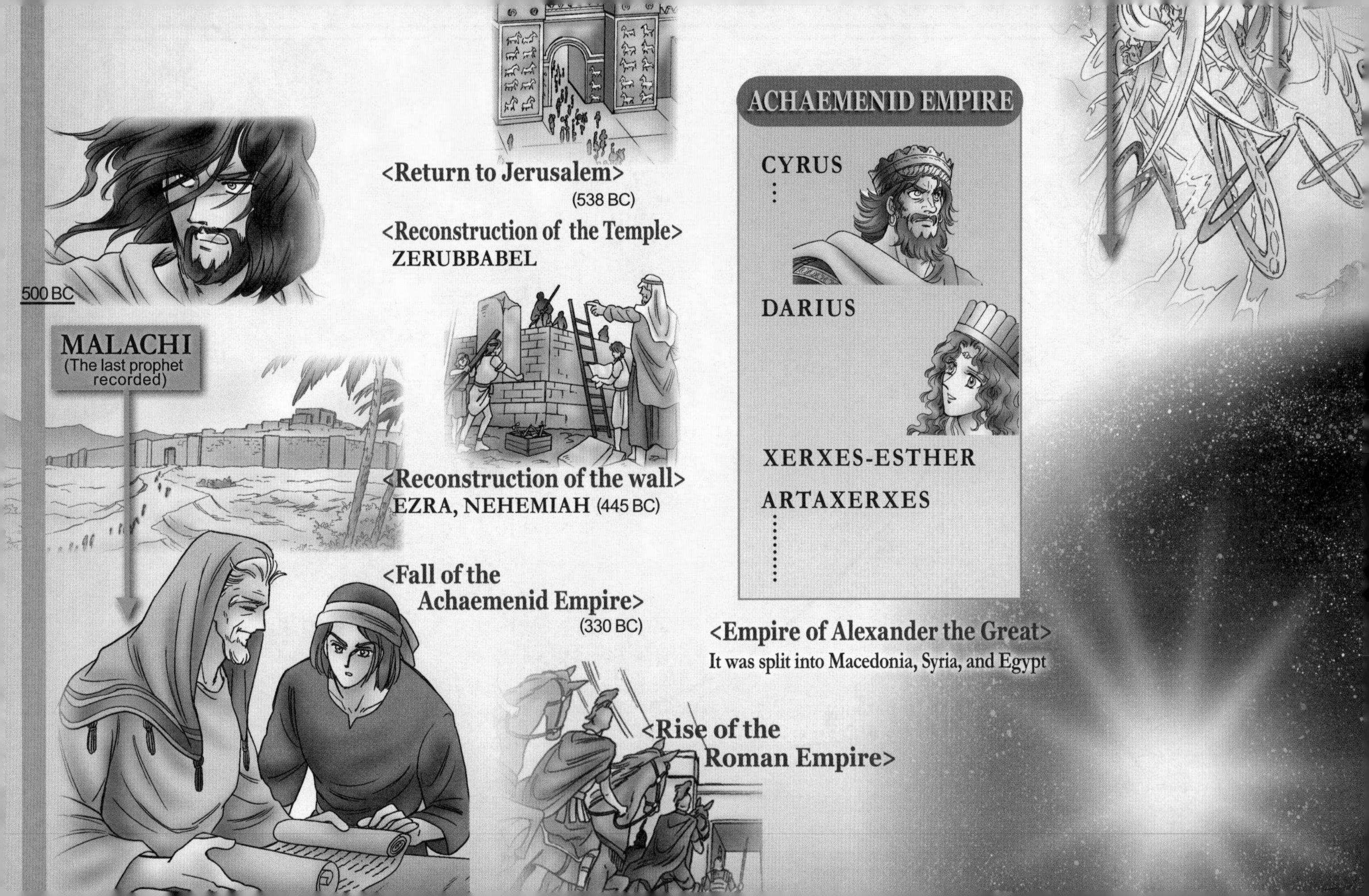
500 BC
MALACHI
(The last prophet recorded)
<Return to Jerusalem>
(538 BC)
<Reconstruction of the Temple>
ZERUBBABEL
<Reconstruction of the wall>
EZRA, NEHEMIAH (445 BC)
<Fall of the Achaemenid Empire>
(330 BC)
ACHAEMENID EMPIRE
CYRUS
DARIUS
XERXES-ESTHER
ARTAXERXES
<Empire of Alexander the Great>
It was split into Macedonia, Syria, and Egypt
<Rise of the Roman Empire>

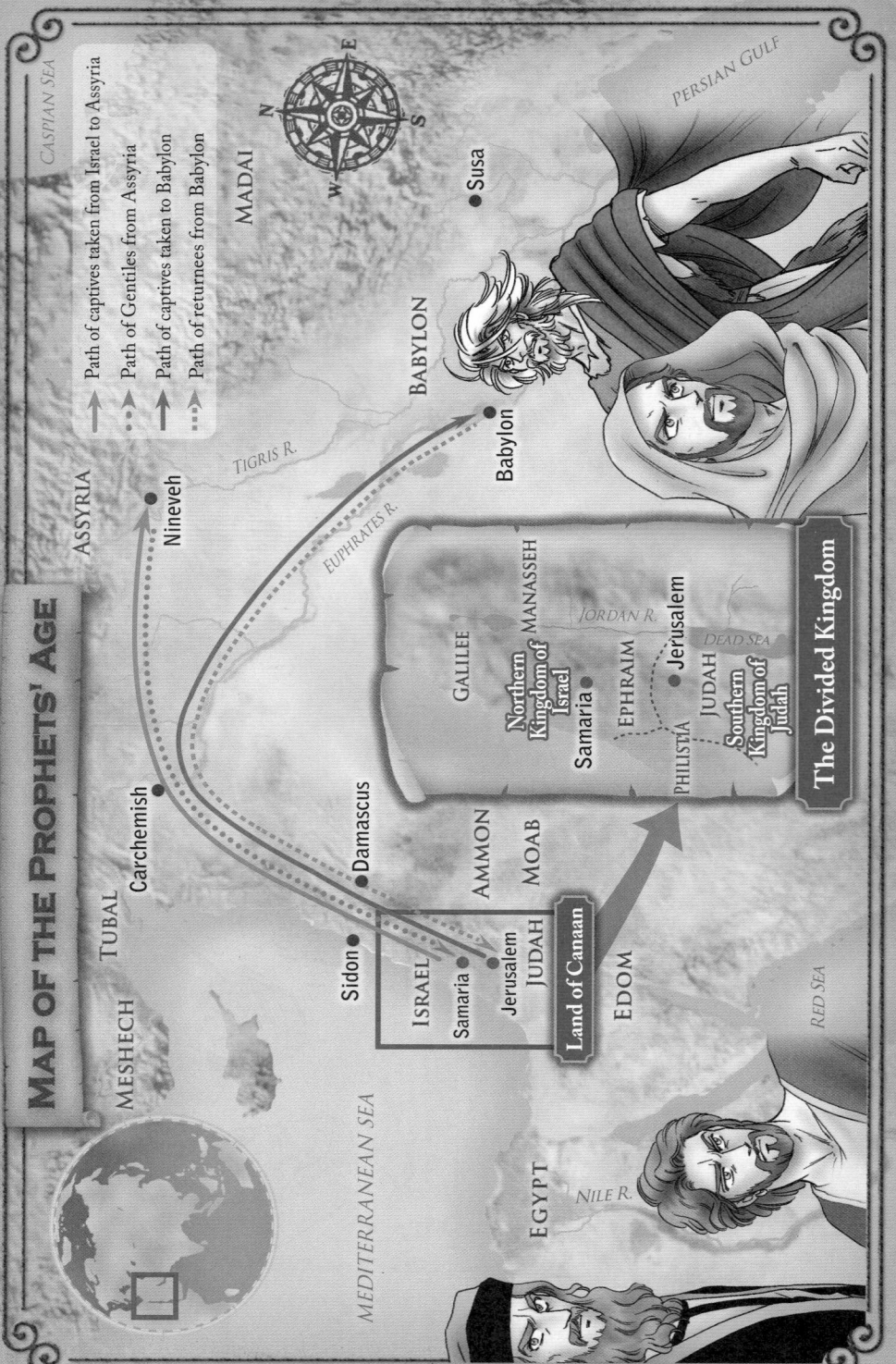

Map of the Prophets' Age

Path of captives taken from Israel to Assyria
Path of Gentiles from Assyria
Path of captives taken to Babylon
Path of returnees from Babylon

CASPIAN SEA

MADAI

PERSIAN GULF

Susa

N E
W S

BABYLON

ASSYRIA

Nineveh

Babylon

TIGRIS R.

EUPHRATES R.

TUBAL

MESHECH

Carchemish

Damascus

Sidon

ISRAEL
Samaria
Jerusalem
JUDAH

AMMON

MOAB

Land of Canaan

EDOM

The Divided Kingdom

GALILEE

MANASSEH

JORDAN R.

Northern
Kingdom of
Israel
Samaria

EPHRAIM

Jerusalem

DEAD SEA

JUDAH
Southern
Kingdom of
Judah

PHILISTIA

The Divided Kingdom

MEDITERRANEAN SEA

EGYPT

NILE R.

RED SEA